■ second edition

# finding
# OUT

HOME

# ■ second edition
# finding OUT

## An Introduction to LGBT Studies

### Michelle A. Gibson
*University of Cincinnati*

### Jonathan Alexander
*University of California, Irvine*

### Deborah T. Meem
*University of Cincinnati*

**⑤SAGE**

Los Angeles | London | New Delhi
Singapore | Washington DC

Los Angeles | London | New Delhi
Singapore | Washington DC

FOR INFORMATION:

SAGE Publications, Inc.
2455 Teller Road
Thousand Oaks, California 91320
E-mail: order@sagepub.com

SAGE Publications Ltd.
1 Oliver's Yard
55 City Road
London EC1Y 1SP
United Kingdom

SAGE Publications India Pvt. Ltd.
B 1/I 1 Mohan Cooperative Industrial Area
Mathura Road, New Delhi 110 044
India

SAGE Publications Asia-Pacific Pte. Ltd.
3 Church Street
#10-04 Samsung Hub
Singapore 049483

Acquisitions Editor: Matthew Byrnie
Editorial Assistant: Stephanie Palermini
Production Editor: Brittany Bauhaus
Copy Editor: Pam Schroeder
Typesetter: C&M Digitals (P) Ltd.
Proofreader: Jennifer Gritt
Indexer: Rick Hurd
Cover Designer: Gail Buschman
Marketing Manager: Liz Thornton
Permissions Editor: Karen Ehrmann

Copyright © 2014 by SAGE Publications, Inc.

Printed in the United States of America

*Library of Congress Cataloging-in-Publication Data*

Meem, Deborah T. (Deborah Townsend),
1949-Finding out : an introduction to LGBT studies / Michelle A. Gibson, University of Cincinnati; Jonathan Alexander, University of California, Irvine; Deborah T. Meem, University of Cincinnati.— Second edition.

pages cm
Revised edition of: Finding out : an introduction to LGBT studies / Deborah T. Meem, Michelle A. Gibson, Jonathan F. Alexander, published c2010.
Includes bibliographical references and index.

ISBN 978-1-4522-3528-8 (pbk.)

1. Homosexuality—History. 2. Gays—History.
3. Bisexuals—History. 4. Transgender people—History. I. Gibson, Michelle. II. Alexander, Jonathan, 1967-III. Title.

HQ76.25.M45 2014
306.76′6—dc23          2012041939

This book is printed on acid-free paper.

13 14 15 16 17 10 9 8 7 6 5 4 3 2 1

# Brief Contents

# Detailed Contents

# Preface

The first edition of this book appeared in January 2009. In that same month, Barack Obama was inaugurated President of the United States. Obama brought with him a Democratic Congress (for the first two years of his presidency) and a firm commitment to progressive politics. In the few short years since then, much has occurred that impacts LGBT lives, both at home and worldwide. Some of these events have been positive, sometimes stunningly so. Consider, for instance, the repeal of Don't Ask, Don't Tell in the United States, the election of a lesbian prime minister in Iceland, and the re-credentialing of the International Lesbian and Gay Association (ILGA) as part of the United Nations Economic and Social Council. But other events have been shockingly negative. Here we think of the rash of suicides among teens perceived to be queer, or the evangelically inspired Anti-Homosexuality Bill in Uganda, or the refusal of Republican senators to support the Violence Against Women Act as long as it acknowledges LGBT victimization. None of this material appeared in the first edition of *Finding Out*, and the rapid pace of global change (compounded by the vast and instantaneous sharing of electronic information) necessitates continual reconsideration of the cultural, political, and personal experiences of LGBT people. So we offer you this second edition, updated but also theoretically deepened, in an attempt to fill gaps created by dizzying change.

While history continues to unfold around us, we remain committed to the pedagogical approach with which we began writing this book. The impulse to author *Finding Out* originated in our own classroom experiences. In teaching Introduction to LGBT Studies, we found that students ranged in background from advanced undergraduate Women's Studies majors well-versed in the rudiments of queer history and basic interdisciplinary methodology to first-year students who enrolled in the course after having met the first person they knew to be gay, lesbian, bisexual, or transgender. Before writing *Finding Out*, we noticed that much of what was available for use in sexuality studies courses was either too simplistic (celebratory texts that did little to engage students in theoretical analyses of issues related to sexuality) or too advanced (anthologies of theoretical articles that assumed a basic knowledge of the theories themselves and of general LGBT history and culture). Our students encountered the first type of text with enthusiasm, but as instructors, we felt frustrated by the absence in the texts themselves of tools for teaching analysis and encouraging more sophisticated thinking. The latter type of text had the students feeling frustrated; we spent much of the time in our courses simply helping students understand what they had read, a reality that left us wishing for more time to engage students in discussions that critiqued and connected those texts.

As far as we knew, no book existed that offered a general introduction to this subject matter grounded in an accessible theoretical framework. So we created *Finding Out* principally out of our own need to bring together texts and materials to facilitate the teaching of LGBT Studies at the introductory level. In other words, we designed *Finding Out* to lie between what we might call the *oversimplification* extreme and the *undersimplification* extreme. This has meant offering in each chapter analyses that penetrate below the surface to underlying ideas and ideologies while, at the same time, presenting the material clearly and accessibly enough to be interesting to a reader new to the subject matter. It has also meant foregrounding primary sources in the end-of-chapter readings. In fact, one of the most significant changes we made for this second edition concerns this very use of primary material. In many chapters, we removed descriptive newspaper article–type readings, replacing them with documents contemporaneous or directly related to events or people discussed in the chapter. For example, at the end of Chapter 6, Inclusion and Equality, we retained the excerpts from the South African Constitution but eliminated articles from the *New York Times* and the *Washington Blade*. In their place, we have included Secretary of State Hillary Rodham Clinton's 2011 International Human Rights Day speech in which she argued eloquently for the unity of gay rights and human rights. In general, we have tried to avoid including so much theoretical material as to render the discussion obscure and impenetrable by first- and second-year college students.

At the same time, our revision for this edition blends clear and understandable language with increased attention to theoretical implications. We attend to the resonance of our own ideas as well as to current theories of queerness that are often employed in academic analysis. In Chapter 11, Queer Transgressions, for instance, we have removed a literary selection in favor of two related pieces, Eve Kosofsky Sedgwick's groundbreaking 1993 article "Queer and Now" (a very early work of academic queer theory) and Michael Warner's 2012 rumination on the history and current condition of queer theory titled "Queer and Then." We feel these pieces illuminate and clarify the discussion of queer theory in Chapter 11 and prepare students for deeper work with theoretical texts in more advanced courses.

We recognize that LGBT Studies is a fairly new area of academic endeavor, and these courses still elicit strong negative reactions in certain places. It is not uncommon to make attempts at mitigating these reactions by approaching courses with LGBT content as attempts to educate toward tolerance, thereby garnering support for LGBT people. We begin with the assumption that teaching about diversity, including sexual and affectional diversity, needs no justification. Thus, as you will see, our language is not about tolerating diversity but about honoring it. We support organizations like Teaching Tolerance[1] which teach students about difference—including some nonnormative sexualities—as a way of becoming more tolerant citizens. We are concerned, though, that the notion of tolerance presupposes certain assumptions that we hope *Finding Out* challenges. The very idea of tolerance, for instance, to borrow Wendy Brown's words, "is necessitated by something one would prefer did not exist. It involves managing the presence of the undesirable" (25). The very act of tolerating, then, is an act of subordination, which places one group in the position of power—the power to confer tolerance— and another in the position of subordination—the desire to be tolerated. We hope for much more than this. In writing *Finding Out*, we have sought an intellectual approach that analyzes how sexuality has become a central component in contemporary self-understanding—individually, culturally, and politically. We also desire a recognition of how many queer cultures bring substantive, potentially transformative insights to bear on mainstream and dominant modes of being. Put simply, we value how our queer visions help us see the world in intellectually, politically, and personally capacious ways. We have tried to create an accessible introductory text—and doing so has entailed its own particular risks.

In aiming this book at a general audience, including those new to the academy, we have risked the criticism of being too introductory. While we intend *Finding Out* to be used in introductory-level college classes (in Sexuality Studies, of course, but also possibly in English composition, sociology, or other areas), we have taken pains not to condescend to our readers; we have sought to include considerable detail as well as in-depth discussion and theoretical grounding in order to maintain the intellectual challenge throughout. You may regret that many of the readings are excerpted rather than reproduced in their entirety. We have had to bow to the economic reality of word count requirements. These requirements may also mean that readers will not see everything they hope for in the text. We have tried

---

[1]Teaching Tolerance "provides educators with free educational materials that promote respect for differences and appreciation of diversity in the classroom and beyond" ("About Teaching Tolerance"). Supported by the Southern Poverty Law Center, this organization maintains a website that is accessed by educators whose desire is to help their students learn about and honor difference.

to choose topics that allow us to discuss issues through selected examples rather than exhaustive lists. *Finding Out* is, after all, a textbook, not an encyclopedia, and we have attempted to elucidate principles and ideas, knowing that much will be left out, even in a revised and updated edition.

Through our weaving together of primary documents, secondary sources, and our own commentary, we hope not only to illuminate events and ideas, but also to raise the vexed issue of who is empowered to tell the stories of LGBT lives. To be sure, from the time of Plato and Sappho through Walt Whitman and Gertrude Stein and James Baldwin to Sarah Schulman and Manuel Muñoz, homo-sexed individuals have written their stories. But the queer aspect of these stories has often been denied in a bid for safety and respect, or coded to avoid general understanding, or subsumed under the culture's dominant narratives, or produced in a location far from home and friends. Only in the last few decades have LGBT people—in a few particular places in the world—had the luxury of expressing their queerness publicly. In writing *Finding Out,* we claim the privilege of writing about our own people in our own language from our own point of view.

## Works Cited

"About Teaching Tolerance." *Tolerance.org: A Web Project of the Southern Poverty Law Center.* N.d. Web. <http://www.tolerance.org/teach/about/index.jsp>.

Brown, Wendy. *Regulating Aversion: Tolerance in the Age of Identity and Empire.* Princeton, NJ: Princeton UP, 2006. Print.

# Acknowledgments

From the very beginning, *Finding Out* has been a collaborative effort. Not only were we writing the book collaboratively (no mean feat!), but we have relied on the help of many colleagues, students, and friends in bringing this project to fruition.

For invaluable assistance in preparation of the first edition, we would like particularly to thank the following folks:

- Kimberly Campanello, the Queen of Permissions, without whom we might not have finished this project;
- Kai Kohlsdorf, the Knave of Permissions, who got the permissions ball rolling before passing it on to Kimberly;
- Matthew Conley, LaNaya Freeman, Nicole Karr, Emily Schweppe, Emma Southard, and Tracie Williams, undergraduate students in Deb's LGBT Studies class at the University of Cincinnati in Winter 2008, who produced the first version of the glossary that appears at the end of this book;
- Maika Arnold, David Bailey, Hannah Bare, Scott Cahall, Sarah Charlesworth, Kersha Deibel-Trotter, Jessica Elliott, Lucas Hartman, Eric Holtel, Tara King, Jane Meek, Keyra Miller, Lura Miller, Emma Plikerd, Jennifer Poon, Jamie Royce, Sarah Szekeresh, and Angelina Venti, the remainder of the Winter 2008 LGBT Studies class, who offered helpful suggestions and put up with small inconveniences as we field-tested *Finding Out*;
- Mary Bucklin and her Introduction to LGBT Studies class at Northern Kentucky University, who field-tested *Finding Out* during Fall 2007;
- Anne Runyan and the Department of Women's, Gender, and Sexuality Studies at University of Cincinnati, for general practical and moral support as we prepared the first edition of *Finding Out*;
- The Friends of Women's Studies, University of Cincinnati, for a grant to help with permissions;
- John Bryan, former Dean of University College at University of Cincinnati, for supporting our intention to offer Sexuality Studies courses;
- Janet Reed, former Head of the Language Arts Department in University College at the University of Cincinnati, for making sure LGBT Studies was consistently scheduled;

- Dorothy Smith, archivist extraordinaire, for teaching us how to produce high-resolution photos;
- Stuart Blersch, Professor Emeritus of English at University of Cincinnati, for information on gays and lesbians under the Nazi regime;
- Jana Braziel, Professor of English, University of Cincinnati, for references concerning diaspora;
- Liz Roccoforte (Women's Studies MA, 2005) for the insight that *Shrek 2* is at root a "home-to-meet-the-folks" coming-out story;
- Todd Armstrong, Editor of the first edition at Sage, and also Aja Baker, Katie Grim, Sarah Quesenberry, and Camille Herrera, Editorial Assistants at Sage;
- Reviewers of the text, who provided insightful and helpful comments throughout this project:

  Mary A. Armstrong (Department of Women's Studies, California Polytechnic State University, San Luis Obispo)

  John C. Beynon (Department of English, California State University, Fresno)

  Stephanie Brzuzy (Department of Social Work, Xavier University)

  Dane S. Claussen (Department of Journalism and Mass Communication, Point Park University)

  Stefanie K. Dunning (Department of English, Miami University)

  Bradley Gangnon (Department of Communication and Theatre Arts, College of St. Scholastica)

  Carol Guess (Department of English and American Cultural Studies, Western Washington University)

  David M. Halperin (Department of English, University of Michigan)

  Laura A. Harris (Department of English, World Literature, and Black Studies, Pitzer College)

  Keguro Macharia (Department of Rhetoric, University of Illinois, Urbana-Champaign)

  Sarah-Hope Parmeter (Department of Writing, University of California, Santa Cruz)

  David A. Powell (LGBT Studies Program, Hofstra University)

  Meredith Raimondo (Department of Comparative American Studies, Oberlin College)

  Joyleen Valero Sapinoso (Women's Studies and LGBT Studies, University of Maryland)

  Cole Woodcox (Department of English, Truman State University)

  Gust A. Yep (Department of Speech & Communication Studies, San Francisco State University)

  Naida Zukic (Department of Speech Communication, Southern Illinois University, Carbondale)

For assistance in preparing the second edition of *Finding Out*, we thank:

- Matthew Byrnie, our Editor at Sage, who guided us through the revisions for this new edition;
- Stephanie Palermini, also at Sage, who diligently and scrupulously tracked down information about readings and pictures;

- Loraine Hutchins, who provided insights into our coverage of bisexuality;
- Deb's numerous students, in particular those enrolled in the winter 2012 LGBT Studies class, who read the book carefully and offered copious and helpful feedback.

Finally, we wish to thank the people in our lives who have supported us while we have worked on this multiyear project: Deb thanks her mother, Barbara T. Meem, for reading and commenting on a draft of the manuscript; Michelle thanks her sister Julie Edwards, whose courage and strength continue to inspire; and Jonathan thanks his husband, Mack McCoy, for living with this project for many years.

# Introduction: To the Reader

In the Middle Ages, the Catholic Church prescribed the death penalty for same-sex erotic behavior, but also created liturgies for same-sex marriages. In the late 19th century, European sexologist Richard von Krafft-Ebing argued for same-sex desire as an illness to be "cured" at the same time that his contemporary Havelock Ellis saw it as a variation of human typology. In 1977, Anita Bryant's Save Our Children organization successfully defeated a gay positive human rights ordinance in Dade County, Florida; at the same time, Harvey Milk was elected as the first openly gay member of the San Francisco Board of Supervisors. And, in the first decade of the 21st century, U.S. President George W. Bush supported a constitutional amendment banning gay marriage while his counterparts in other nations—such as Spain, South Africa, and Canada—enacted constitutional protections for lesbian and gay people. So much of what we know to be "fact" about lesbian, gay, bisexual, and transgender (LGBT) life and culture is given to us as story, as narratives that transmit ideas, information, and values about who queer people are. But who tells those stories, and what do they tell us?

*Finding Out* is a book about these and many other questions. It narrates and analyzes some of the ways LGBT and queer people have been represented—and have come to represent themselves—in a variety of fields: literature, history, the arts, the sciences, media, and politics. But if *Finding Out* is, as its subtitle indicates, an introduction to LGBT Studies, then what does that mean, exactly? The very act of introducing a topic is often about the telling of stories. One common assignment given by instructors who want students to see the connections between what they are studying in the classroom and the world outside is the interview. The storytelling involved in the interview process creates connections between teller and listener and often between past and present. We hope that the stories we tell in *Finding Out* will help create (or, in the case of readers who are already somewhat familiar with LGBT culture and history, capitalize upon) a similar kind of connection.

But we also recognize that the process of telling and retelling these stories is challenging. As you can see in the examples above, narratives of LGBT experience have often embodied a simultaneity of coexisting, yet conflicting, forces. Given this, we have written *Finding Out* to enact a kind of theorized storytelling, a simultaneous offering and critique of narratives that contribute to our understanding of terms like *lesbian, gay, bisexual,* and *transgender.* As you read, you will see this theorized storytelling consistently at work. On one hand, we have the opportunity to highlight the many ways same-sex desires and gender nonconformity have existed throughout history. On the other hand, the stories told about those desires and about that nonconformity are often very complex. At different times and in different locations, people tell very different stories about their desires, even if, on the surface, the similarities tempt us to understand their stories as like our own. Paying attention to critical differences, however, is an important part of understanding not only how same-sex desires and gender variance were experienced in the past, but also how they have come to exist today.

## Some Theoretical Starting Places

As you can see, our approach to LGBT history, culture, and politics is not simply to record facts. History is rarely, if ever, as simple as the recorded facts. Like most students and scholars, we begin with theories about what forces have impacted the evolution of LGBT histories and the emergence of LGBT cultures. We assume first that any historical survey must be undertaken with great care and caution. In writing about the history of same-sex desires and the formation of LGBT identities, we acknowledge a lineage of queer thinking. We attempt to attend carefully to Judith Halberstam's notion of *perverse presentism*. Halberstam warns that anyone writing about the past needs to consider carefully how contemporary notions and constructions of desire and identity can easily be imposed on past persons, incidents, or issues. She argues instead for a "perversely presentist model of historical analysis, a model, in other words, that avoids the trap of simply projecting contemporary understandings back in time, but one that can apply insights from the present to conundrums of the past" (52-3). When we write about the past, we do not assume that contemporary labels are necessarily useful to describe past desires. What looks like a gay, lesbian, bi, or trans identity from our current perspective may have meant something very different to people in the past.

Second, we have attempted to highlight the diversity of same-sex desire and gender variance. Understanding that queer experiences are complex, we honor the varieties and diversities of that experience by looking not only at gay and lesbian lives but also at bisexual and trans lives. Terminology takes on particular importance in this context, for the attempt to avoid constructing the past in contemporary terms often means taking great care with the way we choose to name. *Lesbian,* for instance, shifts in meaning over time from a geographical term to a poetic style to an identity marker. *Gay* as a slang term originally referred to a (female) prostitute. The meaning has since slipped to delineate a sexually transgressive subculture, a black lesbian, and a homosexual man. *Bisexual* originally functioned as a synonym for what we now call *heterosexual,* a term that was itself originally coined to describe nonprocreative sexuality between men and women. Today, the term *bisexual* refers to a person who experiences sexual desire for both men and women. The terms *transgender, transsexual, transman, tranny boi, FtM, MtF,* and so forth describe varieties of role nonconformism based on either biological sex or gender, assuming that these are not only socially constructed but also fluid. *Queer* is perhaps the most elusive of such terms. Once a taunt used against homosexuals, queer has been reclaimed by a variety of activists and theorists as an umbrella term to signify the diversity of LGBT identities and to assert positively the value of difference. However, many object to the term, arguing that it erases important differences among the L, the G, the B, and the T.

Third, we believe that the same awareness needs also to be applied when we think cross-culturally; while same-sex desires might imply gay, lesbian, or bisexual identity in the United States, this is not necessarily true in other cultures, particularly outside of the Global North. We reject the notion of a global gay identity, and we believe that it is imperative to understand sexual and gendered experiences as contextualized by the time and place in which they occur. We refuse, for instance, to fix the term *gay* as a prerequisite for global interaction and coalition. For it is in the permutations of this term and its legacies, as they circulate around the globe in queer organizations and gatherings, from Mexico City's Semana Cultural Lésbico-Gay to New Delhi's Campaign for Lesbian Rights and Beijing's International Women's Conference, from Buenos Aires's Marcha de Orgullo Gay to the diasporic South Asian and Latino Lesbian and Gay Pride Parade in Queens, New York, that the future of the human and civil rights of queers also lies (Cruz-Malavé and Manalansan 4).

We hope, in other words, to examine same-sex and nonnormative desires in various locations worldwide not with the purpose of fitting them into a grand **teleological** narrative linking globalization with sexual freedom. Rather, we identify connections and similarities among movements and experiences as we observe them, and where possible, we allow agents to tell their own stories. We intend these stories to trouble **monolithic** social narratives, believing with Gayatri Gopinath that "essentialized concepts of national and diasporic identity are most fruitfully contested from a 'queer diasporic' positionality" (150). However, while we attempt to offer a sense of the global experience of LGBT people, same-sex practices, and gender variance, we must acknowledge that our strengths as scholars lie in the history and culture of LGBT people in the Global North in general and in the United States in particular. Still, *Finding Out* ranges widely across major events, issues, and ideas pertaining to nonnormative sexualities and gender variance around the world.

Fourth, we believe that the experiences of race, social class, and sexuality are intertwined in compelling ways, and we have attempted throughout *Finding Out* to represent those intersections. Too often, LGBT and Sexuality Studies have been dominated by scholars who have paid scant attention to issues of race and social class. Failing to pay such attention, however, robs our understanding of same-sex histories, identities, and issues of important dimensions. Our experiences are multiply inflected—not just by sexuality but also by race, ethnicity, and social class. For instance, to understand gays and lesbians participating as artists in the Harlem Renaissance of the 1920s is to see those artists not just as gays and lesbians but also as African-American gays and lesbians living in a racist and homophobic culture. In terms of social class, it is important to understand that the primary participants in the Stonewall Riots of 1969 were working-class drag queens; the riots occurred in a specifically working-class context. However, since 1969, gay and lesbian rights organizations in the United States have come to be dominated by middle-class people and middle-class concerns. How did this happen? Answering that question involves looking critically not only at issues of sexuality but also at issues of social class. Doing so, however, can be intellectually—and personally—challenging.

In *Disidentifications: Queers of Color and the Performance of Politics*, José Esteban Muñoz writes, "Subjects who are outside the purview of dominant public spheres encounter obstacles in enacting identifications. Minority identifications are often neglectful or antagonistic to other minoritarian positionalities" (8). In the United States, for instance, we generally see identity in binary terms—of color or white, gay or straight. A person occupying multiple identity categories may be met with incomprehension and even hostility both from the society in general and from the minority groups with which one identifies. A working-class Asian-American lesbian, for instance, may have her queer identification overlooked by a dominant culture that sees her first and foremost as *not white*, while some in her ethnic community may find her queerness disgraceful to herself, to her family, and to Asian-Americans in general. Examining such complexities is crucial if we are to honor the varieties of LGBT and queer experience as well as understand some of the difficulties that people face, individually and collectively, in their searches for equality, freedom, and community. To enrich our understanding of these dimensions of experience, *Finding Out* actively marks class, race, and ethnicity both in general discussion and separated out for deeper analysis.

Finally, because of the complexities we have discussed, we assume that the study of LGBT sexualities, same-sex desires, and gender variance is necessarily an interdisciplinary enterprise, and *Finding Out* borrows extensively from scholarship in fields including history and the social sciences, the arts and humanities, popular culture and media studies, and politics and law. We have attempted to represent as carefully as possible both the methodologies and the findings generated by scholars in these various fields—and we have learned much ourselves from thinking about queer lives and cultures from an interdisciplinary perspective. When we talk about *identity* and *culture,* we are talking about constructs that are simultaneously personal, aesthetic, social, cultural, and political. Stated in political terms, what individual LGBT people experience is important—but not just to the individual—it is important for the way it speaks to and interacts with the experiences of others.

## About this Book

We initially envisioned *Finding Out* as a textbook for use in a wide variety of college courses that focus on LGBT identities, communities, and sexualities. To that end, we have included in the text a number of features designed to advance your thinking— whether you are reading this book for a class, as part of a reading group, or on your own—as you find out more about LGBT/ queer lives and cultures. For instance, throughout the chapters, Lambda Links—indicated by lambda (λ) signs—alert readers that an issue under discussion is related to a similar topic in another chapter. You can use these like "hot links" on a website to follow threads of content through- out the book. Then, at the end of each chapter, you will find sets of questions and suggestions for further reading. These are designed as teaching tools for use by stu- dents in classroom environments or by individual readers who wish to think or read more deeply about issues addressed in the chapter. They are not intended to be comprehensive; they will not address all of the issues in a given chapter. We urge you to use the discussion questions to continue your own exploration of the many con- texts in which same-sex desires and gender variance exist. Finally, **boldfaced** terms in each chapter are defined in the glossary at the end of *Finding Out.*

Part of the challenge of writing *Finding Out* has been recognizing the interdis- ciplinary nature of LGBT Studies. To address this interdisciplinarity, *Finding Out* has four large sections: History, Politics, Literature and the Arts, and Media. These four sections are subdivided into chapters. The first section, History, introduces you to and surveys the various ways sexuality has been configured in a variety of cultural, scientific, and psychological arenas from ancient Greek and Roman culture to the contemporary world. Chapter 1, Before Identity: The Ancient World Through the 19th Century, focuses on same-sex relationships, gender bending, and other aspects of queerness from antiquity to the 19th century, specifically elucidating the pre-identity history of queerness that either helped shape or stood in opposition to later, more formal, claims to queer identity. Picking up the historical thread in the late 19th century, Chapter 2, Sexology: Constructing the Modern Homosexual, describes how medical and sexological models at the **fin de siècle** pathologized a wide variety of sexual "deviances." This chapter explores some of the pressures that led to the development of this model. In the context of the pathologization of homosexuality by the psychological establishment in the early 20th century, Chapter 3, Toward Liberation, examines the rise of queer liberation movements. We end this chapter with the removal of homosexuality from the *Diagnostic and Statistical Manual of Mental Disorders.* Then, recognizing that many LGBT people in the English-speaking world view the Stonewall riots in New York City as a kind of turning point in LGBT history, Chapter 4, Stonewall and Beyond, focuses on queer Americans as we integrated the lessons learned from other liberation movements into our own struggles for human and civil rights.

The second section, Politics, explores how sex and sexuality—particularly queer sexualities—remain a hot topic in contemporary political arenas. Chapters in this section challenge you to think deeply and critically about the political dimensions of LGBT life and culture, with discussions ranging from LGBT identity politics to a consideration of the challenges queer theory issues to such a politics. These chapters also provide an examination of the uses (and abuses) of strategies of assimilation as well as exploration of intersections among LGBT and other marginalized identities and communities. Chapter 5, Nature, Nurture, and Identity, focuses on one of the central ongoing debates about queerness: whether homosexuality is a biological essence or a social construction. Chapter 6, Inclusion and Equality, examines a related set of debates regarding the integration or exclusion of queers in society, focusing particularly on the complex and sometimes conflicting attitudes that create the tensions within the discussion. Such debates about inclusion and exclusion also occur within queer communities, and Chapter 7, Queer Diversities, details the parameters of some of those debates. Finally, Chapter 8, Intersectionalities, looks specifically at how race, social class, gender, and sex are aspects of identity that intersect with queerness. This chapter highlights common struggles across different identities as well as divergences in how multiply identified individuals and groups understand and represent their experiences.

In Section 3, Literature and the Arts, we consider how the arts have long been a space in which homo-, bi-, and trans-erotic desires and identities have been explored and interrogated. Chapters in this section include a number of primary texts—both literary and graphical—that highlight how many artists, working in a variety of forms and genres, have grappled with the meaning of queer sexualities. Our critical introductions and discussions frame each literary or artistic text. Chapter 9, Homo-sexed Art and Literature, ranges from Walt Whitman to Audre Lorde, Michelangelo to Frida Kahlo. Our focus is on art and literature that is well-known in LGBT communities, and we include examples of political and activist art in addition to purely aesthetic work. Moving away from the realm of "high" art, Chapter 10, Lesbian Pulp Novels and Gay Physique Pictorials, focuses on the two main forms of popular homo-sexed entertainment during the middle of the 20th century in the United States; this chapter illustrates how popular culture helps solidify a sense of queer identity. Chapter 11, Queer Transgressions, notes how some works of art and literature intentionally challenge our understanding of sexuality with highly provocative images and rhetoric. This chapter presents material that encourages analysis of sexuality that runs deeper than traditional distinctions among sexual preferences; such work questions normalizing assumptions. Chapter 12, Censorship and Moral Panic, considers controversies about homo-sexed art and documents particular cases of censorship motivated by homophobia.

Chapters in the final section, Media, discuss mass media, including television, movies, the Internet, and alternative publications. Chapter 13, Film and Television, examines the long and complicated history of queers in film and TV in the 20th century. The explosion of lesbian and gay images beginning in the 1990s represented a turning point in queer visibility. In this chapter, we approach this history by considering the ways visibility can operate as a double-edged sword, diluting the power of underground community while ostensibly promoting mainstream acceptance. We also know that contemporary LGBT people find representation and community through the Internet, which can provide queer community in a virtual world. Chapter 14, Queers and the Internet, discusses myths about the Internet as well as social networking and activist sites and their uses. And, Chapter 15, The Politics of Location: Alternative Media and the Search for Queer Space, describes how a variety of nonmainstream media have assisted LGBT people in developing both identity and community. We situate our discussion of such media in terms of how a variety of queer people use them to foster and develop a livable space in which to encounter, explore, and build a queer culture.

We hope that you will experience *Finding Out* as lively, provocative, and challenging. You will not agree with everything you read, and at times, you will probably feel that there is much we have left out—and you will be right. But we believe that *Finding Out* offers a substantive and critical approach to thinking about the history of sexuality, the emergence of LGBT identities, and the development of a queer culture. If it prompts you to find out more about queerness, then it will have accomplished its primary goal. So, with that in mind, we invite you to start finding out. . . .

# Works Cited

Cruz-Malavé, Arnaldo and Martin F. Manalansan IV. "Introduction: Dissident Sexualities/ Alternative Globalisms." *Queer Globalizations: Citizenship and the Afterlife of Colonialism.* Ed. Arnaldo Cruz-Malavé and Martin F. Manalansan IV. New York: NYU P, 2002. 1–10. Print.

Gopinath, Gayatri. "Local Sites/Global Contexts: The Transnational Trajectories of Deepa Mehta's *Fire.*" *Queer Globalizations: Citizenship and the Afterlife of Colonialism.* Ed. Arnaldo Cruz-Malavé and Martin F. Manalansan IV. New York: NYU P, 2002. 149–161. Print.

Halberstam, Judith. *Female Masculinity.* Durham, NC: Duke University Press, 1998. Print.

Muñoz, José Esteban. *Disidentificantions: Queers of Color and the Performance of Politics.* Minneapolis: U of Minnesota P, 1999. Print.

# SECTION I

# History

To understand contemporary formations of identity and community clustering around sex and sexuality, it is important to have a historical understanding of how sexuality has been produced, constructed, and contested. This section introduces students to and surveys the various ways in which sexuality has been configured in a variety of cultural, scientific, and psychological arenas from ancient Greek and Roman culture to the contemporary world.

# CHAPTER 1

# Before Identity

## The Ancient World Through the 19th Century

> This chapter focuses on same-sex relationships, gender bending, and other aspects of queerness from antiquity to the 19th century, focusing specifically on elucidating the complex pre-identity history of queerness that either helped shape or stood in opposition to later, more formal claims to queer identity.

Homosexuality has been conceived of as an innate or acquired identity only in the past century and a half, but same-sex practices, desires, and intimacies, as well as gender variance, can be found in nearly every culture in recorded history. Until the "invention" of homosexual identity, these practices and desires typically were not described in written records; instead, their existence is revealed in words in national lexicons (such as *skesana*, or boy-wife, in South Africa or *kojobesia* in Ghana) or in laws against same-sex sexual practices (such as the "ignorance" forbidden in Qur'an 27:55). In some communities, including many in the pre-Columbian Americas and in India, males who adopted female gender had special shamanic or ceremonial places in cultural practice. In ancient Egypt, two men who served as manicurists to the king were buried together, pictured in the same stylized embrace that characterized the depiction of husband-wife pairs in formal funerary art.

In Greece, the social and sexual relationship between an older man and a youth represented the ideal form of love. A 2,000-year-old rock painting in Zimbabwe shows male-male sex. This chapter presents a brief glimpse into historical records that imply the existence of same-sex intimacies in various cultures prior to the 19th-century conceptualization of homosexual identity.

We do not claim that these historical records attest to the presence of homosexuality or gay identity across cultures and time. Contemporary scholars debate whether such is the case. Some thinkers—Charley Shively and Blanche Wiesen Cook, to name two—have operated on the assumption that the sexual categories observable in the Global North today are "universal, static, and permanent, suitable for the analysis of all human beings and all societies" (Padgug 56). Others argue that sexuality has a history and has evolved over time. Robert Padgug, for instance, observes that "[s]exuality is relational" (58)—in other words, how any given social group or culture thinks of sexuality relates to historical time and place. Historian Stephen Garton argues that "sexuality has emerged as a major field of historical inquiry" over the past half century; thus, "instead of being something natural, [sexuality] came to be seen by historians as subject to historical change" (28–29). One major consequence of this shift in our understanding about sexuality is that most historians are careful not to read historical records of same-sex desire as gay or homosexual in the contemporary sense.

**Figure 1.1**  Court manicurists Niankhkhnum and Khnumhotep, from the necropolis at Saqqara, Egypt.

We should keep in mind that casting an eye to the past to find evidence of gay, lesbian, or trans identity is to assume that history can and should be read through contemporary lenses. It is also to assume that people and groups of the past understood their sexual intimacies in the same way we do. These are problematic assumptions. This is one moment when it might be useful to refer back to the theory of perverse presentism discussed in the introduction to this book [λ Introduction]. It highlights the need to avoid imposing current ideas about and constructions of sexuality on the past at the same time that it acknowledges the historical expression of sexual intimacies and practices that seem connected to current LGBT identifications and practices. To understand past sexual practices—and to honor them—we, like many contemporary historians of sexuality, refrain from identifying historical representations of same-sex desires as specifically gay, lesbian, or homosexual. Likewise, regarding past instances of apparent gender variance, we avoid the terms *transgender* and *transsexual*.

At the same time, while the Egyptian manicurists who were buried together may not be gay in contemporary parlance, we acknowledge that it has been very important and empowering for many contemporary LGBT people to discover and identify what looks like same-sex intimacy and gender variance in the annals of history. Such identification has been a crucial part of finding out about ourselves as contemporary queers and LGBT folk. It has at times provided a sense of history to those who have found themselves left out of world histories that stigmatize or simply ignore **gender** and sexual "outlaws" or nonconformists.

## Greek Paiderastia

Gay men and lesbians often cite the ancient Greeks as their historical forbears—and for good reason. The ancient Greeks developed ways of recognizing and even honoring same-sex desires. Probably the principal source for ancient Greek *paiderastia* (or **pederasty**: love between a man and a boy) is Homer's *Iliad*. In that epic, likely composed in the eighth or ninth century BCE, the Greek hero Achilles, feeling slighted by the king, withdraws from the fighting outside Troy. His youthful lover Patroclus, fearing that Achilles is losing honor, puts on Achilles's armor and goes out to fight in his place. The less powerful Patroclus is killed; his death spurs Achilles to return to the battlefield and defeat the Trojan Hector.

This model of heroic love was absorbed into Greek cultural life in the centuries following the *Iliad*. In Plato's *Symposium*, written in 360 BCE, Phaedrus declares, "I know not any greater blessing to a young man who is beginning life than a virtuous lover or to the lover than a beloved youth" (5). A Greek same-sex pair included the *erastes*, or older man, and an *eromenos*, or youth. The eromenos was typically a postadolescent between the ages of about 12 and 18; once a young man's beard sprouted, he was considered past the age of eromenos. The Greeks did not favor same-sex relationships between men of similar age; the erastes-eromenos pairing was designed to provide pleasure and friendship for the older erastes in exchange for protection, training, and social advantage for the younger eromenos. Same-sex attachments did not preclude heterosexual marriage, but the pederastic combination of spiritual and physical connection represented a higher kind of love, more conducive to the military, political, and educational responsibilities of the (male) citizen of the Greek state.

Nearly all literary production was accomplished by men, and women in the classical world were generally depicted as "goddesses, whores, wives, and slaves" (Pomeroy). Ancient Greek women were certainly not invisible in their lives, but they might as well have been if all we knew of them was what the literature contained. A notable exception was the poet Sappho, who lived in the seventh century BCE on the island of Lesbos (thus the word *lesbian*). Sappho was known in her day as an unparalleled lyric poet, meaning that her poems were written to be accompanied by a lyre. Her refinements upon common lyric meter led poets after her time to attempt writing in *Sapphic meter*. Little of Sappho's work has survived, and that which has is mostly in fragments, yet she is still known for her sensuous and personal poetic voice. Many young, wealthy Greek women were sent to Lesbos to study the arts with Sappho. Much of Sappho's surviving poetry is love lyrics to these young women.

**Find Out More** in the Sappho poems at the end of this chapter.

## Pederasty in Other Early Cultures: The Middle East and Asia

The Qur'an sends a mixed message concerning same-sex desires. On one hand, it specifically forbids same-sex intercourse on earth; on the other, the virtuous man will be surrounded by beautiful boys in Paradise. Indeed, historically, a long tradition of man-boy love exists in the Arab world. The practice of *liwat* (pederasty) involved a relationship between a *luti* (a man with a predilection for beardless boys) and an *amrad* (unpaid beardless boy) or a *murd mu'ajirin* (paid boy). Abu Nuwas, well-known Iraqi poet of the eighth to ninth century CE, began his career as amrad to the older poet Walibah ibn al-Hubab. By the time of Sultan Mahmud of Ghazni (in present-day Afghanistan) around 1000 CE, liwat had come to represent a type of ideal love. Sultan Mahmud and his slave Ayaz were devoted partners; Mahmud later appointed Ayaz ruler of Lahore (in present-day Pakistan). Like Greek pederasty, liwat signified passion and pleasure for the luti as well as affection and social advancement for the amrad.

**Find Out More** in the Abu Nuwas poem at the end of this chapter.

In Japan, endorsed courtly same-sex desire was known as *wakashu-do,* or the way of the boy. It first appears in written records beginning in the Heian (Peace and Tranquility) period (794–1185 CE). Its rise in popularity

**Figure 1.2** Sultan Mahmud and his slave Ayaz.

**Find Out More** in the selection from "Bamboo Clappers Strike the Hateful Number" at the end of this chapter.

in the 12th century seems to have coincided with that of the *No* and *Kabuki* theater traditions, which featured boy actors. Wakashu-do, like Greek and Islamic pederasty, was built around the pedagogic relationship between an adult man and a youth. Like the others, it also flourished in the upper classes of society; it was specifically valued among the samurai in the 16th and 17th centuries. Beginning around 1600, as Japan began to be influenced by Western Christianity, wakashu-do gradually lost favor; when the Americans arrived, armed and wealthy, in 1854, Japanese same-sex desires sank into invisibility.

**Find Out More** in the "Song of Beau Wang" at the end of this chapter.

In China, a powerful male-male culture surrounding opera performers lasted throughout the Qing dynasty (1644–1911). Upper-class opera patrons saw the attractive adolescents playing female roles as models of feminine beauty; these young men were also trained as catamites, or boys for hire. In postimperial 20th-century China, the opera (and, by extension, its connection with male-male love) was scorned as a throwback to the time of feudal excesses.

## Gender Variance in Pre-Columbian America and India

**Figure 1.3** We-wha, c. 1886.

In many Native American tribes, before first contact with white missionaries or settlers, a person who possessed characteristics of both genders was thought of as a *two-spirit,* one who understands male and female. This border knowledge carried with it spiritual and physical power; thus, two-spirit individuals were particularly suited to function as shamans or healers and were valued in some tribal groups accordingly. In the centuries before contact with Europeans, tribal languages developed various words for the two-spirit person: *nadle* (Navajo), *lhamana* (Zuñi), *winkte* (Lakota), and so on. European explorers brought with them the term *berdache,* now often used to describe Native American post-contact gender nonconformists. A berdache typically switched gender entirely. We-wha (c. 1849–1896), a Zuñi, dressed as a woman and did women's work exclusively. We-wha was highly skilled in weaving and pottery making and was also a central figure in the pueblo's spiritual life. In 1886, she accompanied her white friend, anthropologist Matilda Coxe Stevenson, to Washington, DC; no one, including Stevenson, knew at the time that We-wha was born male. While some recorded instances exist of females appropriating male roles as berdaches, this seems to have been rare and less demarcated (Roscoe).

Like berdaches, *hijras* in India and Pakistan are biological males who live as women. Hijras trace their existence to the **eunuchs** who served as guards to nobility during the Mughal Empire (1526–1858). Some hijras are intersexed, some are transsexual, and some are castrated; many have been rejected by their families of origin and form communities with other hijras, earning their livings by prostitution. They often live in communal settings in households comprising several *chelas* (disciples) and supervised by a *guru*. Hijras play a cultural role in the larger community, frequently appearing uninvited to dance and sing at weddings and births of male children. Their role is to entreat the deities to bestow fertility on the husband or male child (Thadani).

# Same-Sex Relationships and Desires in Judeo-Christian Cultures

The Torah includes 613 laws (365 prohibitions and 248 positive commandments), which are known as the Mosaic code. Two of these, Leviticus 18:22 and 20:13, prohibit a man from lying "with mankind as with womankind," calling this practice "abomination" and stating the penalty as death. In addition, the story of Sodom and Gomorrah (Genesis 19) is often read as describing God's punishment of Sodom for homosexuality (thus gay men have been called *sodomites*), although some commentators, notably John Boswell, have pointed out that the men of Sodom appear to sin more through failure of hospitality than sexual depravity. In the New Testament, Jesus is silent on the subject, but Paul in his epistles (Romans 1:25–27, I Corinthians 6:9) castigates both men and women who engage in same-sex sexual acts. Some scholars cast doubt on Paul's intention, saying that the Greek words he uses for those engaging in same-sex sexual behaviors (*malakoi* and *arsenokoitai* rather than the more common term *paideraste*) are ambiguous in meaning. Moreover, some biblical stories seem to honor same-sex affection and intimacy. The friendship between David and Jonathan, as well as the close relationship between Ruth and Naomi, frequently have been cited by lesbian and gay people as instances of same-sex intimacy that are depicted in the Bible as idealized and worthy of respect. Still, it is clear that Judeo-Christian tradition generally forbids same-sex sexual practices for both men and women.

During the first centuries of the Roman Empire, the Lex Scantinia (or Scantinian Law) governed sexual practices. It seems to have stipulated that most forms of same-sex sexual activity were illegal and punishable by a fine. After the *Constantinian change*, whereby the emperor Constantine christianized the Roman Empire in the fourth century CE, the punishment for same-sex sexual behavior (then classified as a "crime against nature" following Paul's charge in Romans 1:26) was upgraded to death. In the Middle Ages, such behavior, particularly **sodomy**, was reclassified as heresy, and during the 15th century, a number of men were beheaded or burned at the stake for having committed the "crime of Sodom." This period also saw sodomy referred to as the *peccatum mutum* or silent sin, that is, a transgression that could not be spoken of. Most of what was written on this subject focused on men exclusively, although as early as the fifth century, St. Augustine warned his sister not to indulge in carnal or immodest love in the convent where she was a nun (Betteridge). In general, female-female sexuality

**Find Out More** in Sophia's spell at the end of this chapter.

was regarded as a lesser offense than male-male sexuality for various reasons: lacking a penis, a woman could not commit the sin of "spilling the seed." Lesbian sex was widely considered to be merely a preliminary activity preparing a woman for marriage; a sexually aggressive woman was thought to be emulating men—in other words, aspiring to a more perfect state of nature. Still, proto-lesbian sexuality was not condoned, especially when it appeared to function as a throwback to pre-Christian Wiccan or pagan religions. For example, early Church fathers (third and fourth centuries CE) disapproved of and ridiculed "binding spells" used by Upper Egyptian women to attract other women (Brooten). Later, a woman could be severely punished for **cross-dressing,** and it is now believed that during the so-called burning times (the prosecution and killing of witches in Europe between the 14th and 18th centuries CE), many of the female victims were women who violated accepted gender practice.

At the same time as the Church excoriated same-sex "heresy" and executed some of its practitioners, certain liturgical elements within it acknowledged, even cele-

**Figure 1.4**   Icon of Sts. Serge and Bacchus, seventh century CE.

brated, same-sex relationships. Saints Serge and Bacchus, Roman soldiers of the third century CE, and also Christian converts and martyrs, are said to have been "joined in life." A document from the 10th century describes Serge as the "sweet companion and lover" of Bacchus; their image is depicted on an icon found in the monastery of St. Catherine on Mt. Sinai, with Jesus appearing as *pronubus* or best man between them.

In fact, a number of Offices of Same-Sex Union exist, dating from the 7th to the 16th centuries CE; most of these were written in Greek or Serbian Slavonic (and thus originate in Eastern Orthodox Christianity), although a very few are in Latin. It is not clear exactly what kind of partnership was envisioned by the authors of these rituals, but certainly they indicate an ecclesiastical acceptance of binding same-sex relationships as part of Church history (Boswell, *Same-Sex Unions*).

> **Find Out More** in the "Order for Solemnization of Same-Sex Union" at the end of this chapter.

## Desires for Identity

In the year 1101 CE, Anselm, Archbishop of Canterbury, issued a decree against clerical marriage. Commentators immediately observed an increase in sodomy among priests; offenders were excommunicated, and their crimes and sentences were published weekly in churches throughout England. Instead of eliminating sodomy by shaming the perpetrators, publishing the crimes seems to have caused heightened interest among male parishioners, who spent considerable time discussing who did what to whom. As a result, the publication ceased but not before revealing the existence of a subculture of men who would be glad for an excuse to gather (Betteridge).

Most intriguing about this story is the persistence of the unspoken community, even in an atmosphere of condemnation and harsh punishment. Extremely severe consequences were the norm in cases of sodomy. The 1598 case of Ludwig Boudin serves as a dramatic example. Boudin, a married pastry baker from Frankfurt, Germany, was accused of sodomy by a jealous competitor. The witnesses mostly recalled events from years in the past, speaking of Boudin as propositioning them when he was drunk; none of them described any activity more serious than an unwelcome advance on Boudin's part. Unable to prove the charge but inclined to find the defendant guilty, the city council subjected Boudin to extensive torture, hoping to force a confession. Repeated applications of the leg screw and the rack failed to achieve the desired result, although they did weaken Boudin to the point where the council decided that further torture would be counterproductive. Boudin was ultimately sentenced to time in the pillory, followed by banishment for life from Frankfurt (Hergemöller).

The Italian Renaissance (15th century) led to a somewhat more open attitude toward male-male sexuality as the revival of classical standards for art and literature rekindled ancient Greek and Roman ideas about, for instance, male beauty and pederasty. Despite the Inquisition breathing down his neck, the Franciscan friar Antonio Rocco wrote *Alcibiades the Schoolboy* in about 1631. This book is the story of the attempted (and finally successful) seduction of a youth by his teacher Filotimo; it is a type of extended Socratic argument in which the two parties engage in prolonged intellectual and flirtatious give-and-take before the teacher's inevitable victory. Alcibiades of Rocco's novel is named after Socrates's young lover in Plato's *Symposium,* and Filotimo argues for a return to socially sanctioned pederasty as practiced by the Greeks. Various modern writers have called *Alcibiades the Schoolboy* the first gay novel because Filotimo describes himself as a man who loves other men rather than women. Filotimo, then, does more than perform homosexual acts; he identifies himself as a homosexual, an early example of a man whom we in the contemporary world might understand as gay.

In the Middle Ages—and through the 19th century, in fact—women had little access to either schools or public establishments, and their general disenfranchisement from church or government tended to isolate them in their homes. Church doctrine pictured women as sexually insatiable and accordingly created rules confining them to the "natural" purpose of sex—that is, procreation. A woman who wished to move freely in the world and initiate sexual activity with another woman would of necessity have to pass as a man, and indeed passing women were most frequently punished for the sin of *mulier cum muliere fornicatio* (woman-with-woman fornication). For example, in 1477, a German woman named Katherina Hetzeldorfer was drowned in the Rhine River after being convicted of an unnamed crime, which involved dressing as a man and "abducting" and seducing at least two women using a leather **dildo**. So skillful was Hetzeldorfer in the use of this device that both her female partners testified in court that they believed her to be a man; of course, had they admitted they knew she was female, they might have shared her fate (Puff). Hetzeldorfer was an early example of a passing woman unlucky enough to get caught; her case and others like it illustrate the difficulties facing women who sought either freedom of movement or sex with other women. Though they could operate in the world as men, they lacked a community of women with similar desires.

If Professor Filotimo in Antonio Rocco's *Alcibiades the Schoolboy* represented the first modern (i.e., self-conscious) gay man, then Anne Lister (1791–1840) was the first modern lesbian. Lister was a wealthy Yorkshire landowner whose social class provided her with the freedom to dress as she pleased and to court women and with the education she needed to write down her exploits in elaborate, coded journals. Like Filotimo, Lister describes her predilection for same-sex desire as part of her nature: "I love and only love the fairer sex and thus beloved by them in turn, my heart revolts from any love but theirs" (145).

## Romantic Friendships and Boston Marriages

Contemporary historians of sexuality have recorded and discussed a variety of same-sex sexual and romantic arrangements between women. While a passing working-class **Tommy** or a wealthy Anne Lister possessed the ability to move around fairly freely in the world, most women before the 20th century did not. Yet middle- and upper-class women had long participated in socially sanctioned romantic friendships, characterized by love letters and poetry, emotional intimacy, and even physical affection. In *Surpassing the Love of Men*, Lillian Faderman gives examples of both French and British women of the 17th century—Mme. de La Fayette, Katherine Philips, and others—who openly expressed their love for other women. She also cites Michel de Montaigne as an example of a man who declared that his romantic love for his friend Éstienne de la Boëtie constituted a "sacred bond" between them. By the 18th century, such romantic friendships had become fashionable, especially among women. Probably the most well-known pair was Sarah Ponsonby and Eleanor Butler, Irish gentlewomen who eloped to Wales in 1778 and lived there together for 53 years. Their cozy, idyllic retreat became a fashionable destination

**Figure 1.5** Eleanor Butler and Sarah Ponsonby, *The Ladies of Llangollen.*

for travelers who were anxious to meet the Ladies of Llangollen. Although the Ladies themselves wrote that their relationship had nothing to do with sex (which they euphemistically called *Vulgar Eros*), it is nevertheless true that such literary proto-lesbians as Anna Seward and Anne Lister visited them and wrote admiringly of their Welsh ménage, and the writer Hester Thrale Piozzi called them "damned sapphists" (Stanley 163). Ponsonby and Butler represent a success story for early female romantic couples in contrast to, for instance, Marianne Woods and Jane Pirie, Scottish schoolmistresses whose livelihood was entirely undermined when they were accused by a student of having engaged in "improper and criminal conduct" with each other. They went to court in 1811 to claim the charge was libelous and won, but their school for girls nonetheless closed because of the scandal.

Woods and Pirie won their libel case in part because Lord Gillies, the judge, believed that "the crime here alleged has no existence" (Faderman, *Scotch Verdict* 282). In the 19th century, romantic friendship was seen as benign, even salutary. In contrast to the Middle Ages, people regarded middle- and upper-class women as asexual, and even if they were not, without a penis present, sex "has no existence." Given this view of privileged women, it is not surprising that Queen Victoria, when asked if she thought the 1885 Criminal Law Amendment Act outlawing same-sex acts between men should also apply to women, expressed her disbelief that such acts between women were physically possible (Castle). This attitude allowed some women to express their love for other women without being suspected of sexual deviance. The poet Emily Dickinson, for example, wrote to her friend and future sister-in-law Sue

Gilbert, "If you were here—and Oh that you were, my Susie, we need not talk at all, our eyes would whisper for us, and your hand fast in mine, we would not ask for language" (Faderman, *Surpassing* 175). Interestingly, Dickinson's niece Martha Dickinson Bianchi cut this passage from her 1924 edition of Emily Dickinson's letters; by that time, the popularization of Freud had put an end to the assumption of female innocence [λ Chapter 3].

In the second half of the 19th century, as a few fortunate (white, upper-class) women gained the opportunity to attend college and embark on careers outside the home, a new phenomenon arose: the Boston marriage. Lillian Faderman defines a Boston marriage as "a long-term monogamous relationship between two otherwise unmarried women" (Faderman, *Surpassing* 190). The reference to Boston resulted from the many women's colleges in that area. At a time when marriage to a man always meant retirement from the public sphere and exclusive focus on home and family, many educated professional women chose to remain unmarried. They formed intense, loving relationships with other women, often combining their work and home lives. Katharine Lee Bates, professor of English at Wellesley College and author of "America the Beautiful," lived with economics professor Katharine Coman for 25 years. Jane Addams, founder of Hull House in Chicago, lived with coworker Mary Rozet Smith for more than 30 years. These women and others in similar circumstances could form same-sex "marriages" precisely because they lived during the romantic friendship era, when such relationships were assumed to be beneficial and asexual.

## Molly-Houses: Early Homoerotic Subculture in England

The first **Buggery** Act outlawing male sodomy was passed in England in 1533, and during the 16th century, some prosecutions took place. Popular sentiment held, however, that Rome, not London, was the "cistern full of sodomy," and there was little evidence of a cohesive subculture. Rictor Norton claims that in the early 17th century, the court of James I was "very nearly a gay subculture unto itself" for the first 15 years of his reign (21). James's most notorious favorite was George Villiers, Duke of Buckingham. So marked were his attentions to Buckingham that the Privy Council held an acrimonious debate in 1617 concerning the moral nature of James's affections. James responded openly, "I love the Earl of Buckingham more than anyone else" and compared their relationship to that of Jesus and St. John. "Christ had his son John," wrote the king, "and I have my George" (qtd. in Norton 21). At the same time, we should remember that James I was married and had very cordial relations with his wife with whom he fathered children.

The open male-male intimacy at court waned in the last years of James's reign, and during the Puritan years, there is little evidence of the growth of urban subcultures. By the turn of the 18th century, however, much had changed. In 1700, the Royal Exchange was the prime cruising ground in London, where so-called Swarthy Buggerantoes ogled handsome young men. By 1720, the negative publicity against same-sex behavior originating from the Society for Reformation of Manners had sent some men to trial but also advertised places and practices for others. In 1726, the police raided an establishment known as Mother Clap's Molly House and took 40 men to Newgate prison. The resulting trial led to three executions, one death in prison, one acquittal, one reprieve, and many gone into hiding. More than this, the British press was full of the subject for months, and enterprising reporters located and revealed dozens of molly houses and cruising areas. As the Reformation Society became increasingly accused of officious meddling in the years that followed the Mother Clap raid, cruising for sex and meeting in particular public houses became safer and relatively routine (Norton ch. 3). An active molly subculture developed in England during the 18th century, whereby effeminate men *(mollies)* engaged in transgressive gender play. Male-male sexuality was thought to run rampant in boys' schools and universities as well. In *The Construction of Homosexuality,* David Greenberg mentions that this phenomenon occurred throughout Europe at that time: there were **transvestite** balls in Portugal, men in ribbons and powder in France, men with female nicknames in Holland, and cross-dressers in Italy.

**Find Out More** in the Wadham limericks at the end of this chapter.

Lest it seem as if these men gained meaningful acceptance in London in the 1700s, it is important to consider that homophobia grew along with awareness of homoeroticism. Public hangings, confinement to the pillory, imprisonment, and heavy fines were common. Men were convicted and punished for sodomy at a far higher rate than for other crimes. For example, in 1811, the first year criminal statistics were compiled by the Home Office, 80% of convicted sodomists were executed, as compared with 13% of other capital offenders (Norton 132). Mob violence against pilloried *sods* (sodomites) was common.

The gradual urbanizing trend of the 19th century led to sufficient growth of many cities in Europe and the United States to provide the anonymity needed for more modern homosexual cultures to develop. Cabarets and clubs in Berlin, specialized houses of prostitution in Amsterdam, molly taverns in New York and London—these and many other places catered to men looking for contact with others. By the last decades of the 1800s, nearly every big city in the Western world had its cruising areas and entertainment houses, and the word *gay* had slipped from its mid-century meaning of prostitute to include men interested in sex with other men and *gay girls,* or lesbians. Mollies developed elaborate codes to signal their availability to other men. Tommies, that is, boyish or passing women, might also be found in gay establishments. In many ways, what we would recognize as a gay subculture was coming into being. Contemporary historians interpret such cultures as signaling the beginning of a recognizably modern gay culture or identity. How such identities solidified into the forms we actually recognize today— both in the eyes of those invested in homoerotic love and in the eyes of larger societies—is the subject of the next chapter.

## QUESTIONS FOR DISCUSSION

1. Thinking seriously about the theory of perverse presentism, recall some of the conversations you have had with friends about the issue of homosexuality in history. What historical figures have you heard are homosexual? What are their birth and death dates? Knowing what you know after reading this chapter, how accurate do you think it is to claim these historical figures as homosexual? Do some Internet research about these figures, and then try to come up with ways of talking about their sexual identities or performances that are more historically accurate.

2. Throughout this chapter, we have mentioned a number of historical figures who have become important in tracing the history of same-sex desires and nonnormative gender identities and performances. Pick one figure who interests you and find out more about that individual's biography. Pay particular attention to that person's importance in the history of same-sex sexuality. As you browse through a variety of biographical and critical materials—on the Web, in histories, in journal articles—keep track of how the individual is labeled. Is he or she or ze referred to as *gay? Homosexual? Queer?* What do the labels suggest not only about the individual in question but about the assumptions of the author of the biographical or critical materials you are reading?

3. In this chapter, we have tried to acknowledge the different terms used at different points in history and in different cultures to refer to people practicing same-sex desires or engaging in gender-variant performances. What are *contemporary* terms for such desires, identities, and performances? Research some of the historical and contemporary terms to find out more about the contexts in which they were—and are—used.

## REFERENCES AND FURTHER READING

Abelove, Henry, Michèle Aina Barale, and David M. Halperin, eds. *The Lesbian and Gay Studies Reader.* New York: Routledge, 1993. Print.

Betteridge, Tom. *Sodomy in Early Modern Europe.* Manchester, UK: Manchester UP, 2002. Print.

Boswell, John. *Christianity, Social Tolerance, and Homosexuality.* Chicago: U of Chicago P, 1980. Print.

———. *Same-Sex Unions in Premodern Europe.* New York: Vintage, 1994. Print.

Brooten, Bernadette J. *Love between Women: Early Christian Responses to Female*

*Homoeroticism.* Chicago: U of Chicago P, 1996. Print.

Castle, Terry. *The Apparitional Lesbian.* New York: Columbia UP, 1995. Print.

Cook, Blanche Wiesen. "'Women Alone Stir My Imagination': Lesbianism and the Cultural Tradition." *Signs* 4.4 (Summer 1979): 718–39. Print.

Dover, K. J. *Greek Homosexuality.* 1978. Cambridge, MA: Harvard UP, 1989. Print.

Downing, Christine. *Myths and Mysteries of Same-Sex Love.* New York: Continuum, 1989. Print.

Duberman, Martin Bauml, Martha Vicinus, and George Chauncey Jr., eds. *Hidden from History: Reclaiming the Gay and Lesbian Past.* New York: New American Library, 1989. Print.

Epprecht, Marc. *Hungochani: The History of a Dissident Sexuality in Southern Africa.* Montreal: McGill-Queen's UP, 2004. Print.

Faderman, Lillian. *Scotch Verdict.* New York: Columbia UP, 1993. Print.

———. *Surpassing the Love of Men: Romantic Friendship and Love between Women from the Renaissance to the Present.* New York: William Morrow, 1981. Print.

Fone, Byrne R. S., ed. *Hidden Heritage: History and the Gay Imagination.* New York: Avocation, 1980. Print.

Garton, Stephen. *Histories of Sexuality: Antiquity to Sexual Revolution.* New York: Routledge, 2004. Print.

Greenberg, David E. *The Construction of Homosexuality.* Chicago: U of Chicago P, 1988. Print.

Hergemöller, Berndt-Ulrich. *Sodom and Gomorrah: On the Everyday Reality and Persecution of Homosexuals in the Middle Ages.* Trans. John Phillips. London: Free Association Books, 2001. Print.

Kugle, Scott. "Sultan Mahmud's Makeover: Colonial Homophobia and the Persian-Urdu Literary Tradition." *Queering India: Same-Sex Love and Eroticism in Indian Culture and Society.* Ed. Ruth Vanita. New York: Routledge, 2002. 30–46. Print.

Lister, Anne. *I Know My Own Heart: The Diaries of Anne Lister (1791–1840).* Ed. Helena Whitbread. London: Virago, 1988. Print.

Murray, Stephen O., and Will Roscoe. *Boy-Wives and Female Husbands: Studies of African Homosexualities.* New York: St. Martin's, 1998. Print.

———. *Islamic Homosexualities: Culture, History, and Literature.* New York: NYU P, 1997. Print.

Norton, Rictor. *Mother Clap's Molly House: The Gay Subculture in England 1700–1830.* London: GMP, 1992. Print.

Padgug, Robert. "Sexual Matters: Rethinking Sexuality in History." *Hidden from History: Reclaiming the Gay and Lesbian Past.* Ed. Martin Duberman, Martha Vicinus, and George Chauncey Jr. New York: Penguin, 1989. 54–64. Print.

Plato. *Symposium.* Trans. Benjamin Jowett. N.d. Web. 19 July 2008. <http://www.lyon.edu/webdata/users/mbeck/Plato/Symposium,%201.doc>.

Pomeroy, Sarah. *Goddesses, Whores, Wives, and Slaves: Women in Classical Antiquity.* New York: Shocken, 1975. Print.

Puff, Helmut. *Sodomy in Reformation Germany and Switzerland 1400–1600.* Chicago: U of Chicago P, 2003. Print.

Reeder, Greg. "Same-Sex Desire, Conjugal Constructs, and the Tomb of Niankhkhnum and Khnumhotep."

*World Archaeology* 32.2 (Oct. 2000): 193–208. Print.

Rocco, Antonio. *Alcibiades the Schoolboy.* Trans. J. C. Rawnsley. Amsterdam: Entimos, 2000. Print.

Roscoe, Will. *The Zuñi Man-Woman.* Albuquerque: UNM P, 1992. Print.

Shively, Charley. *Drum Beats: Walt Whitman's Civil War Boy Lovers.* San Francisco: Gay Sunshine, 1989. Print.

Stanley, Liz. "Epistemological Issues in Researching Lesbian History: The Case of 'Romantic Friendship.'" *Working Out: New Directions for Women's Studies.* Ed. Hilary Hinds, Ann Phoenix, and Jackie Stacey. London: Falmer, 1992. 161–72. Print.

Thadani, Giti. *Sakhiyani: Desire in Ancient and Modern India.* London: Cassell, 1996. Print.

Vanita, Ruth, ed. *Queering India: Same-Sex Love and Eroticism in Indian Culture and Society.* New York: Routledge, 2002. Print.

Watanabe, Tsuneo, and Jun'ichi Iwata. *The Love of the Samurai: A Thousand Years of Japanese Homosexuality.* Trans. D. R. Roberts. London: GMP, 1989. Print.

Wu, Cuncun. *Homoerotic Sensibilities in Late Imperial China.* London: Routledge-Curzon, 2004. Print.

# READINGS

## ➢ Sappho

(c. Seventh Century BCE), Ancient Greece

### "To a Maiden"

Peer of gods he seemeth to me, the blissful
Man who sits and gazes at thee before him,
Close beside thee sits, and in silence hears thee
      Silverly speaking,

Laughing love's low laughter. Oh this, this only
Stirs the troubled heart in my breast to tremble!
For should I but see thee a little moment,
      Straight is my voice hushed;

Yea, my tongue is broken, and through and through me
'Neath the flesh impalpable fire runs tingling;
Nothing see mine eyes, and a noise of roaring
      Waves in my ear sounds;

Sweat runs down in rivers, a tremor seizes
All my limbs, and paler than grass in autumn,
Caught by pains of menacing death, I falter,
      Lost in the love-trance.

Rictor Norton, "The John Addington Symonds Pages" © 1997. Trans. John Addington Symonds (1840–1893), 1885. Available at http://www.infopt.demon.co.uk/translat.htm.

### "Hymn to Aphrodite"

Glittering-throned, undying Aphrodite,
Wile-weaving daughter of high Zeus, I pray thee,
Tame not my soul with heavy woe, dread mistress,
      Nay, nor with anguish!

But hither come, if ever erst of old time
Thou didst incline, and listenedst to my crying,
And from thy father's palace down descending,
      Camest with golden

Chariot yoked: thee fair swift-flying sparrows
Over dark earth with multitudinous fluttering,
Pinion on pinion, through middle ether
        Down from heaven hurried.

Quickly they came like light, and thou, blest lady,
Smiling with clear undying eyes didst ask me
What was the woe that troubled me, and wherefore
        I had cried to thee:

What thing I longed for to appease my frantic
Soul: and Whom now must I persuade, thou askedst,
Whom must entangle to thy love, and who now,
        Sappho, hath wronged thee?

Yea, for if now he shun, he soon shall chase thee;
Yea, if he take not gifts, he soon shall give them;
Yea, if he love not, soon shall he begin to
        Love thee, unwilling.

Come to me now too, and from tyrannous sorrow
Free me, and all things that my soul desires to
Have done, do for me, queen, and let thyself too
        Be my great ally!

---

Rictor Norton. Selection copyright © 1997.

## ➤ Abu Nuwas

(756–c. 815 CE), Persia

---

### "In the Bath-house"

In the bath-house, the mysteries hidden by trousers
        Are revealed to you.
All becomes radiantly manifest.
        Feast your eyes without restraint!
You see handsome buttocks, shapely trim torsos,
        You hear the guys whispering pious formulas
          to one another

        ("God is Great!" "Praise be to God!")

Ah, what a palace of pleasure is the bath-house!
    Even when the towel-bearers come in
        And spoil the fun a bit.

Abu Nuwas. *Carousing with Gazelles: Homoerotic Songs of Old Baghdad*. Trans. Jaafar Abu Tarab. New York: iUniverse, Inc., 2005.

### "My Lover Has Started to Shave"

Jealous people and slanderers overwhelm me with sarcasm
because my lover has started to shave.
I answer them: friends, how wrong you are!
Since when has fuzz been a flaw?
It enhances the splendor of his lips and his teeth,
like silk cloth which is brightened by pearls.
And I consider myself fortunate that his sprouting beard
preserves his beauty from indiscreet glances:
it gives his kisses a different flavor
and makes a reflection glisten on the silver of his cheeks.

Quoted in Greenberg, *The Construction of Homosexuality* (174). Greenberg's source: Daniel, Marc. "Arab Civilization and Male Love." Trans. Winston Leyland. *Gay Sunshine* 32 (1977): 1–11, 27.

## ➢ Zulali Khwansari

(d. 1615 CE), Iran

### From the Epic Poem *Masnavi:*

Mahmud, Sultan of Ghazna, has purchased young Ayaz as a slave.

Mahmud set a cup beside him and a decanter before him
Full of burgundy wine, as if distilled from his own heart

He filled the cup with wine like his love's ruby lips
Entangled in the curls of Ayaz, Mahmud began to lose control

He filled the cup with wine from the clouds of forgetfulness
The glow of Ayaz set the glass aflame with scintillating colors

He lifted the cup to Ayaz and bade him drink
His heart melted as he held the cup to his lips

Mahmud urged him to drink wine from his own hand
Yet a complaint showed in the eyes of Ayaz, a fear of intoxication

But as a servant, Ayaz drank from the cup
As a ruby droplet rolled from his lip to his shirt

His words lay in jumbles as the drop rolled to his foot
And the wine sent him spinning in drunkenness

Hard of breath, Mahmud said, "In this intimacy one can pursue desire
But I can only utter sighs while watching you delicately drink!

Tonight, I'm in the mood to finally reach you
How long has my only wish from God been delayed

Your lips have become ruby red, as intense as the wine
Such a ruby spells the death of better discretion

Your mouth is a wine bottle overflowing
Since the color of wine flows over your lips

Those are not black curls nestled against your cheeks
Since your glance is aflame they must be wisps of smoke

Gazing at you, they seem not like musk-scented curls
For where there is burning desire there must be smoke

Come to me now, bare all, that I may kiss your lips
Those very rose petals that make a beard tender and soft

Your lip is a single drop of wine distilled
My heart's desire is only to taste it unconstrained

Against the black lashes, how bright are your eyes
Am I fated to glimpse them only from a distance?

You never look at me directly in the eye
Though with one glance you will rob me of my heart

This is the last breath I will release from my soul
Without your beauty open before me, I will surely die

If you let me embrace your full form
From my grave stately box-trees will grow tall like you

That idol of Kashmir, like a rose blooming in a graceful cypress
From head to toe your elegant form has set me boiling!"

Ayaz's sweet mouth drawing close, closer
His smile fully prepared, his lip set for the charge

Then from his smile, sweetness boiled over
He took the wine-cup from the Sultan's hand

From that moment, Ayaz was the cupbearer of Mahmud
Whose whole world became drunk with his playful grace.

---

Scott Kugle. "Sultan Mahmud's Makeover: Colonial Homophobia and the Persian-Urdu Literary Tradition." Trans. Scott Kugle. *Queering India: Same-Sex Love and Eroticism in Indian Culture and Society*. Ed. Ruth Vanita. New York: Routledge, 2002, 30–46 (selection pp. 33–34).

## ➢ **Ihara Saikaku**

(1642–1693), Japan

---

### "Bamboo Clappers Strike the Hateful Number"

A monk's hermitage papered with love letters.

Boy actors hide their age.

A pushy samurai loses his whiskers.

When being entertained by a kabuki boy actor, one must be careful never to ask his age.

It was late in autumn, and rain just light enough not to be unpleasant had been falling since early morning. It now lifted and the afternoon sun appeared below the clouds in the west, forming a rainbow over Higashiyama. Just then a group of boy actors appeared wearing wide-striped rainbow robes of satin. The most handsome among them was an actor in the Murayama theater troupe, a jewel that sparkled without need of polishing, named Tamamura Kichiya.[1] He was in the full flower of youth, and every person in the capital was in love with him.

On that particular day, a well-known lover of boys called Ko-romo-notana Shiroku had invited him to go mushroom picking at Mt. Shiroyama in Fushimi, so a large group of actors and their spirited companions left Shijo-gawara and soon arrived at Hitsu-kawa. Leaves of the birch cherries, the subject of a long-ago poem,[2] had turned bright red, a sight more beautiful even than spring blossoms. After spending some time gazing at the scene, the group continued past the woods at Fuji-no-mori, where the tips of the leaves were just beginning to turn brown, and moved south up the mountain.

They parked their palanquins at the base and alighted, heads covered with colorful purple kerchiefs. Since pine trees were their only observers, they removed their sedge hats and revealed their lovely faces. Parting the tangled pampas grass, they walked on with sighs of admiration. The scene was reminiscent of the poem, "My sleeves grow damp since first entering the mountain of your love,"[3] for these were boys at the peak of physical beauty. An outsider looking at them could not but have felt envious of their gentleman companions. A certain man well acquainted with the ways of love once said, "In general, courtesans are a pleasure once in bed; with boys, the pleasure begins on the way there."

It was already close to dusk by the time they began hunting for mushrooms. They found only a few, which they carried like treasures back to an isolated thatched hut far from any village. Inside, the walls were papered at the base with letters from actors. Their signatures had been torn off and discarded. Curious, the boys looked more closely and discovered that each letter concerned matters of love. Each was written in a different hand, the parting messages of kabuki boy actors. The monk who lived there must once have been a man of some means, they thought. He apparently belonged to the Shingon sect, for when they opened the Buddhist altar they found a figure of Kaba Daishi adorned with chrysanthemums and bush clover, and next to it a picture of a lovely young actor, the object no doubt of this monk's fervent devotion.

When they questioned him, the monk told them about his past. As they suspected, he was devoted body and soul to the way of boy love.

"I was unhappy with my strict father and decided to seclude myself in this mountain hermitage. More than two years have passed, but I have not been able to forget about boy love even in my dreams." The tears of grief he wept were enough to fade the black dye of his priestly robes. Those who heard it were filled with pity for him.

"How old are you?" someone asked.

"I am no longer a child," he said. "I just turned 22."

"Why then, you are still in the flower of youth!" they exclaimed.

All of the actors in the room dutifully wrung the tears from their sleeves, but their expressions seemed strangely reticent. Not one of them was under 22 years of age! Among them was one boy actor who, judging from the time he worked the streets, must have been quite old. In the course of the conversation, someone asked him his age.

"I don't remember," he said, causing quite some amusement among the men.

Then, the monk who lived in the cottage spoke up.

"By good fortune, I have here a bamboo clapper that has the ability to tell exactly how old you are."

He gave the clapper to the boy actor and had him stand there while the monk himself gravely folded his hands in prayer. Shortly, the bamboo clappers began to sound. Everyone counted aloud with each strike.

At first, the actor stood there innocently as it struck seventeen, eighteen, nineteen, but beyond that he started to feel embarrassed. He tried with all his strength to separate his right hand from his left and stop the clappers from striking, but, strangely, they kept right on going. Only after striking 38 did the bamboo clappers separate. The boy actor's face was red with embarrassment.

"These bamboo clappers lie!" he said, throwing them down.

The monk was outraged.

"The Buddhas will attest that there is no deceit in them. If you still have doubts, try it again as many times as you like."

The other actors in the room were all afraid of being exposed, so no one was willing to try them out. They were beginning to lose their party mood.

When sake had been brought out and the mushrooms toasted and salted, they all lay back and began to entertain their patrons. One of the boy actors took the opportunity to request a new jacket, another was promised a house with an entrance six ken wide, and still another was presented right there with a short sword. (It was amusing to see how nimbly he took the sword and put it away!)

Into the midst of this merry-making came a rough samurai of the type rarely seen in the capital. He announced his arrival with the words, "Part, clouds, for here I am!" as if to boast of his bad reputation. He forced his way through the twig fence and into the garden, handed his long sword to an attendant, and went up to the bamboo veranda.

"Bring me the sake cup that Tamamura Kichiya is using," he demanded.

Kichiya at first pretended he had not heard, but finally he said, "There is already a gentleman here to share my cup."

The samurai would not tolerate such an answer.

"I will have it at once," he said angrily, "and you will be my snack!"

He took up his long sword mentioned earlier and waved it menacingly at the boy's companion. The poor man was terrified and apologized profusely, but the samurai refused to listen.

"What an awful fellow," Kichiya laughed.

"I won't let him get away with this."

"Leave him to me," he told the others and sent them back home.

When they had gone, Kichiya snuggled up to the foolish samurai.

"Today was so uninteresting," he said.

"I was just having a drink with those boring merchants because I had to. It would be a real pleasure to drink with a lord like yourself."

Kichiya poured cup after cup of sake for the man and flattered and charmed him expertly. Soon, the fool was in a state of waking sleep, unaware of anything but the boy. The man was ready to make love, but Kichiya told him: "I can't go any further because of your scratchy whiskers. It hurts when you kiss me."

"I wouldn't dream of keeping anything on my face not to your liking, boy. Call my servant and have him shave it off," the samurai said.

"If you don't mind, please allow me to improve my lord's good looks with my own hands." Kichiya picked up a razor and quickly shaved off the whiskers on the left side of the samurai's face, leaving the mustache intact on his upper lip. He also left the right side as it was. The samurai just snored loudly, completely oblivious to what was going on.

Kichiya saw his opportunity and escaped from the place as quickly as possible. He took the man's whiskers with him as a memento. Everyone laughed uproariously when he showed them the hair.

"How in the world did you get hold of that! This deserves a celebration!" they said. Akita Hikosabura[4] invented an impromptu "whisker dance" and had the men holding their sides with laughter.

Later, when the samurai awoke, he was furious at the loss of his whiskers. Without his beard he had no choice but to quit living by intimidation. Rather than seek revenge, he decided to act as if the whole thing had never happened.

When they saw him some time later, he was making his living as a marksman with his bow. Recalling how he had lost his beard, they could not help but laugh at the man.

## Notes

1. Tamamura Kichiya was an actor of female roles from 1658 to 1660 in the Kyoto Ebisuya Theater, where he scored a great success as Yang Kuei Fei in the play *Hanaikusa* (Yang Kuei Fei: legendary beauty and consort of the Chinese T'ang emperor T'ai Tzung). In 1661, he moved to the Inishie Theater in Edo, but nothing is known of him after 1673.

2. Fubokusho poem 11307 by Fujiwara no Ieyoshi: "Fragrant on the banks of the Hitsukawa, the late-blooming birch cherries drop their petals, signaling the blossoms' final end."

3. Shinchokusen poem 657 by Minamoto no Tamenaka: "Since first parting the luxuriant growth of dew-covered grass on the mountain of your love, how damp my sleeves have grown."

4. Founder of the Akita dynasty of actors, Hikosabura played jester roles in Kyoto and Osaka in the years 1661 to 1680. Yakusha hyaban gejigeji (1674) describes him as a master of mime, acrobatics, and humorous monologues.

Ihara Saikaku (1642–1693). *Nanshoku Okagami* (*The Great Mirror of Male Love*). Trans. Paul Gordon Schalow, Copyright © 1990 by the Board of Trustees of the Leland Stanford Jr. University.

## ➢ Wu Meicun
### (1609–1671 CE), China

### "Song of Beau Wang"[1]

Beau Wang reappears on the capital's stage in his thirties,
He has grown up and sings sentimental tunes for the former dynasty.
Oh, his face is even more endearing than in the old days,
Dark pupils darting from his white jade eyes.
All the young dandies from the great families of Wuling
Vie to give their life for Beau Wang.
Calmly missing appointments with the imperial ministers,
How they suffer over missing Beau Wang.
Unhurried by the approach of evening curfews,
How they all rush to be on time for Beau Wang.
None before succeeded in calming an audience's cheers and waves,
But just a peep from Beau Wang brings the whole theatre to a hush.
Everybody jostles and leans to gaze upon Beau Wang
Like looking over someone never seen before.
The old capital was fascinated with Little Song
Who entertained in the household of Duke Tian.
Hearing once more the strains of Beau Wang's song,
We no longer grieve for the emperor of yore.

### Note

1. Wang Zijia (c. 1622–54) was a famous boy actor during the late Ming dynasty, whom the poet met again in Beijing in 1651, the eighth year of the Qing dynasty.

Wu Cuncun. *Homoerotic Sensibilities in Late Imperial China*. Trans. Wu Cuncun. London: RoutledgeCurzon, 2004.

# ➢ **Ancient Egyptian Binding Spell**

## (c. Third/Fourth-Century CE), Upper Egypt

"An oval-shaped lead tablet from Hermoupolis Magna (known today as el-Ashmunen) in Upper Egypt contains a sixty-two-line spell inscribed in a third- or fourth-century CE script. . . . The ten lines at the beginning and the ten lines at the end taper off to form an oval-shaped inscription.

A woman named Sophia used this tablet to attract another woman, Gorgonia."

Fundament of the gloomy darkness, jagged-tooth dog, covered with coiling snakes, turning three heads, traveler in the recesses of the underworld, come, spirit-driver, with the Erinyes, savage with their stinging whips; holy serpents, maenads, frightful maidens, come to my wroth incantations. Before I persuade by force this one and you, render him immediately a fire-breathing daemon. Listen and do everything quickly, in no way opposing me in the performance of this action; for you are the governors of the earth.

By means of this corpse-daemon inflame the heart, the liver, the spirit of Gorgonia, whom Nilogenia bore, with love and affection for Sophia, whom Isara bore. Constrain Gorgonia, whom Nilogenia bore, to cast herself into the bath-house for the sake of Sophia, whom Isara bore; and you, become a bath-woman. Burn, set on fire, inflame her soul, heart, liver, spirit with love for Sophia, whom Isara bore. Drive Gorgonia, whom Nilogenia bore, drive her, torment her body night and day, force her to rush forth from every place and every house, loving Sophia, whom Isara bore, she, surrendered like a slave, giving herself and all her possessions to her, because this is the will and command of the great god, Blessed lord of the immortals, holding the scepters of Tartaros and of terrible, fearful Styx and of life-robbing Lethe, the hair of Kerberos trembles in fear of you, you crack the loud whips of the Erinyes; the couch of Persephone delights you, when you go to the longed bed, whether you be the immortal Sarapis, whom the universe fears, whether you be Osiris, star of the land of Egypt; your messenger is the all-wise boy; yours is Anoubis, the pious herald of the dead. Come hither, fulfill my wishes, because I summon you by these secret symbols, swallowing the tip of the tail.

Constrain Gorgonia, whom Nilogenia bore, to cast herself into the bath-house for the sake of Sophia, whom Isara bore, for her. Aye, lord, king of the chthonic gods, burn, set on fire, inflame the soul, the heart, the liver, the spirit of Gorgonia, whom Nilogenia bore, with love and affection for Sophia, whom Isara bore; drive Gorgonia herself, torment her body night and day; force her to rush forth from every place and every house, loving Sophia, whom Isara bore, she, Gorgonia surrendered like a slave, giving herself and all her possessions. Aye, lord, king of the chthonic gods, carry out what is inscribed on this tablet, for I adjure you who divided the entire universe, a single realm.

So, do not disobey my request, but cause Gorgonia, whom Nilogenia bore, force her to cast herself into the bath-house for the sake of Sophia, whom Isara bore, for her. Burn, set on fire, inflame the heart, the liver, the spirit of Gorgonia, whom Nilogenia bore, with love and affection for Sophia, whom Isara bore, for a good end.

Burn, set on fire the soul, the heart, the liver, the spirit of Gorgonia, whom Nilogenia bore, with love and affection for Sophia, whom Isara bore, because this is the will of the great god.

Force Gorgonia, whom Nilogenia bore, to cast herself into the bath-house for the sake of Sophia, whom Isara bore, for her, so that she love her with passion.

Burn, set on fire the soul, the heart, the liver, the spirit of Gorgonia, whom Nilogenia bore, with love and affection for Sophia, whom Isara bore, with passion, longing, love.

Drive, Sun, honey-holder, honey-cutter, honey-producer, drive Gorgonia, whom Nilogenia bore, to love Sophia, whom Isara bore; burn, set on fire the soul, the heart, the liver, the spirit of burned, inflamed, tortured Gorgonia, whom Nilogenia bore, until she casts herself into the bath-house for the sake of Sophia, whom Isara bore; and you, become a bath-woman.

Bernadette J. Brooten. *Love between Women: Early Christian Responses to Female Homoeroticism*. University of Chicago Press, 1996. 81–82.

## ➢ Order for Solemnization of Same-Sex Union
### (13th Century CE), Medieval Europe (Greek) Translation

**i.**

Those intending to be united shall come before the priest, who shall place the Gospel on the center of the altar, and the first of them that are to be joined together shall place his hand on the Gospel, and the second on the hand of the first. And thus sealing them, the priest sayeth the litany.

**ii.**

In peace we beseech Thee, O Lord.
For heavenly peace we beseech Thee, O Lord.
For the peace of all the world, [we beseech Thee, O Lord].
For these servants of God, N. and N., and their love in Christ, we beseech Thee, O Lord.
That they be granted love in the spirit and honor each other, we beseech Thee, O Lord.
That the Lord our God grant them blameless life and pleasing conduct.
That they and we be saved from all [danger, need, and tribulation].

**iii.**

Receive us. Save us. Have mercy upon us.
Mindful of our lady, the all-holy, undefiled, most blessed and glorious ever-virgin Mary, mother of God, and all the saints, we commend ourselves and one another and all that liveth unto Christ our God.

**iv.**

Let us pray.
Lord our God and ruler, who madest humankind after thine image and likeness and didst bestow upon us power of life eternal, whom it pleased that thine holy apostles Philip and Bartholomew be joined together, not bound by the law of nature, but in the mode of faith, who didst commend the union of thy holy martyrs Serge and

Bacchus, not bound by the law of nature, but in a holy spirit and the mode of faith, do Thou vouchsafe unto these thy servants grace to love one another and to abide unhated and not a cause of scandal all the days of their lives, with the help of the Holy Mother of God and all thy saints. Forasmuch as Thou art our unity and certainty and the bond of peace, and thine is endless glory, Father, Son, and Holy Spirit.

### v.

Peace be with you.
*<Bow> your heads*.

O Lord our God, who hast favored us with all those things necessary for salvation and hast commanded us to love one another and to forgive one another our failings, [bless], kind Lord and lover of good, these thy servants who love each other and are come unto this thy holy church to receive thy benediction. Grant unto them unashamed faithfulness, true love, and as Thou didst bestow upon thy holy disciples and apostles thy peace and love, grant also unto these, O Christ our God, all those things necessary for salvation and eternal life.

For Thou art the light, the truth, and life eternal, and thine is the glory.

### vi.

O Lord our God, who in thine ineffable providence didst deem it fit to call brothers the holy apostles and heirs of thy kingdom, accept now these thy servants, N. and N., to be united in spirit and faith, and find them meet to abide unscathed by the wiles of the devil and of his evil spirits, to prosper in virtue and justice and sincere love, that through them and through us may be glorified thine all-holy name, the Father, the Son, and the Holy Spirit, now and forever.

### vii.

Lord our God, magnified in the congregation of the saints, great and awesome ruler over all that is round about Thee, bless these thy servants N. and N., grant unto them knowledge of thy Holy Spirit. Guide them in thy holy fear, bestow upon them joy in thy power, that they be joined together more in spirit than in flesh. Forasmuch as it is Thou who dost bless and sanctify all things, and thine is the glory.

### viii.

O Lord our God, who dwellest in the heavens and dost look down upon those things below, who for the salvation of the human race didst send thine only-begotten son, our Lord, Jesus Christ, and didst choose Peter and Paul (Peter from Caesarea of Philippi, Paul from Tarsus of Cilicia), joining them together in holy spirit, make these thy servants like unto those two apostles. Keep them blameless all the days of their lives, for the sake of thy most venerable and honored name, Father, Son and Holy Spirit, which is thus sanctified and glorified, now and forever.

### ix.

And they shall kiss the holy Gospel and each other, and it shall be concluded.

## ➢ Wadham Limericks

There once was a warden of Wadham
Who approved of the folkways of Sodom,
        For a man might, he said,
        Have a very poor head
But be a fine fellow, at bottom.

When they said to a Fellow of Wadham
Who had asked for a ticket to Sodom,
        "Oh, sir, we don't care
        To send people there,"
He said, "Don't call me Sir, call me Modom."

Well did the amorous sons of Wadham
Their house secure from future flame;
They knew their crime, the crime of Sodom
And judg'd their punishment the same.

# CHAPTER 2

# Sexology

*Constructing the Modern Homosexual*

In the 19th C. the sin model of homosexuality gave way to a medical model which pathologized a wide variety of sexual "deviances." This chapter explores some of the pressures that led to the development of this model.

In 1894, 24-year-old Lord Alfred Douglas, lover of poet and playwright Oscar Wilde, published a poem titled "Two Loves." It depicts an idyllic scene, into which a beautiful young man enters. The poet's persona asks him,

. . . Sweet youth,
Tell me why, sad and sighing, thou dost rove
These pleasant realms?

The young man answers that he is not the "true Love" that fills "the hearts of boy and girl with mutual flame." He is instead, he sighs, "the Love that dare not speak its name" (Douglas). The homoeroticism that saturates the poem suggests that this "Love that dare not speak its name" is love between men or between women. But at the end of the 19th century, that love was nameless in a number of important ways [λ "silent sin," Chapter 1]. First, such love "dare[d] not speak its name" because many same-sex sexual practices were criminalized. For instance, Britain's

Criminal Law Amendment Act, passed in 1885, criminalized sexual touching between men. Anal intercourse (known as *buggery*) was already considered a reprehensible criminal act, once punishable by death; at the time of Douglas's writing, it was punishable by imprisonment from 10 years to life ("Timeline"). Second, little public discourse about homoeroticism and homosexuality existed. In the contemporary world, Western media frequently offer news reports, movies, or conversation about a variety of LGBT issues. This was not the case in 19th-century Europe, where **sexual inversion** was considered an illness and discussed in journals aimed primarily at medical professionals. Finally, Douglas's same-sex "Love" not only "dare not" but could not "speak its name." The term *homosexual* had just been coined and had not gained much public circulation when Douglas composed his poem and committed acts of "gross indecency" with Wilde [λ Chapter 12]. At the time, then, few terms existed that described same-sex relations or acts in any way except as "sinful" or criminal.

In many ways, our contemporary Western understanding of sexuality was constructed at the turn of the 20th century by practitioners of the emerging disciplines of psychiatry, psychology, and sociology. Members of the legal profession, as well as early homosexual rights activists in Europe, also helped disseminate a way of talking about sex and sexuality that prefigured how we talk about sexuality today. Perhaps most important, the work of late 19th-century **sexologists** was crucial in constructing a discourse about sexuality that was scientific rather than laden with religious condemnation or criminal accusation. Such work was not without its own set of judgments and valuations, but our contemporary understanding of homosexuality as an identity begins with the sexologists.

## Victorian Sex: Some Background

I n the late 19th century, there was widespread disagreement about sex and its benefits—or potential hazards—physical, moral, and social. On one hand, according to Jonathan Margolis in *O: The Intimate History of the Orgasm*, "Most Victorian doctors considered sexual desire in women to be pathological and warned that female sexual excitement and indulgence could damage their reproductive organs and urinary system" (282). Similarly, Richard von Krafft-Ebing, in *Psychopathia Sexualis*, "linked masturbation to criminality" and described women "who exhibited 'excessive' sexual desire" as "nymphomaniacs" (Margolis 287). On the other hand, Margolis points out that Havelock Ellis argued that, in marriage, "one should ascertain not just the sexual needs of the husband but of the wife too." (293). What's more, in Europe and the United States, Victorian-era doctors believed that inducing **paroxysm** (or orgasm) was an effective treatment for **hysteria**.

These divergent views are not surprising when we consider the numerous social, cultural, and political upheavals that characterized the turn of the 20th century. Change was in the air. The era was marked by increased urbanization, a growing middle class with greater earning power, continued industrialization, the further development of overseas empires, and along with this, growing colonial unrest. Perhaps most significantly, the rise of scientific thought challenged reliance on biblical or religious modes of understanding the human condition. Scientific upheavals, such as Darwin's theory of evolution or the geological discovery of ancient fossils, suggested that the world was far older than the 6,000 years of recorded biblical history; many people found that scientific discovery could provide a deeper understanding of humanity than scriptural accounts, which were beginning to seem unreliable as sources of knowledge.

These changes affected the way individuals organized and understood their personal lives. As people moved into cities to find jobs and make money, family structures changed. Just a century before, most families consisted of complex and extended kinship networks in mostly rural areas; by the late 19th century, many people were living in smaller familial units, on their own, or in other pairings or groupings. In *Surpassing the Love of Men*, Lillian Faderman describes the emergence of "romantic friendships" among women at that time, such as so-called Boston marriages, in which two professional women set up housekeeping together [λ Chapter 1]. Concomitant with such alternative familial groupings were calls for women's rights, particularly the vote, as women entered the paid workforce in greater numbers. The move to cities also brought individuals into closer contact with prostitution and the *sexual underground*. Urban centers were (and still are, to a large extent) areas in which people could explore and construct a variety of intimate and erotic arrangements. Historian George Chauncey notes that "[i]n the half-century between 1890 and the beginning of the Second World War, a highly visible, remarkably complex, and continually changing gay male world took shape in New York City" (1). Margolis points out that this era also saw an increase in the availability of contraceptives, such as condoms and diaphragms. People were not necessarily having more sex than before, but the available evidence suggests that sex, sexual diversity, and alternative intimate arrangements were more visible and becoming subjects of discussion—and concern.

In fact, a variety of Europeans—ranging from medical professionals and politicians to religious leaders and laypeople—were deeply troubled by the rapid changes they were seeing in family structures and sexual practices. Out of this concern, and motivated by an interest in understanding what people were doing and why, the field of **sexology** was born. It is also important to note that sexology arose in the context of the professionalization of the sciences in the West as part of the grand 19th-century project of discovery and taxonomy. The sexologists' early documentation, theoretical musings, and scientific debates were crucial in providing a language with which to talk about sexuality in general and homosexuality in particular.

# Sexology: Defining a Field of Study

In 1869, the German physician Karl Westphal (1833–1890) noted in the *Archive for Psychiatry and Nervous Diseases* a new abnormality or mental disorder, which he called "contrary sexual feeling," meant to describe men whose sexual feelings were largely for other men and women whose sexual feelings were largely for other women. According to Westphal, such men were generally effeminate and the women "mannish" in behavior and appearance. Westphal and later sexologists called these men and women *inverts* because their gender presentations and, to some degree, their sexual desires seemed to these researchers inverse to the expected norms for their sex ("Invert"). Also in 1869, the writer Karl Maria Kertbeny invented the term *homosexual* to describe similar behaviors ("Karl Maria Kertbeny"). This term was then used by a variety of others in the developing field of sexology to describe same-sex sexual interest.

One of the key characteristics of much sexological thinking about **inversion** was the belief that male inverts were in some way more feminine than "normal" men and that female inverts were more masculine than "normal" women. Iwan Bloch's (1872–1922) *The Sexual Life of Our Times* (1907) offers a striking description of inversion, highlighting this gender "confusion":

> More especially after removing any beard or mustache that be present, we sometimes see much more clearly the feminine expression of face in a male homosexual, whilst before the hair was removed they appeared quite man-like. Still more important for the determination of a feminine habitus are direct physical characteristics. Among these there must be mentioned a *considerable deposit of fat*, by which the resemblance to the feminine type is produced, the contours of the body being more rounded than in the case of the normal male. In correspondence with this the *muscular system* is less powerfully developed than it is in heterosexual men, the skin is delicate and soft, and the complexion is much clearer than is usual in men. (qtd. in Bristow 36)

**Find Out More** about Nature, Nurture, and Identity in Chapter 5.

This kind of thinking about homosexuality was to remain influential, permeating the popular consciousness and seemingly supported by scientific research. The supposed link between deviation from sex and gender norms and homosexuality continues as a fundamental assumption underlying many studies throughout the 20th century and into the 21st [λ Chapter 5].

In *Psychopathia Sexualis,* Krafft-Ebing catalogued, described, and discussed a number of sexual "perversions." According to Krafft-Ebing, "Homosexuals . . . had feelings that represented an 'abnormal congenital manifestation,' and 'the essential feature of this strange manifestation of the sexual life is the want of sexual sensibility for the opposite sex, even to the extent of horror, while sexual inclination and impulse toward the same sex are present'" (Fout 274–75). Krafft-Ebing based his conclusions in large part on numerous case histories of those claiming to have same-sex sexual attractions. His goal in reviewing and analyzing these case histories was in line with much sexological practice: to categorize and provide a taxonomy for the variety of sexual interests and expressions. Krafft-Ebing also studied those whose sexual interests involved **masochism, fetishism,** and **sadism**—all terms that he invented.

Krafft-Ebing generally believed that homosexuality was **congenital,** a condition with which an individual was unfortunately born. At the same time, homosexuality could arise from other **etiologies:** "a hypochondriacal fear of infection during sexual intercourse," fear of pregnancy, and "mental or moral weakness," for instance (qtd. in Bristow 32). Homosexuality was seen as a "perversion"—something to be avoided or at best pitied. Krafft-Ebing's language suggested that homosexuality was a mental illness, a belief many psychologists and psychiatrists supported well into the 20th century [λ Chapter 3]. As a point of clarification, Krafft-Ebing used the term *heterosexual* to describe what he saw as the perverse practice of engaging in sexual relations with a member of the opposite sex without the aim of reproduction. Interestingly, Krafft-Ebing's views on homosexuality as a perversion shifted toward the end of his life; his final edition of *Psychopathia Sexualis* asserted that homosexuality was one manifestation of sexual desire and not necessarily a mental disease ("Krafft-Ebing").

Krafft-Ebing's view may have shifted in part due to the work of other sexologists and writers who were interested in homosexuality and who felt that homosexuals were neither perverse nor mentally ill. Karl Heinrich Ulrichs (1825–1895), a German student of law and theology, believed that homosexuals comprised a "third sex," which he called **Urnings,** a sexological category he described at some length in *The Riddle of "Man-Manly" Love,* a series of pamphlets published from 1864 to 1880. According to Ulrichs's theory, Urnings were the product of heredity and displayed visible, physical differences from heterosexuals. For Ulrichs, the innateness of the Urning condition was the most significant reason that it should not be considered abnormal—hence his insistence that we recognize Urnings as a third sex beyond men and women (Bristow 20–26).

Given the enormous influence of the sexologists in creating a language to discuss homosexuality (and other sexual diversities), some contemporary thinkers have credited the turn of the 20th century with "giving birth" to the modern homosexual.

**Figure 2.1** Magnus Hirschfeld's sexual types: masculine (top), Urning (center), and feminine (bottom).

**Find Out More** in D'Emilio's "Capitalism and Gay Identity" at the end of this chapter.

Most notably, French philosopher Michel Foucault (1926–1984) famously asserted in his *History of Sexuality* (1978 [1976]) that the sexological categorization of sexual diversities in the late 19th century served to create not only new categories of mental illness but also new identities based on sexuality. As Foucault points out, those (e.g., sodomites) who had earlier engaged in homoerotic behavior were frequently condemned for their acts; with the rise of medical classifications and the science of psychology, such people were diagnosed as suffering from mental disorders—and thus "the homosexual was now a species" (43). As David Halperin puts it, "Although there are persons who seek sexual contact with other persons of the same sex in many different societies, only recently and only in some sectors of our society have such persons—or some portion of them—been homosexuals" (qtd. in Jagose 46). Hence, categorization worked not just to pathologize a new species of humans but also to allow those "afflicted" with homosexuality to consider themselves a "species" of people who could describe and talk about their lives beyond the often negative judgments of the medical establishment. Ulrichs, himself an Urning, used the medical classification of inversion and homosexuality to create a reverse discourse that attempted to speak positively about his sexual experiences and insist on the naturalness of the Urning condition as a third sex .

It is important to keep in mind, as Foucault does, that the identity-creating process was enormously complex, involving not only the circulation of discourses in a variety of professional fields (medicine, law, psychiatry) but also the shifting economic circumstances of many European nations at the time. As noted earlier, increased urbanization allowed for greater contact among people with divergent sexual interests, and some scholars—John D'Emilio, for instance—have pointed to such economic shifts as just as important as sexological research in the formation of a modern homosexual identity. As we shall see throughout the rest of this book, complex forces and phenomena always play crucial roles in the development of personal identities as well as the social and political organizations based on those identities.

# A Sexologist in Depth: Havelock Ellis

To understand how sexologists worked, let us look at one famous sexologist in more depth. Havelock Ellis (1859–1939) was a British physician who wrote prolifically about sex and sexuality at the turn of the 20th century. One of his most important works, *Sexual Inversion,* coauthored with the writer John Addington Symonds in 1897, was an important early and relatively sympathetic discussion of homosexual men. Indeed, Ellis wanted to present a fair—and scientific—representation of homosexuality. His *Studies in the Psychology of Sex,* a two-volume work collecting a sampling of his writing on sex (published in 1937 but including work copyrighted as early as 1905), reveals Ellis's interest in a variety of sexual practices, not just homosexuality.

In *Studies in the Psychology of Sex,* Ellis attempts to differentiate between inversion and other kinds of homosexuality. For Ellis, inverts are primarily disposed to sexual attraction to members of the same sex, whereas other forms of homosexual attraction may be due to "accidental absences." For instance, when boys or girls are separated from one another in boarding schools, the "natural" object of sexual attraction (a member of the opposite sex) is absent; hence, sexual attraction "between persons of the same sex" may occur.

Ellis's language is intriguing. He characterizes heterosexual attraction as "natural" while at the same time suggesting that homoerotic attraction is "a phenomenon of wide occurrence among all human races and among most of the higher animals" (1). This curious split—naturalizing heterosexuality but not wanting to condemn homosexuality—appears throughout Ellis's writing. For example, he writes that "[p]rison life develops and fosters the homosexual tendency of criminals; but there can be little doubt that that tendency, or else a tendency to sexual indifference or bisexuality, is a radical character of a very large number of criminals" (26). He goes on to note that "[t]he fact that homosexuality is especially common among men of exceptional intellect was long since noted by Dante" (26). Ellis then spends several pages listing and discussing "famous inverts," such as the writers Oscar Wilde and Edward Fitzgerald. He also reports on some "near misses": "While Shakespeare . . . narrowly escapes inclusion in the list of distinguished inverts, there is much better ground

**Figure 2.2**   Havelock Ellis.

for the inclusion of his great contemporary, Francis Bacon" (44). Ellis then reviews the work of some of the major sexologists of his time; he also presents several cases in which inverts describe their lives in narrative form, offering detailed sexual histories. It is clear that this listing of famous inverts and examples of inversion is designed to somewhat normalize (if not necessarily naturalize) homosexuality. In other words, given its presence among various human (and "higher animal") populations, Ellis believed that homosexuality should probably be treated as another variation in human sexual behavior.

Ellis's treatment of female inverts is similar. He notes that "[h]omosexuality is not less common in women than in men" (195) and that "[i]t has been noted of distinguished women in all ages and in all fields of activity that they have frequently displayed some masculine traits" (196). Ellis holds to the theory of inversion—that homosexual women are more often than not more masculine in presentation. At the same time, Ellis admits that relatively little is known about sexual inversion in women and that the topic needs further study. But he is willing to share some of his initial insights and findings. Most notably, he argues that "[w]hile the use of the clitoris is rare in homosexuality, the use of an artificial penis is by no means uncommon and very widespread" (258). Ellis maintains that "[a]n enlarged clitoris is but rarely found in inversion and displays a very small part in the gratification of feminine homosexuality" (258). Here he repudiates the myth that "mannish" female inverts are endowed by nature with abnormally large sexual organs that can, by themselves, produce "paroxysm" in a female partner.

Despite Ellis's sensible rejection of some ridiculous myths about inverts, one doubts the validity of his scientific method when reading his characterization of some of their more pronounced physical attributes. For instance, he writes that "[a] marked characteristic of many inverts, though one not easy of precise definition, is their youthfulness of appearance, and frequently child-like faces, equally in both sexes" (290). Granted, Ellis qualifies his comments ("one not easy of precise definition"), but many of his other findings are outrageous, such as his belief that female inverts are "very good whistlers" (256) and that male inverts prefer "green garments" (299). At the same time, Ellis maintains, sympathetically, that "[a]ll avocations are represented among inverts" (293). Despite his often quirky conclusions, Ellis wanted to portray inverts in particular and homosexuality in general in a positive light.

A significant issue facing sexologists was the cause of inversion and homosexuality, and Ellis has much to say on this subject, even if he will not commit to one particular or necessary cause. As noted earlier, he believed that lack of a "natural" object of sexual attraction can induce homoerotic attractions. He says that, in the case of women, for instance, "[h]omosexuality is specially fostered by those employments which keep women in constant association, not only by day, but often at night also, without the company of men" (212). Such employments may include the work of nuns in convents or leaders of the "woman movement" (262). Ellis also felt, in line with the received wisdom of his day, that masturbation had deleterious side effects: "I am certainly inclined to believe that an early and excessive indulgence in masturbation, though not an adequate cause, is a favoring condition for the development of inversion, and that this is especially so in women" (277). This would be true because masturbation presupposes sexual desire, which was considered by Ellis and his contemporaries to be exclusively a masculine characteristic. Hence, a masturbating woman would be considered sexually "mannish," and thus, an invert.

In general, Ellis subscribed to three principal causes of homoerotic sexual attraction: (1) the absence of more "natural" objects of affection, (2) significant disappointment in romantic relationships with the opposite sex, or (3) seduction by a member of the same sex. Presumably, a combination of these factors could also induce inversion. At the same time, Ellis did not want to preclude the strong possibility of congenital predisposition to inversion or homosexual attraction. He wrote,

> These three influences, therefore . . . example at school, seduction, disappointment in normal love, all of them drawing the subject away from the opposite sex and concentrating him on his own sex, are exciting causes of inversion; but they require a favourable organic predisposition to act on, while there are a large number of cases in which no exciting cause at all can be found, but in which, from earliest childhood, the subject's interest seems to be turned on his own sex, and continues to be so turned throughout life. (324)

Interestingly, this passage prefigures the nature-versus-nurture debates that would become so important in academic circles throughout the 20th century: are complex behaviors and feelings, such as sexual attraction, biologically innate or the product of social influences or forces [λ Chapter 5]?

For Ellis, discussions of sexual inversion and homosexuality consisted not only of scientific explorations and theories but also of an awareness of the social dimension of the objects under study. He believed he viewed the topic of homosexuality from an unbiased perspective. But Ellis's aim was more than just avoiding an "attitude of moral superiority" (356). He felt that bias against inverts and homosexuals was legally unfounded and untenable. He wrote that "legislation against homosexuality has no clear effect either in diminishing or increasing its prevalence" (350). This view is clearly related to his sense that there is no real "cure" for inversion or homosexuality: "The question of the treatment of homosexuality must be approached with discrimination, caution, and scepticism. Nowadays, we can have but little sympathy with those

**Find Out More** in the Ellis case histories at the end of this chapter.

who, at all costs, are prepared to 'cure' the invert. There is no sound method of cure in radical cases" (327). Given its congenital nature and apparent incurability, legislating against homosexuality seemed to Ellis nonsensical.

## Paving the Way for Freud

In many significant ways, the sexologists paved the way for Sigmund Freud (1856–1939), Austrian neurologist and founder of psychoanalysis. While Freud was not a sexologist per se, his theories of sexuality became guiding principles for many 20th-century approaches to the study of sex, sexuality, identity, and personality. His influence has been tremendous, but it is worth keeping in mind that Freud was working in the same cultural and intellectual milieu that gave rise to the study of sexology. Freud certainly knew the work of the sexologists and was acquainted with many of them personally. He also took very seriously the importance of sex and sexual feeling in the development of the individual. Much of his work focused on tracing "healthy" psychosexual development through various stages (such as oral, anal, genital), and Freud suggested that the failure to navigate a particular stage successfully *(arrested development)* might result in homosexuality. But for Freud, this was not necessarily serious cause for alarm because the successful resolution of each stage and the consequent development of a fully adjusted heterosexual personality and identity is, he felt, a rare achievement. We all get stuck somewhere.

Much of Freud's central thinking about sexuality and its relationship to identity is found in *Three Essays on the Theory of Sexuality,* published in 1905. Freud believed in an innate *polymorphous perversity* that had to be shaped by social forces to achieve reproductive heterosexuality. This theory sharply differentiates Freud's work from that of the sexologists. As Steven Seidman writes, "[w]hereas sexologists defined the sexual instinct as reproductive and naturally heterosexual, Freud argued that the sexual instinct is oriented to pleasure. . . . Freud argued that the body has many erotic areas and that there are many ways of experiencing sexual satisfaction" (7). According to this view, possibilities for sexual excitation were multiple, and the path of one's desire could not be reduced to particular physiological characteristics. British theorist Alan Sinfield notes as well that "[i]n *Three Essays on the Theory of Sexuality . . .* Freud dismisses the sexologists' theories of innate inversion as crude, and disputes the anatomical basis they had been claiming. Even a change-over of 'mental qualities, instincts and character traits' cannot be demonstrated, let alone a physiological cross-over" (164).

Despite these differences, Freud and the sexologists shared some common insights into and beliefs about sexuality. According to Seidman, "Freud opened the way to thinking about sex as a fundamentally psychosocial reality; however, Freud never abandoned the sexological view that sex is natural" (12). David Halperin sees Havelock Ellis's and Freud's theories "separating sexual practices from gender" as representing "a key stage in the development of the possibility of gay identity" (Sinfield 163).

## Sexology and Early Sexual Rights Movements

As Foucault points out, the intense medical, psychiatric, and sexological scrutiny of inversion and homosexuality allowed some of those pathologized as homosexuals to create "reverse discourses" in which they recast their "illness" as positive identification. Ulrichs is a powerful example of this, leading some contemporary theorists to look favorably on the sexological enterprise. Steven Seidman, for instance, argues that "[s]exology has always had a social purpose." He notes that "[s]ome sexologists saw their work as contributing to the creation of a healthy, fit population. . . . Some policies even discouraged active sexual behavior by so-called inferior races and the sexual intermingling of races" (5). Such **eugenic** implications clearly complicate any "positive" intentions on behalf of sexologists to promote sex as a "natural" and "normal" practice, but we should not overlook the early sexual rights activists who used sexological research to fight laws designed to criminalize homoerotic behavior [λ Chapter 4].

Such laws were coming into existence at roughly the same time that sexologists were describing and categorizing homosexual behavior. While practices such as anal sex had previously been punishable in several European nations, a number of homoerotic practices were now coming under legal scrutiny and being not only pathologized but criminalized as well. For instance, the newly formed German state adopted Paragraph 175 in 1871, which banned all sexual activity between men (as well as **bestiality**) ("Germany) [λ Chapter 3]. Paragraph 175 spurred Ulrichs and others to become pro-homosexual activists, essentially creating the first relatively visible homosexual rights groups in Western history. Another prominent activist, the physician Magnus Hirschfeld (1868–1935), wrote pamphlets, books, and even a movie script (*Different from the Others*, 1919) to advocate on behalf of the third sex [λ Chapter 13]. John C. Fout details events of the early sexual rights movements in Germany, noting that "[i]n 1897 Magnus Hirschfeld and his newly created *Wissenschaftlich-humanitares Komittee* (Scientific humanitarian committee, or WhK) petitioned the Reichstag to reform Paragraph 175 of the German penal code, which criminalized sexual acts between males" (265). Fout argues that governments enacted antihomosexual legislation to calm the sociopolitical chaos that seemed to characterize the era.

Other important early sexual rights activists included the British writers Edward Carpenter (1844–1929) and Radclyffe Hall (1880–1943). Carpenter's poetry, pamphlets, and nonfiction works argued forcefully for thinking of sexual freedom for all as a basic right and privilege to be protected by democratic institutions as they slowly moved toward communist-style utopias. Hall is credited with writing the first novel recognizably about a lesbian, *The Well of Loneliness* (1928), which was subsequently banned in Britain and the subject of a censorship trial in the United States. *The Well of Loneliness* is an important document in that it borrows from sexological views circulating at the time; Havelock Ellis himself wrote a preface for the book in which he praised it for its "notable psychological and sociological significance [as] a completely faithful and uncompromising [depiction of] one particular aspect of sexual life as it exists among us to-day" (Hall, preface). Its hero, Stephen Gordon, is clearly a congenital invert in the sense that she is depicted (as Hall described herself) as a woman born with a man's soul. The end of the novel is a passionate and moving plea for tolerance: "Acknowledge us, oh God, before the whole world. Give us also the right to our existence!" (437) [λ Chapters 7 and 12].

Such pleas fell on deaf ears as the European continent drifted toward war spurred by imperial ambitions, economic collapse, the rise of National Socialism and other fascist movements, and yet more global war. Amid this increasing social and political chaos, many politicians sought stability by imposing order based on clear class divides and gender roles. In their view, we should all know our places in the social scheme of things. Unfortunately, the maintenance of the status quo and the attendant social control that such maintenance entailed would keep further Western movements for sexual rights and freedom below the political radar until the 1950s and 1960s.

## Sexology's Legacy

**A**s we think back on the development of sexology as a science, we quickly dismiss some of its practitioners' more audacious claims, such as the predilection of male homosexuals for the color green. In many other ways, though, the sexologists helped shape our contemporary understanding of sex and sexuality. Their classifications of sexuality and the development of the categories *homosexual* and *heterosexual* survive today as *gay* and *straight,* two of the most significant identity markers in contemporary Western culture, society, and politics. Furthermore, Dennis Altman suggests that turn-of-the-century categorizations of sexuality in the West have not only survived into the 21st century but have proliferated across the globe:

> Globalization has helped create an international gay/lesbian identity, which is by no means confined to the western world: there are many signs of what we think of as "modern"

homosexuality in countries such as Brazil, Costa Rica, Poland, and Taiwan. Indeed, the gay world—less obviously the lesbian, largely due to marked differences in women's social and economic status—is a key example of emerging global "subcultures," where members of particular groups have more in common across national and continental boundaries than they do with others in their own geographically defined societies. (87)

We will see examples of this commonality, as well as some striking challenges to it, throughout the remainder of this book, particularly as we look at examples of queerness in countries across the globe.

## QUESTIONS FOR DISCUSSION

1. Sexologists at the turn of the century considered themselves scientists. Whatever the merits of their scientific practices (and those practices are obviously not without their faults), a scientific understanding of homosexuality has continued to be important to this day. In what ways? Do you think a scientific understanding of homosexuality is beneficial to contemporary LGBT people? Why or why not?

2. If you were to write your own case history for a sexologist, what would it look like? Try your hand at such a case history, whatever your sexual orientation, and then compare it with one collected by Ellis. What are the similarities and differences? Look closely at particular ways in which you phrase your experience. Do you find any resemblances between what you have written and what others wrote a century ago?

3. Although we in the contemporary world often think of the Stonewall riots in 1969 as inaugurating the contemporary fight for gay and lesbian civil rights, we have seen in this chapter some much earlier manifestations of sexual rights advocacy. Using the Internet, a local library, or a local LGBT community center, research other late 19th- and early 20th-century homosexual or sexual rights movements. What do those earlier movements have in common with contemporary organizations and movements? What are some of the more striking differences? Consider how the sociopolitical situation today differs from that of a century ago.

## REFERENCES AND FURTHER READING

Altman, Dennis. *Global Sex*. Chicago: U of Chicago P, 2001. Print.

Bristow, David. *Sexuality*. London: Routledge, 1997. Print.

Carpenter, Edward. *The Intermediate Sex: A Study of Some Transitional Types of Men and Women*. c. 1912. New York: Kennerley, 1921. Print.

Chauncey, George. *Gay New York: Gender, Urban Culture, and the Making of the Gay Male World, 1890–1940*. New York: Basic Books, 1994. Print.

Douglas, Lord Alfred. "Two Loves," n.d. Web. 19 July 2008. <http://www.law.umkc.edu/faculty/projects/ftrials/wilde/poemsofdouglas.htm>.

Duberman, Martin Bauml, Martha Vicinus, and George Chauncey Jr., eds. *Hidden from History: Reclaiming the Gay and Lesbian Past.* New York: New American Library, 1989. Print.

Ellis, Havelock. *Studies in the Psychology of Sex.* New York: Random House, 1937. Print.

Faderman, Lillian. *Surpassing the Love of Men: Romantic Friendship and Love between Women from the Renaissance to the Present.* New York: Morrow, 1981. Print.

Foucault, Michel. *The History of Sexuality, Volume 1.* 1976. Trans. Robert Hurley. New York: Vintage, 1978. Print.

Fout, John C., ed. *Forbidden History: The State, Society, and the Regulation of Sexuality in Modern Europe.* Chicago: U of Chicago P, 1992. Print.

Freud, Sigmund. *Three Essays on the Theory of Sexuality.* 1905. Trans. James Strachey. New York: Basic Books, 1975. Print.

"Germany Adopts Paragraph 175." *Timeline: Nations and Laws,* n.d. Web. 19 July 2008. <http://www.gayhistory.com/rev2/factfiles/ff1871.htm>.

*GLBTQ: An Encyclopedia of Gay, Lesbian, Bisexual, Transgender, & Queer Culture.* N.p., n.d. Web. 19 July 2008. <http://www.glbtq.com/>.

Greenberg, David F. *The Construction of Homosexuality.* Chicago: U of Chicago P, 1988. Print.

Hall, Radclyffe. *The Well of Loneliness.* 1928. New York: Avon, 1981. Print.

"Invert." *Words: A Glossary of Words Unique to Modern Gay History,* n.d. Web. 19 July 2008. <http://www.gayhistory.com/rev2/words/invert.htm>.

Jagose, Annamarie. *Queer Theory: An Introduction.* New York: NYU P, 1996. Print.

"Karl Maria Kertbeny." *Timeline: Culture and Identity,* n.d. Web. 19 July 2008. <http://www.gayhistory.com/rev2/factfiles/ffkertbeny.htm>.

Katz, Jonathan Ned. *The Invention of Heterosexuality.* New York: Dutton, 1995. Print.

"Krafft-Ebing, Richard von (1840–1902)." *GLBTQ: An Encyclopedia of Gay, Lesbian, Bisexual, Transgender, and Queer Culture,* n.d. Web. 19 July 2008. <http://www.glbtq.com/socialsciences/krafft_ebing_r.html>.

Krafft-Ebing, Richard von. *Psychopathia Sexualis: A Medico-forensic Study.* 1886. Trans. Harry E. Wedeck. New York: Putnam, 1965. Print.

Margolis, Jonathan. *O: The Intimate History of the Orgasm.* London: Century, 2004. Print.

Oosterhuis, Harry. *Stepchildren of Nature: Krafft-Ebing, Psychiatry, and the Making of Sexual Identity.* Chicago: U of Chicago P, 2000. Print.

Seidman, Steven. *The Social Construction of Sexuality.* New York: Norton, 2003. Print.

Sinfield, Alan. *The Wilde Century: Effeminacy, Oscar Wilde and the Queer Movement.* New York: Columbia UP, 1994. Print.

"Timeline: Nations and Laws." *Timeline: The People and the Stories of Modern Gay History,* n.d. Web. 19 July 2008. <http://www.gayhistory.com/rev2/factfiles/ff1861.htm>.

Weeks, Jeffrey. *Sexuality and Its Discontents: Meanings, Myths, and Modern Sexualities.* London: Routledge, 1985.

## ➤ Havelock Ellis

(1937), United Kingdom

### From "History II," *Studies in the Psychology of Sex*

My parentage is very sound and healthy. Both my parents (who belong to the professional middle class) have good general health; nor can I trace any marked abnormal or diseased tendency, of mind or body, in any records of the family.

Though of a strongly nervous temperament myself, and sensitive, my health is good. I am not aware of any tendency to physical disease. In early manhood, however, owing, I believe, to the great emotional tension under which I lived, my nervous system was a good deal shattered and exhausted. Mentally and morally my nature is pretty well balanced, and I have never had any serious perturbations in these departments.

At the age of 8 or 9, and long before distinct sexual feelings declared themselves, I felt a friendly attraction toward my own sex, and this developed after the age of puberty into a passionate sense of love, which, however, never found any expression for itself till I was fully 20 years of age. I was a day-boarder at school and heard little of school-talk on sex subjects, was very reserved and modest besides; no elder person or parent ever spoke to me on such matters; and the passion for my own sex developed gradually, utterly uninfluenced from the outside. I never even, during all this period, and till a good deal later, learned the practice of masturbation. My own sexual nature was a mystery to me. I found myself cut off from the understanding of others, felt myself an outcast, and, with a highly loving and clinging temperament, was intensely miserable. I thought about my male friends—sometimes boys of my own age, sometimes elder boys, and once even a master—during the day and dreamed about them at night, but was too convinced that I was a hopeless monstrosity ever to make any effectual advances. Later on it was much the same, but gradually, though slowly, I came to find that there were others like myself. I made a few special friends, and at last it came to me occasionally to sleep with them and to satisfy my imperious need by mutual embraces and emissions. Before this happened, however, I was once or twice on the brink of despair and madness with repressed passion and torment. Meanwhile, from the first, my feeling, physically, toward the female sex was one of indifference, and later on, with the more special development of sex desires, one of positive repulsion. Though having several female friends, whose society I like and to whom I am sincerely attached, the thought of marriage or cohabitation with any such has always been odious to me.

As a boy I was attracted in general by boys rather older than myself; after leaving school I still fell in love, in a romantic vein, with comrades of my own standing. Now—at the age of 37—my ideal of love is a powerful, strongly built man, of my own age or rather younger—preferably of the working class. Though having solid sense and character, he need not be specially intellectual. If endowed in the latter way, he must not be too glib or refined. Anything effeminate in a man, or anything of the cheap intellectual style, repels me very decisively. . . .

I cannot regard my sexual feelings as unnatural or abnormal, since they have disclosed themselves so perfectly naturally and spontaneously within me. All that I have read in books or heard spoken about the ordinary sexual love, its intensity and passion, lifelong devotion, love at first sight, etc., seems to me to be easily matched by my own experiences in the homosexual form; and, with regard to the morality of this complex subject, my feeling is that it is the same as should prevail in love between man and woman, namely: that no bodily satisfaction should be sought at the cost of another person's distress or degradation. I am sure that this kind of love is, notwithstanding the physical difficulties that attend it, as deeply stirring and ennobling as the other kind, if not more so; and I think that for a perfect relationship the actual sex gratifications (whatever they may be) probably hold a less important place in this love than in the other.

### From "History XXXVI—Miss H., aged 30," *Studies in the Psychology of Sex*

Among her paternal relatives there is a tendency to eccentricity and to nervous disease. Her grandfather drank; her father was eccentric and hypochondriacal, and suffered from obsessions. Her mother and mother's relatives are entirely healthy, and normal in disposition.

At the age of 4 she liked to see the nates of a little girl who lived near. When she was about 6, the nurse-maid, sitting in the fields, used to play with her own parts, and told her to do likewise, saying it would make a baby come; she occasionally touched herself in consequence, but without producing any effect of any kind. When she was about 8 she used to see various nurse-maids uncover their children's sexual parts and show them to each other. She used to think about this when alone, and also about whipping. She never cared to play with dolls, and in her games always took the part of a man. Her first rudimentary sex-feelings appeared at the age of 8 or 9, and were associated with dreams of whipping and being whipped, which were most vivid between the ages of 11 and 14, when they died away on the appearance of affection for girls. She menstruated at 12.

Her earliest affection, at the age of 13, was for a schoolfellow, a graceful, coquettish girl with long golden hair and blue eyes. Her affection displayed itself in performing all sorts of small services for this girl, in constantly thinking about her, and in feeling deliciously grateful for the smallest return. At the age of 14 she had a similar passion for a girl cousin; she used to look forward with ecstasy to her visits, and especially to the rare occasions when the cousin slept with her; her excitement was then so great that she could not sleep, but there was no conscious sexual excitement. At the age of 15 or 16 she fell in love with another cousin; her experiences with this girl were full of delicious sensations; if the cousin only touched her neck, a thrill went through her body which she now regards as sexual. Again, at 17, she had an overwhelming, passionate fascination for another schoolfellow, a pretty, commonplace girl, whom she idealized and etherealized to an extravagant extent. The passion was so violent that her health was, to some extent, impaired; but it was purely unselfish, and there was nothing sexual in it. On leaving school at the age of 19 she met a girl of about the same age as herself, very womanly, but not much attracted to men. This girl became very much attached to her, and sought to gain her love. After some time Miss H. was attracted by this love, partly from the sense of power it gave her, and an intimate relation grew up. This relation became vaguely physical, Miss H. taking the initiative, but her friend desiring such relations and taking extreme pleasure in them; they used to touch and kiss each other tenderly (especially on the *mons veneris*), with equal ardour. They each experienced a strong pleasurable feeling in doing this, and sexual erethism, but no orgasm, and it does not appear that this ever occurred. Their general behavior to each other was that of lovers, but they endeavoured, as far as possible, to hide this fact from the world. This relation lasted for several years, and would have continued, had not Miss H.'s friend, from religious and moral scruples, put an end to the physical relationship. Miss H. had been very well and happy during this relationship; the interference with it seems to have exerted a disturbing influence, and also to have aroused her sexual desires, though she was still scarcely conscious of their real nature. . . .

She has never masturbated. Occasionally, but very rarely, she has had dreams of riding accompanied by pleasurable sexual emotions (she cannot recall any actual experience to suggest this, though fond of riding). She has never had any kind of sexual dreams about a man; of late years she has occasionally had erotic dreams about women. Her feeling toward men is friendly, but she has never had sexual attraction toward a man. She likes them as good comrades, as men like each other. She enjoys the society of men on account of their intellectual attraction. . . .

She is attracted to womanly women, sincere, reserved, pure, but courageous in character. She is not attracted to intellectual women, but at the same time cannot endure silly women. The physical qualities that attract her most are not so much beauty of face as a graceful, but not too slender, body with beautiful curves. The women she is drawn to are usually somewhat younger than herself. Women are much attracted to her, and without any effort on her part. She likes to take the active part and protecting role with them. She is herself energetic in character, and with a somewhat neurotic temperament. She finds sexual satisfaction in tenderly touching, caressing, and kissing the loved one's body. (There is no *cunnilinctus*, which she regards with abhorrence.) She feels more tenderness than passion. . . .

She believes that homosexual love is morally right when it is really part of a person's nature, and providing that the nature of homosexual love is always made plain to the object of such affection. She does not approve of it as a mere makeshift, or expression of sensuality, in normal women. She has sometimes resisted the sexual expression of her feelings, once for years at a time, but always in vain. The effect on her of loving women is distinctly good, she asserts, both spiritually and physically, while repression leads to morbidity and hysteria. She has suffered much from neurasthenia at various periods, but under appropriate treatment it has slowly diminished. The inverted instinct is too deeply rooted to eradicate, but it is well under control.

Havelock Ellis. *Studies in the Psychology of Sex*. New York: Random House, 1937.

## ➤ John D'Emilio

(1993), United States

### From "Capitalism and Gay Identity"

. . . I believe that a new, more accurate theory of gay history must be part of [the gay and lesbian] political enterprise. When the gay liberation movement began at the end of the 1960s, gay men and lesbians had no history that we could use to fashion our goals and strategy. In the ensuing years, in building a movement without a knowledge of our history, we instead invented a mythology. This mythical history drew on personal experience, which we read backward in time. For instance, most lesbians and gay men in the 1960s first discovered their homosexual desires in isolation, unaware of others, and without resources for naming and understanding what they felt. From this experience, we constructed a myth of silence, invisibility, and isolation as the essential characteristics of gay life in the past as well as the present. Moreover, because we faced so many oppressive laws, public policies, and cultural beliefs, we projected this onto an image of the abysmal past: until gay liberation, lesbians and gay men were always the victims of systematic, undifferentiated, terrible oppression.

These myths have limited our political perspective. They have contributed, for instance, to an overreliance on a strategy of coming out—if every gay man and lesbian in America came out, gay oppression would end—and have allowed us to ignore the institutionalized ways in which homophobia and heterosexism are reproduced. They have encouraged, at times, an incapacitating despair, especially at moments like the present: How can we unravel a gay oppression so pervasive and unchanging?

There is another historical myth that enjoys nearly universal acceptance in the gay movement, the myth of the "eternal homosexual." The argument runs something like this: gay men and lesbians always were and always will be. We are everywhere; not just now, but throughout history, in all societies and all periods. This myth served a positive political function in the first years of gay liberation. In the early 1970s, when we battled an ideology that either denied our existence or defined us as psychopathic individuals or freaks of nature, it was empowering to assert that "we are everywhere." But in recent years it has confined us as surely as the most homophobic medical theories, and locked our movement in place.

Here I wish to challenge this myth. I want to argue that gay men and lesbians have *not* always existed. Instead, they are a product of history, and have come into existence in a specific historical era. Their emergence is associated with the relations of capitalism; it has been the historical development of capitalism—more specifically, its free labor system—that has allowed large numbers of men and women in the late twentieth century to call themselves gay, to see themselves as part of a community of similar men and women, and to organize politically on the basis of that identity. Finally, I want to suggest some political lessons we can draw from this view of history.

What, then, are the relationships between the free labor system of capitalism and homosexuality? First, let me review some features of capitalism. Under capitalism, workers are "free" laborers in two ways. We have the freedom to look for a job. We own our ability to work and have the freedom to sell our labor power for wages to anyone willing to buy it. We are also freed from the ownership of anything except our labor power. Most of us do not own the land or the tools that produce what we need, but rather have to work for a living in order to survive. So, if we are free to sell our labor power in the positive sense, we are also freed, in the negative sense, from any other alternative. This dialectic—the constant interplay between exploitation and some measure of autonomy—informs all of the history of those who have lived under capitalism.

As capital—money used to make more money—expands, so does this system of free labor. Capital expands in several ways. Usually it expands in the same place, transforming small firms into larger ones, but it also expands by taking over new areas of production: the weaving of cloth, for instance, or the baking of bread. Finally, capital expands geographically. In the United States, capitalism initially took root in the Northeast, at a time when slavery was the dominant system in the South and when noncapitalist Native American societies occupied the western half of the continent. During the nineteenth century, capital spread from the Atlantic to the Pacific, and in the twentieth, U.S. capital has penetrated almost every part of the world.

The expansion of capital and the spread of wage labor have effected a profound transformation in the structure and functions of the nuclear family, the ideology of family life, and the meaning of heterosexual relations. It is these changes in the family that are most directly linked to the appearance of a collective gay life.

The white colonists in seventeenth-century New England established villages structured around a household economy, composed of family units that were basically self-sufficient, independent, and patriarchal. Men, women, and children farmed land owned by the male head of household. Although there was a division of labor between men and women, the family was truly an interdependent unit of production: the survival of each member depended on the cooperation of all. The home was a workplace where women processed raw farm products into food for daily consumption, where they made clothing, soap, and candles, and where husbands, wives, and children worked together to produce the goods they consumed.

By the nineteenth century, this system of household production was in decline. In the Northeast, as merchant capitalists invested the money accumulated through trade in the production of goods, wage labor became more common. Men and women were drawn out of the largely self-sufficient household economy of the colonial era into a capitalist system of free labor. For women in the nineteenth century, working for wages rarely lasted beyond marriage; for men, it became a permanent condition.

The family was thus no longer an independent unit of production. But although no longer independent, the family was still interdependent. Because capitalism had not expanded very far, because it had not yet taken over—or socialized—the production of consumer goods, women still performed necessary productive labor in the home. Many families no longer produced grain, but wives still baked into bread the flour they bought with their husbands' wages; or, when they purchased yarn or cloth, they still made clothing for their families. By the mid-1800s, capitalism had destroyed the economic self-sufficiency of many families, but not the mutual dependence of the members.

This transition away from the household family-based economy to a fully developed capitalist free labor economy occurred very slowly, over almost two centuries. As late as 1920, 50 percent of the U.S. population lived in communities of fewer than 2,500 people. The vast majority of blacks in the early twentieth century lived outside the free labor economy, in a system of sharecropping and tenancy that rested on the family. Not only did independent farming as a way of life still exist for millions of Americans, but even in towns and small cities women continued to grow and process food, make clothing, and engage in other kinds of domestic production.

But for those people who felt the brunt of these changes, the family took on new significance as an affective unit, an institution that produced not goods but emotional satisfaction and happiness. By the 1920s, among the white middle class, the ideology surrounding the family described it as the means through which men and women formed satisfying, mutually enhancing relationships and created an environment that nurtured children. The family became the setting for "personal life," sharply distinguished and disconnected from the public world of work and production.

The meaning of heterosexual relations also changed. In colonial New England, the birthrate averaged over seven children per woman of childbearing age. Men and women needed the labor of children. Producing offspring was as necessary for survival as producing grain. Sex was harnessed to procreation. The Puritans did not celebrate *hetero*sexuality but rather marriage; they condemned *all* sexual expression outside the marriage bond and did not differentiate sharply between sodomy and heterosexual fornication. . . .

As wage labor spread and production became socialized, then, it became possible to release sexuality from the "imperative" to procreate. Ideologically, heterosexual expression came to be a means of establishing intimacy, promoting happiness, and experiencing pleasure. In divesting the household of its economic independence and fostering the separation of sexuality from procreation, capitalism has created conditions that allow some men and women to organize a personal life around their erotic/emotional attraction to their own sex. It has made possible the formation of urban communities of lesbians and gay men and, more recently, of a politics based on a sexual identity.

Evidence from colonial New England court records and church sermons indicates that male and female homosexual behavior existed in the seventeenth century. Homosexual *behavior*, however, is different from homosexual *identity*. There was, quite simply, no "social space" in the colonial system of production that allowed men and women to be gay. Survival was structured around participation in a nuclear family. There were certain homosexual acts—sodomy among men, "lewdness" among women—in which individuals engaged, but family was so pervasive that colonial society lacked even the category of homosexual or lesbian to describe a person. It is quite possible that some men and women experienced a stronger attraction to their own sex than to the opposite sex—in fact, some colonial court cases refer to men who persisted in their "unnatural" attractions—but one could not fashion out of that preference a way of life. Colonial Massachusetts even had laws prohibiting unmarried adults from living outside family units.

By the second half of the nineteenth century, this situation was noticeably changing as the capitalist system of free labor took hold. Only when *individuals* began to make their living through wage labor, instead of as parts of an interdependent family unit, was it possible for homosexual desire to coalesce into a personal identity—an identity based on the ability to remain outside the heterosexual family and to construct a personal life based on attraction to one's own sex. By the end of the century, a class of men and women existed who recognized their erotic interest in their own sex, saw it as a trait that set them apart from the majority, and sought others like themselves. These early gay lives came from a wide social spectrum: civil servants and business executives, department store clerks and college professors, factory operatives, ministers, lawyers, cooks, domestics, hoboes, and the idle rich: men and women, black and white, immigrant and native born.

In this period, gay men and lesbians began to invent ways of meeting each other and sustaining a group life. Already, in the early twentieth century, large cities contained male homosexual bars. Gay men staked out cruising areas, such as Riverside Drive in New York City and Lafayette Park in Washington. In St. Louis and the nation's capital, annual drag balls brought together large numbers of black gay men. Public bathhouses and YMCAs became gathering spots for male homosexuals. Lesbians formed literary societies and private social clubs. Some working-class women "passed" as men to obtain better paying jobs and lived with other women—lesbian couples who appeared to the world as husband and wife. Among the faculties of women's colleges, in the settlement houses, and in the professional associations and clubs that women formed one could find lifelong intimate relationships supported by a web of lesbian friends. By the 1920s and 1930s, large cities such as New York and Chicago contained lesbian bars. These patterns of living could evolve because capitalism allowed individuals to survive beyond the confines of the family.

Simultaneously, ideological definitions of homosexual behavior changed. Doctors developed theories about homosexuality, describing it as a condition, something that was inherent in a person, a part of his or her "nature." These theories did not represent scientific breakthroughs, elucidations of previously undiscovered areas of knowledge; rather, they were an ideological response to a new way of organizing one's personal life. The popularization of the medical model, in turn, affected the consciousness of the women and men who experienced homosexual desire, so that they came to define themselves through their erotic life. . . .

# CHAPTER 3

# Toward Liberation

Given the context of the pathologization of homosexuality by the psychological establishment in the early 20th C., this chapter examines the rise of queer liberation movements. We end with the removal of homosexuality from the *Diagnostic and Statistical Manual of Mental Disorders*.

The turn of the 20th century in the United States and in Europe was marked by a continuation of the process of women gaining increasing access to education and autonomy from the interdependency of family life and its many obligations. In the last half of the 19th century, many women's colleges were established in the United States—Mills in 1865, Smith and Wellesley in 1875, Spelman (the first black women's college) in 1881, and Bryn Mawr in 1888. For many women, choosing college was tantamount to refusing heterosexual marriage. Between 1889 and 1908, 53% of women educated at Bryn Mawr were unmarried, and more generally, between 1877 and 1924, 75% of women earning doctorates did not marry (McGarry 52). The eugenicists of their day were alarmed at this development. As early as 1838 (that is, pre-Darwin), Henry F. Harrington had warned that educated women were no more than "mental hermaphrodites" (293). A generation later, Dr. Edward Clarke castigated educated, middle-class, young women in the United States for developing their brains at the expense of their reproductive capacities. By 1900, Dr. William Lee Howard could refer to independent women as "disgusting anti-social being[s] . . .—degenerates" (687). The reaction set in even as progress was taking place. Educated, independent, unmarried women were figured as representing evolutionary decay, and the benign Boston marriage could then be seen as a "degenerate" lesbian sexual relationship.

As we saw in the last chapter, however, some turn-of-the-century psychologists offered more moderate opinions regarding lesbianism in particular and homosexuality in general. For example, Sigmund Freud believed that homosexuality resulted from arrested sexual development, though he refused to go so far as to characterize it as an illness and did not believe that homosexual behavior should be criminalized. In fact, in a letter written to a mother who asked Freud for advice about her son's homosexuality, he wrote,

> Homosexuality is assuredly no advantage, but it is nothing to be ashamed of, no vice, no degradation, it cannot be classified as an illness; we consider it to be a variation of the sexual function produced by a certain arrest of sexual development. Many highly respectable individuals of ancient and modern times have been homosexuals, several of the greatest among them (Plato, Michelangelo, Leonardo da Vinci, etc.). It is a great injustice to persecute homosexuality as a crime, and cruelty too. (Freud, "Letter to an American Mother")

British physician Havelock Ellis, whose work Freud suggests that this mother read, countered popular opinion by writing in *Sexual Inversion* that homosexuality was neither a crime nor a disease, considering it instead an alternative sexual preference probably resulting from a combination of factors related to upbringing and the physical makeup of the individual. German sexologist Magnus Hirschfeld was among the first to argue that homosexuality is not necessarily linked to gender variance: "One thing that often causes a wrong assumption that someone is homosexual is masculine behavior in women and feminine behavior in men. . . . For a long time in many circles it was almost the rule to assume without further ado that women with short hair or men who appeared as female impersonators were homosexual. The matter is just not that simple" (77) [λ Chapter 2].

Freud, Ellis, and Hirschfeld stood in opposition to Howard in seeing homosexuality as neither a sin nor a sign of degeneracy, but simply a natural variation of the human species. Others have argued that in part because it is a variation and not the norm—and also because of the long history of persecution and punishment of those engaging in same-sex (and other non-sanctioned) sexual acts—homosexuality should continue to be restricted or outlawed by the state. Such thinking persists in the contemporary world. For example, in his dissenting opinion to the Court's *Lawrence v. Texas* ruling (2003) [λ Chapter 6] that laws prohibiting sodomy are a violation of "personal dignity and autonomy" Supreme Court Justice Antonin Scalia noted that, in the United States, sodomy laws date back to the Colonial era, and there are "records of 20 sodomy prosecutions and 4 executions during the colonial period" (Scalia). Scalia, in short, was arguing that society needs laws against sodomy because society has always had laws against sodomy—in other words, that a law's prior existence is sufficient reason for it to continue to exist, whether or not the norms of society have evolved in a different direction. Many countries in the world either presently have or have had laws that prohibit homosexual behavior, mostly based on religious beliefs that homosexuality is both abnormal and immoral. In the Western world, these laws have been under continuous scrutiny and discussion, but there are still places in the world—India and Singapore, for instance—where homosexual acts can bring the offender a sentence of life in prison. In Afghanistan and Iran, homosexuality is punishable by execution. However, many countries in the world have either overturned their sodomy statutes or never imposed them at all.

## Medical Models of Homosexuality

In support of arguments that homosexuality is a deviation from the norm, much of the scientific work related to homosexuality is based on a medical model designed to discover the reasons for individuals' homosexual tendencies. Often this work is couched in phraseology that makes it seem as if the goal of such research is to identify homosexuality early in order to develop "cures" for those who "suffer" from it. Because human behavior is seen as closely linked to the brain, many of the medical studies of homosexuals have focused on explaining how the brain of a homosexual works [λ Chapter 5]. This notion that homosexuals are somehow physically different from heterosexuals and that homosexuality is a psychological deviancy has been adopted not only by the medical establishment but also by gay men and lesbians themselves throughout the 20th century. We see it, for instance, in Radclyffe Hall's 1928 novel *The Well of Loneliness* [λ Chapters 2 and 12], and the theme runs back into the 19th century and forward into the late 20th century. For Hall and other lesbian and gay people in the early 20th century, it was important to embrace the medical model despite its emphasis on deviance because this model provided (1) a language with which homosexuals could describe their lives and (2) lists of characteristics homosexuals could use to recognize each other in the world. The notion that homosexuality results from biological factors out of the control of individuals is called **essentialism**, and it has been useful to a gay rights movement that needed to assert the innocence of homosexuals and the naturalness of homosexuality. Most recently, with advances in genetic science, Dean Hamer and others have tried to isolate a "gay gene," but this attempt to discover a biological reason for homosexuality is not new [λ Chapter 5]. To date, no irrefutable evidence exists that homosexuals are biologically different from heterosexuals. Still, gay activists employ **strategic essentialism** as a method whereby homosexuals' presumably fixed identity is deployed as an argument against discrimination. Despite the political usefulness of essentialism, many activists have wondered whether focusing so much on the notion of innate sexuality might fuel a desire among antigay elements to "catch" and perhaps even "cure" homosexuality, and such suspicions are borne out by the existence of programs all over the Western world that promise to make homosexual teens and adults into "ex-gays."

During much of the 20th century, psychiatrists in the United States and throughout the world treated homosexuality as an illness primarily caused by poor parenting—domineering mothers and passive or inadequate fathers. Many prominent psychiatrists—Sandor Rado, Irving Bieber, and Charles Socarides, for example—argued vehemently that homosexuality should be treated as a pathology in need of treatment and cure. In fact, in a 1969 *Time* magazine article that claimed to introduce "the homosexual lifestyle" to American consciousness, Socarides espoused this view in a very public forum.

Around the same time, Cornelia Wilbur, the psychiatrist whose work with "Sybil" (Shirley Ardell Mason) popularized the multiple personality disorder (MPD) diagnosis, also studied lesbian sexuality. Her article "Clinical Aspects of Female Homosexuality" (1965) argued that, like gay men, lesbians typically grew up in families with passive fathers and domineering mothers. The Wilbur study is one of the few analyses of lesbians done by the group of mid-20th-century psychiatrists that scholar Neil Miller calls the "'Gay Is Sick' Shrinks"; most of the studies focused on male sexuality, portraying homosexual men as predatory, effeminate, and emotionally unstable. This notion that "gay is sick" has had enormous negative personal implications for LGBT men and women; as well, the idea has served as justification for laws against "deviant" (nonheterosexual) sexuality. Because of widespread social acceptance of this idea, gay men and lesbians have been subjected to many invasive and traumatic medical interventions, including electroshock convulsive therapy (shock treatments), lobotomies, castration, hormone therapy, aversion therapy, and forced incarceration in mental hospitals.

**Transsexual** individuals have also frequently come under the scrutiny of the medical community. The first male-to-female surgical transformation took place in Germany in the 1930s, and the first radical mastectomy for a female-to-male **transgender** person occurred in the United States in 1917; in 1946, New Zealand surgeon Harold Gillies performed the first sex reassignment surgery from female to male, a more complex surgery than from male to female. But access to surgery has been limited by the fact that few insurance companies provide coverage for sex reassignment procedures, which are typically classified as cosmetic (therefore elective) surgery. Harry Benjamin, influenced by the work of Magnus Hirschfeld, was the best-known physician for patients diagnosed with **gender identity disorder** (**GID**), or what he called **gender dysphoria**. Benjamin developed a set of Standards of Care (1979) for transsexual individuals; these standards require extensive psychotherapy and a letter of support from a psychiatrist before a person seeking sex reassignment can be approved for surgery (Meyerowitz). Transpeople are particularly at the mercy of the medical communities in their countries if they desire any level of sex reassignment—from hormonal therapy to surgery. Even after physical reassignment, transsexuals face a daunting array of legal and social problems as they attempt to adjust to their new lives [λ Chapters 5 and 7].

## Urban Life and Sexual Expression

Despite the uneasy relationship between LGBT people and the medical establishment throughout much of the 20th century, that time also saw the rise of many prominent and visible queer communities. In the United States, the era known as the Harlem Renaissance, which lasted from the Roaring Twenties through the Depression in the 1930s, helped provide meeting places and creative and sexual outlets for many African-American artists and writers [λ Chapter 9]. Known primarily as an era during which African-American art, literature, music, dance, and social commentary flourished in the Harlem section of New York City, the Harlem Renaissance was also marked by the attitude that homosexuality was a personal matter. As a result, artists, actors, musicians, and literati who earned respect for their artistic and scholarly work could be fairly open about their sexuality. Lesbian and gay performers and artists such as Ma Rainey, Mabel Hampton, Alain Locke, and Claude McKay were significant figures in the Harlem Renaissance. Though it is important to understand that the "closet door" was somewhat open for these individuals, their ability to be "out" should not be read in contemporary terms. There was, for these gay men and lesbians, a significant threat should their sexuality become too much of a focus. Discrimination in housing and employment, as well as the threat of institutionalization or imprisonment, were dangers—and for African-American homosexuals, the intertwining of racial discrimination and homophobia intensified these threats. Communities where expressions of nonnormative sexuality were somewhat accepted were also emerging in Europe. In Berlin in 1904, for example, Anna Rüling urged the fledgling women's movement to attend to "Uranian" concerns. In Parisian salons, artists and intellectuals gathered in relative safety to find both intellectual and emotional community, and sexual openness was welcomed. Famous lesbians and **bisexuals** such as Natalie Barney, Gertrude Stein and her partner Alice B. Toklas, Djuna Barnes, and Colette developed a community in which nonjudgmental attitudes and emotional and creative support were offered freely [λ Chapter 9]. The Bloomsbury group in London, which included bisexual and homosexual individuals such as Dora

Carrington, Vita Sackville-West, Virginia Woolf, and E. M. Forster, was known for its plain sex talk, and many of its members openly supported Radclyffe Hall when *The Well of Loneliness* was taken to court on obscenity charges [λ Chapter 12]. While it is true that many LGBT people today see *The Well of Loneliness* as afflicted by self-loathing and internalized homophobia, it was the first novel to present a portrayal of lesbian life, and backing it clearly indicated support of a sexual lifestyle alternative to heterosexuality.

As we can see, popular attitudes about sexuality evolve inconsistently based on the realities of particular moments in time. Contemporary Americans who identify as lesbian, gay, bisexual, transgendered, or even queer might be tempted to look back at the history of their predecessors' treatment and see the past as "the bad old days" and the present as marked by greater openness and liberation. Such a view of history, though, does not take into account the tendency of attitudes toward sexuality to loosen and then tighten again. There have been many historical moments when fairly accepting societies became more restrictive as a result of a particular social crisis. In the United States, the social openness of the 1920s and early 1930s was interrupted by the Depression. Many believed that the Depression was a kind of "retribution" for a generation of American **decadence**, and one response to a growing scarcity of resources and access to the necessities for living was an increasing conservatism in social attitudes. In Germany, the Nazis' rise to power—also related indirectly to the worldwide Depression—led not only to more conservative attitudes toward homosexuals but also to outright persecution.

## World War II and Homosexuality

Due in part to the work of scholars such as Erwin Haeberle, we can see that before World War II, Germany was perhaps the leader in research and activist reform work around the acceptance of homosexuality as a reasonable sexual alternative to heterosexuality. Much of the early sexological research was done by German Jews—Magnus Hirschfeld, for example. During the turbulence of the 1930s, however, much of the sexologists' work was lost when the Nazis destroyed all German sexological research and began their persecution of Jews, homosexuals, and others. Figure 3.1 shows the different badges used to identify groups who were persecuted by the Nazis.

When Germany became a unified nation in 1871, its new legal code included Paragraph 175, which outlawed sodomy. Between 1933 and 1945, the Nazis used this law to arrest approximately 100,000 men they had identified as homosexual (*Paragraph 175*). Before the Nazis came to power, there had been concerted efforts made in Germany to reform the law against sodomy, but the Nazis actually extended the law. One result of this extension was that at the end of World War II, when the remaining prisoners in concentration camps were set free, only the homosexuals were still classified as criminals. Interestingly, Paragraph 175 criminalized sexual activity among men but not among women. It is noteworthy that the pink triangle used to identify homosexuals so that they could be singled out for persecution in the Nazi concentration camps has now become an international symbol for gay liberation.

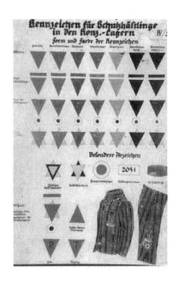

**Figure 3.1** This is a chart of the different badges prisoners of Nazi concentration camps were forced to wear.

Before World War II, there was no formal policy against homosexuals serving in the U.S. military. During the war, American women were called upon to serve in the military and to work outside their homes in ways they never had before; furthermore, since World War I, the armed services had had the reputation of being an "ideal breeding ground" for lesbianism. In the 1940s, the military began to use psychiatrists to keep homosexuals from enlisting and to issue what were called *blue discharges* (because they were often printed on blue paper) to military personnel identified as homosexuals. After the war was over, and when the armed services could afford to remove their homosexual recruits, a *Newsweek* article from 9 June 1947 reported that the United States military now considered the blue discharges "vague and protective" and would no longer use them; from this point on, even homosexuals who had not been "guilty of a definite offense would receive an 'undesirable' discharge" (Miller 241). The article also stated that case histories in Army files revealed, among other things, that homosexual soldiers "topped the average soldier in intelligence, education, and rating," with 10% holding college degrees and only "a handful" being illiterate, and on the "whole [homosexual] army personnel were law-abiding and hard-working" (240). Despite these realities, official policy of the U.S. military was to ferret out homosexuals attempting to enlist by identifying and refusing those men whose looks or behavior seemed effeminate or by testing potential enlistees for knowledge of homosexual customs or vocabulary. Their rationale was that the morale of heterosexual servicemen would be compromised if they were required to live and work with homosexuals, whose supposed uncontrollable and inappropriate sexual desire made them inherently untrustworthy. As Kathleen Parker writes, the prohibition of gay servicemen was based solely on "military objectives: unit cohesion, military discipline, order and morale. It [was] not about the rights of gays to serve, but about the rights of non-gays to be protected from forced intimacy with people who may be sexually attracted to them" (B7).

A number of lesbians who served in the Women's Army Corps (WAC) reported that their direct supervisors were unwilling to push the sexuality issue because their services were so desperately needed. Among these was Johnnie Phelps, whose story is recounted by Elizabeth Lapovsky Kennedy and Madeline D. Davis, Randy Shilts, and several film documentaries. According to Phelps, she was summoned by the general-in-command of her battalion (Dwight D. Eisenhower), who told her that he wanted to rid the battalion of lesbians and commanded that she draw up a list of women who fit that description. Phelps claims she told Eisenhower that she would be willing to draw up such a list as long as he understood that her name would be at its top and that the list would include at least "95%" of the women in the battalion; Eisenhower quickly rescinded the order.

We should remember that World War II was not the first moment when gay men and lesbians visibly served the war effort. World War I was an important turning point for women who wanted to serve in the military. Britain, the United States, Russia, and Germany all allowed women to officially enlist in the military for the first time. Though Britain, the United States, and Germany did not allow women to serve in combat, the Russian military included about 2,000 women soldiers who fought in what was called the "Women's Battalion of Death," formed and commanded by Maria Bochkareva. There are, of course, no data on the number of lesbians serving in the Battalion of Death, and Bochkareva herself was twice married to men. Among women identifying as lesbian who served in some capacity during World War I were Gertrude Stein, Alice B. Toklas, and Radclyffe Hall, all of whom served as ambulance drivers. Stein and Toklas had a Ford shipped to Paris from the United States and outfitted it as an ambulance. Radclyffe Hall's *The Well of Loneliness* and her short story "Miss Ogilvy Finds Herself" tell of lesbians serving in the British military during World War I; both works describe women experiencing for the first time (1) the self-validation involved in serving one's country as a uniformed citizen, and (2) the exhilaration of being recognized as a lesbian in a world of women.

## McCarthy and the Purge of the "Perverts"

The now-infamous Joseph McCarthy was, during the early part of his career, a fairly unknown member of the U.S. Senate. In 1950, he and other political leaders led an attempt to ferret out and purge the country of Communists; they also charged that homosexuals were a threat to national security, publicly referring to them as "perverts" and claiming that they had infiltrated the government and were "perhaps as dangerous as the actual Communists" (McGarry 37). The fear that homosexuals were both emotionally unstable and particularly susceptible to blackmail lay at the core of the argument made by McCarthy and his aide, Roy Cohn [λ Chapter 9], a closeted gay man and the actual architect of the campaign to purge the government of homosexuals. In 1953, President Dwight D. Eisenhower signed Executive Order 10450. This order made "sexual perversion" sufficient reason for exclusion from federal employment; as a result, homosexuals were fired from federal jobs eight times more frequently than before 1950 (McGarry 37).

From the very beginning, the notion that the government was overrun with Communist sympathizers was closely linked to the idea that the Communist threat was related to homosexuality. At about the same time that McCarthy announced to an audience in Wheeling, West Virginia, that he had in his hand a list of 205 members of the Communist Party who were working in the State Department (he later admitted that what he actually waved before that audience was a laundry list), Undersecretary of State John Peurifoy testified before a Senate committee that there were 91 "persons in the shady category" working in the government. He added that "[m]ost of these were homosexuals." Guy George Gabrielson, chairman of the Republican National Committee from 1949 to 1952, warned that "perhaps as dangerous as the actual Communists are the sexual perverts [homosexuals] who have infiltrated the Government in recent years." The connection of Communism to homosexuality became embedded in the popular imagination when a *New York Daily News* political commentator reported that an "all-powerful, super-secret inner circle of highly educated, socially highly placed sexual misfits" had "infiltrated" the State Department and warned that these people were "all easy to blackmail, all susceptible to blandishments by homosexuals in foreign nations" (Miller 258–59).

Ironically, the period of the McCarthy witch hunts was also the time when much of the work took place that finally led to the declassification of homosexuality as a mental illness. Before that time, most American studies of homosexuality had focused on mental patients or prisoners. In the 1950s, Evelyn Hooker did the first extensive study of homosexuals not incarcerated in mental hospitals or prisons. Hooker found that there were few if any clear psychological differences between homosexuals and heterosexuals besides those related to the burdens of oppression and the necessity for hiding one's sexual preferences from family, friends, and coworkers. She also found the psychological diversity of homosexuals to be similar to that of heterosexuals. Many in the psychological community responded to this work with surprise and sometimes skepticism. Other scholars also began to question long-held assumptions about sexuality.

Alfred Kinsey's *Sexual Behavior in the Human Male* (1948) and *Sexual Behavior in the Human Female* (1953), coauthored with Wardell B. Pomeroy and Clyde E. Martin, elicited great interest from the average American. In these books, Kinsey characterized homosexuality as a normally occurring sexual alternative. Because Kinsey was so well known, Americans often see him as the "father of sexology" [λ Chapters 2 and 5].

Kinsey's books popularized the idea of homosexuality as a normal variation of human sexuality. He proposed that all people exist on a heterosexual-homosexual continuum and that approximately 10% of the population is homosexual. Picking up on this work, Donald Webster Cory (a pseudonym for Edward Sagarin) wrote *The Homosexual in America* in 1951. This widely read book was among the first to describe homosexual life, focusing on both emerging gay culture and discrimination.

Kinsey and Cory were liberalizing voices in the repressive postwar years. Such thinking occurred in a cultural context of growing critique, particularly in the United States. Some artists, writers, and social nonconformists were gathering around the term *beat* to describe both a sense of being "beaten down" by conservative views and forces and a desire to "march to the beat of a different drummer," to paraphrase Thoreau. The Beats gained much notoriety in the 1950s, and they were often very sympathetic to the plight of homosexuals. Some among them, such as poet Allen Ginsberg, became outspoken homosexual artists [λ Chapter 9].

Still, the McCarthyite prejudices lingered. Even as countercultural movements arose in the 1960s, some social critics who seemed very different from figures such as McCarthy and Cohn felt free to speak out against homosexuals. Feminist leader Betty Friedan, for instance, lamented "the homosexuality that is spreading like a murky smog over the American scene." Friedan picked up on the "gay is sick" theme by saying that homosexuality was created by the "parasitical motherlove" of women confined to the home by social pressures designed to keep women out of the workforce (Wolfe). Friedan also coined the phrase "The Lavender Menace" to describe lesbians in the feminist movement; this phrase eventually became a rallying call for lesbians who left mainstream organizations such as the National Organization for Women (NOW) to form more welcoming communities around political activism on behalf of lesbians.

# The Homophile Movement

At the close of World War II, some lesbians and gay men began to understand themselves as a social minority oppressed and made invisible by a larger, unfeeling, and wrongheaded heterosexual majority. This new way of seeing homosexuality helped create an environment in which the notion that homosexuality was a sickness or a perversion could be effectively challenged not only by physicians and psychotherapists but also by homosexuals themselves. In a 1948 issue of her self-published newsletter *Vice Versa*, "Lisa Ben" (an anagram for lesbian) proclaimed, "I for one consider myself neither an error of nature nor some sort of psychological freak. Friends of similar tendencies . . . also refuse to regard themselves in this light. . . . Is it not possible that we are just as natural and normal by our standards as so-called 'normals' are by theirs?" (McGarry 142).

In the United States, this kind of resistant thinking gave rise to what is known as the **homophile movement**. The primary goal of homophile organizations was to gain acceptance for gay men and lesbians by heterosexuals. In the early 1950s, Harry Hay founded the Mattachine Society, and Del Martin and Phyllis Lyon founded the Daughters of Bilitis (DOB) [λ Chapter 6]. These and other organizations made some advances in gaining acceptance and rights for lesbians and gay men, and they were successful in increasing visibility. The mainstream media, by contrast, continued to present gay life as seedy, sordid, and dangerous. Consider, for instance, the *Time* article mentioned earlier in this chapter, which presents homosexuals as part of a dark "underground" and features a debate among "experts" about whether homosexuality is an illness. Although it did bring news of the existence of other homosexuals to many nonurban heterosexuals and homosexuals, it also supported the notion that homosexuals were sad, sick, and even sexually predatory.

At this time, police frequently harassed gay men and lesbians—especially those they saw as resisting traditional gender roles—in gay bars and on the streets. Landlords could evict gay men and lesbians without cause. In response, the Veterans' Benevolent Association, founded in New York City in 1945, focused its efforts on helping homosexuals who were arrested or who were discriminated against in employment or housing because of their homosexuality. The Knights of the Clock, founded in Los Angeles in 1950, served as a social group for interracial gay couples who were not comfortable with the bar scene (McGarry 142). The Mattachine Society, founded by Harry Hay in 1950, was perhaps the best-known homophile organization in the country. Hay, a longtime member of the Communist Party, founded the group in response to the anti-Communist and anti-homosexual environment created by McCarthy and his cronies. The group had a complex administrative structure that was developed to maintain the anonymity of its founders and to give it the impenetrable structure Hay thought would protect it against outside assault. The organization adopted the name "Mattachine" in reference to a group of medieval French townsmen who "conducted dances and rituals in the countryside during the Feast of Fools at the vernal equinox" (Miller 334). Generally, the Mattachine Society and the DOB worked toward assimilation of gays and lesbians and argued their similarity to the heterosexual mainstream. In keeping with this philosophy, homophile organizations often asked men participating in gay rights marches to wear business suits complete with ties and women to wear skirts that fell to the knee or below. Some members of the homophile movement did not fully embrace the **assimilationist** goals of Mattachine and DOB. For instance, one subgroup of Mattachine began publishing *One,* a magazine that eventually had a national circulation of 5,000. *One* was less assimilationist in its tone than the official rhetoric of the Mattachine Society. Similarly, the DOB was not a monolithic organization; as the middle-class lesbians in the group began to become more and more political, many working-class lesbians broke away from the DOB to form localized social groups.

The early and mid-20th century saw dramatic challenges that directly affected both popular and political perceptions of LGBT people and the evolving self-perception of gays and lesbians, many of whom were searching for a way to articulate their emerging sense of identity in an often hostile sociocultural and political climate. Americans tend to understand the late 1960s and early 1970s as a time when attitudes about alternative sexualities changed dramatically, fueled in part by the Stonewall riots in 1969 [λ Chapter 4] and the removal of homosexuality from the American Psychiatric Association's *Diagnostic and Statistical Manual* in 1973—two major events we will talk about in depth in Chapter 4. We see similar changes in other countries. In the United Kingdom, although the 1957 Wolfenden Act decriminalized homosexuality, it was classified as a disease there until 1994. In 1992, the World Health Organization stopped classifying homosexuality as a disease. In 2001, the Chinese government did the same ("China"). In short, the efforts of activists working for sexual freedom in the 1950s, 1960s, and early 1970s led to important changes in medical opinion and criminal statutes, many of which have paved the way for later activists to challenge long-held negative opinions about lesbians and gay men. In the next chapter, we will see the profound impact of such activism on more recent history.

## QUESTIONS FOR DISCUSSION

1. The Harlem Renaissance offers us a rich glimpse into a talented, creative, and often politically astute group of writers, musicians, and artists who examined how race works in American society. Several artists who participated in the Harlem Renaissance were also gay, lesbian, or bisexual. Research one artist—a writer, singer, or graphic artist—and find out more about how this person examined both racial and sexual issues in his or her work.

2. View the film *Paragraph 175*. Immediately after you have finished the film, summarize its main factual points in a freely written paragraph or in a list. Mark those facts that you have heard before with a star; then mark the facts that are new to you with an asterisk. Before viewing the film, did you know that homosexuals were persecuted by the Nazis? How does knowing that affect you? What do you feel that you still need to know about this issue? What does it mean to you that the pink triangle, which we now identify as an international symbol of gay power and community, was first used by the Nazis as a way of marking homosexual men for persecution?

3. Read the majority opinion (written by Kennedy) and the concurrence (by O'Connor), as well as the dissenting opinions by Scalia and Thomas, in the case of *Lawrence v. Texas*. Compose a letter to one or more of the Supreme Court justices in the case supporting her or his written opinion. Make sure to refer to aspects of LGBT history and culture that you have learned as you have read chapters from this book. The opinions can be found at the Cornell Law School website (http://www.law.cornell.edu/supct/html/02-102.ZS.html).

## REFERENCES AND FURTHER READING

"China Decides Homosexuality No Longer Mental Illness." *The South China Morning Post,* 8 March 2001. Web. 24 March 2008. <http://www.hartford-hwp.com/archives/55/325.html>.

Clarke, Edward H. *Sex in Education; or, A Fair Chance for the Girls.* Boston: Osgood, 1873. Print.

Cory, Donald Webster. *The Homosexual in America: A Subjective Approach.* New York: Greenberg, 1951. Print.

Duberman, Martin Bauml, Martha Vicinus, and George Chauncey Jr., eds. *Hidden from History: Reclaiming the Gay and Lesbian Past.* New York: New American Library, 1990. Print.

Faderman, Lillian. *Odd Girls and Twilight Lovers: A History of Lesbian Life in Twentieth-Century America.* New York: Columbia UP, 1991. Print.

Freud, Sigmund. "Letter to an American Mother," Web. 19 July 2008. <http://www.psychpage.com/gay/library/freudsletter.html>.

Harrington, Henry F. "Female Education." *Ladies' Companion* 9 (1838): 293. Print.

Hirschfeld, Magnus. *The Homosexuality of Men and Women.* Trans. Michael A. Lombardi-Nash. Amherst, NY: Prometheus, 2000. Print.

Hooker, Evelyn. "The Adjustment of the Male Overt Homosexual." *Journal of Projective Techniques* 21 (1957): 18–31. Print.

Howard, William Lee. "Effeminate Men, Masculine Women." *New York Medical Journal* 71 (1900): 686–687. Print.

Kennedy, Elizabeth Lapovsky, and Madeline D. Davis. *Boots of Leather, Slippers of Gold: The History of a Lesbian Community.* New York: Routledge, 1993. Print.

Kinsey, Alfred and the staff of the Institute for Sex Research, Indiana University. *Sexual Behavior in the Human Female.* Philadelphia: Saunders, 1953. Print.

Kinsey, Alfred, Wardell B. Pomeroy, and Clyde E. Martin. *Sexual Behavior in the Human Male.* Philadelphia: Saunders, 1948. Print.

McGarry, Molly. *Becoming Visible: An Illustrated History of Lesbian and Gay Life in Twentieth-Century America.* New York: Penguin Studio, 1998. Print.

Meyerowitz, Joanne. *How Sex Changed: A History of Transsexuality in the United States.* Cambridge, MA: Harvard UP, 2004. Print.

Miller, Neil. *Out of the Past: Gay and Lesbian History from 1869 to the Present.* New York: Vintage, 1995. Print.

*Paragraph 175.* Dir. Rob Epstein and Jeffrey Friedman. Nar. Rupert Everett, Klaus Müller (III), Karl Gorath, and Pierre Seel. New Yorker Video, 2001. DVD. 2004.

Parker, Kathleen. "Clinton, Gays-in-Military Issue Likely behind Change of Joint Chiefs." *Cincinnati Enquirer,* 14 June 2007: B7. Print.

Scalia, Antonin. Dissent. *Lawrence v. Texas* (02-102) 539 U.S. 558 (2003). Print.

Shilts, Randy. *Conduct Unbecoming: Gays and Lesbians in the US Military.* New York: Ballantine, 1994. Print.

Wilbur, Cornelia. "Clinical Aspects of Female Homosexuality." *Sexual Inversion: Multiple Roots of Homosexuality.* Ed. J. Marmor. New York: Basic Books, 1965. 268–301. Print.

Wolfe, Alan. "The Mystique of Betty Friedan." *Atlantic Monthly* 284.3 (September 1999). Web. 19 July 2008. <http://www.theatlantic.com/issues/99sep/9909friedan.htm>.

---

# READINGS

---

## ➢ "Donald Webster Cory" (Edward Sagarin) and John P. LeRoy

(1963), United States

---

### "Should Homosexuality Be Eliminated?"

The large majority of the population, in America and abroad, being themselves hetero-sexual and being antagonistic for various reasons to homosexuals and to their activities, would like to see this aspect of human life eliminated. They may learn, in time, to tolerate it, but it is tolerance in the literal meaning of the word; that is, something that one is able to stand, but of which one does not approve. But, by and large, their aim is the elimina-tion of all sex activities between members of the same sex.

Unfortunately, although the ends sought by such people may, if placed within a real-istic contemporary context, seem commendable, the motivations that lead them to these ends are frequently less so. For they condemn homosexual activity, not because the peo-ple involved in it are disturbed or unhappy—in fact, just the opposite, because the activi-ties of the hostile community make them more disturbed, more unhappy. They condemn it because it is immoral, or decadent, or ungodly, or for some other equally subjective and entirely unverifiable reason.

Actually, a great deal of the discussion that has been taking place on the question of homosexuality has been centered around the viewpoint that it is a problem, a sign of cultural decadence on a societal level and of immaturity on a personal level; that it is a disease, a maladjustment, or a disturbance. Though some of these descriptive words may be fitting, and others less so, it is entirely possible that it may well be as much of a disturbance in this culture not to accept sexuality—homo-, hetero-, or any other that is voluntarily engaged in among adults.

Upon close observation of the relationship between society and the homosexual, one finds that many people have focused on the neurotic character of individual inverts, while minimizing the social oppression which they must silently bear, while others have ignored the former and emphasized only the latter. Neither should be neglected. . . .

By means of a variety of legal, social, and moral pressures, society makes clear its strong disapproval of homosexuality. But disapproval and punishment do not imply effec-tive diminution. What, if anything, is being done to deter the desire for this activity; to prevent it; to cure it; or to eliminate it? Very little, and for complex reasons that psycholo-gists are beginning to grapple with. The hostile measures of an antagonistic society may even serve to foster the homosexual way of life.

Homosexuality is not deliberately and perversely chosen. A man (or woman) discov-ers that his psychosexual development has progressed in a different direction from that which is regarded as normal and, for better or worse, must adjust his erotic life accord-ingly, if he is to have any erotic life at all. All the legal and social sanctions are usually discovered after the person has realized that he is homosexual and, of course, by then it is too late.

The hostility that society directs toward the invert drives him underground, where he must conceal his erotic preferences, rather than bring those desires out into the open, where they can be dealt with objectively. For some, the existence of a twilight world attracts the adventurous rebel for whom living in immediate proximity to danger serves as a source of excitement in an otherwise drab existence. Aside from forcing many homosexuals into a sub-society, which they frequently abhor and in which they function only with anxiety, the hostility also serves to help some homosexuals hate themselves so thoroughly that they unconsciously get themselves into trouble in order to be punished, thereby convincing themselves that the self-hatred was justified. Those inverts whose self-hatred is bound up with a more general type of paranoia would have to find other ways of getting rejected if society were not so antagonistic, but since the hostility is ready-made, the conditions are there on which the pathology can thrive.

The rejection that homosexuals must endure forces them to pretend to be something they are not. Under such conditions, they have difficulty functioning well, either as humans or as homosexuals. Their self-image is undermined, they must lead a double life. None of these difficulties help to eliminate homosexuality, nor do they keep it from spreading, nor do they deter it, nor do they help people find a cure for it. Hostility serves only to add anxieties to life, not to overcome them. It creates wide chasms between those who would otherwise be close, such as members of the same family. It makes the gathering of accurate information about homosexuality difficult, because homosexuals fear an open avowal of their lives and hence few are available as subjects for research. Worst of all, it makes people hate themselves who do nobody any harm and who might otherwise have led happier, healthier, and more useful lives.

The reasons for the officially expressed hatred of homosexuality are many and varied. In ancient and medieval times, semen was looked upon as a precious substance, for in it was contained the seed for a new human being to be sown in the woman. Sexual activities and activities that were not procreative in aim were seen as deliberate waste of seed, and in societies riddled by war, famine, disease, and tyranny, a high value was placed on procreation and hence on the seminal fluid. The same antagonisms affected masturbation and promiscuity, which aroused the disapproval of the moralists of the time, but (probably because the lawmakers were themselves involved) did not incite the same social condemnation as did male homosexuality.

In relations between two males, one of whom is a receptor and the other the insertor, the receptor was thought to be allowing his body to be used as a substitute for a woman's, while the insertor was lowering or corrupting another man to the level of a woman, hence bringing shame upon the institution of manhood. Because men usually have stronger muscles than women, Western societies have placed man in a superior position to women, and man would not tolerate having that position undermined. Lesbian relationships were seen as trivial by comparison, for there could be no analogy so far as lowering or demeaning the status of one or both participants. . . .

Toward the latter part of the nineteenth century, it was popular to think of homosexuality as an inborn biological phenomenon, linked with genetic imbalance, endocrinological disorder, or intermediate sexuality. The work of [Edward] Carpenter, Havelock Ellis, and [Richard von] Krafft-Ebing [λ Chapter 2] seemed to point up these conclusions.

Twentieth-century psychology and psychoanalysis laid bare certain psychodynamic aspects of the origins of homosexuality, and proliferated elaborate theories, case histories, and emphasis upon the assumption that homosexuality is a learned tendency and, theoretically at least, should be able to be unlearned. Since homosexuality is a form of human behavior, and since all human behavior has as its root cause a combination of heredity and environment, the etiology of homosexuality must be explained in terms of both, which does not imply a return, even in part, to the discarded concept of inborn inversion. Everyone has a biological capacity for sexual expression, an undirected energy that has been termed the libido. Past the age of puberty, this capacity will manifest itself in a heterosexual fashion in the majority of cases if society effectively and intelligently uses its power to promote such relationships. For the undirected sexual drive can, under favorable social conditions, go toward the other sex, if only because men and women are more biologically compatible than persons of the same sex.

In the cases where homosexuality develops, it is seen as a reaction to some form of frustration, the acting out of some defense mechanism, or an attempt to adjust to a difficult situation in which the other sex is viewed with fearfulness or suspicion, or cannot be obtained for gratification at a certain period, or an inability to obtain such gratification is feared.

However, these psychological factors may only be precipitating ones, since it is possible for two different people to respond to the same environment in different ways.

Can heredity explain the reaction to a given environment peculiar to any given individual? For the fact is that certain conditions may precipitate homosexuality for some, but very similar (although never identical) circumstances may not for others. For still others, a similar set of circumstances may make for other types of adjustments, living patterns, or anxieties, sexual or otherwise.

Until more is known, we can only say, in terms that are unfortunately vague, that exclusive homosexuality is a result of reacting to certain types of environmental conditions, usually centering around some traumatic childhood episode, or through continual unhealthful relationships with parents or siblings, usually in which a distorted concept of sexuality is involved. Sometimes these relationships appear to have been the causes for homosexuality, but at other times a different form of maladjustment has resulted.

To define homosexuality as a disease because it is considered socially deviant, with all the consequences of this social attitude, is purely tautological. It is saying that if society considers a phenomenon a disease, it is a disease. But to reduce this to the individual level, one should first determine the prevalence of undefined anxiety, a person's conception of himself, his ability to function realistically and to have positive relationships with other people, in deciding whether or not a given homosexual is to be regarded as neurotic, psychotic, or emotionally disabled. No doubt many of them are, but this is not a good reason to increase their anxieties and disturbances by condemnation.

The problem is made even more confusing by the fact that many of our social conventions and our hectic way of life tend to precipitate neuroses and psychoses to such an extent that, in a recent study conducted in midtown New York, some eighty percent of the population was judged by a competent team of psychiatrists to be suffering from some form of neurosis, and one-quarter of the population was diagnosed as being emotionally or mentally so disabled as to be nonfunctioning.

So a question has been raging: Are homosexuals always, necessarily, and invariably disturbed? And if they are, is such disturbance a symptom of their general personality disorder—or is it inspired by the hostile society and by life in an environment that fosters not only hate but self-hate?

There are many corollaries and side-issues to this question. Are heterosexuals also disturbed? It would seem that they are, but that their sex orientation is not, in and of itself, a symptom or a cause of such anxieties as they harbor. The same cannot be said of the homosexuals. On the other hand, are we still, despite the advances, despite the Mattachine Society and research grants, obtaining a distorted sample, consisting of those who have, because of their compulsive and self-defeating actions, gotten into trouble, or because of their self-rejection sought therapeutic aid?

One knows so little about the homosexuals who do not come for therapy, and objective comparisons with this type of homosexual along with their heterosexual counterparts have been few and far between. It is probable that, within limits, homosexuals vary in their state of mental health. Some function better than the average; others are similar to most people so far as mental health is concerned, but in all likelihood, the average person is disturbed and anxiety-ridden. If significant differences can be shown between the amount of mental illness present in the homosexual and the heterosexual, one would have to conclude that this difference is not due exclusively to social hostility, nor to faulty personality development, but to a combination of both.

To claim that homosexuality is immature is likewise tautological, for it is a refined way of saying that one is biased against homosexuals. The criteria for maturity are always arbitrary, set up differently for each age and for each society. In our society, one cannot be mature unless one marries and raises a family. Not to do so is regarded as being biologically irresponsible. Freudianism and theories of regression, infantile fixation, and arrested development are glibly mentioned in support of this, as well as the opposition to using sex for something other than procreation. It does not occur to many people who argue that homosexuality is immature that one can have sexual preferences different from their own and still conduct one's life in a positive, dedicated, and enlightened manner and meet all other criteria for maturity.

This is sometimes taken to mean that although homosexuals may be mature in other respects they are sexually immature because their form of sexuality does not lead to further offspring. By this line of reasoning, the spinster virgin, the celibate priest, the devout nun, and the responsible, contraceptive-using married pair who cannot afford, and hence do not want, children, are all to be grouped into one category of immature people, where they will join the homosexual. The standards for maturity often reflect the biases of those who adopt them.

Our society is preoccupied with family life, and anyone who is not so preoccupied is seen as a lesser person. Single men and women are looked upon with disfavor, while the family man and the loyal wife are seen as pure, wholesome, and virtuous. We are not trying to disparage the advantages of being married and raising a happy, healthy family, nor are we trying to minimize the gratifications that can be obtained thereby. Are we, therefore, to inflict punishment on one who does not fulfill this function? If so, then society should impartially punish all the unmarried, all the childless, lest one suspect that some are being singled out for reasons entirely extraneous to their non-family statuses.

Most homosexuals do not get married, and do not raise families. This, in and of itself, in a society already suffering from overpopulation, is not a sufficiently good reason for wanting to eliminate homosexuality, but it is a good reason why most people should be heterosexual. But heterosexuality having been the primary form of sexuality since time immemorial, and likely to remain so, there seems to be little danger of the family's dying out as an institution. In fact, there would be no problem of continuing the human species, even if half the population were bisexual half the time! Since we now have a problem of too many people in the world, and with the issue of birth control making headlines, it is untenable that homosexuality should be condemned on the grounds that it is non-procreative. A good deal of time, money, and effort is now going toward making heterosexuality less procreative so that future generations will have enough space on this planet.

Thus, the answer to the question "Should homosexuality be eliminated?" can be made only by clarifying the query itself. A wide variety of sexual experiences, all in non-coercive form, is always desirable, if it helps the individual to explore the many ways of making love and relating to other human beings. Unfortunately, by definition, the homosexuals are not enjoying such a variety, but then, neither are the exclusive heterosexuals. The benefits, if any, accruing to society from such variation are of little help to one who is personally distressed. So the real task should be to eliminate the personal and social unhappiness that is a part of homosexuality in contemporary society, rather than try to do away with the phenomenon itself as an alternative kind of behavior.

Furthermore, all effort should be made to prevent and cure compulsive homosexuality and heterosexuality, so that it will be possible for human beings to function better with either sex. That most people, under most conditions, would choose the other sex, would be inevitable, but this would not make pariahs out of those who choose their own, or both.

American society can begin by examining the totality of its attitudes on all sexual matters. Not bound by outmoded traditions, laws, and customs when they are at variance with scientific tenets, and not hampered by moral codes that are irrelevant and tautological, great progress can be made. With more enlightened attitudes, less hostility, and greater objectivity, we can seek to bring up our children so that they know all that they need to know about sex and its variations, with no shame or guilt associated with them.

America must begin to accept homosexuals as people, and give them whatever prestige, social acceptance, and rewards that are due them on their own merits as individuals, instead of viewing them as curious outcasts. If this is done, perhaps the homosexual will be better able to accept himself, thus alleviating great human distress, but perhaps also laying a foundation for diminished neurotic homosexual activity.

We can encourage therapists to work with their homosexual patients, with the goal of making better people out of them, better suited to lead a happier, healthier existence, less burdened with anxiety, and more capable of dealing with life on its own terms in a positive, realistic fashion. If partial or complete change in sexual orientation is involved in this, then so be it. If it is not, then helping the patient to overcome whatever problems are confronting him and to function in a more psychologically healthy way with himself and the people around him are sufficiently important therapeutic goals, far more important than merely making a heterosexual of him without removing the neuroses and anxieties.

Finally, we can use what resources we have to further enlightened research, so that knowledge about the unknown areas will be forthcoming. If the world powers can afford to spend billions of dollars on armaments, which only serve to destroy people when used, can we not afford to make a worthwhile investment to find out more about the things that may help make life happier for all of us? We can further explore the means for increasing the sexual well-being of the nation, rather than add to our too-high rate of mental illness.

To summarize, should homosexuality be eliminated? We believe:

1. Society should seek to eliminate the personal distress and anxieties that arise as a result of social hostility.

2. Society should cease to define homosexuality per se as immoral, lecherous, or anti-social.

3. Society should aim to isolate those patterns in the contemporary world that are encouraging the development of neurotic and compulsive sexuality.

4. Society should simultaneously seek to make life more pleasurable for those who are homosexual and yet encourage all its growing members to follow the less difficult, more normative path of heterosexuality.

It is a program that is not only, in our opinion, free of contradictions, but it is one that in a practical sense is achievable.

When all is said and done, the important thing is not whether a person is homosexual or heterosexual. The important thing is that he is sexual, that society accepts him as such, and that he accepts himself as such.

---

"Donald Webster Cory" (Edward Sagarin) and John P. LeRoy. *The Homosexual and His Society: A View from Within*. New York: Citadel, 1963.

## ➤ Marilyn Barrow

(1963) United States

---

### "Living Propaganda"

Every person has some prejudices directed against some other person or persons. Prejudices can be numerous in an individual or very few—but they exist in all of us. Some are against ethnic groups, economic classes, physical or mental defects, etc. Some have ludicrous causes, very unreasoning, i.e., "The first blue-spotted person I met offended me; therefore, I hate all blue-spotted people." Silly? Yes, but not very uncommon.

What do prejudices boil down to? Simply a dislike, mistrust or fear of anything alien to individual experience. We are conditioned into prejudice by our parents, or are affected by public opinion; and sometimes, with homosexuality in particular, the prejudice is a reflection of fear of personal involvement. When prejudice is toward a group, it is directed at the stereotype image of the group. Thus every male homosexual is a limp–wristed faggot and every female homosexual is a stomping bull-dike.

The homosexual organizations are working to combat prejudice and concomitant legal injustices. Even allowing for a miraculous legal success in the next few decades, this would hardly lessen the individual prejudice. Indeed, it would undoubtedly increase it somewhat, just as the recent legal strides for Negroes have created much hostility.

If the first blue-spotted person I met hadn't been so unpleasant I doubt if I would dislike them so much, even though my mother warned me against blue-spotted people, and in school everyone made fun of blue-spotted people.

And so with every one of us, we are living propaganda. Everyone we meet who knows we are gay, and likes and respects us, is a potential weapon for our struggle.

The flamboyant Lesbian, free-wheeling exponent of the artificial gay life, is hardly a good public image. On the other hand, living a lie does little good. There has to be some middle ground between these two extremes, especially for those of us who want to be respectable citizens in our communities. What does it benefit my people if I am moral and upright, if my appearance in this guise is assumed to be heterosexually oriented? This is living a lie.

In my city I know many homosexuals who are respectable members of the community. None of them, however, would allude to being homosexual except with other homosexuals. In that sense, they are respectable liars. I am not, of course, advocating a wholesale announcement—it does not have to be this way.

Everyone knows that Monty is a homosexual in the organization where he works. A new employee is told this within a month of arriving. However, instead of sneers or innuendo, the information is always told with additions. "Monty is a wonderful guy, he's worked here for 27 years and everyone loves him." This is really true. He is feminine enough in appearance so that hiding his homosexuality would be difficult. By admitting it and taking some kidding and being a "good guy" and a "wonderful worker" he is unquestionably the most popular employee. He is living propaganda of a very constructive kind.

In the same organization there is Jack, a very masculine fellow, who is quite easily spotted as gay. He takes the opposite tack, is witty and knife-tongued—and loathed. Jack is brilliant, handsome, a good worker, but he is a damaging kind of living propaganda.

In my office there are 15 women and three male supervisors. The work is a form of public relations, and the job requires initiative and literacy. Almost everyone in the office has had some college. An educated group of fairly young women are likely to be pre-disposed to liberal attitudes toward sexual variation. They are "sharp" and hard to fool.

I am the only Lesbian in the room, and there are apparently no others with tendencies in this direction. Everyone in the room (I am sure) knows that I am homosexual. Each reacts differently depending on his individual personality.

To some I am a joke, likable perhaps, but a joke nevertheless. To most, I am the senior member of the group. Most of them come to me with questions about the work. Some of them fear me (I have a bad temper); most of them like me; and for all except one or two I am their first reasonably intimate contact with a homosexual.

There are humorous and even embarrassing moments. But I know that for the most part these people have a more liberal attitude because of this working situation. Since I live a reasonably acceptable life, ergo, perhaps others like me do also. The head of the office automatically invited my roommate to the Christmas party, just as the married women brought husbands and the unmarried their boyfriends. I have privately been asked many questions, ranging from the very serious to the very humorous. The office wag torments me continuously with innuendo, to get a laugh, in which I am more than happy to join, since she is my favorite in the office. Some months ago, when the movie "West Side Story" was showing here, I arrived one morning to have the wag pop her head into my cubicle and serenade me with this paraphrase: "I feel pretty, I feel pretty, I feel pretty and witty and gay. And I pity any girl who isn't queer today."

They know, most of them, that I am not ashamed; somehow they feel that therefore I have nothing to be ashamed of.

With personnel changes, possibly 25 people have been part of the group. And most of them have now had one fairly uneventful and reasonably pleasant work experience with that taboo creature, the Lesbian! I am sure some of them will never need this experience, but some of them will. I am also sure that this will have made them less quick to judge, more understanding in their attitude.

There is a healthy atmosphere when you can be part of the scene as you really are, not as some pretender. It's a good feeling to be honest, and you may help in the good fight. Try it, try living propaganda in your own life!

---

Barrow, Marilyn. "Living Propaganda." *The Ladder* 8.2 (1963): 4-6.

# CHAPTER 4

# Stonewall and Beyond

Recognizing that many LGBT people in the English-speaking world view the Stonewall riots in New York City as a kind of turning point in LGBT history, this chapter focuses on queer Americans as we integrated the lessons learned from other liberation movements into our own struggles for human/civil rights.

On November 27, 1978, former City Supervisor Dan White sneaked into San Francisco City Hall through a basement window, avoiding metal detectors. He entered the office of Mayor George Moscone and shot him dead. White then walked down the hall to Supervisor Harvey Milk's office and killed him too. That night a huge crowd gathered outside City Hall to mourn Milk, the first openly gay member of the San Francisco Board of Supervisors. The candlelight vigil was seen on newscasts around the country and not only elicited sympathy from millions of Americans but also produced a strong outcry against antigay rhetoric and violence.

Milk had been elected to the Board of Supervisors 11 months earlier. He and White had served together on the board, though their relationship was strained. As a supervisor, White had vowed to rid the city of "radicals, social deviates, and incorrigibles" and represented the only actively antigay voice on the board (Sinclair 221). White resigned from the board after serving less than a year because he could not support his family on the low salary.

After the murders, White's lawyers blamed his actions on "diminished capacity" due to depression and convinced a nearly all-white, largely working-class and conservative jury to find the defendant guilty of voluntary manslaughter, not first-degree murder, with a sentence of seven years in prison (Miller 407). After the verdict, the public mood shifted from grief to fury. Angry and disillusioned gays and

**Figure 4.1**    Harvey Milk and George Moscone.

lesbians took to the streets, burning police cars and vandalizing property in what became known as the White Night Riots. In response, the San Francisco police virtually invaded the Castro gay district.

In 1977, the same year Milk was elected to the San Francisco Board of Supervisors, Dade County, Florida, passed a Human Rights Ordinance, including lesbians and gays among those protected from discrimination. In response, former Miss America and Florida orange juice pitchwoman Anita Bryant led a "Save Our Children" campaign seeking to repeal the ordinance. Bryant's group marched under the catchphrase, "Homosexuals cannot reproduce, so they must recruit," to which Milk's campaign responded, "My name is Harvey Milk, and I'm here to recruit you." Forging alliances with fundamentalist Christian ministers and mobi-

lizing antigay voters throughout Florida, the Save Our Children campaign won a resounding victory in June 1977, overturning the Human Rights Ordinance with nearly 70% of the vote (Miller 403). Save Our Children was a response to the growing gay and lesbian liberation movement, which saw visibility as an avenue to increased political power. Bryant's organization folded in 1979, but during its brief existence, it came to represent the new tactics of a resurgent religious right.

Milk's election and the furor after his assassination on one hand and Bryant's antigay campaign on the other

**Figure 4.2**    Anita Bryant after an activist threw a pie in her face.

*[handwritten annotation: pay attention to these for]*

characterize the tumultuous history of increasing LGBT visibility in the United States during the second half of the 20th century. As LGBT people moved into mainstream institutions and claimed both greater visibility and political power, reactionaries and social conservatives redoubled efforts to promote so-called traditional values. Reactions among LGBT people and progressive allies have been varied, with numerous positions and stances, sometimes conflicting, evolving as the debate over gay rights has taken shape. In this chapter, we look at the social and political events that have shaped queer visibility and activism since the late 1960s. In many ways, this period saw some of the most significant gains in civil rights, protections, and enfranchisement for LGBT people; in other ways, it saw significant social and political challenges that continue to face queer people today.

## Emerging Visibility and Activism

**M**any LGBT people identify the beginning of a highly visible gay rights movement in the United States with the Stonewall riots, which occurred on June 27 and 28, 1969, in New York City. The riots erupted in response to police harassment of patrons of the Stonewall Inn, a popular gay bar. Having experienced decades of consistent raids on gay bars by police, customers who had been in the Stonewall Inn when the police shut it down that night gathered outside the building, cheering whenever another person was released by the police and emerged. Most of the bar patrons were eventually released, but the bar staff, three drag queens, and two male-to-female transgendered people were held and eventually escorted outside to be loaded into a paddy wagon. The crowd's jovial irreverence quickly gave way to anger and protest as others swarmed around the Stonewall Inn, throwing bricks and trash cans and initiating several days of riots in the area (Duberman). The Stonewall riots immediately took on a significance disproportionate to the actual events, and within a month, the Gay Liberation Front had formed and begun organizing for gay rights and liberation, calling specifically for job protection for gay employees, an end to police harassment, and the decriminalization of sodomy.

**Find Out More** Screaming Queens (2005), a film by Victor Silverman and Susan Stryker, argues that the Compton Cafeteria riot in 1966 was the "first known act of collective, violent resistance to the social oppression of queer people in the United States" ("Screaming"). The riots involved a number of transpeople.

As we saw in the preceding chapter, organizing for lesbian and gay visibility and rights was not new; the Mattachine Society and the Daughters of Bilitis (DOB), among others, made important attempts during the 1950s to organize gays and lesbians politically and to educate American society about discrimination against queer people. Mattachine and DOB frequently argued that gays and lesbians were "normal" Americans, and these groups encouraged members to dress and behave in ways that conformed to middle-class gender norms. In contrast, the Stonewall riots represented a more spontaneous form of direct action and civil unrest, carried out primarily by working-class people. Hence, the Stonewall rioters in some ways resembled many youth, antiwar, and civil rights movements engaging in political activism at that time. Furthermore, coming at the end of the 1960s, the Stonewall riots occurred at a time when a variety of American citizens were questioning sexual mores and traditional values. The time seemed ripe for gays, lesbians, and gender nonconformists to articulate their political desires in more direct and even confrontational ways. Many of these countercultural movements began in grassroots working-class rebellion and subsequently morphed into rights organizations with middle-class leadership and gradually less radical goals. In many ways, the Stonewall riots have served as an important symbol of the fight for greater queer visibility and political power. LGBT social and political organizations around the world use Stonewall in their names, and annual pride parades in June across the globe celebrate the uprisings (Manalansan). But what kind of political action did the riots suggest was emerging in the late 1960s and early 1970s?

The Gay Liberation Front (GLF) took its activist energy from other left-leaning movements, specifically socialist organizations and those protesting the Vietnam War. The name of the organization derived from North Vietnam's National Liberation Front and thus served to mark the group as confrontationally countercultural. Among their positions, the GLF sought to raise consciousness about the capitalist systems that they felt oppressed gays, lesbians, and others. In their view, the "GAY LIBERATION FRONT is a revolutionary group of homosexual women and men formed with the realization that complete sexual liberation for all people cannot come about unless existing social institutions are abolished" (McGarry 163). In publications such as COME OUT! and Carl Wittman's "Refugees from Amerika: A Gay Manifesto," the GLF strongly encouraged gays and lesbians to assert their visibility and claim political power. More specifically, they felt that social institutions such as the heteronormative nuclear family and persistent sexism were responsible for the oppression of gays and lesbians and that these institutions should be actively challenged and overthrown. Making common cause with blacks, workers, and the Vietnamese, among others, the GLF figured itself as fighting American imperialism in addition to the homophobia that seemed so much a part of it (D'Emilio). In 1970, meetings of a London-based GLF, soon followed by similar meetings in France, signaled the spread of gay activism in Europe. Front Homosexuel d'Action Revolutionnaire, following on the heels of widespread student riots across France in 1968, fought for both homosexual rights and access to free abortion and contraception (Miller).

The rise of lesbian feminism suggested that some activists and thinkers at this time agreed in part with the GLF's aims but wanted to critique social structures and institutions from more specific and challenging perspectives. The women's movement had already introduced feminism and feminist concerns to the popular consciousness, and lesbian feminism highlighted the connection between feminist theory and lesbian practice. A rallying call of lesbian feminism, commonly attributed to Ti-Grace Atkinson, was "Feminism is the theory; lesbianism is the practice." In 1969, activist and author Rita Mae Brown and two of her colleagues resigned from the National Organization of Women (NOW) because Betty Friedan, one of NOW's founders, warned of a "lavender menace" of lesbians who might co-opt the organization for their own ends and, worse, undermine potential public sympathy [λ Chapter 3]. Emerging lesbian feminist collectives, such as The Furies and Radicalesbians, argued specifically for a separate "Lesbian Nation" (Johnston). In a manifesto titled "The Woman-Identified Woman," Radicalesbians praised the "primacy of women relating to women" as a way of achieving unity. In 1973, the message was "Lesbian, lesbian, any woman can be a lesbian" (from the album *Lavender Jane Loves Women*, Alix Dobkin). After all, they reasoned, if the term woman-identified woman was substituted for the troublesome term lesbian, more women could be gathered under their radical umbrella.

**Figure 4.3** Original album cover, Alix Dobkin's *Lavender Jane Loves Women*.

Lesbian feminists believed that the antiwar movement was sexist and the women's movement homophobic, so they advocated for social and political separatism. Believing that all men, including gay men, were sexist, they argued that "working with men only takes away valuable time that should be spent working with lesbians" (McGarry 179). In significant ways, a vibrant and varied women's culture emerged out of such activist work; women-only music festivals, such as the National Women's Music Festival and the Michigan Womyn's Music Festival [λ Chapter 15], as well as women-centered publishers such as Naiad, Crossing, Kitchen Table, and Aunt Lute, promoted lesbian feminist thinking and activism. Clearly, lesbian feminism highlighted many lesbians' feeling that an enormous political and social divide existed between their worlds and goals for liberation movements and those of their male counterparts. Not all lesbians were separatists, however, and not all gay men were misogynists. The Combahee River Collective specifically rejected separatism for black lesbians.

Liberation politics gave progressive lesbians and gay men a sense of belonging to a community that was both political and social, and activism had a positive

**Find Out More** in "The Woman-Identified Woman" at the end of this chapter.

impact on the day-in-and-day-out treatment of bar owners and their patrons. The gay bar—including the newly popular discotheque—became a safer meeting place than it had been during the 1950s and 1960s. Nonetheless, a sense at the time was that there was a clear and strongly policed divide between "the bar" and the more political LGBT work being done outside the bar. It was not uncommon for LGBT activists to critique those they believed "wasted time" on the bar scene as being unconcerned about larger political issues; as well, it was not uncommon for disco queens and bar dykes to see the earnest activists as outsiders and downers. The reality is, though, that the bars and the political organizations served different, though equally important, purposes: the bar tended to be a source of information about local clinics, a place for gay candidates to distribute campaign brochures, and a venue in which people could share advertisements and addresses for gay-friendly businesses. Outside the bar, activists began to organize campaigns to gain visibility for LGBT people and to help further national and international political goals.

In October 1979, 75,000 to 100,000 people converged on Washington, DC, to hold the first National March on Washington for Lesbian and Gay Rights. Featured speakers included "Allen Ginsberg and Audre Lorde, feminist activist and writer Kate Millett, D.C. Mayor Marion Barry, San Francisco Supervisor Harry Britt, ousted gay U.S. Army Sgt. Leonard Matlovich, and U.S. Rep. Ted Weiss, the chief sponsor of a House gay rights bill" (Chibbaro). After much contentious debate, organizers decided to invite radical black writer and activist Angela Davis as a speaker, a move that indicated that issues of race and social class were on the minds of at least some of the leaders at the time. Davis declined to speak at the march because the Communist Party, of which she was a member, did not want to lend tacit support to homosexual rights. The 1979 march had been a pet project of the late Harvey Milk, part of his vision of a truly national LGBT movement.

**Find Out More** in "The Combahee River Collective Statement" at the end of this chapter.

## AIDS Activism

In the early 1980s, doctors in some large urban centers in the United States began reporting a syndrome affecting an individual's ability to fight disease. The syndrome, which seemed viral in nature, was appearing predominantly among gay men, prompting doctors and health officials to call it *gay-related immune deficiency* (GRID) or *gay cancer*. Eventually, reports spread about other affected groups, mostly prostitutes and intravenous drug users, and the syndrome was relabeled AIDS—acquired immune deficiency syndrome. Initial reports about the disease were largely confined to gay or large urban news sources, but AIDS reached national awareness when actor Rock Hudson, looking emaciated and frail, held a press conference in 1985 to announce that he had AIDS—and was gay. In addition, some early cases of the disease resulting from blood transfusions, such as the illness of teenager Ryan White, helped to spread publicity; the Ryan White CARE Act, which provided services for people living with HIV (human immunodeficiency virus, which can lead to AIDS) and AIDS, was signed on August 18, 1990.

Panic spread first among gay men and then among the larger public, prompting some officials to close bathhouses. Some politicians argued for quarantining gay men, or at least those diagnosed with AIDS. HIV is passed from person to person through semen, blood, breast milk, or vaginal secretions, and the virus can lie dormant for several years before compromising an individual's immune system, resulting in the syndrome itself, AIDS. Because the disease is primarily transmitted through anal sex and intravenous drug use, government officials during the 1980s, particularly in the Reagan-controlled White House, were reluctant to identify it as a public health concern. In fact, President Reagan himself never mentioned the term AIDS until after the death of Rock Hudson, and even then, his administration never supported meaningful funding for AIDS research (Shilts).

In the face of government apathy, a variety of gay and lesbian activists began organizing politically both to protest the government's inaction and to assist those with AIDS. They were aided in the popular consciousness by revelations that certain well-known, presumably straight figures, such as athletes Arthur Ashe and Magic Johnson, had contracted AIDS as "innocent victims" (Ashe from a blood transfusion, Johnson from heterosexual sex). The AIDS epidemic galvanized gay and lesbian people in ways that more abstract political issues such as repeal of sodomy laws had not (Miller). Organizations such as Gay Men's Health Crisis (GMHC) responded directly to both health concerns and political necessities around AIDS. ACT UP—the AIDS Coalition to Unleash Power—was formed in 1987. Using direct action techniques, ACT UP employed tactics that were often confrontational and controversial. For instance, ACT UP activists yelled slogans and threw condoms during a 1989 mass held by Cardinal John Henry O'Connor, a New York priest who outspokenly opposed gay and lesbian rights. Spin-off groups from ACT UP, such as Queer Nation and Lesbian Avengers, continued this work into the 1990s, holding kiss-ins and zaps and popularizing one of the major slogans protesting the government's reluctance to deal with AIDS: "Silence = Death." At

**Figure 4.4**   AIDS activism slogans. Photo by Scott Lloyd DeWitt and Ryan Trauman.

this time, many gay activists started using the term queer to describe their politics and identities; the term suggested an unwillingness to conform and a desire to oppose the norms that called for silence around gay and lesbian sexualities [λ Chapter 7].

**Find Out More** in Douglas Crimp's book, *AIDS: Cultural Analysis, Cultural Activism* (Cambridge, MA: MIT Press, 1988).

Randy Shilts estimates that "[o]n the day the world learned that Rock Hudson was stricken [1985], some 12,000 Americans were already dead or dying of AIDS and hundreds of thousands more were infected with the virus that caused the disease" (xxii). A quarter century later, the official United Nations Global Report on the worldwide AIDS epidemic stated that, after a peak in new HIV infections in the late 1990s, "the overall growth of the global AIDS epidemic appears to have stabilized." The 2.6 million newly infected people reported in 2009 represented a 19% decrease from the 3.1 million infected in 1999. In the United States and the Global North, advanced retroviral drugs have greatly improved the quality of life for people living with HIV. In parts of sub-Saharan Africa, where HIV/AIDS was so prevalent as to virtually paralyze national economies, a combination of available drugs, "the impact of HIV prevention efforts, and the natural course of HIV epidemics" have led to a 25% drop in new infections since 2001 (Global Report).

U.S. AIDS advocacy groups were astonishingly successful at promoting public awareness of the epidemic and at raising money for patient services and research. Nonetheless, widespread publicity and increased visibility led to a backlash against gay men in particular, who were seen as the cause of AIDS, despite the fact that the disease had been identified as a health problem in Africa in the 1970s. In 1982, for instance, a Georgia man named Michael Hardwick was arrested for sodomy; his lawyers argued the case during the same years that AIDS was causing national panic in the United States, and in 1986, the Supreme Court, by a 5–4 vote, upheld Georgia's sodomy statute and, by extension, the right of states to outlaw sodomy. In the years following the Bowers v. Hardwick decision, a number of states, mostly in the South, refined their laws to criminalize only homosexual, not heterosexual, sodomy. Fear of AIDS was clearly leading to a polarization of national opinion, for which homosexuality served as a fulcrum.

## Antigay Backlash and Hate-Crimes Legislation

The election of conservative governments throughout the West, as well as the fall of communist states in Eastern Europe and the former Soviet Union at the end of the 1980s, signaled a mass cultural shift toward more conservative values and ideas. As early as the late 1960s, the phrase "family values" began to be used to describe ideals related to a valuing of the "traditional" heterosexual, intact family unit. The phrase came to function as a euphemism for various antiabortion, anti-sex education, antifeminist, and anti-LGBT ideologies. Among such ideologies is Abstinence-Only Education, a cornerstone of George W. Bush's presidency (2001–2009). It assumed that a refusal to mention sexuality in school curricula leads to less teen sex and fewer out-of-wedlock births. Operating on the assumption that teenagers should refuse categorically to engage in sexual activity, abstinence-only programs denied young people basic information about sexual safety. For instance, it has been implicated in the rise of unprotected sex among young people ("Dangers"). Also notable for LGBT people are movements such as the above-mentioned Save Our Children campaign and the ex-gay movement, which has given rise to a rhetoric of healing through programs designed to convince gay and lesbian youth and adults to pursue heterosexual lifestyles. Avoiding the essentialist argument about whether LGBT people are born with their sexualities, these programs have been successful in employing a "gay is a choice" ideology to connect homosexuality to sin and to assert the righteousness of allowing active discrimination against LGBT people.

In 1991, the Colorado for Family Values organization wrote the following proposed amendment to the state constitution:

> No Protected Status Based on Homosexual, Lesbian, or Bisexual Orientation. Neither the State of Colorado, through any of its branches or departments, nor any of its agencies, political subdivisions, municipalities or school districts, shall enact, adopt or enforce any statute, regulation, ordinance or policy whereby homosexual, lesbian or bisexual orientation, conduct, practices or relationships shall constitute or otherwise be the basis of or entitle any person or class of persons to have or claim any minority status, quota preferences, protected status or claim of discrimination.

Colorado voters passed this amendment in 1992 by a 54% to 47% margin. However, after a protracted legal battle, the Supreme Court overturned the amendment in 1996, stating that Colorado could not pass laws making homosexuals "unequal to everyone else. . . . A State cannot so deem a class of persons a stranger to its laws" (Robinson). A similar ordinance passed in Cincinnati, Ohio, in 1993, but the Supreme Court refused to hear an appeal against the discriminatory Article XII of that city's charter. Eventually, voters in Cincinnati overturned Article XII in 2004, swayed more by economic arguments (a boycott against bringing convention business to town, for example) than by fairness arguments.

During Bill Clinton's presidency (1993–2001), several particularly gruesome cases of gay bashing received wide publicity, and the nation saw the devastating results of homophobic violence. In December 1993, Brandon Teena, a 21-year-old transman, was killed—along with his friends Lisa Lambert and Philip DeVine—in

Lambert's home in Humboldt, Nebraska. Teena was killed by John Lotter and Tom Nissen in an attempt to keep him from testifying against them for raping him during an attack motivated by their discovery of Teena's biological sex. After the brutal murder of Matthew Shepard, a gay University of Wyoming student, in October 1998, Clinton's attempt to widen the definition of hate crimes to include lesbians and gays was defeated in Congress. A year later, in 1999, Wyoming also tried to add lesbians and gays to its hate crimes statute; that measure was defeated after a 30–30 tie in the Wyoming House of Representatives. That same year, Billy Jack Gaither, an Alabama man, was killed by two men after Gaither allegedly showed sexual interest in them. The murderers attempted what has come to be known as the *gay panic* legal defense, claiming that Gaither's "talking queer stuff" caused them to respond with uncontrollable violence ("Assault"). The two men were sentenced to life in prison without possibility of parole. President Clinton compared Gaither's killing to Shepard's and also to that of James Byrd, an African-American man dragged to death in a racially motivated attack in Texas the year before. In 2002, lesbians Carla Grayson and Adrienne Neff, along with their 22-month-old son, barely escaped after arsonists set fire to their Montana home. The fire was apparently set in retaliation for a lawsuit filed against the University of Montana by Grayson and other employees that called for the extension of domestic partner benefits to same-sex couples [λ Chapter 6].

Public opinion and legislative and executive will finally coincided to address the hate-crime issue after the inauguration of President Barack Obama in 2009. In October of that year, Obama signed the Matthew Shepard and James Byrd Jr. Hate Crimes Prevention Act, which was intentionally included by Democrats in a defense spending bill in order to forestall anticipated Republican opposition. At the signing, Obama said, "[W]e must stand against crimes that are meant not only to break bones but to break spirits—not only to inflict harm but to instill fear" (Zeleny). Despite this more progressive legal context, antigay bullying of young people continues and has led some activists, such as Dan Savage, to set up the It Gets Better Project to provide encouragement for LGBT youth [λ Chapter 14].

Battles over gay rights have occurred in a global context that has witnessed the spread of religious fundamentalism, which is notoriously hostile to gays, lesbians, and bisexuals. These belief systems work against progressive impulses to enhance freedoms and life choices. In the United States, the word *fundamentalist* normally refers to right-wing Christians. In Iran, however, a conservative Muslim government arrests and at times

**Figure 4.5**    Iranian teens hanged.

executes those convicted of sodomy. In 2005, two Iranian teens were hanged, the government claiming that they were guilty of raping a 13-year-old boy; gay rights organizations around the world claimed that the "crime" they were "guilty" of was really consensual sodomy. In an article about the hanging, Homan, a Los Angeles–based Iranian LGBT group, quotes OutRage!, which asserts that "according to Iranian human rights campaigners, over 4000 lesbians and gay men have been executed since the Ayatollahs seized power in 1979" ("Execution").

## Gays in the Military and the Marriage Issue

Two cases that show the difficulty faced when a progressive political agenda in favor of LGBT rights meets political opposition can be seen in the efforts to end the ban on gays in the military and to allow same-sex couples the right to marry. A frequent flashpoint for debates about LGBT rights has been the issue of gays in the military. A number of nations—Israel, Canada, Denmark, Great Britain, and others—have for years allowed LGB people to serve openly in the armed forces. Until recently, the United States implemented a Don't Ask, Don't Tell (DADT) policy, which neither pro-gay nor antigay groups much liked. In 1993, public opinion seemed primed for a reversal of the rules instituted during World War II stipulating that homosexuals be discharged from the armed forces [λ Chapter 3]. During his 1992 presidential campaign, candidate Bill Clinton promised to lift the ban on gays in the military, but after his election, he encountered stiff opposition from the Pentagon and Republican leadership. To the intense disappointment of many LGBT activists, Clinton instituted a compromise policy officially named Don't Ask, Don't Tell, Don't Pursue, Don't Harass. This policy did not succeed in integrating homosexual people into the military; what it did was mandate punishment for those who came out while serving. Under this policy, members of the armed services could not "make a statement that they are lesbian, gay or bisexual; engage in physical contact with someone of the same sex for the purposes of sexual gratification; or marry, or attempt to marry, someone of the same sex" (Human Rights Campaign). Ironically, this policy, which was supposed to be a progressive move designed to end the U.S. military's practice of ferreting out or actively pursuing LGBT people, actually extended the "offenses" that could result in expulsion from the military. While DADT was in force, approximately 14,000 people were discharged from the military; the minimum estimated cost of the policy was $288 million (Servicemembers United, Warren). Congress voted to repeal DADT in December 2010. President Obama, Secretary of Defense Leon Panetta, and Chairman of the Joint Chiefs of Staff Admiral Mike Mullen certified that repeal would not harm military readiness, and DADT was officially repealed as of September 2011.

DADT stipulated that military personnel must not marry a person of the same sex. Absent DADT, what will happen to the issue of same-sex marriage in the United States? Let us begin by considering events of the last two decades. The national Defense of Marriage Act (DOMA), which defines marriage as the legal union of one man and one woman, was enacted in 1996 during the Clinton administration, partly in response to increasing agitation (in Hawaii, for instance) for same-sex marriage. Since then, there has been a proliferation of state-level DOMAs that have led some legislators to talk about a national constitutional amendment restricting marriage to one man and one woman. Efforts to accomplish this failed during the George W. Bush administration. Still, as of May 2012, 39 states have either an amendment or a law against same-sex marriage ("Defining Marriage"). Conversely, 15 states and the District of Columbia permit either full marriage (Connecticut, Iowa, Massachusetts, New Hampshire, New York, and Vermont) or state-sanctioned civil unions or domestic partnerships (California, Delaware, Hawaii, Illinois, New Jersey, Nevada, Oregon, Rhode Island, Washington, and the District of Columbia ("Same-Sex"). The drive to restrict marriage to heterosexual partici-pants seemed to reach its zenith in the first decade of the 21st century. However, in this same period, the U.S. Supreme Court overturned sodomy laws (Lawrence v. Texas [2003]), and more recently, President Obama has decided that his administration will no longer defend the constitutionality of the federal DOMA ("Obama: DOMA Unconstitutional").

> **Find Out More** about the repeal of DADT in the readings at the end of this chapter.

> **Find Out More** about DOMA and the Obama administration's stance on it in the readings at the end of this chapter.

Internationally, the Netherlands (2001) and Belgium (2003) were among the first European nations to legalize gay marriage. Such moves built on a global push to extend basic civil rights to LGBT people; in 1996, the new constitution of South Africa was the first in the world to specifically prohibit discrimination on the grounds of sexual preference. Since then, several nations have legalized same-sex marriage; as of this writing, 10 countries have legalized full marriage equality for their lesbian and gay citizens: Argentina, Belgium, Canada, Iceland, Netherlands, Norway, Portugal, South Africa, Spain, and Sweden ("Timeline"). The context in which same-sex marriage is legalized often underscores the tensions between progressive and conservative impulses; debates about gay marriage are often volatile, even when countries move to secure marriage rights for lesbians and gays. As a compromise position, some countries, as well as some states within the United States, have adopted civil unions that guarantee some of the marriage rights given to heterosexual couples.

Debates about gay marriage, and LGBT rights in general, elicit strong reac-tions. What can get lost in discussions of ideals and values is the personal cost to

*[handwritten margin note: Answer these questions!]*

individual lives when rhetoric touches reality. For instance, who pays when Jerry Falwell calls AIDS "God's punishment for homosexuality"? Who pays when legislation or policy insists on drawing a connection between sex education and immorality? These examples of antigay, antisex rhetoric seem to condone, even encourage, verbal, moral, or physical violence against sexual minorities and nonconformists. Furthermore, since HIV disease is still spread primarily through sexual contact, the disease has sparked calls for greater and more comprehensive sex education both in the West and throughout the world. In the United States, however, such calls have prompted heated debates among politicians and their constituents about promoting alternative lifestyles.

In many ways, the treatment of gays, lesbians, bisexuals, and the transgendered has come to mark how progressive a particular country is—or is not. In his book *The Rise of the Creative Class,* Richard Florida notes that the presence of an open, vibrant gay subculture is one of the markers of intellectual and creative stimulation in U.S. cities. In *Maneuvers,* Cynthia Enloe proposes a connection between LGBT rights and a progressive national image on the global stage. While some cultures have begun to recognize LGBT and queer lives through progressive laws and attitudes, the battle over what rights to extend to LGBT people continues around the world.

*[handwritten margin note: Queers are cool!]*

## Questions for Discussion

1. Earlier in this chapter, we pointed out how different organizations across the world have used the name Stonewall in the titles of a variety of LGBT social and political organizations. Research one of these organizations on the Internet and examine how exactly the term Stonewall is used. Is reference made to the Stonewall riots of 1969? What other markers of LGBT identity are used that are familiar to you? What markers are new to you?

2. The manifestos of the early gay rights and lesbian feminist activists make for provocative and challenging reading even today. If you had to write your own contemporary manifesto about LGBT, queer, or sexual issues, what would you put in it? What form would it take? To whom would you address it? Try your hand at writing such a manifesto and compare your writing with the manifestos of early gay and lesbian feminist thinkers.

3. Take a look at the AIDS Memorial Quilt website at www.AIDSQuilt.org and think about how people who have died of AIDS have been memorialized in this creative and emotionally evocative way. Thinking about the LGBT people and issues we have discussed in the past four chapters, choose either one person or one event to memorialize in a creative way. What form will your memorial take? How will you creatively talk about the past in ways that will be educational, relevant, and meaningful for contemporary audiences?

"Assault on Gay America: The Life and Death of Billy Jack Gaither." *Frontline.* Web. 2 Feb. 2008. <http://www.pbs.org/wgbh/pages/frontline/shows/assault/>.

Chibbaro, Lou. "Gay Movement Boosted by '79 March on Washington." *The Washington Blade,* 5 November 2004. Web. 2 Feb. 2008. <http://www.washblade.com/2004/11-5/news/national/movement.cfm>.

Crimp, Douglas. *AIDS: Cultural Analysis, Cultural Activism.* Cambridge, MA: MIT Press, 1988. Print.

"The Dangers of Abstinence-Only Education." Planned Parenthood Fact Sheet, n.d. Web. 25 Mar. 2008. <http://www.ppacca.org/site/pp.asp?c=kuJYJeO4F&b=139536>.

D'Emilio, John. "After Stonewall." *Making Trouble: Essays on Gay History, Politics, and the University.* New York: Routledge, 1992. 234–74. Print.

"Defining Marriage: Defense of Marriage Acts and Same-Sex Marriage Laws." *National Conference of State Legislatures,* 24 Feb. 2012. Web. 29 March 2012. <http://www.ncsl.org/issues-research/human-services/same-sex-marriage-overview.aspx>.

Duberman, Martin Bauml. *Stonewall.* New York: Plume, 1994. Print.

Enloe, Cynthia. *Maneuvers: The International Politics of Militarizing Women's Lives.* Berkeley: U of California Press, 2000. Print.

"Execution of Two Teenagers Accused of Homosexual Acts." Homan: The Iranian Gay, Lesbian, Bisexual, & Transgendered Organization, Incorporated, 2005. Web. 31 Jan. 2008. <http://www.homanla.org/New/executions.htm>.

Florida, Richard L. *The Rise of the Creative Class.* New York: Basic Books, 2004. Print.

*Global Report: UN AIDS Report on the Global AIDS Epidemic 2010.* N.p., 2010. Web. 29 Mar. 2012. <http://www.unaids.org/globalreport/documents/20101123_GlobalReport_full_en.pdf>.

Human Rights Campaign. N.p., n.d. Web. 2 Feb. 2008. <http://www.hrc.org/Content/NavigationMenu/HRC/GetInformed/Issues/Military2/Fact_Sheets>.

Johnston, Jill. *Lesbian Nation: The Feminist Solution.* New York: Touchstone, 1973. Print.

Kennedy, Elizabeth Lapovsky, and Madeline D. Davis. *Boots of Leather, Slippers of Gold: The History of a Lesbian Community.* New York: Penguin, 1994. Print.

Lawrence v. Texas. 539 U.S. 558 (2003).

Manalansan, Martin. "In the Shadows of Stonewall: Examining Gay Transnational Politics and the Diasporic Dilemma." *GLQ: A Journal of Lesbian and Gay Studies* 2.4 (1995): 425–38. Print.

McGarry, Molly. *Becoming Visible: An Illustrated History of Lesbian and Gay Life in Twentieth-Century America.* New York: Penguin Studio, 1998. Print.

Miller, Neil. *Out of the Past: Gay and Lesbian History from 1869 to the Present.* New York: Vintage, 1995. Print.

"Obama: DOMA Unconstitutional, DOJ Should Stop Defending in Court." *The Huffington Post,* 5 May 2011. Web. 29 Mar. 2012. <http://www.huffingtonpost

.com/2011/02/23/obama-doma-uncon stitutional_n_827134.html>.

Patton, Cindy. *Sex and Germs: The Politics of AIDS*. Boston: South End, 1985. Print.

Reese, R. "The Socio-political Context of the Integration of Sport in America." *Journal of African American Men* 4.3 (1999). Web. 2 Feb. 2008. <http://www .csupomona.edu/~rrreese/INTEGRA TION.HTML>.

Robinson, B. A. "Targeting Gays and Lesbians: Ruling by the U.S. Supreme Court in *Romer v. Evans*." Religious Tolerance. org, 16 Sept. 2004. Web. 2 Feb. 2008. <http://www.religioustolerance.org/ hom_laws7.htm>.

"Same-Sex Relationship Recognition Laws: State by State." Human Rights Campaign, 23 March 2012. Web. 29 Mar. 2012. <http://www.hrc.org/resour ces/entry/same-sex-relationship-recognition-laws-state-by-state>.

"Screaming Queens: The Riot at Compton's Cafeteria." Frameline, n.d. Web. 25 Mar. 2008. <http://cart.frameline.org/Pro ductDetails.asp?ProductCode=T636>.

Servicemembers United. *The DADT Digital Archive Project*. N.p., 2012. Web. <http://dadtarchive.org>.

Shilts, Randy. *And the Band Played On: Politics, People and the AIDS Epidemic*. New York: St. Martin's, 1987. Print.

Sinclair, Mick. *San Francisco: A Cultural and Literary History*. Northampton, MA: Interlink, 2004. Print.

Smith, Barbara, ed. *Home Girls: A Black Feminist Anthology*. New York: Kitchen Table Women of Color Press, 1983. Print.

Smith, R. R., and R. R. Windes. *Progay/ Antigay: The Rhetorical War over Sexuality*. Thousand Oaks, CA: Sage, 2000. Print.

"Timeline of Gay and Lesbian Marriage, Partnership or Unions Worldwide." *UK Gay News*, 21 Sept. 2011. Web. 29 Mar. 2012. <http://www.ukgaynews .org.uk/marriage_timeline.htm>.

Warren, Jay. "Fact Check: How Much Did DADT Cost." N.p., 8 Feb. 2011. Web. 29 Mar. 2012. <http://www2.wsls.com/ news/2011/feb/08/fact-check-how-much-did-dadt-cost-ar-828927/>.

Zeleny, Jeff. "Obama Signs Hate Crimes Bill." *New York Times*, 28 Oct. 2009. Web. 29 Mar. 2012. <http://thecaucus .blogs.nytimes.com/2009/10/28/ obama-signs-hate-crimes-bill/>.

## READINGS

### ➢ **Radicalesbians**

(c. late 1960s–early 1970s), United States

#### "The Woman-Identified Woman"

What is a lesbian? A lesbian is the rage of all women condensed to the point of explosion. She is the woman who, often beginning at an extremely early age, acts in accordance with her inner compulsion to be a more complete and freer human being than her society— perhaps then, but certainly later—cares to allow her. These needs and actions, over a period of years, bring her into painful conflict with people, situations, the accepted ways of thinking, feeling and behaving, until she is in a state of continual war with everything around her, and usually with her self. She may not be fully conscious of the political implications of what for her began as personal necessity, but on some level she has not been able to accept the limitations and oppression laid on her by the most basic role of her society—the female role. The turmoil she experiences tends to induce guilt proportional to the degree to which she feels she is not meeting social expectations, and/or eventually drives her to question and analyze what the rest of her society more or less accepts. She is forced to evolve her own life pattern, often living much of her life alone, learning usually much earlier than her "straight" (heterosexual) sisters about the essential aloneness of life (which the myth of marriage obscures) and about the reality of illusions. To the extent that she cannot expel the heavy socialization that goes with being female, she can never truly find peace with herself. For she is caught somewhere between accepting society's view of her—in which case she cannot accept herself—and coming to understand what this sexist society has done to her and why it is functional and necessary for it to do so. Those of us who work that through find ourselves on the other side of a tortuous journey through a night that may have been decades long. The perspective gained from that journey, the liberation of self, the inner peace, the real love of self and of all women, is something to be shared with all women—because we are all women.

It should first be understood that lesbianism, like male homosexuality, is a category of behavior possible only in a sexist society characterized by rigid sex roles and dominated by male supremacy. Those sex roles dehumanize women by defining us as a supportive/ serving caste in relation to the master caste of men, and emotionally cripple men by demanding that they be alienated from their own bodies and emotions in order to perform their economic/political/military functions effectively. Homosexuality is a by-product of a particular way of setting up roles (or approved patterns of behavior) on the basis of sex; as such it is an inauthentic (not consonant with "reality") category. In a society in which men do not oppress women, and sexual expression is allowed to follow feelings, the categories of homosexuality and heterosexuality would disappear.

But lesbianism is also different from male homosexuality, and serves a different function in the society. "Dyke" is a different kind of put-down from "faggot," although both imply you are not playing your socially assigned sex role . . . are not therefore a "real woman" or a "real man." The grudging admiration felt for the tomboy, and the queasiness felt around a sissy boy point to the same thing: the contempt in which women—or those who play a female role—are held. And the investment in keeping women in that contemptuous role is very great. Lesbian is a word, the label, the condition that holds women in line. When a woman hears this word tossed her way, she knows she is stepping out of line. She knows that she has crossed the terrible boundary of her sex role. She recoils, she protests, she reshapes her actions to gain approval. Lesbian is a label invented by the Man to throw at any woman who dares to be his equal, who dares to challenge his prerogatives (including that of all women as part of the exchange medium among men), who dares to assert the primacy of her own needs. To have the label applied to people active in women's liberation is just the most recent instance of a long history; older women will recall that not so long ago, any woman who was successful, independent, not orienting her whole life about a man, would hear this word. For in this sexist society, for a woman to be independent means she can't be a woman—she must be a dyke. That in itself should tell us where women are at. It says as clearly as can be said: women and person are contradictory terms. For a lesbian is not considered a "real woman." And yet, in popular thinking, there is really only one essential difference between a lesbian and other women: that of sexual orientation—which is to say, when you strip off all the packaging, you must finally realize that the essence of being a "woman" is to get fucked by men.

"Lesbian" is one of the sexual categories by which men have divided up humanity. While all women are dehumanized as sex objects, as the objects of men they are given certain compensations: identification with his power, his ego, his status, his protection (from other males), feeling like a "real woman," finding social acceptance by adhering to her role, etc. Should a woman confront herself by confronting another woman, there are fewer rationalizations, fewer buffers by which to avoid the stark horror of her dehumanized condition. Herein we find the overriding fear of many women toward being used as a sexual object by a woman, which not only will bring her no male-connected compensations, but also will reveal the void which is woman's real situation. This dehumanization is expressed when a straight woman learns that a sister is a lesbian; she begins to relate to her lesbian sister as her potential sex object, laying a surrogate male role on the lesbian. This reveals her heterosexual conditioning to make herself into an object when sex is potentially involved in a relationship, and it denies the lesbian her full humanity. For women, especially those in the movement, to perceive their lesbian sisters through this male grid of role definitions is to accept this male cultural conditioning and to oppress their sisters much as they themselves have been oppressed by men. Are we going to continue the male classification system of defining all females in sexual relation to some other category of people? Affixing the label lesbian not only to a woman who aspires to be a person, but also to any situation of real love, real solidarity, real primacy among women, is a primary form of divisiveness among women: it is the condition which keeps women within the con-fines of the feminine role, and it is the debunking/scare term that keeps women from forming any primary attachments, groups, or associations among ourselves.

Women in the movement have in most cases gone to great lengths to avoid discus-sion and confrontation with the issue of lesbianism. It puts people up-tight. They are hostile, evasive, or try to incorporate it into some "broader issue." They would rather not talk about it. If they have to, they try to dismiss it as a "lavender herring." But it is no side issue. It is absolutely essential to the success and fulfillment of the women's liberation movement that this issue be dealt with. As long as the label "dyke" can be used to frighten women into a less militant stand, keep her separate from her sisters, keep her from giving primacy to anything other than men and family—then to that extent she is controlled by the male culture. Until women see in each other the possibil-ity of a primal commitment which includes sexual love, they will be denying themselves the love and value they readily accord to men, thus affirming their second-class status.

As long as male acceptability is primary—both to individual women and to the move-ment as a whole—the term lesbian will be used effectively against women. Insofar as women want only more privileges within the system, they do not want to antagonize male power. They instead seek acceptability for women's liberation, and the most crucial aspect of the acceptability is to deny lesbianism—i.e., to deny any fundamental challenge to the basis of the female. It should also be said that some younger, more radical women have honestly begun to discuss lesbianism, but so far it has been pri-marily as a sexual "alternative" to men. This, however, is still giving primacy to men, both because the idea of relating more completely to women occurs as a negative reaction to men, and because the lesbian relationship is being characterized simply by sex, which is divisive and sexist. On one level, which is both personal and political, women may withdraw emotional and sexual energies from men, and work out various alternatives for those energies in their own lives. On a different political/psychological level, it must be understood that what is crucial is that women begin disengaging from male-defined response patterns. In the privacy of our own psyches, we must cut those cords to the core. For irrespective of where our love and sexual energies flow, if we are male-identified in our heads, we cannot realize our autonomy as human beings.

But why is it that women have related to and through men? By virtue of having been brought up in a male society, we have internalized the male culture's definition of ourselves. That definition consigns us to sexual and family functions, and excludes us from defining and shaping the terms of our lives. In exchange for our psychic servicing and for performing society's non-profit-making functions, the man confers on us just one thing: the slave status which makes us legitimate in the eyes of the society in which we live. This is called "femininity" or "being a real woman" in our cultural lingo. We are authentic, legitimate, real to the extent that we are the property of some man whose name we bear. To be a woman who belongs to no man is to be invisible, pathetic, inauthentic, unreal. He confirms his image of us—of what we have to be in order to be acceptable by him—but not our real selves; he confirms our womanhood—as he defines it, in relation to him—but cannot confirm our person-hood, our own selves as absolutes. As long as we are dependent on the male culture for this definition, for this approval, we cannot be free.

The consequence of internalizing this role is an enormous reservoir of self-hate. This is not to say that the self-hate is recognized or accepted as such; indeed most women would deny it. It may be experienced as discomfort with her role, as feeling empty, as numbness, as restlessness, as a paralyzing anxiety at the center. Alternatively, it may be expressed in shrill defensiveness of the glory and destiny of her role. But it does exist, often beneath the edge of her consciousness, poisoning her existence, keep-ing her alienated from herself, her own needs, and rendering her a stranger to other women. They try to escape by identifying with the oppressor, living through him, gaining status and identity from his ego, his power, his accomplishments—and by not identifying with other "empty vessels" like themselves. Women resist relating on all levels to other women who will reflect their own oppression, their own secondary status, their own self-hate. For to confront another woman is finally to confront one's self—the self we have gone to such lengths to avoid. And in that mirror we know we cannot really respect and love that which we have been made to be.

As the source of self-hate and the lack of real self are rooted in our male-given iden-tity, we must create a new sense of self. As long as we cling to the idea of "being a woman," we will sense some conflict with that incipient self, that sense of I, that sense of a whole person. It is very difficult to realize and accept that being "feminine" and being a whole person are irreconcilable. Only women can give to each other a new sense of self. That identity we have to develop with reference to ourselves, and not in relation to men. This consciousness is the revolutionary force from which all else will follow, for ours is an organic revolution. For this we must be available and supportive to one another, give our commitment and our love, give the emotional support necessary to sustain this movement. Our energies must flow toward our sisters, not backward toward our oppressors. As long as woman's liberation tries to free women without facing the basic heterosexual structure that binds us in one-to-one relationship with our oppressors, tremendous energies will continue to flow into trying to straighten up each particular relationship with a man, into finding how to get better sex, how to turn his head around—into trying to make the "new man" out of him, in the delusion that this will allow us to be the "new woman." This obviously splits our energies and commitments, leaving us unable to be committed to the construction of the new patterns which will liberate us.

It is the primacy of women relating to women, of women creating a new consciousness of and with each other, which is at the heart of women's liberation, and the basis for the cultural revolution. Together we must find, reinforce, and validate our authentic selves. As we do this, we confirm in each other that struggling, incipient sense of pride and strength, the divisive barriers begin to melt, we feel this growing solidarity with our sisters. We see ourselves as prime, find our centers inside of ourselves. We find receding the sense of alienation, of being cut off, of being behind a locked window, of being unable to get out what we know is inside. We feel a realness, feel at last we are coinciding with ourselves. With that real self, with that consciousness, we begin a revolution to end the imposition of all coercive identifications, and to achieve maximum autonomy in human expression.

---

Karla Jay and Allen Young. From *Out of the Closets: Voices of Gay Liberation,* 1970, edited by Karla Jay and Allen Young © 1972, 1977, and 1992. Reprinted with permission of the editors.

## ➢ Combahee River Collective
### (1974–1980), United States

---

### "The Combahee River Collective Statement"*

We are a collective of Black feminists who have been meeting together since 1974.[i] During that time we have been involved in the process of defining and clarifying our politics, while at the same time doing political work within our own group and in coalition with other progressive organizations and movements. The most general statement of our politics at the present time would be that we are actively committed to struggling against racial, sexual, heterosexual, and class oppression, and see as our particular task the development of integrated analysis and practice based upon the fact that the major systems of oppression are interlocking. The synthesis of these oppressions creates the conditions of our lives. As Black women we see Black feminism as the logical political movement to combat the manifold and simultaneous oppressions that all women of color face.

We will discuss four major topics in the paper that follows: (1) the genesis of contemporary Black feminism; (2) what we believe, i.e., the specific province of our politics; (3) the problems in organizing Black feminists, including a brief herstory of our collective; and (4) Black feminist issues and practice.

## 1. *The Genesis of Contemporary Black Feminism*

Before looking at the recent development of Black feminism we would like to affirm that we find our origins in the historical reality of Afro-American women's continuous life-and-death struggle for survival and liberation. Black women's extremely negative relationship to the American political system (a system of white male rule) has always been determined by our membership in two oppressed racial and sexual castes. As Angela Davis points out in "Reflections on the Black Woman's Role in the Community of Slaves," Black women have always embodied, if only in their physical manifestation, an adversary stance to white male rule and have actively resisted its inroads upon them and their communities in both dramatic and subtle ways. There have always been Black women activists—some known, like Sojourner Truth, Harriet Tubman, Frances E. W. Harper, Ida B. Wells Barnett, and Mary Church Terrell, and thousands upon thousands unknown—who have had a shared awareness of how their sexual identity combined with their racial identity to make their whole life situation and the focus of their political struggles unique. Contemporary Black feminism is the outgrowth of countless generations of personal sacrifice, militancy, and work by our mothers and sisters.

A Black feminist presence has evolved most obviously in connection with the second wave of the American women's movement beginning in the late 1960s. Black, other Third World, and working women have been involved in the feminist movement from its start, but both outside reactionary forces and racism and elitism within the movement itself have served to obscure our participation. In 1973, Black feminists, primarily located in New York, felt the necessity of forming a separate Black feminist group. This became the National Black Feminist Organization (NBFO).

Black feminist politics also have an obvious connection to movements for Black liberation, particularly those of the 1960s and 1970s. Many of us were active in those movements (Civil Rights, Black Nationalism, the Black Panthers), and all of our lives were greatly affected and changed by their ideologies, their goals, and the tactics used to achieve their goals. It was our experience and disillusionment within these liberation movements, as well as experience on the periphery of the white male left, that led to the need to develop a politics that was anti-racist, unlike those of white women, and anti-sexist, unlike those of Black and white men.

There is also undeniably a personal genesis for Black feminism, that is, the political realization that comes from the seemingly personal experiences of individual Black women's lives. Black feminists and many more Black women who do not define themselves as feminists have all experienced sexual oppression as a constant factor in our day-to-day existence. As children we realized that we were different from boys and that we were treated differently. For example, we were told in the same breath to be quiet both for the sake of being "ladylike" and to make us less objectionable in the eyes of white people. As we grew older we became aware of the threat of physical and sexual abuse by men. However, we had no way of conceptualizing what was so apparent to us, what we knew was really happening.

Black feminists often talk about their feelings of craziness before becoming conscious of the concepts of sexual politics, patriarchal rule, and most importantly, feminism, the political analysis and practice that we women use to struggle against our oppression. The fact that racial politics and indeed racism are pervasive factors in our lives did not allow us, and still does not allow most Black women, to look more deeply into our own experiences and, from that sharing and growing consciousness, to build a politics that will change our lives and inevitably end our oppression. Our development must also be tied to the contemporary economic and political position of Black people. The post World War II generation of Black youth was the first to be able to minimally partake of certain educational and employment options, previously closed completely to Black people. Although our economic position is still at the very bottom of the American capitalistic economy, a handful of us have been able to gain certain tools as a result of tokenism in education and employment which potentially enable us to more effectively fight our oppression.

A combined anti-racist and anti-sexist position drew us together initially, and as we developed politically we addressed ourselves to heterosexism and economic oppression under capitalism.

## 2. *What We Believe*

Above all else, our politics initially sprang from the shared belief that Black women are inherently valuable, that our liberation is a necessity not as an adjunct to somebody else's but because of our need as human persons for autonomy. This may seem so obvious as to sound simplistic, but it is apparent that no other ostensibly progressive movement has ever considered our specific oppression as a priority or worked seriously for the ending of that oppression. Merely naming the pejorative stereotypes attributed to Black women (e.g., mammy, matriarch, Sapphire, whore, bulldagger), let alone cataloguing the cruel, often murderous, treatment we receive, indicates how little value has been placed upon our lives during four centuries of bondage in the western hemisphere. We realize that the only people who care enough about us to work consistently for our liberation are us. Our politics evolve from a healthy love for ourselves, our sisters and our community which allows us to continue our struggle and work.

This focusing upon our own oppression is embodied in the concept of identity politics. We believe that the most profound and potentially most radical politics come directly out of our own identity, as opposed to working to end somebody else's oppression. In the case of Black women this is a particularly repugnant, dangerous, threatening, and therefore revolutionary concept because it is obvious from looking at all the political movements that have preceded us that anyone is more worthy of liberation than ourselves. We reject pedestals, queenhood, and walking ten paces behind. To be recognized as human, levelly human, is enough.

We believe that sexual politics under patriarchy is as pervasive in Black women's lives as are the politics of class and race. We also find it difficult to separate race from class from sex oppression because in our lives they are most often experienced simultaneously. We know that there is such a thing as racial-sexual oppression which is neither solely racial nor solely sexual, e.g., the history of rape of Black women by white men as a weapon of political repression.

Although we are feminists and Lesbians, we feel solidarity with progressive Black men and do not advocate the fractionalization that white women who are separatists demand. Our situation as Black people necessitates that we have solidarity around the fact of race, which white women of course do not need to have with white men, unless it is their negative solidarity as racial oppressors. We struggle together with black men against racism, while we also struggle with black men about sexism.

We realize that the liberation of all oppressed peoples necessitates the destruction of the political-economic systems of capitalism and imperialism as well as patriarchy. We are socialists because we believe that work must be organized for the collective benefit of those who do the work and create the products, and not for the profit of the bosses. Material resources must be equally distributed among those who create these resources. We are not convinced, however, that a socialist revolution that is not also a feminist and anti-racist revolution will guarantee our liberation. We have arrived at the necessity for developing an understanding of class relationships that takes into account the specific class position of Black women who are generally marginal in the labor force, while at this particular time some of us are temporarily viewed as doubly desirable tokens at white-collar and professional levels. We need to articulate the real class situation of persons who are not merely raceless, sexless workers, but for whom racial and sexual oppression are significant determinants in their working/economic lives. Although we are in essential agreement with Marx's theory as it applied to the very specific economic relationships he analyzed, we know that his analysis must be extended further in order for us to understand our specific economic situation as Black women.

A political contribution which we feel we have already made is the expansion of the feminist principle that the personal is political. In our consciousness-raising sessions, for example, we have in many ways gone beyond white women's revelations because we are dealing with the implications of race and class as well as sex. Even our Black women's style of talking/testifying in Black language about what we have experienced has a resonance that is both cultural and political. We have spent a great deal of energy delving into the cultural and experiential nature of our oppression out of necessity because none of these matters has ever been looked at before. No one before us has ever examined the multilayered texture of Black women's lives. An example of this kind of revelation/conceptualization occurred at a meeting as we discussed the ways in which our early intellectual interests had been attacked by our peers, particularly Black males. We discovered that all of us, because we were "smart" had also been considered "ugly," i.e., "smart-ugly." "Smart-ugly" crystallized the way in which most of us had been forced to develop our intellects at great cost to our "social" lives. The sanctions in the Black and white communities against Black women thinkers is comparatively much higher than for white women, particularly ones from the educated middle and upper classes.

As we have already stated, we reject the stance of Lesbian separatism because it is not a viable political analysis or strategy for us. It leaves out far too much and far too many people, particularly Black men, women, and children. We have a great deal of criticism and loathing for what men have been socialized to be in this society: what they support, how they act, and how they oppress. But we do not have the misguided notion that it is their maleness, per se—i.e., their biological maleness—that makes them what they are. As Black women we find any type of biological determinism a particularly dangerous and reactionary basis upon which to build a politic. We must also question whether Lesbian separatism is an adequate and progressive political analysis and strategy, even for those who practice it, since it so completely denies any but the sexual sources of women's oppression, negating the facts of class and race.

### 3. *Problems in Organizing Black Feminists*

During our years together as a Black feminist collective we have experienced success and defeat, joy and pain, victory and failure. We have found that it is very difficult to organize around Black feminist issues, difficult even to announce in certain contexts that we are Black feminists. We have tried to think about the reasons for our difficulties, particularly since the white women's movement continues to be strong and to grow in many directions. In this section we will discuss some of the general reasons for the organizing problems we face and also talk specifically about the stages in organizing our own collective.

The major source of difficulty in our political work is that we are not just trying to fight oppression on one front or even two, but instead to address a whole range of oppressions. We do not have racial, sexual, heterosexual, or class privilege to rely upon, nor do we have even the minimal access to resources and power that groups who possess any one of these types of privilege have.

The psychological toll of being a Black woman and the difficulties this presents in reaching political consciousness and doing political work can never be underestimated. There is a very low value placed upon Black women's psyches in this society, which is both racist and sexist. As an early group member once said, "We are all damaged people merely by virtue of being Black women." We are dispossessed psychologically and on every other level, and yet we feel the necessity to struggle to change the condition of all Black women. In "A Black Feminist's Search for Sisterhood," Michele Wallace arrives at this conclusion:

> We exist as women who are Black who are feminists, each stranded for the moment, working independently because there is not yet an environment in this society remotely congenial to our struggle—because, being on the bottom, we would have to do what no one else has done: we would have to fight the world.[ii]

Wallace is pessimistic but realistic in her assessment of Black feminists' position, particularly in her allusion to the nearly classic isolation most of us face. We might use our position at the bottom, however, to make a clear leap into revolutionary action. If Black women were free, it would mean that everyone else would have to be free since our freedom would necessitate the destruction of all the systems of oppression.

Feminism is, nevertheless, very threatening to the majority of Black people because it calls into question some of the most basic assumptions about our existence, i.e., that sex should be a determinant of power relationships. Here is the way male and female roles were defined in a Black nationalist pamphlet from the early 1970s:

> We understand that it is and has been traditional that the man is the head of the house. He is the leader of the house/nation because his knowledge of the world is broader, his awareness is greater, his understanding is fuller and his application of this information is wiser . . . After all, it is only reasonable that the man be the head of the house because he is able to defend and protect the development of his home . . . Women cannot do the same things as men—they are made by nature to function differently. Equality of men and women is something that cannot happen even in the abstract world. Men are not equal to other men, i.e. ability, experience or even understanding. The value of men and women can be seen as in the value of gold and silver—they are not equal but both have great value. We must realize that men and women are a complement to each other because there is no house/family without a man and his wife. Both are essential to the development of any life.[iii]

The material conditions of most Black women would hardly lead them to upset both economic and sexual arrangements that seem to represent some stability in their lives. Many Black women have a good understanding of both sexism and racism, but because of the everyday constrictions of their lives, cannot risk struggling against them both.

The reaction of Black men to feminism has been notoriously negative. They are, of course, even more threatened than Black women by the possibility that Black feminists might organize around our own needs. They realize that they might not only lose valuable and hardworking allies in their struggles, but that they might also be forced to change their habitually sexist ways of interacting with and oppressing Black women. Accusations that Black feminism divides the black struggle are powerful deterrents to the growth of an autonomous Black women's movement.

Still, hundreds of women have been active at different times during the three-year existence of our group. And every Black woman who came, came out of a strongly-felt need for some level of possibility that did not previously exist in her life.

When we first started meeting early in 1974 after the NBFO first eastern regional conference, we did not have a strategy for organizing, or even a focus. We just wanted to see what we had. After a period of months of not meeting, we began to meet again late in the year and started doing an intense variety of consciousness-raising. The overwhelming feeling that we had is that after years and years we had finally found each other. Although we were not doing political work as a group, individuals continued their involvement in Lesbian politics, sterilization abuse and abortion rights work, Third World Women's International Women's Day activities, and support activity for the trials of Dr. Kenneth Edelin, Joan Little, and Inéz García. During our first summer, when membership had dropped off considerably, those of us remaining devoted serious discussion to the possibility of opening a refuge for battered women in a Black community. (There was no refuge in Boston at that time.) We also decided around that time to become an independent collective since we had serious disagreements with NBFO's bourgeois-feminist stance and their lack of a clear political focus.

We also were contacted at that time by socialist feminists, with whom we had worked on abortion rights activities, who wanted to encourage us to attend the National Socialist Feminist Conference in Yellow Springs. One of our members did attend and despite the narrowness of the ideology that was promoted at that particular conference, we became more aware of the need for us to understand our own economic situation and to make our own economic analysis.

In the fall, when some members returned, we experienced several months of comparative inactivity and internal disagreements which were first conceptualized as a Lesbian-straight split but which were also the result of class and political differences. During the summer those of us who were still meeting had determined the need to do political work and to move beyond consciousness-raising and serving exclusively as an emotional support group. At the beginning of 1976, when some of the women who had not wanted to do political work and who also had voiced disagreements stopped attending of their own accord, we again looked for a focus. We decided at that time, with the addition of new members, to become a study group. We had always shared our reading with each other, and some of us had written papers on Black feminism for group discussion a few months before this decision was made. We began functioning as a study group and also began discussing the possibility of starting a Black feminist publication. We had a retreat in the late spring which provided a time for both political discussion and working out interpersonal issues. Currently we are planning to gather together a collection of Black feminist writing. We feel that it is absolutely essential to demonstrate the reality of our politics to other Black women and believe that we can do this through writing and distributing our work. The fact that individual Black feminists are living in isolation all over the country, that our own numbers are small, and that we have some skills in writing, printing, and publishing makes us want to carry out these kinds of projects as a means of organizing Black feminists as we continue to do political work in coalition with other groups.

### 4. *Black Feminist Issues and Projects*

During our time together we have identified and worked on many issues of particular relevance to Black women. The inclusiveness of our politics makes us concerned with any situation that impinges upon the lives of women, Third World and working people. We are of course particularly committed to working on those struggles in which race, sex and class are simultaneous factors in oppression. We might, for example, become involved in workplace organizing at a factory that employs Third World women or picket a hospital that is cutting back on already inadequate health care to a Third World community, or set up a rape crisis center in a Black neighborhood. Organizing around welfare and daycare concerns might also be a focus. The work to be done and the countless issues that this work represents merely reflect the pervasiveness of our oppression.

Issues and projects that collective members have actually worked on are sterilization abuse, abortion rights, battered women, rape and health care. We have also done many workshops and educationals on black feminism on college campuses, at women's conferences, and more recently for high school women.

One issue that is of major concern to us and that we have begun to publicly address is racism in the white women's movement. As Black feminists we are made constantly and painfully aware of how little effort white women have made to understand and combat their racism, which requires among other things that they have a more than superficial comprehension of race, color, and Black history and culture. Eliminating racism in the white women's movement is by definition work for white women to do, but we will continue to speak to and demand accountability on this issue.

In the practice of our politics we do not believe that the end always justifies the means. Many reactionary and destructive acts have been done in the name of achieving "correct" political goals. As feminists we do not want to mess over people in the name of politics. We believe in collective process and a nonhierarchical distribution of power within our own group and in our vision of a revolutionary society. We are committed to a continual examination of our politics as they develop through criticism and self-criticism as an essential aspect of our practice. In her introduction to Sisterhood Is Powerful Robin Morgan writes:

> I haven't the faintest notion what possible revolutionary role white heterosexual men could fulfill, since they are the very embodiment of reactionary-vested-interest-power.

As Black feminists and Lesbians we know that we have a very definite revolutionary task to perform and we are ready for the lifetime of work and struggle before us.

## Notes

*The Combahee River Collective was a black feminist group in Boston whose name came from the guerilla action conceptualized and led by Harriet Tubman on June 2, 1863, in the Port Royal region of South Carolina. This action freed more than 750 slaves and is the only military campaign in American history planned and led by a woman.

  i. This statement is dated April 1977.
 ii. Michele Wallace. "A Black Feminist's Search for Sisterhood," *The Village Voice,* July 28, 1975, pp. 6–7.
iii. Mumininas of Committee for Unified Newark, Mwanamke Mwananchi (The Nationalist Woman), Newark, NJ © 1971, pp. 4–5.

---

The "Combahee River Collective Statement," 1977, appeared originally in *Capitalist Patriarchy and the Case for Socialist Feminism,* edited by Zillah R. Eisenstein, published by Monthly Review Press.

# ➤ US CONGRESS Repeal of Don't Ask, Don't Tell

H.R.2965

### One Hundred Eleventh Congress of the United States of America

### *At the Second Session*

*Begun and held at the City of Washington on Tuesday, the fifth day of January, two thousand and ten*

### *An Act*

To amend the Small Business Act with respect to the Small Business Innovation Research Program and the Small Business Technology Transfer Program, and for other purposes.

*Be it enacted by the Senate and House of Representatives of the United States of America in Congress assembled,*

### *Section 1. Short Title.*

This Act may be cited as the "Don't Ask, Don't Tell Repeal Act of 2010".

### *Sec. 2. Department of Defense Policy Concerning Homosex-Uality in the Armed Forces.*

(a) COMPREHENSIVE REVIEW ON THE IMPLEMENTATION OF A REPEAL OF 10 U.S.C. 654.—

   (1) INGENERAL.—On March 2, 2010, the Secretary of Defense issued a memorandum directing the Comprehensive Review on the Implementation of a Repeal of 10 U.S.C. 654 (section 654 of title 10, United States Code).

   (2) OBJECTIVES AND SCOPE OF REVIEW.—The Terms of Reference accompanying the Secretary's memorandum established the following objectives and scope of the ordered review:

(A) Determine any impacts to military readiness, military effectiveness and unit cohesion, recruiting/retention, and family readiness that may result from repeal of the law and recommend any actions that should be taken in light of such impacts.

(B) Determine leadership, guidance, and training on standards of conduct and new policies.

(C) Determine appropriate changes to existing policies and regulations, including but not limited to issues regarding personnel management, leadership and training, facilities, investigations, and benefits.

(D) Recommend appropriate changes (if any) to the Uniform Code of Military Justice.

(E) Monitor and evaluate existing legislative proposals to repeal 10 U.S.C. 654 and proposals that may be introduced in the Congress during the period of the review.

(F) Assure appropriate ways to monitor the workforce climate and military effectiveness that support successful follow-through on implementation.

(G) Evaluate the issues raised in ongoing litigation involving 10 U.S.C. 654.

*H.R.2965—2*

(b) EFFECTIVE DATE.—The amendments made by subsection (f) shall take effect 60 days after the date on which the last of the following occurs:

(1) The Secretary of Defense has received the report required by the memorandum of the Secretary referred to in subsection (a).

(2) The President transmits to the congressional defense committees a written certification, signed by the President, the Secretary of Defense, and the Chairman of the Joint Chiefs of Staff, stating each of the following:

   (A) That the President, the Secretary of Defense, and the Chairman of the Joint Chiefs of Staff have considered the recommendations contained in the report and the report's proposed plan of action.

   (B) That the Department of Defense has prepared the necessary policies and regulations to exercise the discretion provided by the amendments made by subsection (f).

   (C) That the implementation of necessary policies and regulations pursuant to the discretion provided by the amendments made by subsection (f) is consistent with the standards of military readiness, military effectiveness, unit cohesion, and recruiting and retention of the Armed Forces.

(c) NO IMMEDIATE EFFECT ON CURRENT POLICY.—Section 654 of title 10, United States Code, shall remain in effect until such time that all of the requirements and certifications required by subsection (b) are met. If these requirements and certifications are not met, section 654 of title 10, United States Code, shall remain in effect.

(d) BENEFITS.—Nothing in this section, or the amendments made by this section, shall be construed to require the furnishing of benefits in violation of section 7 of title 1, United States Code (relating to the definitions of "marriage" and "spouse" and referred to as the "Defense of Marriage Act").

(e) NO PRIVATE CAUSE OF ACTION.—Nothing in this section, or the amendments made by this section, shall be construed to create a private cause of action.

(f) TREATMENTOF1993 POLICY.—

(1) TITLE10.—Upon the effective date established by sub-section (b), chapter 37 of title 10, United States Code, is amended—

   (A) by striking section 654; and

   (B) in the table of sections at the beginning of such chapter, by striking the item relating to section 654.

(2) CONFORMING AMENDMENT.—Upon the effective date established by subsection (b), section 571 of the National

*H.R.2965—3*

Defense Authorization Act for Fiscal Year 1994 (10 U.S.C. 654 note) is amended by striking subsections (b), (c), and (d).

   *Speaker of the House of Representatives.*
   *Vice President of the United States and President of the Senate.*

# ➤ U.S. CONGRESS Original Defense of Marriage Act Legislation

H.R.3396

---

**One Hundred Fourth Congress of the United States of America**

*At The Second Session*

*Begun and held at the City of Washington on Wednesday, the third day of January, one thousand nine hundred and ninety-six*

*An Act*

To define and protect the institution of marriage.

*Be it enacted by the Senate and House of Representatives of the United States of America in Congress assembled,*

## Section 1. Short Title.

This Act may be cited as the "Defense of Marriage Act".

## Sec. 2. Powers Reserved to the States.

(a) IN GENERAL.—Chapter 115 of title 28, United States Code, is amended by adding after section 1738B the following:

**§1738C. Certain acts, records, and proceedings and the effect thereof**

"No State, territory, or possession of the United States, or Indian tribe, shall be required to give effect to any public act, record, or judicial proceeding of any other State, territory, possession, or tribe respecting a relationship between persons of the same sex that is treated as a marriage under the laws of such other State, territory, possession, or tribe, or a right or claim arising from such relationship.".

(b) CLERICAL AMENDMENT.—The table of sections at the beginning of chapter 115 of title 28, United States Code, is amended by inserting after the item relating to section 1738B the following new item:

"1738C. Certain acts, records, and proceedings and the effect thereof."

## Sec. 3. Definition Of Marriage.

(a) IN GENERAL.—Chapter 1 of title 1, United States Code, is amended by adding at the end the following:

**"§7. Definition of 'marriage' and 'spouse'**

"In determining the meaning of any Act of Congress, or of any ruling, regulation, or interpretation of the various administrative bureaus and agencies of the United States, the word 'marriage' means only a legal union between one man and one woman as husband and wife, and the word 'spouse' refers only to a personof the opposite sex who is a husband or a wife.".

*H.R.3396—2*

(b) CLERICAL AMENDMENT.—The table of sections at the beginning of chapter 1 of title 1, United States Code, is amended by inserting after the item relating to section 6 the following new item:

"7. Definition of 'marriage' and 'spouse'.".

*Speaker of the House of Representatives.*

*Vice President of the United States and President of the Senate.*

## ➢ Obama Administration Statement on the Defense of Marriage Act

Department of Justice

Office of Public Affairs

FOR IMMEDIATE RELEASE

Wednesday, February 23, 2011

### *Statement of the Attorney General on Litigation Involving the Defense of Marriage Act*

WASHINGTON – The Attorney General made the following statement today about the Department's course of action in two lawsuits, Pedersen v. OPM and Windsor v. United States, challenging Section 3 of the Defense of Marriage Act (DOMA), which defines marriage for federal purposes as only between a man and a woman:

In the two years since this Administration took office, the Department of Justice has defended Section 3 of the Defense of Marriage Act on several occasions in federal court. Each of those cases evaluating Section 3 was considered in jurisdictions in which binding circuit court precedents hold that laws singling out people based on sexual orientation, as DOMA does, are constitutional if there is a rational basis for their enactment. While the President opposes DOMA and believes it should be repealed, the Department has defended it in court because we were able to advance reasonable arguments under that rational basivs standard.

Section 3 of DOMA has now been challenged in the Second Circuit, however, which has no established or binding standard for how laws concerning sexual orientation should be treated. In these cases, the Administration faces for the first time the question of whether laws regarding sexual orientation are subject to the more permissive standard of review or whether a more rigorous standard, under which laws targeting minority groups with a history of discrimination are viewed with suspicion by the courts, should apply.

After careful consideration, including a review of my recommendation, the President has concluded that given a number of factors, including a documented history of discrimination, classifications based on sexual orientation should be subject to a more heightened standard of scrutiny. The President has also concluded that

Section 3 of DOMA, as applied to legally married same-sex couples, fails to meet that standard and is therefore unconstitutional. Given that conclusion, the President has instructed the Department not to defend the statute in such cases. I fully concur with the President's determination.

Consequently, the Department will not defend the constitutionality of Section 3 of DOMA as applied to same-sex married couples in the two cases filed in the Second Circuit. We will, however, remain parties to the cases and continue to represent the interests of the United States throughout the litigation. I have informed Members of Congress of this decision, so Members who wish to defend the statute may pursue that option. The Department will also work closely with the courts to ensure that Congress has a full and fair opportunity to participate in pending litigation.

Furthermore, pursuant to the President's instructions, and upon further notification to Congress, I will instruct Department attorneys to advise courts in other pending DOMA litigation of the President's and my conclusions that a heightened standard should apply, that Section 3 is unconstitutional under that standard and that the Department will cease defense of Section 3.

The Department has a longstanding practice of defending the constitutionality of duly-enacted statutes if reasonable arguments can be made in their defense. At the same time, the Department in the past has declined to defend statutes despite the availability of professionally responsible arguments, in part because – as here – the Department does not consider every such argument to be a "reasonable" one. Moreover, the Department has declined to defend a statute in cases, like this one, where the President has concluded that the statute is unconstitutional.

Much of the legal landscape has changed in the 15 years since Congress passed DOMA. The Supreme Court has ruled that laws criminalizing homosexual conduct are unconstitutional. Congress has repealed the military's Don't Ask, Don't Tell policy. Several lower courts have ruled DOMA itself to be unconstitutional. Section 3 of DOMA will continue to remain in effect unless Congress repeals it or there is a final judicial finding that strikes it down, and the President has informed me that the Executive Branch will continue to enforce the law. But while both the wisdom and the legality of Section 3 of DOMA will continue to be the subject of both extensive litigation and public debate, this Administration will no longer assert its constitutionality in court.

---

11-222 Attorney General

Available at http://www.justice.gov/opa/pr/2011/February/11-ag-222.html.

# SECTION II

# Politics

Sex and sexuality—particularly queer sexualities—remain a "hot" topic in contemporary political arenas, and this section challenges students to think deeply and critically about the political dimensions of LGBT life and culture. Discussions in this section range from a careful consideration of LGBT identity politics to a consideration of the challenges queer theory poses to such politics. These chapters also provide an examination of the uses (and abuses) of strategies of assimilation, and an exploration of intersections among LGBT and other marginalized identities and communities.

# CHAPTER 5

# Nature, Nurture, and Identity

One of the central ongoing debates about queerness deals with whether homosexuality is a biological essence or a social construction. This chapter examines arguments relative to that debate.

For more than a century, scientists and scholars have sought to identify the combination of factors that makes a person feel sexual desire for someone of the same sex. This quest began in the 19th century, as Western medicine claimed status as a profession, with standardized training academies, curricula, and practices. The professionalization of medicine evolved through a number of developments in science at that time, including (1) refinement of scientific methods, (2) significant advances in technology, (3) a mania for taxonomy, and (4) a new understanding of human behavior as pathology. Chapters 2 and 3 of this text focused on the early sexologists and their often gender-stereotypical ideas about homosexuality, culminating in a discussion of the popularization of Freudian terms and ideas in Europe and the United States. This chapter discusses more recent biological and psychological theories purporting to explain the etiology of same-sex desire, gender nonconformity, or both, as well as the impact of these theories on contemporary social and political arenas. We will also see how science and other seemingly "objective" sexual research can be motivated by social and political interests.

# Kinsey

**B**efore turning his attention to human sexuality in the 1940s, zoologist Alfred Kinsey was best known for his meticulously researched study of the gall wasp. In 1940, he and his research team at Indiana University began the massive undertaking that culminated in publication of *Sexual Behavior in the Human Male* in 1948 and *Sexual Behavior in the Human Female* in 1953. The group interviewed thousands of men and women, taking detailed sexual histories. When the 1948 volume appeared, public reaction was intense. Many were shocked and displeased by Kinsey's frank and unapologetic discussion of sexual matters ("Kinsey in the News"). Others were glad to see puritan America exposed as a "nation of sexual hypocrites" (Reisman). Still others were simply titillated. In any case, the country echoed Kinsey's name. About 200,000 copies of *Sexual Behavior in the Human Male* sold in the first two months after it appeared in January 1948. Popular magazines featured articles and cartoons about Kinsey's book. Singer and comedienne Martha Raye had a hit tune in 1949 titled "Ooh, Dr. Kinsey!" Archie "Stomp" Gordon recorded a blues number, "What's Her Whimsy, Dr. Kinsey," after *Sexual Behavior in the Human Female* appeared in 1953:

> I had a gal named Mabel, she used to call me her Hon, But since your book came out, old Mabel always carries a gun.
>
> What is her whimsy, Dr. Kinsey? Won't you tell me if you could, Why she ain't behavin' the way your book says she would.

In fact, the rage for Kinsey has continued nearly unabated for 60 years. As Bob Kanefsky's 1988 parody "Kinsey Scale" and Momus's 2001 song "Psychopathia Sexualis" attest, Kinsey's reputation for opening the Pandora's Box of sex has not diminished (Kanefsky, Currie). In 2004, the feature film *Kinsey* met with reasonable popular success, and Kinsey was profiled in 2005 as part of PBS's *American Experience* series.

One element of Kinsey's work on sexuality that distinguished it from

*"Is there a Mrs. Kinsey?"*

**Figure 5.1** "Is there a Mrs. Kinsey?"

that of his sexologist predecessors was his absolute refusal to allow moral or medical concerns to enter into his examination. Kinsey insisted that human sexuality in all its variations was simply a matter of stimulus and response—given sufficient stimulus, human beings experience sexual arousal. Kinsey took the same approach to men and women as he had taken to gall wasps a decade earlier: gather an extraordinary amount of raw data, keep careful records, and draw no conclusions not directly supported by the data. Another element that distinguished Kinsey's work was that his goal was primarily descriptive; he sought to chronicle American men's and women's sexual histories and practices, but he was far less interested in why they behaved as they did. He included almost no discussion of the etiology of homosexuality in the *Human Male* volume and, in the *Human Female* follow-up, relegated the topic to a single footnote reviewing previous published work proposing causes of lesbianism.

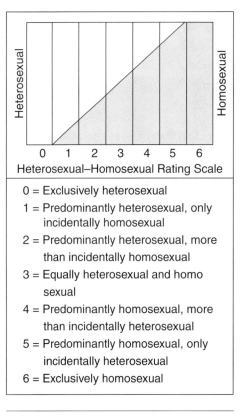

**Figure 5.2**   Kinsey scale.

Kinsey's stimulus-and-response approach to sexuality in general and homosexuality in particular flew in the face of the *congenital sexual inversion* theories of Richard von Krafft-Ebing and Havelock Ellis [λ Chapter 2]. Kinsey rejected the idea of a fixed, inborn (homo)sexual identity. "Only the human mind," he wrote, "invents categories and tries to force facts into separate pigeon-holes" (*Male*, 639). But because "nature rarely deals with discrete categories," and because he believed that "the capacity of an individual to respond erotically to any sort of stimulus, whether it is provided by another person of the same or of the opposite sex, is basic in the species" (660), Kinsey devised a seven-point scale upon which people could chart their degree of homo- or heterosexual inclination and experience.

## Kinsey Scale

Since the appearance of *Human Male*, the Kinsey scale has become a common measure for psychologists and others to gauge an individual's tendency toward same-sex or different-sex attraction; the scale seemed to provide a flexible way of understanding the diversity of human sexual expression. More than this, however, the enormous popularity of Kinsey's sexual behavior books among laypeople has placed the Kinsey scale at the fulcrum of contemporary debates about the nature of homosexuality. Kinsey saw homosexuality as a fluid position on a continuum of possible sexual experiences, and all his conclusions were reached on the basis of self-reported personal statements. His sexual history interviews led him to conclude that "40 to 50 percent of the male population" (*Male* 660) has some homosexual experience, and roughly 5% to 22% of the male population and 2% to 6% of the female population is located at 5 or 6 on the Kinsey scale, or "± exclusively homosexual" (*Female* 488). He found that 10% of males were predominantly homosexual between the ages of 16 and 55 (*Male* 651). This is the source of the "one in ten" concept that figures so prominently in gay rights discussions today.

## After Kinsey

**K**insey did not invent his sexuality scale out of thin air. As early as 1896, Magnus Hirschfeld had constructed two elaborate schemata for measuring the intensity of sexual attraction. The first chart laid out a 10-point scale indicating the strength of an individual's "Love Drive," irrespective of object. The second chart used that scale to plot the degree of attraction to the same sex or a different sex. Hirschfeld's results, which are conveniently symmetrical, identify three sexual "types": the *total man* or *total woman* (heterosexual), the *psychological hermaphrodite* (what we would call *bisexual* today), and the *complete Uranian* (homosexual) [λ Chapter 2]. Kinsey adapted this continuum format to demonstrate the range and diversity of human sexual behavior. As a scientist studying observable behaviors, he sought to move the topic of homosexuality out of the realm of the soft sciences (e.g., psychology) and into the hard sciences (e.g., biology). Some scientists have taken issue with Kinsey's research methods, pointing out that his interviewees were not truly randomly chosen and thus may not have reflected a reliable cross section of the population.

Still, many researchers in a variety of fields have found a continuum approach to sexuality and gender useful in theorizing varieties of human experience, behavior, and identification. A decade after Kinsey's death (1956), Dr. Harry Benjamin's book *The Transsexual Phenomenon* introduced the Gender Disorientation Scale. Benjamin's scale has six stages:

**Figure 5.3** An expression of gay pride, this button shows the way Kinsey's scale has become part of the popular consciousness.

Group 1
- Type I: Transvestite (Pseudo)
- Type II: Transvestism (Fetishistic)
- Type III: Transvestism (True)

Group 2
- Type IV: Transsexual (Nonsurgical)

Group 3
- Type V: True Transsexual (Moderate Intensity)
- Type VI: True Transsexual (High Intensity)

Benjamin breaks each of these six classifications down into eight subcategories: gender feeling, dressing habits and social life, sex object and sex life, Kinsey scale, conversion operation, estrogen medication, psychotherapy, and remarks. For example, Benjamin discusses the Type VI "True Transsexual" as follows:

**Gender Feeling:** Feminine. Total psycho-sexual inversion.

**Dressing Habits and Social Life:** May live and work as a woman. Dressing gives insufficient relief. Gender discomfort intense.

**Sex Object Choice and Sex Life:** Intensely desires relations with normal male as female if young. May have been married and have children, by using fantasies in intercourse.

**Kinsey Scale:** 6

**Conversion Operation:** Urgently requested and usually attained. Indicated.

**Estrogen Medication:** Required for partial relief.

**Psychotherapy:** Psychological guidance or psychotherapy for symptomatic relief only.

**Remarks:** Despises his male sex organs. Danger of suicide or self-mutilation, if too long frustrated.

Benjamin's classification system was specifically designed to serve as a diagnostic tool for gender dysphoric men, and not until later did anyone seriously consider the situation of gender dysphoric women. Such sexism—a lack of attention to born women undergoing sexual-reassignment therapies and procedures—is all too common in both scientific research and medical practice. Still, the Benjamin standards, as they are known, have come to represent threshold requirements for approval of sex reassignment surgery. The Gender Disorientation Scale references the Kinsey scale; thus the Benjamin Type VI, or True Transsexual, measures Kinsey 6 (exclusively homosexual). Benjamin assumes that male homosexuality involves effeminacy; in so doing, he maintains the inversion model of homosexuality favored by the 19th-century sexologists.

According to Benjamin's interpretation of this model, gender—that is, learned behaviors and attitudes supposed to correspond with biological sex—serves as an indicator of sexuality and transsexuality. Benjamin also assumes that all appropriate sexual desire is heterosexual. Therefore, a man whose gender is "feminine" and who desires other men exclusively possesses one of the indicators for sex reassignment surgery, which would "correct" his sexual attractions by making him into a woman who desires a man. The original Benjamin standards required that a candidate for the "conversion operation" score high on the Kinsey scale because this would indicate that the individual's gender was already feminine. So, even though transsexuals often do not consider themselves to be homosexual, many lied to their therapists knowing they needed to present as close to total psycho-sexual inversion as possible to be eligible for surgery. Erwin Haeberle criticizes the early sexologists for making an "arbitrary linkage of erotic inclination and gender role." The Benjamin standards, though applied somewhat less stringently today than in the past, are characterized by this same "arbitrary linkage."

### Klein Sexual Orientation Grid

| Variable | Past | Present | Ideal |
|---|---|---|---|
| A. Sexual Attraction | | | |
| B. Sexual Behavior | | | |
| C. Sexual Fantasies | | | |
| D. Emotional Preference | | | |
| E. Social Preference | | | |
| F. Self-Identification | | | |
| G. Straight/Gay Lifestyle | | | |

| 1 | 2 | 3 | 4 | 5 | 6 | 7 |
|---|---|---|---|---|---|---|
| Other sex only | Other sex mostly | Other sex somewhat more | Both sexes equally | Same sex somewhat more | Same sex mostly | Same sex only |

**Figure 5.4**   Klein Sexual Orientation Grid.

# Klein's Sexual Orientation Grid

In the years following the 1969 Stonewall uprising [λ Chapter 4] and the 1973 removal of homosexuality from the *Diagnostic and Statistical Manual* of mental illnesses [λ Chapter 3], psychologists attempted to devise more complex schemata for charting sexuality, in part due to calls from LGBT activists for more gay-positive approaches. In 1978, psychiatrist Fritz Klein introduced the Klein Sexual Orientation Grid (KSOG), which was based on the Kinsey scale but with the addition of multiple dimensions (such as sexual fantasies and perception of lifestyle) designed to produce unique results for each person. The KSOG builds upon the Kinsey scale (bottom row) but operates by plugging those numbers into a chart built from sexual and emotional categories and three time scales. The user is asked to average her or his responses on the 21 items to arrive at a single Kinsey number. It has become common over the years, however, to dispense with the final average and use the chart to emphasize the multifaceted nature of sexual identity.

## The Storms Sexuality Axis

The Kinsey scale, the Benjamin standards, and the KSOG have been criticized for their assumption of an inevitable homosexual-heterosexual binary. Contemporary sexuality researchers have faced considerable difficulty thinking about sexuality in a way that truly challenges that binary. In 1981, psychologist Michael Storms positioned bisexuality as the area between homosexuality and heterosexuality, rather than encompassing all sexuality (as implied by Kinsey). The Storms Sexuality Axis (SSA) positions homosexuality and heterosexuality on x- and y-axes, with bisexuality representing points in between. The SSA also accounts for **asexuality** in its attempt to offer a more individualized set of identifiers. In 1990, a group of University of Dayton psychologists offered still another variation on the Kinsey scale, the Multidimensional Scale of Sexuality (MSS). The MSS asks 45 true-false questions, then proposes a scoring scheme based on a combination of Kinsey 0–6 and the SSA. (To take the MSS, go to http://www.psych.wright.edu/Kurdek01/MSS.htm.) It was designed to produce ratings of both the behavioral and the cognitive/affective components of sexuality (Berkey, Perelman-Hall, and Kurdek). A recent attempt at a post-Kinsey explication of gradations in sexuality comes from psychiatrist Michael Kauth, whose 2006 article in the *Journal of Bisexuality* aims "to

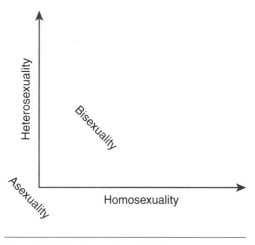

**Figure 5.5** The Storms Sexuality Axis.

unmask implicit social beliefs about same-sex attraction and attraction to both sexes and to promote reliable, testable models of sexual orientation" with an ultimate goal "to expand and standardize the concept of sexual orientation" (79). Like Benjamin, Klein, Storms, and Berkey before him, Kauth begins with Kinsey's (experience-based, not psychological) continuum, applies it to the psychological study of sexuality, and tweaks it to achieve a more wide-ranging and descriptive method of identifying sexual orientations.

Recognizing the sociopolitical dimensions affecting and in some cases shaping desire, Vivian Cass and Adrienne Rich adapted the continuum format to overtly political purposes, and they thus may be thought of as distant cousins to Kinsey. In 1979, Australian psychiatrist Cass introduced a six-stage model of sexual identity integration:

- Stage I: Identity Confusion
- Stage II: Identity Comparison
- Stage III: Identity Tolerance
- Stage IV: Identity Acceptance
- Stage V: Identity Pride
- Stage VI: Identity Synthesis

Cass's model is restricted to mapping the identity development of lesbian and gay people, not those who are transgender or bisexual. Because the focus is on internal self-recognition and growth, this model is assumed to be particularly useful for college students and other young people, although the basic progression is supposed to be more or less the same for all ages. A notable feature of Cass's model is Stage VI, Identity Synthesis, in which the fully adapted homosexual transcends a primarily gay consciousness to reach a stage in which she or he recognizes that various aspects of identity are equally important and should be blended. Other homosexual identity models have occasionally omitted this last stage, assuming that Identity Pride is a sufficient goal in itself, but Cass argues that a person must transcend anger and rebelliousness (characteristics of Stage V) to achieve healthy **self-actualization**. Another notable feature of this model is Cass's recognition of lesbian and gay culture and community. In 1979, when she published "Homosexual Identity Formation," few resources were available to assist lesbian and gay people as they came out. Still, Cass understood (especially in Stages III–V) that a homosexual community existed and represented a key part of the coming-out process. Later models, such as Susan Meyer and Alan Schwitzer's continuum that appeared in 1999, keep Cass's six stages but refer to more established community institutions. Meyer and Schwitzer's Stage 6 (Networking and Connecting) differs from Cass's Stage VI (Identity Synthesis) in that the final identity is validated through connection with other subcultural individuals and institutions. The other primary difference between Cass and Meyer and Schwitzer is that the former focused only on lesbian and gay people, proposing that the model could apply to any age group; Meyer and Schwitzer, by contrast, refer to "college students with gay, lesbian, bisexual, and other minority sexual orientations" (41). As sensitive as these thinkers are to the importance of queer culture, none of them really address the issues of transgendered people, whose struggle for acceptance or at least tolerance is sometimes complicated by the fact that they are often shunned both by the larger, heterosexist culture and by many in the lesbian and gay community with whom they supposedly share common cause as sexual and gender "outsiders."

While many researchers have approached the nature–nurture question through biological and psychological research, others approached the question from a more theoretical or philosophical angle. Adrienne Rich, award-winning poet and longtime lesbian activist, introduced the concept of a lesbian continuum in her important essay "Compulsory Heterosexuality and Lesbian Existence" in 1980. Rich hoped to find a way to lessen the conflict between heterosexual and lesbian feminists in the women's movement [λ Chapter 4]. She also hoped to unearth lesbian existence from the centuries of neglect in which it had been buried. Rich's primary strategy for accomplishing these goals was the concept of the lesbian continuum: "I mean the term *lesbian continuum* to include a range—through each woman's life and through-out history—of woman-identified experience, not simply the fact that a woman has had or consciously desired genital sexual experience with another woman" (239). Rich's continuum bears some resemblance to the "Woman Identified Woman" (WIW) [λ Chapter 4] but differs in one significant respect: the WIW idea was designed to expand the definition of *lesbian* by including women who experienced primary relationships with other women. The lesbian continuum posited a deep and abiding connection among women across time and geography, such that a woman might recognize herself as occupying a position on a preexisting and ongoing time-line. "If we consider the possibility," wrote Rich, "that all women . . . exist on a lesbian continuum, we can see ourselves as moving in and out of this continuum, whether we identify ourselves as lesbian or not" (240). Rich hoped that this recognition would have the power to unify women across superficial differences that divide them and to empower women to rebel against the compulsory heterosexuality imposed upon them by every culture in the world: "We begin to observe behavior, both in history and in individual biography, that has hitherto been invisible or misnamed, behavior which often constitutes . . . radical rebellion. And we can connect these rebellions and the necessity for them with the physical passion of woman for woman which is central to lesbian existence: the erotic sensuality which has been, precisely, the most violently erased fact of female experience" (241). Rich's lesbian continuum has been criticized—she even attaches a letter challenging it to later editions of the essay—for indulging a privileged white woman's vision of the unity of "all women" when all women do not enjoy the same benefits or acknowledge the same needs. Still, it represented a stunning indictment of the phenomenon of compulsory heterosexuality, and by removing the concept *lesbian* from an exclusively sexual definition, it created a vision of a politically viable movement based on femaleness. Rich's vision is far from Kinsey's scale because its examples come from neither the "hard" nor the "soft" sciences but rather from philosophy and literature, but it nonetheless reveals the power of the continuum format in conceptualizing sexual connection.

## The Quest for the Gay Gene

In *Human Male,* Kinsey warned future researchers that discovering "Factors Accounting for the Homosexual" (660) was going to be a daunting task. Psychologists, he wrote, must be aware that "it is one thing to account for an all-or-none proposition, as heterosexuality and homosexuality have ordinarily been taken to be. But it is a totally different matter to recognize factors which will account for the continuum which we find existing between the exclusively heterosexual and the exclusively homosexual history" (661). Scientists seeking to locate a biological basis for homosexuality must show that "the fluctuations in preferences for female or male partners are related to fluctuations in the hormones, the genes, or the other biologic factors which are assumed to be operating" (661). Kinsey went on to lay out a detailed set of conditions that would need to be met in order to prove that homosexuality is an inherited condition in humans:

1. It would be necessary to define strictly what is meant in the study by the term homosexual. . . .

2. There should be a determination of the incidence of the phenomenon in groups of siblings in which the complete sexual history of every individual in each family is known. . . .

3. Especial attention should be paid to the balance between the homosexual and the heterosexual behavior in the histories of each of the siblings in such a study.

4. The recognition of homosexuality in any individual should not be considered sufficient unless a complete sexual history is available. . . .

5. Similarly, the heterosexuality of any individual who enters into the calculations should be determined through complete sex histories. In nearly all studies to date, heterosexuality has been assumed . . . when there was no public knowledge of homosexuality. These are, of course, untrustworthy sources of information. . . .

6. There should be data on enough cases of siblings to be statistically significant. . . .

7. The incidence of the homosexual, as it is defined in the study, should be shown to be higher among siblings than it is in the histories of the nonsiblings in the study. Inasmuch as our present data indicate that more than a third (37%) of the white males in any population (or probably, for that matter, among anyone's ancestors) have had at least some homosexual experience, and inasmuch as the data indicate that a quarter of the males in the population (and a quarter of the males in anyone's ancestry) may have more than incidental homosexual experience in the course of their lives, it would be necessary to show that the incidence of the homosexual in groups of siblings is higher than that. This, of course, has never been shown in any study on the inheritance of the homosexual.

8. Whatever the hereditary mechanisms which are proposed, they must allow for the fact that some individuals change from exclusively heterosexual to exclusively homosexual patterns in the course of their lives, or vice versa, and they must allow for frequent changes in ratings of individuals on the heterosexual-homosexual scale. (662–63)

Kinsey's layout of the requirements scientists would need to fulfill in order to ascertain a link between biology and homosexuality has structured much of the biological research in the 60+ years since the appearance of *Human Male*. This is interesting because Kinsey's conditions, especially those dealing with sibling samples, make a point of alerting researchers to issues that he believes will make it close to impossible to gather valid data. Nevertheless, a host of studies both before and after Kinsey have attempted to identify genetic, hormonal, or anatomical factors linked to homosexuality in humans.

A number of these studies have used animals. One of the earliest seems to have been Richard Goldschmidt's 1917 study of what he called *intersexuality* in insects. Goldschmidt's observations of the gypsy moth *Lymantria* identified a number of intermediate types between male and female; he reasoned that these types demonstrated a hereditary basis for homosexuality in humans. Kinsey, among others, dismissed Goldschmidt's findings because "he identified homosexual males and females in the human species as **intersexes**" (*Male* 661) rather than simply as people engaging in a spectrum of sexual experiences. Still, scientists have continued to attempt to extrapolate from animals to people. I. L. Ward's work with rats, Roselli, Larkin, Resko, Stellflug, and Stormshak's work with rams, and Ebru Demir and Barry Dickson's work with fruit flies all suggest genetic explanations for homosexuality in humans. The Demir and Dickson study of *Drosophila* identifies one gene, named *fruitless* or *fru,* that they believe appears to control sexual orientation. It is true that when a female fruit fly is engineered to **splice** *fru* in a male-specific fashion, she approaches and attempts to copulate with other females. It has not been demonstrated, however, that any similar gene operates in humans.

Sibling studies—particularly of twins—were seen by Kinsey as promising in terms of establishing a hereditary pattern of homosexuality. Indeed, an early study from Kinsey's era reported a concordance rate (the likelihood that if one monozygotic—or identical—twin is gay, the other will be too) near 100% (Kallmann). More recent studies make much less extravagant claims: J. Michael Bailey and Richard C. Pillard's research, for instance, shows concordance rates of 52% and 48% for male and female monozygotic twins, respectively, and 22% and 16% for male and female dizygotic (fraternal) twins, respectively. Because the concordance results for monozygotic twins are less than 100%, it is impossible to conclude that genes absolutely determine sexual orientation; but these studies seem to indicate the possibility of a genetic influence on sexuality. Using pairs of gay brothers, a research group led by Dean Hamer attempted to locate a "gay gene" that controls sexual orientation. They reported finding a promising site in an area called Xq28 on the X chromosome, but a later group failed to confirm the discovery. A 2005 study by Brian Mustanski et al. found possible sites on chromosomes 7, 8, and 10 but did not present firm evidence of an actual connection between the gene and homosexuality. Simon LeVay asserts that "sexual orientation is . . . partly inherited, at least in men" ("Biology" 6); however, no irrefutable genetic evidence has surfaced.

A number of studies have focused on hormones as a cause of homosexuality in men and women. German neuroendocrinologist Günter Dörner's prenatal hormonal theory of homosexuality proposed that the brains of pre-homosexual fetuses develop in a sex-atypical way due either to unusual amounts of hormones or to specific brain responses to hormones. Another set of hormone studies claims that the ring finger (D4) in lesbians is significantly longer than the index finger (D2), whereas in most women, D2 is nearly the same length as D4. The relatively low D2:D4 ratio in lesbians is similar to most men; the theory postulates that these individuals were exposed prenatally to high androgen, or male hormone, levels.

**Find Out More** in "Differences in Finger Length Ratios between Self-Identified 'Butch' and 'Femme' Lesbians" at the end of this chapter.

One of the most important and controversial hormone studies was undertaken by Simon LeVay in 1991. In an autopsy study of gay men, LeVay found that the third interstitial nucleus of the anterior hypothalamus (INAH3) was smaller than in straight men—in fact, similar in size to women's. The hypothalamus is a part of the brain that serves a number of functions, among which is hormonal and neurotransmitter regulation. Therefore, a man with a smaller-than-usual INAH3 might be expected to have developed in a sex-atypical way. LeVay's study was verified in 2001 and is probably the most plausible of the biological studies of homosexuality. Nevertheless, LeVay's sample of gay men, most of whom had died from AIDS, points to two problems with his study. First, it is not clear what effect AIDS may have on the human hypothalamus, and therefore, the possibility exists that its unusual size in these men results from disease and has no relationship to sexual orientation. Second, the sample itself is suspect. LeVay's own definition of homosexuality—"a dissociation between anatomical sex and sex-typical sexual orientation" ("Biology" 4)—presupposes subjects who self-identify as gay since, unlike skin color, for example, homosexuality is not visibly marked on the human body. The sample problem is not unique to LeVay, of course. Kinsey anticipated it in 1948 by urging future researchers in this area to undertake detailed sexual histories and to resist the assumption that homosexuals and heterosexuals are somehow distinct and opposite. Many have ignored his warning, and it is common practice to assemble a research sample of sexual minority individuals through suspect means, such as *snowballing*—beginning with people the researcher knows personally, then asking them to recruit their friends into the study—or using LGBT political or social groups. These methods produce samples that tend to be skewed with respect to (1) race, (2) social class, (3) outness, and (4) attitude toward gayness and gay rights issues.

A third problem with LeVay's study that is not related to the AIDS sample—and that is common to virtually all sexual orientation research—is the assumption that what he calls "sex-typical" orientation is based on traditional ideas of what constitutes maleness and femaleness. The androgen receptor gene, for instance, "plays the key role in mediating testosterone's influence on the body and brain" (LeVay, "Biology" 6). Testosterone increases behaviors identified in many cultures as "male" (e.g., sexual aggressiveness and propensity toward violence). Therefore, researchers reason, if a woman is sexually aggressive or a man is gentle, they are sex atypical and might be lesbian or gay. In other words, much of the research on sexual orientation seems tied to the **gender inversion** models that were in fashion over a century ago but that are today seen as limiting to both men and women. It should also be noted that these researchers have focused on homosexuality as it is constructed in the United States and the Global North. Attention to non-Western constructions of sexuality will surely problematize the assumptions upon which

**Find Out More** in "Essentialism" at the end of this chapter.

these scientific studies are based. For instance, how might researchers collect interviews in a culture in which *homosexual* and *heterosexual* are not common terms of identity? It may be tempting for Western-trained researchers to apply sexual orientation identity terms to people who do not self-identify as *gay* or *straight*, but would such terms adequately reflect the interviewees' experiences and desires?

## Nature–Nurture: What's at Stake?

Let us conclude this chapter by considering what is at stake in the nature–nurture debate. LeVay argues that "the continued search for the responsible genes [for sexual orientation] and their mechanism of action is certainly warranted" ("Biology" 6), and many LGBT activists have employed a kind of "strategic essentialism" [λ Chapter 3] in their ongoing quest for civil rights; this has meant adopting the position that homosexuality is inherited in the same way that race or brown eyes are inherited. If one is simply born a homosexual, then discrimination is not morally justifiable. Proving that sexual orientation is a genetic trait thus seems to support the rights movement. One might expect that LGBT activists would unhesitatingly embrace the genetic explanation. Indeed, strategic essentialism has proven useful, and some still support it. But many LGBT people distrust the biological approach. For one thing, some prefer liberationist politics (supporting sexual freedom) to those that emphasize biological determinism. Interviewees throughout Vera Whisman's *Queer by Choice: Lesbians, Gay Men, and the Politics of Identity* assert that a central component of their sense of identity is not so much gay identity as sexual self-determination, the right to choose how, when, and why they engage with other people intimately. Some also fear that the genetic explanation leads back to the gay-is-sick [λ Chapter 3] philosophy, where the medical establishment made draconian attempts to "cure" LGBT people. Some imagine fetuses genetically marked as homosexual being aborted or otherwise eliminated in families that prefer heterosexual children. Some critique the science as flawed due to the elision of racial diversity from virtually all research studies. Still others simply reject the sexist ideas of "gender confusion" and the pathologization of the "masculine female or the non-masculine male" (Pickering and Saunders 7).

Those who do not support gay rights use combinations of both nature and nurture arguments to oppose queer activists. The Concerned Women for America (CWA) charge, for instance, that "LeVay is an open homosexual, and ... he had an agenda from the outset" (Chun). CWA criticizes LeVay's work as bogus science undertaken to support the "gay agenda." Probe Ministries traces the biology argument back to Kinsey's 10% estimate, which was used by "Harry Hay, the father of the homosexual 'civil rights' movement, urging that homosexuality be seen no longer as an act of sodomy but as a 10% minority class" [λ Chapter 3] (Bohlin 1). Probe counters by including homosexuality among "sexual sins" that may be genetically influenced but must be resisted because they are immoral; they use Leviticus 18 and 20 [λ Chapter 1] to link homosexuality to incest, adultery, bestiality, and child sacrifice. So, from Probe's standpoint, the nature argument is irrelevant; homosexuality, even if "natural," should still be resisted, much as one might resist other socially "unacceptable" impulses. Arguing from a nurture position, Dr. Paul Cameron of the Family Research Institute maintains that "homosexual behavior is learned" (1) and therefore can be unlearned, through psychotherapy and "ex-gay ministries" (6). The argument that homosexuality is a chosen set of behaviors has been deployed frequently in the fight against LGBT civil rights.

**Find Out More** in "Is Your Baby Gay?" at the end of this chapter.

Whatever side one may occupy in the nature–nurture debate, it is clear that, even in the realm of science, political investments often influence the type and nature of research projects undertaken as well as the way those projects are understood, interpreted, and used by a variety of activists—both pro- and anti-queer. Both Kinsey and LeVay, for instance, pursued their research not just to understand human sexuality but to make room for a more capacious appreciation for sexual diversity. The fact that scientists such as LeVay, among many others, have argued for a biological basis for homosexuality suggests the power and cultural capital of science in Western societies. Such research is pursued in an effort to cash in on that capital, demonstrating the seeming naturalness of sexual behaviors found in all cultures throughout history. Still, as persuasive as some of the biological research seems to be in arguing for a genetic basis for homosexuality, and despite the fact that "five decades of psychiatric evidence demonstrate that homosexuality is immutable, and nonpathological" (Burr 65), no one appears to regard the issue as definitively settled. Methodological weaknesses have been perceived in both biological and psychological research, not the least of which is that both still assume heterosexuality as the default position. We can see heteronormativity at work in scientific inquiry; researchers look for a "gay gene," but why do they not attempt to isolate a "straight gene"? Presumably, only the nonnormative—the queer—needs to be explained, while the normative goes unremarked as obviously and unquestionably natural. In addition, both the gay agenda and the antigay agenda weigh in on the debate, typically ignoring what the scientists are saying entirely (Mucciaroni and Killian).

## QUESTIONS FOR DISCUSSION

1. This chapter has included a number of instruments designed to measure a person's homosexuality (the Kinsey scale, the Benjamin Gender Disorientation Scale, the KSOG, and so forth). Take several of these tests yourself. What are your results? Is one instrument more accurate than another in expressing how you feel about your own sexual identity? What questions or measurements seem most effective to you? What might be missing from these instruments? If you were to design your own scale, what would it look like?

2. In this chapter, we have asserted that a number of biological and psychological studies about homosexuality rest on some typically dualistic assumptions about gender: men normally act a certain way and women another. Such assumptions are founded on cultural beliefs about what "normal men" and "normal women" are supposed to be like. As you read the Find Out More article by Brown, Finn, Cooke, and Breedlove analyzing the D2:D4 finger length ratio in butch and femme lesbians, attempt your own gender critique. What unstated assumptions about gender underlie the authors' argument?

3. There are those who argue that some scientists pursuing work that examines the relationship of nature and nurture to sexuality are supporting what they call the *gay agenda,* and it cannot be denied that much scientific research is done with an eye toward answering questions related to larger social issues. Can it not be argued that groups who accuse scientists such as Simon LeVay of having a gay agenda might have agendas of their own? Do some investigative work to find out more about organizations such as the CWA, Probe Ministries, and the Family Research Institute. Do they have agendas? If so, describe them.

## REFERENCES AND FURTHER READING

Bailey, J. M., and R. C. Pillard. "Genetics of Human Sexual Orientation." *Annual Review of Sex Research* 6 (1995): 126–50. Print.

Bailey, J. M., R. C. Pillard, M. C. Neale, and Y. Agyei. "Heritable Factors Influence Sexual Orientation in Women." *Archives of General Psychiatry* 50 (1993): 217–23. Print.

Benjamin, Harry. *The Transsexual Phenomenon.* N.p., 1966. Web. 19 July 2008. <http://www.transgenderzone.com/downloads/tphenom.htm>.

Berkey, B. R., T. Perelman-Hall, and L. A. Kurdek. "The Multidimensional Scale of Sexuality." *Journal of Homosexuality* 19 (1990): 67–87.

Bohlin, Sue. "Homosexual Myths." Probe Ministries, n.d. Web. 19 July 2008. <http://www.probe.org/content/view/699/72/>.

Brown, Windy M., Christopher J. Finn, Bradley M. Cooke, and S. Marc Breedlove. "Differences in Finger Length Ratios between Self-Identified 'Butch' and 'Femme' Lesbians." *Archives of Sexual Behavior* 31.1 (2002): 123–27. Print.

Burr, Chandler. "Homosexuality and Biology." *The Atlantic Monthly* 271.3 (1993): 47–65. Print.

Cameron, Paul. "What Causes Homosexual Desire and Can It Be Changed?" N.p., n.d. Web. 19 July 2008. <http://www.biblebelievers.com/Cameron3.html>.

Cass, Vivian C. "Homosexual Identity Formation: A Theoretical Model." *Journal of Homosexuality* 4.3 (1979): 219–35. Print.

Chun, Trudy. "Born or Bred? The Debate over the Cause of Homosexuality." Concerned Women for America, 1 June 2000. Web. 19 July 2008. <http://www.cwfa.org/articledisplay.asp?id=1097&department=CWA&categoryid=family>.

Currie, Nick (Momus). "Psychopathia Sexualis." N.p., 2001. Web. 19 July 2008 <http://www.phespirit.info/momus/20010112.htm>.

Demir, E., and B. J. Dickson. "*fruitless* Splicing Specifies Male Courtship Behavior in *Drosophila.*" *Cell* 121 (2005): 785–94. Print.

Dörner, Günter. "Hormone Dependent Differentiation, Maturation and Function of the Brain and Sexual Behavior." *Endokrinologie* 69 (1977): 306–20. Print.

Goldschmidt, Richard. "Intersexuality and the Endocrine Aspect of Sex." *Endocrinology* 1 (1917): 433–56. Print.

Gordon, Archie "Stomp." "What's Her Whimsey, Dr. Kinsey?" N.d. Web. 19

July 2008. <http://www.theonlineblues. com/archie-stomp-gordon-what-s-her-whimsey-dr-kinsey-lyrics.html>.

Haeberle, Erwin J. "Bisexuality: History and Dimensions of a Modern Scientific Problem." N.p., 1998. Web. 19 July 2008 <http://www2.hu-berlin.de/sexology/ GESUND/ARCHIV/SEXOR4.HTM>.

Hamer, D. H., S. Hu, V. L. Magnuson, N. Hu, and A. M. L. Pattatucci. "A Linkage between DNA Markers on the X Chromosome and Male Sexual Orientation." *Science* 261 (1993): 320–26. Print.

Hirschfeld, Magnus. *Sappho und Sokrates: Wie erklärt sich die Liebe der Männer und Frauen zu Personen des eigenen Geschlechts?* 2nd ed. Leipzig: Max Spohr, 1902. Print.

Kallmann, E. J. "Comparative Twin Studies on the Genetic Aspects of Male Homosexuality." *Journal of Nervous and Mental Disease* 115 (1952): 283–98. Print.

Kanefsky, Bob. "Kinsey Scale." N.p., 1988. Web. 19 July 2008. <http://www.song worm.com/lyrics/songworm-parody/ KinseyScale.html>.

Kauth, Michael R. "Revealing Assumptions: Explicating Sexual Orientation and Promoting Conceptual Integrity." *Journal of Bisexuality* 5.4 (2006): 79–105. Print.

Kinsey, Alfred, and the staff of the Institute for Sex Research, Indiana University. *Sexual Behavior in the Human Female.* Philadelphia: W. B. Saunders, 1953. Print.

Kinsey, Alfred, Wardell B. Pomeroy, and Clyde E. Martin. *Sexual Behavior in the Human Male.* Philadelphia: W. B. Saunders, 1948. Print.

"Kinsey in the News." N.p., n.d. Web. 19 July 2008. <http://www.pbs.org/wgbh/ amex/kinsey/sfeature/sf_response_ male.html>.

Klein, Fritz. *The Bisexual Option: A Concept of One Hundred Percent Intimacy.* New York: Arbor House, 1978. Print.

LeVay, Simon. "The Biology of Sexual Orientation." 2003. N.p., April 2009. Web. 22 May 2012. <http://www.simonlevay.com/ the-biology-of-sexual-orientation>.

———. "A Difference in Hypothalamic Structure between Heterosexual and Homosexual Men." *Science* 253 (1991): 1034–37. Print.

Meyer, Susan, and Alan M. Schwitzer. "Stages of Identity Development among College Students with Minority Sexual Orientations." *Journal of College Student Psychotherapy* 13.4 (1999): 41–66. Print.

Mohler, R. Albert, Jr. "Is Your Baby Gay? What If You Could Know? What If You Could Do Something About It?" N.p., n.d. Web. 19 July 2008. <http://www.albertmohler .com/blog_print.php?id=891>.

Mucciaroni, Gary, and Mary Lou Killian. "Immutability, Science and Legislative Debate over Gay, Lesbian and Bisexual Rights." *Journal of Homosexuality* 47.1 (2004): 53–77. Print.

Munsey, David. "The Love That Need Not Name Its Speaker." *National Journal of Sexual Orientation Law* 2.1 (1996). Web. <http://www.ibiblio.org/gaylaw/ issue3/issue3.html>.

Mustanski, B. S., M. G. Dupree, C. M. Nievergelt, S. Bockland, N. J. Schork, and D. H. Hamer. "A Genomewide Scan of Male Sexual Orientation." *Human Genetics* 116 (2005): 272–78. Print.

Norton, Rictor. "Essentialism." N.p., n.d. Web. 19 July 2008. <http://www.ric tornorton.co.uk/social03.htm>.

Pickering, Rachael, and Peter Saunders. "What Causes Homosexuality?" *Nucleus* (Oct. 1997). Web. <http://www.cmf.org.uk/literature/content.asp?context=article&id=630>.

Reisman, Judith. "Kinsey and the Homosexual Revolution." N.p., n.d. Web. 19 July 2008. <http://www.leaderu.com/jhs/reisman.html>.

Rich, Adrienne. "Compulsory Heterosexuality and Lesbian Existence." *The Lesbian and Gay Studies Reader.* 1980. Eds. H. Abelove, M. Aina Barale, and D. Halperin. New York: Routledge, 1993. 227–54. Print.

Roselli, C. E., K. Larkin, J. A. Resko, J. N. Stellflug, and F. Stormshak. "The Volume of a Sexually Dimorphic Nucleus in the Ovine Medial Preoptic Area/Anterior Hypothalamus Varies with Sexual Partner Preference." *Endocrinology* 145.2 (2004): 478–83. Print.

Storms, Michael. "A Theory of Erotic Orientation Development." *Psychological Review* 88.4 (1981): 340–53. Print.

Ward, I. L. "Prenatal Stress Feminizes and Demasculinizes the Behavior of Males." *Science* 175.17 (1972): 82–84. Print.

Whisman, Vera. *Queer by Choice: Lesbians, Gay Men, and the Politics of Identity.* New York: Routledge, 1996. Print.

# READINGS

## ➤ Windy M. Brown, Christopher J. Finn, Bradley M. Cooke, and S. Marc Breedlove

(2002), United States

### "Differences in Finger Length Ratios between Self-Identified 'Butch' and 'Femme' Lesbians"

In nonhuman mammals, sexual differentiation of behavior seems largely driven by exposure to steroid hormones during the perinatal period (Breedlove, Cooke, & Jordan, 1998). The Y chromosome in males causes the undifferentiated gonads to develop as testes, and the testes to secrete androgen, which masculinizes the structure of the brain, permanently molding the animal's behavior to a male-like form (Phoenix, Goy, Gerall, & Young, 1959). Whether early androgen exposure also directly alters the structure of the developing human brain, and thereby adult behavior, remains undetermined.

In the study of sexual orientation, there is little direct evidence that individual differences in early androgen exposure affect the sexual preferences of men. In women, however, there have been several reports of a difference between heterosexual and homosexual women in purported markers of prenatal or neonatal androgen exposure. McFadden and Champlin (2000) found that auditory evoked potentials (AEP) are more masculine in lesbians than in heterosexual women. Because the sex difference in AEP is present in newborn humans, and because other somatic sex differences in newborns appear to be due to the masculinizing influence of androgen in males, presumably AEP are influenced by, and can therefore serve as markers for, fetal androgen exposure. Thus the AEP results suggest that homosexual women were exposed to more fetal androgen than were heterosexual women. McFadden and Champlin also found that the AEP of homosexual men suggested that they, if anything, had experienced significantly higher levels of perinatal androgen than did heterosexual men. McFadden and Pasanen (1998) also found that otoacoustic emissions, which are also sexually dimorphic at birth (and therefore may also serve as markers for fetal androgen), are significantly more male-like in homosexual women than in heterosexual women. This result is a further indication that lesbians may have been exposed to higher fetal androgen levels than heterosexual women (for an overview, see McFadden, 2002).

Another purported somatic marker of fetal androgen is the ratio of the length of the index finger (2D) to the ring finger (4D). This ratio, 2D:4D, is smaller in men than in women (Ecker, 1875), a sex difference that is stable from 2 years of age to adulthood (Manning, Scott, Wilson, & Lewis-Jones, 1998). As most somatic differences between young boys and girls have been attributed to differences in exposure to androgen before and just after birth (George & Wilson, 1994), the sex difference in 2D:4D was presumed to reflect sex differences in early androgen.

We have tested this hypothesis by examining the 2D:4D of people with congenital adrenal hyperplasia (CAH). CAH is a disorder that causes the adrenals to produce excessive androgens beginning prenatally and extending to treatment, which usually begins shortly after birth following an accurate diagnosis. We found that the ratios were indeed smaller in CAH females than in control females, and were also smaller in CAH males than in control males (Brown, Hines, Fane, & Breedlove, 2001). The difference between CAH males and control males was especially prominent when comparing relatives, suggesting that genetic background can affect the finger length ratios but that, within a particular genetic background, greater early androgen exposure reduces the finger ratios. We have also found a similar sex difference in the digit length ratios of mice: rear paw 2D:4D is smaller in males than in females at weaning and in adulthood (Brown, Finn, & Breedlove, 2001), which suggests that adult digit length ratios may provide a retrospective indication of perinatal androgens in many mammalian species.

Accordingly, the report of Williams et al. (2000) that the 2D:4D of homosexual women was more masculine (smaller) than that of heterosexual women indicates again that lesbians are, on average, exposed to more prenatal androgen than are heterosexual women. If so, then increased exposure to fetal androgen may increase the probability of homosexuality in human females. This study found no differences in the 2D:4D of heterosexual versus homosexual men.

If early hormone levels affect human sexual orientation in the same manner as they do other sex dimorphic behaviors in other animals, this influence would be expected to be organizational in nature such that the behavior pattern affected is set from a young age and remains constant throughout the life span. There is some evidence, however, that some women have a heterosexual orientation during certain periods of their lives and a homosexual orientation at other periods (Diamond, 1998). This suggests that other factors, including social influences, can also affect sexual orientation in women. Therefore, presumably some of the lesbians studied in the previously cited reports were exposed to low levels of androgen in development, i.e., perinatal androgens played no role in the development of their sexual orientation. Because other, nonandrogenic factors influence female sexual orientation, the experimental detection of effects of early androgen, especially via indirect measures, requires large sample sizes. We therefore wondered whether it would be possible to subdivide lesbian participants into groups in which perinatal androgen exposure might be more or less likely to have played a role in the development of a homosexual orientation. Because some lesbians consider themselves to be more masculine ("butch") than other women, we tested whether the finger length ratios of "butch" lesbians would show evidence of greater perinatal androgen exposure than those of "femme" lesbians.

## Methods

A booth was rented for the August 2000 Gay Pride Mardi Gras in Oakland, CA. All adult participants were offered a California Lottery "scratcher" ticket in return for answering an anonymous survey that asked their age, sex at birth, and number of older brothers and sisters.

*Participants and Measures.* Participants identified themselves as "exclusively heterosexual," "predominantly heterosexual," "bisexual," "predominantly homosexual," or "exclusively homosexual." They were also asked the gender of their sexual partners ("exclusively males," "predominantly males," "males and females equally," "predominantly females," or "exclusively females") and the gender of sexual partners in their fantasies. These latter two questions were asked to confirm self-reports of orientation and, in this study, all participants gave answers that were consistent with their reported sexual orientation. They were also asked to answer the following question: "If I had to describe myself as one of the two types below, I would consider my overall outlook to be (circle one)": with the choices butch and femme on the line beneath. The questionnaire informed them that answering any question was voluntary and would not affect their receipt of a ticket. Participants were not asked to report their ethnicity.

The participants then had their hands copied on a portable photocopier. A clear Plexiglas form was placed on the glass platen. This form had two posts, 6 mm in diameter, 147 mm apart. Participants were asked to place their hands flat, palm-down, thumbs near each other, fingers on each hand together, on the form with the posts between the index and middle fingers of each hand, snug against the junction of the two fingers. A millimeter scale was present 12 mm lateral to the posts and the participants' middle fingers were aligned on this scale. A white plastic bag, filled with rice for ballast, was placed over the hands before photocopying. Matching numbered stickers were affixed to the back of each questionnaire and photocopy to discern which answers were associated with each photocopy.

Finger lengths were measured by an experimenter, without knowledge of any participant's group membership. If the tip of either finger was obscured in the photocopy, then no ratio was available for that hand for that participant. Measures were taken for each finger to the nearest 0.5 mm, based on their alignment to the photocopied ruler running along the middle finger. This method of measuring finger length differs slightly from other recent reports, but is much more efficient than the method we used previously (Williams et al., 2000). It also more closely matches the measurement method reported by George (1930), confirming Ecker's report (Ecker, 1875). Two mixed-design ANOVAs, with an independent factor of either male/female (to evaluate sex differences) or butch/femme (to evaluate lesbian subgroups), and right and left hand finger ratios as repeated measures, were conducted. Further analysis of differences between groups were evaluated by Student's $t$ tests, with all reported $p$ values two-tailed.

### Results

The present measurement method detected the previously reported sex difference in 2D:4D between the 267 female and 168 male participants. ANOVA revealed a sex difference in which ratios were greater in females than in males, $F(1, 432) = 28.3$, $p < .001$, a laterality effect in which the ratios were greater on the right than on the left, $F(1, 432) = 6.0$, $p < .02$, and a significant interaction of the two factors, $F(1, 432) = 18.6$, $p < .001$. Student's $t$ tests indicated that the interaction was due to a greater sex difference on the right than on the left. For the right hand, the ratio was $0.994 \pm 0.003$ (*SEM*) for women, $0.958 \pm 0.004$ for men, $t(431) = 6.6$; $p < 10^{-10}$; for the left hand, the ratio was $0.967 \pm 0.003$ for women and $0.938 \pm 0.004$ for men, $t(431) = 5.9$, $p < 10^{-8}$. Our previous report (Williams et al., 2000) also found the sex difference in 2D:4D to be greater on the right hand than on the left hand.

Of the 267 women, 29 identified themselves as heterosexual (either "predominantly heterosexual" or "exclusively heterosexual"), 28 as bisexual, 207 as homosexual (either "predominantly homosexual" or "exclusively homosexual"), and one declined to answer the questions about sexual orientation. The data from bisexuals were not examined. Among the homosexual women, 89 identified themselves as femme, 87 as butch, whereas 31 declined to answer the question. Self-identified butch versus femme lesbians were not significantly different in age (femme: mean of $39.41 \pm .98$ years, range, 22–58; butch: $41.12 \pm .90$ years, range, 24–66). . . .

## Discussion

We found that it was possible to classify homosexual women into two self-reported categories: those who regard themselves as having a "butch" outlook and those who regard themselves as having a "femme" outlook. Although there is debate over the validity of segregating homosexual women into these categories (Laner & Laner, 1980), most participants in this study appeared to intuitively understand what we were referring to by these classifications and most of them, when asked, appeared to readily identify more with one than the other. These two groups differed significantly in the 2D:4D ratio of the right hand, suggesting that the femme group had been exposed to less prenatal androgen than had the butch group. Nevertheless, the overlap between the two groups for this measure was considerable. The data thus indicate that there are more factors influencing sexual orientation than simply early androgen exposure.

The finding that women who identify themselves as either butch or femme lesbians differ in this biological marker for androgen suggests that it may be worthwhile to try to more rigorously define subgroups of individuals regarded as either heterosexual or homosexual. The present classification was simple (an answer to a single, rather amorphous question) and therefore surely crude. It should be possible, with more extensive probing of personality traits, to more accurately classify homosexual women. Such refined classifications might reveal a greater difference in 2D:4D, or might reveal personality traits that co-vary with finger ratios, which might shed light on the butch-femme distinction. For example, after conducting the study we learned of the report by Wilson (1983) regarding women who answered a newspaper survey. Those who reported that their index finger was shorter than their ring finger were more likely to describe themselves as "assertive and competitive" than those whose index finger was longer than the ring finger. Again, the sample size was large (985 women), so it is not a question of whether early androgens determine this personality style, only whether they increase the probability of such a personality developing. It is possible that the present differences in 2D:4D reflect a difference in assertiveness between butch and femme lesbians.

The 2D:4D difference between butch and femme lesbians is consistent with the idea that early androgens have some influence on later sexual orientation, at least in females. The present findings also conform to the report from Singh, Vidaurri, Zambarano, and Dabbs (1999) that butch lesbians had a higher waist-to-hip ratio, higher salivary testosterone levels, and more reports of childhood gender-atypical behavior than did femme lesbians. These results and the previously discussed auditory system measures suggest that early exposure to androgen can increase the probability of a homosexual orientation in human females.

We have so far detected no difference between heterosexual and homosexual men in 2D:4D, suggesting that early androgens do not differ between the two groups and may not play a role in the development of male sexual orientation. But the present findings suggest that it might be possible to classify homosexual men into categories that might reveal a difference in early androgen exposure. For example, some homosexual men report a history of gender nonconformity as children, whereas others do not. It is possible that a relative lack of early androgen exposure might contribute to the development of homosexuality in the former, and/or that a relative surplus of early androgen might contribute to homosexuality in the latter. Robinson and Manning (2000) in fact report that the finger ratios of gay men differ according their score on the Kinsey sexual orientation scale.

We have several times found the sex difference in 2D:4D to be greater on the right hand than on the left (Williams et al., 2000, the present study, and unpublished observations), as have other groups (Manning et al., 1998). We also found that the difference between CAH and control women was greater on the right hand than on the left (Brown, Hines, et al., 2001). These data suggest that the right hand finger ratios are more sensitive to prenatal androgen than are those on the left. We can offer no explanation for why androgen would affect the developing right hand more than the left.

While reviewing the proofs for this article, we learned that Tortorice (2001) recently reported 2D:4D to be smaller in self-rated butch lesbians than in femme lesbians.

## References

Breedlove, S. M., Cooke, B., & Jordan, C. L. (1998). The orthodox view of sexual differentiation of the brain. *Brain, Behavior and Evolution*, *54*, 8–14.

Brown, W. M., Finn, C., & Breedlove, S. M. (2001). A sex difference in the digit length ratio in mice [Abstract]. *Hormones and Behavior*, *39*, 325.

Brown, W. M., Hines, M., Fane, B., & Breedlove, S. M. (2001). Masculinized finger length ratios in humans with congenital adrenal hyperplasia (CAH) [Abstract]. *Hormones and Behavior*, *39*, 325–326.

Diamond, L. M. (1998). Development of sexual orientation among adolescent and young adult women. *Developmental Psychology*, *34*, 1085–1095.

Ecker, A. (1875). Einige bemerkungen über einen schwankenden character in der hand des menschen. [Some remarks about a varying character in the hand of humans.] *Archiv für Anthropologie*, *8*, 68–74.

George, F. W., & Wilson, J. D. (1994). Sex determination and differentiation. In E. Knobil & J. D. Neil (Eds.), *The physiology of reproduction* (pp. 3–28). New York: Raven Press.

George, R. (1930). Human finger types. *Anatomical Record*, *46*, 199–204.

Laner, M. R., & Laner, R. H. (1980). Sexual preference or personal style? Why lesbians are disliked. *Journal of Homosexuality*, *5*, 339–356.

Manning, J. T., Scott, D., Wilson, J., & Lewis-Jones, D. I. (1998). The ratio of 2nd to 4th digit length: A predictor of sperm numbers and concentrations of testosterone, luteinizing hormone and oestrogen. *Human Reproduction*, *13*, 3000–3004.

McFadden, D. (2002). Masculinization effects in the auditory system. *Archives of Sexual Behavior*, *31*, 93–105.

McFadden, D., & Champlin, C. A. (2000). Comparison of auditory evoked potentials in heterosexual, homosexual, and bisexual males and females. *Journal of the Association of Research in Otolaryngology*, *1*, 89–99.

McFadden, D., & Pasanen, E. G. (1998). Comparison of the auditory systems of heterosexuals and homosexuals: Click-evoked otoacoustic emissions. *Proceedings of the National Academy of Sciences of the United States of America*, *95*, 2709–2713.

Phoenix, C. H., Goy, R. W., Gerall, A. A., & Young, W. C. (1959). Organizing action of prenatally administered testosterone propionate on the tissues mediating mating behavior in the female guinea pig. *Endocrinology*, *65*, 369–382.

Robinson, S. J., & Manning, J. T. (2000). The ratio of 2nd to 4th digit length and male homosexuality. *Evolution and Human Behavior*, *21*, 333–345.

Singh, D., Vidaurri, M., Zambarano, R. J., & Dabbs, J. M. (1999). Lesbian erotic role identification: Behavioral, morphological, and hormonal correlates. *Journal of Personality and Social Psychology, 76,* 1035–1049.

Tortorice, J. (2001). Gender identity, sexual orientation, and second-to-fourth-digit ratio in females [Abstract]. *Human Behavior and Evolution Society Abstracts, 13,* 35.

Williams, T. J., Pepitone, M. E., Christensen, S. E., Cooke, B. M., Huberman, A. D., Breedlove,

T. J., Jordan, C. L., et al. (2000). Finger length patterns indicate an influence of fetal androgens on human sexual orientation. *Nature, 404,* 455–456.

Wilson, G. D. (1983). Finger-length as an index of assertiveness in women. *Personality and Individual Differences, 4,* 111–112.

---

Brown, Windy M., Christopher J. Finn, Bradley M. Cooke, and S. Marc Breedlove. "Differences in Finger Length Ratios between Self-Identified 'Butch' and 'Femme' Lesbians." *Archives of Sexual Behavior* 31 (February 2002): 123–27.

# ➢ Albert Mohler

(March 2, 2007), United States

---

### "Is Your Baby Gay? What If You Could Know? What If You Could Do Something about It?"

What if you could know that your unborn baby boy is likely to be sexually attracted to other boys? Beyond that, what if hormonal treatments could change the baby's orientation to heterosexual? Would you do it? Some scientists believe that such developments are just around the corner.

For some time now, scientists have been looking for a genetic or hormonal cause of sexual orientation. Thus far, no "gay gene" has been found—at least not in terms of incontrovertible and accepted science. Yet, it is now claimed that a growing body of evidence indicates that biological factors may at least contribute to sexual orientation.

The most interesting research along these lines relates to the study of sheep. Scientists at the U.S. Sheep Experiment Station are conducting research into the sexual orientation of sheep through "sexual partner preference testing." As William Saletan at *Slate.com* explains:

A bare majority of rams turn out to be heterosexual. One in five swings both ways. About 15 percent are asexual, and 7 percent to 10 percent are gay.

Why so many gay rams? Is it too much socializing with ewes? Same-sex play with other lambs? Domestication? Nope. Those theories have been debunked. Gay rams don't act girly. They're just as gay in the wild. And a crucial part of their brains—the "sexually dimorphic nucleus"—looks more like a ewe's than like a straight ram's. Gay men have a similar brain resemblance to women. Charles Roselli, the project's lead scientist, says such research "strongly suggests that sexual preference is biologically determined in animals, and possibly in humans."

What makes the sheep "sexual partner preference testing" research so interesting is that the same scientists who are documenting the rather surprising sexual behaviors of male sheep think they can also change the sexual orientation of the animals. In other words, finding a biological causation for homosexuality may also lead to the discovery of a "cure" for the same phenomenon.

That's where the issue gets really interesting. People for the Ethical Treatment of Animals [PETA] has called for an end to the research, while tennis star Martina Navratilova called the research "homophobic and cruel" and argued that gay sheep have a "right" to be homosexual. No kidding.

Homosexual activists were among the first to call for (and fund) research into a biological cause of homosexuality. After all, they argued, the discovery of a biological cause would lead to the normalization of homosexuality simply because it would then be seen to be natural, and thus moral.

But now the picture is quite different. Many homosexual activists recognize that the discovery of a biological marker or cause for homosexual orientation could lead to efforts to eliminate the trait, or change the orientation through genetic or hormonal treatments.

Tyler Gray addresses these issues in the current issue of *Radar* magazine. In "Is Your Baby Gay?," Gray sets out a fascinating scenario. A woman is told that her unborn baby boy is gay. This woman and her husband consider themselves to be liberal and tolerant of homosexuality. But this is not about homosexuality now; it is about their baby boy. The woman is then told that a hormone patch on her abdomen will "reverse the sexual orientation inscribed in his chromosomes." The *Sunday Times* [London] predicts that such a patch should be available for use on humans within the decade. Will she use it?

This question stands at the intersection of so many competing interests. Feminists and political liberals have argued for decades now that a woman should have an unrestricted right to an abortion, for any cause or for no stated cause at all. How can they now complain if women decide to abort fetuses identified as homosexual? This question involves both abortion and gay rights—the perfect moral storm of our times.

Homosexual activists have claimed that sexual orientation cannot be changed. What if a hormone patch during pregnancy will do the job?

As Gray suggests:

> In a culture that encourages us to customize everything from our Nikes to our venti skinny lattes, perhaps it is only a matter of time before baby-making becomes just another consumer transaction. Already have a girl? Make this one a boy! Want to impress your boho friends? Make a real statement with lesbian twins!

More to the point, Gray understands that such a development would reshape the abortion and gay-rights debates in America:

> Conservatives opposed to both abortion and homosexuality will have to ask themselves whether the public shame of having a gay child outweighs the private

sin of terminating a pregnancy (assuming the stigma on homosexuality survives the scientific refutation of the Right's treasured belief that it is a "lifestyle choice.)" Pro-choice activists won't be spared either. Will liberal moms who love their hairdressers be as tolerant when faced with the prospect of raising a little stylist of their own? And exactly how pro-choice will liberal abortion-rights activists be when thousands of potential parents are choosing to filter homosexuality right out of the gene pool?

The development of Preimplantation Genetic Diagnosis [PGD] is one of the greatest threats to human dignity in our times. These tests are already leading to the abortion of fetuses identified as carrying unwanted genetic markers. The tests can now check for more than 1,300 different chromosomal abnormalities or patterns. With DNA analysis, the genetic factors could be identified right down to hair and eye color and other traits. The logic is all too simple. If you don't like what you see on the PGD report . . . just abort and start over. Soon, genetic treatments may allow for changing the profile. Welcome to the world of designer babies.

If that happens, how many parents—even among those who consider themselves most liberal—would choose a gay child? How many parents, armed with this diagnosis, would use the patch and change the orientation?

Christians who are committed to think in genuinely Christian terms should think carefully about these points:

1. There is, as of now, no incontrovertible or widely accepted proof that any biological basis for sexual orientation exists.

2. Nevertheless, the direction of the research points in this direction. Research into the sexual orientation of sheep and other animals, as well as human studies, points to some level of biological causation for sexual orientation in at least some individuals.

3. Given the consequences of the Fall and the effects of human sin, we should not be surprised that such a causation or link is found. After all, the human genetic structure, along with every other aspect of creation, shows the pernicious effects of the Fall and of God's judgment.

4. The biblical condemnation of all homosexual behaviors would not be compromised or mitigated in the least by such a discovery. The discovery of a biological factor would not change the Bible's moral verdict on homosexual behavior.

5. The discovery of a biological basis for homosexuality would be of great pastoral significance, allowing for a greater understanding of why certain persons struggle with these particular sexual temptations.

6. The biblical basis for establishing the dignity of all persons—the fact that all humans are made in God's image—reminds us that this means *all* persons, including those who may be marked by a predisposition toward homosexuality. For the sake of clarity, we must insist at all times that all persons—whether identified as heterosexual, homosexual, lesbian, transsexual, transgendered, bisexual, or whatever—are equally made in the image of God.

7. Thus, we will gladly contend for the right to life of all persons, born and unborn, whatever their sexual orientation. We must fight against the idea of aborting fetuses or human embryos identified as homosexual in orientation.

8. If a biological basis is found, and if a prenatal test is then developed, and if a successful treatment to reverse the sexual orientation to heterosexual is ever developed, we would support its use as we should unapologetically support the use of any appropriate means to avoid sexual temptation and the inevitable effects of sin.

9. We must stop confusing the issues of moral responsibility and moral choice. We are all *responsible* for our sexual orientation, but that does not mean that we freely and consciously *choose* that orientation. We sin against homosexuals by insisting that sexual temptation and attraction are predominately chosen. We do not always (or even generally) choose our temptations. Nevertheless, we are absolutely responsible for what we *do* with sinful temptations, whatever our so-called sexual orientation.

10. Christians must be very careful not to claim that science can never prove a biological basis for sexual orientation. We can and must insist that no scientific finding can change the basic sinfulness of all homosexual behavior. The general trend of the research points to at least some biological factors behind sexual attraction, gender identity, and sexual orientation. This does not alter God's moral verdict on homosexual sin (or heterosexual sin, for that matter), but it does hold some promise that a deeper knowledge of homosexuality and its cause will allow for more effective ministries to those who struggle with this particular pattern of temptation. If such knowledge should ever be discovered, we should embrace it and use it for the greater good of humanity and for the greater glory of God.

Albert Mohler. Excerpt from "Was It Something I Said? Continuing to Think about Homosexuality" (16 March 2007). c Albert Mohler, 2 March, 2007, United States.

# ➢ Rictor Norton
(1997), United States

### From "Essentialism"

My traditionalist historical position is termed "essentialism" by postmodern theorists, which they regard with contempt, in the same way that I regard social constructionist theory as the main impediment to the understanding of queer history. The history of ideas (and ideologies) can be interesting and valuable, but it is tragic that homosexuals have been subsumed *totally* within the idea of the 'homosexual construct'. The result is little better than intellectual ethnic cleansing.

In the social constructionist view, knowledge is constructed, deconstructed, and reconstructed through ideological discourse. In my traditionalist or essentialist view, knowledge is discovered, repressed, suppressed, and recovered through history and experience. **Social constructionism** emphasizes revolutionary development (the dialectic); I emphasize evolutionary development, cultural growth and permutation, and sometimes mere change in fashion. Rather than the word 'construct', which implies building from scratch according to an arbitrarily chosen blueprint, I prefer the words 'consolidate' or 'forge', implying that the basic material already exists but can be subjected to shaping and polishing.

'Cultural constructs' are sometimes set up in opposition to 'universal truths' in an effort to force traditionalists/essentialists into an impossibly idealistic corner, but 'culture' is a concept that can be claimed by essentialists as well as by social constructionists. The essentialist position is that queer culture is organic rather than artificial. Social constructionists see culture as a construct whose arbitrary foundation is determined by the builder; I see culture as the cultivation of a root, and I shall be developing the ethnic view that queer culture grows naturally from personal queer identity and experience and is self-cultivated by queers rather than by the ideology and labels of straight society.

I cannot reasonably object if critics wish to label me an 'essentialist' pure and simple, because I believe that homosexuals are born and not made, and that homosexuality is hard-wired. However, I also believe that queers fashion their own culture (using their own resources rather than being imposed upon by society), and this is a significant focus of my own version of essentialism, which might be called 'queer cultural essentialism'. I take the view that there is a core of queer desire that is transcultural, transnational, and transhistorical, a queer essence that is innate, congenital, constitutional, stable or fixed in its basic pattern. However, I distinguish between queer persons, queer sexual acts and behaviour, and queer social interactions, and try not to confuse the constancy of the desire with the variability of its expression. Personal queer identity arises from within, and is then consolidated along lines suggested by the collective identity of the queer (sub)culture.

In the theoretical literature it is generally assumed that essentialism is the same as uniformism/conformism (often made explicit in lesbian-feminist theory). But the view that homosexuality is a monolith is not at all an essential feature of essentialism. The essentialist does not say there is only *one* gay root: in fact a *diversity of roots* has been a key feature of essentialism since the early 1970s—witness the plural title of the two-volume collection of essays from *Gay Sunshine: Gay Roots.* It is really social constructionist theorists who have forced traditionalism into this straightjacket, just as they have forced gay experience into the political straitjacket.

I have no problem in reconciling the view that queer desire is innate but that it expresses itself in sexual or social actions and (sub)cultures that may reflect to a greater or lesser degree the time and place in which they occur. Self-presentation can be carefully constructed even though it is founded upon an innate self-conception.

---

Rictor Norton. Adapted from *The Myth of the Modern Homosexual.* London: Cassell, 1997. Available at http://www.rictornorton.co.uk/social03.htm/.

# CHAPTER 6

# Inclusion and Equality

There are a number of highly visible debates regarding the integration or exclusion of queers in society. This chapter highlights some of these debates, focusing particularly on the complex and sometimes conflicting attitudes that create tensions within the discussion.

A crucial distinction to make when talking about notions related to inclusion and equality is between civil rights (the rights of citizenship) and human rights (the rights many assume that we should have because we are human). LGBT activists in the Global North are sometimes criticized because, in our efforts to garner civil rights for sexual and gender nonconformists, we can become blinded to the needs of people (including LGBT people) who lack access to food, shelter, and health care. This critique assumes that human rights are more basic than civil rights in that they focus on the bedrock conditions of existence rather than on legislative mechanisms. And granted, the fight for civil rights only occurs in contexts where many or most citizens generally enjoy freedom of association, speech, and religion—freedoms that many consider fundamental but are not necessarily respected as civil rights by some governments.

But as we shall see, a focus internationally on human rights has also been helpful as LGBT people have fought for inclusion and equality in their respective countries. Just after World War II (1948), as the post-Holocaust world attempted to come to grips with what had just occurred, the United Nations (UN) announced the Universal Declaration of Human Rights, which writer Donn Mitchell interprets as establishing "a right to be free from discrimination of *any kind.*" The Universal Declaration states that "everyone is entitled to all the rights and freedoms set forth in this Declaration, without distinction of any kind, such as race, colour, sex, origin, property, birth or other status" (qtd. in Mitchell 13). Mitchell argues that the use of the phrase "such as" allows for expansion of the protections offered by the declaration. It seems reasonable to assume that the declaration applies to gender nonconformists and sexual minorities, particularly because it was a response to the Holocaust, and homosexuals were among the groups persecuted by the Nazis. Richard Schneider points out that "[a]t a time when our enemies are able to score points by charging 'special rights,' perhaps a shift toward a broader definition of human rights, one that encompasses the rights of all oppressed groups in society, would make sense" (4) [λ Chapter 8]. One of the great challenges in creating a movement that works for LGBT people around the world has been to articulate the connections between local organizations and priorities and the concept of universal human rights. Schneider's advocacy of "a broader definition of human rights" implies an insistence on others viewing LGBT people as fully human, working with other fully human individuals for the benefit of "all oppressed groups in society."

## Civil and Human Rights in a Global Context

One way to understand our local work for inclusion and equality in a global context is to think seriously about the mythology that has grown up around the U.S. LGBT civil rights struggle. The common assumption is that the United States is a leader in the quest for LGBT inclusion and equality; in reality, however, our efforts have occurred in a global context of similar and related struggles. Much is made in this country of the dangers faced by lesbian and gay people before and during the 1960s. The story is that the Stonewall riots occurred partly in response to systematic police harassment of lesbian and gay people who met in bars and other social spaces. While this is true, that harassment was not unique to the United States. For instance, as Joe Knowles points out, in the 1960s, Cuban homosexuals "were rounded up and put to work in military camps. This was also the time when the Cuban government passed Resolución Número 3, which mandated that homosexuals working in the arts be fired and reassigned jobs in hard labor" (19). *Lawrence v. Texas* [λ Chapter 4], the 2003 case in which the U.S. Supreme Court ruled that state laws against sodomy were unconstitutional, followed two decades after the 1981 European Court of Human Rights decision that bans on homosexual sex violated the European Convention on Human Rights. Dian Killian argues that, while the "Republic of Ireland is still perceived by many Americans as a bog island of thatched cottages and donkey carts, and the United States as the

**Find Out More** in the excerpt from the Constitution of the Republic of South Africa at the end of this chapter.

gay-mythologized land of Stonewall," stringent hate crimes laws in Ireland "make it an offense even to incite violence against lesbians or gay men." Ireland has amended its Unfair Dismissals Act to protect gays in the workplace, and Ireland's national gay paper is "partially funded" by the state (24–25). Denmark also has national hate crimes legislation and other protections against discrimination on the basis of sexual orientation, although that country still denies LGBT people the right to adopt children, except for the biological children of partners (Jensen). In 2006, however, Danish legislators ruled that lesbians and single women were entitled to the same access to artificial insemination in public hospitals as heterosexual women (Wockner, "International News").

African struggles for LGBT inclusion and equality are perhaps the best illustration of the mixed attitudes toward LGBT people internationally. South Africa was the first country in the world to write LGBT equality into its constitution. Under the leadership of Nelson Mandela [λ Chapter 8] and others attempting to create a post-Apartheid liberal government, South Africa adopted a constitution that protects its people from discrimination based on "race, gender, sex, pregnancy, marital status, ethnic or social origin, colour, sexual orientation, age, disability, religion, conscience, belief, culture, language and birth." What's more, South Africa's sodomy laws have been struck down. In stark contrast, across the border in neighboring Zimbabwe, President Robert Mugabe has referred to homosexuals as "dogs and pigs" and said, "Animals in the jungle are better than these people because at least they know how to distinguish between a male and a female" (Monifa 41). Similarly, the prime minister of nearby Swaziland, Sibusiso Dlamini, called homosexuality an "abnormality and sickness," and one of his predecessors, Princh Bhekimpi, proclaimed that "homosexuality is regarded as satanic in Swaziland. Therefore, I am forced to evict all gays and lesbians in my area" (Monifa 41). The official position in Zambia is that gays are to be arrested. More drastically, Uganda's Parliament is considering an anti-homosexuality bill that would increase the penalties already in place by creating a new category of offense called "aggravated homosexuality." According to the text of the bill, aggravated homosexuality covers same-sex sexual assault against, for instance, minors, people with disabilities, or family members (Fodden). The penalty for such assault is extreme, as a person found guilty of aggravated homosexuality would face the death penalty; thus, the proposed bill has been referred to as the "Kill the Gays Bill." A troubling aspect of the Ugandan anti-gay movement has been the involvement of American evangelicals, specifically a group known as The Family, a "secretive American evangelical organization whose members include Senators James Inhofe, Jim DeMint, and Tom Coburn" (Goldberg). The American Family members lent an extreme antigay ideology to their Ugandan associates, sponsoring seminars designed to inflame homophobic passions. Cooler heads, both at home in Uganda and worldwide, have spoken out against the bill—see, for instance, Secretary of State Hillary Rodham Clinton's speech in favor of LGBT rights in the readings at the end of this chapter—but this narrative indicates the deep divisions between progressive and fundamentalist forces globally.

Many African countries have organizations that work to address the needs of and provide some protections for LGBT people, but in national climates where homosexuality is officially demonized, protections are limited and providers of such services place themselves in physical danger. These widely varying situations in Africa exemplify the inconsistent practice of governments around the world toward their LGBT citizens and highlight the difficulty of crafting policy for positive change.

## Inclusion Versus Assimilation: Two Approaches to Securing Rights

In the United States, one way the problem of public policy fairness plays out is in questions about the approach rights-based organizations take to securing civil rights for LGBT people [λ Chapter 4]. The Human Rights Campaign (HRC), the largest and best-funded American civil rights organization, describes its mission in this way:

> By inspiring and engaging all Americans, HRC strives to end discrimination against LGBT citizens and realize a nation that achieves fundamental fairness and equality for all. HRC seeks to improve the lives of LGBT Americans by advocating for equal rights and benefits in the workplace, ensuring families are treated equally under the law and increasing public support among all Americans through innovative advocacy, education and outreach programs. HRC works to secure equal rights for LGBT individuals and families at the federal and state levels by lobbying elected officials, mobilizing grassroots supporters, educating Americans, investing strategically to elect fair-minded officials and partnering with other LGBT organizations. ("About HRC")

In the last decade, HRC has focused much of its energy and financial resources on advocating the rights of gays and lesbians to marry, to serve openly in the military, and to feel secure and free from discrimination in the workplace. HRC has also initiated dialogues with religious leaders in an effort to address homophobia in church communities. In general, despite the words *human rights* in its name, HRC is a civil rights organization, which works to obtain for LGBT people the same rights that are enjoyed by heterosexual citizens of the United States.

Some U.S. gay organizations take a more in-your-face approach, even though their work shares the HRC's focus on civil rights. A leaflet distributed in 1990 at a New York pride march by an organization called Queers announced, "I Hate Straights." The authors advocated a forceful approach marked by pride in sexuality and "sexualness." While the pamphlet is not as "anti-straight" as the title might suggest, the tone is aggressive:

> The next time some straight person comes down on you for being angry, tell them that until things change, you don't need any more evidence that the world turns at your expense. You don't need to see only hetero couples grocery shopping on your TV. . . . You don't want any more baby pictures shoved in your face until you can have or keep your own. No more weddings, showers, anniversaries, please, unless they are our own brothers and sisters celebrating. And tell them not to dismiss you by saying, "You have rights," "You have privileges," "You are overreacting," or "You have a victim's mentality." Tell them "Go away from me, until you change." Go away and try on a world without the brave, strong queers that are its backbone, that are its guts and brains and souls. Go tell them go away until they have spent a month walking hand in hand in public with someone of the same sex. After they survive that, then you'll hear what they have to say about queer anger. (Anonymous Queers 148)

The HRC and Queers strategies couldn't be more different. HRC's approach has consistently emphasized the need for equality with straights, arguing that anything less is unfair and unjust. Queers, in contrast, provocatively ask straights to examine their own privilege, their lives, and their behavior. HRC wants to ensure that queers are treated as well as heterosexuals. Queers suggests LGBT people have much to teach heterosexuals about sexuality and gender.

An example of how these different philosophies approach a specific issue may be useful. Many queer activists and theorists have criticized the push among some Western gays and lesbians for the right to marry and thus to assimilate into the mainstream of society; they feel that strategizing for marriage rights, while laudable in many ways, distracts us from more fundamentally questioning the institution of marriage itself. Marriage, they argue, honors commitments between two people (same sex or "opposite" sex), but what about intimate arrangements that don't fit those parameters? Is marriage an institution designed specifically to channel sexual expression into monogamous, sexist, and heterosexist forms? Marital rights extended to gays and lesbians, as the HRC imagines them, might honor some nontraditional relationships but would most likely still be limited in significant ways. Thus, it is important to look beyond the civil rights paradigm and critique institutional systems, asking who is served by them and who is excluded.

## Exclusion, Inequality, and Physical Violence

nevitably, the battle over inclusion and equality is fought not only at the state level but also at the local or personal level. In the United States, for example, there are myriad stories of violence perpetrated against individuals who work for—or sometimes just assume the "rightness" of—inclusion and equality for LGBT people. The stories of Barry Winchell and Fred C. Martinez are fairly representative. These two stories demonstrate the local and personal impact of a national climate of exclusion and inequality in which official policy at the local and federal levels denies LGBT people the right to protection from discrimination—in housing, employment, family matters such as marriage and adoption, and other areas.

The 1999 death of Private First Class Barry Winchell focused attention on the military policy popularly referred to as Don't Ask, Don't Tell [λ Chapter 4]. While stationed at Fort Campbell, Kentucky, Winchell began going to a Nashville club that featured transgendered performers. There Winchell met Calpernia Addams, a male-to-female transgendered woman, with whom he later became romantically involved (France). The relationship between Winchell and Addams eventually became known to Winchell's peers, and many began to think of him as a homosexual, though he seems not to have self-identified as such. On July 4, 1999, after hours of drinking on the base, Winchell and Calvin Glover began to argue; as the argument escalated, the two men became engaged in a physical altercation, which culminated in Winchell punching Glover. According to Glover, over the next few hours, Justin Fisher (Winchell's roommate) taunted him, saying that he had been bested by a gay man. In the early morning hours of July 5, after hours of harassment by Fisher, Glover used a baseball bat to beat Winchell into unconsciousness (Sciolino). Eventually, Winchell died.

After the killing, many gay rights activists claimed Winchell as a kind of gay martyr whose death symbolized all that was wrong with the DADT policy in the military. In 2000, Addams told David France of the *New York Times,* "I'm disappointed in a lot of ways with almost every organization that I thought would help me with this. A lot of things I don't want to go in print—speaking out against these major national gay and lesbian organizations—but a lot of them I thought would come and help me or say something, or do a press release or give me some advice. And they just didn't." The tone of France's article, titled "An Inconvenient Woman," indicates his concern that gay rights activists ignored Addams because she was transsexual, in effect sacrificing her in their quest to overturn DADT. This critique exemplifies the difficulties faced by organizations such as the National Gay and Lesbian Task Force presently working to secure rights for LGBT people. Many argue that a more complex view of sexuality—moving beyond gay and lesbian to other less well understood sexual minorities—is necessary to significantly lessen gender and sexual oppression.

A 21-month Army investigation of the Winchell murder resulted in the exoneration of all officers involved and a finding that "no climate of homophobia existed at the base" in Fort Campbell, Kentucky (Sciolino). Nonetheless, in 2002,

**Figure 6.1**   Private First Class Barry Winchell.

the *New York Times* reported the following: "The number of military discharges of gays has risen to its highest level in 14 years, and reported incidents of anti-gay harassment have climbed by 23 percent in a year" (Marquis). On August 15, 2006, the Associated Press reported that in 2005 Fort Campbell had the second highest DADT dismissal rate of all bases in the country, with more than twice the number of dismissals as in 2004 ("Missouri"). If we assume a correlation between higher DADT dismissal rates and an increasing frequency of bias incidents toward LGBT people on U.S. military bases, then it becomes clear that "official" policing of sexuality and gender creates a sense that unofficial policing through intimidation and other types of violence is not only acceptable but also desirable. What's more, it is hard to imagine how military officials could deny that this kind of environment is not only homophobic but also transphobic.

Fred C. Martinez, who was 16 years old at the time of his murder, identified as gay, transgender, and "two-spirited." A Native American living in the town of Cortez, Colorado, Martinez was a gender nonconformist. He was sent home from school on several occasions for carrying a purse and wearing makeup and fingernail polish. In addition, he was consistently harassed by peers. In 2001, Martinez was murdered by 18-year-old Shaun Murphy, who claimed to have acted in self-defense but, in the days after the murder, bragged to friends that he had "bug-smashed a fag" (Rostow). An *Advocate* article about the murder quotes Denise de Percin, executive director of the Colorado Anti-Violence Project, as saying, "Everything so far leads us to believe [Martinez] was targeted for transgressing gender.... People who transgress gender and whose expression is not considered normal are the ones who are most often targeted for bias-motivated violence" (Quittner 2). At the time of Martinez's murder, federal hate crimes legislation in the United States did not include language regarding LGBT people, so it would have been outside the purview of the Department of Justice and the Federal Bureau of Investigation (FBI) to become involved in a case where sexual orientation or gender nonconformity were the motivations for murder; hence, Murphy was charged with (and pled guilty to) second-degree murder, not with the commission of a hate crime. Even after his sentencing, Murphy told officials that he was acting in self-defense when he murdered Martinez, whom he said attacked him first; this claim, as well as his mother's that Murphy was not homophobic, both seem spurious in light of the "bug-smashed a fag" comment.

In both the Martinez and Winchell murder cases, official policies of exclusion and unequal treatment were complicit in the crimes committed by individuals. The omission of provisions explicitly addressing gender and sexual orientation in hate crimes legislation sent a strong message to citizens that violence against certain individuals was, if not condoned, at least less serious than other crimes motivated by prejudice. Social systems that impose standards of gender conformity—as administrators at Martinez's high school did when they sent him home for wearing makeup and carrying a purse—create a circumstance in which gender nonconformists are seen as deserving harassment and in which peers consider it their right (and perhaps subconsciously their responsibility) to police one another's gender behaviors. Social restrictions on behavior related to gender and sexuality, as well as a perception that LGBT people are predatory outsiders, have contributed to exclusionary attitudes based on a sense of the inherent inferiority of LGBT people as compared with gender conformists and heterosexuals; those restrictions have also encouraged perpetrators of violence to claim self-defense when their victims were lesbian, gay, bisexual, or transgendered. Of course, these three elements of the Martinez case were interrelated, for they arise from a social structure that assumed that sexual and gender difference were threatening.

## Exclusion and Inequality—Both "Outside" and "Inside"

The preceding cases give us a sense of the difficulties facing queer people seeking inclusion and equality—difficulties that many LGBT people experience as a mixture of exclusion and inequality both from mainstream culture and, at times, from queer culture or communities. Consider the following examples:

- In 1990, the Manhattan chapter of the Ancient Order of Hibernians denied the Irish Lesbian and Gay Organization (ILGO) the right to march in New York City's St. Patrick's Day parade. In 2006, the ban was still in effect, and the organizer of the event, John Dunleavy, commented, "If we let the ILGO in, is it the Irish Prostitute Association next?" During the parade, protesters pointed out the uniqueness of the ban on their participation with the following chant: "We can march in Dublin, we can march in Cork, why can't we march in New York?" (Dobnik).
- "Avowed homosexuals" are banned from participation in the Boy Scouts of America (BSA) at any level. According to a BSA spokesman, "An avowed homosexual wouldn't be a role model for [traditional family] values" (Snyder A2).

- In the 1990s and early 2000s, gay men were not explicitly excluded from the Million Man March or the Millions More Movement march, but the executive director of the latter event, the Reverend Willie Wilson, delivered a blisteringly antigay sermon just three months before the Millions More event. The sermon resulted in the resignation of Reverend Dr. Amina Binta, cochair of the local organizing committee for the march. Binta said, "They're not serious about allowing us to sit at the table. . . . And if they are, I don't care to eat their fare, because they're serving up a steady diet of homophobia that is very venomous" (Volin and Chibbaro).

These successful efforts to exclude take on enormous import when we consider their connections to violence perpetrated against LGBT people. Exclusionary practices such as these send the clear message to a society that the policing of gender and adult sexuality is both necessary and desirable.

We can see such policing at work in responses to the AIDS pandemic. Historically, discussions around AIDS—in the United States and in the rest of the world—have focused on the notion that homosexual sex spreads disease. As we mentioned in Chapter 4, the disease was initially called *gay-related immune deficiency* (GRID), and throughout most of the 1980s, it was assumed that only gay people got AIDS. In fact, in the late 1980s, Sebastian Bach of the band Skid Row appeared

**Figure 6.2**  Logo displayed on Sebastian Bach's T-shirt.

on stage wearing a T-shirt that read "AIDS: Kills Fags Dead," a parody of the popular slogan for the spray insecticide Raid, which was, "RAID: Kills Bugs Dead."

Though Bach issued a public apology for the incident and claimed he had no idea what was written on the T-shirt, the slogan was then popularized—to the point where the Westboro Baptist Church in Topeka, Kansas (infamous for its God Hates Fags campaign), adopted it as a slogan when they protested at the funeral of Matthew Shepard (Rosen) [λ Chapter 4]. Even today, some people still believe that HIV and AIDS are "gay diseases." The American Red Cross is among the many organizations that have attempted to correct this flawed assumption. According to the Red Cross fact sheet on HIV/AIDS,[1]

As of July 2002, the Joint United Nations Programme on HIV/AIDS (UNAIDS) estimated that about 18 million women were living with HIV/AIDS worldwide, accounting for 47 percent of the 37.2 million adults living with HIV/AIDS. In many countries, HIV spreads mostly through sex between men and women. And in the United States, the number of people with HIV/AIDS who became infected through sex between men and women continues to grow. ("This Month's")

Nonetheless, antigay activists continue to equate HIV and AIDS with homosexuality. As an extreme example, the God Hates Fags crusade claims that those who die from complications related to HIV/AIDS, as well as American casualties of war, are being punished by a higher power to make the United States suffer for becoming a "fag nation" (Westboro Baptist Church). In a controversial decision, the U.S. Supreme Court's chief justice, John Roberts, said in his majority opinion that the court protects "even hurtful speech on public issues to ensure that we do not stifle public debate" (Sherman).

Indeed, the issue of sexual freedom is not as simple as it might seem on the surface. LGBT activist groups, even as they fight for inclusion in society, have historically disputed issues of inclusion and equality within their own ranks. Consider the following examples:

- Transgender and transsexual individuals have argued for at least a generation that lesbian and gay organizations do not recognize and respond to their struggle for inclusion and equality.
- In the late 20th century, many lesbian feminists believed butch and femme lesbians were replicating "the heterosexual institution with its role playing dualities" (Johnston 155).
- LGBT people who also identify as **sadomasochist** have historically been seen as outside the mainstream in the larger LGBT movement.
- In many ways and over many years, white-led LGBT political and social groups have engaged in overtly and covertly racist behavior. Bars, for example, have refused to admit black patrons ("Director's Finding"). Even online chat room participants describe eliciting more responses if they claim to be white rather than of color (Gosine).
- In the 1970s, some radical lesbian groups articulated negative feelings toward bisexual women, who they claimed, "take energy from women and give it to men" (Moore).

The debates around these issues and others have consistently arisen within organizations whose work it is to fight for inclusion and equality. In "Messages of Exclusion: Gender, Movements, and Symbolic Boundaries," Joshua Gamson describes and theorizes controversies surrounding two groups, the Michigan Womyn's Music Festival (MWMF) and the ILGA as they attempt to police the boundaries of their own communities.

One highly visible debate among lesbians grew up around what many saw as the exclusionary practices of the MWMF [λ Chapters 4 and 15]. The MWMF was founded by Lisa and Kristie Vogel and Mary Kindig in 1976. Conceived as a space for female performers to showcase their work in a supportive and nurturing environment, the festival draws thousands of women each year and has become a legendary cultural event for lesbian feminists throughout the United States. Throughout its history, the MWMF has undergone repeated critiques from women who challenged the festival to be more inclusive. Some claimed the MWMF needed to respond more fully to the specific needs of women of color, women with disabilities, poor women, and others. And, in many cases, organizers made significant changes to the festival in order to address those concerns. The most heated debate concerning MWMF, however, began in 1991 when a *festie-goer* (as attendees are called) was removed from the land after revealing that she was transsexual. Nancy Burkholder, who by all reports had attended the festival the year before without difficulties, came to represent what many believe is the inappropriately exclusionary MWMF policy that only women-born-women (WBW) be allowed to attend the festival. After the Burkholder incident, a group of women within the festival began protesting the WBW policy. In 1993, some women who practiced S&M approached the protesters and offered their services as security. In 1999, under the leadership of trans activist Riki Wilchins, a group of transwomen established Camp Trans, an annual protest outside the festival grounds. Of the controversy, Lisa Vogel says, "It's our right and it's our responsibility to say who we want the event to be for and . . . who we're organizing it for; it's not making a judgment or a statement . . . about anybody else. It wasn't back in 1976 when we said it was women only, and it's not in 2005 when we want it to be for women-born-women. Our queer community is diverse, and I support separate and whole space for anybody who wants it" (Lo). Vogel clearly does not see exclusionary practices as problematic in this instance. Her argument seems to be that this process of exclusion highlights the complexities that arise when groups are oppressed on a number of different levels. In this case, Vogel argues that WBW, as a result of living a lifetime of oppression related to their sex, experience femaleness very differently than do transwomen, who bring with them to women-only environments the experience of privilege born of living as males in a sexist society. Trans activists counter this argument by pointing out that many male-to-female transgendered and transsexual individuals face a type of sexist discrimination similar to that faced by girls and women. Choosing to live as women in a sexist world, they argue, neutralizes any previous male privilege they may have enjoyed earlier in their lives. Moreover, they claim the right to define their womanness outside of exclusionary terms such as *women-born-men*. This ongoing controversy foregrounds the complexities of identity and identity politics.

A very different debate concerning inclusion and equality in organizations fighting for sexual freedom has to do with the distinction between the freedoms adults should enjoy with other consenting adults and the freedoms adults should enjoy in their relationships with children. The North American Man/Boy Love Association (NAMBLA), for example, has argued for decades that its members are treated as outsiders in the LGBT movement, and debates about whether NAMBLA's concerns fall within or outside the parameters of the larger fight for sexual freedom are intense, emotional, and politically significant. In 1993, the ILGA became the first

LGBT group to receive consultative status in the UN Economic and Social Council; a year later, the ILGA lost its consultative status because UN members complained about its connections to **pedophile** groups such as NAMBLA and the Dutch group Vereniging Martijn. ILGA responded by expelling NAMBLA, Vereniging Martijn, and a group called Project Truth from its ranks and began the work of regaining its consultative status (Gamson). Partly in response to the ILGA situation, Gregory King of the Human Rights Campaign Fund declared, "NAMBLA is not a gay organization. They are not part of our community and we thoroughly reject their efforts to insinuate that pedophilia is an issue related to gay and lesbian civil rights" (qtd. in Gamson 179). Finally, in 2011, ILGA regained consultative status with the UN's Economic and Social Council ("UN Economic"). Some would argue that ILGA's expulsion of NAMBLA is tantamount to retreating from a liberationist view of sexuality that would question long-held attitudes that create sexually repressive environments. Others counterargue that supporting pedophiles who want to legalize sexual relationships between children and adults means condoning the oppression of children who are not prepared to make sexual decisions that serve their own best interests.

As Gamson points out, there is an odd relationship between the MWMF and the ILGA and NAMBLA controversies. The situations are, of course, extremely different, for it is impossible to equate the desire of male-to-female transsexual and transgendered people to be accepted as women with the efforts of a group whose goal is to secure the right for adult men to engage in sexual activity with boys. But in both cases, important questions are being asked about the issue of inclusion and exclusion. Gamson articulates these questions in this way: "Who is calling the question of public exclusion and for what political purposes? Who are the audiences being targeted and how do they (or the perception of them by those attacking and defending versions of collective identity) shape the outcome?" (192). In the case of MWMF, the question was called by participants in the festival, women who believed strongly that in a sexist culture, women-born-men would bring with them to women's space the sexist values and attitudes that women in such a space were attempting to resist. In the case of the ILGA, the question was called by the American religious right in the person of Jesse Helms, who proposed a bill (signed into law by Bill Clinton) that would withhold $119 million in donations to the UN until the U.S. president could determine that no organizations supporting pedophilia were granted any "official status, accreditation, or recognition" within the UN (Gamson 185).

For as long as there has been a gay rights movement, gay rights opponents have asserted a connection between homosexuality and pedophilia; despite consistent refutation of such correlation by the psychiatric community, the notion has persisted that gay men are sexual predators who pose a danger to children. The power of this myth showed up in the popular support for Anita Bryant's Save Our Children Campaign; in the argument made by many in the Catholic Church that the problem of child sexual abuse by priests would be solved by purging the priesthood of all homosexuals; in the argument by the Boy Scouts of America that gay scout leaders pose a threat to scouts; in the efforts across the United States and throughout the Global North to keep LGBT people from teaching, adopting, and raising children; and in the myriad other circumstances in which pedophilia and homosexuality are conflated. These attempts to link LGBT people with pedophiles are rooted in the notion that all sexual difference is equivalent—and dangerous.

Amnesty International's statement on the oppression of LGBT people includes the following:

> In virtually every part of the globe, LGBT lives are constrained by a web of laws and social practices which deny them an equal right to life, liberty and physical security, as well as other fundamental rights such as freedom of association, freedom of expression and rights to private life, employment, education and health care. While the degree to which discrimination is institutionalized varies from country to country, almost nowhere are LGBT people treated as fully equal before the law. ("Crimes")

In many cases, the struggle of LGBT people for inclusion and equality focuses on eliminating discrimination in the most basic areas of human life. We struggle for the fundamental freedoms granted to our heterosexual counterparts—to raise our families, to enjoy the civil liberties our governments provide for their citizens, and to have our basic human rights protected. But issues related to inclusion and equality have as much to do with the way people treat one another on a daily basis as they have to do with "rights." Governments and other institutions—LGBT organizations included—that engage in exclusionary practices and treat groups of citizens unequally establish and maintain an environment that sharply delineates between insiders and outsiders.

# Note

1. Despite the Red Cross's efforts to "support the use of rational, scientifically-based deferral periods," the Department of Health and Human Services Secretary's Advisory Committee on Blood Safety and Availability maintains a lifetime ban on blood donations from men who have had sex with men ("Joint Statement").

## QUESTIONS FOR DISCUSSION

1. Rhetoric about individual cases of bullying against people perceived to be LGBT sometimes "impl[ies] that homophobia can be rooted out, one bad apple at a time" (Gray). News reports about homophobic violence often assume that such incidents are individual, isolated cases. Does addressing homophobia one person at a time improve (or not) the social climate for sexual minorities? Think in particular about societies, like those discussed in this chapter, where homophobia is legislated. Consider specific cases.

2. In most of American popular culture, the discussion of gay marriage is framed as a debate about whether lesbian and gay people should have the right to the social, political, and material benefits that heterosexual married people already enjoy. This pro-con framing, though, tends to beg deeper questions about the institution of marriage—its efficacy in the contemporary world, its use as a social control, and the materialism and conspicuous consumption promoted by the "wedding industry" in the United States. Choose an article or other media representation (television or radio, for instance) of the gay marriage debate from the popular culture and identify several questions that the piece does not ask. How is not asking these questions an implicit endorsement of certain values and ideas?

3. While the repeal of DADT is rightly celebrated as an advance in the fight for gay rights, we wonder what happened to those who were discharged under the policy. Did some service people rejoin the military? What happened to those who did not? Research the biographies of LGBT service people expelled from the military under DADT, and consider the different life paths taken by people once subject to a homophobic policy.

## REFERENCES AND FURTHER READING

"About HRC." *Human Rights Campaign,* n.d. Web. 13 Oct. 2007. <http://www.hrc.org/about_us/>.

Anonymous Queers. "Queers Read This: I Hate Straights." *Queer Cultures.* Eds. Deborah Carlin and Jennifer DiGrazia. Upper Saddle River, NJ: Prentice Hall, 2004. 138–48. Print.

"Crimes of Hate, Conspiracy of Silence: Torture and Ill-Treatment Based on Sexual Identity." Amnesty International, n.d. Web. 25 Mar. 2008. <http://www.ai-lgbt.org/ai_report_ torture.htm#impunity>.

"Director's Finding." San Francisco Human Rights Commission, 26 Apr. 2005. Web. 25 Mar. 2008. <http://www.sflnc.com/binary.php/528/Badlands%20Finding%20.pdf>.

Dobnik, Verena. "NYC Parade Protested for Antigay Stance." *The Boston Globe,* 18 Mar. 2006. Web. 25 Mar. 2008. <http://www.boston.com/news/nation/articles/2006/03/18/nyc_parade_protested_for_antigay_stance/>.

Fodden, Simon. "Text of the Ugandan Anti-Homosexuality Bill." *Slaw,* 27 Nov. 2009. Web. 30 Mar. 2012. <http://www.slaw.ca/2009/11/27/text-of-the-ugandan-anti-homosexuality-bill/>.

France, David. "An Inconvenient Woman." *New York Times,* 28 May 2000. Web. 25 Mar. 2008. <http://query.nytimes.com/gst/fullpage.html?res=9902E5DB1E3AF93BA15756C0A9669C8B63&scp=2&sq=barry+winchell&st=nyt>.

Gamson, Joshua. "Messages of Exclusion: Gender, Movements, and Symbolic Boundaries." *Gender & Society* 11.2 (1997): 178–99. Print.

Goldberg, Michelle. "The Uganda Anti-Gay Bill's U.S. Roots." *The Daily Beast.* 11 May 2011. Web. 30 Mar. 2012. <http://www.thedailybeast.com/articles/2011/05/11/uganda-anti-homosexual-bill-inspired-by-american-evangelicals.html>.

Gosine, Andil. "Brown to Blonde at Gay.com: Passing White in Queer Cyberspace." *Queer Online: Media Technology and Sexuality*. Eds. Kate O'Riordan and David J. Phillips. New York: Peter Lang, 2007. Print.

Gray, Mary L. "Stop Blaming Dharun Ravi: Why We Need to Share Responsibility for the Loss of Tyler Clementi." *Huffington Post,* 2 Mar. 2012. Web. 30 Mar. 2012. <http://www.huffington post.com/mary-l-gray-phd/tyler-cleme nti_b_1317688.html>.

Jensen, Steffen. "Denmark: The Nordic Model." *Harvard Gay and Lesbian Review* 6.1 (1999): 36–37. Print.

Johnston, Jill. *Lesbian Nation: The Feminist Solution.* New York: Touchstone, 1973. Print.

"Joint Statement before the Advisory Committee on Blood Safety and Availability." American Red Cross, 15 June 2010. Web. 30 Mar. 2012. <http://www.aabb .org/pressroom/statements/Pages/state ment061510.aspx>.

Killian, D(ian). "Ireland's Fast Track to Equality." *Harvard Gay and Lesbian Review* 6.1 (1999): 24–26. Print.

Knowles, Joe. "The Boys in Havana." *Harvard Gay and Lesbian Review* 6.1 (1999): 19–20. Print.

Koyema, Emi. "Michigan/Trans Controversy Archive." N.p., 2000–2008. Web. 29 Mar. 2008. <http://eminism.org/mich igan/documents.html>.

Lawrence v. Texas. 539 U.S. 558 (2003).

Lo, Malinda. "Behind the Scenes at the Michigan Womyn's Music Festival." *After Ellen,* 20 Apr. 2005. Web. 25 Mar. 2008. <http://www.afterellen.com/archive/ ellen/Music/2005/4/michigan3.html>.

Marquis, Christopher. "Military Discharges of Gays Rise, and So Do Bias Incidents." *New York Times,* 14 Mar. 2002. Web. 25 Mar. 2008. <http://query.nytimes.com/ gst/fullpage.html?res=9C00E2DC1039 F937A25750C0A9649C8B63>.

"Missouri Army Base Leads 'Don't Ask, Don't Tell' Dismissal Rate." Associated Press, 14 Aug. 2006. Web. 25 Mar. 2008. <http://www.foxnews.com/story/ 0,2933,208247,00.html>.

Mitchell, Donn. "Get to Know the Universal Declaration." *Harvard Gay and Lesbian Review* 6.1 (1999): 13–14. Print.

Monifa, Akilah. "Sub-Saharan Africa and South Africa." *Harvard Gay and Lesbian Review* 6.1 (1999): 41–42. Print.

Moore, Jennifer. "A Few Key Political Issues for Bi People." N.d., n.p. Web. 25 Mar. 2008. <http://www.uncharted-worlds .org/bi/bipol.htm>.

"Queers Read This." N.p., June 1990. Web. 25 Mar. 2008. <http://www.qrd.org/qrd/ misc/text/queers.read.this>.

Quittner, Jeremy. "Death of a Two Spirit." *The Advocate,* 28 Aug. 2001. Web. 25 Mar. 2008. <http://findarticles.com/ p/articles/mi_m1589/is_2001_August _28/ai_77660063/>.

Rosen, Craig. "How Do You Spell Hate?" N.p., 31 July 2003. Web. 25 Mar. 2008. <http://www.lacitybeat.com/cms/ story/detail/?id=148&IssueNum=8>.

Rostow, Ann. "Martinez's Killer Gets 40 Years." N.p., 3 June 2002. Web. 29 Mar. 2008. <http://www.tgcrossroads.org/news/?AI D=221&IID=31&type=Headlines>.

Schneider, Richard. "Human Rights around the World." *Harvard Gay and Lesbian Review* 6.1 (1999): 4. Print.

Sciolino, Elaine. "Army Exonerates Officers in Slaying of Gay Private." *New York Times.* 19 July 2000. Web. <http://query .nytimes.com/gst/fullpage.html?res=9D 0DE3DC113BF93AA25754C0A9669C8 B63&sec=&spon=&pagewanted=all>.

Sherman, Mark. "Westboro Baptist Church Wins Supreme Court Appeal Over Funeral Protests." *Huffington Post,* 2 Mar. 2011. Web. 30 Mar. 2012. <http://www.huffingtonpost.com/2011/03/02/westboro-baptist-church-w_n_830209.html>.

Snyder, David. "Court Ruling Spurs Protest of Boy Scouts in Baltimore." *Washington Post* 6 July 2000: A2. Print.

"This Month's HIV/AIDS Facts." American Red Cross, July 2002. Web. 19 July 2008. <http://www.redcross.org/services/hss/tips/gaydisease.html>.

"UN Economic and Social Council vote grants consultative status to ILGA." *Fridae: Empowering Gay Asia,* 27 July 2011. Web. 30 Mar. 2012. <http://www.fridae.asia/newsfeatures/2011/07/27/11056.un-economic-and-social-council-vote-grants-consultative-status-to-ilga?n=sec>.

Volin, Katherine, and Lou Chibbaro Jr. "Minister's Fiery Anti-gay Sermon Riles Activists." *The Washington Blade,* 15 July 2005. <http://www.washblade.com/print.cfm? content_id=6077>.

Westboro Baptist Church. "God Hates America." 25 March 2008. <http://www.godhatesamerica.com/>.

Wilets, James D. "The Human Rights of Sexual Minorities: A Comparative and International Law Perspective." *Human Rights: Journal of the Section of Individual Rights & Responsibilities* 22.4 (1995): 22–27.

Wockner, Rex. "Gay Sex Legal across Europe." *Bay Windows,* 2003. 21.34: 11. Print.

———. "International News." *San Francisco Bay Times,* 14 Sept. 2006. Web. 18 Sept. 2006. <http://www.sfbaytimes.com>.

# READINGS

## ➢ From the Constitution of the Republic of South Africa

(1996), South Africa

### Preamble

We, the people of South Africa,

Recognise the injustices of our past;

Honour those who suffered for justice and freedom in our land;

Respect those who have worked to build and develop our country; and

Believe that South Africa belongs to all who live in it, united in our diversity.

We therefore, through our freely elected representatives, adopt this Constitution as the supreme law of the Republic so as to

> Heal the divisions of the past and establish a society based on democratic values, social justice and fundamental human rights;
>
> Lay the foundations for a democratic and open society in which government is based on the will of the people and every citizen is equally protected by law;
>
> Improve the quality of life of all citizens and free the potential of each person; and
>
> Build a united and democratic South Africa able to take its rightful place as a sovereign state in the family of nations.

May God protect our people.

*Nkosi Sikelel' iAfrika. Morena boloka setjhaba sa heso.*

*God seën Suid-Afrika.* God bless South Africa.

*Mudzimu fhatutshedza Afurika. Hosi katekisa Afrika.*

### Section on Equality From the Bill of Rights

#### *Equality*

(1) Everyone is equal before the law and has the right to equal protection and benefit of the law.

(2) Equality includes the full and equal enjoyment of all rights and freedoms. To promote the achievement of equality, legislative and other measures designed to protect or advance persons, or categories of persons, disadvantaged by unfair discrimination may be taken.

(3) The state may not unfairly discriminate directly or indirectly against anyone on one or more grounds, including race, gender, sex, pregnancy, marital status, ethnic or social origin, colour, sexual orientation, age, disability, religion, conscience, belief, culture, language and birth.

(4) No person may unfairly discriminate directly or indirectly against anyone on one or more grounds in terms of subsection (3). National legislation must be enacted to prevent or prohibit unfair discrimination.

(5) Discrimination on one or more of the grounds listed in subsection (3) is unfair unless it is established that the discrimination is fair.

## ➢ Hillary Clinton's International Human Rights Day Speech

(December 6, 2011), Geneva, Switzerland

Good evening, and let me express my deep honor and pleasure at being here. I want to thank Director General Tokayev and Ms. Wyden along with other ministers, ambassadors, excellencies, and UN partners. This weekend, we will celebrate Human Rights Day, the anniversary of one of the great accomplishments of the last century.

Beginning in 1947, delegates from six continents devoted themselves to drafting a declaration that would enshrine the fundamental rights and freedoms of people everywhere. In the aftermath of World War II, many nations pressed for a statement of this kind to help ensure that we would prevent future atrocities and protect the inherent humanity and dignity of all people. And so the delegates went to work. They discussed, they wrote, they revisited, revised, rewrote, for thousands of hours. And they incorporated suggestions and revisions from governments, organizations, and individuals around the world.

At three o'clock in the morning on December 10th, 1948, after nearly two years of drafting and one last long night of debate, the president of the UN General Assembly called for a vote on the final text. Forty-eight nations voted in favor; eight abstained; none dissented. And the Universal Declaration of Human Rights was adopted. It proclaims a simple, powerful idea: All human beings are born free and equal in dignity and rights. And with the declaration, it was made clear that rights are not conferred by government; they are the birthright of all people. It does not matter what country we live in, who our leaders are, or even who we are. Because we are human, we therefore have rights. And because we have rights, governments are bound to protect them.

In the 63 years since the declaration was adopted, many nations have made great progress in making human rights a human reality. Step by step, barriers that once prevented people from enjoying the full measure of liberty, the full experience of dignity, and the full benefits of humanity have fallen away. In many places, racist laws have been repealed, legal and social practices that relegated women to second-class status have been abolished, the ability of religious minorities to practice their faith freely has been secured.

In most cases, this progress was not easily won. People fought and organized and campaigned in public squares and private spaces to change not only laws, but hearts and minds. And thanks to that work of generations, for millions of individuals whose lives were once narrowed by injustice, they are now able to live more freely and to participate more fully in the political, economic, and social lives of their communities.

Now, there is still, as you all know, much more to be done to secure that commitment, that reality, and progress for all people. Today, I want to talk about the work we have left to do to protect one group of people whose human rights are still denied in too many parts of the world today. In many ways, they are an invisible minority. They are arrested, beaten, terrorized, even executed. Many are treated with contempt and violence by their fellow citizens while authorities empowered to protect them look the other way or, too often, even join in the abuse. They are denied opportunities to work and learn, driven from their homes and countries, and forced to suppress or deny who they are to protect themselves from harm.

I am talking about gay, lesbian, bisexual, and transgender people, human beings born free and given bestowed equality and dignity, who have a right to claim that, which is now one of the remaining human rights challenges of our time. I speak about this subject knowing that my own country's record on human rights for gay people is far from perfect. Until 2003, it was still a crime in parts of our country. Many LGBT Americans have endured violence and harassment in their own lives, and for some, including many young people, bullying and exclusion are daily experiences. So we, like all nations, have more work to do to protect human rights at home.

Now, raising this issue, I know, is sensitive for many people and that the obstacles standing in the way of protecting the human rights of LGBT people rest on deeply held personal, political, cultural, and religious beliefs. So I come here before you with respect, understanding, and humility. Even though progress on this front is not easy, we cannot delay acting. So in that spirit, I want to talk about the difficult and important issues we must address together to reach a global consensus that recognizes the human rights of LGBT citizens everywhere.

The first issue goes to the heart of the matter. Some have suggested that gay rights and human rights are separate and distinct; but, in fact, they are one and the same. Now, of course, 60 years ago, the governments that drafted and passed the Universal Declaration of Human Rights were not thinking about how it applied to the LGBT community. They also weren't thinking about how it applied to indigenous people or children or people with disabilities or other marginalized groups. Yet in the past 60 years, we have come to recognize that members of these groups are entitled to the full measure of dignity and rights, because, like all people, they share a common humanity.

This recognition did not occur all at once. It evolved over time. And as it did, we understood that we were honoring rights that people always had, rather than creating new or special rights for them. Like being a woman, like being a racial, religious, tribal, or ethnic minority, being LGBT does not make you less human. And that is why gay rights are human rights, and human rights are gay rights.

It is violation of human rights when people are beaten or killed because of their sexual orientation, or because they do not conform to cultural norms about how men and women should look or behave. It is a violation of human rights when governments declare it illegal to be gay, or allow those who harm gay people to go unpunished. It is a violation of human rights when lesbian or transgendered women are subjected to so-called corrective rape, or forcibly subjected to hormone treatments, or when people are murdered after public calls for violence toward gays, or when they are forced to flee their nations and seek asylum in other lands to save their lives. And it is a violation of human rights when life-saving care is withheld from people because they are gay, or equal access to justice is denied to people because they are gay, or public spaces are out of bounds to people because they are gay. No matter what we look like, where we come from, or who we are, we are all equally entitled to our human rights and dignity.

The second issue is a question of whether homosexuality arises from a particular part of the world. Some seem to believe it is a Western phenomenon, and therefore people outside the West have grounds to reject it. Well, in reality, gay people are born into and belong to every society in the world. They are all ages, all races, all faiths; they are doctors and teachers, farmers and bankers, soldiers and athletes; and whether we know it, or whether we acknowledge it, they are our family, our friends, and our neighbors.

Being gay is not a Western invention; it is a human reality. And protecting the human rights of all people, gay or straight, is not something that only Western governments do. South Africa's constitution, written in the aftermath of Apartheid, protects the equality of all citizens, including gay people. In Colombia and Argentina, the rights of gays are also legally protected. In Nepal, the supreme court has ruled that equal rights apply to LGBT citizens. The Government of Mongolia has committed to pursue new legislation that will tackle anti-gay discrimination.

Now, some worry that protecting the human rights of the LGBT community is a luxury that only wealthy nations can afford. But in fact, in all countries, there are costs to not protecting these rights, in both gay and straight lives lost to disease and violence, and the silencing of voices and views that would strengthen communities, in ideas never pursued by entrepreneurs who happen to be gay. Costs are incurred whenever any group is treated as lesser or the other, whether they are women, racial, or religious minorities, or the LGBT. Former President Mogae of Botswana pointed out recently that for as long as LGBT people are kept in the shadows, there cannot be an effective public health program to tackle HIV and AIDS. Well, that holds true for other challenges as well.

The third, and perhaps most challenging, issue arises when people cite religious or cultural values as a reason to violate or not to protect the human rights of LGBT citizens. This is not unlike the justification offered for violent practices towards women like honor killings, widow burning, or female genital mutilation. Some people still defend those practices as part of a cultural tradition. But violence toward women isn't cultural; it's criminal. Likewise with slavery, what was once justified as sanctioned by God is now properly reviled as an unconscionable violation of human rights.

In each of these cases, we came to learn that no practice or tradition trumps the human rights that belong to all of us. And this holds true for inflicting violence on LGBT people, criminalizing their status or behavior, expelling them from their families and communities, or tacitly or explicitly accepting their killing.

Of course, it bears noting that rarely are cultural and religious traditions and teachings actually in conflict with the protection of human rights. Indeed, our religion and our culture are sources of compassion and inspiration toward our fellow human beings. It was not only those who've justified slavery who leaned on religion, it was also those who sought to abolish it. And let us keep in mind that our commitments to protect the freedom of religion and to defend the dignity of LGBT people emanate from a common source. For many of us, religious belief and practice is a vital source of meaning and identity, and fundamental to who we are as people. And likewise, for most of us, the bonds of love and family that we forge are also vital sources of meaning and identity. And caring for others is an expression of what it means to be fully human. It is because the human experience is universal that human rights are universal and cut across all religions and cultures.

The fourth issue is what history teaches us about how we make progress towards rights for all. Progress starts with honest discussion. Now, there are some who say and believe that all gay people are pedophiles, that homosexuality is a disease that can be caught or cured, or that gays recruit others to become gay. Well, these notions are simply not true. They are also unlikely to disappear if those who promote or accept them are dismissed out of hand rather than invited to share their fears and concerns. No one has ever abandoned a belief because he was forced to do so.

Universal human rights include freedom of expression and freedom of belief, even if our words or beliefs denigrate the humanity of others. Yet, while we are each free to believe whatever we choose, we cannot do whatever we choose, not in a world where we protect the human rights of all.

Reaching understanding of these issues takes more than speech. It does take a conversation. In fact, it takes a constellation of conversations in places big and small. And it takes a willingness to see stark differences in belief as a reason to begin the conversation, not to avoid it.

But progress comes from changes in laws. In many places, including my own country, legal protections have preceded, not followed, broader recognition of rights. Laws have a teaching effect. Laws that discriminate validate other kinds of discrimination. Laws that require equal protections reinforce the moral imperative of equality. And practically speaking, it is often the case that laws must change before fears about change dissipate.

Many in my country thought that President Truman was making a grave error when he ordered the racial desegregation of our military. They argued that it would undermine unit cohesion. And it wasn't until he went ahead and did it that we saw how it strengthened our social fabric in ways even the supporters of the policy could not foresee. Likewise, some worried in my country that the repeal of Don't Ask, Don't Tell would have a negative effect on our armed forces. Now, the Marine Corps Commandant, who was one of the strongest voices against the repeal, says that his concerns were unfounded and that the Marines have embraced the change.

Finally, progress comes from being willing to walk a mile in someone else's shoes. We need to ask ourselves, "How would it feel if it were a crime to love the person I love? How would it feel to be discriminated against for something about myself that I cannot change?" This challenge applies to all of us as we reflect upon deeply held beliefs, as we work to embrace tolerance and respect for the dignity of all persons, and as we engage humbly with those with whom we disagree in the hope of creating greater understanding.

A fifth and final question is how we do our part to bring the world to embrace human rights for all people including LGBT people. Yes, LGBT people must help lead this effort, as so many of you are. Their knowledge and experiences are invaluable and their courage inspirational. We know the names of brave LGBT activists who have literally given their lives for this cause, and there are many more whose names we will never know. But often those who are denied rights are least empowered to bring about the changes they seek. Acting alone, minorities can never achieve the majorities necessary for political change.

So when any part of humanity is sidelined, the rest of us cannot sit on the sidelines. Every time a barrier to progress has fallen, it has taken a cooperative effort from those on both sides of the barrier. In the fight for women's rights, the support of men remains crucial. The fight for racial equality has relied on contributions from people of all races. Combating Islamophobia or anti-Semitism is a task for people of all faiths. And the same is true with this struggle for equality.

Conversely, when we see denials and abuses of human rights and fail to act, that sends the message to those deniers and abusers that they won't suffer any consequences for their actions, and so they carry on. But when we do act, we send a powerful moral message. Right here in Geneva, the international community acted this year to strengthen a global consensus around the human rights of LGBT people. At the Human Rights Council in March, 85 countries from all regions supported a statement calling for an end to criminalization and violence against people because of their sexual orientation and gender identity.

At the following session of the Council in June, South Africa took the lead on a resolution about violence against LGBT people. The delegation from South Africa spoke eloquently about their own experience and struggle for human equality and its indivisibility. When the measure passed, it became the first-ever UN resolution recognizing the human rights of gay people worldwide. In the Organization of American States this year, the Inter-American Commission on Human Rights created a unit on the rights of LGBT people, a step toward what we hope will be the creation of a special rapporteur.

Now, we must go further and work here and in every region of the world to galvanize more support for the human rights of the LGBT community. To the leaders of those countries where people are jailed, beaten, or executed for being gay, I ask you to consider this: Leadership, by definition, means being out in front of your people when it is called for. It means standing up for the dignity of all your citizens and persuading your people to do the same. It also means ensuring that all citizens are treated as equals under your laws, because let me be clear – I am not saying that gay people can't or don't commit crimes. They can and they do, just like straight people. And when they do, they should be held accountable, but it should never be a crime to be gay.

And to people of all nations, I say supporting human rights is your responsibility too. The lives of gay people are shaped not only by laws, but by the treatment they receive every day from their families, from their neighbors. Eleanor Roosevelt, who did so much to advance human rights worldwide, said that these rights begin in the small places close to home—the streets where people live, the schools they attend, the factories, farms, and offices where they work. These places are your domain. The actions you take, the ideals that you advocate, can determine whether human rights flourish where you are.

And finally, to LGBT men and women worldwide, let me say this: Wherever you live and whatever the circumstances of your life, whether you are connected to a network of support or feel isolated and vulnerable, please know that you are not alone. People around the globe are working hard to support you and to bring an end to the injustices and dangers you face. That is certainly true for my country. And you have an ally in the United States of America and you have millions of friends among the American people.

The Obama Administration defends the human rights of LGBT people as part of our comprehensive human rights policy and as a priority of our foreign policy. In our embassies, our diplomats are raising concerns about specific cases and laws, and working with a range of partners to strengthen human rights protections for all. In Washington, we have created a task force at the State Department to support and coordinate this work. And in the coming months, we will provide every embassy with a toolkit to help improve their efforts. And we have created a program that offers emergency support to defenders of human rights for LGBT people.

This morning, back in Washington, President Obama put into place the first U.S. Government strategy dedicated to combating human rights abuses against LGBT persons abroad. Building on efforts already underway at the State Department and across the government, the President has directed all U.S. Government agencies engaged overseas to combat the criminalization of LGBT status and conduct, to enhance efforts to protect vulnerable LGBT refugees and asylum seekers, to ensure that our foreign assistance promotes the protection of LGBT rights, to enlist international organizations in the fight against discrimination, and to respond swiftly to abuses against LGBT persons.

I am also pleased to announce that we are launching a new Global Equality Fund that will support the work of civil society organizations working on these issues around the world. This fund will help them record facts so they can target their advocacy, learn how to use the law as a tool, manage their budgets, train their staffs, and forge partnerships with women's organizations and other human rights groups. We have committed more than $3 million to start this fund, and we have hope that others will join us in supporting it.

The women and men who advocate for human rights for the LGBT community in hostile places, some of whom are here today with us, are brave and dedicated, and deserve all the help we can give them. We know the road ahead will not be easy. A great deal of work lies before us. But many of us have seen firsthand how quickly change can come. In our lifetimes, attitudes toward gay people in many places have been transformed. Many people, including myself, have experienced a deepening of our own convictions on this topic over the years, as we have devoted more thought to it, engaged in dialogues and debates, and established personal and professional relationships with people who are gay.

This evolution is evident in many places. To highlight one example, the Delhi High Court decriminalized homosexuality in India two years ago, writing, and I quote, "If there is one tenet that can be said to be an underlying theme of the Indian constitution, it is inclusiveness." There is little doubt in my mind that support for LGBT human rights will continue to climb. Because for many young people, this is simple: All people deserve to be treated with dignity and have their human rights respected, no matter who they are or whom they love.

There is a phrase that people in the United States invoke when urging others to support human rights: "Be on the right side of history." The story of the United States is the story of a nation that has repeatedly grappled with intolerance and inequality. We fought a brutal civil war over slavery. People from coast to coast joined in campaigns to recognize the rights of women, indigenous peoples, racial minorities, children, people with disabilities, immigrants, workers, and on and on. And the march toward equality and justice has continued. Those who advocate for expanding the circle of human rights were and are on the right side of history, and history honors them. Those who tried to constrict human rights were wrong, and history reflects that as well.

I know that the thoughts I've shared today involve questions on which opinions are still evolving. As it has happened so many times before, opinion will converge once again with the truth, the immutable truth, that all persons are created free and equal in dignity and rights. We are called once more to make real the words of the Universal Declaration. Let us answer that call. Let us be on the right side of history, for our people, our nations, and future generations, whose lives will be shaped by the work we do today. I come before you with great hope and confidence that no matter how long the road ahead, we will travel it successfully together. Thank you very much.

---

This is a transcript of U.S. Secretary of State Hillary Clinton's Human Rights Day speech, delivered in Geneva. Available at http://www.state.gov/secretary/rm/2011/12/178368.htm.

# CHAPTER 7

# Queer Diversities

Within queer communities, intense debates have raged over who is "OK," who belongs under the queer umbrella. This chapter details some of the parameters of those debates.

I magine a Gay Pride Day parade. A sunny weekend in mid-June, crowds bustling, vendors hawking their rainbow-striped goods. The parade features floats, marching bands, and costumed characters filing past. There go the leaders of the local gay rights organization. Then proud families from Parents, Families, and Friends of Lesbians and Gays (PFLAG). A growling rumble ushers in the Dykes on Bikes, followed by a leathermen troop. A gaggle of drag queens, bringing up the rear, draws the largest number of shouts, catcalls, and whistles as the parade draws to a close.

Of course, numerous other folks, organizations, and groups may march past you in such a parade—all attesting to the diversity of those who identify as LGBT. But the good cheer and festivities of a pride day parade conceal tensions within that diversity, the kind of strain that exists when any large "family" gathers together to make—and define—a community. In the process of defining a community, the place or even desirability of some is called into question. For instance, the equality and rights activists at the front of the parade might frown a bit at the presence of the leathermen and drag queens; after all, the more flamboyant members of our community might strike an unsettling chord with sympathetic straight voters and dispel the sense that we queers are "normal folk," just like everyone else. Conversely, that woman, marching with the drag queens, the one transitioning from

**Figure 7.1**   A Gay Pride parade in Cincinnati, Ohio.

being a man who likes men to a straight-identified woman, may be wondering if she is in the right parade. Will her queer community accept her once she has completed her transition and married her sweetheart? Will she still be queer?

We can trace the expansion of the LGBT community by looking at some work that has attempted to capture the richness of who we are as a people. It is remarkably easy to leave out, either by accidental oversight or unexamined prejudice, potential allies or others who could make common cause with us. When attempting to chronicle gay life in America in his 1980 book, *States of Desire: Travels in Gay America*, author Edmund White had to admit, "I criticize my book for concentrating on gay men in big cities and for ignoring lesbians as well as small-town or rural life" (336). In 400 pages, he could only cover so much of our diversity, and he ended up leaving out any significant discussion of women. Over a decade later, anthropologist Gilbert Herdt's collection, *Gay Culture in America: Essays from the Field (1992)*, attempted a more comprehensive view of what it means to be gay in the United States; his book contains essays on black men, "nonghetto," or suburban gays, and

**Figure 7.2**   A Gay Pride parade in Cincinnati, Ohio.

gay Mexican Americans. Still, bisexuals and the transgendered were largely ignored by the authors in Herdt's collection.

Diversity enriches our communities, our sense of what it means to be a member of the LGBT family. It also complicates matters. Just as feminists have debated whether pornography has a place in feminism, many queers have debated at different times whether challenging or controversial aspects of our community deserve a place. Within queer communities, intense debates have raged over who is really queer, who belongs under the queer umbrella. Of course, what is called "challenging" or "controversial" and decisions about who "belongs" often change over time and as contexts change. This chapter details the parameters of some of the most visible debates about diversity and what it means for queer communities.

In some societies, homosexuality and queerness are assumed to be nonexistent; in others, complex social roles have grown up around expressions of nonnormative sexuality and gender. It is important, then, to realize that diversity—and even the notion that diversity is important and desirable—is socially constructed. This means that the very decision to present a chapter on queer diversity in a text such as this is dependent on (1) a social setting in which diversity is acknowledged, (2) persistent attention to differences among those who identify as queer, and (3) resistance to monolithic thinking about queerness. Hence, this chapter focuses on some of the visible points of contestation in the emergence of self-consciously queer communities. One way we can develop a sense of how diversity problematizes—and enriches— a queer community is by examining the common label—LGBT—used to describe who we are and whom we include. Some commentators and comedians quip that the alphabetic shorthand of "LGBT" itself is insufficient to encompass the diversity of queers seeking community, shelter, or acknowledgment. Some have suggested, for instance, that we are LGBTQ (Q for queer . . . or is it Q for questioning?), LGBTQA (A for allies), LGBTQIA (I for intersexuals), and so forth. With this in mind, let us consider how diversity complicates the sense of community—in some challenging but ultimately productive ways.

## L . . . G . . . T . . . : A Story of Push and Pull

As we have noted in previous chapters, some lesbian feminists have promoted lesbian separatism [λ Chapter 4], understanding that sexism is as significant an issue to lesbians as homophobia. The idea of separatism has sparked debates about definitions of woman and womanhood itself. Monique Wittig, a French philosopher and feminist, is famous for arguing that "lesbians are not women." Following Simone De Beauvoir, the French existentialist who argued that "one is not born a woman" but learns the cultural expectations of womanhood and femininity as part of her lived experience, Wittig argues that, in heterosexist patriarchal systems, the category *woman* only makes sense in relation to men. Lesbians invested in woman-to-woman relationships thus abandon significant relations to men and are therefore not women. As Wittig explains, "[I]t would be incorrect to say that lesbians associate, make love, live with women, for 'woman' has meaning only in heterosexual systems of thought and heterosexual economic systems. Lesbians are not women" (32). Of course, many other women and lesbian thinkers, such as Adrienne Rich, disagree, stating that lesbians are women who must confront both homophobia and sexism in patriarchal and male-dominated societies [λ Chapter 5].

Other lesbians have made stark distinctions between different kinds of lesbians. In the introduction to her dystopian novel, *Doc and Fluff,* Pat Califia, writing as a lesbian, says that it is "about dykes, not lesbians" (xiv). Califia characterizes lesbians as assimilationists: "To affiliate with lesbians is to select a strategy of mainstreaming, emphasizing what one has in common with straight people, working for the recognition of domestic partnership, and basically accepting a heterosexual and capitalist model for the good life"; "uncritically adopting those standards and those ideals"; and failing to focus on the "real enemy—the institution of heterosexuality." "Dykes," on the other hand, "have no choice about being visible," and "Dyke culture is about confrontation, acquiring and protecting territory, and taking care of your own" (xv–xvi).

As you can see, definitional debates about identity—who we are and what our identities mean—can create provocative positions and disagreements. Recognition and discussion of transgenderism and transsexualism, for instance, have resulted in significant challenges to the parameters of the identity of *woman.* Are male-to-female (**MtF** or **M2F**) transsexuals actually women [λ Chapter 6]? Because they once lived as men, can they truly understand the sexism that many women find to be a key experience of women in patriarchal societies? What about those who become involved intimately with transsexuals? A lesbian activist friend of ours recently married a female-to-male (**FtM** or **F2M**) transsexual activist. Is the lesbian still a lesbian? Her husband once lived as a woman but now lives as a man; how does such a change affect the way our friend feels about her own identity—and about how others perceive her identity?

Debates about lesbian-identified women undergoing transition to become men have raged within the lesbian community. Some feel that FtMs should be excluded from lesbian communities, even if they lived for years as lesbian-identified women. Alix Dobkin, writing in "The Emperor's New Gender," suggests that the rise and appeal of transgenderism is tempting some women to reject their womanhood and embrace gender ambiguity (at best) or male identification (at worst); she sees such changes as ongoing symptoms of sexism and misogyny:

> Gays and lesbians have struggled for decades to be able to name ourselves and to BE ourselves. But now, in our own community we are expected to applaud Dykes rejecting

womanhood and embrace men taking it over. In our smart, brave and compassionate community, being "different" is the unifying thread holding us together in a diverse crazy quilt of which queers are justifiably proud.

But while we're at it, let's also honour our identity and history. And our women. Then maybe our girls won't be so eager to run. So let's put away the knives. Can we talk?

Pat Califia herself was a self-identified butch dyke who transitioned from female to male; he lives with another FtM transsexual and now goes by the name Patrick Califia-Rice.

*Speaking Sex to Power: The Politics of Queer Sex,* written by Califia-Rice post-transition, includes a chapter in which he considers the MWMF [λ Chapter 4], Alix Dobkin, and the challenges that transpeople sometimes pose to lesbians. The chapter titled "Sexual Politics, FtMs, and Dykes: Who Will Leap out of Bed First?" poignantly details Califia-Rice's own personal struggles to maintain connections with the lesbian communities that nurtured her and were her first home:

> I think lesbians have a right to ask why FTM's who pass fully as male want to be given the right to participate in all-women events. It's legitimate to ask if this is simple opportunism. Yes, it can be difficult to clarify one's identity; sometimes simply saying you are a man or a woman is not entirely accurate. . . . Since the FTM community is much smaller than the lesbian community, and many of us maintain friendship ties or erotic connections there, it can be painful and frightening to have to give up these resources. (117)

Califia-Rice also points out that FtMs have a difficult time fitting into gay male communities if they identify as gay or bi men. He writes in the chapter "Trannyfags Unzipped" that "[g]ay/bisexual female-to-male transsexuals (FTMs) are just starting to become more visible. This can be pretty jarring for gay men who base their common identity on having a dick" (132). Even other FtMs balked at Califia-Rice and his partner's decision to interrupt the partner's transition so he could give birth, since "real men" aren't really "supposed" to want to bear children. Califia-Rice, writing in an article titled "Family Values," says that he and his partner received verbal taunts from "a handful of straight-identified homophobic FtMs online who started calling Matt by his girl name, because real men don't get pregnant. One of these bigots even said it would be better for our baby to be born dead than be raised by two people who are 'confused about their gender.'"

In an attempt to bridge the gap between his various communities, Califia-Rice has suggested that female-to-male transsexuals and butch dykes may have much in common, such as having to grapple with what typically "masculine" interests or gender presentation might mean for their lives. Vik Savage, self-described as a "Butch Dyke not FTM," sharply disagrees, saying that past lesbians "had good boundaries around men and oppression. We don't. We're all freakin' wishy-washy with our B***SH*T about 'oh but they're SO like us!'. Fuck that! They're MEN, dudes! MEN, MEN, MEN, MEN. Hello!!!!!" Despite Califia-Rice's eloquence and his insistence that he has not "renounced" his history as a dyke, questions of community still haunt his discussions about transmen, transwomen, lesbianism, and feminism. Diverse experiences of sexuality and gender have complicated intimacies and identities within and among these communities.

## Bisexual Erasure in the LGBT Community

B isexuality has been among the most vexed internal issues facing Western queer communities. For years, the letter *B* has been tacked onto the *L* and the *G*, with *T* coming a bit more recently; but many *B*s have never found themselves particularly welcome in or a part of their lesbian and gay communities. Many gays and lesbians have suggested that bisexuals are just "going through a phase" on their way to "true" gayness or lesbianism or that they are trying to hold on to straight privilege while fooling around with people of their own sex. And, in fact, a controversial article published in 2005 in the *New York Times* pointedly asked, "Gay, Straight, or Lying? Bisexuality Revisited." The article's author, Benedict Carey, reported on some studies suggesting that "[p]eople who claim bisexuality . . . are usually homosexual, but are ambivalent about their homosexuality or simply closeted." Despite such negativity and bad press, bisexual activists have formed groups locally, nationally, and even throughout the world to educate others about bisexuality and bisexual identity. In the United States, BiNet USA (http://www.binetusa.org/) is perhaps the largest and most politically active of organizations for bisexual people.

Bi-eroticism is a transhistorical and transcultural phenomenon, argues Marjorie Garber in her influential 1995 book, *Vice Versa: Bisexuality and the Eroticism of Everyday Life*, which traces the representation of bi-erotic intimacies in over two millennia of Western art, texts, and media. Garber carefully avoids labeling bi-eroticism as *bisexual identity*, and she thus avoids the fallacy of presentism. Rather, Garber carefully and exhaustively documents how numerous major artists, actors, thinkers, and philosophers—from Shakespeare to Wilde, from Sappho to Frida Kahlo—explored in their works attraction and intimate affection that are neither exclusively straight nor gay. Shakespeare's acclaimed sonnet sequence, for instance, contains sets of love poems written about and to a woman (the "dark lady" of the sonnets) as well as to a young male friend (the actual subject of the famous sonnet often used in weddings, "Let me not to the marriage of true minds"). Garber's work ultimately asks that we question our assumptions about the sexual identities of past figures. Oscar Wilde, for instance, has long been thought of as a gay icon, but he was also a loving father who deeply cared for his children and his wife. Is Wilde then gay?

What do his bi-erotic investments say about his sexuality and his identity? Along the same lines, other scholars and writers, such as Wayne Bryant and his 1997 book *Bisexual Characters in Film: From Anaïs to Zee*, as well as Loraine Hutchins and Lani Ka'ahumanu and their 1991 collection of bisexual coming-out stories, *Bi Any Other Name*, document the presence of bi-eroticism in a variety of media products and nonfiction narratives. *Bi Any Other Name* in particular shows the difficulties faced by those attempting to assert an identity as bisexuals; such individuals often face hostility from both gays and straights, who deny their existence as bisexuals and question their right to name themselves and their attractions.

Some scholars note that the seemingly persistent unwillingness to acknowledge or discuss bisexuality and bi-eroticism throughout the West has roots in both a general fear of sexuality and an attempt to delineate clear distinctions between gays and straights. Bisexuals, existing somewhere apart from the two, pose a threat to the binary construct that gives both homosexuality and heterosexuality their meaningfulness in relation to one another. Along these lines, Yale law professor Kenji Yoshino has argued provocatively in "The Epistemic Contract of Bisexual Erasure" that bisexuality should be contrasted to **monosexuality**, or the erotic and affectional investment in loving either people of the same sex or the opposite sex—but not both. For Yoshino, monosexuals have much to gain not just by ignoring bisexuality but by actively denying its existence:

> The first investment monosexuals have in bisexual erasure is an interest in stabilizing sexual orientation. The component of that interest shared by both straights and gays is an interest in knowing one's place in the social order: both straights and gays value this knowledge because it relieves them of the anxiety of identity interrogation. Straights have a more specific interest in ensuring the stability of heterosexuality because that identity is privileged. Less intuitively, gays also have a specific interest in guarding the stability of homosexuality, insofar as they view that stability as the predicate for the "immutability defense" or for effective political mobilization. . . . Bisexuality is thus threatening to all monosexuals because it makes it impossible to prove a monosexual identity.

Yoshino also suggests that monosexuals are troubled by the specter of bisexual "nonmonogamy," which many gays, lesbians, and straights assume to be a key aspect of bisexuality. Gays and lesbians seeking to be accepted by mainstream Western society, which figures intimate relationships as ideally monogamous, fear that bisexual nonmonogamy threatens gays' ability to pass as "normal." The truth, of course, is much more complicated. Many bisexually identified people are indeed monogamous, just as many gays, lesbians, and straights are most decidedly not monogamous. Furthermore, many gays and lesbians fear bisexuality because it seems to suggest that one can choose one's sexuality. In contrast, many gays and lesbians (as well as some straights) want to argue that their sexuality is not chosen and is thus natural—a powerful argument in some people's eyes for extending civil rights and protections to gays and lesbians [λ Chapter 5]. Bisexuality, then, is an intolerable position in the eyes of many gays, lesbians, and straights.

We can see the extent of bisexual erasure in reactions to Ang Lee's controversial film about an erotic relationship between two male cowboys, *Brokeback Mountain* (2005). Both cowboys are married and have intimate relations with women in addition to their stormy and complex decades-long affair with one another. Amy Andre, in an article for *American Sexuality Magazine,* proposes that

> *Brokeback Mountain* is not a movie about gay people, and there are no gay people in it. There. I said it. Despite what you may have read in the many reviews that have come out about this new cowboy feature film, *Brokeback Mountain* is a bisexual picture. Why can't film reviewers say the word "bisexual" when they see lead characters with sexual and romantic relationships with both men and women?

Andre's assertion that the film is actually about two bisexual men, not just two closeted gay men, may be debatable. But her point that discussion about the film largely avoided any consideration of the potential bisexuality of the characters speaks to the extent to which bisexuality and bi-eroticism are seldom taken seriously or even acknowledged in the larger culture. When bisexuality is noticed by the media, it is often depicted in damaging and noxious ways. In the introduction to their edited collection *Bisexual Men in Culture and Society,* Brett Beemyn and Erich Steinman assert that "[n]ot only are there relatively few cultural images of men who are attracted to more than one gender, but the representations that do exist often focus on how behaviorally bisexual men supposedly pose a hidden HIV threat to heterosexual women" (3) [λ Chapter 8]. According to the myth, then, married bisexual men are on the down low, sneaking off for secret liaisons with other men and potentially bringing home sexually transmitted diseases. Such representations, as well as the persistent attempts to erase bisexuality from the culture, are frequent targets of bisexual activists. The American Institute of Bisexuality, for instance, has pledged to raise awareness of not only the existence of bisexuality but also the many contributions that bisexuals make to culture, society, the arts, and the numerous communities to which they belong (http://www.bisexual.org).

# Intersexuality

Intersexuals may be the newest to find voice in the LGBT community. Intersexuals are individuals who in the past would have been labeled hermaphrodites; they are typically born with both male and female genitalia or sex organs or with indeterminate genitalia—that is, genitals that are not clearly male or female sex organs, such as large clitorises that resemble small penises. Many intersexuals in the West are subject to surgery as infants to "correct" their gender indeterminacy and to "fix" them as either clearly male or clearly female. While some intersexuals are not aware that their hermaphroditism was corrected, others report being shocked to discover that they were subjected to such surgical procedures as infants.

The Intersex Society of North America (ISNA) advocates for an end to these surgeries and, in their words, "is devoted to systemic change to end *shame, secrecy,* and *unwanted genital surgeries* for people born with an anatomy that someone decided *is not standard for male or female.*" ISNA believes firmly that "[i]ntersexuality is primarily a problem of *stigma and trauma,* not *gender,*" and that "[p]*arents' distress* must not be treated by surgery on the child." Many intersexed activists argue that their fight is comparable to that of queers who advocate for individual self-determination and freedom from normative gender constructions. We can hear the connections between intersexed and queer activists in the following quotation from Morgan Holmes's essay "Queer Cut Bodies": "Intersexed adults are first intersexed minors who have been subjected to the wills of their families and doctors. Avoidance of surgeries serving no purpose except to make the intersexed child more appealing to parents and to their culture is a fine place to start reconceptualizing the intersexed body" (106). Many queers can identify with Holmes's characterization of children "subjected to the wills of their families" and to being forced to become "more appealing" (i.e., less queer). But more than such similarities, the intersexed and many queers collectively fight the imposition of heteronormative values and ideas—not only on the way we choose to love and to be intimate but on our very bodies as well.

# *Q*: Beyond Sexual Identity

The letter Q is sometimes added to the LGBT grouping to signify either those who are "questioning" or those who prefer the term *queer* to describe their sexual identities or affinities. Some use the word *queer* as a catchall for the LGBT conglomerate, but many others prefer *queer* as a political term. Specifically, *queer* is used to mark those whose sexualities, sexual practices, or erotic and affectional investments lie outside the mainstream of normative heterosexuality. Some activists in the 1990s (and to this day) use the term *queer* aggressively, signaling that they have taken a term once used to stigmatize homosexuals and other "perverts" and are now using it proudly, even defiantly. We are queer—so what? The reclamation of the word *queer,* then, serves to defy normative, conventional society and its bigoted exclusions. As David Halperin puts it in *Saint Foucault,* "Queer is by definition whatever is at odds with the normal, the legitimate, the dominant" (62).

Some writers have explored the usefulness of *queer* as a marker of the transgressive margins, while others have developed different terms to promote a queer ethos—the celebration of sexual difference and nonnormative eroticism. For instance, Carol Queen and Lawrence Schimel use the term *pomosexual* to describe a postmodern sexuality that is free, exploratory, and unwilling to confine itself to specific labels. In their edited collection, *Pomosexuals: Challenging Assumptions about Gender and Sexuality,* they note the similarity between the terms *pomosexual* and *queer:*

> the "pomosexual," who, like the queer s/he closely resembles, may not be tied to a single sexual identity, may not be content to reside within a category measurable by social scientists or acknowledged by either rainbow-festooned gays or by Ward and June Cleaver. (23)

For many writers such as Queen, a well-known sex activist, *queer* foregrounds not only difference but also pleasure, an aspect of sexual politics that many pomosexuals feel is often overlooked or under-considered in public discussions of sex and sexuality.

Along similar lines, others in the LGBTQ community have attempted to emphasize the diversity of sexual interests and erotic styles by forming subcultural groups focused on particular identifications. For instance, some gay men identify strongly with "bear culture" and call themselves "bears" (men a bit larger or hairier than the norm) or "bear cubs" (men who love men who are a bit larger or hairier than the norm). Bears break out of the consumerist stereotype, fostered by shows such as *Queer Eye for the Straight Guy,* which figures gay men as slim, super health-conscious, interior-decorating gurus; bears, in contrast, are large men whose interests tend to be typically (even stereotypically) masculine, such as sports, camping, and roughhousing. In *The Bear Book II,* Les Wright notes that bears challenge any sense of normative gayness or queerness: "All of these Ur-springs of the bearstream trickled along because in the invention of 'gaymen' and 'gay culture,' ideas and concepts required the invention of a new vocabulary to describe categories and subcategories inside the love that so long had dared not speak its name" (xlii).

While groups such as the bears highlight the diversity of erotic interest and lifestyles within the LGBT community, many queers do not necessarily experience queer communities as stylistic free-for-alls. For some, the challenge of diversity is finding a comfortable place within the diversity, and some critics and scholars worry about the establishment of hierarchies that oppress people who do not fit into particular groups. For instance, in some gay male communities, men who are "straight-acting" are more valued and sought after as sexual partners than others. Wayne Martino argues that discriminating hierarchies may be evolving within gay male communities around the notion of straight-acting, particularly "[w]ithin a sociocultural context in which specific discourses about straight-acting masculinities gain a particular authoritative status or ascendancy—for example, from 'Bears' who claim that they don't engage in 'faggoty sex' to 'gainers' who deliberately put on weight to adopt a particular way of being masculine that challenges the idealization of the gay male body" (Kendall and Martino 58). In general, the seeming freedom implied in terms such as *queer* or *pomosexual* needs to be considered against the often restrictive, even oppressive social and sexual practices in which people actually engage.

Conforming to certain styles, fashions, or self-presentations may be one way to deal with the diversity within LGBTQ communities, but the pressure to conform has created a fair amount of backlash. For example, Christy Calame and Robbie Scott Phillips capture some of the frustration with conformity. In their provocative manifesto, "Fuck Your Healthy Gay Lifestyle (The FRINGE Manifesto—Freaks, Radicals, and Inverts Nail Gay Elite!)," they argue that "[g]ays and lesbians do not exist—there are only queers and straights. Those known as 'gay and lesbian people' are essentially straight assholes who sleep with members of their same sex and have nothing to do with queerness except their fear and rape of it. Queers are twisted and disgusting, beautiful and glamorous, extreme and alive. We live outside the margin and move to keep working edges, surviving co-optations, decimation, and attack by those so-called gay and lesbian people" (233). Scholars such as Michael Warner have taken such critiques seriously; his book, *The Trouble with Normal*, analyzes how some gays and lesbians seek political favor by attempting to demonstrate that little difference exists between gays and straights; they argue that rights should be equitably distributed because we are all, essentially, the same. For instance, the Log Cabin Republicans, a national group of U.S. lesbian and gay Republicans, advocate primarily for legalizing gay marriage and open military service because extending these rights will bring gays into the American mainstream— thus promoting a sense of queers as "normal" citizens. Many other queers, such as Calame and Phillips, argue strongly that access to rights should not hinge on sameness but should be available to all irrespective of difference.

Historian John D'Emilio, writing in "Gay Politics, Gay Community," notes that the "[g]rowth [of the lesbian and gay community] has also meant differentiation, diversity, and divisions. Gay communities around the country are coming to mirror the society at large with all of the conflicting interests that stem from differences of gender, race, and class" (94). This recognition prompts many questions. In particular, when we attempt to capture the diversity of the LGBT and queer community, we still need to ask, "Who is not represented by the LGBTQ label?" Is the experience, for instance, of African-American gays and lesbians in the United States the same as their white counterparts? What about Latin@s and Asian-Americans? What about

**Find Out More** in Amber Hollibaugh's article "Queers without Money" at the end of this chapter.

queers in different national contexts? We will have much more to say about the intersections among different identity categories (queerness, race, ethnicity, social class, and gender) in the following chapter.

For now, we can consider briefly how the experience of social class often intersects with and complicates the experience of queerness. Some critics have—with no small justification—claimed that LGBT communities and rights organizations have been dominated by white, middle-class interests, values, and people. Social class has long been overlooked as an important consideration when understanding and representing oneself as queer. Amber Hollibaugh writes eloquently about the enforced silences imposed on working-class LGBT people. A recent documentary film, *Small Town Gay Bar*, poignantly demonstrates Hollibaugh's point: the film depicts queer life in rural Mississippi, where LGBT people only feel safe identifying themselves in bars, many of which are not visibly marked as queer and are found by word of mouth. Nicola Field, in her book *Over the Rainbow: Money, Class and Homophobia*, summarizes the importance of considering social class as a significant dimension of one's experience of queerness:

> Demonstrating as lesbians and gay men, many of us would not dare to wear our working clothes. We may be afraid of being recognised, of facing repercussions at work where we are isolated and alone. . . . We are visible in a crowd but we remain largely invisible in our daily lives. The sense of solidarity that comes with marching and mingling as part of a mass of gay people is therefore a welcome relief from the isolation of everyday life. When we march we say that this is the one day of the year that belongs to "us." However, it is impossible to sustain this sense of political power once the carnival is over. (152)

Indeed, the "invisibility" experienced by many working-class queers is at times a necessary component of moving out of the working class. Many working-class queers, for instance, consider service in the armed forces a way to obtain money for a college education. The U.S. military's DADT [λ Chapters 4 and 6] policy once made being queer in the military much more challenging, complicating class mobility for many queers.

## *A* for Allies

The queer community has also had complex, productive, and at times troubled relationships with those who might be potential allies. These allies have much to offer the queer community in terms of support and insight, but alliances have not always been easy. For instance, people throughout the *kink* community, including a wide variety of fetishists and sadomasochists interested in alternative forms of sexual expression, may not necessarily be interested in homo- or bi-erotic behavior, but their nonnormative sexualities make them likely allies with queers. Many of them consider themselves queer in the broadest sense of the word. **Sadomasochists** (S/M), in particular, face social stigmas comparable to those of many in the LGBT community; in "The Joy of S/M," Susan Wright suggests that "[t]he biggest burden for s/m practitioners is the social stigma. I've come to expect that the Christian Right will attack us for our sexual choices, deriding us and labeling our behavior as wrong because it is not what they would choose to do." While such discrimination might make practitioners of S/M seemingly natural allies with queers, Wright notes that many in the LGBT community actively discriminate against those who are vocal about their kink interests. She cites a 1994 survey that "found that 56% of the 539 s/m women surveyed had been the victim of violence—harassment, discrimination, or assault—by fellow lesbians because of their s/m orientation. Clearly s/m practitioners have a long fight ahead for equal protection and our civil rights." Of course, some queers are themselves actively invested in S/M, both as an erotic practice and as a vehicle for forming community with other like-minded individuals. Califia-Rice has long been a strong advocate for S/M, and queer authors such as Dennis Cooper have written extensively—and provocatively—about fringe, fetish, and sadomasochistic sexual practices [λ Chapter 11]. Still, many in the LGBT community find such interests repugnant, particularly as they seem "abnormal," and give the lie to arguments that queers are much like straights. What is ironic about such objections is the reality that many in S/M communities are themselves straight.

Another group that has both supporters and detractors within the larger LGBT community is sex workers. The International Union of Sex Workers has identified a number of demands that would benefit sex workers throughout the world. These include the following:

- Clean and safe places to work.
- The right to choose whether to work on our own or co-operatively with other sex workers.
- The absolute right to say no.
- Access to training—our jobs require very special skills and professional standards.
- Access to health clinics where we do not feel stigmatised.
- Re-training programmes for sex workers who want to leave the industry.
- An end to social attitudes which stigmatise those who are or have been sex workers. (http://www.iusw.org/start/index.html)

Certainly, many queers have similarly argued for access to health services, the right to feel safe at work, and freedom from stigmatization. Amber Hollibaugh asks why it has taken so long for the needs of sex workers to attract the attention of feminist thinkers and activists—those who are invested in protecting the rights of women. Her answer underscores the social class division that frequently exists between middle- and upper-class feminists and many female sex workers: "Maybe because it's hard to listen—I mean really pay attention to—a woman who, without other options, could easily be cleaning your toilet? Maybe because it's intolerable to listen to the point of view of a woman who makes her living sucking off your husband?" (181). Hollibaugh suggests that ignorance about queer sex workers is even more acute: "If the world of sex work is usually concealed, the world of lesbian sex workers is completely invisible. Throughout every part of the sex-trade business, there are lesbians working as hookers and dancers, as dykes who function in massage parlors and as the lesbian madams of brothels and escort services—and as prostitutes' rights organizers around the world" (183).

As you can see, the issue of diversity within the LGBT and queer community is complex and often vexed. In significant ways, we are queer because of that diversity, because of our difference from normative cultural conceptions of appropriate gender behavior and accepted sexual practice. Still, many queers, when encountering sexual diversity, act much as many straights do when encountering queerness— with hesitation, skepticism, and sometimes hostility. Whether such skepticism and hostility are warranted varies from issue to issue, identity to identity, and community to community. In his apologia for homosexuality titled *Corydon,* French author André Gide requests that we do not "understand" him too quickly—that we do not assume that what seems different can be honored by viewing it as less complex than it actually is. The diversity within the LGBT and queer community ensures that any understanding of queerness that jumps to quick conclusions is likely to be foiled upon closer examination. This diversity—this complexity— makes our experiences in many ways all the richer, particularly as we are prompted to think more deeply and critically about what queer is—and could be.

## QUESTIONS FOR DISCUSSION

1. One myth of American culture suggests that we in the United States comprise a melting pot of different nationalities, identities, and communities. In what ways is the queer or LGBT community in this country a melting pot? Is the metaphor of the melting pot appropriate or even accurate? Try to generate a list of other or better metaphors. Consider your experiences or those of queers you might know. Record your own and others' reflections on queerness and the melting pot metaphor.

2. Certainly, issues of diversity complicate unified and collective political action, particularly in that different identity groups may want to promote different agendas addressing their own particular issues or experiences. At the same time, a variety of different queers—ranging from gay men and intersexuals to FtM transsexuals and lesbian separatists—might have commonalities around which to organize politically. What are

they? Are there queer values that many diverse members of LGBT and queer communities might be able to advance as a political agenda?

3. Early in this chapter, we raised the *alphabet issue*—the expanding string of letters used to identify the diversity within queer communities. As we noted, some people prefer to use the term *queer* as a catchall for this diversity, while others, particularly some feminists, feel that the word *queer* erases or elides women's interests and focuses on men. Can you think of another word or phrase to replace *queer* or *LGBT* to represent the LGBT and queer community? What are the advantages of your chosen word or phrase? What are its potential disadvantages? Who is likely to support it? Who not? Why?

## REFERENCES AND FURTHER READING

Andre, Amy. "Bisexual Cowboys in Love." *American Sexuality Magazine,* Winter 2006. Web. <http://nsrc.sfsu.edu/Mag Article.cfm?Article=554>.

Beemyn, Brett, and Erich Steinman, eds. *Bisexual Men in Culture and Society.* New York: Harrington Park Press, 2002. Print.

*Bisexual Foundation.* N.d. Web. <http://www.bisexual.org>.

Bryant, Wayne M. *Bisexual Characters in Film: From Anaïs to Zee.* New York: Haworth Press, 1997. Print.

Calame, Christy, and Robbie Scott Phillips. "Fuck Your Healthy Gay Lifestyle (The FRINGE Manifesto—Freaks, Radicals, and Inverts Nail Gay Elite!)." *Generation Q: Gays, Lesbians, and Bisexuals Born around 1969's Stonewall Riots Tell Their Stories of Growing Up in the Age of Information.* Eds. Robin Bernstein and Seth Clark Silberman. Los Angeles: Alyson Publications, 1996. 233–36. Print.

Califia, Pat. *Doc and Fluff.* Boston: Alyson Publications, 1990. Print.

Califia-Rice, Patrick. "Family Values." *The Village Voice,* 20 June 2000. Web. 19 July 2008. <http://villagevoice.com/2000-06-20/news/family-values/>.

———. *Speaking Sex to Power: The Politics of Queer Sex.* San Francisco: Cleis Press, 2002. Print.

Carey, Benedict. "Gay, Straight, or Lying? Bisexuality Revisited." *New York Times,* 5 July 2005. Web. 19 July 2008. <http://select.nytimes.com/gst/abstract.html?res=F20714FB3B550C768CDDAE089 4DD404482>.

D'Emilio, John. "Gay Politics, Gay Community: San Francisco's Experience." *Making Trouble: Essays on Gay History, Politics, and the University.* New York: Routledge, 1992. Print.

Dobkin, Alix. "The Emperor's New Gender." *Off Our Backs.* April 2000. Web. 19 July 2008. <http://www.raperelief shelter.bc.ca/issues/newgender .html>.

*Eulenspiegel Society.* N.d. Web. 19 July 2008. <http://www.tes.org/>.

Field, Nicola. *Over the Rainbow: Money, Class and Homophobia.* East Haven, CT: Pluto Press, 1995. Print.

Garber, Marjorie. *Vice Versa: Bisexuality and the Eroticism of Everyday Life.* New York: Simon & Schuster, 1995. Print.

Gide, André. *Corydon.* New York: Farrar, Straus, Giroux, 1983. Print.

Halperin, David M. *Saint Foucault: Towards a Gay Hagiography.* New York: Oxford University Press, 1995. Print.

Herdt, Gilbert, ed. *Gay Culture in America: Essays from the Field.* Boston: Beacon, 1992. Print.

Hollibaugh, Amber L. *My Dangerous Desires: A Queer Girl Dreaming Her Way Home.* Durham, NC: Duke University Press, 2000. Print.

Holmes, Morgan. "Queer Cut Bodies." *Queer Frontiers: Millennial Geographies, Genders, and Generations.* Ed. *Queer Frontiers* Editorial Collective (Joseph A. Boone, Martin Dupuis, Martin Meeker, Karin Quimby, Cindy Sarver, Debra Silverman, and Rosemary Weatherston). Madison: University of Wisconsin Press, 2000. 84–110. Print.

Hutchins, Loraine, and Lani Ka'ahumanu, eds. *Bi Any Other Name: Bisexual People Speak Out.* Boston: Alyson Publications, 1991. Print.

*International Union of Sex Workers.* N.d. Web. <http://www.iusw.org/start/index.html>.

*Intersex Society of North America.* N.d. Web. <http://www.isna.org/>.

Kendall, Christopher, and Wayne Martino, eds. *Gendered Outcasts and Sexual Outlaws: Sexual Oppression and Gender Hierarchies in Queer Men's Lives.* New York: Harrington Park Press, 2006. Print.

Martino, Wayne. "Straight-Acting Masculinities: Normalization and Gender Hierarchies in Gay Men's Lives." *Gendered Outcasts and Sexual Outlaws: Sexual Oppression and Gender Hierarchies in Queer Men's Lives.* Eds. Christopher Kendall and Wayne Martino. New York: Harrington Park Press, 2006. 35–60. Print.

Ochs, Robyn. *Getting Bi: Voices of Bisexuals around the World.* Boston: Bisexual Resource Center, 2005. Print.

Queen, Carol, and Lawrence Schimel, eds. *Pomosexuals: Challenging Assumptions about Gender and Sexuality.* San Francisco: Cleis Press, 1997. Print.

Savage, Vik. "Point/Counterpoint: Reactions to Pat Califia." Technodyke.com, n.d. Web. 19 July 2008. <http://www.techno dyke.com/features/point_cp_pat.asp>.

Warner, Michael. *The Trouble with Normal: Sex, Politics, and the Ethics of Queer Life.* New York: The Free Press, 1999. Print.

White, Edmund. *States of Desire: Travels in Gay America.* New York: Dutton, 1980. Print.

Wittig, Monique. *The Straight Mind.* Boston: Beacon, 1992. Print.

Wright, Les K., ed. *The Bear Book II: Further Readings in the History and Evolution of a Gay Male Subculture.* New York: Harrington Park Press, 2001. Print.

Wright, Susan. "The Joy of S/M." Fetish Information Exchange, 10 September 1999. Web. 19 July 2008. <http://www .fetishexchange.org/joyofsm.shtml>.

Yoshino, Kenji. "The Epistemic Contract of Bisexual Erasure." *Stanford Law Review,* 1 January 2000. Web. 19 July 2008 <http://www.kenjiyoshino.com/ articles/epistemiccontract.pdf>.

# READINGS

## ➢ Amber Hollibaugh

(2001), United States

**"Queers Without Money: They Are Everywhere. But We Refuse to See Them."**

I mean, homosexuals have high incomes, they have high levels of education; they're owners of major credit cards. There was a survey done. So you're not talking about poor people, homeless people living under a bridge.

—Reverend Lou Sheldon, a conservative Christian leader

I lived the first year of my life in a converted chicken coop in back of my grandmother's trailer. The coop was hardly tall enough for my 6' 4" father and 5' 8" mother to stand up in. My dad, a carpenter, tore out the chickens' egg-laying ledges and rebuilt the tiny inside space to fit a bed, a table, two chairs, a basin they used as a sink (there was no running water), a shelf with a hot plate for cooking, and a small dresser. They used the hose outside to wash with, and ran extension cords in from my grandmother's trailer for light and heat. My bed, a dresser drawer, sat on top of the table during the day. At night it was placed next to where they slept.

I was sick the entire first year of my life. So was my mother, recovering from a nasty C-section and a series of ensuing medical crises. By the time she and I were discharged, three months later, whatever money my parents had managed to save was used up, and they were deeply in debt. They had been poor before my birth, and poor all of their lives growing up, but this was the sinker.

After my first year, we moved from the chicken coop into a trailer. My father worked three jobs simultaneously, rarely sleeping. My mother took whatever work she could find: mending, washing, and ironing other people's clothes. But we never really recovered. We were impoverished. Growing up, I was always poor. I am also a lesbian.

This, then, is my queer identity: I am a high-femme, mixed-race, white-trash lesbian. And even after all these years of living in a middle-class gay community, I often feel left outside when people speak about their backgrounds, their families. And if you listen to the current telling of "our" queer tale, people like me would seem an anomaly. Because, we are told—and we tell ourselves—queerness can't be poor.

Yet this seeming anomaly is the tip of the proverbial iceberg. It represents hundreds of thousands of us who come from poor backgrounds, or are living them still—and are very, very queer.

That would seem obvious when you combine the proportion of the population reputed to be queer (between 4 and 10 percent) with the 37 million poor people in America. Yet the early surveys done on gay and lesbian economic status in this country told a different tale: that queers had more disposable income than straights, lived more luxurious lives, and were all DINKs (Dual Income No Kids). "My book begins as a critique of those early surveys, which were done largely to serve the interests of gay and lesbian publications and a few marketing companies," says economist M. V. Lee Badgett in her new book, *Money, Myths, and Change: The Economic Lives of Lesbians and Gay Men.* "Those surveys are deeply flawed."

Badgett notes that "opposition to gay people is often based on the perception that queers are better off than everybody else; that we're really asking for 'special rights'—and that breeds resentment." Badgett's research shows something else. It constitutes the first true picture of queer economic reality. Among other things, Badgett found that:

- Gays, lesbians, and bisexuals do *not* earn more than heterosexuals, or live in more affluent households.
- Gay men earn 13 to 32 percent less than similarly qualified straight men (depending on the study).
- Though lesbians and bisexual women have incomes comparable to straight women—earning 21 percent less than men—lesbian couples earn significantly less than heterosexual ones.

But . . . try finding representations of poor or working-class gay people on *Will & Grace.* See how hard you have to search for media images of queers who are part of the vast working poor in this country. Find the homeless transgendered folks. Find stories of gay immigrants, lesbian moms working three jobs, bisexual truckers falling asleep from too many hours on the road, gay men in the unemployment line. Try finding an image of queer people who are balancing on the edge—or have fallen off.

The myth of our wealth goes deep, so deep that even other gay people seem to believe it. We have tried to protect ourselves from the hard truths of our economic diversity by perpetuating the illusion of material wealth, within the confines of male/female whiteness. This is a critical aspect of how we present ourselves in this country at this point in time. We treat the poverty that exists among us—as well as the differences of class—as a dirty secret to be hidden, denied, repelled. We treat economic struggle as something that functions outside the pull of queer desires, removed from our queerly lived lives.

As Badgett notes, by celebrating the myth of queer affluence, we have "drawn attention to exactly the kind of picture that Lou Sheldon is drawing of gay and lesbian people." There is a richer—and ultimately more sympathetic—queer reality: "We are everywhere—but we're all different."

Why is it so hard to acknowledge this? Why is poverty treated as a queer secret? And why does it produce a particular kind of homosexual shame? Bear with me. Imagine what you've never allowed yourself to see before.

When I directed the Lesbian AIDS Project at Gay Men's Health Crisis, stories of the hundreds of HIV-positive lesbians who were a part of that project literally came roaring out of those women's mouths. These were lesbians who had almost never participated in queer politics or visited any of New York City's queer institutions. On those rare occasions when they had tried, they quickly departed, unseen and unwelcomed.

Andrew Spieldenner, a young gay organizer of color who has worked for years with men who have sex with men, has a name for this phenomenon. He calls it "a queer and invisible body count." It is made up of poor lesbians and gay men, queer people of color, the transgendered, people with HIV and AIDS and—always and in large numbers—the queer young and the queer elderly.

The Metropolitan Community Church, a largely gay denomination, reports that the demand for food at its New York pantry has doubled since the beginning of welfare reform in 1996. The Lesbian & Gay Community Services Center says that homeless people in their addiction programs have tripled since then. The Hetrick-Martin Institute, which serves "gay and questioning youth," estimates that 50 percent of homeless kids in New York City are queer.

"We are entering a time when the economy is going into a slump," says Joseph De Filippis, who coordinates the Queer Economic Justice Network. "This isn't going to be like the '90s, when it was easy for employers to give things like domestic-partner benefits. There are going to be more and more of us who are affected by joblessness and economic crisis. And the welfare reform law expires in 2002. It's our issue, damn it. It has always been our issue."

Ingrid Rivera, director of the Racial & Economic Justice Initiative of the National Gay and Lesbian Task Force, has lived this issue. "I was on welfare, I was homeless, I thought I'd be lucky if I finished high school. I am a woman of color, I am a mother, and I am queer. I've worked and lived in a poor world and I've worked in queer organizations that are primarily white. I've seen it from both perspectives, and there's a kind of disconnect. In the gay, mostly white world, race and economic justice isn't talked about as a queer issue. And because of that split, queerness becomes a white thing."

Poverty and outright destitution can happen to anyone—and the queerer you are, the fewer safety nets exist to hold you up or bounce you back from the abyss. Queerness intensifies poverty and compounds the difficulty of dealing with the social service system. The nightmares—even in this city, with its gay rights law—include:

- Being separated from your partner if you go into the shelter system. Straight couples can remain together by qualifying for the family system.
- Being mandated into homophobic treatment programs for drug or drinking problems and having the program decide to treat your queerness instead of your addiction. If you leave the program, you lose any right to benefits—including Medicaid.
- Being unable to apply as a family for public housing.
- Ending up a queer couple in the only old-age home you can afford and being separated when you try to share a room.

Barbara Cassis came from a wealthy Long Island family. But when he began to understand and acknowledge his transgendered nature, his parents kicked him out. He was homeless, young, and broke. "Thank God for drag queens," she says, looking back. "A drag queen found me crying in Times Square and took me home. She talked to me about what I was going through, let me stay with her in her apartment, taught me how to support myself, how to get clients as a prostitute or in the gay bars where I could work as I transitioned. But then she died of AIDS and I was homeless again."

The homeless shelters were the worst experience of all for Barbara as a transwoman. Often, it felt easier to just stay on the streets. If you're homeless, and you haven't transitioned—which costs a fortune—you're forced to go to a shelter based on birth gender. The risk of violence and danger is always high for everyone; the shelters are crowded, short of staff, and the staff that is there has no training in how to deal with trans or gay issues. So if you are a transperson, just taking a shower means that you're taking your life in your hands.

"It took me years to get on my feet," says Cassis, now an administrative assistant at the Positive Health Project, "to start dealing with being HIV-positive, and get the training and education I needed to find a decent job. It has also taken years for me to reconcile with my family, which I have. If it hadn't been for the kind of people the gay community often discounts and despises, I wouldn't be here today."

Like my mother said, the only difference between a poor drunk and a rich one is which drunk can hide it. The shame of being poor is an acutely public shame, difficult to hide. And *queer* homosexuality—the kind of queerness that makes gender differences and radical sexual desires crystal clear—this queerness triggers similar ruinous social perils.

We punish people in this country for being poor and we punish homosexuality. When both are combined, it does more than double the effect: It twists and deepens it, gives it sharper edges, and heightens our inability to duck and cover or slide through to a safer place. It forces you to live more permanently outside than either condition dictates.

The problem intensifies when you realize what queers are in the mind of America. We stand for the culture's obsession with the erotic. It is we who are portrayed as always doing it or trying to, we who quickly become the sexual criminals at the heart of any story. We are the ones who are dangerous; our sexuality is more explosive, more explicit, more demanding, more predatory.

And so it goes for poor people: part stereotype (read trailer trash or welfare queen), part object of blame for being too stupid not to have done better. The underlying assumption is that the only appropriate desires are those that rest comfortably atop plenty of money. The desires and needs afforded by wealth—and plenty of it, earned or not—are appropriate, acceptable, good. But messy desires? Desires that combine with class and color? Desires and needs that ricochet around the erotic? These needs are not acceptable. They are condemned.

No wonder the gay movement can't see the poverty in its midst. The one thing this culture longs for and seems to value in queer life is the image of wealth. It appears to be the only thing we do right. And it is the only piece of our queerness that we can use when our citizenship is at stake. We learned this at the beginning of the AIDS crisis, when we activated that wealth to do what the government wouldn't: We built institutions to care and protect and serve our own. It is a riveting example of how we have claimed our own and valued what the mainstream culture despised about our lives. We could do the same with queer poverty.

"If the community got involved in the issues of being queer and poor," says Jay Toole, a lesbian in the LGBT caucus of the Coalition for the Homeless, "it would be like the community saying, 'I'm here, and here's my hand. You can go further, I'm here.'"

Toole is finishing school now. She plans to work as a substance abuse counselor, to go back into the shelters and bring gay people into the community, "so that they don't have to be so alone as I was. Because when Ann Duggan [from the Coalition] brought me back down to the Lesbian & Gay Center from the shelter, it was finally like coming home."

## ➤ John Aravosis

(October 8, 2007), United States

### "How Did the T Get in LGBT?"

Like an ever-expanding mushroom cloud of diversity, every few years America's gay leaders and activists welcome a new category of member to the community. Wikipedia walks us through our complicated family history:

"LGBT [lesbian, gay, bisexual and transgendered] or GLBT are the most common terms [to describe the gay community]. . . . When not inclusive of transgender people it is shortened to LGB. It may also include two additional Qs for queer and questioning (sometimes abbreviated with a question mark) (LGBTQ, LGBTQQ, GLBTQ2); a variant being LGBU, where U stands for 'unsure', an I for intersex (LGBTI), another T for transsexual (LGBTT), another T (or TS or the numeral 2) for two-spirited people, and an A for straight allies or asexual (LGBTA). At its fullest, then, it is some permutation of LGBTTTIQQA."

In simpler times we were all gay. But then the word "gay" started to mean "gay men" more than women, so we switched to the more inclusive "gay and lesbian." Bisexuals, who were only part-time gays, insisted that we add them too, so we did (not without some protest), and by the early 1990s we were the lesbian, gay and bisexual, or LGB community. Sometime in the late '90s, a few gay rights groups and activists started using a new acronym, LGBT—adding T for transgender/transsexual. And that's when today's trouble started.

America's gay community, or rather, its leadership, is apoplectic over the imminent passage of the first federal gay civil rights legislation, the Employment Non-Discrimination Act, or ENDA. ENDA would make it illegal for an employer to fire, or refuse to hire or promote, an otherwise qualified candidate simply because of their sexual orientation (gay, straight, lesbian or bisexual). (Contrary to popular belief, it is legal to fire someone for being gay under federal law and in 31 states.) You'd think this would be cause for celebration, but not so much.

ENDA was first introduced 30 years ago. In all that time, it only protected sexual orientation and never included gender identity. This year, that changed, and gender identity was added to the bill. Coincidentally, this year is also the first time that ENDA actually has a real chance of passing both the House and Senate—but only if gender identity isn't in the bill. So the bill's author, openly gay Rep. Barney Frank, D-Mass., dropped the transgendered from the bill, and all hell broke loose. Gay activists and 220 national and local gay rights groups angrily demanded that gender identity be put back in the bill, guaranteeing its defeat for years to come. Many of them, suddenly and conveniently, found all sorts of "flaws" with legislation that they had embraced the previous 29 years. They convinced House Democratic leaders to delay action on ENDA till later in October. They'd rather have no bill at all than pass one that didn't include the transgendered.

Then an odd thing happened. I started asking friends and colleagues, ranging from senior members of the gay political/journalistic establishment to apolitical friends around the country to the tens of thousands of daily readers of my blog, if they thought we should pass ENDA this year even without gender identity. Everyone felt bad about taking gender identity out of ENDA, everyone supported transgender rights, and everyone told me "pass it anyway."

Their main argument, which I support: practical politics. Civil rights legislation— hell, all legislation—is a series of compromises. You rarely get everything you want, nor do you get it all at once. Blacks, for example, won the right to vote in 1870. Women didn't get that same right until 1920. The Civil Rights Act of 1964 provided a large umbrella of rights based on race, religion, sex and national origin, but failed to mention gays or people with disabilities. People with disabilities were finally given specific rights under the Americans with Disabilities Act of 1990, but gays as a class have still to be granted a single civil right at the federal level. If we waited until society was ready to accept each and every member of the civil rights community before passing any civil rights legislation, we'd have no civil rights laws at all. Someone is always left behind, at least temporarily. It stinks, but it's the way it's always worked, and it's the way you win. . . .

I have a sense that over the past decade the trans revolution was imposed on the gay community from outside, or at least above, and thus it never stuck with a large number of gays who weren't running national organizations, weren't activists, or weren't living in liberal gay enclaves like San Francisco and New York. Sure, many of the rest of us accepted de facto that transgendered people were members of the community, but only because our leaders kept telling us it was so. A lot of gays have been scratching their heads for 10 years trying to figure out what they have in common with transsexuals, or at the very least why transgendered people qualify as our siblings rather than our cousins. It's a fair question, but one we know we dare not ask. It is simply not p.c. in the gay community to question how and why the T got added on to the LGB, let alone ask what I as a gay man have in common with a man who wants to cut off his penis, surgically construct a vagina, and become a woman. I'm not passing judgment, I respect transgendered people and sympathize with their cause, but I simply don't get how I am just as closely related to a transsexual (who is often not gay) as I am to a lesbian (who is). Is it wrong for me to simply ask why? . . .

I know firsthand that it's not safe in the gay community to ask questions about how the transgendered fit in. I also know that I am not alone in my questions, or my fear of asking them. While I've been taking abuse for my position, I've also been amazed by the number of phone calls, e-mails and people stopping me on the street here in Washington, both straight and gay, thanking me for asking the questions I did, for voicing the doubts that they share. (Not surprisingly, many of these expressions of solidarity have been off-the-record.) . . .

Conservatives understand that cultural change is a long, gradual process of small but cumulatively deadly victories. Liberals want it all now. And that's why, in the **culture wars**, conservatives often win and we often lose. While conservatives spend years, if not decades, trying to convince Americans that certain judges are "activists," that gays "recruit" children, and that Democrats never saw an abortion they didn't like, we often come up with last-minute ideas and expect everyone to vote for them simply because we're right. Conservatives are happy with piecemeal victory, liberals with noble failure. We rarely make the necessary investment in convincing people that we're right because we consider it offensive to have to explain an obvious truth. When it comes time to pass legislation, too many liberals just expect good and virtuous bills to become law by magic, without the years of legwork necessary to secure a majority of the votes in Congress and the majority support of the people. We expect our congressional allies to fall on their swords for us when we've failed to create a culture in which it's safe for politicians to support our agenda and do the right thing. ENDA, introduced for the first time 30 years ago, is an exception to that rule. It took 30 years to get to the point where the Congress and the public are in favor of legislation banning job discrimination against gays. . . .

That's why James Dobson, Tony Perkins and the men at the Concerned Women for America are so hell-bent on defeating ENDA. To the religious right, ENDA without gender identity isn't a weak, meaningless bill fraught with loopholes. Our enemies know that passage of any federal gay civil rights legislation is a legislative and cultural milestone that would make it that much easier for all of us—gays and lesbians, bisexuals and eventually even the transgendered—to realize all of our civil rights in our lifetime.

I'll take that half-a-loaf any day.

## ➤ Susan Stryker

(October 11, 2007), United States

### "Why the T in LGBT Is Here to Stay"

Pity poor John Aravosis, the gay rights crusader from AmericaBlog whose "How Did the T Get in LGBT?" essay, in reference to the controversy over gender identity protections in the pending Employment Non-Discrimination Act, was published on Salon a few days ago.

To hear Aravosis tell it, he and multitudes of like-minded gay souls have been sitting at the civil rights table for more than 30 years, waiting to be served. Now, after many years of blood, sweat, toil and tears, a feast in the form of federal protection against sexual orientation discrimination in the workplace has finally been prepared. Lips are being licked, chops smacked, saliva salivated, when—WTF!?!—a gaunt figure lurches through the door.

It is a transgender person, cupped hands extended, begging for food. Seems somebody on the guest list—maybe a lot of somebodies—let this stranger in off the streets without consulting everyone else beforehand, claiming he-she-it-or-whatever was a relative of some sort. Suddenly, what was supposed to be a fabulous dinner party starts surreally morphing into one of those OxFam fundraisers dramatizing third-world hunger whose sole function is to make the "haves" feel guilty for the plight of the "have-nots."

Maitre d' Barney Frank offers an elegant pretext for throwing the bum out. The establishment's new management, Speaker Nancy Pelosi, is caught off-guard by the awkward turn of events, but deftly shuffles the hubbub into the wings and starts working the room, all smiles, to reassure the assembled guests that a somber and long-sought civil rights victory will be celebrated in short order.

Aravosis and those who share his me-first perspective are not so sure. Seeing half a loaf of civil rights protection on the table before them, and sensing that the soirée might come to a premature and unexpected denouement, they make a grab, elbows akimbo, for said truncated loaf. This is, after all, their party.

In my line of work—teaching history and theory of sexuality and gender—we've invented a polysyllabic technical term applicable to Aravosis & Co., which is homocentric, whose definition Aravosis supplies when he asserts, as he did in his recent essay, that gay is the term around which the GLBT universe revolves. By gay he means gay men like himself, to which is added (in descending order of importance), lesbian, bisexual and transgender, beyond which lies an even more obscure region of poorly understood and infrequently observed identities.

Aravosis isn't questioning the place of the T in the GLBT batting order; he's just concerned with properly marking the distinction between "enough like me" and "too different from me" to merit inclusion in the categories with which he identifies. . . .

Aravosis, not being one to mince words when it comes to mincing meat, wants to know what he, as a gay man, has "in common with a man who wants to cut off his penis, surgically construct a vagina, and become a woman." The answer is "gender." The last time I checked my dictionary, homosexuality had something to do with people of one gender tending to fall in love with people of the same gender. The meaning of homosexuality thus depends on the definition of gender. However much Aravosis might wish to cut the trannies away from the rest of his herd, thereby preserving a place free of gender trouble for just plain gay guys such as himself, that operation isn't conceptually possible. Gender and sexuality are like two lines intersecting on a graph, and trying to make them parallel undoes the very notion of homo-, hetero- or bisexuality. . . .

Without solid theoretical ground to stand on, Aravosis resorts to flights of rhetorical fancy in lieu of an argument against gender protections. He characterizes the more than 300 GLBT organizations nationwide now on record as supporting a gender-inclusive ENDA, which collectively speak on behalf of hundreds of thousands if not millions of people, as plotting something of a palace coup. They attempt, he claims, to force the gay movement—along with the country that is poised to embrace them—to crawl unwillingly into bed with a big bunch of tranny whatevers. Aravosis positions himself as a man giving voice to an oppressed silent majority, a majority too cowed by their fear of appearing "politically incorrect" to express their true feelings, in order to proclaim "that over the past decade the trans revolution was imposed on the gay community from outside, or at least above."

. . .

Transgender people have their own history of civil rights activism in the United States, one that is in fact older, though smaller and less consequential, than the gay civil rights movement. In 1895, a group of self-described "androgynes" in New York organized a "little club" called the Cercle Hermaphroditos, based on their self-perceived need "to unite for defense against the world's bitter persecution." Half a century later, at the same time some gay and lesbian people were forming the Mattachine Society and the Daughters of Bilitis, transgender people were forming the Society for Equality in Dress. When gay and lesbian people were fighting for social justice in the militant heyday of the 1960s, transgender people were conducting sit-in protests at Dewey's lunch counter in Philadelphia, fighting in the streets with cops from hell outside Compton's Cafeteria in San Francisco's Tenderloin, and mixing it up at Stonewall along with lots of other folks.

There was a vibrant history of transgender activism and movement building through the 1970s, when it suddenly became fashionable on the left to think of transgender people as antigay and antifeminist. Gay people were seen as freeing themselves from the straitjacket of psychopathology, while transgender people were clamoring to get into the Diagnostic and Statistical Manual of the American Psychiatric Association; feminists were seen as freeing themselves from the oppressiveness of patriarchal gender, while transgender people were perpetuating worn-out stereotypes of men and women. It's a familiar refrain, even now. Transgender arguments for access to appropriate healthcare, or observations that no one is ever free from being gendered, fell on deaf ears.

Until the early 1990s, that is, when a new generation of queer kids, the post-baby boomers whose political sensibilities had been forged in the context of the AIDS crisis, started coming into adulthood. They were receptive to transgender issues in a new way—and that more-inclusive understanding has been steadily building for nearly two decades.

Aravosis and those who agree with him think that the "trans revolution" has come from outside, or from above, the rank-and-file gay movement. No—it comes from below, and from within. The outrage that many people in the queer, trans, LGBT or whatever-you-want-to-call-it community feel over how a gender-inclusive ENDA has been torpedoed from within is directed at so-called leaders who are out of touch with social reality. It has to do with a generation of effort directed toward building an inclusive movement being pissed away by the clueless and the phobic. That's why every single GLBT organization of any size at the national and state levels—with the sole exception of the spineless Human Rights Campaign—has unequivocally come out in support of gender protections within ENDA, and has opposed the effort to pass legislation protecting only sexual orientation.

What happens in Congress in the weeks ahead on this historic issue is anybody's guess. I urge all of you who support the vision of an inclusive ENDA to contact your representatives in government and let your views be known.

# CHAPTER 8

# Intersectionalities

Race, social class, gender, and sex are aspects of identity that intersect with queerness. This chapter highlights common struggles across different aspects of identities.

Audre Lorde is known for describing herself as "Black, lesbian, feminist, mother, warrior, poet." For Lorde, these markers interacted with and affected her life simultaneously.

Today, feminists, other activists, and those involved in the professions of law and social work use the term **intersectionality** to describe our complex awareness that we inhabit—and are inhabited by—multiple categories of identity and that our experience of several identities taken together may be emotionally, culturally, and materially different than the experience of any one particular identity category by itself. A white gay man, for instance, might feel oppressed by society's negative attitudes toward LGBT people at the same time that he enjoys privilege connected to being a white man. Conversely, a black gay man may experience his queerness not only as a gay man but as a black man; that is, he negotiates two minoritized categories in U.S. culture. His experience, however, is not necessarily one of just "doubled" oppression; rather, he may experience both a dominant culture and an African-American culture that code gayness as a white phenomenon, so his queerness may be invisible to many in his different communities. His experience of himself as a black gay man assumes complexities and nuances that are intrinsic to how this culture understands and constructs both race and sexuality. At the same time,

**Find Out More** about Marlon Riggs's view of his documentary, *Tongues Untied,* in Chapter 12 of this text.

intersectionality also allows us to see not only how multiple identities complicate our lives but also how the very aspects of our identity that are sources of oppression in one environment serve as sources of privilege in another. A butch lesbian, for example, may experience sexist and heterosexist oppression associated with her femaleness and her homosexuality; that same sexism may also transform her perceived masculinity into a kind of power (Gibson, Marinara, and Meem). And intersectionality is inescapable; we are all, as Lorde points out, influenced by a number of different (and sometimes even oppositional) aspects of our identities—whether we are conscious of it or not.

Let us consider a more specific example of how this may work. A New York court case known as *In the Matter of the Adoption of Evan* ruled that a nonbiological lesbian parent (Diane F.) could adopt the artificially inseminated child of her partner (Valerie C.). In reaching this ruling, the court found the adoption to be in the best interest of the child Evan and also cited other lesbian adoption decisions. The highest rationale seemed to be the validation of the nuclear family: "While noting financial and emotional reasons favoring the adoption, the court clearly viewed the legitimization of Evan's family as primary" (Rosenblum 98). The court officer made it clear that the class position of Evan's mothers was a strong supporting factor in his ruling: "Diane, age 39, is an Assistant Professor of Pediatrics and an attending physician at a respected teaching hospital. Valerie, age 40, holds a Ph.D. in psychology and teaches at a highly regarded private school" (Rosenblum 104). We may note the subjective inclusion of value judgments here: the hospital is "respected" and the school is "highly regarded." In contrast, let us consider the Mississippi case *White v. Thompson*. In this case, lesbian mother White lost custody of her children to her ex-husband's parents. Part of the stated reason for this ruling was that the court found White and her partner to be "unfit, morally and otherwise" to raise children because they were lesbians (Rosenblum 105). But a strong corroborating factor was social class. White worked in a convenience store, occasionally leaving the children unsupervised while they slept because she could not afford a babysitter. In addition, wrote the court, "[s]he and her lover . . . lived together in a trailer with their children" (qtd. in Rosenblum 105). Did Valerie and Diane win their adoption petition partly because of their class privilege? Did White and her partner lose custody partly because they were poor? Certainly, these cases raise questions about the way social class affects individuals' ability to show what in our culture is considered to be a "stable family environment" and to marshal the resources necessary to wage a protracted legal battle. The intersection of lesbianism and social class—and geographical location—had strong bearing on the legal outcomes of both of these cases.

Feminist scholars Gwyn Kirk and Margo Okazawa-Rey define **intersectionality** as "an integrative perspective that emphasizes the intersection of several attributes, for example, gender, race, class, and nation" (G-3). This definition seems straightforward, but as the two cases described above indicate, the impact on the personal lives of individuals can be quite complicated and varied because the complex of attributes differs from person to person. Within the intersectional paradigm, a lesbian is never just a lesbian, a gay man is never just a gay man, and so forth. The focus on intersectionality as a tool for conceptualizing the nature of interlocking oppressions arose in the late 1980s, when legal scholar Kimberlé Crenshaw used the idea specifically "to articulate the intersection of racism and patriarchy" and "to describe the location of women of color both within overlapping systems of subordination and at the margins of feminism and anti-racism" ("Mapping" 1265). Crenshaw pointed out that these "problems of exclusion cannot be solved simply by including Black women within an already established analytical structure. Because the intersectional experience is greater than the sum of racism and sexism, any analysis that does not take intersectionality into account cannot sufficiently address the particular manner in which Black women are subordinated" ("Demarginalizing" 140). Here she seems to be rejecting then-popular *inclusion theories,* such as multiculturalism. She implies that thinking in terms of intersectionality means doing important critical work that thinking in terms of inclusion does not. In an inclusive environment, individuals are encouraged to represent categories (a black man speaks for black men, or a lesbian speaks for lesbians, for example); inclusivity, in other words, involves the habitual use of essentializing, even stereotypical, attributes.

**Find Out More** about queer theory and identity in Chapter 11.

Intersectional analyses, on the other hand, attempt to de-essentialize identity by assuming multiple and shifting identifications; they also pick up on queer theory's postmodern notion of strategic identity performance. We recall that the women of the Combahee River Collective articulated their experience of multiple oppressions and general invisibility as black lesbians in the 1970s [λ Chapter 4]. In that spirit, using examples from law, literature, domestic violence discourse, and sensational public debate (the Anita Hill testimony at Clarence Thomas's confirmation hearing, for example), Crenshaw challenges antiracism and antisexism groups to rethink "the entire framework that has been used as a basis for translating 'women's experience' or 'the Black experience' into concrete policy demands" ("Demarginalizing" 140).

The introduction of intersectionality as a schema for approaching the study of queer oppression has developed as LGBT people have become increasingly aware of the ways in which attributes other than sexuality create intellectual, emotional, and material diversity. In the previous chapter, Queer Diversities, we discussed specific instances of how LGBT people are tolerated or discriminated against for their specific queerness [λ Chapter 7]. Intersectionality allows us to see an even more complex picture of how individuals are included or excluded by considering their queerness in its relationship to other identity categories, such as race, class, age, and nationality. In fact, we have come to see that the very notion of LGBT community is problematic because every member of the groups represented by those letters has had experiences that might not be shared or experienced similarly by the others based on their complex and multiple identities.

Keeping in mind these rich sociocultural contexts is crucial if we are to understand what sexual behavior means to individuals and to groups and if we are to avoid the trap of presentism [λ Introduction]. When collecting data about sexual behaviors in the 1940s and 1950s, Alfred Kinsey interviewed whites and blacks, rich and poor, but his analysis never focused on how sexuality is experienced differently across race and social class [λ Chapter 5]. Why are such omissions problematic? We know, for instance, that historically and contemporaneously, some people engage in homoerotic behavior without adopting gay or lesbian identities. It is also the case that, in some African-American and Latino cultures, a man can penetrate another man in a sexual encounter and not consider himself—or be considered by others—gay. In those cultures, men are figured as *penetrators* and women or gay men as the *penetrated*. Such examples clearly demonstrate that how one understands his or her sexuality is deeply rooted in other social and cultural contexts. Understanding the intersection of those contexts provides us a richer sense of how sexuality, race, class, gender, nationality, and other identity markers function simultaneously. We need to develop this sense if we are to understand better how sex and sexuality function in people's lives.

## The "Down Low" and Applied Intersectional Theory

Near the beginning of his article "Some Queer Notions about Race," Samuel R. Delany admits that he has "always felt a difficulty in discussing the problems [of race and sexuality] together." Specifically, he feels that "[t]o speak of gay oppression in the context of racial oppression always seemed an embarrassment. Somehow it was to speak of the personal and the mechanics of desire in the face of material deprivation and vast political and imperialist and nationalist systemics" (201). While we respect Delany's point of view and observe that he complicates the argument as the article goes on, we believe that our discussion of the importance of intersectional analyses demonstrates that issues such as race and sexuality cannot easily be separated. Claiming that one issue (such as race) is about "material deprivation" whereas another (sexuality) is about the "mechanics of desire" fails to account for the many ways in which sexuality issues are entangled in economic issues as well as the many ways in which racial issues are entangled in cultural notions about sex. Moreover, Delany's statement ignores the core feminist insight that "the personal is political" and that separating them elides the experiences of women and other "muted groups" (Ardener).

We can see the intersection of the personal and the political, and of race and sexuality, in representations of the phenomenon of the *down low,* a slang term describing what many (J. L. King, for instance) identify as a sexual phenomenon among some black men. The popular media tell us that these men form secretive groups whose purpose is providing opportunities to have clandestine sexual encounters with one another. The idea has been so intriguing to the American public that it became a topic on *The Oprah Winfrey Show* and *Law and Order: Special Victims Unit.* Between February and December 2001, the down low was the subject of feature stories in newspapers all over the country and in magazines such as *VIBE, Essence,* and *Jet.* Most of these stories portrayed black women as the unknowing victims of black men engaging in sexual behavior with one another and connected the down low with the spread of HIV/AIDS to these straight black women. Gay author and activist Keith Boykin, who doubts the truth of much down low mythology, writes, "The down low fit perfectly into larger cultural dynamics because it confirmed stereotypical values that many of us already believed. For some whites, it confirmed their hypersexualized perception of black people, and for some blacks it confirmed their hypersexualized perception of gay men. Given society's stereotypical view of black men combined with societal beliefs about homosexuality, the story became more believable because it vilified a group of people we did not understand and many of us did not want to know" (151).

Boykin's discussion is intersectional in that it deploys an analysis of race, sexuality, social class, and gender dynamics to help us understand why a phenomenon such as the down low so fully captured the American imagination. The enormous interest in the idea of black men meeting regularly to engage in sexual acts—and the idea that such behavior was somehow predatory and that it threatened the precarious hold many believed the United States had on the spread of HIV/AIDS—confirmed myths about black men that have been part of the public

**Figure 8.1**  Keith Boykin.

consciousness in this country since slavery. It also helped confirm what many people believed about gay men—namely, that sexually insatiable homosexual men spread disease through their behavior, which constitutes a sin punishable by painful death. What's more, stories about families affected by men on the down low confirmed what many have come to believe about heterosexual relationships by portraying women as the unwitting victims of men's sexual promiscuity. A single-issue analysis of media hype around the down low might have encouraged LGBT people to "adopt" the men portrayed in the coverage as gay men oppressed by a society that provides few outlets for the more open expression of their sexuality and pushes them into heterosexual relationships. And the statistics delivered by the Centers for Disease Control and Prevention (CDC), which seemed to indicate that more black women were getting AIDS than at any other point in the history of the disease, appeared to confirm the existence of a covert down low. However, Boykin points out that the CDC reported 4,000 fewer new cases of AIDS among blacks in 2001 than in 1991, while the percentage of AIDS cases among black women rose because the number of AIDS cases among white women decreased sharply during that same period (167). A misreading of the statistics, particularly the percentages, seemed to indicate a widespread down low phenomenon, while a closer look at the numbers challenged this assumption.

J. L. King, who is a primary focus of Boykin's criticism, as well as other men interviewed for stories on the down low, disagree with Boykin's claim that "America's recent obsession with the down low is not about the truth" (5), but it seems obvious that, whether or not the cultural phenomenon exists, Boykin's point about the reasons for its prominence in the collective American psyche makes some sense. After all, as the discussion of Kinsey in Chapter 5 illustrates, thinking about the private sexual lives of our neighbors titillates many Americans. What's more, on a very real level, confirmation of our stereotypes is comforting. When we examine the issue intersectionally—that is, when we consider how not only queerness but also race are understood and constructed in American society—we can easily see how panic about the down low arises. Many in the United States fear not only queer sexualities but also people of color; the combination of queerness and blackness, coupled with basic assumptions of male aggressiveness, led to a scenario in which it was easy to imagine covert black gay male predators infecting women at an alarming rate. The reality, of course, is not nearly so simple.

## Women, Class, and Internationality

Other important sexuality issues, particularly those involving the locations of women and lesbians, are best understood through intersectional analyses. In "Spirit and Passion," Carmen Vazquez argues that many gay rights strategies do not sufficiently or critically take into account "those of us who happen to be female, of color, working-class, or poor" (697). For Vazquez, political strategies that argue that gays and lesbians should be "mainstreamed" and given exactly the same rights as heterosexuals fail to recognize the economic injustices that many women throughout the world already face. Put another way, she asks us to reconsider the "mainstream" and whether or not it is worth joining. Gays, for instance, may seek the right to marry, but if the right to marry occurs in a context in which women are at a persistent economic disadvantage to men, then how do lesbians materially benefit from the right to marry? Marriage, too, is a double-edged sword, because in many countries, it is the primary vehicle of women's social and economic disempowerment.

**Figure 8.2** Carmen Vazquez.

The importance of considering such issues intersectionally becomes clear when examining marriage in an international context. In Bulgaria, for example, marriage is an economic imperative for women. A young woman typically goes directly from her parents' house to her husband's, never living on her own. This life trajectory militates against the development of lesbian relationships and cultures. Monika Pisankaneva writes that Bulgarian women "encounter more difficulties than men in starting a career; they are driven to low-rank professions like teachers, secretaries, nurses or shop-assistants; these 'female' professions are so poorly paid that no one could live independently earning so little" (139). Pisankaneva acknowledges that "young lesbians are more motivated than heterosexual women to leave their homes" but may be hampered in finding work if they appear too masculine. Thus, "[i]n long-term lesbian relationships it is usually the more feminine partner who becomes the breadwinner" while "[m]asculine-looking women usually find low-paid jobs such as shop assistants, construction or service workers" (139). This pattern resembles some typical **butch-femme** relationships in the United States in the 1950s, where the femme (because she enacted gender-normative female behavior) often functioned as the primary family wage earner (Kennedy and Davis). In both cases, the "employable" woman was invisible as a lesbian and merely put up with the economic deprivations associated with femaleness in her culture.

Both Pisankaneva and Kennedy and Davis link butch-femme gender presentation to nonelite class positioning. Alison Murray's analysis of Indonesian lesbian life points out that "[t]here is no lesbian 'community' in Jakarta, since class overdetermines both gender and sexuality" (166). At the same time, "lower class lesbians" are associated with "butch-femme roles, promiscuity, and insalubrious nightlife" (175). Murray interprets the correlation of lower social class with more rigid gender roles as an indicator of outness: "For the lower class without privileges to lose, overt signifiers of 'deviance' within a subcultural street milieu suggest a source of resistance to power" 166). Here again, we see that it is impossible to understand what it means to be lesbian in Indonesia without an intersectional analysis that includes gender and class in addition to sexuality.

We must not assume, however, that only women are restricted by cultural norms and economic placement from easy access to a queer life. Shivananda Khan describes the relationship between "high levels of sexual repression" and "urgent sexual release" for men in India. Sexual expression, writes Khan, must take place in a context of absolute lack of privacy. A man in New Delhi commented, "Privacy? What privacy? I share a room with my three older brothers, and I have had sex with all of them. The other room is where my parents and grandparents sleep. There is no lock on the door. In the hallway, my uncle and aunt sleep. It's like this everywhere in India" (110). Similarly, Tomás Almaguer writes that "[t]he constraints of family life often prevent homosexual Mexican men from securing unrestricted freedom to stay out late at night, to move out of their family's home before marriage, or to take an apartment with a male lover. Thus their opportunities to make homosexual contacts in other than anonymous locations, such as the balconies of movie theaters or certain parks, are severely constrained" (260). These examples highlight customs that work against male independence in ways that parallel the traditional cloistering of women within family space. In some cultures, familial identifications override other identity categories. In China, as Wah-Shan Chou argues, the traditional culture "simply refuses to classify people into homo or hetero because individuals (both women and men, homo or heterosexually inclined ones) are first and foremost members of the family and wider society" (34). Both parents and children internalize this way of being in the world. Thus, if a child comes out as a *tongzhi* (homosexual), parents feel "the shame of losing face for having a deviant child who does not get married." The young person, too, feels pain because "[i]n a society where filial piety is given the utmost importance in defining a person, hurting one's parents can be the most terrible thing for a *tongzhi* to experience" (34). Here, the intersection of non-endorsed sexuality and a powerful family-centric social organization works against individual agency. This pattern may occur even in a space of relative freedom such as the United States, where individualism is a central value. Ann Allen Shockley, for instance, writes of the fictional Roz, a black woman who brings her white lover Marge "Home to Meet the Folks." Roz's mother is surprised and disappointed, but her Black Nationalist brother and his wife are overtly hostile; they castigate Roz not only for being a lesbian but for being a race traitor.

**Find Out More** about the link between nationalism and homophobia in Sonnet Gabbard's article in the readings at the end of this chapter.

We have already seen how conservative social and sexual values have been used to bolster a nationalist agenda [λ Chapter 3]. In Russia, after the 1917 revolution, the Bolshevik state considered homosexuality a "degenerative disease of the terminally bourgeois" and urged prominent gay men to marry women or leave the country. According to Laurie Essig, "Under the Soviets, . . . [h]omosexuality was a crime not just against 'nature' but against society. Homosexual acts were treasonous in the (dis)utopia of the Workers' State" (5). Similarly, in Cuba during the 1960s (and to some extent still today), homosexuals were defined as second-class citizens. They were excluded from membership in the Communist Party, which in itself guaranteed an inability to rise in the social order. Fidel Castro reportedly refused to believe that any homosexual could be "a true Revolutionary, a true Communist militant" (Lockwood 124). Ian Lumsden feels that the real sin was never homosexuality per se but rather male resistance to the powerful cult of *machismo,* or hypermasculinity. The Cuban state seems to have worried less about bourgeois corruption than about effeminacy. In Cuba, Lumsden writes, "[s]exual orientation is inferred from gender identity rather than vice versa, as tends to be the case in North America" (132). Therefore, a man who exhibits even the slightest "effeminate" behavior (crossing one leg at the knee or gesturing expressively while talking) is assumed to be homosexual. Here again, we see how an intersectional analysis reveals linkages among sexuality, gender, cultural and social organization, and citizenship.

## Tools for Intersectional Analysis

The concept of intersectionality is often difficult to grasp until we think simultaneously—and critically—about our own multiple identities. When we consider our personal traits and characteristics in relation to one another, in relation to varying cultural contexts in which those identities occur, and in relation to changes in those identities over time, we can understand how the concept of intersectionality applies to our own lives. Scholars have invented several different diagrams and exercises designed to enhance our understanding of intersectionality. These diagrams offer us a picture of how identities, sociocultural contexts, and political realities intersect.

A popular self-classification tool from the feminist consciousness-raising movement of the 1970s (with some modifications by us) asks its users to position themselves within a hierarchical model according to their multiple identifications and their experience of privilege or oppression associated with each (see Figure 8.3).

| Most Relative Privilege | Male | Middle Class | Heterosexual | White | Young | Able-bodied | Thin | Christian | Butch |
|---|---|---|---|---|---|---|---|---|---|
| Less Relative Privilege | Female | Working Class | Lesbian, Gay | Of Color | Middle-Aged | Differently Abled | Larger | Religion other than Christian | Femme |
| Least Relative Privilege | Gender not easily pegged as female or male | Poor | Bisexual, Transgender | | Old | Disabled | Fat | | |

**Figure 8.3** Relative Privilege and Oppression.

Users of this tool mark characteristics of their own identities then think about them in terms of the privilege or oppression they experience in relation to those identifications. As you may notice, when you try this exercise for yourself, the outcome is more complicated than you might expect. For instance, someone who performs the intersectional identification female, lesbian, of color, and butch might find that the butch identification, when combined with other factors, does not necessarily translate into a greater degree of privilege than the femme, as the table indicates it should.

In "Thinking Sex: Notes for a Radical Theory of the Politics of Sexuality," Gayle Rubin observes that "the realm of sexuality . . . has its own internal politics, inequities, and modes of oppression" (4). Rubin describes a "sex hierarchy" composed of an inner "charmed circle" and the "outer limits." She characterizes the charmed circle as comprising "normal, natural, healthy, holy" sex and the outer circle as "abnormal, unnatural, sick, sinful" sex (14). (See Figure 8.4.)

Rubin observes that "[t]his kind of sexual morality . . . grants virtue to the dominant groups, and relegates vice to the underprivileged." This particular way of doing intersectionality simultaneously analyzes political, legal and moral usage; we may recall the value judgments that lay behind the New York and Mississippi adoption and custody decisions discussed earlier in this chapter. Rubin makes the point that this way of figuring sexuality resembles what she calls "ideologies of racism" (15), and if you examine Rubin's charmed circle carefully, you will see how it also recognizes ideologies of classism in our society. Monogamous married heterosexual sex at

**The charmed circle:**
Good, Normal, Natural, Blessed Sexuality
Heterosexual
Married
Monogamous
Procreative
Non–commercial
In pairs
In a relationship
Same generation
In private
No pornography
Bodies only
Vanilla

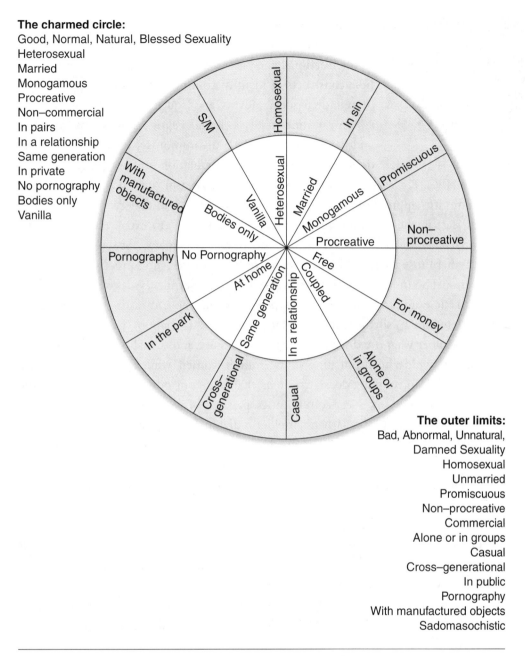

**The outer limits:**
Bad, Abnormal, Unnatural,
Damned Sexuality
Homosexual
Unmarried
Promiscuous
Non–procreative
Commercial
Alone or in groups
Casual
Cross–generational
In public
Pornography
With manufactured objects
Sadomasochistic

**Figure 8.4** Gayle Rubin's charmed circle.

home is far closer to the center of the circle as opposed to sex for money or in public. What assumptions are made here? Certainly, the economic stability of married home life is privileged over alternative forms of sexual expression, and the close connection of sexuality with economic stability (you should have sex in the privacy of your own home) stigmatizes those who cannot afford such a luxury as privacy or who need to supplement low incomes through sex work. Rubin assumes that sexuality and class

**Find Out More** in Kathy Y. Wilson's "Just a Closer Walk with Thee" in the readings at the end of this chapter.

intersect to promote certain kinds of lives and intimacies and to disparage others.

Intersectional analyses provide a valuable sense of how multiple constructs of identity, community, and ideology combine to reinforce social norms and squelch dissent. Patricia Hill Collins, writing in *Black Sexual Politics,* argues that "[r]acism and heterosexism . . . share a common set of practices that are designed to discipline the population into accepting the status quo" (96). For example, both racism and heterosexism draw boundaries around whom it is appropriate to love and be intimate with, and they reinforce the norm (at least in the West) as predominantly white and heterosexual. Indeed, crossing racial lines in love is still culturally discouraged in many parts of the world—whether those relationships are hetero- or homoerotic. And so too is crossing generational boundaries. Age intersects sexuality in powerful ways, as we demonstrated with the example of ancient Greek pederasty and the contrasting example of the contemporary North American Man/Boy Love Association (NAMBLA). But in many other ways, we draw boundaries around age and sexuality; we are often disturbed by older men pursuing younger adult women, while an older woman and younger man coupling doesn't seem as challenging or odd. Why is this so? At the same time, in many queer communities, pairings of older and younger people are not uncommon, particularly as an older individual can assist a younger individual financially and in getting a start in adulthood. Examining such dynamics offers us a richer sense of how people organize—and are allowed to imagine—their lives.

Thinking about race, gender, class, age, and sexuality simultaneously shows us how ideologies based on them serve particular political interests and agendas. Understanding these matrices provides us a way to analyze—and critique—interlocking oppressions. In the following chapters, we will continue to represent queerness as it intersects a variety of other significant markers of identity, community, and ideology. Doing so not only will allow us to represent queerness with the complexity it deserves but will also show us how many different members of LGBT communities throughout the world construct their identities, form communities, and critique the sociocultural pressures that frequently oppress them.

## QUESTIONS FOR DISCUSSION

1. Intersectional analyses offer us ways to understand queerness in particular and sexuality in general as they are embedded in other sociocultural and political contexts. Look back at some of the ways in which we, the authors of this textbook, have represented queerness in earlier chapters. Where might some of our representations, in specific cases, have become all the richer with additional intersectional analysis? Try your hand at rewriting some of our examples with that added emphasis.

2. Some critics have argued that intersectional analyses are so complex that they work against the possibility of cogent political action. That is, if identities are so complex, then how can we argue for and achieve broad political change based on them? How might you address such a criticism? What are the ways in which intersectional analyses might actually support political change?

3. Richard Ford's article "What's Queer about Race?" in the readings at the end of this chapter describes the liberating feel of a queer theoretical approach to notions of race. Think about Ford's point. Do you agree? If gayness and gender (as well as marriage) can be subject to "corrosive critique" via the concept of queer, can race also be fruitfully analyzed in this way?

## REFERENCES AND FURTHER READING

"About Audre Lorde." *The Audre Lorde Project Inc.* Web. 19 July 2008. <http://www.alp.org/about/audre>.

Almaguer, Tomás. "Chicano Men: A Cartography of Homosexual Identity and Behavior." *The Lesbian and Gay Studies Reader.* Eds. H. Abelove, M. Barale, and D. Halperin. New York: Routledge, 1993. 255–73. Print.

Ardener, Shirley, ed. *Perceiving Women.* London: Malaby Press, 1975. Print.

Boykin, Keith. *Beyond the Down Low.* New York: Carroll & Graf, 2005. Print.

Chou, Wah-Shan. "Homosexuality and the Cultural Politics of *Tongzhi* in Chinese Societies." *Gay and Lesbian Asia: Culture, Identity, Community.* Eds. G. Sullivan and P. Jackson. Binghamton, New York: Harrington Park Press, 2001. 27–46. Print.

Collins, Patricia Hill. *Black Sexual Politics: African Americans, Gender, and the New Racism.* New York: Routledge, 2005. Print.

Crenshaw, Kimberlé. "Demarginalizing the Intersection of Race and Sex: A Black Feminist Critique of Antidiscrimination Doctrine, Feminist Theory and Antiracist Politics." *The University of Chicago Legal Forum* (1989): 139–67. Print.

———. "Mapping the Margins: Intersectionality, Identity Politics, and Violence against Women of Color." *Stanford Law Review* 43 (July 1991): 1241–99. Print.

Delany, Samuel R. "Some Queer Notions about Race." *Queer Cultures.* Eds. D. Carlin and J. DiGrazia. Upper Saddle River, NJ: Pearson/Prentice Hall, 2004. 199–219. Print.

Essig, Laurie. *Queer in Russia: A Story of Sex, Self, and the Other.* Durham, NC: Duke UP, 1999. Print.

Fellows, Will. *Farm Boys: Lives of Gay Men from the Rural Midwest.* Madison: U of Wisconsin P, 1998. Print.

Ford, Richard Thompson. "What's Queer about Race?" *South Atlantic Quarterly* 106.3 (Summer 2007): 477–84. Print.

Gabbard, Sonnet. "Preserving the Nation: Transitional Serbia, the European Union, and Homophobia." Unpublished MA Thesis. 2012. Print.

Gibson, Michelle, Martha Marinara, and Deborah T. Meem. "Bi, Butch, and Bar Dyke: Pedagogical Performances of Class, Gender, and Sexuality." *College Composition and Communication* 52.1 (2000): 69–95. Print.

Kennedy, Elizabeth Lapovsky, and Madeline Davis. "Living Arrangements and the Organization of Domestic Life." *Boots of Leather, Slippers of Gold: The History of a Lesbian Community.* New York: Routledge, 1993. 283–93. Print.

Khan, Shivananda. "Culture, Sexualities, and Identities: Men Who Have Sex with Men in India." *Gay and Lesbian Asia: Culture, Identity, Community.* Eds. G. Sullivan and P. Jackson. Binghamton, NY: Harrington Park Press, 2001. 99–115. Print.

King, J. L. *On the Down Low: A Journey into the Lives of "Straight" Black Men Who Sleep with Men.* New York: Broadway, 2004. Print.

Kirk, Gwyn, and Margo Okazawa-Rey. *Women's Lives: Multicultural Perspectives.* New York: McGraw-Hill, 2000. Print.

Lockwood, Lee. *Castro's Cuba, Cuba's Fidel.* New York: Macmillan, 1967. Print.

Lumsden, Ian. *Machos, Maricones, and Gays: Cuba and Homosexuality.* Philadelphia: Temple UP, 1996. Print.

Murray, Alison J. "Let Them Take Ecstasy: Class and Jakarta Lesbians." *Gay and Lesbian Asia: Culture, Identity, Community.* Eds. G. Sullivan and P. Jackson. Binghamton, NY: Harrington Park Press, 2001. 165–84. Print.

Nichols, Jean Brashear. "The Friday Night Bunch: A Lesbian Community in West Texas." *Journal of Lesbian Studies* 9 (2005): 73–80. Print.

Pisankaneva, Monika. "Reflections on Butch-Femme and the Emerging Lesbian Community in Bulgaria." *Femme/Butch: New Considerations of the Way We Want to Go.* Eds. M. Gibson and D. Meem. Binghamton, NY: Harrington Park Press, 2002. 135–44. Print.

Rosenblum, Darren. "Queer Intersectionality and the Failure of Recent Lesbian and Gay 'Victories.'" *Law & Sexuality* 4 (1994): 83–122. Print.

Rubin, Gayle. "Thinking Sex: Notes for a Radical Theory of the Politics of Sexuality." *The Lesbian and Gay Studies Reader.* Eds. H. Abelove, M. Barale, and D. Halperin. New York: Routledge, 1993. 3–44. Print.

Seo, Dong-Jin. "Mapping the Vicissitudes of Homosexual Identities in South Korea." *Gay and Lesbian Asia: Culture, Identity, Community.* Eds. G. Sullivan and P. Jackson. Binghamton, NY: Harrington Park Press, 2001. 65–79. Print.

Shockley, Ann Allen. "Home to Meet the Folks." *The Black and White of It.* Weatherby Lake, MO: Naiad, 1980. 51–59. Print.

Vazquez, Carmen. "Spirit and Passion." *Queer Cultures.* Eds. D. Carlin and J. DiGrazia. Upper Saddle River, NJ: Pearson/ Prentice Hall, 2004. 689–98. Print.

Wilson, Kathy Y. "Just a Closer Walk with Thee." *Cincinnati Magazine,* July 2008. Web. 21 November 2008. <http://www .cincinnatimagazine.com/article.aspx? id=54522>.

# READINGS

## ➢ Kathy Y. Wilson

(July 2008), United States

### "Just a Closer Walk with Thee"

Call her a radical. Call her an upstart. Call her a lesbian BaptiMethoCostal. Just don't call Pastor Lesley E. Jones's Truth & Destiny Covenant Ministries a gay church.

The chrome-studded motorcycle should be a dead giveaway. So should the lovers' casual touch during service. But at first blush, little about Truth & Destiny Covenant Ministries in Northside is easily reconcilable or recognizable if yours is a—let's get this out of the way right now—homophobic, fire-and-brimstone church experience.

Not the motorcycle out front on warm Sundays driven there by a black lesbian; not the same-gender couples who share Bibles and blithely brush against one another like intimates; not the teenagers who run the aisles with abandon, dancing and shouting in Pentecostal fits of Holy Spirit calisthenics. And certainly not the Rev. Lesley E. Jones, the lesbian pastor who cofounded Truth & Destiny Covenant Ministries (TDCM) in 2003. Adorned in a cassock and square-toed patent leather loafers, Jones sings, sweats, prays, shouts, and leads her congregation of 100-plus members through to salvation.

Worship at TDCM is different from worship at mainline white churches; different from worship at many black churches, too. Rest assured, at Truth & Destiny, no one will ever use the lame analogy about God creating "Adam and Eve, not Adam and Steve." If you're gay or lesbian, you will not be preached about in the third person; you won't be told to change your ways or risk eternal damnation. All gender identities, races, sexual orientations, and even faiths are embraced at TDCM. Jones's business card states the mission clearly: "Preaching the Radically Inclusive Gospel." The banner hanging outside above the door trumpets a similar message: "Boldly Proclaiming God's Love For All People."

TDCM exists despite, and maybe even because of, the homophobia and misogyny ensconced in some segments of the black church, whether Baptist, Pentecostal, Episcopal, or Methodist, and it's on its way to being a groundbreaking model of "radically inclusive" worship for congregations struggling to adopt more progressive practices. This small church is gearing up for nothing short of a revolution. And Reverend Jones, a 41-year-old lesbian mother who dedicated her life to Christ during childbirth—*she shall lead them.*

"You wanna know how to stay on the battlefield?" Reverend Jones asks rhetorically, surveying her congregation. "Listen to a good soldier. Don't just study the Bible, study the people of God."

Her robe is cinched at the waist by a wide purple sash. She's skulking across the pulpit, wiping her brow and gripping the microphone. Directly behind her, seven small glass block windows form a cross in the wall. To the left, there's a full drum kit. A center aisle leads directly to the pulpit. The church is casual, with worshipers wearing jeans, shorts, and sneakers and walking around during songs, sermons, and passages of personal testimony.

They call out "Pastor Lesley" while she's preaching or making announcements. In turn, she is relaxed, confident, straightforward. Of average height and build, she is a brown-skinned woman with thick, shoulder-length black hair that she wears tied back until, in a moment of particular fire and fervor, she unleashes it for effect.

It's the first Sunday in April and the small, spare church is nearly full. There are teenagers, elderly women from the neighborhood, lesbian couples, and several single men all sitting on straight-back chairs. The congregants are rapt and responsive. Some fidget with Holy Spirit tics—rocking, pushing to the edges of their seats, hands flapping mid-air. They are filled with religious energy waiting to be uncorked by the right scripture, the perfect intonation, the well-placed hymn.

"I can tell who's saved and who's carnal-minded," she says.

"C'm*ooon*, pastor," someone pleads.

"And just because you're carnal-minded doesn't mean you're not saved. It means you're nominal . . ."

"*Huh!*" someone hiccups in a James Brown punctuation.

". . . you're doing just enough," Jones finishes.

Then Jones mixes the sin of Saturday night with the redemption of Sunday morning. "Some of y'all need to git *loooow*!" she exhorts, dramatically stomping back to the corner of the pulpit and squatting low to the ground. It's the lyric from a strip club anthem, the song directed at strippers dancing for cash, but she's flipped it into an admonition for the heaven-bound: *Get low to avoid being beaten down by life.*

Then Jones redirects the sermon. She's responding to the way some people—Christian folks—gossip about TDCM. She's talking about the way the community-at-large whispers that her church is "The Gay Church."

"I keep telling you this ain't a *gay* thing. It's a *God* thing," Jones says. Therein lies the mission and founding tenet of Truth & Destiny Covenant Ministries: Everyone is welcome here. The fact that outsiders translate that as "gay church" is a testament to how unwelcome gay and lesbian Christians feel in other churches.

"Some churches make you fill out applications," Jones points out to her congregation. "They want to know your income and they make you show a W-2, ask you about your roommate," she says, pantomiming air quotes when she says *roommate.* "'Well, how many bedrooms you got?'"

This mockery of other, less tolerant congregations draws titters. "God is creating a movement of the radically inclusive," she tells them. "When we go out into the world we need to be careful that we're teaching people not what we *think* is right, but what we *know* is right. And that is that God has always been radically inclusive."

Jones's proclamation is the antidote to long-held beliefs among some Christians about what constitutes abomination (homosexuality); who goes to hell for it (homosexuals); and even who is welcome in the church (homosexuals generally aren't, unless they are choir members or musicians). Reconciling faith and sexuality for blacks is no more difficult than it is for white believers. However, blackness can cloud and confound that reconciliation. Some black Christians believe homosexuality is an "attack" on the black family; some feel the fight for gay rights distracts from racial equality; others believe homosexuality is just plain wrong, or it's "the white man's problem." Conversely, progressive black theologians say all discriminatory thought and practice is wrong, and they call for the black church to return to its role as the center of unbiased social and faith works.

Meeting Jones and visiting her church blurs all the right/wrong/heaven/hell absolutes, the judgment, theory, and theology. A conversation with her could be subtitled "How To Reconcile Faith and Sexuality For Bigoted Dummies." That's what her church is about.

But don't call it "the Gay Church."

"Pastoring can take a toll on your relationship, especially if you're pastoring alone," says Jones. We're sitting in the cold and cramped supply room that doubles as the church office. She's dressed casually in a gray T-shirt, loafers, and slacks with a faint pinstripe. In person she is warm and forthcoming, even-keeled and funny. But her pulpit and her personal life have commingled with difficulty. She explains that she and her partner of nine years, Rosa Jones, the woman with whom she founded TDCM, separated in December. (They are now in the process of reconciling.)

"Planning a church is like any other business," Jones says. "The first five years you work to build." And in building her church, she says, "one of the things I failed at was publicly acknowledging my spouse."

In that way, Jones isn't so different from many mainline pastors who struggle to balance their public and private lives. Except that most pastors don't have to put so much energy into explaining that what they do is, indeed, the Lord's work. "Everybody here is not lesbian, gay, bisexual, trans, questioning, or queer," she says. "There are straight folks who are here because the gospel is taught and they believe in inclusion. They also believe in the social justice [work] we do here. We take care of the poor, the sick—and that attracts a lot of people. We purposely don't wave a [gay] pride flag."

Further, in the sanctuary there's no picture of Christ—He of the flowing dark hair, sandals, and robes who could double as a Grateful Dead fan. Why? "We can't put Jesus up on the wall until we can find a rainbow Jesus of every hue, image, and nationality," Jones says. "That white male dogma? That's not the Jesus I know."

Searching for that Jesus, six years ago Jones and Rosa gathered 20 friends for dinner at their home. "What would your church look like?" the two women asked. Then they scribbled notes on newsprint they hung around the room.

"They wanted a place where their family could be celebrated," Jones says. "A place where youth and children were valued, a variety in the worship style—a blend of liturgical and freestyle. They wanted a multi-ethnic and multi-racial [church] . . . a place where people valued people. I remember this one," she recalls. "They said, 'If I'm not at church, I want someone to miss me.'"

Despite the passion and specificity of those worship wishes, after dinner the pages were rolled up and slid beneath the bed. Jones attended several racially diverse, gay-friendly congregations in Cincinnati, but never felt satisfied. She hungered for something more deeply rooted in the black church tradition of bombast and pageantry. After three years and deep consultation with the Rev. Darlene Franklin, pastor of Full Truth Ministries in Detroit, Michigan's oldest predominantly black radically inclusive congregation, and with the Rev. Bonnie Daniel, now retired from New Spirit Metropolitan Community Church in Northside, Jones took the next step. She and Rosa started TDCM in 2003 as "a place to worship in the full truth of our life that also met our spiritual needs."

"I didn't one day plant myself and just say, 'I'm gonna pastor me a church,'" Jones jokes. She started her career as a teacher—first in Cincinnati Public Schools and then at Marva Collins Preparatory School in Silverton. Fans of 1320 AM WCVG, a now-defunct gospel station, may remember her; she was the station's morning show announcer and sales manager from 1995 to 2000. She also worked as a program director at the YMCA. In 2000 she joined the Hamilton County Human Relations Commission, ultimately ascending to director, a post she held until 2006. Jones has a bachelor's degree in social sciences from Miami University and certificates in ministry and pastoral counseling from Light University, an online pastoral program, but she is also working on a certificate of ministry from New York Theological Seminary, from which she intends to ultimately receive a master's degree in divinity. When people ask about her credentials, she likes to say, "I got a SBG degree—Sent By God!"

A self-described "BaptiMethoCostal," Jones was born in North Carolina but raised off and on in Middletown, where she graduated from Middletown High School. Her father is Baptist, her mother Methodist, and one of her grandmothers was a Pentecostal evangelist. She's the only child of her parents' marriage, but has two teenaged adopted stepbrothers. Coming out to her family was "a challenge," she says; she didn't do it until she was 33. She knew she was gay as a teenager. But she was also sexually curious, and she got pregnant at 19 as a freshman at Kentucky State University. The birth of her son Blake, now a student at Cincinnati State, was her "coming to know Jesus experience," as she calls it.

"I really prayed for a son," she says. "I was reading the story of Hannah and she prayed for a son [Samuel], so I prayed that prayer. It was during a time when I was really being beaten down in the church."

The judgment leveled at her by church members made Jones more spiritually determined. In 1988, when she turned 21, she rededicated her life to Jesus Christ. However, revealing her sexuality to her family didn't come so easily. When she did finally come out to her mother, she did it in a letter. With a letter, she says, "I could say what I needed to say without being interrupted." Her mother's initial reaction was to declare that she was going to have her daughter "kidnapped and deprogrammed." Jones accepted it as an emotional and visceral response to life-altering news. "Although my mother has struggled with who I am, she's come to church, she's participated," she says. Her mother's way of letting Jones know that she was OK with her daughter's sexuality was by bringing Jones's brothers to church, too. "We have to realize our parents are grieving," she says. "They're coming out, too."

Jones, however, has less patience for the myopia of some black ministers and their churches. "They're so comfortable in their chauvinism, [and] in their homophobia," she says. "Misogyny and homophobia [are] prevalent in ministry across the board. They're comfortable with the 'Don't ask/Don't tell' policy."

Jones wants to be part of changing that. She wants her church to make people stand up and take notice. "We're a revolutionary concept," she says. "I believe it's in process."

The chasm between traditional black churches and their gay and lesbian brethren is part of the complicated history of black Christianity in America.

Theologian and author Kelly Brown Douglas, the Elizabeth Connolly Todd Distinguished Professor of Religion at Goucher College in Baltimore, Maryland, knows the subject well. In 1985, Douglas was the first black woman—and only the fifth nationwide—ordained an Episcopal priest in the Southern Ohio Diocese. She is straight, but the Dayton native's path was sometimes made arduous by a black male bishop who "stopped my ordination a few times for no other reason than that I was a woman," she says. She notes that, paradoxically, early black Christians incorporated the oppression, repression, and bigotry they saw in white churches into their own.

"Most black people became Christian during the Great Awakenings, the Evangelical revivals of the late 1700s and the early 1800s," Douglas says. In the Evangelical view, "You had to overcome the passion of the body. Paul's edict in Corinthians—it's better to marry than to burn with passion—speaks to that."

In 1999, Douglas published *Sexuality and the Black Church: A Womanist Perspective,* a seminal text outlining the far-reaching roots of homophobia and sexism throughout the black faith community. "We must take into account how black people have been caricatured in this country and that is sexualized," she says. "To be 'normal sexually' is to abide by the norms and standards of white patriarchal narratives—however they do it." And that includes using religion as a weapon of oppression.

"The black church's own history is ironic," she says. "They weren't allowed to be who they are and now they're not allowing [gay and lesbian] people to be who they are."

However, the black church clearly is not a monolith. "The 'capital C' black Church is made up of multitudinous, disparate churches, diverse by congregational size," she explains. "You can have megachurches and storefronts; you can have very sedate and very rapturous. It is rural, suburban, urban, AME, CME. What makes black churches part of the black Church is what roots them to history."

The Rev. Damon Lynch Jr., the brazenly progressive 69-year-old pastor of New Jerusalem Baptist Church in Carthage, a 2,200-member "megachurch," is one such minister rooted to history. He says that he was galvanized to support and protect gay rights by the historical events that unfolded during his lifetime. "I was fortunate to come along when the country was on fire," he says. "When the Kings and the Andy Youngs and the Abernathys came to town, I was the one who went to the airport to go get them."

Lynch sits back in his spacious church office, its walls crammed with images: Nelson Mandela, Malcolm X, the Rev. Martin Luther King Jr., framed clips of Lynch marching, several city proclamations, and a strange photo of Lynch and the Rev. Donald Jordan stiffly flanking George W. Bush. "I've been a proponent for gay rights for years—during the days when this city was intolerant," says Lynch. "Me coming up in Cincinnati and Georgia before that, I know what that was about. Discrimination of any kind isn't right."

From 1996 to 1999, Lynch was president of the Baptist Ministers' Conference of Greater Cincinnati and Vicinity. Lynch would intermittently come to public logger-heads with the Rev. Fred Shuttlesworth, the proudly conservative civil rights stalwart who has opposed gay rights. The disagreement reached its apex in the battle over Cincinnati's human rights ordinance, which culminated in 2004 with the repeal of Article XII, the city's so-called "anti-gay amendment."

"I became the bad guy within the black ministers," Lynch recalls. "'Reverend—you go out there for those homosexuals and those sissies!'" he adds, mocking black preachers who questioned his loyalties. "Shuttlesworth was saying, 'If Martin was alive, he'd be siding with us.' Miss Coretta King came here and said, 'That's not true, Fred,'" his voice affecting that of a genteel southern woman's.

Despite some public grilling for his beliefs, Lynch doesn't mince words about the homophobia still rampant in some black churches. "I think we're the most homopho-bic going," he says. "We can be as liberal as we wanna be on social issues but when it comes to sexuality issues, we're hypocrites."

Lynch says Jones has visited his church; he also knows her because of her involve-ment with the Human Relations Commission. Her work is "exemplary," he says. "It's impeccable."

In Lynch's view, there are black preachers who are simply stultified by their own homophobia. Scripture in their hands is a tactic. "The Bible says 'unequally yoked' and it has nothing to do with sexuality, it has to do with unbelievers," he says. "But they will take it and make it any other thing."

Like Brown-Douglas, Lynch weaves the ugly dangling threads between black homophobia and white supremacy. "White folks used [religion] against black and white," he says. "When people are working out of emotion and don't know the Bible, you've got a helluva problem on your hands."

For her own support and continued growth, Jones attends a Bible study every Monday along with eight theologians—all female. She says being a woman in the black church is as groundbreaking as being a lesbian, but it's those inherent differences that make women (gay or straight) effective church leaders.

"Women bring balance to the church when they're in leadership roles. Pastoring among men is mainly competitive. In the black church you're not considered a great preacher unless you can tune"—an old-school, singsong-y practice that blends preaching with singing. "Women tend to be more theologically sound because they have something to prove. Men compete: 'How big is your church?' That size thing is for real," she says. "Being women in the church allows us to be more sensitive. Women bring a balance to that hard, direct kind of way and we balance men in their competitiveness."

Jones feels that women have historically been "unwelcome" in the pulpit. She cites Isaiah 54, an account of "the future glory of Zion," which begins: "Sing, O barren woman, you who never bore a child."

"[There] we'll get into the unwelcome, the unclean, the unproven," she says, paraphrasing Isaiah 56: 3–5. "God speaks to the eunuch and says, *Because of your faithfulness I will make your home greater than my sons and daughters in Israel.* When I read that, God obviously was looking for something different in the heart of man. That's where my faith journey toward God really speaks to me. As a woman I've been relegated to second-class citizen in the church."

TDCM is part of The Fellowship, a 100-member trans-denominational network of congregations practicing radical inclusion. It's led by Bishop Yvette Flunder, pastor of San Francisco's City of Refuge Church. Terry Hocker, TDCM's associate pastor, sees Jones taking a leadership role in an organization like The Fellowship, perhaps even becoming a bishop herself. "When I look at it from the outside, yes, I believe [TDCM] is revolutionary," Hocker says. "It is the stuff denominations are made of."

For Jones, a woman whose church started in her heart and then her living room, it's a noteworthy progression. The historical ramifications of being in the vanguard of a fledgling movement with such personal investments at stake aren't lost on her. "We're forerunners in this," she says. "I don't think the congregation has gotten it yet, but we're on the cusp."

She believes that ultimately other people of faith will open the doors of their sanctuaries to this new idea and to the brothers and sisters they've cast aside. "I can still go to a Baptist church and meet Jesus in my heart," she says. "But if my heart doesn't change about people, I'll never see the people for who they are."

Kathy Y. Wilson. Originally published in the July 2008 issue of *Cincinnati Magazine*.

## ➤ Richard Thompson Ford

(2007), United States

### "What's Queer about Race?"

When I announced my engagement to be married, almost everyone offered the obligatory congratulations and best wishes and left it at that. Marriage is, of course, a social ritual of script and conscription—there is a very limited range of polite reactions one can have to the announcement of a marriage engagement. Decidedly not among them: "Married? You're *getting married*? Hold on a minute, I need a drink." This was precisely the reaction of a very dear friend to my happy news. But I was expecting it. She, a scholar who had studied the institution with the beady-eyed, corrosive curiosity of a coroner establishing the cause of a death, was a rare critic (not to say *opponent*) of marriage. She knew more about matrimony than most—certainly more than I. My impression was less that she thought I was making a life-altering and potentially catastrophic mistake, like enlisting in the Marine Corps—though she may have thought that too—than that I was taking the safe and boring way out. "I'd always thought of you two as a hip unmarried couple," she mused.

Later, this same friend was visiting and noticed our "engagement photos." (For the uninitiated: these are photos of the happy couple in staged romantic natural settings and vaguely suggestive "candid" poses; intended to convey to the viewer the dewy optimism of love's first bloom, they customarily involve beaches at sunset, sylvan landscapes, and the couple gazing longingly into each other's eyes or lounging in precoital bliss.) To the chagrin of our wedding photographer, we insisted on taking ours at a bar, martinis in hand, evoking companionship, we thought, but also insisting on the cosmopolitan and profane side of the erotic—more film noir than romantic comedy. The photos were in black and white, a medium suited to invoke instant nostalgia and to highlight stark contrasts in tone, such as the black bar top and the white cocktail napkins, the reflective gleam of the silver shaker and the light-absorbing matte black of a leather jacket, or the deep chestnut tone of my skin and the almost luminescent blond peach of hers. My friend (let's call her "Janet") scrutinized the photos and then remarked, approvingly, "You *really are* an interracial couple. It's easy to forget because I know you so well, but looking at this picture. . . . It's still pretty transgressive, isn't it?"

I take it as almost axiomatic that queer theory embraces, even celebrates transgression; it seeks the sublime not in resistance—that's too damn bristly and self-serious—but in blithe and gleeful disregard for social convention. While its matronly stepsister gay rights wants equal access to mainstream social conventions—however ramshackle and dilapidated or procrustean they may be—queer theory is interested in shaking them up so we can see which ones aren't fit for human habitation. The normalization strategy of gay rights is to merge so seamlessly and imperceptibly into mainstream institutions that it seems impossible to imagine it could ever have been any other way; by contrast, queer theory opts for bullying, razzing, and mocking social conventions until it's hard to imagine them in the same way. So queer theory has always had a potentially broad applicability. If gay rights would say of marriage, "You have it; why shouldn't we?" (an uninteresting claim, but one that's hard to argue with), queer theory would say, "Married? You're getting *married*? Hold on a minute, I need a drink."

The not-too-subtle insinuation that marriage—not its hetero-exclusivity but marriage itself—might be the appropriate target of critique makes queer theory portable to foreign and exotic social contexts in a way that gay rights discourse cannot be. Despite what right-wing paranoiacs like Tom DeLay might believe, gay marriage really has little to do with my heterosexual marriage one way or the other. By contrast, a queer theory critique of marriage generally applies to me and mine as much as to Ellen DeGeneres and Rosie O'Donnell.

But why stop there? After all, marriage is a sitting duck; as Laura Kipnis points out, its critique is almost as much a part of the culture as its incessant celebration—before lit-crit attacks on holy matrimony, there was Al Bundy, before him Jackie Gleason,

Henry VIII, Agamemnon.[1] No, queer theory's radical attack targets not marriage, but identity. Here's what Janet Halley has written apropos:

> One is a lesbian not because of anything in oneself, but because of social interactions, or the desire for social interactions: it takes two women . . . to make a lesbian. . . . Similar things can be said about gay men, homosexuals, bisexuals . . . transvestite . . . transsexual/ transgendered people . . . and sexual dissidents of various . . . descriptions. Even more complex challenges to the coherentist assumptions about identity politics emerge when attention focuses on the question of the merger, exile, coalition, and secession of these constituencies. . . . Sexual orientation and sexuality movements are perhaps unique among contemporary identity movements in harboring an unforgivingly corrosive critique of identity itself. . . . The term "queer" was adopted by some movement participants in part to frustrate identity formation around dissident sexualities.[2]

So *queer* denotes not an identity but instead a political and existential stance, an ideological commitment, a *decision* to live outside some social norm or other. At the risk (the certainty) of oversimplification, one could say that even if one is born straight or gay, one must decide to be queer.

Queer theory's anti-identitarianism is the key to its portability: just as the queer critique targets marriage generally—not just its straights-only exclusivity—so too the queer critique of (nominally) gay identity politics would seem to apply to identity politics generally. If gay identity is problematic and subject to a corrosive critique, mightn't other social identities be as well? Obviously, the next domino vulnerable to toppling is gender. It's easy enough to read some aspects of gay, lesbian, and transgendered politics as partially—perhaps even fundamentally—critical of gender identity. And as Halley suggests, this is potentially disruptive of other identities: doesn't a critique of gender destabilize the woman-in-a-man's-body/man-in-a-woman's-body idea of transsexual identity? Unlike Judith Butler's idea of drag as resistance to gender identity,[3] the goal of this type of transsexual identity is not to do gender badly but to do it well; indeed, to *get it right*, to correct nature's mistake and make the body correspond to an intrinsically gendered soul. But, of course, the idea that gender is something one could get right is anathema to much of modern sexuality discourse as well as much of modern feminism. It would seem that one can't take both the critique of gender and the man-in-a-woman's-body transgender identity seriously. Bye-bye, mutually supportive coalition politics; hello, civil war.

As our row of dominos succumbs to gravity, racial identity has been the last to fall. Why the last? Unlike sex difference, which is still widely taken for granted as real, biologically determined, fixed, and intrinsic, it is now widely acknowledged that racial identity is fictitious: the political Right now champions a norm of color blindness, while the postmodern Left insists that race is a social and ideological construction. So

---

[1]Laura Kipnis, *Against Love: A Polemic* (New York: Pantheon, 2003).

[2]Janet E. Halley, "'Like Race' Arguments," in *What's Left of Theory: New Work on the Politics of Literary Theory*, ed. Judith Butler, John Guilory, and Kendall Thomas (New York: Routledge, 2000), 41.

[3]Judith Butler, *Gender Trouble: Feminism and the Subversion of Identity* (New York: Routledge, 1990).

one would expect a critique of racial identity politics to follow hard on the stilettos of queer theory's critique of sexual identity politics.

But racial identity has proven remarkably resistant to critique. Even hard-core social constructionists backpedal, hastening to add to their critiques the caveat that racial identities—however constructed and inessential—are the product of the "real lived experience" of racial discrimination, of social and political communities, and of distinctive cultural norms, all of which are, of course, as real as the hand in front of your face (which is poised to bitch-slap you if you deny it), even if race itself isn't. And while the Right sings a stridently anti-identitarian gospel of "color blindness" when resisting affirmative action, they change their tune when it comes to profiling criminals, diagnosing diseases, or choosing spouses.

The resulting schizoid relationship to race is the stuff of farce. Race-conscious progressives insist that generalizations about race are valid for purposes of university admissions but not for stopping terrorists from boarding commercial aircraft or interdicting drug couriers on the nation's freeways; conservatives insist just the opposite. Advocates of multiracial identity beat up relentlessly on racial essentialism when pressed to choose one and only one race, but their solution is to insist on multiracial categories and designations to reflect their "true" racial identity.

So Left and Right have an interest in protecting racial identity, albeit for different purposes. And also for the same purposes: an unexamined psychological commitment to race as an intrinsic identity motivates Left identity politics and the right-wing bigotry underlying *The Bell Curve* or William Bennett's offhand suggestion that the crime rate would drop if all black infants were aborted.[4] Most people want to believe that races are real. It seems that race, like the presumption of innocence, the Hippocratic oath, or "till death do us part," is too useful a fiction to dispense with.

Racial identity, like sex identity, comes with a set of norms attached; there are (politically) correct ways of exhibiting black, Asian, Latino, and white race—what Anthony Appiah calls racial "scripts"[5]—just as there are established norms for male and female gender. As with gender, many of these norms are very difficult to distinguish from common stereotypes. In socially fluid and insecure environments—cities, large corporations, universities—conventional racial scripts enjoy a magnetic pull. Strangers need easy sources of identification. Alienated and isolated individuals crave belonging. Race supplies these: provided everyone keeps to the script, you can count on a community in almost any unfamiliar setting. Just as an American tourist seeks out McDonald's for a reliable taste of home, so too people look for standardized racial norms as an anchor in alien territory— safe, predictable, comforting.

But maybe not all that healthy. And definitely not all that interesting.

Cruising along at high speed on the momentum of the canon wars, by the 1990s multiculturalism had influenced Left liberal legal theory in a big way. Civil rights law reform proposals had taken a sharp identitarian turn; the vogue was to emphasize the ineluctable nature of group cultural difference and insist that law should account for, embrace, and enforce it. According to a raft of law review articles written since the early 1990s, race discrimination laws should be expanded to require employers to

---

[4]Richard Herrnstein and Charles J. Murray, *The Bell Curve: Intelligence and Class Structure in American Life* (New York: Free Press, 1994); William Bennett, Morning in America, radio program, September 28, 2005.

[5]Kwame Anthony Appiah, "Identity, Authenticity, Survival," in *Multiculturalism: Examining the Politics of Recognition*, ed. Amy Gutmann (Princeton, NJ: Princeton University Press, 1994), 160–61.

accommodate racially specific cultural and social practices. The logic of these proposals consistently asserted the unambiguous and uncomplicated relationship between race and behavior: racial scripts exist, and to resist or challenge them—even to neglect them—is invidious discrimination on the basis of race.

Queer theory's destabilizing agenda offered me a way to resist the super-sizing of identity politics at a moment when it seemed at its most preeminent. In my recent book *Racial Culture*,[6] I advanced an attack from the Left on racial identity politics in legal theory. I argued that the cultural rights law reform proposals either asserted or implied a "repressive hypothesis" that assumed that racial power was exercised exclusively in the attempt to censor or repress expressions of racial difference. Following Foucault, I insisted that this conception of power was inadequate: the production of racial expression and racial norms was also an exercise of power, one made all the more potent by its ability to blend into a background landscape of seemingly unregulated and voluntary family and leisure-time social relationships. Stripped of this naturalistic camouflage, politically correct norms of racial conduct could be seen as mechanisms of coercion:

> The necessary correlative to this unearned solidarity is an unwarranted presumption about the entailments of group membership. There is a peculiar variant of political correctness, one that regulates, not what can be said about a minority group by outsiders, but instead the behavior of group members. This political correctness requires and duly produces opprobrium for people who miss their cue: we encounter "Oreos"—blacks on the outside who don't "act black" and therefore presumably aren't black "on the inside"—and quickly enough other racial groups acquire similar figures (for some odd reason all refer to food): Asian "bananas," Latino "coconuts," Native American "apples." These figures of scorn imply that there is a particular type of behavior that is appropriate to a given race, and thereby censure deviation from it. (39–40)

*Racial Culture's* approach to questions of race and racial justice was heavily influenced by queer theory. Queer theory not only offered a new theoretical frame within which to understand and analyze the often severely coercive aspects of Left liberal racial identity politics; just as important, it also offered an alternative attitude, tone, or "stance" to occupy in relation to it. As I argued, "One of the most effectively spellbinding aspects of [identity politics] has been its somber and weighty sanctimoniousness, which has intimidated those who might puncture its pretensions and deterred deserved critique" (211). Pretentious and preachy diction has become one of the hallmarks of identity politics scholarship. The hushed and respectful tones of the cemetery and the sonorous oratory of the pulpit both serve an important rhetorical function: to preempt from the outset the possibility that what is being said might be trivial or laughable. Worse yet, the etiquette of the funeral and of the sermon rules out the important stylistic mode of playfulness, the devices of satire and lampoon, the analytics of irony, and the aesthetics of wit.

Queer theory offered me an alternative mode—indeed, an antagonistic mode—of engagement with identity politics scholarship and with racial identity itself. Rather than a Hobson's choice between polite and reserved acquiescence—a sort of forced

---

[6]Richard Thompson Ford, *Racial Culture: A Critique* (Princeton, NJ: Princeton University Press, 2005). Subsequent citations will be given parenthetically by page number.

conscription into institutions of social regulation—or a shrill and angry reaction, queer theory offered a third way, one I find liberating and creative. Instead of insincere congratulations and best wishes or angry denunciation, one could begin by reaching for the Jack Daniels and highball glass.

Modern identity politics has old and deep roots, but it blossomed in the social movements of the 1960s. The politics of the new Left became institutionalized in law reform, in the academy, and in the set of prescriptions and admonishments that travel under the title "Morality." This is by and large a success story, but it has a melancholy subplot. The energy, joy, sexiness, and fun of the counterculture was largely—perhaps inevitably— stripped away as the politics of the new Left became mainstream. Ideas became dogmas, rebellion was reduced to rules, commitments became cages. The mainstreaming of identity politics made it routine rather than spontaneous; made it more prescriptive and less liberating; swapped the tang of volunteerism for the bland flavor of obligation.

And, perhaps worst of all, academic identity politics became the domain of the expert. As the term *political correctness* suggests, identity politics developed an increasingly intricate sense of decorum: there was a right way to go about things and a million ways for the novice and the dilettante to screw up. The controversies over terminology were the most striking example of this preciousness. Quick, which is correct: Negro, Black, black, Afro-American, African American, colored person, person of color? Gay, queer, gay men and lesbians, gay, lesbian, bisexual, and transgendered? Ladies, women, womyn? Is the gendered pronoun okay? S/he (or does that suggest the female gender is just adjunctive to the male)? He/she? It? Maybe it's better that you just sit in the back of the room and listen. The acknowledged message behind all of this correctness was loud and clear: social justice was the domain of the professional—don't try this at home, kids.

Queer theory offered a way to take race politics back from the professionals. It had—at least it seemed to me—a closer and fresher connection with the everyday life of a counterculture, with its contradictions, its sweaty struggles, its passions, its screwups, its street styles and fashion faux pas. Queer theory, with its open-handed conflicts and negotiations between gay men, lesbians, trannies, butch and lipstick lesbians, tops, bottoms, clean-shaven Chelsea boys and bearded burly "bears," felt like London's music scene in 1979, with its allied, agonistic, and frantically creative relationship between punks, mod revivalists, teddys, skinheads, rude boys, two-tones, new romantics. By contrast, the bloated academic conventions of race and gender identity politics slipped into self-parody worthy of Spinal Tap; the scripted rebellion of the academic new Left looked as uncomfortable as Bob Dylan in a tuxedo. My ambition in *Racial Culture* was to write about race without regard to the professional conventions of the genre—to just grab a guitar and play what sounded good. I wanted to say all of the things I had always thought and then censored, without regard to whether they would be received as "liberal" or "conservative"; I wanted to ignore orthodoxies—not self-consciously challenge them but just write as if they weren't relevant.

So queer theory offered three tools important to my work: the substantive critique of identity; critique as a *style* (much in the way Susan Sontag famously described camp as a style,[7] and with many affinities—satire, lampoon, irony, and wit) that could be used

---

[7]Susan Sontag, "Notes on 'Camp,'" in *Against Interpretation and Other Essays* (1966; New York: Anchor Books, 1990), 275–92.

in discussing serious political and social questions; and the liberation from professional orthodoxies: the virtues of apostasy over piety, the productive clash of ideas being worked out, "cults" being formed and broken apart, the energy of an avant-garde (to use an archaic term) in constant motion. That's better than any wedding gift I can imagine.

Ford, Richard Thompson. 2007. "What's Queer about Race?" *South Atlantic Quarterly* 106(3): 477-84.

## ➢ **Sonnet Gabbard**

(2012), United States

### **"Preserving the Nation: Transitional Serbia, the European Union, and Homophobia"**

October 2, 2011 stood to be yet another litmus test for lesbian, gay, bisexual and transgender (LGBT) rights in Serbia. Could Belgrade's LGBT communities safely gather publicly for a second consecutive Gay Pride Parade? One year earlier, LGBT community members, activists, and allies held the first Gay Pride Parade in ten years. While the freedom to gather publicly and protection from Serbian police were certainly steps forward for LGBT rights, participants and the police protecting them faced violent outbursts in 2010 from homophobic soccer hooligans and nationalists. Organizers were anxiously awaiting the parade, hoping that the negative aspects of 2010 would be assuaged, given support from the European Union, international aid and non-governmental organizations (NGOs), the Ministry of Interior, and local human rights activists and organizations. Unfortunately, October 2, 2011 came and went without a Pride Parade in Belgrade. The week leading up to the event, the Minister of Interior, a former member of Slobodan Milosevic's party[1], announced that his forces would not and could not protect Pride participants from potential anti-gay violence, thus motivating the Serbian parliament to ban the parade.[2] European Union members and delegates were all but silent[3]. After nearly a year of preparation and anticipation, Pride organizers and participants were left to decide whether to move forward with the already planned parade in spite of its attendant insecurities. Rather than having a formal pride event without police protection, the group decided to do a visibility action by walking to the square. The event lasted only an hour, and was not well attended. The sudden cancellation was a blow to LGBT activists and organizers, particularly considering the strides for LGBT rights that had been made during the previous year.

[1] Ivica Dačić, along with the first openly gay Serbian politician, Boris Milicevic, is a member of the Socialist Democratic Party.

[2] CNN Staff Writer. "Serb Authorities Prohibit Gay Pride Parade." *CNN.com.* Accessed October 2, 2011. <http://www.cnn.com/2011/10/01/world/europe/serbia-gay-pride/>

[3] In fact, the reaction from the EU delegation was tepid at best. The head of the EU delegation, Vincent Degert, said to the Serb radio station B92, "There is no condition for Serbia to hold one, two, five or ten parades in order to join the EU. That's not the way we think." "Pride Parade not condition for EU – EU rep." B92. 26 Sept. 2011. Web. 12 Apr. 2012. <http://www.b92.net/eng/news/politics-article.php?yyyy=2011>.

The homophobic rhetoric and threats of antigay violence surrounding the 2010 and 2011 Belgrade Gay Pride Parades serve as a snapshot of the many challenges facing LGBT communities in Serbia, and reflect the broader "gender norms"[4] crisis underway in the post-conflict transition[5]. Not only are community members under regular attack by nationalist and right-wing leaders, they are also constantly negotiating a somewhat precarious relationship with the Serbian government. The government wavers in its support for gay rights by implementing laws and policies in-name-only in order to line up with neoliberal-inspired European Union mandates and policy recommendations.[6] As one Serbian LGBT activist put it, "the [2010] pride parade was a really significant event because for the first time there was a successful public showing of differences in a collective manner. It was a success because it happened, it occurred. It wasn't a success at the same time because there were a lot of attacks. . .so it was like a war zone. . . but it happened."[7] In this sense, LGBT responses to homophobic violence in post-conflict Serbia offer two inter-related sets of dilemmas. First, the way in which heteronormative notions of gender and sexuality are understood and negotiated in Serbia reflects a broader set of transnational disputes concerning "the family" underway throughout the world today. From the passage of same-sex partner recognition policies in both the global North and South (e.g., Netherlands, Canada, South Africa, Argentina), to homophobic state responses including the near passage of the death penalty for individuals considered "homosexual" in Uganda, homosexuality itself has become a terrain of dispute in broader struggles concerning national sovereignty, democratization and transitional justice. This is indeed the case in Serbia, a country undergoing dramatic political and economic change following an intense period of conflict. Second, and in relation to this, the Serbian state is simultaneously contending with nationalism (which tends to be protectionist and inward-looking) and economic/political integration into the EU (which tends to orient the state and nation outwards, to the regional/global market and global political community). In Serbia, as elsewhere, struggles concerning "the family" are heightened in an increasingly hyper-heteronormative nation, one that

---

[4]By gender norms crisis I am referring to the tensions brought about by Serbia's integration into the European Union. This state of transition has created new forms of xenophobia and homophobia by highlighting the EU's entry requirements, such as Serbia's adoption of equal rights laws for the LGBT community. Thus, joining the EU has triggered resurgence in a heterocentric pro-family agenda for many, resulting in a perceived need to reestablish traditional masculine and feminine roles and a heterosexual nuclear family structure.

[5]Following nearly a decade of armed conflict, Serbia is now in a post-conflict state, and transitioning from an authoritarian socialist governance and economic structure to a neoliberalized democracy and economy. Serbia's application to join the European Union is one example of the ways in which the country is attempting to shed its socialist and conflict-riddled past and become a part of a neoliberal democratic and economic entity.

[6]Amy Lind provides a working definition of neoliberalism: "'Neoliberalism' is not easy to define. This is so, I have found, because neoliberalism does not refer only to a set of economic policies—as some might believe—but rather to a political strategy which relies upon an ideology of the market and implementing a certain set of policies." Amy Lind, "Making Feminist Sense of Neoliberalism: The Institutionalization of Women's Struggles for Survival in Ecuador and Bolivia." *Journal of Developing Societies* 18.2-3 (2002): 228-58.

[7]See Nenad Popovic interview transcript.

seeks to define itself as "different from" the "imposing" EU. The EU's top-down policy recommendations and suggested strategies for implementation of equal and human rights[8] create a dualistic, contradictory result for Serbia's LGBT communities. While the EU's mandates for equal rights and protection create space for public dialogue, recognition, and potential "security" for LGBT communities, the disconnect between public policy and public opinion has created an increase in anti-gay rhetoric and violence.

Focusing on post-conflict transitional Serbian society allows me to examine the lasting effects of war, militarism, and nationalism not only on those who fought in and were victims of the conflicts, but also on the civilians who survived the war. Therefore it is imperative to discuss post-conflict Serbian civil society, especially the challenges and changes confronting the women's movement and newly targeted groups such as gays and lesbians, in light of historic nationalism and Serbia's bid to join the European Union and generally "integrate" its economy into the global market.

Coupled with both governmental transitions, Serbia's economy has experienced a wave of transnational neoliberal capitalist investment over the past few years. What was formerly a somewhat isolated socialist economy is swiftly becoming a liberalized economy with foreign investors at the helm.[9] Together with the rise in privatization of industry is the elevating of the importance of civil society to the democratization of Serbia both on the local level and through foreign aid and development. While this trend to privatize industry and promote welfare through privately funded civil society is not unique to countries in transition[10], what is particularly striking about the Serbian case are the various vehicles[11] being used to promote neoliberalism. For example, the European Union strongly encourages the passing of certain types of laws in an effort to "democratize" Serbia, such as anti-discrimination laws, with the carrot being entry into new economic markets.

### Nationalism and the Rise of Homophobia in Serbia

In order to understand Serbia's unique transitional state, a brief historical context is needed. A decade following the most recent bloody ethnic conflict in Kosovo, the breakup and wars in the former Yugoslavia[12] (and the arrest and trial of the former Serbian leader Slobodan Milošević for war crimes) Serbia is slowly rebuilding. During this time of transition, many women's organizations and lesbian and gay organizations have reported a continuance of ultra-nationalism and xenophobic radicalism (Bakić 2009). Despite these ugly trends, the Serbian government is making attempts to transition towards international recognition as a peaceful democracy with hopes of joining the EU, as demonstrated by their recent cooperation with the search, arrest, and finally handover to the International Court of Justice in The Hague of Radovan

---

[8]E.g. Serbian Parliament's passing and implementation of the non-discrimination acts, organizing of the Serbian Gay Pride Parades, and other attempts to create and implement equal rights legislation.

[9]See Zoran Ristić. "Privatisation and Foreign Direct Investment in Serbia." *South-East Europe Review* (2004): 121-36.

[10]Ibid.

[11]Ibid.

[12]For more information on the most recent Balkan Wars see Silber and Little. *The Death of Yugoslavia.* London: BBC Books, 1996.

Karadžić, Ratko Mladić, and Goran Hadžić[13] following years of pressure from the international community. Proponents of joining the European Union argue that becoming a member would create significant improvement to Serbia's post-socialist economy. In addition to the economic gains, supporters also argue that entry to EU would further legitimize Serbian democracy and help reposition the state from a post-conflict society to a fully functioning democracy.

Serbia is on the brink of major change of status in the international community. While these efforts symbolize a break from the ultra-nationalist past, Serbia is still wrestling with waves of radical nationalism, xenophobia, sexism, and homophobia. Political scientist Sarah Correia discusses the rise in nationalism in Serbia among Serbian youth, saying, "Extremist right-wing groups define themselves as 'patriots' defending national independence and integrity both from outside threats and internal denigration" (Correia 2010). With the promise of EU integration looming, there has been a resurgence in efforts to preserve the national identity, and by extension, to promote reinvestment in the "national family." We see this manifested in Serbian nationalist rhetoric of "family values" coupled with homophobic sentiments.

Serbian politicians have hardly welcomed EU pressure to integrate LGBT rights into Serbian government. This is particularly evident in looking at politicians' public statements to Serb media outlets. Labris, one of Serbia's oldest lesbian organizations, published a report on the status of the LGBT population in Serbia in 2010 looking specifically at the media coverage of the 2010 Belgrade Pride Parade. The report serves as a snapshot of some of the opponents to LGBT rights and the challenges imposed on individuals who identify as lesbian, gay, bisexual, and transgender in Serbia. In their analysis of the media coverage of the Pride Parade, Labris writes that prior to 2010, most news stories focusing on LGBT issues appeared in *Entertainment* sections. However, in the months leading up to and following the 2010 Pride Parade, LGBT issues gravitated to *Politics and Society* columns. This movement represents a shift in the overall social and cultural dialogue around recognition and legitimization of LGBT politics and issues. That being said, the report is quick to point out that overall balance and representation of both LGBT communities and anti-gay forces is lacking (Labris report 2010: 9). According to the report, homophobic discourse was increasingly reported in the months leading up to the Parade, with few responses solicited from LGBT organizations or community members. One frequent topic was the homophobic rant *du jour* from Dragan Marković Palma ("Palma"), president of the parliamentary party Serbia United and mayor of the Central Serbian city, Jagodina. When asked about his opposition to the Pride Parade, Palma said:

> "[My political party] is opposed to displays of sexual orientation in public places. One of the most democratic countries—France, has recently banned the wearing of the burqa in public places, although it is the Muslim tradition for over 1,000 years. Do we really have to agree to something that has no tradition whatsoever? Since when is it considered a Serbian brand for men in thongs and vibrators to strut around in the streets. I have nothing against them doing what they please within their own four walls, let them rent a convention space and do what they want. This has nothing to do with the violation of human rights,

---

[13]The Bosnian Serb war criminals charged with engineering and leading the execution of unarmed Muslim Bosniak men and boys in Srebenica, Bosnia during the war.

seeing how the gay parade was banned in Moscow last year. This has everything to do with mocking the Serbian Orthodox Church and Serbian people, and we at JS cannot ban the parade, but we will not support it either" (Palma, Alo, July 26, 2010, Labris publication 10).

Here Palma is attempting to compare Serbian politics to French secularism while in the same breath drawing on notions of Serbian religious tradition. Additionally, his desire to contain what he interprets as blatant displays of non-heterosexual love and desire for private spaces further supports the fundamental purpose of Pride Parades, that is, to promote political, social, and cultural visibility, to come out of various metaphorical closets.

As the Labris report mentions, Palma was not alone in 2010 in his anti-gay sentiments. According to the report, media outlets regularly published homophobic slurs by Serbian politicians, such as Jovan Marić's statement that the parade "significantly demolishes the traditional values of the traditional values of the Serbian people, the Serbian Orthodox Church and the Patriarch are against it, and the Patriarch has the last say" (Dnevnik September 26, 2010, Labris report 2010:10). Bora Đjođević's more aggressive statement to Kurirborders on hate speech: "I have nothing against fags, I apologize for using that old term for them, but let them fuck in the ass at home. Dick in the ass till they rupture, it's totally fine, it's gay culture. . ." (Kurir, October 3, 2010, Labris report 2010 10). These examples demonstrate that homophobia is still rampant in Serbian politics and culture.

It is important to note that sentiments similar to Đjođević's, Palma's, and Marić's are not new to Serbian political and public discourse regarding LGBT issues. Irene Dioli writes, "LGBTIQ individuals in (former) Yugoslavia have a history of being denied a space—first because of the invisibility cloak forced upon them (socially and legally) during the socialist regime, and then because of hegemonic nationalistic ideologies enforcing the traditional hierarchic gender binary and preventing or limiting, with propaganda as well as sheer violence, the safe, natural expression of sexual diversity" (Dioli 2009: 1). Dioli's account highlights the wave-like process whereby homophobia has afflicted Serbian society. What began as keeping LGBT individuals and identities in the closet during socialist Yugoslavia has morphed into a new form of homophobia couched in preserving an ultra-nationalist notion of Serb identity. That which threatens the proliferation of the Serb race (whether it be Serb integration into the EU, non-Serbs, or LGBT individuals) faces resistance.

Dioli posits that Yugoslavia's gendered violence during the ethnic conflicts has further solidified hyper-gendered norms and expectations, which grew out of militarism, violence, and propaganda. In referring to the post-Yugoslav states (such as Serbia), she writes, "In the former Yugoslav context, the rise of nationalist trends after the demise of Yugoslavia and the ethnically framed wars of the nineties have violently brought normative gender enforcement to the surface of public discourse" (Dioli 2009: 3). Dioli's recognition of the relationship among militarism, war, and gender norms is useful, particularly when considering the rhetoric ultra-nationalists use to stoke both anti-gay and anti-EU fires. The same people who regularly use xenophobic language, warning of foreigners, Albanians, Muslims, Croats, Roma, homosexuals, etc. as threats to the Serb nation, are those who had ties to Serb paramilitaries and nationalist leaders during the wars.

The case of transitional Serbia and LGBT rights is just one slice of a broader consideration of the "globalization of homophobia" (Bosia and Weiss, forthcoming). It is important to inject a sexuality studies perspective into the debates surrounding post-conflict studies and nationalism. I attempt to do so in three ways. First,

I incorporate theories on nationalism, violence, and extremism developed during the ethnic conflicts and apply them to a post-conflict society, where, as evidenced by the recent outbreak of violence against the Serb LGBT community, they are still pertinent. Second, foregrounding emergent theories of feminist security studies, transitional justice theory, and gender and sexual violence, I inject a gender and sexuality perspective into discussions regarding Serbia's transition into EU membership, which has the potential to influence policy for the betterment of women and the LGBT community. Third, I hope to reframe international discussions of peace transformation and extreme nationalism towards a gender and sexuality perspective. Considering the number of nations coming out of ethnic and sectarian violence and on the brink of peace, the findings in my analysis could possibly help provide suggestions for transitioning into a peaceful inclusive society.

## Bibliography

Bakić, Jovo. "Extreme-Right Ideology, Practice and Supporters: Case Study of the Serbian Radical Party." *Journal of Contemporary European Studies* 17.2 (2009): 193-207. Print.

Bosia, Michael J. and Meredith L. Weiss. *The Globalization of Homophobia: Perspectives and Debates.* Forthcoming.

Correia, Sarah. "Nationalist Violence in Post-Milosevic Serbia: Extremist Right-Wing Youth Groups as Instruments of Intimidation of Civic-Minded Individuals and Organizations." *Transnational Terrorism, Organized Crime and Peace-building: Human Security in the Western Balkans.* By Wolfgang Benedek. New York: Palgrave Macmillan, 2010. Print.

Dejan Jović, "The Disintegration of Yugoslavia —A Critical Review of Explanatory Approaches." *European Journal of Social Theory.* 4.1 (2001): 101-120. Print.

Derrida, Jacques, "On Absolute Hostility: The Cause of the Philosophy and the Specter of the Political," *The Politics of Friendship* by Jacques Derrida. London, New York: Verso, 2005, p. 112-138. Print.

Dioli, Irene. "Back to a Nostalgic Future—The Queeroslav Utopia." *Sextures* 1.1 (2009). Web. <http://sextures.net/dioli-queeroslav-utopia>.

Duhaček, Daša. "Feminist Perspectives on Democratization in Serbia/Western Balkans." *Signs: Journal of Women in Culture and Society* 31.4 (2006): 923-28. Print.

Duggan, Lisa. *The Twilight of Equality?: Neoliberalism, Cultural Politics, and the Attack on Democracy.* Boston: Beacon, 2003. Print.

Gavrilovic, Jelena. *Labris Annual Report.* Belgrade, 2010. Print.

"Gej Lezbejski Info Centar | Beograd - Srbija." *GayEcho—Regionalni Gej Lezbejski Info Portal.* Web. 20 Jan. 2011. <http://gayecho.com/glic/>.

Judah, Tim. *The Serbs: History, Myth, and the Destruction of Yugoslavia.* New Haven: Yale UP, 2000. Print.

Jauhola, Marjaana. "Building Back Better?—Negotiating Normative Boundaries of Gender Mainstreaming and Post-tsunami Reconstruction in Nanggroe Aceh Darussalam, Indonesia." *Review of International Studies* 36 (2010): 29-50. Print.

Lind, Amy. *Development, Sexual Rights and Global Governance.* London: Routledge, 2010. Print.

Lewis, Desiree. "Rethinking Nationalism in Relation to Foucault's History of Sexuality and Adrienne Rich's 'Compulsory Heterosexuality and Lesbian Existence'." *Sexualities* 11.1/2 (2008): 104-09. Print.

Peterson, V. Spike and Anne Sisson Runyan. *Global Gender Issues.* 3rd ed. Boulder, CO: Westview, 2010. Print.

Ristić, Zoran. "Privatisation and Foreign Direct Investment in Serbia." *South-East Europe Review* (2004): 121-36. Print.

Silber, Laura, and Allan Little. *The Death of Yugoslavia.* London: BBC Books, 1996. Print.

Todosijević, Bojan. "The Structure of Political Attitudes in Hungary and Serbia." *East European Politics and Societies* 22.4 (2008): 879-900. Print.

# SECTION III

# Literature and the Arts

The arts have long been a space in which homo-, bi-, and trans-erotic desires and identities have been explored and interrogated. This section provides students with a number of primary texts—both literary and graphical—that highlight how many artists, working in a variety of forms and genres, have grappled with the meaning of queer sexualities. Critical introductions and discussions of all artworks frame each "text."

# CHAPTER 9

# Homosexed Art and Literature

This chapter gives an overview of homosexed art and literature, spanning from Sappho to Mabel Maney. The focus will be on art and literature that is well-known in LGBT communities. We include examples of political and activist art in addition to purely aesthetic work.

LGBT supporters and activists have claimed many great artists, musicians, and writers of the past as gay despite the fact that they lived before, to use Foucault's phrase, "the homosexual was . . . a species" (43). During the Renaissance in Europe, for example, one aspect of classical Greek and Roman culture that was reborn was homoerotic art. Italian artists Donatello (1386–1466), Leonardo da Vinci (1452–1519), and Michelangelo (1475–1564) created sculptures of young men that were clearly designed to showcase the male body. There is in fact evidence indicating that all three men were what we would today call "gay": Donatello, it was claimed, had love affairs with his male apprentices; da Vinci was arrested for sodomy in 1476; and Michelangelo's great-nephew carefully changed all the pronouns in the love sonnets from male to female as he was editing the artist's poetry in 1623. One artist was even popularly known as "Il Sodoma" (the sodomite: Giovanni Antonio Bazzi, 1477–1549).

Still, it is important to remember that, although these men, like many others in their time, engaged in homosexual acts, they lived prior to consciousness of a homosexual identity [λ Chapter 1]. Thus, we risk slipping into the practice of presentism if we insist upon interpreting their art as expressing something essentially gay [λ Introduction]. Nonetheless, these artists are just a few of the well-known figures—including Shakespeare, Emily Dickinson, and countless others—who regularly appear on Internet lists of famous lesbians and gay men in history. Clearly, there has been no lack of encomiums—both popular and scholarly—praising the influence of queers (especially gay men) on Western culture. With tongue in cheek, Cathy Crimmins, playing on this idea, titled her book about gay male aesthetic culture *How the Homosexuals Saved Civilization: The True and Heroic Story of How Gay Men Shaped the Modern World.*

This chapter makes no attempt to re-hike that well-trodden path. Instead, we focus here on art, literature, and public performance that have contributed directly to building queer culture. We

**Figure 9.1**  "Il Sodoma," St. Sebastian, 1525.

must warn you, however: no single chapter can do justice to the range, diversity, and depth of queer art. We can only provide a sampling, highlights, of LGBT artistic production. (Given their immense impact on contemporary culture, television and movies will be discussed separately in Chapters 13 through 15.) Because self-consciously homosexed art came into existence with the emergence of sexological terms for sexual identity, our initial focus will be on the work of 19th-century artists in the West, who exerted a great influence on artistic production by a variety of queer artists throughout the 20th century. Proceeding chronologically, we also turn our attention to the development of self-conscious queer art in a variety of national contexts, particularly as notions of LGBT identity have spread around the world meeting both acceptance and resistance as diverse people attempt to represent their lives, intimacies, and experiences.

## Whitman and His Descendants

Walt Whitman (1819–1892) is generally acknowledged to be among the very finest of 19th-century American poets. To some, Whitman was the "good grey poet" singing an epic of America and placing himself at the center of its national life. To others, he was the notorious Mr. Whitman, whose unabashed descriptions of the human "body electric" shocked buttoned-up Victorian-era Americans, who virtuously forbade their innocent daughters from reading him. To still others, his long free-verse lines and philosophy of personal liberation positioned him as a harbinger of literary modernism. And finally, to a small but growing cadre of late 19th-century men, Whitman was the prophet of homosexuality, openly celebrating love between men. From his own time through today, gay advocates have pointed to Whitman's life and work as important expressions of early gay consciousness.

Whitman's principal life work was *Leaves of Grass,* a collection of poems first published in 1855 and subsequently revised, enhanced, and expanded to the point that, at the poet's death in 1892, it had appeared in at least seven different versions. The 1860 edition of *Leaves of Grass* introduced a group of poems under the title "Calamus," referring to the phallus-shaped calamus plant, which in turn is associated with the ancient Greek god Kalamos, who was transformed through grief at the death of his male lover ("Walt Whitman"). The Calamus poems openly celebrate what Whitman called "adhesiveness," the "love that fuses, ties and aggregates, making the races comrades, and fraternizing all," as distinguished from "individualism, which isolates" (*Poetry and Prose* 973). In Calamus 1, "In Paths Untrodden," the poet describes himself as

> Resolved to sing no songs to-day but those of manly attachment,
> . . . To tell the secret of my nights and days,
> To celebrate the needs of comrades. (268)

Throughout *Leaves of Grass,* Whitman proclaims his "adhesive" love for men and refers to God in the same terms:

> My rendezvous is appointed, it is certain.
> The Lord will be there and wait till I come on perfect terms,
> The great Camerado, the lover true for whom I pine will be there. (241)

Within the context of 19th-century Western culture, intimate expressions between men (and women, for that matter) were not uncommon, even if not explicitly sexual in nature. The idea of romantic (nonsexual) friendship can be traced through much writing of the period. But Whitman's gestures move beyond the platonically romantic; in fact, the poet suggests that the uncensored language of sexuality, particularly in the Calamus poems, will doubtless shock and offend some potential readers:

> Through me forbidden voices,
> Voices of sexes and lusts . . . voices veiled, and I remove the veil,
> Voices indecent by me clarified and transfigured. (50)

"Who but I," wrote Whitman in "Starting from Paumanok" in 1860, "should be the poet of comrades?" (179).

The open secret of his homoerotic interests, plainly articulated from the first appearance of *Leaves of Grass,* revolted many contemporary critics and reviewers. Rufus Griswold, for example, reviewing *Leaves of Grass* for the New York *Criterion* in 1855, excoriated Whitman for indulging in a "degrading, beastly sensuality that is fast rotting the healthy core of all the social virtues" (24). Still, Whitman and his poetry fascinated people far and near. John Addington Symonds, an Englishman a generation younger than Whitman, declared himself a "Whitmanian" and initiated in 1871 a correspondence with the older poet that was to last until Whitman's death in 1892. In his biography of Symonds, Rictor Norton sees the writer's obsession with Whitman as part of a lifelong effort to make sense of his own homosexuality. It took Symonds 20 years to work up the courage to ask Whitman directly whether, as the Calamus poems clearly "prais[ed] and propagat[ed] a passionate affection between men," the "delicate difficulties" surrounding physical sex might properly be left to "the persons' own sense of what is right and fit" (Norton). In other words, Symonds hoped that Whitman was making a place for physical sex between men. Imagine Symonds's disappointment when Whitman wrote back that his "morbid inferences" concerning homosexuality "are disavow'd by me & seem damnable" (Katz 349). Despite Whitman's refusal during his lifetime to advocate publicly for the new sexual inversion identity named by the sexologists [λ Chapter 2], his practice of "adhesive" love combined with his vast fame to humanize homosexuality.

We can see Whitman's influence on the beginnings of "gay" art in the last part of the 19th century. Two significant figures from this period are Americans Winslow Homer (1836–1910) and Thomas Eakins (1844–1916). Homer typically portrayed the camaraderie of men doing "masculine" things: hunting, laboring, boxing, and so on. This can also be said of Eakins, who specifically intended much of his art of the 1890s to convey the ideas of Whitman. Richard Mann writes that "Eakins' carefully composed images of naked youths in arcadian landscape settings (such as *The Swimming Hole,* 1885) constitute visual equivalents of Whitman's poems, celebrating male beauty and comradeship." (See Figure 9.2.) While Homer and Eakins expressed Whitman's "adhesiveness," they, like the poet, never self-consciously identified with the new homosexual identity described

**Figure 9.2**   Thomas Eakins, *The Swimming Hole.*

by the sexologists. Whitman's influence continued into the 20th century. English painter David Hockney (b. 1937) openly referenced Whitman throughout his early career. He titled a 1960 painting *Adhesiveness* and included lines from Whitman's poetry in other works (e.g., "We Two Boys Together Clinging" [1961]).

Among the many 20th-century poets who identified with Whitman was Portuguese Modernist Fernando Pessoa (1888–1935). Actually, it is misleading to attribute the poem "Saudação a Walt Whitman" ("Greetings to Walt Whitman," 1915) to Pessoa because, like most of his work, "Saudação" appeared under the name of one of Pessoa's *heteronyms,* or aliases—in this case, Álvaro de Campos. (Even Pessoa's core identity is suspect as *pessoa* means "person" or "persona" in Portuguese.) The Álvaro de Campos who composed "Saudação" was a Whitman-esque *pessoa* who could write in "Tabacaria" (Tobacco Shop), *"tenho em mim todos os sonhos do mundo"* ("I hold in myself all the dreams of the world"). In "Saudação," Campos addresses Whitman as a *"grande pederasta"* and exclaims, *"Quantas vezes eu beijo o teu retrato!"* ("How many times I kiss thy portrait!"). Here we see Campos insisting upon a connection to his *"grande herói . . . Cantor da fraternidade"* ("great hero . . . singer of brotherhood").

Just as Symonds and Pessoa/Campos imagined a link with Whitman, gay literary critic Newton Arvin (1900–1963) unmasked the poet's "abnormal sexuality" (273) to de-pathologize and empower it. In 1938, when Arvin wrote *Whitman,* the phenomenon of sexual inversion had emerged from sexological obscurity into the popular consciousness and was considered an illness [λ Chapter 3]. The first four chapters of Arvin's book argue for a view of Whitman as a social progressive, even a radical; then, in the fifth chapter, Arvin switches gears and takes up the issue of Whitman's homosexuality, a daring move at that time. He points to the preface to the 1876 edition of *Leaves of Grass,* where Whitman announces that "the special meaning of the *Calamus* cluster . . . mainly resides in its Political significance" (*Selected Poems* 359). Arvin concludes that, although Whitman was "unmistakably homosexual" (274), he was no "mere invert" (277) but rather a transcendent "poet of fraternity" (280) in whose hands sexual inversion became "as strong and normal an emotion in men as love between the sexes" (272). Arvin, in short, pleads for a critical interpretation of Whitman that rehabilitates homosexuality. Sadly, in 1960, Arvin was arrested for possession of pornographic material (most of which consisted of physique pictorial magazines such as those discussed in Chapter 10) and fired from his teaching position at Smith College.

The combination of Whitman's proto-gay "adhesiveness" and his unmistakable poetic style exerted a powerful influence on generations of 20th-century queer poets. Langston Hughes (1902–1967), arguably the finest of the Harlem Renaissance poets, wrote with a decidedly Whitmanesque sensibility, especially in his early poems, which adopt Whitman's use of colloquial language and his concern with democratic inclusiveness to address the position of blacks in a racist society. The Beat poets of the 1950s, particularly Allen Ginsberg (1926–1997), praised and emulated Whitman's expansive vision of a humanistic America [λ Chapter 11]. Ginsberg's "A Supermarket in California" (1955) specifically addresses Whitman the lover of boys, and his epic "Howl" (written in 1955) echoes Whitman's self-styled "barbaric yawp" (Whitman, *Poetry and Prose* 247). Judy Grahn's (b. 1940) *Common Woman* poems (1969) and *A Woman Is Talking to Death* (1974) embody some of the same Whitmanian content and style. June Jordan (1936–2002), activist poet, writer, and teacher, praised the "politicizing significance of bisexual affirmation . . . to insist upon the equal validity of all the components of social/sexual complexity" ("June Jordan"). Jordan's poetry also references Whitman's style; we see this clearly in "Poem for South African Women" (1980). We can see it as well in Audre Lorde's poem "A Woman Speaks" and her biomythography, *Zami*, through their relentless expansiveness and their reimagining of the outside world with respect to the inner reality of the same-sex-loving person. We also see it in the use to which later writers, such as Charley Shively, put Whitman's life and work. Shively, a fiery gay activist and scholar known for burning a Bible during his keynote speech at the 1977 Boston Gay Pride rally and for serving as founding editor of the early gay publication *Fag Rag*, edited two collections of Whitman's letters to young men. In these volumes, *Calamus Lovers* (1987) and *Drum Beats* (1989), Shively insists upon Whitman's overt homosexuality, not hesitating to use late 20th-century terms (such as *butch, basket, gay, boyfriend, queen, queer,* and the like) anachronistically to argue for an essentialist reading of Whitman. While Shively may be committing the presentist fallacy, Lorde's and Jordan's uses of Whitman speak to their desire to expand a powerful poetic tradition, particularly in their cases by directly addressing issues of race and gender that Whitman did not.

> **Find Out More** about Whitman and his influence on contemporary queer poets by reading the poetry in the readings at the end of this chapter.

# The Expatriates

For 19th-century women and men seeking to develop same-sex relationships and an artistic life, Rome, Paris, and other European capitals seemed to

**Figure 9.3**   Edmonia Lewis.

represent freedom from sex, gender, and racial constraints that inhibited them at home. Homosexual British and American men often traveled to Italy seeking the lost tradition of classical Greek and Roman homoeroticism [λ Chapter 1]. Women, who were for the first time testing the waters of personal and artistic freedom, had no such ready-made models and had to invent new ways of being. The community of artistic proto-lesbians that coalesced around actress Charlotte Cushman (1816–1876) in Rome in the 1850s was one such significant experiment in same-sex living. Cushman and writer Matilda Hays (1823–1908) migrated together to Rome in 1852, where Elizabeth Barrett Browning described their relationship as "a female marriage" (qtd. in Browning 27). They were soon followed by sculptor Harriet Hosmer (1830–1908) and other expatriate women artists: sculptors Emma Stebbins (1815–1882), Edmonia Lewis (1845–c. 1911), and Mary Lloyd (1819–1896); actress Fanny Kemble (1809–1893) and her sister, singer Adelaide Kemble Sartoris (c. 1814–1879); and others. Both Cushman and Hosmer possessed confident and powerful personalities, and both had been described (by Barrett Browning and Nathaniel Hawthorne, among others) as decidedly mannish in behavior and dress. Henry James raised the specter of deviant sexuality when he called the group a "strange sisterhood"; he also implied that they were cold and celibate by referring to them as "a white, marmoreal flock" (1: 257). The intense and shifting relationships within the group gave the lie to James's assumption of female frigidity. Their consistent production of fine and marketable art bespoke the power of freedom for women artists from the shackles imposed by family and mid-Victorian social mores.

By the beginning of the 20th century, the prime locale for expatriate homosexual artists was no longer Rome but Paris. Led by wealthy American writer Natalie Barney (1876–1972) and British poet Renée Vivien (1877–1909), an intense, prolific, and decidedly nonmonogamous coterie of lesbian expatriates took up residence there during the ***Belle Époque***. Among these were American writer Gertrude Stein (1874–1946) and her partner Alice B. Toklas (1877–1967). Both Stein and Barney were as well known for the salons at which they entertained other (usually poorer) artists of their day as for their own published work. Journalist Solita Solano (1888–1975) wrote of Barney's entertainments, "Natalie did not collect modern art, she collected people, and you could be sure of being dazzled any Friday (her day) you dropped in for tea" (Solano). Stein, by contrast, did collect modern art—by Picasso, Renoir, Gauguin, and others—but she also felt that her European home and expatriate artist friends fueled a kind of artistic genius in her. "I have lived half my life in Paris," she wrote, "not the half that made me but the half in which I made what I made" (Stein 62). Other notable lesbian or bisexual expatriate women who turned up at Barney's gatherings at 20 Rue Jacob included American painter Romaine Brooks (1874–1970); Radclyffe Hall (1880–1943), British author of the enormously influential novel *The Well of Loneliness* [λ Chapters 2 and 12]; American journalist Janet Flanner (1892–1978); American author Djuna Barnes (1892–1982); and Polish Art Deco painter Tamara de Lempicka (1898–1980).

**Figure 9.4**    Portrait of the Duchess de la Salle, 1925, by Tamara de Lempicka (1898–1980).

Many African-American artists emigrated to Paris during the 20th century to escape American racism. Those who were gay, lesbian, or bisexual had even more reason to leave, as France was far more accepting of homosexuality than the United States. Gay poet Claude McKay (1889–1948) wrote acidly about New York while in "European self-exile" (Lewis xxvii). Bisexual performer Josephine Baker (1906–1975) was far more popular in Paris than she ever was at home. After being called a "Negro wench" by the *New York Times* during an American tour in the 1930s (*The Official Josephine*), she returned to France, saying bitterly, "[The Eiffel Tower] looked very different from the Statue of Liberty, but what did that matter? What was the good of having the statue without the liberty?" (Vorotova). The best known of the black expatriates was James Baldwin (1924–1987), who moved to Europe in 1948 for a combination of reasons: "strained relations with his stepfather, problems over sexual identity, suicide of a friend, and racism" (Liukkonen). While in Paris, Baldwin wrote what Henry Louis Gates Jr. calls "his most successfully crafted and fully realized novel" (xxvi), *Giovanni's Room* (1956), which describes a young white man's struggle with his homosexuality. After his initial exploration of homosexuality, Baldwin turned in later novels, such as *Another Country* (1962) and *Tell Me How Long the Train's Been Gone* (1968), to complex examinations of both sexuality and race. In *Another Country,* for instance, Baldwin takes on some of the sociocultural difficulties of men loving across racial lines.

# Performing Queer: Theater

The limp-wristed **aesthete,** swishing into a drawing room or contemplating a lily, was a figure of fun before Oscar Wilde came to be his ideal embodiment. William S. Gilbert and Arthur Sullivan's operetta *Patience* (1881), for instance, tells the love story of Reginald Bunthorne, who admits to being an "aesthetic sham." Bunthorne instructs the audience precisely how to affect the persona of a "fleshly poet" by walking

… down Piccadilly with a poppy
or a lily in your medieval hand.
And ev'ryone will say,
As you walk your flow'ry way,
"If he's content with a vegetable love
which would certainly not suit me,
Why, what a most particularly pure young man
this pure young man must be!" (*Patience* No. 6)

**Figure 9.5**    George Grossmith as Bunthorne, 1881.

Bunthorne was a satirical rendering of the poet and noted aesthete Algernon Swinburne (1837–1909). But it was through the witty and epigrammatical Wilde that the figure of the aesthete solidified into the popular image of the homosexual man. Early in 1895, just weeks before the trials that were to end Wilde's successful career as a dramatist—and that led directly to his death five years later—his satirical comedy of manners, *The Importance of Being Earnest,* opened at the St. James Theatre in London [λ Chapter 12]. The play's two male leads, Algernon and Jack, are both clever young men who seek wives, believing all the while that "[d]ivorces are made in Heaven." Both men engage in the practice of *Bunburying,* which permits them to escape from tedious obligations. As Algernon remarks,

I have invented an invaluable permanent invalid called Bunbury, in order that I may be able to go down into the country whenever I choose. Bunbury is perfectly invaluable. If it wasn't for Bunbury's extraordinary bad health, for instance, I wouldn't be able to dine with you at Willis's to-night.

While not an explicitly sexual term, Bunburying seems to serve as a metaphor for living a double life, as Wilde himself (married and carrying on homosexual affairs) certainly needed to do.

The British artist Aubrey Beardsley (1872–1898) was part of Wilde's circle of aesthetes and illustrated Wilde's play *Salome* in 1893. Beardsley's distorted pen-and-ink erotic drawings earned him notoriety during his short life. As he wrote, "I have one aim—the grotesque. If I am not grotesque I am nothing" ("Aubrey Beardsley"). The *Salome* illustrations included "naked figures, hermaphroditic men, ugly, deformed dwarfs and sinister women" (Cooper 80). Like Beardsley, the Russian Léon Bakst (1866–1924) received his first boost to fame through connection to a circle of artists and writers—in this case, one led by impresario Sergei Diaghilev (1872–1929). This

**Figure 9.6**  Aubrey Beardsley's "Woman in the Moon."

group founded a journal, *Mir iskusstva* (*World of Art*), which promoted the principles of Art Nouveau. Through Diaghilev, Bakst became associated with the Ballet Russes, which formed in Paris in 1909. As artistic director of the ballet, Bakst designed sets and costumes; his famous painting of dancer Vaslav Nijinsky (1890–1950) in costume for Debussy's *L'après-midi d'un faune* (*Afternoon of a Faun*) reveals at once his homoerotic

gaze and the Beardsley-like grotesquerie of the costume. We should note that all of these artistic endeavors, from Wilde's plays to Diaghilev's ballet, were generally part of a privileged "high art" cultural scene that was somewhat tolerant of homoerotic gestures—provided that they could be passed off as "artistic" (as in Beardsley's case) or laughable (as in Wilde's).

In contrast, the American stage at the time was more conservative than its European counterparts. *The God of Vengeance* (1907), by Yiddish playwright Sholem Asch (1880–1957), enjoyed a successful run in Berlin in 1910, before Asch emigrated from Germany to the United States in 1914. But when the play (in English translation) opened in New York in 1922, its lesbian theme, combined with its setting in a brothel, so offended

**Figure 9.7**  Bakst Nijinsky.

local censors that the producer, director, and 12 actors were arrested and later found guilty of presenting an indecent play. British writer Ronald Firbank's (1886–1926) three-act comedy *The Princess Zoubaroff* (1920), which deals with a lesbian convent, avoided the censors by having no major public performances in Europe and no performances at all in the United States. When *The Captive,* by French author Edouard Bourdet (1887–1945), opened on Broadway in 1926, Mayor Jimmy Walker signed the now-infamous Padlock Law, whereby city authorities would literally padlock the doors and arrest the cast of any theater that dared to present homosexuality, sex outside of marriage, or prostitution (Whittaker 278). From this time through the next four decades, censorship kept most LGBT-themed drama off the stage in American cities [λ Chapter 12]. To be sure, Lillian Hellman's (1905–1984) 1934 play, *The Children's Hour,* had a long run at New York's Maxine Elliot Theatre, but the play might well have won the Pulitzer Prize had not the selection committee refused to see it. Furthermore, its core plot involving a teacher accused of lesbianism by a student [λ Chapter 1, the 1811 Pirie and Woods case] simply vanished in the 1936 film version, replaced by a heterosexual love triangle. The Breen Office, charged with enforcing adherence to the Motion Picture Production Code, excised the homosexual references from Tennessee Williams's (1911–1983) *A Streetcar Named Desire* (1947) when it was made into a film in 1951. In London, however, despite state censorship that officially continued into the 1960s, gay-themed plays such as Noel Coward's (1899–1973) *Design for Living* (1934) and Robert Anderson's (1917–2009) *Tea and Sympathy* (1953) escaped prosecution for obscenity, probably because they took low-key approaches, not directly tackling homophobia, as had Hellman's play (Morley).

By the late 20th century, especially in the United States, the concerns and attitudes of a newly empowered gay movement were beginning to be reflected onstage. Plays such as *Boys in the Band* (1968), *Bent* (1979), and *Torch Song Trilogy* (1981) brought gay men to center stage as never before. The devastation of AIDS, ironically, seems to have contributed to the success of dramas such as Larry Kramer's (b. 1935) *The Normal Heart* (1984), Tony Kushner's (b. 1956) *Angels in America* (1991), and Jonathan Larson's (1960–1996) *Rent* (1996). The change over a decade from the searing accusatory tone of Kramer's play to the slick mainstream appeal of *Rent* reflected the way AIDS had positioned gay men as protagonists in a great national tragedy; moreover, organizing against the scourge provided gay male artists with access to media and entertainment power brokers.

Not surprisingly, lesbian drama was absent from high-visibility venues, reflecting the ongoing exclusion of women in public performance generally. Carolyn Gage (b. 1952) attributes lesbian invisibility in theater to lesbian playwrights' tendency to focus on socially threatening "uncolonized women." Gage's one-woman play, *The Second Coming of Joan of Arc* (1986), is one such threatening play: "We watch as [Joan] decolonizes herself—from the church, from the military, from the state—and at the end names and separates herself from her internalized misogyny," states Gage in an interview. This play, Gage's best known, was performed in church basements and at festivals for years before receiving any wide attention.

A similar erasure is Sarah Dreher's (b. 1937) award-winning play *8 × 10 Glossy* (1985), which is seldom performed—in fact, it has never been performed by anyone outside the author's own drama circle. Like Gage, Dreher focuses on sexual abuse, which wreaks lifelong damage upon women and enforces oppressive silence. Both these plays, and many others by lesbians, are overtly political, even polemical, and this appears to have stood in the way of their gaining wide crossover recognition. It is important to note,

**Figure 9.8**  Carolyn Gage as Joan of Arc.

however, that these and other lesbian plays never aimed for such recognition but focused instead on reaching lesbians oppressed by homophobic culture. As Gage says, "Telling the truth is always disruptive. And theatre, of all the art forms, is a particularly powerful medium for truth-telling. Playwrights historically have ended up in hot water, because the nature of live theatre is inherently political" (Cramer 7).

## Homosexed Literature: Global Disruptions

Given that gay identity is largely a construct of American and European civilization, the treatment of the homoerotic outside the West and the Global North reveals tensions and issues surrounding sex and sexuality that are particular to their contexts. At times, we may note some similarities between Western and non-Western understandings of queerness. Japanese ultratraditionalist author Yukio Mishima (1925–1970), for example, staked out new territory with his 1948 *Bildungsroman Confessions of a Mask,* which is assumed to be at least semiautobiographical. We might compare this book with American Rita Mae Brown's (b. 1944) *Rubyfruit Jungle* (1973) or with Sri Lankan Shyam Selvadurai's (b. 1965) *Funny Boy* (1994); all three novels offer unapologetic, reality-based accounts of young people recognizing their homo- or bisexuality, coming out, and growing into adulthood. Still, their cultural specificity must be noted. Mishima's and Selvadurai's protagonists face cultural and familial pressures that may seem similar to those of comparable gay characters in the West but are not necessarily equivalent. Mishima's Japanese characters, for instance, face cultural pressures not just to conform to certain gendered and sexual roles but to rebuild a country that has lost a world war. The account of the closet in *Confessions of a Mask* is nuanced not just by family politics but by national politics at a time when Japan's international reputation had been devastated by military defeat; in this context, homosexuals seemed not only like sexual deviants but national deviants by not engaging in the kinds of relationships that would help to restore and repopulate the country.

Although some Latin countries tolerate fairly open expressions of homosexuality, many do not. Hostile cultural environments have produced three characteristic types of LGBT literature in the Latin world. One response to such hostility is a highly coded literature; the Spanish Majorcan author Carme Riera (b. 1948), for instance, uses a prison cell to symbolize the closeted lesbian life in her story *I Leave You the Sea* (1975). A second type of Latin LGBT literature reflects the forced exile of many gay men to more accepting locations. Here we think of gay Uncle Sergio in Puerto Rican Magali García Ramis's (b. 1946) novel *Felices Días, Tío Sergio* (*Happy Days, Uncle Sergio*, 1986) or Eduardo in Brazilian Silviano Santiago's (b. 1936) *Stella Manhattan* (1994). Perhaps most notably, Cuban author Reinaldo Arenas (1943–1990) recounts in his memoir *Before Night Falls* the widespread oppression of homosexuals in Castro's Cuba and the author's eventual immigration to the United States as a refugee. In Arenas's account of communist Cuba, homosexuality is cast as a Western decadence, a self-indulgence contrary to the spirit of working collectively to build a strong nation. Finally, some Latin authors have chosen an intersectional approach, burying LGBT plotlines within discussions of social or political struggles. Sara Levi Calderón (b. 1942), for example, writes about a lesbian relationship between two Jewish women in Mexico in her 1990 novel *Dos Mujeres* (*Two Women*). This book, set in the context of the North American Free Trade Agreement (NAFTA) and Mexico's efforts to become a "first-world" nation, raises issues of **diaspora**—Jewish and lesbian. Chilean author Pedro Lemebel (b. about 1955) uses the 1986 anti-Pinochet tensions in Santiago to contextualize the gay relationship in his novel *Tengo Miedo Torero* (*My Tender Matador,* 2001). And Antonio José Ponte's (b. 1964) *Contrabando de Sombras* (*Smuggled Shadows,* 2002) envisions the Spanish Inquisition and the Cuban Revolution as parallel events that encouraged the persecution of homosexual men.

In South Africa, a mostly white LGBT community has developed a visible subculture on the Euro-American model. But elsewhere in sub-Saharan Africa, LGBT literature is almost unknown. Works such as Nigerian Wole Soyinka's (b. 1934) novel *The Interpreters* (1965) and Senegalese Mariama Bâ's (1929–1981) *Scarlet Song* (1981) mention same-sex love but only negatively and among minor characters.

A notable exception to LGBT invisibility in African literature is *No Past, No Present, No Future* (1973) by Sierra Leonean Yulisa Amadu Maddy (b. 1936). In this novel, one of the three main characters is a gay man who leaves Africa for Europe; this is a case of racial and homosexual expatriation that recalls Baldwin's work.

## Fine Art: From the Beautiful to the Political

American Charles Demuth (1883–1935) was best known during his lifetime as a Precisionist. That is, as Robert Hughes writes, he was "painting a functional American landscape refracted through a deadpan modernist lingo." But among his images of "grain elevators, water towers, and factory chimneys" are brightly colored paintings of Greenwich Village bathhouses. His *Turkish Bath with Self-Portrait* (1918) reveals the existence—and the allure—of the thriving gay subculture in New York City (see Figure 9.9).

Bright colors also characterize the art of Mexican Frida Kahlo (1907–1954). Kahlo lived in pain after a gruesome bus accident in 1925; many of her paintings combine visions of her physical agony with the cheerful reds and golds and yellows associated with much Mexican folk art and culture. In fact, over a third of her works are self-portraits, often emphasizing the disfigurements of her body. Kahlo was bisexual, and in her well-known painting *Two Nudes in the Jungle* (1939), she presents same-sex intimacy as a comforting release from pain and tension.

French Surrealist photographer Claude Cahun (1894–1954), like Kahlo, executed many self-portraits. These elaborately staged photographs memorialized Cahun's flamboyant transvestism; along with her open lesbianism and her Stein-like salon, they created for Cahun a reputation as a transgressive and theatrical figure.

**Figure 9.9** Charles Demuth's *Turkish Bath with Self-Portrait*.

**Figure 9.10** Claude Cahun portrait, 1928.

Beginning roughly at the time of the Stonewall riots in 1969, LGBT art in the United States took on an overtly political purpose. Harmony Hammond, for instance, defines *lesbian art* as "art that comes out of a feminist consciousness and reflects the experience of having lesbian relationships or being lesbian in patriarchal culture" (8). Unlike art by men, claims Arlene Raven, "None of it was developed exclusively in the rarefied world of art" (6). Photographers such as Ann Meredith, Bettye Lane, and Joan E. Biren (b. 1944) used the camera to freeze and celebrate moments in the development of Lesbian Nation [λ Chapter 4]. Kate Millett's (b. 1934) monumental papier mâché *Naked Ladies* (1977) spoke to the necessity for women to take up physical space in a world controlled by men. Louise Fishman's (b. 1939) *Angry Painting* (1973) embodied an attitude common to many lesbians of that era. And of course, even in that period when representations of sex were seen as problematic, Tee A. Corinne (b. 1943) and others produced images of female genitalia. In Australia, the galvanizing event for lesbian art was police violence at the 1978 Sydney Mardi Gras parade. Over the following decade, homosexuals in Australia gradually obtained rights and freedom from most harassment; visibility in the art world grew as well. Artists such as Maree Azzopardi, Fiona Lawry, and Jane Becker came into their own in the 1990s.

Some artists, such as Andy Warhol (1928–1987), became as famous for their lifestyles as for their art. One of the principal proponents of Pop Art in the 1960s, Warhol's famous canvases, many silk-screened, took items from popular culture—such as Campbell's soup cans or pictures of Marilyn Monroe—and recast them as art objects intended for contemplation in museums. While such work was not explicitly queer or even homoerotic, it quickly became associated with a gay aesthetic, perhaps in that it valued the typically undervalued or cast a sympathetic light on objects normally cast off or ignored. Warhol's portraits of Monroe, Liza Minelli, Elizabeth Taylor, and Judy Garland seemed gay in the sense that they idolized figures popular among gay male subcultures. Such work seemed to validate for many gay men the value of their cultural icons. But Warhol's lesser-known work, such as the film *Blow Job* (1964), is frankly homoerotic. *Blow Job* focuses our attention on the face of a handsome young man as he supposedly receives fellatio from another man. Blurring the boundary between pornography and art, Warhol challenged viewers to consider the beauty in the homoerotic.

Beginning in the 1980s, the AIDS epidemic led to a rush of new political art. The powerful image "Silence = Death" [λ Chapter 4] was the most widely recognized but by no means the only production by political graphics collectives such as Gran Fury and Visual AIDS in New York and General Idea in Toronto. Their immediate goal was to raise money for AIDS research because their governments were slow in responding to the crisis. Simultaneously, activist Cleve Jones (b. 1954) conceived of the NAMES Project Quilt, which has "ballooned into the largest gay art project in history"

(Saslow 279). Keith Haring (1958–1990) drew cartoonlike figures that came to stand for AIDS activism. The photographer Robert Mapplethorpe (1946–1989) created deliberately provocative images that raised right-wing hackles and led to calls for censorship and elimination of funding for the National Endowment for the Arts [λ Chapter 12]. These powerful images elicited sympathy for AIDS victims while often refusing to soften the confrontational queer effect.

In the early 21st century, at least in some parts of the United States and the Global North, queer art links aesthetic production to cultural and political concerns. An art project titled "Hey Hetero!" performs an educational function on buses and billboards in Australia. The artist created large posters featuring straight couples with captions like, "Hey Hetero! Get married because you can!" (Kelly and Fiveash). Pulitzer Prize–winning cartoonist Jim Borgman (b. 1954) used the bully pulpit of his syndicated newspaper connection to argue for an end to gay bashing in the wake of the murder of Matthew Shepard in 1998 with a cartoon featuring a religious figure standing next to a grave and the caption, "Gay Rites" (Borgman). And Chicana artist Ester Hernández (b. 1944) overlays the iconic image of the Virgin of Guadalupe upon a lesbian figure (*La Ofrenda*, 1990). In short, queer artists producing queer-themed art and literature have made a significant impact on cultures worldwide.

## Questions for Discussion

1. In her 1998 book *Stagestruck*, Sarah Schulman describes recognizing plot and characters from her novel *People in Trouble* (1987) in the smash Broadway hit *Rent*. More than the issue of plagiarism, Schulman raises other questions: "How is AIDS going to be represented in this society? What is the result of the cultural appropriation of gay and lesbian work? What happens when an individual artist is dominated by a corporate product?" (2). Read *People in Trouble* and see *Rent* (film version 2005). How might you answer Schulman's questions?

2. This chapter offered you a broad overview of homosexed art and literature, and inevitably, we had to leave out discussion of much worthy and important art. Several online resources readily provide useful introductions to queer art and literature. Locate one, perhaps starting with a search on Google, glbtq.com, or Wikipedia, and find an artist whom we have not covered in this chapter. Investigate his, her, or ze's life and art, paying particular attention to the social and historical contexts in which that person worked. Write a proposal in which you explain why the artist you have researched should be included in a new edition of this book.

3. In this chapter, we identified Whitman as a poet who has descendants—that is, artists and writers coming after him who were influenced by his work enough either to imitate him, such as Edward Carpenter and Allen Ginsberg, or to expand on issues, such as race and gender, that he didn't explore in great depth, like Langston Hughes and Audre Lorde. Consider why it has been important for some LGBT and queer artists to engage previous artists—aesthetically, culturally, and politically. What do they gain by doing so? What do their readers or viewers gain? How might such conversations among artists across time

create a sense of tradition, and how can such a sense be important for LGBT and queer people? At the same time, keep in mind the risk of presentism we have discussed at earlier points in this book. What are the dangers in contemporary LGBT artists claiming past artists as queer?

## REFERENCES AND FURTHER READING

Anderson, Nancy Fix. *Woman against Women in Victorian England: A Life of Eliza Lynn Linton*. Bloomington: Indiana UP, 1987. Print.

Arvin, Newton. *Whitman*. New York: Macmillan, 1938. Print.

"Aubrey Beardsley." N.p. 23 July 2008. Web. 8 Aug. 2008. <http://en.wikipedia.org/wiki/Aubrey_Beardsley>.

Baldwin, James. "Preservation of Innocence." 1949. *Collected Essays*. Ed. Toni Morrison. New York: Library of America, 1998. 594–600. Print.

Borgman, Jim. "Gay Rites." *The Cincinnati Enquirer*. 16 Oct. 1998. Web. 26 Mar. 2008. <http://borgman.enquirer.com/>.

Browning, Robert. *Dearest Isa: Robert Browning's Letters to Isabella Blagden*. Ed. Edward C. McAleer. Austin: U of Texas P, 1951. Print.

Cooper, Emmanuel. *The Sexual Perspective: Homosexuality and Art in the Last 100 Years in the West*. London: Routledge & Kegan Paul, 1986. Print.

Cramer, Pat. "Interview with Carolyn Gage." *Off Our Backs* (Jan.–Feb. 2002). Web. 8 August 2008. <http://findarticles.com/p/articles/mi_qa3693/is_200201/ai_n9067922>.

Crimmins, Cathy. *How the Homosexuals Saved Civilization: The True and Heroic Story of How Gay Men Shaped the Modern World*. New York: Tarcher, 2004. Print.

Foucault, Michel. *The History of Sexuality, Volume 1: An Introduction*. Trans. Robert Hurley. New York: Vintage, 1990. Print.

Gage, Carolyn. Telephone interview with D. Meem. 23 Apr. 2007.

Gates, Henry Louis, Jr. "Introduction." *The Annotated Uncle Tom's Cabin*. New York: W. W. Norton, 2007. Print.

Gilbert, William S. (libretto). *Patience, or, Bunthorne's Bride*. N.d. Web. 8 Aug. 2008. <http://www.karadar.com/Librettos/sullivan_PATIENCE.html>.

Griswold, Rufus. "Review of *Leaves of Grass*." *Criterion* 1 (10 Nov. 1855): 24. Print.

Hammond, Harmony. *Lesbian Art in America: A Contemporary History*. New York: Rizzoli, 2000. Print.

Henderson, Mae. "James Baldwin: Expatriation, Homosexual Panic, and Man's Estate." *Callaloo* 23.1 (2000): 313–27. Print.

Hughes, Robert. *American Visions: The Epic History of Art in America*. Quoted on *Artchive*. N.d. Web. 8 Aug. 2008. <http://www.artchive.com/artchive/D/demuth.html>.

James, Henry. *William Wetmore Story and His Friends: From Letters, Diaries, and Recollections*. 2 vols. Boston: Houghton Mifflin, 1903. Print.

"June Jordan." N.p, 2002. Web. 8 Aug. 2008. <http://sunsite.berkeley.edu/gaybears/jordan/>.

Katz, Jonathan Ned. *Gay American History: Lesbians & Gay Men in the U.S.A.*

Rev. ed. New York: Meridian, 1992. Print.

Kelly, Deborah, and Tina Fiveash. "Hey, Hetero!" N.p. 2003. Web. 26 Mar. 2008. <http://www.abc.net.au/arts/design/stories/s455304.htm>.

Lewis, David Levering. *The Portable Harlem Renaissance Reader.* New York: Penguin, 1995. Print.

Liukkonen, Petri. "James (Arthur) Baldwin." N.p., 2002. 8 Aug. 2008. Web. <http://www.kirjasto.sci.fi/jbaldwin.htm>.

Mann, Richard G. "American Art: Gay Male, Nineteenth Century." *glbtq: An Encyclopedia of Gay, Lesbian, Bisexual, Transgender, and Queer Culture.* 2002. Web. 8 Aug. 2008. <www.glbtq.com/arts/am_art_gay_19c.html>.

Morley, Sheridan. "Minimalist View of a Gay Scene." *International Herald Tribune.* 10 Feb. 1999. Web. 8 August 2008. <http://www.iht.com/articles/1999/02/10/lon.t_0.php>.

Norton, Rictor. *The John Addington Symonds Pages.* 1997. Web. 8 Aug. 2008. <http://rictornorton.co.uk/symonds/index.htm>.

Pessoa, Fernando. "Saudação a Walt Whitman." *Poesias de Álvaro de Campos.* N.d. Web. 8 Aug. 2008. <http://www.secrel.com.br/jpoesia/facam05.html>.

———. "Tabacaria." *Poesias de Álvaro de Campos.* N.d. Web. 8 Aug. 2008. <http://www.insite.com.br/art/pessoa/ficcoes/acampos/456.html>.

Raven, Arlene. "Los Angeles Lesbian Arts." *Art Paper* 18.6 (Nov.–Dec. 1994): 6. Print.

Saslow, James M. *Pictures and Passions: A History of Homosexuality in the Visual Arts.* Harmondsworth, UK: Penguin, 1999. Print.

Schulman, Sarah. *Stagestruck: Theater, AIDS, and the Marketing of Gay America.* Durham, NC: Duke UP, 1998. Print.

Shively, Charley. *Calamus Lovers: Walt Whitman's Working Class Comerados.* Gay Sunshine P, 1987. Print.

———. *Drum Beats: Walt Whitman's Civil War Boy Lovers.* Gay Sunshine P, 1989. Print.

Solano, Solita. "1920s Expats on Natalie's Salon." *The World of Natalie Clifford Barney.* N.d. Web. 8 Aug. 2008. <http://www.natalie-barney.com/1920swriters.htm>.

Stein, Gertrude. "An American and France." *What Are Masterpieces.* Ed. Robert Bartlett Haas. New York: Pitman, 1970. 59–70. Print.

*The Official Josephine Baker Website.* CMG Worldwide. N.d. Web. 8 Aug. 2008. <http://www.cmgww.com/stars/baker/index.php>.

Vorotova, Katerina. "Josephine Baker." 2008–2012. Web. 8 Aug. 2008. <http://www.harlemlive.org/shethang/profiles/josephinebaker/jbaker.html>.

"Walt Whitman." 5 August 2008. N.p. Web. 8 Aug. 2008. <http://en.wikipedia.org/wiki/Walt_Whitman#_note-4>.

Whitman, Walt. *Poetry and Prose.* Ed. Justin Kaplan. New York: Library of America, 1996. Print.

———. *Selected Poems 1855–1892: A New Edition.* Ed. Gary Schmidgall. New York: St. Martin's, 1999. Print.

Whittaker, Donald E., III. *Subversive Aspects of American Musical Theatre.* Diss. Louisiana State University, 2002. Web. 21 Aug. 2012. <http://etd.lsu.edu/docs/available/etd-0418102173116/unrestricted/Whittaker_III_dis.pdf>.

Wilde, Oscar. "The Importance of Being Earnest: A Trivial Comedy for Serious People." Project Gutenberg eBook. N.d. Web. 8 Aug. 2008. <http://www.gutenberg.org/files/844/844-h/844-h.htm>.

# READINGS

## ➢ Walt Whitman

(1819–1892), United States

### "We Two Boys Together Clinging"

We two boys together clinging,
One the other never leaving,
Up and down the roads going—North and South excursions making,
Power enjoying—elbows stretching—fingers clutching,
Arm'd and fearless—eating, drinking, sleeping, loving,
No law less than ourselves owning—sailing, soldiering, thieving, threatening,
Misers, menials, priests alarming—air breathing, water drinking, on the turf or the sea-beach dancing,
Cities wrenching, ease scorning, statutes mocking, feebleness chasing,
Fulfilling our foray.

Walt Whitman. From *Leaves of Grass*.

## ➢ Michael Field

(Katherine Bradley, 1848–1914 and Edith Cooper, 1862–1913), Great Britain

### "Sometimes I do despatch my heart"

Sometimes I do despatch my heart
Among the graves to dwell apart:
On some the tablets are erased,
Some earthquake-tumbled, some defaced,
And some that have forgotten lain
A fall of tears makes green again;
And my brave heart can overtread
Her brood of hopes, her infant dead,
And pass with quickened footsteps by
The headstone of hoar memory,
'Till she hath found
One swelling mound
With just her name writ and beloved,
From that she cannot be removed.

### "It was deep April"

It was deep April, and the morn
Shakespere was born;
The world was on us, pressing sore;
My love and I took hands and swore,
Against the world, to be
Poets and lovers evermore,
To laugh and dream on Lethe's shore,
To sing to Charon in his boat,
Heartening the timid souls afloat;
Of judgement never to take heed,
But to those fast-locked souls to speed,
Who never from Apollo fled,
Who spent no hour among the dead;
Continually
With them to dwell,
Indifferent to heaven and hell.

---

Michael Field. Penname for Katherine Bradley and Edith Cooper.

## ➢ **Edward Carpenter**
### (1844–1929), Great Britain

---

### "Love's Vision"

At night in each other's arms,
Content, overjoyed, resting deep deep down in the darkness,
Lo! the heavens opened and He appeared—
Whom no mortal eye may see,
Whom no eye clouded with Care,
Whom none who seeks after this or that, whom none who has not
escaped from self,
There–in the region of Equality, in the world of Freedom no
longer limited,
Standing as a lofty peak in heaven above the clouds,
From below hidden, yet to all who pass into that region most
clearly visible—
He the Eternal appeared.

## ➢ Langston Hughes

(1902–1967), United States

### "I, Too, Sing America"

I, too, sing America.
I am the darker brother.
They send me to eat in the kitchen
When company comes,
But I laugh,
And eat well,
And grow strong.

Tomorrow,
I'll be at the table
When company comes.
Nobody'll dare
Say to me,
"Eat in the kitchen,"
Then.
Besides,
They'll see how beautiful I am
And be ashamed—

I, too, am America.

## ➢ Judy Grahn

(1940– ), United States

### "A History of Lesbianism"

How they came into the world,
the women-loving-women
came in three by three
and four by four
the women-loving women

came in ten by ten
and ten by ten again
until there were more
than you could count

> they took care of each other
> the best they knew how
> and of each other's children,
> if they had any.

How they lived in the world,
the women-loving-women
learned as much as they were allowed
and walked and wore their clothes
the way they liked
whenever they could. They did whatever
they knew to be happy or free
and worked and worked and worked.
The women-loving-women
in America were called dykes
and some liked it
and some did not.

> they made love to each other
> the best they knew how
> and for the best reasons

How they went out of the world,
the women-loving-women
went out one by one
having withstood greater and lesser
trials, and much hatred
from other people, they went out
one by one, each having tried
in her own way to overthrow
the rule of men over women,
they tried it one by one
and hundred by hundred,

until each came in her own way

to the end of her life

and died:

> The subject of lesbianism
> is very ordinary; it's the question
> of male domination that makes everybody
> angry.

Judy Grahn. "A History of Lesbianism" from *The Work of a Common Woman*.

## ➢ **June Jordan**
### (1936–2002), United States

### **"Poem about My Rights"**

Even tonight and I need to take a walk and clear

my head about this poem about why I can't

go out without changing my clothes my shoes

my body posture my gender identity my age

my status as a woman alone in the evening/

alone on the streets/alone not being the point/

the point being that I can't do what I want

to do with my own body because I am the wrong

sex the wrong age the wrong skin and

suppose it was not here in the city but down on the beach/

or far into the woods and I wanted to go

there by myself thinking about God/or thinking

about children or thinking about the world/all of it

disclosed by the stars and the silence:

I could not go and I could not think and I could not

stay there

alone

as I need to be

alone because I can't do what I want to do with my own

body and

who in the hell set things up

like this

and in France they say if the guy penetrates

but does not ejaculate then he did not rape me
and if after stabbing him if after screams if
after begging the bastard and if even after smashing
a hammer to his head if even after that if he
and his buddies fuck me after that
then I consented and there was
no rape because finally you understand finally
they fucked me over because I was wrong I was
wrong again to be me being me where I was/wrong
to be who I am
which is exactly like South Africa
penetrating into Namibia penetrating into
Angola and does that mean I mean how do you know if
Pretoria ejaculates what will the evidence look like the
proof of the monster jackboot ejaculation on Blackland
and if
after Namibia and if after Angola and if after Zimbabwe
and if after all of my kinsmen and women resist even to
self-immolation of the villages and if after that
we lose nevertheless what will the big boys say will they
claim my consent:

Do You Follow Me: We are the wrong people of
the wrong skin on the wrong continent and what
in the hell is everybody being reasonable about
and according to the Times this week
back in 1966 the C.I.A. decided that they had this problem
and the problem was a man named Nkrumah so they
killed him and before that it was Patrice Lumumba
and before that it was my father on the campus
of my Ivy League school and my father afraid
to walk into the cafeteria because he said he
was wrong the wrong age the wrong skin the wrong
gender identity and he was paying my tuition and
before that
it was my father saying I was wrong saying that
I should have been a boy because he wanted one/a
boy and that I should have been lighter skinned and
that I should have had straighter hair and that
I should not be so boy crazy but instead I should

just be one/a boy and before that
it was my mother pleading plastic surgery for
my nose and braces for my teeth and telling me
to let the books loose to let them loose in other
words
I am very familiar with the problems of the C.I.A.
and the problems of South Africa and the problems
of Exxon Corporation and the problems of white
America in general and the problems of the teachers
and the preachers and the F.B.I. and the social
workers and my particular Mom and Dad/I am very
familiar with the problems because the problems
turn out to be
me

I am the history of rape
I am the history of the rejection of who I am
I am the history of the terrorized incarceration of
myself

I am the history of battery assault and limitless
armies against whatever I want to do with my mind
and my body and my soul and
whether it's about walking out at night
or whether it's about the love that I feel or
whether it's about the sanctity of my vagina or
the sanctity of my national boundaries
or the sanctity of my leaders or the sanctity
of each and every desire
that I know from my personal and idiosyncratic
and indisputably single and singular heart
I have been raped
be-
cause I have been wrong the wrong sex the wrong age
the wrong skin the wrong nose the wrong hair the
wrong need the wrong dream the wrong geographic
the wrong sartorial I
I have been the meaning of rape
I have been the problem everyone seeks to
eliminate by forced

penetration with or without the evidence of slime and/
but let this be unmistakable this poem
is not consent I do not consent
to my mother to my father to the teachers to
the F.B.I. to South Africa to Bedford-Stuy
to Park Avenue to American Airlines to the hardon
idlers on the corners to the sneaky creeps in
cars
I am not wrong: Wrong is not my name
My name is my own my own my own
and I can't tell you who the hell set things up like this
but I can tell you that from now on my resistance
my simple and daily and nightly self-determination
may very well cost you your life

---

June Jordan. From *Directed by Desire: The Collected Poems of June Jordan*. Port Townsend, WA: Copper Canyon Press, 2005. Copyright © 2005 June Jordan Literary Estate trust; reprinted by permission. www .junejordan.com.

## ➢ **Audre Lorde**

(1934–1992), United States

---

### **"A Woman Speaks"**

Moon marked and touched by sun
my magic is unwritten
but when the sea turns back
it will leave my shape behind.
I seek no favor
untouched by blood
unrelenting as the curse of love
permanent as my errors
or my pride
I do not mix
love with pity
nor hate with scorn
and if you would know me
look into the entrails of Uranus
where the restless oceans pound.

I do not dwell within my
birth nor my divinities
who am ageless and half-grown
and still seeking
my sisters
witches in Dahomey
wear me inside their coiled cloths
as our mother did
mourning.
I have been woman
for a long time
beware my smile
I am treacherous with old magic
and the noon's new fury
with all your wide futures
promised
I am
woman
and not white.

---

# CHAPTER 10

# Lesbian Pulp Novels and Gay Physique Pictorials

Focusing on the main forms of popular homosexed entertainment during the early part of the 20th century in the United States, this chapter illustrates the manner in which popular culture helped solidify a sense of identity.

In Chapter 1, we discussed the attempts of Anselm, Archbishop of Canterbury in England, to shame priests found guilty of sodomy by excommunicating them and publishing their crimes and sentences. As we noted, these publications eventually ceased because they drew extraordinary attention from male parishioners whose primary interest was in discussing who did what to whom [λ Chapter 1]. Clearly, one of the unintended consequences of making sodomy public was that a community of "interested parties" formed around a practice meant to punish men who engaged in sodomy. Nearly 900 years later, in the mid-20th century, a similar phenomenon began to emerge in the United States with the publication of physique pictorials and lesbian and gay male pulp novels. In the case of physique pictorials, magazines chock-full of photos of nearly nude male bodybuilders and ostensibly intended for a heterosexual, health-conscious readership, soon became favorites of a largely gay male audience. In the case of lesbian pulp novels and exposé texts written to titillate heterosexual males with innuendo of lesbian sex and that purported to warn of the dangers of lesbians and lesbianism, the books were so widely read by lesbians that, very early on, lesbian authors began writing them, knowing full well that they were reaching out to readers very much like themselves. Gay male pulp novels, even those published as "literary" texts and in cloth before their publication as cheap paperbacks, served a similar function for gay men.

The 1950s and early 1960s in the United States were marked by a number of important cultural contradictions. On one hand, the popular culture was focused on policing strict gender roles; women were encouraged to refocus their creative energies and labor on the home and (heterosexual) family because men had returned from World War II and needed employment in the factories that had used women's labor during the war. On the other hand, many women had learned during the war that they were capable of doing the high-paying industrial work hitherto reserved for men and wanted to continue in that work and contribute to the support of their families or to support themselves outside the constraints of the heterosexual family. The McCarthy era was in full swing, and much attention was paid to ferreting out Communists and "perverts" in the government, to which end Executive Order 10450 was signed by President Eisenhower in 1953. At the same time, the Mattachine Society and the DOB were formed, and both Alfred Kinsey and Evelyn Hooker were studying human sexuality in more objective ways than ever before [λ Chapter 3]. The physique pictorials and lesbian and gay pulp novels straddled these oppositional cultural forces and became conduits through which lesbian, gay male, and transgender culture passed.

## Physique Magazines

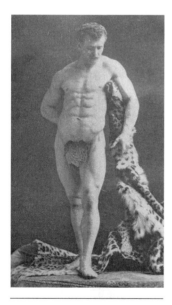

**Figure 10.1**   Eugen Sandow
Getty caption: "British muscle man Eugen Sandow in pose of The Farnese Hercules" (front view).

Physique magazines began in the late 19th century when Prussian bodybuilder Eugen Sandow (1867–1925) established *Physical Culture Magazine* in London to help publicize his Institute for Physical Culture. According to writer Jim Webber, Sandow's magazine, "along with the Boy Scouts and the Olympics, which were founded at about the same time, became part of the 'muscular Christian' movement, which promoted nationalism, racial purity, and brazen heterosexuality."

Bernarr Macfadden began publishing the U.S. version of *Physical Culture* at the beginning of the 20th century for a heterosexual male audience interested in diet, exercise, and overall physical fitness. By the end of World War II, physique magazines had gained a significant audience among physical fitness buffs. These magazines, and the fitness craze of which they were a part, met the demands of a culture in which more and more working men were employed in fairly sedentary office jobs and in which technological advances—particularly in domestic appliances—were reducing the physical requirements of maintaining a home. Charles Atlas, whom *Physical Culture* called "The World's Most Handsome Man," had by the mid-20th century posed for 30 years in scanty clothing; Atlas, an Italian whose real name was Angelino Siciliano, turned 62 in 1955, and advertisements for his exercise method, Dynamic Tension, were commonplace at that time in the United States (Waldron).

In 1956, the issue of fitness became a public concern when a study was released showing that American children were less physically fit than their European counterparts; accordingly, the President's Council on Physical Fitness and Sports

**Figure 10.2**   Charles Atlas, strongman.

was formed. In fact, the bodybuilding, diet, and fitness boom so generally permeated American culture that Alan Miller (writing for the gay magazine *Body Politic*) remembers being initiated to the pleasures of beefcake magazines in a barbershop:

> I first encountered *Physique Pictorial* in 1960. Several issues were thrown among the magazine collection of Top's Barber Shop hidden behind a variety store on Queen Mary Road in Montreal. The six barbers were—or so I vaguely remember—not the least bit embarrassed at having these things about, let alone that a young boy would be flipping through them. . . . Even when blatantly erotic, physique magazines were excused (one is not sure how successfully) as works for those interested in bodybuilding, art or nudism—anything to avoid labels being applied to the purchasers.

As Miller's experience indicates, bodybuilding and beefcake magazines soon became popular homoerotica.

According to David Bianco, though, Bernarr Macfadden "didn't intend his magazine for sexual titillation. When he became aware of its homosexual following, he publicly denounced his gay readers as 'painted, perfumed, kohl-eyed, lisping, mincing youths,'" whom he encouraged other men to "beat up." Nonetheless, the popularity of bodybuilding magazines helped create a climate that allowed photographer Bob Mizer to begin publishing gay-oriented *Physique Pictorial* in 1951. As early as 1948, Mizer distributed a catalog of photographs he advertised as "invaluable for artists, inspirational for bodybuilders" (McGarry and Wasserman 117). Mizer and others capitalized on bodybuilding magazines' underground gay male following. James M. Saslow says, "Under cover of the venerable physical culture movement, monthlies like *Tomorrow's Man* and *Adonis* printed reams of bodybuilders and sportsmen in the scantiest G-strings that would pass censorship. Bob Mizer . . . set up [the] Athletic Model Guild . . . to connect would-be poster-boys with artists and photographers" (252–253). U.S. postal codes, though vague, were generally interpreted as prohibiting full-frontal nudity, so models in Mizer's original catalogs and in *Physique Pictorial* wore posing straps and showed no body hair below the neck (McGarry and Wasserman 121). Bianco points out that the number of physique magazines aimed at a gay male readership grew until, by 1958, there were "several dozen" with as many as 70,000 readers.

Tom of Finland, whose given name was Touko Laaksonen, was probably the best-known illustrator to contribute work to physique magazines. He began publishing in *Physique Pictorial* when Mizer used one of his drawings for the cover of the spring 1957 issue. Micah Ramakers claims that Bob Mizer invented Laaksonen's pseudonym, though other sources claim that Laaksonen chose the name "Tom" himself because he worried that Touko would be difficult for the American tongue. Tom of Finland would eventually publish more than 100 images in Mizer's publication and in other physique magazines, and many of those appeared on the covers (Ramakers 4).

Highly stylized pieces featuring muscled men with enlarged penises and torsos, Tom's work often portrayed men engaged in sexual acts with one another. Many of his subjects wore uniforms—law enforcement, military, athletic—signaling a masculinity at odds with some sexologists' assertions that homosexual men had the souls of women trapped in male bodies [λ Chapter 2]. The drawings were often inspired by the photos appearing in the very magazines for which Tom was working and, as Ramakers points out, were "intended to complement the photos of desirable young men, which were the basis of the physique magazines' success" (48).

Clearly, beefcake magazines served a particular function for white gay men. However, they also reflected the pervasive racism that has so plagued U.S. constructions of maleness and, by extension, male homosexuality. Tracy Morgan points out that when the Mattachine Society and the DOB were protesting the McCarthy purges of

**Figure 10.3** Tom of Finland drawing (www
.Tomsparties.com/Galleries/ToF/index.html).

white homosexuals from government jobs, "few Black people were federally employed" at all (284). Morgan notes that the kind of racism that excluded blacks from government employment was reflected as well in the pages of physique magazines, where the portrait of masculinity was "patriotic, strong, and white" (284) and that gay men who found these images sexually arousing might enjoy the magazines less if the images were more racially diverse. This does not mean, however, that no men of color appeared as models in physiques. Of the three main types of magazines Morgan found—those using a Grecian metaphor, the "all-American" style directed at fitness buffs, and those that served as "early homophile publications" (287)—the second type was the most (though not significantly) racially integrated. Morgan says,

> Black men were generally underrepresented in physique publications in relation to their actual numbers in U.S. society during the years 1955–60. . . . The "all-American"-style physique magazines I surveyed included more than four times as many images of Black men as did the Grecian publications. In the latter category, in approximately twenty-six volumes published over a five-year period (1955–60), a paltry four images of Black men made it into print. . . . In contrast, the magazines oriented toward bodybuilding . . . included an average of one Black male image per issue, and often more. (289)

To understand the presence of black men in some physique magazines as indicative of any kind of effort to resist the racism in the larger culture would be a mistake. As Morgan notes, black men were often photographed with "props" like heavy chains and cargo crates, and the few Latino men who appeared in the pages of physiques, though "generally represented with fewer accoutrements, occasionally don straw hats while surrounded by rum bottles" (290). As is clear, the racial stereotypes of the mid-century United States and the tendency to exoticize the racial other were reflected in these magazines, and as we will see in a later chapter, Robert Mapplethorpe's homoerotic photographs of black men in the 1980s may represent a later version of this practice [λ Chapter 12].

# Lesbian Pulp Novels

The first modern paperbacks appeared in 1939 but did not proliferate until World War II when the military distributed them to soldiers on the front as entertainment. These books, known as *pulps* because of the cheap paper used in their production, were designed to appeal to mainstream (as opposed to "literary") readers, so they tended to focus on topics and use story lines that would enrapture a reader from the very first page. This meant that they were generally formulaic Westerns, detective fiction, romance, and ripped-from-the-headlines sensational texts that tended to reinforce ideas popularly held in the culture. Pulp novels had their heyday between 1950 and 1965, and they were sold on newsstands, as well as in drugstores and bus terminals, usually for about 25 cents. Their low price and pocket-sized format meant that most people considered them disposable in the same way that their predecessors, pulp magazines, had been. Scholar Yvonne Keller describes lesbian pulps as "typically lurid, voyeuristic and frequently homophobic, easily the opposite of 'high literature.' At the time, they were called 'trashy,' or 'dirty books'; they are somewhat like *National Enquirer* in book form" ("Ab/Normal" 177–78). Initially, lesbian pulps were written with a heterosexual male audience in mind, an audience that would find their contents titillating and would read them with a voyeuristic gaze. Hence, many of the early authors of lesbian-themed pulps were men.

The covers of lesbian pulp novels, as Jaye Zimet shows in *Strange Sisters: The Art of Lesbian Pulp Fiction, 1949–1969,* often featured illustrations of busty, scantily clad, traditionally beautiful, almost always white women, and most often there were two women on the cover—one kneeling or lying on the floor or a bed and the other standing above her or sitting nearby, either looking at the first woman or gazing out at the viewer/reader. With titles like *Women's Barracks* (1950), *Female Convict* (1952), *Women in Prison* (1953), *Women without Men* (1957), and *Reformatory Girls* (1960), these books promised to reveal the sultry underside of environments where nontraditional women—soldiers, prisoners, and wayward teens—lived together as emotional and sexual companions. Of the women portrayed on pulp covers, Ann Bannon says,

> Who were these "girls"? Gazing at the pulp-art covers of lesbian fiction published half a century ago is like reconnecting with old acquaintances; I hesitate to call them friends, since I never really recognized them as such. In fact, over the years as my own books [the Beebo Brinker series] were published, I looked in astonishment at the choices the editors and art directors had made. The books arrived in brown packets, for the very good reason that they were deliberately evocative of shady sex. With only small adjustments, and sometimes none at all, the young women I was looking at could easily have walked off those pulp covers and onto the pages of *Harper's Bazaar* to sell the "New Look." Many could have graced the ladies' undies section of the Sears, Roebuck catalog just as they were. (qtd. in Zimet 9)

The covers of lesbian-themed pulps, then, were not the lesbians with whom most women—those who knew they knew lesbians, that is—were familiar, especially early on; these were the lesbians of heterosexual male fantasies.

*Women's Barracks*, by Tereska Torres, was the book that started "the golden age of paperback originals" (Stryker 49). The novel is based at least partially on Torres's experiences serving in Charles de Gaulle's Free French army during World War II.

Though *Women's Barracks* deals openly with the sexual dalliances among the military women who are its characters, that is not its primary focus.

The book sold over a million copies in 1950, and eventually, it gained such notoriety that it became the focus of obscenity trials in Canada and the United States. Noting that, after World War II, Canadian newsstands "were opened to a huge range of mass market publications from the United States," Mary Louise Adams explains that Crown Attorney Raoul Mercier showed no interest in "the parts where heterosexual women find themselves pregnant, or where they discuss their plans to sleep with married men or where they attempt suicide. The definition of immorality was too narrow to include them. For Mercier, what made this book obscene was its discussion of lesbianism" (111).

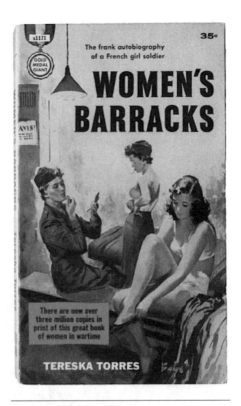

**Figure 10.4** *Women's Barracks* cover, Photo by Yvonne Keller.

In 1952, *Women's Barracks* was brought before a U.S. House of Representatives committee led by Congressman Ezekiel Candler Gathings; the committee "refused to quote it in their *Report of the Select Committee into Current Pornographic Materials*, claiming that its lesbian passages—which were restrained by contemporary standards—were too graphic to be included in a government document" (Stryker 51). According to Stryker, the report from the Gathings Committee resulted in publishers attempting to tone down the sexual content of their books and placing "greater emphasis on stories that drove home the generally tragic consequences of straying from the straight and narrow path" (51).

Some lesbians, most writing under pseudonyms, began to author lesbian-themed pulp novels specifically for a lesbian audience. Vin Packer, whose given name is Marijane Meaker and whose other pennames were Ann Aldrich and M. E. Kerr, wrote what was probably the first of these novels, *Spring Fire*. The novel is about Leda and Mitch, two sorority sisters who become involved in a dramatic, sexually charged romance marked by overwrought drama and betrayal. The story ends tragically with Leda lapsing into psychosis and Mitch clearly "scared straight" by the entire sordid affair.

Meaker is quick to point out that previous to the publication of *Spring Fire,* a lesbian market was not evident to anyone at Fawcett (the book's publisher), which was merely spurred on to publish more lesbian-themed paperbacks by the economic success of *Women's Barracks:*

> [*Spring Fire*] was not aimed at any lesbian market, because there wasn't any that we knew about. I was just out of college. I was gay . . . it wasn't a prurient book . . . Tereska Torres wasn't aiming [*Women's Barracks*] at any market either—just telling her experiences the best she could, as I was. We were amazed, *floored,* by the mail that poured in. That was the first time that anyone was aware of the gay audience out there. (qtd. in Keller, "Was It Right" 390)

Stryker echoes Meaker's characterization of the impact of *Spring Fire,* claiming that it "called attention to an enthusiastic lesbian readership whose extent had not been appreciated previously but one to which Fawcett and other mainstream paperback publishers would cater for the next fifteen years" (57). Perhaps for the first time, and clearly by accident, a lesbian market had emerged.

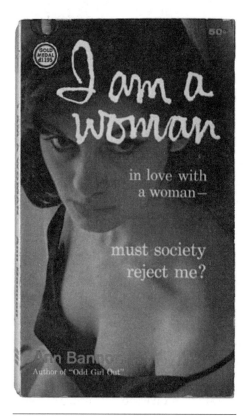

**Figure 10.5**   *I Am a Woman* by Ann Bannon, Photo by Yvonne Keller.

Roberta Yusba notes that "perhaps 40 or 50 lesbian novels were written by women and were also good enough to become underground classics. Dog-eared copies of books by Ann Bannon, Valerie Taylor, Artemis Smith, and Paula Christian were passed among friends in lesbian communities . . . and also reached isolated, small-town lesbians who could read them and see that they were not the only lesbians in the world" (qtd. in Nealon 748). Though the publishers still had ultimate control over the covers of the books, the stories between the covers tended to act as "tour guides" to places where lesbians seemed to congregate and interact with one another—places such as Greenwich Village, where much of Bannon's Beebo Brinker series takes place.

They also functioned as what Joan Nestle has called *survival literature* in that they helped provide a sense of what romantic relationships between women might look like. In her anthology of excerpts from lesbian-themed pulp novels, Katherine V. Forrest explains that very little biographical information exists for the novelists who produced these books because many of "the pulp fiction lesbian writers were deeply closeted, and some have dissolved into the mists like Cheshire cats, leaving only their printed words behind" (xi).

**Figure 10.6**   Ann Bannon.

Two authors who did not exactly dissolve into the mists were Patricia Highsmith (Mary Patricia Plangman) and Ann Bannon (Ann Weldy). Highsmith, writing as Claire Morgan, produced what many claim to be the first lesbian novel to end "happily"—that is, with the possibility that the two main characters, Therese and Carol, might enjoy an ongoing lesbian relationship with one another. *The Price of Salt* was not a paperback original, but it reached the height of its popularity after it appeared in paperback in 1952. Because it was published first by a mainstream publisher, Highsmith's novel had less of the potboiler character of paperback originals and more of the relative complexity of mainstream literature. Although a popular novelist, Highsmith (author of *Strangers on a Train, The Talented Mr. Ripley,* and other books) did not acknowledge until 1984 that she was indeed the Claire Morgan who wrote *The Price of Salt*; the fact that it sold a million copies indicates that it met a need for a lesbian readership hungry for representation.

**Figure 10.7**   Patricia Highsmith.

By contrast, Ann Bannon's Beebo Brinker novels were published as paperback originals; they tended to have more fully developed, less stereotypical lesbian characters and plots as well as slightly more hopeful endings than

**Find Out More** about lesbian pulps by reading a selection from Ann Bannon's *I Am a Woman*, the reading at the end of this chapter.

many of the pulps. Bannon's novels were rereleased in the 1980s and 1990s by well-known lesbian publishing house Naiad Press and in the 2000s by Cleis Press, and all of Highsmith's novels were recently rereleased by W. W. Norton.

## Gay Male Pulp Novels

Like their lesbian-themed counterparts, which were much "more numerous and popular than those that dealt with male homosexuality," gay male-themed pulps "represent, beneath a veneer of enticing exploitation, a compendium of the not-so-hidden preoccupations and fears of the tempestuous and socially unstable postwar years" (Bronski, *Pulp Friction* 3). Michael Bronski notes, though, that the "trajectory for gay male pulps is very different [from that of lesbian-themed pulps]. There was no burgeoning market for gay male novels in the 1950s because they apparently had little crossover appeal for a substantial heterosexual readership" (*Pulp Friction* 4). Although some gay male-themed pulp novels were published as paperback originals, many were republications of earlier novels originally published in hardback by mainstream houses.

**Figure 10.8** *Twilight Men* cover.

A few gay male books were written and published in hardback during the 1930s and republished in paperback format after World War II. For instance, André Tellier's *Twilight Men* was originally published in 1931 and republished in paperback by Greenberg in 1948 and by Pyramid Books in 1957; Blair Niles, a woman best known at the time for the travel and nature writing she wrote collaboratively with her husband, wrote *Strange Brother*, also originally published in 1931, then republished in 1952. Forman Brown's *Better Angel*, published in 1933, was republished in 1951 as *Torment* under the pseudonym Richard Meeker. Novels by mainstream authors such as Gore Vidal (*The City and the Pillar*, 1948) and Truman Capote (*Other Voices, Other Rooms*, 1948) received critical attention and notoriety because of their gay male content—explicit in the case of Vidal and implicit in the case of Capote.

We should not assume, however, that Vidal's fame and connections granted his gay-themed novel immunity from homophobia in the publishing business. *The City and the Pillar* "so unnerved *The New York Times* it refused even to print the publisher's ads" (Young). This rejection was surely a factor in how Vidal composed the original ending of his novel. The first edition of *The City and the Pillar* ends with the main character, Jim, murdering Bob, the childhood friend with whom he has been in love ever since their sexual encounters in the woods when both were teens. The murder occurs in the context of Jim's realization of Bob's homophobia. The 1965 version of *The City and the Pillar* was revised by Vidal and ends with Jim raping rather than murdering Bob, ostensibly because Vidal no longer needed to conform to publisher mandates that the book end in the death of one of the main characters. Capote's *Other Voices, Other Rooms* focuses on Joel Knox, who is sent to live in a rural Alabama mansion with his estranged father and a cast of other characters, including Randolph, who is a transvestite. Near the end of the novel, the reader is led to believe that Randolph is also the character described by Joel earlier as the "queer lady" who appears in one of the mansion's windows. *Other Voices, Other Rooms* did not enjoy great critical success because reviewers saw it as contrived and lacking in narrative structure. However, the implicit homosexual themes in the novel, combined with the provocative jacket photo—Capote lounging on a sofa and giving the camera a come-hither look—caused a controversy that helped make Capote a literary star. Vidal's novel was republished in paperback in 1950 and Capote's in 1949, making theirs among the first gay-themed novels to appear in paperback format.

Like *The City and the Pillar* and *Other Voices, Other Rooms*, James Baldwin's *Giovanni's Room* (1956) [λ Chapter 9] appeared in paperback after experiencing little success in its initial hardback printing. *Giovanni's Room* is a book Michael Bronski characterizes as among those gay "self-hating novels ... which end in either murder or self-destruction" ("Queer Eye"). As a Signet pulp, however, featuring a sexy Giovanni on the cover and a pseudo-journalistic subscript ("A daring novel that treats a controversial subject

**Figure 10.9**  Truman Capote's jacket photo for *Other Voices, Other Rooms*.

**Figure 10.10** James Baldwin.

with honesty and compassion"), *Giovanni's Room* sold much better than before—signaling, perhaps, a growing mainstream interest in frank treatments of homosexual lives.

We should also note that some of the women writing lesbian pulps were also writing books with gay male themes. Vin Packer (Marijane Meaker), for example, published *Whisper His Sin* in 1954. Stryker says of this novel, "Prior to the mid-1960s there were simply no mass-market books that dealt with male-male desire that did not somehow couch it in terms of bisexual conflict, illustrate it with misleading cover art containing both men and women, or hide it behind pathologizing marketing blurbs. This was certainly the case with *Whisper his Sin* . . . which did a little of all three" (107).

## Transgender Novels

At mid-century, North American and Western European ideas about the nature of homosexuality—which deeply affected the packaging of pulp novels—still reflected the influence of the German sexologists' ideas about gender inversion [λ Chapter 2]. As a result, post-World War II pulp novels often portrayed lesbians and gay men as possessing the qualities commonly associated with the "opposite sex." What's more, U.S. popular media and culture, profoundly affected by advances in technology, were asking ethical questions often associated with technological progress—How far is too far for science to go in altering nature? What is the relationship between science and nature? In previous generations, these questions had manifested themselves in fascination with the human potential to create monsters in the name of science—as in, for instance, Mary Shelley's *Frankenstein*. In 1952, this type of fascination focused on transsexuality when the news broke that Christine Jorgensen, formerly George, had received successful sex reassignment surgery in Denmark. According to Stryker, though Jorgensen's autobiography (with an introduction by Harry Benjamin) [λ Chapter 5] would not be published until 1967, the "journalism trade publication *Editor and Publisher* announced in the spring of 1954 that more newsprint had been generated about

Jorgensen during the previous year than about any other individual—over a million and a half words" (73).

As is evidenced in the work of B-movie director Edward D. Wood Jr. (featured in the 1994 bio-pic *Ed Wood,* by Tim Burton), in 1950s U.S. popular culture, almost no distinction was made among transvestitism, transsexuality, and intersexuality. Capitalizing on the Jorgensen media frenzy, Wood directed *Glen or Glenda* based on Jorgensen's sex change operation. Humorously dubbed the "Worst Director of All Time," Wood supplemented his income as a producer by writing pulp novels, most of which contained transvestite characters or focused exclusively on transvestitism. Among the titles are *Black Lace Drag* (1963), featuring a transvestite hit man named Glen and his drag persona, Glenda, and its sequel, *Death of a Transvestite* (1967). Wood's quickly composed, sensationalist work— both in film and in print—has gained such a following in recent years that there is currently an Internet religion called The Church of Ed Wood, which boasts a membership of more than 3,000.

Stryker points out that some "novels written in the late 1940s, well before the Jorgensen media blitz, suggest that transgender issues were actually quite central to postwar American anxieties about sexuality, and to the paperback phenomenon itself" (77). One example of how these anxieties were expressed is Stuart Engstrand's *The Sling and the Arrow.* Engstrand's sensational novel is about a man who not only cross-dresses but asks his wife to do the same; he eventually becomes psychotic, imagines that he has transformed into a woman, kills his wife, and "drives off into the night where he takes his place near the head of a long line of gender-bent pop culture killers" (Stryker 78).

Lesbian pulp novels were seen for at least a decade following the advent of feminism as having very little positive to say to women wishing to build identities not constricted by stereotypes and sexist constructions of gender. However, queer pulps and, more recently, pulp cover art have reemerged as popular artifacts. The current use of pulp covers as refrigerator magnets, postcards, and T-shirt transfers celebrates campy images that recall, if not a more difficult time, then at least a more closeted time. The celebration of pulp reveals a sense of connection to a past today's LGBT people both eschew and embrace. Many critics focus on the unhappy endings and bizarre characterizations in these books, but Katherine Forrest proclaims, "Their words reached us, they touched us in different and deeply personal ways, and they helped us all" (xix). Though it is clear that most pulp texts were meant to teach readers that queers were . . . well, queer, and therefore doomed to difficult lives filled with sleaze and shame, our predecessors found in them important connections to one another.

## Questions for Discussion

1. Works of pulp fiction, despite their often tragic endings, can be great fun to read, particularly as they offer an insight into what gay, lesbian, bisexual, and transgendered lives might have been like in mid-century America. Read a few pulp fiction stories from Katherine V. Forrest's anthology of lesbian pulps or Michael Bronski's anthology of gay male pulps. What characterizes the representation of gay and lesbian lives or homoerotic desire in these novels and stories? For instance, what bisexual plots do you see? Are there any similarities between these pulp representations and contemporary figurings of queer life in mainstream media?

2. The art of Tom of Finland typically eroticizes uniformed, jackbooted, muscular men in scenarios where they dominate other men. What do you believe the artist intended viewers to experience? Is there any political or social meaning to Tom's art?

3. The selection from Ann Bannon's pulp novel *I Am a Woman* included in the readings for this chapter focuses on the coming-out conversation between Laura and her controlling and abusive father. During the course of this conversation, Laura accuses her father of having caused her to become a lesbian. Consider this idea in light of the discussion of 1950s pop Freudianism in Chapter 3. What are some of the major narratives purporting to explain why people are L, G, B, or T?

## References and Further Reading

Adams, Mary Louise. "Youth, Corruptibility, and the English-Canadian Postwar Campaigns against Indecency, 1948–1955." *Journal of History of Sexuality* 6.1 (1995): 89–117. Print.

Barale, Michéle Aina. "When Jack Blinks: Si(gh)ting Gay Desire in Ann Banno's *Beebo Brinker*." *Feminist Studies* 18.1 (1992): 533–49. Print.

Bianco, David. "Physique Magazines." *PlanetOut History,* 2007. Web. 8 August 2008. <www.planetout.com/news/history/archive/09271999.html>.

Brandt, Kate. *Happy Endings: Lesbian Writers Talk about Their Lives and Work.* Tallahassee, FL: Naiad, 1993. Print.

Bronski, Michael. *Pulp Friction: Uncovering the Golden Age of Gay Male Pulps.* New York: St. Martin's Griffin, 2003. Print.

———. "Queer Eye for the 50s Guy." *Utne Reader,* January/February 2004. Web. 8 August 2008. <http://www.utne.com/2004-01-01/Queer-Eye-for-the-50s-Guy.aspx>.

Cruikshank, Margaret. *Lesbian Studies: Present and Future.* New York: Feminist Press, 1982. Print.

Duberman, Martin, Martha Vicinus, and George Chauncey, eds. *Hidden from History: Reclaiming the Gay and Lesbian Past.* New York: Meridian, 1990. Print.

Foote, Stephanie. "Deviant Classics: Pulps and the Making of Lesbian Print Culture." *Signs: Journal of Women in*

*Culture and Society* 31.1 (2005): 169–90. Print.

Forrest, Katherine V. *Lesbian Pulp Fiction: The Sexually Intrepid World of Lesbian Paperback Novels, 1950–1965.* San Francisco: Cleis, 2005. Print.

Foster, Jeannette H. *Sex Variant Women in Literature.* Tallahassee, FL: Naiad, 1985. Print.

Goldman, Jason. "The Golden Age of Gay Porn: Nostalgia and the Photography of Wilhelm von Gloeden." *Gay and Lesbian Quarterly* 12.2 (2006): 237–58. Print.

Grier, Barbara. *The Lesbian in Literature.* Tallahassee, FL: Naiad, 1981. Print.

Hooven, Valentine. "Tom of Finland: A Short Biography." *Tom of Finland.* Tom of Finland Foundation. 2003–2006. Web. 7 April 2007. <www.tomoffinlandfoundation.org/ foundation/touko.html>.

Keller, Yvonne. "Ab/Normal Looking: Voyeurism and Surveillance in Lesbian Pulp Novels and US Cold War Culture." *Feminist Media Studies* 5.2 (2005): 177–95. Print.

———. "Was It Right to Love Her Brother's Wife So Passionately? Lesbian Pulp Novels and U.S. Lesbian Identity, 1950–1965." *American Quarterly* 57.2 (2005): 385–410. Print.

McGarry, Molly, and Fred Wasserman. *Becoming Visible: An Illustrated History of Lesbian and Gay Life in Twentieth-Century America.* New York: Penguin, 1998. Print.

Miller, Alan. "Beefcake before Blueboy." *The Body Politic,* 90 Jan.–Feb. 1983. Web. 8 August 2008. <http://www.clga.ca/Material/PeriodicalsLGBT/docs/beefcake.htm>.

Morgan, Tracy. "Pages of Whiteness: Race, Physique Magazines, and the Emergence of Public Gay Culture." *Queer Studies: A Lesbian, Gay, Bisexual, and Transgender Anthology.* Eds. Brett Beemyn and Mickey Eliason. New York: NYU P, 1996: 280–97. Print.

Nealon, Christopher. "Invert-History: The Ambivalence of Lesbian Pulp Fiction." *New Literary History* 31 (2000): 745–64. Print.

Nestle, Joan. *A Restricted Country.* New York: Firebrand, 1987. Print.

Ramakers, Micah. *Dirty Pictures: Tom of Finland, Masculinity, and Homosexuality.* New York: St. Martin's, 2000. Print.

Saslow, James M. *Pictures and Passions: A History of Homosexuality in the Visual Arts.* New York: Penguin/Putnam, 1999. Print.

Stryker, Susan. *Queer Pulp: Perverted Passions from the Golden Age of the Paperback.* San Francisco: Chronicle Books, 2001. Print.

Waldron, Gail. "Charles Atlas: A Brief Biography." *Charles Atlas.* Charles Atlas, Ltd. 2000. Web. 3 April 2007. <www.sandowplus.co.uk/Competition/Atlas/atlasindex.htm>.

Walters, Suzanna Danuta. "As Her Hand Crept Slowly Up Her Thigh: Ann Bannon and the Politics of Pulp." *Social Text* 23 (1989): 83–101. Print.

Webber, Jim. "Physique Magazines: Beefcake and the Origins of Gay Male Adult Magazines." *Lavendar Library.* N.d. Web. 2 April 2006. <www.lavenderlibrary.org/pages/Physique.htm>.

Wheeler, Elizabeth. *Uncontained: Urban Fiction in Postwar America.* New Brunswick, NJ: Rutgers, 2001. Print.

Young, Ian. "The Paperback Explosion: How Gay Paperbacks Changed America." N.d. Web. 8 August 2008. <www.ianyoungbooks.com/GayPbks/Paperbacks.htm>.

Zaborowska, Magdalena J. "Giovanni's Room." *The Literary Encyclopedia.* The Literary Dictionary Company, 13 June 2003. Web. 8 August 2008. <http://www.litencyc.com/php/sworks.php?rec=true&UID=4964>.

Zimet, Jaye. *Strange Sisters: The Art of Lesbian Pulp Fiction, 1949–1969.* New York: Viking, 1999. Print.

Zimmerman, Bonnie. *The Safe Sea of Women: Lesbian Fiction, 1969–1989.* Boston: Beacon, 1990. Print.

# READING

## ➢ Ann Bannon

(1959–), United States

### From *I Am a Woman*

He didn't know, and she didn't want him to know. She was the one who cared about their relationship, who wanted love and trust and gentleness between them. Not her father. He didn't give a damn, as long as she minded him. "You said you had no daughter," she repeated bitterly.

"You wanted it that way, Laura."

She turned to stare at him, incredulous. "I?" she said. "*I* wanted it that way?"

"You denied my existence before I ever denied yours," he said. "You ran away from me."

"You *forced* me to."

"I did no such thing."

"You made life intolerable for me."

"I didn't mean to." It was an extraordinary admission, completely unexpected, and she looked at him speechless for a moment.

"Then why didn't you show me some kindness?" she said. "Just a very little would have gone a long way, Father."

He crushed out his cigarette in the heavy ashtray with an expression of contempt on his face. "You women are all alike, I swear to God," he said. "Give you a little and you demand a lot."

"What's wrong with a lot?" she said, trembling. "You're my father."

"Yes, exactly!" he said, so roughly that she ducked. "I'm your father!"

"Did you treat my mother this way?" she whispered. "Her life must have been hell."

He looked for a minute as if he would strangle her. She stood her ground, pale and frightened, until he relented suddenly and turned his profile to her, looking out the window. "Your mother," he said painfully, "was my wife. I adored her."

Laura was absolutely unable to answer him. She sat down weakly in the stuffed chair by the dresser and put her face in her hands. Her father—her enormous gruff harsh father—had never spoken such a tender word in her presence in all her life.

"I could never marry again, when she died," he said. Laura felt frightened as she always did when her mother's death was mentioned. She expected him to turn on her unreasonably as he had so often before. "I never struck her."

"Then why me?" she implored out of a dry throat.

He turned and looked at her, his mouth twisted a little, running a distraught hand through his hair. "You needed it," was all he would say.

"What for?"

"You *needed* it, that's what for!" And she was afraid to push him further. After some minutes he said, "Laura, you're coming back to Chicago with me."

"No Father, I can't. I won't."

"That's why I waited for you," he went on, as if she had said nothing.

"I won't go to Chicago or anywhere else with you. I'm through with you."

"You could look for work with a radiologist, if you like it so well. I won't insist on journalism. You have a flair for it, it's a waste to leave the field, but I won't insist. You see, Laura, I can be human enough."

She stared at him. She had never heard him talk like this. He glanced at her, annoyed by the look on her face. "I've made reservations," he said, "for June first. That's Saturday. I could probably get earlier ones."

"Father." She stood up. "I can't come with you."

"Don't say that!" he commanded her, so sharply that she started.

"I can't," she whispered.

"You can, and you will. That's all I want to hear on the subject." As she started once again to protest he held his hands up for silence. "No more discipline, Laura. I promise you that. I was a fool. You were too, but never mind that now. I was too hard on you, it's true. I see that. Well, you're more or less grown up by this time. I guess we can dispense with spanking."

"Spanking! It was more than that and you know it!"

"Don't argue with me, Laura." He turned on her, his voice low and fierce. Then, making a visible effort to calm himself, he said, "Get your things together and I'll see about the reservations."

"No."

"Don't fight me, Laura."

"Father, there's something you don't know about me." *I have to tell him. I'll never be free from him till I tell him. Till he knows what he's made of his only child.* "There's something you don't know about me," she whispered.

"I don't doubt it. Now hurry up, we've wasted enough time."

"Father . . . listen to me." It was almost too hard to say. Her legs were trembling and her heart was wild.

"Well, out with it, for God's sake! Jesus, Laura, you go through more agony . . . Well? What is it?" He frowned at her tense face.

"I—I'm a—homosexual."

His mouth dropped open and his whole body went rigid. Laura shut her eyes and prayed. She held her lower lip in her teeth, ready for the blow, and felt the humiliating tears begin to squeeze through her shut lids. She moaned a little.

He made up his mind fast and his voice cracked out like a lash. "Nonsense!" he snarled.

"It's true!" Her eyes flew open and she cried again, passionately, "It's true!" It was her bid for freedom; she had to show this courage, this awful truth to him, or she would never walk away from him. She would spend all her life in a panic of fear lest he find her out. "I'm in love with my roommate. I've made love—"

"All right, all right, all right!" he shouted. His voice was rough and his face contorted. He turned away from her and put his hands over his face. She watched him, every muscle tight and aching.

At last he let his hands drop and said quietly, "Did I do that to you, Laura?"

Without hesitating, without even certain knowledge, but only the huge need to hurt him, she said, "Yes."

He turned slowly around and faced her and she had never seen his face like that before. It was pained and full of gentleness. Perhaps it looked that way to her mother now and then. "I did that to you," he said again, to himself. "Oh, Laura. Oh, Laura." His heavy brow creased deeply over his eyes. He walked to her and put his hands on her shoulders and felt her jerk with fear. "Laura," he said, "have you ever loved a man?"

She shook her head, unable to speak.

"Have you ever wanted a man?"

Again she shook her head.

"Do you know what it's like to want a man?"

"No," she whispered.

"Do you want to know?" His eyes were wide and intense, his grip on her shoulders was very hard.

"I'm so afraid of them, Father. I don't want to know."

He seemed to be in another world. Laura was utterly mystified by his strange behavior, blindly grateful for his sudden warmth, and she let herself weep softly.

"Laura," he said, as if he derived some private pleasure from saying her name over and over. "Your mother—you look so much like your mother. You never looked like me at all. Every time I look at you I see her face. Her fragile delicate face. Her eyes, her hair." He put his arms around her. "Come back to Chicago with me," he said gently. "You don't have to love a man, Laura. I don't want you to. I don't want you to be like other girls, I don't want you to go off with some young ass and give him your youth and your beauty. I don't mind if you're different from the rest. I can take that if you are able to."

Laura clung to him, astonished, fearful, grateful, anxious, a whirlwind of confused feelings churning inside her.

"I want you to stay with me," he said. "I always did. I won't let you go."

"You made me go, Father. You punished me so."

"No, no Laura! Don't you see, it was myself." He was holding her so hard now, as if to make up for years of avoiding her, that she ached with it. She began to cry on his shoulder.

"Oh, Father, Father," she wept. "You never told me you wanted me to stay with you. You made me believe you hated me."

"No," he said. "I never hated you." He spoke in a rush, as if he couldn't help himself, as if it were suddenly forcing its way out of him after years of suppression. "Never, Laura, it was just that I was so lonely, so terribly lonely; I wanted her so much and she was gone. And there was only you, and you tormented me."

"I?" She tried to see his face, but he held her too close.

"You were so much like her, even when you were a child. Every time I looked at you, I—oh, Laura, it's myself I should have punished all this time. I *was* punished. I've suffered. Believe me. Laura, please believe me."

Laura was suddenly shocked rigid to feel his lips on her neck. He put his hand in her hair and kissed her full on the mouth with such agonized intensity that he electrified her. He released her just as suddenly and turned away with a kind of sob. "Ellie! Ellie!" he cried, his hands over his face.

Laura was shaking almost convulsively. At the sound of her mother's name she grabbed the thick and heavy glass ashtray from the dresser, picking it up with both hands. She rushed at him, unable to think or reason, and brought the ashtray down on the crown of his head with all the revolted force in her body. He slumped to the floor without a sound.

Laura gaped at him for a sick second and then she turned and fled. She left the door wide open and ran in a terrible panic to the elevators. She sobbed frantically for a few moments, and then she pushed the down button. She jabbed it over and over again hysterically, unable to stop until an elevator arrived and the doors opened. She stumbled in and pressed into a back corner, helpless in the grip of the sickness in her. The operator and his two other passengers stared at her, but she paid them no heed, even when one asked if he could help her. At the ground floor the operator had to tell her, "Everybody out."

She turned a wild flushed face to him and he said, "Are you all right, Miss?" And she glared at him, violently offended by his manner, his uniform, his question.

"Don't you know those pants won't make a man of you?" she exclaimed acidly. And rushed out, leaving him gaping open-mouthed after her.

---

Ann Bannon. *I Am a Woman*. Tallahassee, FL: Naiad, 1986 [1959]. Reprinted by Cleis in 2002

# CHAPTER 11

# Queer Transgressions

Transgressive art and literature challenge our understanding of sexuality with highly provocative images and rhetoric. This chapter presents material that encourages analysis of sexuality that runs deeper than traditional distinctions among sexual preferences. This is work that questions normalizing assumptions for (and about) both gays and straights.

The work we will be considering in this chapter is work by artists, designers, and cultural producers who use transgression consciously as a mode of social or political critique and resistance. Such work is often edgy, sometimes even erotic—but it is also very public, addressing many audiences and challenging their assumptions and values. Transgressive art and literature have played increasingly important roles in shaping the contemporary queer imagination, especially as such art foregrounds the ways queers resist dominating, normalizing, and homophobic narratives about their lives and loves. The works of authors such as Kathy Acker, Dennis Cooper, Gary Indiana, and Jeanette Winterson often portray characters engaging in acts of transgressive resistance—acts that simultaneously work against the restrictive identities that we are called to adopt in a heteronormative world and that, through their resistance, transgress the dichotomies, binaries, and boundaries that attempt to order identity, culture, and social interaction along delimiting lines of patriarchal and heterosexist ideologies. These works provide much-needed imaginative models for carving queer spaces, identities, and lives out of an often hostile political and cultural matrix. But, as Winterson notes in a refrain repeated throughout her collection of experimental fiction, *The World and Other Places,* "What you risk reveals what you value." While acts of transgression are often deployed as acts of resistance, they are also acts of assertion, performances of the transgressors' investments and values both against and within the social matrix they are transgressing. In addition to discussing political, literary, and erotic queer transgressions, this chapter also presents some material that invites an analysis of sexuality that runs deeper than traditional distinctions among sexual preferences and affiliations. This is work that questions normalizing assumptions for both queers and straights.

# Theoretical Transgressions: The Emergence of Queer Theory

In many ways, queer theory has been among the most challenging movements within the academy. Growing out of feminism, gay and lesbian studies, and postmodern literary theory, queer theory asks that we take very seriously the representation—and construction—of sex and sexuality in a wide variety of cultural venues. Gay and lesbian studies began to take shape in the 1970s and 1980s, focused on identifying and analyzing representations of the homoerotic and the homosexual in the canons of literature. A queer approach, beginning with Eve Kosofsky Sedgwick's *Epistemology of the Closet* (1990), substantively shifted the question of representation to a radical reunderstanding of Western culture as principally preoccupied with the construction and control of identities based on sexual orientation. Sedgwick argues that "virtually any aspect of modern Western culture must be, not merely incomplete, but damaged in its central substance to the degree that it does not incorporate a critical analysis of modern homo/heterosexual definition" (1). Following the work of Michel Foucault (1926–1984), thinkers such as Sedgwick (1950–2009) and Judith Butler (b. 1956) wanted not just to "find" homosexuals but to analyze the power constructs that divide us in the modern and contemporary world, at least in the West, into two categories: gay and straight. These theorists question and often even reject the binary construction of the species into gay/ straight, even male/ female, in such a way that one pole of the binary (straight, often male) is valorized, privileged, and normalized over the other (gay, often female).

Probing what had been assumed to be a given—our identification based on sexual orientation—is certainly a transgressive move, prompting scholars to reconsider basic assumptions about identity, community, and politics. If the way we understand sexual orientation isn't a natural given, then neither are heterosexuality, homophobia, or bias against those who engage in alternative or nonnormative intimate and filial practices. Such thinking called for a mode of critique and an activist politics that insisted that we question the "norm" or anything that is socially constructed as "natural" or "normal." As David Halperin put it in *Saint Foucault: Toward a Gay Hagiography,*

> Resistance to normativity is not purely negative or reactive or destructive; it is also positive and dynamic and creative. It is by resisting the discursive and institutional practices which, in their scattered and diffuse functioning, contribute to the operation of heteronormativity that queer identities can open a social space for the construction of different identities, for the elaboration of various types of relationships, for the development of new cultural forms. (66–67)

"Resistance to normativity," encapsulated in embracing the term *queer,* is a transgressive move. It asks that we reconsider the desirability of the "normal," of being "normal," and that we transgress boundaries of taste, belief, and values to "open a social space" for considering and valuing different tastes, beliefs, and values. More recently, bisexual and transgender activists and scholars have been using the basic tenets of queer theory to challenge constructions of **monogamy** and gender.

How does queer theory challenge academic work? Let's take an example from literary studies. Working with a gay and lesbian studies approach, a literary scholar might look for past representations of gay and lesbian people in works of literature or for how an author's supposed gayness influenced his or her literary output. For instance, William Shakespeare wrote a series of powerful sonnets, some addressed to a close male friend and others to a "dark lady." Some of the sonnets addressed to his friend contain, by contemporary standards, fairly loaded romantic language, and the poet declares about his male friend, "Let me not to the marriage of true minds admit impediment"—the opening lines of a sonnet often used in wedding ceremonies today. One might assume, given Shakespeare's language, that the sonnets represent a bisexual consciousness or identity. A queer theorist might argue that such an interpretation is *presentist*— that is, viewing past behaviors anachronistically through current identity categories. Queer theorists would argue instead for a *perverse presentism* that would look for expressions of desire, intimacy, and eroticism but not assume that such resemble contemporary categories of gay, lesbian, bisexual, or trans identity [λ Introduction]. Rather, the queer theorist would seek to understand how such expressions are related to constructs of power and social relations. In Shakespeare's case, for instance, perhaps his "romantic" language about his friend suggests not an erotic relationship but a privileging of friendship between men,

**Find Out More:** *See the readings by Eve Kosofsky Sedgwick and Michael Warner at the end of this chapter for additional discussion of queer theory.*

with women being relegated to love objects, not true equals. We might view Shakespeare's intriguing sonnet through Sedgwick's lens in *Between Men: English Literature and Male Homosocial Desire* (1985); there she proposes that male-male intimacy in pre-20th-century Western culture is only intelligible as it elides spaces occupied by women.

## Art and Consumerism

Queer artists have been producing work that challenges assumptions about sex, gender, sexuality, and identity. As we have seen in previous chapters, ACT UP's various kiss-ins and demonstrations in Catholic churches in New York were designed to be provocative and transgressive. The point was to insert queer into spaces where people either felt safe from queerness or were not expecting displays of sexuality [λ Chapter 4]. In transgressing social norms about when and where sexuality, particularly queer sexualities, can be performed, ACT UP hoped to remind a complacent, indifferent, and even hostile culture that queer people and their issues, such as the AIDS epidemic, are part of the larger social and political fabric. In an effort to be recognized as citizens demanding ethical treatment, queer activists transgressed some of the West's "sacred" spaces, such as churches and shopping malls.

A clearly discernible, public, and even somewhat queer transgressive aesthetic in American culture became apparent in the writings of those who identified with **Beat culture** in the 1950s. Authors such as Jack Kerouac, Gregory Corso, and Diane DiPrima urged their readers, through a variety of experimental forms and free-form genres, to question what they saw as an emerging culture dominated by consumerism, political complacency, and repressive norms, particularly around sex and sexuality. This work would eventually contribute to revolutionary youth cultures of the 1960s, particularly the so-called sexual revolution. A founding figure of the Beat movement and a lifelong proponent of sexual freedom was the gay poet Allen Ginsberg (1926–1997), whose work understood democracy as enabling a variety of expressions of intimate freedom [λ Chapter 9]. In one of his most famous poems, "Howl" (written in 1955), Ginsberg laments the devastation wreaked on creative youth by a cramped, uptight, repressive society:

I saw the best minds of my generation destroyed by madness, starving hysterical naked,

dragging themselves through the negro streets at dawn looking for an angry fix,

angelheaded hipsters burning for the ancient heavenly connection to the starry dynamo in the machinery of night . . .

A bit later in the poem, Ginsberg speaks frankly of homosexuals as victims of a sexually repressive consumerist society, of those

> who let themselves be fucked in the ass by saintly motorcyclists, and screamed with joy,
>
> who blew and were blown by those human seraphim, the sailors, caresses of Atlantic and Caribbean love . . .
>
> who lost their loveboys to the three old shrews of fate the one eyed shrew of the heterosexual dollar the one eyed shrew that winks out of the womb and the one eyed shrew that does nothing but sit on her ass and snip the intellectual golden threads of the craftsman's loom . . . (23)

"Howl" was so inflammatory that shortly after its publication, the poem was the subject of a censorship trial. Fellow poet and publisher Lawrence Ferlinghetti, who published "Howl" as part of his City Lights series, noted that "[t]he 'Howl' that was heard around the world wasn't seized in San Francisco in 1956 just because it was judged obscene by cops, but because it attacked the bare roots of our dominant culture, the very Moloch heart of our consumer society" (qtd. in Ginsberg, xi). Ginsberg's transgression lay not only in depicting homosexuality but also in linking the repression of queerness and other forms of alternative, nonnormative behavior to the desires of a consumerist culture intent on squelching transgressive creativity and enforcing conformity.

More recent LGBT and queer artists have used a comparable transgressive energy to enliven their work and offer cultural critiques within the consumer culture that the Beats sought to reject. Perhaps most famously in the late 20th century, the artist Robert Mapplethorpe [λ Chapter 12] produced a series of photographs of queer sex acts—some frankly sadomasochistic—that simultaneously shocked and titillated a variety of viewers, both queer and straight. We discuss Mapplethorpe in more detail in the next chapter, but an obvious question one must ask about him is whether an artist whose work becomes familiar in the popular culture can still be considered transgressive; the same question could be asked of photographer Annie Leibovitz, who was named "America's Best-Known Photographer" by *Newsweek* in 2007. Leibovitz began her career shooting for the fledgling *Rolling Stone,* and among her most familiar photographs, shot for that magazine, is one of Yoko Ono and John Lennon taken only hours before Lennon's murder in 1980. In 1991, a Leibovitz photograph of Demi Moore seven months pregnant and nude appeared on the cover of the mainstream magazine *Vanity Fair.* Except in New York City, that issue of the magazine appeared on bookstore shelves wrapped in a white envelope, with only Moore's eyes showing above (Anderson). In *Pregnant Pictures,* Sandra Matthews and Laura Wexler argue that "Leibovitz crossed a boundary at a ripe cultural moment, and with her image of the pregnant woman, pregnant pictures crossed over into the public visual domain" (qtd. in Bartlett 3). Leibovitz's work also seems to find "ripe cultural moments" for transgressing normative sexual boundaries with photographs of lesbian and gay celebrities such as Melissa Etheridge, Martina Navratilova, and Leibovitz's long-time partner, Susan Sontag.

Leibovitz has enjoyed great popularity, much of it in mainstream culture and, most recently, in advertising. This fact highlights some important questions about transgression: if, as often happens in capitalist societies, art is commodified and accepted as part of the popular culture, can it still be considered transgressive? Are there ways in which art popularized and commodified in a culture can transgress traditional boundaries by reaching an audience that would not necessarily seek exposure to that which is more clearly transgressive?

Desiring to collapse the boundaries between the public and the private, or perhaps to show the artificiality of such boundaries in a consumerist culture that uses sex to sell merchandise, some gay designers have created controversy with public advertisements depicting gays, lesbians, and bisexuals together, often holding hands or kissing. This kind of representation can be both mainstream-oriented and transgressive. For example, a widely-distributed 2012 J.C. Penney catalog shows a wholesome and casually dressed gay male couple playing affectionately with their children. More confrontational is the Italian photographer Oliviero Toscani, who has produced controversial advertising images that aim not only to sell products, such as clothing for Benetton, but also to level pointed social critiques at war, capital punishment, racism, and homophobia. One reporter chronicles Toscani's mixing of advertising and activism:

> In 1990, Toscani's "United Colors of Benetton" campaign launched a ten-year span [of] symbolic, poignant, jarring, and controversial ads that the man and the company became known for: a priest kissing a nun; a bloody baby fresh from the womb; a black stallion mounting a white mare; a colorful mix of condoms spread over a bright background; a white infant suckling a black woman's breast; the exposed pulsing hearts of three different races shown during surgery; the body of an AIDS victim moments before death; frightened refugees clawing for food at a ship's cargo net; and the bloody uniform of a dead Bosnian soldier. (Lyman)

Toscani's advertisements for the clothing company Ra-Re have stirred protest in some countries, particularly the photographer's home country of Italy. The advertisements are frank depictions of male-male intimacy; in one photo, an older man clutches a younger man's crotch, and in another photo, the pair embrace on a couch (McMahon). According to reports from Italy, some parents and conservative citizens have complained vociferously about these advertisements, saying that they do not know how to explain such flagrant displays of homosexuality to children. But creating such dilemmas may be the aim of Toscani's work: to provoke consideration and discussion of that which still, in much of the West, remains hidden, closeted, and out of the public view. Toscani's photos transgress those boundaries, forcing the queer into public consciousness.

## From Pornography to Sadomasochism

While some LGBT and queer artists may transgress the norms and expectations of the larger cultures in which they work and live, other queer artists focus attention on troubling normative expectations within communities. These artists, writers, and designers often feel that queer people are too quick to assimilate into larger cultures unwilling to examine their sexual prejudices and repressions. Some of these artists also believe that queers have simply become another commodity market, full of consumers who are eager to buy the latest cars, don the latest fashions, and sport the latest "must-have" gadgets, knickknacks, and art.

A number of books on "how to be gay" poke fun at normative constructions of LGBT identity. For instance, *So You Want to Be a Lesbian? A Guide for Amateurs and Professionals*, by Liz Tracey and Sydney Pokorny, covers a variety of topics from coming out, flirting, and the promises (and pitfalls) of monogamy to lesbian culture, lesbian cuisine, lesbian vehicles, and "dyke cult heroes." Full of humor and fun "facts," *So You Want to Be a Lesbian?*, much like its companion volume, *The Unofficial Gay Manual*, is largely a parody of a popular genre, the self-help book. While these books are mostly tongue-in-cheek, the popularity of such "guides" suggests a relatively normative sense of what it means to be gay or lesbian. Recently, a comparable book has appeared for bisexuals, *The Bisexual's Guide to the Universe: Quips, Tips, and Lists for Those Who Go Both Ways*, by Nicole Kristal and Mike Szymanski. More seriously, books such as *Virtually Normal* by Andrew Sullivan and *A Place at the Table* by Bruce Bawer argue that gays and lesbians should strive to fit into the dominant culture, adopting its nonhomophobic norms in an effort to increase tolerance for homosexuals.

British writer Mark Simpson's edited collection, provocatively titled *Anti-Gay*, soundly critiques such assimilationist moves and argues for valuing a more transgressive kind of queerness:

> That many non-heterosexuals were already itching to escape from gay's clingy, cartoony embrace has already been demonstrated with queer. . . . [There was] initially at least a strong strain of punkish transgression running through queer which was quite liberating for many. Groups like Homocult, the situationist art collective in Manchester, who specialized in "negative" images of homosexuality; North American zinesters like *Bimbox* who arguably invented queer; the work of film directors like Bruce LaBruce, Tom Kalin, and Todd Haynes who, as Kalin put it, aimed to put the "homo" back in "homicide"; and Queercore, a bad-attitude trash sound attracting a younger generation

of deviants who didn't want or weren't wanted by what they took to be heterosexuality but didn't want to sip cappuccino on Old Compton Street or Santa Monica Boulevard either. (xv)

Many "established" gay and queer artists, such as Ginsberg and Mapplethorpe, have exhibited just such "punkish" traits in their work, which troubles gay and lesbian people who hope to fit into mainstream Western culture. Ginsberg's pro-communist, pro-drug politics, for instance, were unsettling to many in the broader LGBT community. Moreover, not only certain sectors of the public but also some other queer authors and activists were disturbed by Mapplethorpe's work. In these cases, what is being transgressed is a sense of how a larger LGBT or queer community wants to represent itself to itself. As we grapple with our own values, with what is important to us in our diverse and often divergent communities, conflicts inevitably arise [λ Chapter 7].

Dorothy Allison (b. 1949), award-winning author of *Bastard Out of Carolina*, has written provocatively about the importance of recognizing and honoring our sexual desires, particularly for lesbians. In her collection of essays, *Skin,* she writes about pornography, a touchy subject among those feminists who see porn as degrading to women. Allison maintains a **sex-positive** approach, arguing that "the word queer means much more than lesbian. Since I first used it in 1980 I have always meant it to imply that I am not only a lesbian but a transgressive lesbian—femme, masochistic, as sexually aggressive as the women I seek out, and as pornographic in my imagination and sexual activities as the heterosexual **hegemony** has ever believed" (23). Pat Califia, writing as a sex-positive lesbian long before he transitioned to a transman, wrote about recognizing the divergent sexual tastes of queer communities. Califia's erotic fiction often transgressed self-imposed norms of sexual behavior among gays and lesbians, particularly as it depicted intense sadomasochistic sex acts and bisexual intimacy. In the essays in *Public Sex: The Culture of Radical Sex,* Califia challenged conceptions of the place, role, and variety of sexuality within queer cultures. In "A Secret Side of Lesbian Sexuality" (1979), Califia argued that "[t]he sexual closet is bigger than you think" (157) and announced, "I identify more strongly as a sadomasochist than as a lesbian. I hang out in the gay community because that's where the sexual fringe starts to unravel" (158). What Califia most appreciates about "gay community" is that it can be a space in which boundaries of normative sex and sexuality are transgressed [λ Chapter 7].

One artist whose work challenges what he sees as a prudishness lurking within some parts of the larger LGBT/queer community is Dennis Cooper (b. 1953). A stylistic maverick, Cooper works in many forms, including the novel, poetry, and journalism. The content of his work, though, has disturbed a variety of audiences, queer and nonqueer alike. Cooper's themes and plots focus on homoerotic sadomasochism, and some elements of his work are reminiscent of **snuff** porn, in which people are killed for the erotic pleasure of others. Noted gay novelist Edmund White calls Cooper's writing "obsessive" and "far from ordinary morality"; he "meditates ceaselessly on violence and perversion [and seems] dedicated to drugs, kink, and a fragile sense of beauty fashioned out of the detritus of American suburbs" (282). One of Cooper's most famous novels is *Frisk,* the second book in a five-novel sequence depicting the underlife of young men engaging in a variety of sexual practices, taking drugs, and sometimes hustling their bodies to make money for food or the next quick fix. These young people are often used and abused by older men who pay them to perform sexual services. In this sense, the books are reminiscent of the works of authors such as John Rechy, whose 1963 novel, *The City of Night,* sympathetically chronicled the lives of street hustlers servicing men.

But Cooper's aim in writing is not just to chronicle a queer underlife; it is rather to explore the erotic imagination at its most transgressive and boundary pushing. *Frisk,* for instance, is a bizarre coming-of-age story, tracing the sexual development of one young man, ironically named Dennis, and his interest in sexual torture and snuff. In one passage, Dennis reflects on his desires:

> It wasn't that I didn't fantasize murdering hustlers. It's just that I tend to be too scared or shy the first few times I sleep with someone to do what I actually want. The worst that could, and did, happen was I'd get a little too rough. But the hustler would stop me, or I'd stop myself, before things became more than conventionally kinky, as far as he knew. (36)

During a trip to Holland, Dennis begins sending letters to his friends back home that describe sexual exploits in which he becomes more than a "little rough" and actually murders his tricks. For Dennis, such sexual murder is driven by his desire to know, to possess the objects of his attraction; meditating on the contradiction between loving and killing, he tells a friend of his, "I can actually imagine myself inside the skins I admire. I'm pretty sure if I tore some guy open I'd know him as well as anyone could, because I'd have what he consists of right there in my hands, mouth, wherever. . . . I want to know *everything* about you. But to really do that, I'd have to kill you, as bizarre as that sounds" (51, 67).

Novels such as *Frisk,* like most of Cooper's work, have been decried by numerous gay activists who see artists like Cooper as validating a homophobic society's belief that queers are predatory, sick, and sinful. At the very least, such activists maintain, presenting a seedy underside of gay life makes it more difficult for LGBT people to assimilate into the dominant culture and to claim that queer people are, essentially, just like everyone else. But Cooper's goals in novels such as *Frisk* are precisely to trouble the desire to fit in, the desire to be normal. At the end of the book, we learn that Dennis has not in fact killed anyone; we've just been reading, like the friends who received his letters, about fantasies that he has no intention of fulfilling. Cooper draws our attention to how most people have fantasies that they will not enact and how the content of our imaginations is often far from normative. As he puts it in an interview, *Frisk* "is about the difference between what is possible in one's fantasy life, and what is possible in one's real life. . . . It tries, in various ways, to seduce the readers into believing a series of murders are real, then announces itself as a fiction, hopefully leaving readers responsible for whatever pleasure they took in believing the murders were real. . . . Murder is only erotic in the imagination, if at all" (Reitz). *Frisk,* then, points out that the transgressive lies, often latently, behind most any façade of normalcy and that ignoring it is to ignore part of what makes us complex and interesting. Cooper also insinuates that transgressive and normalizing impulses coexist uneasily and that any ethical life will have to acknowledge their interrelationship and negotiate carefully between them. Novelists such as Cooper show us that the transgressive lies not just at the fringes of the mainstream; it is often at its center, critiquing the normative lives many of us build for ourselves.

## Transgression and Politics

Throughout this chapter, we have outlined how many different LGBT and queer artists have used the transgressive to question the values, norms, and assumptions of both dominant cultures and LGBT communities. At this point, though, we must ask, what are the limits of transgression as a form of political agency? More broadly, to what political use can transgression be put, and is it a politically efficacious strategy? Certainly, artists such as Cooper, as well as other gay writers such as Bret Easton Ellis (*Less Than Zero* and *American Psycho*) and Jeanette Winterson (*Written on the Body* and *Oranges Are Not the Only Fruit*) challenge us with difficult topics, inviting us to identify with transgression and transgressive acts. In the process, these writers question our assumptions about what is normal and, through our periodic identifications with nonnormative characters, provoke us to reconsider our tendencies to prejudge. At the same time, there are limits. Winterson, at the end of her novel *Art and Lies,* depicts the relationship between a priest and a young boy whom the priest has gelded so that he can be a *castrato,* remaining boy-like and retaining his high-pitched singing voice. While Winterson's writing is beautiful and often moving, to what extent can we identify with the priest? Moreover, do we want to identify with such characters? What are our limits in questioning and stretching our own values?

Other questions about transgressive aesthetic practices and their ability to promote change have surfaced around drag performances and their exploration of gender. Judith Butler, in her ground-breaking book *Gender Trouble* (1990), which helped form the queer theoretical approach, argued that drag performances show us that gender isn't a given, that it is a "performance" to which people are called and that must be repeated again and again to pass as "normal." A drag queen can perform femininity, for instance, showing up femininity as a cultural construct. But does drag performance transgress gender norms and our understanding of gender as essential? Or does it reinforce normative notions of gender? Some critics believe that drag performers might actually disparage femininity and feminine behavior rather than celebrate them in their performances. In *The Drag King Book* (1999), Judith Halberstam argues that

> [t]he future of gender ... remains uncertain. Gender rebellion seems to be standard fare in popular magazines, sitcoms, cartoons, mainstream film and it is in full display on many a college campus. But somehow the bending of gender has failed actually to shift the dominance of male and female as the binary poles of gender definitions. Gender play offers us, paradoxically, much room for trial and error, but also little prospect for momentous change. Girls and boys are still raised to be normal men and women, and gender experimentation is far from encouraged. (150)

In *The Sexual Citizen*, academics David Bell and Jon Binnie take up the issue of transgressive approaches, arguing ultimately that it is important, even imperative, that we question—and transgress—the boundaries that keep sex and sexuality private. They ask, "How can we think about intimacy without reinstating the public/private divide; without keeping intimacy's link to privacy intact? How do we think love in ways other than those hegemonically scripted by mainstream culture? What is it that we talk about when we talk about love?" (124).

One still wonders, though, if figuring queerness as "necessarily oppositional" (138), as transgressive, really works. Certainly, some will be alienated by such an approach. And it is important to keep in mind that understanding queerness as a mode of transgressive political agency is a very Western concept. In other cultures, in which queerness and the homoerotic are understood differently, opening up a space for transgressive politicking is difficult, if not impossible. Tom Boellstorff, for example, identifies how constructions of queerness in non-Western cultures problematize strategies for resistance. In Indonesia, he writes,

> *Gay* men and *lesbi* do not "come out of the closet" but speak of being "opened" ... or "shut." ... We find not an epistemology of the closet but an epistemology of life worlds, where healthy subjectivity depends not on integrating diverse domains of life and having a unified, unchanging identity in all situations but on separating domains of life and maintaining their borders against the threat of gossip and discovery. (228)

In Indonesia, then, queer transgression as we have described it might not register with the same amount of combined provocation and titillation. It might be rejected outright as simply an unhealthy management of identities, and thus the space for considering renegotiation of boundaries and values might not open up. More pointedly, in some countries, such as Iran, the appearance of open homosexuality may be considered transgressive enough to warrant the death penalty [λ Chapter 4]. A thorough understanding of a sociocultural and political context, including what boundaries can be pushed and how hard, is necessary if transgression is to help open up a space for reconsidering cultural values. Some boundaries pushed too hard may create backlash, counterresistance, and unintended consequences. And at many times, the pushing of boundaries around sex and sexuality, particularly homoerotic sexuality, has resulted in moral panics, even censorship—key subjects of the following chapter.

## QUESTIONS FOR DISCUSSION

1. Transgressive tactics are dependent for their efficacy on particular contexts, and in some circumstances, transgression is an ineffective way to raise consciousness and spark debate. Interview an LGBT activist in your locale and ask him, her, or ze about the use of transgressive tactics in promoting awareness of LGBT and queer issues and concerns. You might easily find such an activist by calling an LGBT center in your area.

2. What is the line between the pornographically and the transgressively erotic? Some would argue that certain kinds of pornography are in fact transgressive in that they force us to rethink attitudes about sex and sexuality and to consider new forms of sexual pleasure and desire. Write about this idea, highlighting the distinction between the pornographic and the transgressively erotic. As part of your thinking, you might consider the binary present in this question: Are there clear boundaries between the erotic and the pornographic?

3. Sometimes we learn not just by reading and thinking about a subject but by doing and participating in it as well. Try your hand at creating some transgressive art. Create a collage in which you attempt to transgress a particular notion, idea, or norm. What norms would you choose to transgress? Gender norms? Sexual norms? Norms surrounding public and private behavior? Think of your collage as an advertisement that would be posted around your local community. How would that community respond? What kinds of transgressive collages would be particularly provocative in your community? That is, what kinds of transgressive tactics would be politically useful without so alienating community members that they simply ignore your message?

## REFERENCES AND FURTHER READING

Allison, Dorothy. *Skin: Talking about Race, Sex and Class.* New York: Firebrand, 1994. Print.

Anderson, Susan Heller. "Chronicle." *New York Times,* 11 July 1991. Web. 8 Aug. 2008. <http://query.nytimes.com/gst/fullpage.html?res=9D0CE3D8173AF932A25754 C0A967958260&sec=&spon=&partner=permalink&exprod=permalink>.

Bartlett, Alison. "Madonnas, Models, and Maternity: Icons of Breastfeeding in the Visual Arts." N.p., n.d. Web. 8 Aug. 2008. <www.usq.edu.au/resources/bartlettpaper.pdf>.

Bawer, Bruce. *A Place at the Table: The Gay Individual in American Society.* New York: Poseidon, 1993. Print.

Bell, David, and Jon Binnie. *The Sexual Citizen: Queer Politics and Beyond.* Malden, MA: Blackwell, 2000. Print.

Boellstorff, Tom. "The Perfect Path: Gay Men, Marriage, Indonesia." *Queer Studies: An Interdisciplinary Reader.* Ed. Robert J. Corber and Stephen Valocchi. Malden, MA: Blackwell, 2003. 218–36. Print.

Bronski, Michael, ed. *Pulp Friction: Uncovering the Golden Age of Male Pulps.* New York: St. Martin's Griffin, 2003. Print.

Butler, Judith. *Gender Trouble: Feminism and the Subversion of Identity.* New York: Routledge, 1990. Print.

Califia, Pat. *Public Sex: The Culture of Radical Sex.* Pittsburgh, PA: Cleis, 1994. Print.

Cooper, Dennis. *Frisk.* New York: Grove, 1991. Print.

DiLallo, Kevin, and Jack Krumholtz. *The Unofficial Gay Manual.* New York: Main Street, 1994. Print.

Ensler, Eve. "The Little Coochi Snorcher That Could." Deleted scene from *The Vagina Monologues.* N.p., n.d. Web. 9 Aug. 2008. <www.sacerdoti.com/jonathan/vaginas/coochie.html>.

Ginsberg, Allen. "Howl." *Howl on Trial.* Eds. Bill Morgan and Nancy J. Peters. San Francisco: City Lights, 2006. 16–30. Print.

Halberstam, Judith and Del LaGrace Volcano. *The Drag King Book.* London: Serpent's Tail, 1999. Print.

Halperin, David. *Saint Foucault: Toward a Gay Hagiography.* New York: Oxford UP, 1995. Print.

Kristal, Nicole, and Mike Szymanski. *The Bisexual's Guide to the Universe: Quips, Tips, and Lists for Those Who Go Both Ways.* New York: Alyson, 2006. Print.

Lyman, Eric J. "The True Colors of Oliviero Toscani." N.p., Aug. 2001. Web. 26 May 2007. <http://www.ericjlyman.com/adageglobal.html>.

McMahon, Barbara. "Italy Snaps over Gay Poster Excess." *The Observer,* 18 Sept. 2005. Web. 26 May 2007. <http://observer.guardian.co.uk/international/story/0,6903,1572822,00.html>.

Reitz, Daniel. "Dennis Cooper." *Salon,* 4 May 2000. Web. 26 May 2007. <http://archive.salon.com/people/feature/2000/05/04/cooper/index.html>.

Sedgwick, Eve Kosofsky. *Epistemology of the Closet.* Berkeley: U California P, 1990. Print.

Simpson, Mark. *Anti-Gay.* London: Freedom, 1996. Print.

Sullivan, Andrew. *Virtually Normal: An Argument about Homosexuality.* New York: Knopf, 1995. Print.

Tracey, Liz, and Sydney Pokorny. *So You Want to Be a Lesbian? A Guide for Amateurs and Professionals.* New York: St. Martin's Griffin, 1996. Print.

White, Edmund. *The Burning Library: Essays.* New York: Random House, 1994. Print.

Winterson, Jeanette. *Art and Lies.* New York: Knopf, 1995. Print.

———. *The World and Other Places.* New York: Knopf, 1999. Print.

## READING

> ## Eve Kosofsky Sedgwick

(United States), 1993

### From "Queer and Now"

**Christmas Effects** What's "queer"? Here's one train of thought about it. The depressing thing about the Christmas season—isn't it?—Is that it's the time when all the institutions are speaking with one voice. The Church says what the Church says. But the capital State says the same thing: maybe not (in some ways it hardly matters) in the language of theology, but in the language the State talks: legal holidays, long school hiatus, special postage stamps, and all. And the language of commerce more than chimes in, as consumer purchasing is organized ever more narrowly around the final weeks of the calendar year, the Dow Jones aquiver over Americans' "holiday mood." The media, in turn, fall in triumphally behind the Christmas phalanx: ad-swollen magazines have oozing turkeys on the cover, while for the news industry every question turns into the Christmas question—Will the hostages be free *for Christmas?* What did the flash flood or mass murder (umpty-ump people killed and maimed) do to those families' *Christmas?* And meanwhile, the pairing "family/Christmas" becomes increasingly tautological, as families more and more constitute themselves according to the schedule, and in the endlessly iterated image, of the holiday itself constituted in the image of "the" family.

The thing hasn't, finally, so much to do with propaganda for Christianity as with propaganda for Christmas itself. They all—religion, state, capital, ideology, domesticity, the discourses of power and legitimacy—wind up with each other so neatly once a year, and the monolith so created is something one can come to view without happy eyes. What if instead there were a practice of valuing the ways in which meanings and instructions can be at loose ends with each other? What if the richest junctures weren't the ones where *everything means the same thing?* Think of the entity "the family," and impacted social space in which all of the following are meant to line up perfectly with each other:

a surname

a sexual dyad

a legal unit based on state-regulated marriage

a circuit of blood relationships

a system of companionship and succor

a building

a proscenium between "private" and "public"

an economic unit of earning and taxation

a prime site of economic consumption

a prime site of cultural consumption

a mechanism to produce, care for, and acculturate children

a mechanism for accumulating goods over several generations

a daily routine

a unit in a community of worship

a site of patriotic formation

and of course the list could go on. Looking at my own life, I see that—probably like most people—I have valued in pursuit of these various elements of family identity to quite differing degrees (e.g., no use at all for worship, much need of companionship). But what's been consistent in this particular life isn't interest in *not* letting very many of these dimensions line up directly with each other at one time. I see it's been a ruling intuition for me that the most productive strategy (intellectually, emotionally) might be, whenever possible, to *dis*articulate them from one another, to *dis*engage them—the bonds of blood, of law, of habitation, of privacy, of companionship and succor—from the lockstep of their unanimity in the system called "family."

Or think of all the elements that are condensed in the notion of sexual identity, something that the common sense of our time presents as a unitary category. Yet, exerting any pressure at all on "sexual identity," you see that its elements include

your biological (e.g. chromosomal) sex, male or female;

your self-perceived gender assignment, male or female (supposed to be the same measure biological sex);

the preponderance of your traits of personality and appearance, masculine or feminine (supposed to correspond to your sex and gender);

the biological sex of your preferred partner;

the gender assignment of your preferred partner (supposed to be the same as her/his biological sex);

the masculinity or femininity of your word partner (supposed to be the opposite[1] of our own);

your self-perception as gay or straight (supposed to correspond to whether your preferred partner is your sex or the opposite);

your preferred partner's self-perception as gay or straight (supposed to be the same as yours);

your procreative choice (supposed to be yes if straight, no with gay);

your preferred sexual act(s) (supposed to be inserted but fewer male or masculine, receptive if you're female or feminine);

your most eroticized sexual organs (supposed to correspond to the procreative capabilities of your sex, and to your insert if/receptive assignment);

your sexual fantasies (supposed to be highly congruent with your sexual practice, but stronger in intensity);

your main locus of emotional bonds (supposed to reside in your preferred sexual partner);

your enjoyment of power in sexual relations (supposed to be low if you are female or feminine, high if male or masculine);

the people from whom you learn about your own gender and sex (supposed to correspond to yourself in both respects);

your community of cultural and political identification (supposed to correspond to your own identity);

and—again—many more. Even this list is remarkable for the silent presumptions it has to make about a given person's sexuality, presumptions that are true only to varying degrees, and for many people not true at all: that everyone "has a sexuality," for instance, and that it is implicated with each person's sense of overall identity in similar ways; that each person's most characteristic erotic expression will be oriented toward another person and not autoerotic; that if it is alloerotic, it will be oriented toward a single partner or kind of partner at a time; that its orientation will not change over time.[2] Normatively, as the parenthetical prescriptions in the list above suggest, it should be possible to deduce anybody's entire set of specs from the initial datum of biological sex alone—if one adds only the normative assumption that "the biological sex of your preferred partner" will be the opposite of one's own. With or without that heterosexist assumption, though, what's striking is the number and *difference* of the dimensions that "sexual identity" is supposed to organize into a seamless univocal whole.

And if it doesn't?

That's one of the things that "queer" can refer to: the open mesh of possibilities, gaps, overlaps, dissonances and resonances, lapses and excesses of meaning when the constituent elements of anyone's gender, of anyone's sexuality aren't made (or *can't be* made) to signify monolithically. The experimental linguistic, epistemological, representational, political adventures attaching to the very many of us who may at times be moved to describe ourselves as (among many other possibilities) pushy femmes, radical faeries, fantasists, drags, clones, leatherfolk, ladies in tuxedoes, feminist women or feminist men, masturbators, bulldaggers, divas, Snap! queens, butch bottoms, storytellers, transsexuals, aunties, wannabes, lesbian-identified men or lesbians who sleep with men, or . . . people able to relish, learn from, or identify with such.

Again, "queer" can mean something different: in light of the way I have used so far in this dossier is to denote, almost simply, same-sex sexual object choice, lesbian or gay, whether or not it is organized around multiple criss-crossings of definitional lines. And given the historical and contemporary force of the prohibitions against *every* same-sex sexual expression, for anyone to disavow those meanings, or to displace them from the term's definitional center, would be to dematerialize any possibility of queerness itself.

At the same time, a lot of the most exciting recent work around "queer" spins the term outward along dimensions that can't be subsumed under gender and sexuality at all: the ways that race, ethnicity, postcolonial nationality criss-cross with these *and other* identity-constituting, identity-fracturing discourses, for example. Intellectuals and artists of color whose sexual self-definition includes "queer"—I think of an Isaac Julien, a Gloria Anzaldúa, a Richard Fung—are using the leverage of "queer" to do a new kind of justice to the fractal intricacies of language, skin, migration, state.

Thereby, the gravity (I mean the *gravitas*, the meaning but also the *center* of gravity) of the term "queer" itself deepens and shifts.

Another telling representational effect. A word so fraught as "queer" is—fraught with so many social and personal histories of exclusion, violence, defiance, excitement—never can only denote; nor even can it only connote; a part of its experimental force as a speech act is the way in which it dramatizes locutionary position itself. Anyone's use of "queer" about themselves means differently from the use of it about someone else. This is true (as it might also be true of "lesbian" or "gay") because of the violently different connotative evaluations seem to cluster around the category. But "gay" and "lesbian" still present themselves (however delusively) as objective, impure goal categories governed by empirical rules of evidence (however contested). "Queer" seems to hinge much more radically and explicitly on a person's undertaking particular, performative acts of experimental self-perception and filiation. A hypothesis worth making explicit: that there are important senses in which "queer" can signify only *when attached to the first person*. One possible corollary: that what it takes—all it takes—to make the description "queer" a true one is the impulsion *to* use it in the first person.

### Notes

1. The binary calculus I'm describing here depends on the notion that the male and female sexes are each other's "opposites," but I do want to register a specific demurral against that bit of easy common sense. Under no matter what cultural construction, women and men are more like each other than chalk is like cheese, then ratiocination is like raisins, than up is like down, or than I is like o. The biological, psychological, and cognitive attributes of men overlap with those of women by vastly more than they differ from them.

2. A related list that amplifies some of the issues raised in this one appears in the introduction to *Epistemology of the Closet*, pp. 25-26.

---

Sedgwick, Eve Kosofsky. "Queer and Now." *Tendencies*. Duke UP: Durham. 1993 (1–20).

## ➢ **Michael Warner**

(2012), United States

---

#### From "Queer and Then?"

. . . From the moment of the first reports of queer politics and queer theory, many gay men and lesbians hated the idea. For using the term positively, I was denounced by *The New York Native* as "the gay Lyndon LaRouche." Lo these many years later, straight and gay people alike continue to deride queer theory as the ultimate joke of a debased and fraudulent academy. The playwright Larry Kramer, without showing much sign of understanding queer theory, nevertheless bewails that "gay people are the victims of an enormous con job, a tragic heist." In his view, people throughout history have been gay in exactly the way we understand the term today, and the purpose of gay studies should be to celebrate them. Queer theory's attention to the historical variety and complexity of sexual cultures is, for Kramer, a betrayal of gay people and common sense alike.

One thing that language registers is that queer theory opened up a conceptual divergence from lesbian and gay studies (ironically at a time when that field was just coming into its own), as well as a political divergence from the lesbian and gay movement (which also burst into mainstream politics with the 1992 presidential campaign of Bill Clinton).

The intellectual part of queer theory had in fact begun long before, at least with Foucault's *History of Sexuality* (first published in French in 1976). Foucault's book was clearly unassimilable to movement politics. Early debates about it within gay studies focused on its critique of psychoanalysis and its turn to a constructionist account of gay identity. Foucault's remark that "the nineteenth-century homosexual became a personage" became the most famous phrase in the book. But the bigger challenge, one that took longer to digest, was the way Foucault had flipped the lens on the whole project of studying sexuality. Instead of starting with sexual identities, he wanted to think about the prior structuring of sexuality by several techniques distinctive to modern societies. He drew attention to the way sexuality is stabilized for us by secular expert knowledge and anchored in individuals both by genres of therapy and self-representation. In his account, sexuality became visible as a field of regulation, therapy, and liberation simultaneously. He opened new questions about the deep ties between modern knowledge of sexuality and various forms of what he called "state racism," including colonialism and, in the extreme forms, genocide and eugenics; the process by which the categories of experts can be taken up as mobilizations by the individuals to whom they are applied; the kinds of normalization specific to modern societies; and the variety of alternative formations throughout history in which the pleasures of the body have been developed within entirely different purposes and imperatives.

The politics of sexuality, in Foucault's treatment, led not just to an affirmative study of sexual minorities, but to a thorough and radical re-evaluation of the techniques of defining modernity. Lesbian and gay studies quickly took on board Foucault's constructionist account of the hetero-homo opposition, but the rest of his argument necessarily lay beyond the study of same-sex attraction, and indeed beyond the study of sexuality as a stable object.

Eve Sedgwick accomplished something similar in her early work. Her 1985 book *Between Men* was a watershed, for me at least. Published just when I was completing graduate school, it approached homophobia—the organizing problematic of lesbian and gay studies—as a constitutive byproduct of modern styles of straight-male homosociality. Sedgwick was envisioning a way for gay studies and feminism to find a common perspective on straightness, masculinity, and the dynamics of domination in modern culture. Like Foucault's, her analysis flipped the lens: The real problem, for her, was the mechanism of male sociability that, in envisioning the domination of women, made its own homoerotic dimensions abject, projecting the homosexual as a failed but dangerous and repudiated version of itself.

In that turn, Sedgwick was already beginning to imagine what she would boldly declare in the first paragraph of her 1990 *Epistemology of the Closet:* "An understanding of virtually any aspect of modern Western culture must be, not merely incomplete, but damaged in its central substance to the degree that it does not incorporate a critical analysis of modern homo/heterosexual definition." If any-thing, subsequent queer theory has tended to argue an even stronger version of that claim, suggesting that the normative field of sexuality is so dispersed that it requires us to understand such things as racialization, the dynamic between devel-oped countries and colonies or postcolonies, the stabilization of sex biomorphism, and so on.

Those last questions had also been raised by Judith Butler before they had come to be called queer theory. Butler's 1990 *Gender Trouble,* in addition to its well-known (but still widely misunderstood) arguments about performativity of gender, had its deepest impact through the same kind of shift in perspective. Instead of starting with the nature of sex, she urged us to analyze the normative frameworks by which gender and sexuality are constituted and inhabited in the first place. Fusing insights from phenomenology and Pierre Bourdieu's practice theory together with a long history of feminist thought, Butler foregrounded a problem that has still not been fully grasped in most philosophy or the social sciences. Where most accounts of norms imagine an agent who acts on the basis of beliefs or desires and reflects on what ought to be done, Butler called attention to the ways we find ourselves already normatively organized as certain kinds of agents, for example by having gender in ways that must be intelligible to others. The problem, she said, was the "regulatory fiction of heterosexual coherence," which "disguises itself as a developmental law regulating the sexual field that it purports to describe."

That approach immediately opened up new problems, occasioning, for example, a debate about "antinormativity" within queer theory. (Does the embrace of queerness entail a romantic opposition to all normativity whatsoever? Is there something inher-ently antisocial in the experience of sexuality?) But it also gave a vocabulary for a kind of analysis that the disciplines otherwise lacked.

In all these ways, the tremendous intellectual energy of what would come to be called queer theory was already casting a much broader net than lesbian and gay studies. One result over the years has been a succession of movements in which the critical project is joined and adapted by those who have different constituencies in view: trans studies, postcolonial queer studies, queer race studies. Each of those—like the parallel development of queer affect studies, which was not as closely tied to any political constituency—often begin by distancing themselves from what they take to be a narrower version of queer theory. Thus queer theory has often seemed, from its very inception, to be elsewhere or in the past. . . .

A good example of queer theory's ambivalence about itself is Jasbir K. Puar's influential 2007 book *Terrorist Assemblages.* Puar does battle with a succession of polemical opponents: queer liberalism, queer neoliberalism, queer exceptionalism, etc. If all of one's identities "must be constantly troubled," she points out, one imagines "an impossible transcendent subject who is always already conscious of the normativizing forces of power and always ready and able to subvert, resist, or transgress them." That seems undeniable as far as it goes, but it also restates one of the generative problems in Butler's early work. So while Puar seems to want to associate queer theory with a liberal imperial imagination, she does so in terms that she takes from queer theory itself. Despite its criticisms of (some) queer theory, then, Puar's book is itself an example of the kind of vital work that queer theory enables, with or without the rubric. *Terrorist Assemblages* would very likely sit on any queer-theory syllabus today.

Queer theory in this broader sense now has so many branches, and has developed in so many disciplines, that it resists synthesis. The differences have often enough become bitter, sometimes occasioning the kind of queerer-than-thou competitiveness that is the telltale sign of scarcity in resources and recognition. That impulse can be seen, for example, in the title of a special issue of *Social Text* called "What's Queer About Queer Studies Now?" And given queer theory's strong suspicion of any politics of purity, it is ironic that queer theorists can often strike postures of righteous purity in denouncing one another. The Gay Shame Conference at the University of Michigan at Ann Arbor in 2003, for instance—to discuss aspects of lesbian and gay male sexuality, history, and culture that "gay pride" had suppressed—featured a remarkable amount of mutual shaming, as though everyone had missed the point.

The scarcity of resources that feeds such a dynamic has a lot to do with university structure. At many colleges, queer theory is now institutionalized as a minor subfield of LGBT studies. Some projects, such as queer ethnography, flourish in this structure better than others. The broader provocation to the disciplines has been neatly compartmentalized, with the consequence that many of queer theory's greatest challenges—for example, in the analysis of normativity, which should have become central to philosophy and the social sciences, but has been scrupulously ignored by them, or the connections between sexuality and secularism that are central to so many kinds of conflict around the world—remain undeveloped. Thus to my mind, the widespread impression that queer theory is a thing of the past, that we are now at some point "After Sex," seems tragically mistaken.

At its best, queer theory has always also been something else—something that will be left out of any purely intellectual history of the movement. Like [the rant] "I want a dyke for president," it has created a kind of social space. Queer people of various kinds, both inside and outside academe, continue to find their way to it, and find each other through it. In varying degrees, they share in it as a counterpublic. In this far-too-limited zone, it has been possible to keep alive a political imagination of sexuality that is otherwise closed down by the dominant direction of gay and lesbian politics, which increasingly reduces its agenda to military service and marriage, and tends to remain locked in a national and even nationalist frame, leading gay people to present themselves as worthy of dignity because they are "all-American," and thus to forget or disavow the estrangements that they have in common with diasporic or postcolonial queers.

That effect has been possible not just because of the theories themselves, but because of the space of belonging and talk in which theory interacts with ways of life. Much of the social effervescence is only indirectly felt on the page. But it has always been also there on the page, in the work of writing.

That might seem like an odd thing to say, since for mainstream journalists (as for Larry Kramer) queer theory is the extreme case of "difficult" academic prose, and Judith Butler and Eve Sedgwick were both singled out for mockery by the self-appointed guardians of accessibility. We are often told that queer theory lacks "clarity." But technical clarity and journalistic accessibility are not the same, and the attack on difficult style has often been a means to reassert the very standards of common sense that queer theory rightly challenged. Moreover, even the most difficult prose has given people room for being serious in ways sanctioned nowhere else.

And so much of the writing is remarkable. Think of Sedgwick's bristling, coiled paragraphs; or Berlant's ability to work so unpredictably across registers to produce a knowledge that is both live and speculative (as in "Beyonding is a rhetoric people use when they have a desire not to be stuck"); or all those astonishing shoes-on-the-table moments like the opening sentence of Bersani's still-controversial essay "Is the Rectum a Grave?": "There is a big secret about sex: most people don't like it."

Sex, as Bersani astutely observed, distresses people, and they don't like to be reminded of it. Perhaps he had already noticed, at a moment when "queer theory" was not yet the name for what he was doing, the very reason why people seem to long for a present in which they can be postqueer.

---

Warner, Michael. "Queer and Then?" *The Chronicle of Higher Education*, 1 January 2012. <http://chronicle.com/article/QueerThen-/130161/>.

# CHAPTER 12

# Censorship and Moral Panic

Controversies about homosexed art—the Mapplethorpe controversy in Cincinnati, for instance— are highlighted, as are particular cases of censorship motivated by homophobia. Beyond censorship, we also examine attempts to mainstream queer art.

In Chapter 10, we talked about the attempted censorship of the novel *Women's Barracks,* pointing out that the Canadian Crown's attorney identified the lesbian passages in Torres's book as obscene but ignored equally racy mention of heterosexual sex and sexuality. The public uproar that provided the context for the *Women's Barracks* trial had to do with a general sense in Canadian culture that obscene and sexually provocative material from the United States would corrupt Canadian youth [λ Chapter 10]. This impulse to focus on an offending object in order to encourage and perpetuate public outcry against transgressive behavior can create what Stan Cohen has termed *moral panic.* In a period of moral panic,

[a] condition, episode, person or group of persons emerges to become defined as a threat to societal values and interests. . . . Sometimes the panic is passed over and forgotten, but at other times it has more serious and long term repercussions and it might produce changes in legal and social policy or even in the way in which societies conceive themselves. (9)

Not all censorship is the result of moral panic, but most censorship of homosexed art and literature occurs at cultural moments when the fear of corruption by sexually deviant material is framed as a pervasive social problem. It is tempting to equate censorship only with the banning of books or with historical attempts to eradicate what the Nazis called "degenerate art," but we will focus on campaigns or trials that fit Cohen's definition of moral panic in an attempt to elucidate the larger social and cultural complexities of the censoring impulse. Censorship often arises from a desire to protect the innocent, often women and children, from sexual values that certain queer art seems to propagate—**sexual libertarianism**, sexual freedom, and even transcendence or obliteration of sexual boundaries. We hope to show that attempts to censor queer art often represent contradictory motivations and constituencies. In this chapter, we focus attention on several high-profile moral panics triggered by homosexed art and literature.

## Oscar Wilde

T he three trials of Oscar Wilde in 1895 were among the most widely covered and discussed legal proceedings of their time. A large part of the public interest in them arose from the celebrities involved—primarily the author and playwright Oscar Wilde, who was enjoying great success in London's theater district with sold-out performances of *The Importance of Being Earnest,* and the hot-headed Marquess of Queensbury, father of Lord Alfred Douglas ("Bosie"), with whom Wilde had been in a multiyear relationship.

Already famous for his brilliant conversation, controversial writings, and flamboyant public behavior, Wilde paraded around London with Bosie, inciting Queensbury to call him a "Somdomite," a misspelling of "Sodomite." In response, Wilde injudiciously decided to bring a libel suit against Queensbury. Wilde's suit was dismissed; during the deliberations, however, Queensbury's lawyers unearthed evidence that Wilde had consorted with a variety of young working-class men. Wilde was arrested on charges of "gross indecency," pursuant to a relatively recent law that criminalized sexual conduct between men. Wilde's first trial with him as the defendant ended in a hung jury, but at the second trial, he was convicted and sentenced to the maximum punishment, two years of hard labor. Three years after being released from Reading Gaol, Wilde died in France a broken and impoverished man.

**Figure 12.1** Oscar Wilde and Lord Alfred Douglas.

During the trials, prosecutors focused on locating passages from Wilde's writings to corroborate other testimony supporting his supposed "gross indecency." Prosecutor Edward Carson read portions of the author's early poems and letters to Bosie where Wilde wrote romantically, even effusively, about their friendship. Carson also quoted from Wilde's novel, *The Picture of Dorian Gray,* in which the artist Basil Hallward accuses the increasingly corrupt Dorian of deleterious influences on his acquaintances. Hallward asks Dorian, "Why is your friendship so fatal to young men?[1] There was that wretched boy in the Guards who committed suicide. You were his great friend. There was Sir Henry Ashton, who had to leave England with a tarnished name" (Wilde 117). Carson pressed Wilde to name the "unnatural vice" alluded to in these passages, strongly insinuating that literature depicting immoral acts or feelings could contribute to the degradation of those reading it:

> C[arson]—Am I right in saying that you do not consider the effect [when writing] in creating morality or immorality?
>
> W[ilde]—Certainly, I do not.
>
> C—So far as your works are concerned, you pose as not being concerned about morality or immorality? . . .
>
> W—. . . I have no pose in this matter. In writing a play or a book, I am concerned entirely with literature—that is, with art. I aim not at doing good or evil, but in trying to make a thing that will have some quality of beauty. ("The Trials of Oscar Wilde")

Wilde's attempt to focus purely on aesthetic concerns proved an unfortunate strategy for his defense, making it appear that he had something to hide.

Carson's efforts to conflate the man and the work in order to damn them both led Wilde to defend his book, even implying that Dorian's demise at the end of the novel suggested that the story had a moral end. But the damage had already been done. In the famous Preface to *Dorian Gray,* Wilde had written that "[t]here is no such thing as a moral or an immoral book. Books are well written, or badly written. That is all" (3). By the time of the trial, many in the public were fully willing to believe that Wilde was not only writing about but also involved in a variety of immoral activities, particularly with other men, and that he was a potential danger to society. His writing and celebrity created nothing less than a moral panic, and some members of the public expressed relief when the author was sent off to prison. Author Eliza Lynn Linton, for example, remarked in late 1895, "Happily here the chief offender seems to have suddenly subsided—to have gone out like some noxious vapour which flared for a time over fetid marshes, luring the unwary into perils worse than death itself. The world is the cleaner by his absence—the cleaner and less ugly" (41).

Wilde's trials seem to presage future public debates and moral panics about homosexed art and literature; they helped position government agencies as protective of their citizens, safeguarding them against "unnatural" influences. In Carson's words, the public should be protected from books with "perverted moral views" (qtd. in Wilde 355). As sexologists were developing categories that helped to create a visible homosexual identity [λ Chapter 2], legal structures began containing its expression, particularly its potential spread to the innocent.

# Radclyffe Hall

Radclyffe Hall's novel *The Well of Loneliness* was the first to insist upon a literary space for the female sexual invert. The obscenity trials that resulted in the suppression of the book in England portrayed its subject as dangerous. Even more, the *Well of Loneliness* trials represented a moral panic in that an entire potential subject for literature—lesbianism—was prohibited for half a century afterward. First published by Jonathan Cape in late July 1928, *The Well of Loneliness* contained an introduction-cum-endorsement by sexologist Havelock Ellis [λ Chapter 2] and was generally recognized as a "long and very serious novel entirely upon the subject of sexual inversion" (Hall, qtd. in Doan 1). After a few weeks of thoughtful reviews in the press and relatively brisk sales at bookstores, the London *Sunday Express* printed a sensational editorial by journalist James Douglas. "I would rather give a healthy boy or a healthy girl a phial of prussic acid than this novel," wrote Douglas; "Poison kills the body, but moral poison kills the soul" (10). Suddenly the terms of the debate were altered, and many Britons took sides. Generally speaking, conservative traditionalists such as Home Secretary William Joynson-Hicks took the view that Hall's novel should be suppressed in order to protect the innocent "young generation" from so much as recognizing the existence of a potentially "polluting" practice such as lesbianism. Liberals, free-speech advocates, and literary figures, by contrast, supported the book as a "work of art finely conceived and finely written" ("Review" 13).

In the wake of Douglas's broadside, publisher Cape took a rash action: he sent a copy of the book to the Home Office, accompanied by a letter promising to withdraw it should it be found obscene. Presumably, Cape thought that Douglas's hypocritical "social purity" argument would fall flat with Joynson-Hicks. He could not anticipate that Joynson-Hicks would discuss the

**Figure 12.2**  Radclyffe Hall.

book with Sir Archibald Bodkin, the director of public prosecutions, and with Sir Chartres Biron, the Bow Street magistrate; all three men were members of what Laura Doan calls "fringe organizations, with narrow interests in reviving religious values and policing public morality" (21). Joynson-Hicks, feeling that "there must be some limit to the freedom of what a man may write or speak in this great country of ours," especially when, in his opinion, "what is written or spoken makes one of the least of these little ones offend," ruled that *The Well of Loneliness* should be suppressed (qtd. in Souhami 208). This would have been the end of the matter had not the prescient Cape arranged to have *Well* reprinted and sold under a French imprint. The French edition began appearing in London bookstores, and the police were finally directed to impound all copies they could find. The book (not the author) was put on trial for obscenity.

In the two weeks between the announcement and the trial, battle lines were drawn. Although some appeared to fall in with the obscenity faction, many found the court's procedures and opinions repulsive. The *Daily Herald* made fun of Joynson-Hicks and Bodkin: "They, stifling their natural horror and disgust, plough through all the naughty books, heroically risking any possible shocks to their chaste minds in order to safeguard the innocent British public" ("Gadfly"). Publisher Geoffrey Faber complained that, if the censors had their way, "the whole of the content of English literature is to be restricted in future to such stuff as Sir William thinks it safe to put in the hands of a schoolgirl" (qtd. in Souhami 208). Such protests were unavailing. In what Marc Vargo calls "arguably the most biased obscenity trial in the history of Great Britain" (63), in which Magistrate Biron refused to hear the testimony of expert witnesses, *Well* was found to be obscene and all copies were ordered destroyed. The appeal two weeks later was denied by the same court, and that was that. Interestingly, nothing in the book itself was actually found to be obscene (its sexiest line is probably "And that night they were not divided," referring to the hero Stephen Gordon and her lover Mary Llewellyn). It was the subject of lesbianism that was potentially corrupting; indeed, after the British trial in 1928, openly lesbian literature did not appear in England again for more than 50 years.

In the United States, *Well* fared considerably better. It was challenged in late 1928, but the trial differed from its British predecessor in two important

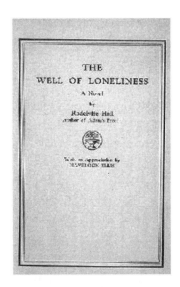

**Figure 12.3**  Image of 1928 *The Well of Loneliness* cover by Radclyffe Hall, published by Jonathan Cape.

ways: (1) discussion of literary merit and testimony of expert witnesses were permitted, and (2) the justices assigned to decide the case made a point of reading the book before they passed judgment. They concluded that the accusation of obscenity was a matter of literary taste because *Well* did not violate any existing obscenity laws. Therefore, they found it not obscene and not subject to any limitation concerning sale or distribution.

It is worthwhile to consider the trials of *The Well of Loneliness* in the context of other widely publicized literary obscenity cases of the 1920s. In 1921, in a case brought by the New York Society for the Suppression of Vice, a trial court found James Joyce's novel *Ulysses* obscene; it was also banned in England. D. H. Lawrence's novel *Lady Chatterley's Lover* was banned in 1928 (its year of publication) in both the United States and the United Kingdom; its classification as obscene was not overturned for 30 years. The *Well* American trial bears on the *Ulysses* case in that the finding that *Well* was not obscene rested on it being found not to be pornographic. The same legal logic obtained in 1933 when a U.S. court overturned the obscenity ruling against *Ulysses,* declaring it not pornographic and therefore not obscene. The U.S. *Lady Chatterley* and *Well* cases provide a point of fruitful comparison. The origins of the complaints against these texts are similar in that the complainants attempt to create a moral panic around sexual expression represented in literature. However, the two trials highlight the contingent nature of the outcomes of the censoring impulse; different books, different judges, and slightly different times produce different results.

The suppression of *The Well of Loneliness* in the United Kingdom seems to have had a number of long-term negative effects. Radclyffe Hall herself was ill off and on for years after the trials; she attributed her bouts of poor health to residual stress from them. She also wrote no more lesbian novels after *Well.* Nor, it might be added, did anyone else; potential authors of books about love between women seemed to have been temporarily scared off by the hysteria around *Well.* Most seriously, writes Diana Souhami, "By this trial, the government stigmatized and criminalized a kind of love. Its idiocy echoed down the years, silencing writers, consigning people to concealment of their deepest feelings and to public scorn" (237). The obscenity ruling, like the Pirie-Woods libel suit from 1811 [λ Chapter 1] and the recasting of the lesbian plot of Lillian Hellman's *The Children's Hour* as a heterosexual love triangle in the 1930s [λ Chapter 9], contributed to the erasure of lesbian art and lesbian lives from the popular consciousness.

The conflation of literature and life that contributed to the gross indecency conviction of Oscar Wilde in 1895 and the Home Office's obscenity finding concerning *The Well of Loneliness* in 1928 represented legal milestones functioning to suppress LGBT writing throughout much of the first half of the 20th century in the

United States and the United Kingdom. Some literature of the early to mid-century, to be sure, appeared despite the censors. Lesbian works such as Virginia Woolf's *Orlando* (1928), Djuna Barnes's *Ladies Almanack* (1928), and Gertrude Stein's *The Autobiography of Alice B. Toklas* (1936) avoided suppression through use of an intensely coded style that obscured the homosexed content. Certain gay male writers—Truman Capote (1924–1984) and Gore Vidal (b. 1925–2012), for example—parlayed their maleness and their access to publishing venues into contracts with big-name companies. Still, even they were stymied by the McCarthy anticommunist, anti-homosexual witch hunts of the early 1950s [λ Chapter 3], during which some books (*The Well of Loneliness,* Vidal's *The City and the Pillar* from 1948), previously available in handsome cloth bindings, vanished from upscale bookstores and reappeared in pulp editions at bus stations and drugstores [λ Chapter 10].

The fever broke in the 1960s, partly through new legislation that legalized a wider range of literary expression and partly through the rise of countercultural movements that established their own small presses. The 1959 Obscene Publications Act in the United Kingdom was found not to apply if the challenged work possessed so-called literary merit. In the United States, an obscenity ruling against the film version of *Lady Chatterley's Lover* was overturned by the Supreme Court in 1959 on the basis of the First Amendment guarantee of freedom of speech. The lifting of these restrictions led directly to the general availability of previously suppressed (heterosexual) works such as *Lady Chatterley* and Henry Miller's *Tropic of Cancer.* Soon thereafter, new presses specializing in LGBT subjects—Daughters, Gay Sunshine, Naiad, Crossing, and others—brought out hundreds of books, both originals and reprints, and helped build a body of homosexed literature in the 1970s and 1980s. In Chapter 4, we described the right-wing backlash against newly visible gay and lesbian movements that began with Anita Bryant in the late 1970s. Bryant, like journalist James Douglas nearly a century earlier, framed her Save the Children campaign as an effort to protect the innocent from the corrupting influence of homosexuality. By the end of the 1980s, this antigay impulse, now embodied in U.S. Senator Jesse Helms (R-NC), had gained sufficient momentum to challenge the principle of artistic freedom in Congress.

## Sapphire, Mapplethorpe, and Riggs

An example of a conservative, right-wing attempt to create a moral panic under the guise of protecting the American public from homosexed art was a resolution sponsored by Senator Helms in 1989. Helms's bill proposed prohibiting the use of funds by the National Endowment for the Arts or the National Endowment for the Humanities to promote, disseminate, or produce materials that may be considered obscene, including but not limited to, depictions of sadomasochism, homoeroticism, the sexual exploitation of children, or individuals engaged in sex acts and which, when taken as a whole, do not have serious literary, artistic, political or scientific value. (HR 2788)

Defining such value required making highly contingent judgments. What might be considered devoid of literary value and merely obscene in one circumstance and by one group might be seen very differently in another circumstance or by another group. For instance, Senator Helms intended passages such as this, from Sapphire's "Wild Thing" (which he read out loud to the Senate) to disgust his colleagues:

> I remember when
> Christ sucked my dick
> behind the pulpit,
> I was 6 years old
> he made me promise
> not to tell no one.

Sapphire's poetry is indeed provocative, but she seeks here to speak the truth about the experience of child molestation in a racist, patriarchal society.

Another of Helms's targets was a posthumous exhibition of Robert Mapplethorpe's photography, titled *Robert Mapplethorpe: The Perfect Moment*. The exhibition had been slated to appear at art galleries across the nation over an 18-month period, beginning at the Institute of Contemporary Art in Philadelphia, which had organized it, and moving to Chicago, Washington DC, Hartford, Berkeley, Cincinnati, and Boston. The show met with positive response in Philadelphia and Chicago, but its appearance in Washington was canceled because Corcoran Art Gallery Director Christina Orr-Cahall hoped to avoid giving Senator Helms ammunition for his battle against National Endowment for the Arts (NEA) funding for the work of controversial artists. So, by the time the exhibit moved to Cincinnati's Contemporary Arts Center (CAC) in 1989, much ado had been made of its contents, and local conservative forces, particularly those connected to Citizens for Community Values (the same organization that would later spearhead the successful effort to remove sexual orientation from the city's human rights ordinance [λ Chapter 4]), were prepared for a full-blown assault against the CAC.

On the day the Mapplethorpe exhibit opened in Cincinnati, according to one local newspaper, "Hundreds of people waited in the arcade outside the CAC while police closed the facility and videotaped the exhibit to use as evidence in criminal cases against [Museum Director Dennis] Barrie and the center. The crowd became agitated, chanting and booing the cops who remained stationed at the center's front doors" (Fox). Local prosecutors charged Barrie with obscenity, and while Barrie and the CAC were eventually acquitted in a jury trial, the fuss underscored Mapplethorpe's reputation as a provocative, boundary-pushing, transgressive artist.

Though these efforts to outlaw public exhibitions of Mapplethorpe's work have been at the forefront of recent debates about obscenity, it would be misleading to argue that conservative politicians and activists are alone in their objections to the work. Liberal and left-leaning critics, though usually not inclined to argue for censorship, have had problems with Mapplethorpe's photographs. For instance, gay African-American author and poet Essex Hemphill was deeply disturbed by the apparent objectification of black male bodies in some of Mapplethorpe's photographs. Cultural critic Kobena Mercer also voiced concern about those Mapplethorpe photographs that feature African-American men, saying that his first impulse when viewing the photos was to be "immediately disturbed by the racial dimension of the imagery and, above all, angered by the aesthetic objectification that reduced these individual black men to purely abstract 'things,' silenced in their own right as subjects and serving mainly as aesthetic trophies to enhance Mapplethorpe's privileged position as a white gay male artist in the New York avant-garde" (464).

> **Find Out More** in Steven Dubin's "Art's Enemies" in the readings at the end of this chapter.

Noting that the popular discussion of Mapplethorpe's work tended to be framed as a "straightforward opposition between censorship and freedom of artistic expression," Mercer warns against reducing that discussion to a "neat dichotomy between bigoted Philistines and enlightened cultural liberals" (472). In his essay, "Just Looking for Trouble," Mercer describes how cultural conservatives sometimes use seemingly progressive stances to forward their own agendas:

> In his original proposal to regulate public funding of art deemed "obscene and indecent," Jesse Helms went beyond the traditional remit of moral fundamentalism to add new grounds for legal intervention on the basis of discrimination against minorities. Helms wanted the state to intervene in instances where artistic and cultural materials "denigrate, debase or revile a person, group or class of citizens on the basis of race, creed, sex, handicap or national origin." By means of this rhetorical move, he sought to promote a climate of opinion favorable to new forms of coercive intervention. In making such a move, the strategy is not simply to win support from black people and ethnic minorities, nor simply to modernize the traditional "moral" discourse against obscenity, but to broaden and extend the threshold of illegitimacy to a wider range of cultural texts. (473)

The desire to protect the public from offensive material and the move to protect minorities from discrimination become conflated in censoring transgressive art. In other words, some cultural conservatives try to use politically progressive rhetoric to advance a conservative agenda. This move was not unprecedented; it had proved somewhat successful during the so-called sex wars of the 1980s, when feminists allied with conservative forces to create legislation that would allow women and other minorities to seek damages against producers and distributors of pornography.

The work of filmmaker Marlon Riggs (1957–1994) proved less easily manipulable for this kind of recasting. Riggs's *Tongues Untied*, a 1989 documentary about being both gay and black, provoked a firestorm of protest. Funded in part through federal grants, the film outraged conservatives who did not want taxpayers' money supporting explorations of homosexuality. In a powerful scene in the film, a Pride Day parade features a group of black men carrying a banner proclaiming, "Black Men Loving Black Men Is a Revolutionary Act." The film's boldness was simply too much for conservatives such as Pat Buchanan, who called *Tongues Untied* "pornographic art" (Smith). Riggs's counterclaim was both eloquent and pointed in its acknowledgment of how dominant cultures often elide any humane recognition of the diversity within them: "Implicit in the much overworked rhetoric of community standards is the assumption of only one central community (patriarchal, heterosexual and usually white) and only one overarching cultural standard (ditto)" (Riggs).

# Queering Children's Books

Today it is possible to locate literally hundreds of queer-themed books for children, most aimed at young adult readers, that is, ages 12 and up. The problems arise around books aimed at elementary school-aged children. Diana Schemo writes, "According to a 2004 national poll by the Kaiser Family Foundation, Harvard University's Kennedy School of Government and National Public Radio, roughly three out of four parents say it is appropriate for high schools to teach about homosexuality, but about half say it is appropriate in middle school." Only tiny percentages approve of introducing LGBT subject matter to younger children. Lesbian author Lesléa Newman knows of no attempt to censor her young adult or adult writing, but her children's book, *Heather Has Two Mommies* (1989), has had quite a different history. When New York adopted the multicultural curriculum guide "Children of the Rainbow" in 1992, *Heather Has Two Mommies,* along with Michael Willhoite's *Daddy's Roommate* (1991), became flashpoints for angry discussions about making books with homosexual themes available in schools. New York City School Chancellor Joseph Fernandez suspended the school board of District 24, which had refused to endorse the new curriculum for fear of "promot[ing] a homosexual lifestyle" (Duberman 589). Eventually, Fernandez was forced out as chancellor over the controversy.

Even today, *Heather Has Two Mommies* and *Daddy's Roommate* regularly appear on lists of banned books; see, for instance, Wikipedia's "List of Most Commonly Challenged Books in the U.S." or Herbert Foerstel's *Banned in the USA: A Reference Guide to Book Censorship in Schools. Heather* and *Roommate* have come to stand in for claims that "gay agenda" advocates seek to corrupt children. Conservative organizations position themselves as protectors of the innocent, using Newman's and Willhoite's books as examples of the corrupting influence of homosexuality. For instance, Peter LaBarbera's articles, "How to Protect Your Children from Pro-homosexuality Propaganda in Schools" and "When Silence Would Have Been Golden," cast curricula that promote tolerance or diversity as dangerously pro-gay, even as "brainwashing kindergartners." Antigay demonizing of *Heather Has Two Mommies* and *Daddy's Roommate,* as well as of such more recent books as *King & King* (2002) and *Antonio's Card* (2005), seeks to initiate a moral panic, which can in turn invest received moral authorities with the responsibility—and, more to the point, with the power—to protect innocent, less powerful people from ideas they do not like.

## Deepa Mehta

We can see the deployment of multiple protectionist rhetorics to censor queer art in the moral panic surrounding the release of Canadian Indian Deepa Mehta's 1996 film, *Fire*. The film tells the story of the evolving relationship between two sisters-in-law whose unhappiness in their marriages and growing attraction to one another take place in an oppressive environment where families live together in confined spaces and where women's lives are controlled by their social circumstances. Previous to the release of *Fire*, Daniel Lak of BBC Online, while clarifying that the film is "not meant to be about gay life," acknowledged that "one group of people in [India] is awaiting this film eagerly—the Indian lesbian community, which for years has maintained a silent, almost secret existence." Perhaps partly as an effort to maintain that silence, protesters reacted strongly to the film's 1998 release in India, claiming that it represented an affront not only to Indian sexual mores but to Indian culture and nationhood. Conservative Hindu activists called the film "un-Indian" and warned that portraying lesbianism will "spoil our women" ("Deepa").

**Find Out More** in the excerpt from Gayatri Gopinath's "Local Sites/Global Contexts: The Transnational Trajectories of *Fire* and 'The Quilt'" in the readings at the end of this chapter.

This notion is reminiscent of the 1928 suppression of *The Well of Loneliness,* not on the grounds of obscenity but solely on account of its lesbian subject matter. The intersectional moral panic around *Fire* raised issues of nationalism, sexism, and heterosexism. As in other countries where homosexuality has been silenced until very recently, the Hindu protesters figure India as a land of heterosexuals, where gay men and lesbians present a powerful challenge to the national self-image. Moreover, as a danger to "our women," the film is seen as an "attack on the privileges of patriarchy" in India (Morris). *Fire,* however, gave voice to the "unhappiness of women in traditional families" ("Deepa") and thus exposed the pervasive sexism and misogyny of the culture. Finally, the vandalism and violence attending *Fire*'s release in Bombay revealed profound homophobia—disguised as a concern that the movie would "corrupt Indian women"—and unleashed a spate of gay bashing. This homophobic backlash occurred in the context of a general belief in the sanctity of marriage and related disapproval of pre- and extramarital sex.

The Indian Censor Board's decision to allow *Fire* to be shown may have led in the short term to right-wing protests and vandalism. But in the long run, it opened the door for other homosexed art in India. We note, for instance, that *Girlfriend,* a Bollywood film about a lesbian relationship, opened in 2004. The same right-wing protesters claimed that "such movies pollute the culture and should not be made" (Singh). However, Censor Board approval of *Girlfriend* and state protection of theaters showing it suggest that the moral panic around *Fire* did not completely squelch lesbian-themed filmmaking in India. We argue that this trajectory typically follows moral panics; the very rhetoric designed to muzzle transgressive art also tends to spur the creation of new work with similar themes. Even in the case of the *Well of Loneliness* trials, which resulted in the temporary erasure of lesbian-themed work from public view, the book itself has become a central lesbian text that has remained in print since its pulp version appeared in the 1950s. *The Picture of Dorian Gray* has also enjoyed enormous popularity and has been continuously available, and the hullabaloo over Mapplethorpe's work made him a popular, even an iconic, figure in the Western art world. As we will see in the final three chapters of this book, moral panics have failed to suppress the impulse to create queer community through transgressive artistic expression.

# Note

1. In the version of *The Picture of Dorian Gray* that appeared in *Lippincott's Monthly Magazine* in July 1890, Hallward asks, "Why is your friendship so <u>fateful</u> to young men?" (258). Wilde changed the word to *fatal* for the revised, expanded version of the novel published by Ward, Lock and Company in 1891.

## QUESTIONS FOR DISCUSSION

1. Consider the way this chapter has defined *censorship* and *moral panic*. Brainstorm a list of moral panics that have been initiated by or have resulted in the impulse to censor—instances in which books have been banned from libraries, in which there have been calls for the removal of advertisements or programming from television, or in which a media outlet has refused to publish specific kinds of material. List several of these and try to identify the players involved in each situation. Identify each player's issues or concerns. If the issue was finally resolved in one way or another, write a short description of the resolution. Once you have compiled a list of notes about these moral panics, answer these questions: Who benefits if the material is censored? Who benefits from the panic around the issue? Who benefits from the resolution? Try to avoid easy answers. For instance, sometimes a moral panic seems to benefit only the person or group creating it, but try to consider the possibility that the moral panics you identified might have benefited the person or group whose work was initially censored. How does that work?

2. As we discussed earlier in this chapter, some of the moral panic surrounding the public revelation of Oscar Wilde's homosexuality and his subsequent trials was fueled by discussion in newspapers and reviews of Wilde's novel, *The Picture of Dorian Gray*. Reviews of this novel are easily accessible on the World Wide Web. Find a few reviews and critically examine the language used either to condemn or to support this book. Does any of the rhetoric seem familiar? You might compare the language that circulated in response to Wilde's novel with language used in contemporary debates about homosexed art and literature. For instance, find an interview online in which Sapphire comments about Jesse Helms's condemnation in Congress of her poem "Wild Thing." How similar is the language in these two public debates, separated by nearly 100 years? How is it different? What might account for the similarities and differences?

3. Censorship can take many forms other than suppression of works and themes in public art and entertainment. For example, until recently discussions of bullying in schools and of teen suicide typically elided mention of LGBT young people, who are disproportionately victimized by bullying and at risk for suicide. Even today there is considerable reluctance among some groups to acknowledge the very existence of LGBT kids, much less the chronic problems they face. Do some research about one or both of these phenomena and try to locate the source of the censorship. Why are children and teens perceived to be LGBT not included in the discussion, and who stands to benefit from such censorship?

## REFERENCES AND FURTHER READING

Cohen, Stan. *Folk Devils and Moral Panics.* London: MacGibbon and Kee, 1972. Print.

"Deepa Mehta's *Fire* Creates Controversy and Protests in India." N.p., 19 Aug. 1999. Web. 8 Aug. 2008. <http://www .sawnet.org/news/fire.html>.

de Haan, Linda, and Stern Nijlund. *King & King.* Berkeley, CA: Tricycle P, 2002. Print.

Doan, Laura. *Fashioning Sapphism: The Origins of a Modern English Lesbian Culture.* New York: Columbia UP, 2001. Print.

Douglas, James. "A Book That Must Be Suppressed." *Sunday Express* 19 August 1928: 10. Print.

Duberman, Martin. Introduction to "Families, Values, and the Rainbow Curriculum: A Roundtable Discussion." *A Queer World: The Center for Lesbian and Gay Studies Reader.* Ed. Martin Duberman. New York: NYU P, 1997. 589. Print.

Foerstel, Herbert N. *Banned in the USA: A Reference Guide to Book Censorship in Schools.* 2nd ed. Westport, CT: Greenwood, 2006. Print.

Fox, John. "Then and Now: Mapplethorpe and the CAC." *CityBeat,* 6.19 (2000). Web. 9 Aug. 2008. <http://citybeat.com/2000-03-30/cover.shtml>.

"Gadfly." *Daily Herald* 7 March 1929: 7. Print.

González, Rigoberto. *Antonio's Card.* San Francisco: Children's Book P, 2005. Print.

Hall, Radclyffe. *The Well of Loneliness.* New York: Anchor, 1990. Print.

Hemphill, Essex. *Ceremonies: Prose and Poetry.* New York: Penguin, 1992. Print.

HR 2788. Summary as of 10/3/1989. Web. 8 Aug. 2008. <http://thomas.loc.gov/cgi-bin/bdquery/z?d101:HR02788:@@@D&summ2=m&>.

LaBarbera, Peter J. "How to Protect Your Children from Pro-homosexuality Propaganda in Schools." *The Fountain Gateway: The Christian Resource and Index Directory.* Family Research Council in Focus. 2 July 2006. Web. 8 Aug. 2008 <http://www.fountaingate

way.com/SpecialsNMessages/messageindex/index.html>.

———. "When Silence Would Have Been Golden: Acts of Homosexual Promotion to Youth That We Wish Had Never Happened." *Concerned Women for America.* Culture and Family Issues, 10 Apr. 2002. Web. 8 Aug. 2008 <http://www.cultureandfamily.org/articledisplay.asp?id=2580&department=CFI&categoryid=papers#propaganda>.

Lak, Daniel. "Lesbian Film Sets India on Fire." *BBC Online,* 13 Nov. 1998. Web. 8 Aug. 2008. <http://news.bbc.co.uk/2/hi/south_asia/213417.stm>.

Wilde, Oscar. *The Picture of Dorian Gray.* Ed. Donald L. Lawler. New York: W. W. Norton, 1988. Print.

Linton, Eliza Lynn. "The Philistine's Coming Triumph." *National Review* (Sept. 1895): 40–49. Print.

"List of Most Commonly Challenged Books in the U.S." N.d., 11 July 2008. Web. 8 Aug. 2008. <http://en.wikipedia.org/wiki/List_of_most_commonly_challenged_books_in_the_U.S.>.

Mercer, Kobena. "Just Looking for Trouble: Robert Mapplethorpe and Fantasies of Race." *Feminism and Pornography.* Ed. Drucilla Cornell. Oxford, UK: Oxford UP, 2000. 460–76. Print.

Morris, Gary. "Burning Love: Deepa Mehta's Fire." *Bright Lights Film Journal,* 2000. Web. 8 Aug. 2008. <http://www.brightlightsfilm.com/30/fire.html>.

Newman, Lesléa. *Heather Has Two Mommies.* Los Angeles: Alyson, 1989. Print.

Rev. of *The Well of Loneliness. The Daily Telegraph,* 17 Aug. 1928: 13. Print.

Riggs, Marlon. "Tongues Re-tied?" N.p., 15 Ap. 1997. Web. 8 Aug. 2008.

<http://www.current.org/prog/prog 114g.html>.

Sapphire. "Wild Thing." *American Dreams.* New York: Vintage, 1997: 141–51. Print.

Schemo, Diana Jean. "Lessons on Homosexuality Move into the Classroom." *New York Times,* 15 Aug. 2007. Web. 8 Aug. 2008 <http://www.nytimes .com/2007/08/15/education/15edu cation.html>.

Senate Report 105-086. "Arts & Humanities Amendments of 1997." N.p., 24 Sept. 1997. Web. 8 Aug. 2008. <http://thomas .loc.gov/cgibin/cpquery/?&sid=cp105w 2SuW&refer=&r_n=sr086.105&db_ id=105&item=&sel=TOC_0&>.

Singh, Jupinderjit. "Protest in City against Screening of 'Girlfriend.'" N.p., 16 June 2004. Web. 8 Aug. 2008. <http://www .tribuneindia.com/2004/20040616/ ldh1.htm>.

Smith, Justin. "Tongues Untied Screening and Panel Discussion." *GBMNews,* 3 Mar. 2008. Web. 9 Aug. 2008. <http:// www.gbmnews.com/articles/3034/1/ Tongues-UntiedScreening-and-Panel-Discussion/Page1.html>.

Souhami, Diana. *The Trials of Radclyffe Hall.* New York: Doubleday, 1999. Print.

"The Trials of Oscar Wilde." N.p., n.d. Web. 8 Aug. 2008. <http://www.law.umkc.edu/ faculty/projects/ftrials/wilde/wilde.htm>.

Vargo, Marc E. *Scandal: Infamous Gay Controversies of the Twentieth Century.* Binghamton, NY: Harrington Park/ Haworth, 2003. Print.

Willhoite, Michael. *Daddy's Roommate.* Los Angeles: Alyson, 1991. Print.

# READINGS

## ➢ Steven C. Dubin
(1994), United States

### From "Art's Enemies: Censors to the Right of Me, Censors to the Left of Me"

Those on the political right believe that many elements in contemporary culture are menacing, capable of contaminating pure minds. Reverend [James] Wildmon discovers these dangers everywhere, and expressions of his concern range from his fear that Mighty Mouse was giving youngsters lessons on how to snort cocaine to his authoritative appraisal of what he labels pornography: this stuff is so powerful you may be "hooked with one look." What he dreads most is imitation without reflection, without mediation.

From time to time, those on the left uncannily reflect the same sentiments. For *some* antipornography feminists, the motto is "Porn is the theory; rape the practice." In pragmatic terms this led prominent feminists to condemn Bret Easton Ellis's *American Psycho* (1991) as a guidebook on how to brutalize women. And gays similarly protested *Cruising* (1980), *Silence of the Lambs* (1991), and *Basic Instinct* (1992)—to the point of disrupting the shooting of these films on several occasions—fearing that each movie perpetuated negative stereotypes and could provoke actual violence toward gays.

These reactions are understandable but facile. They reflect a search for a "quick fix" to complex problems and disregard the historical and structural roots of discrimination and violence toward "the other." If eliminating violence were as uncomplicated as eradicating representations of it, a large part of the populace would undoubtedly support such a drive. Absolutists comfort themselves by seeking a magic-bullet-type solution. Yet their assumptions about society and the individual are simplistic and not very flattering. Humans are far more enigmatic than Pavlovian dogs.

### Ideologues Possess a Sense of Apocalypse

Many of the issues ideologues struggle over may seem trivial. But to them, they are not. Absolutists clutch a *Weltanschauung* that perceives the forces of darkness and light coming to critical blows. Even minor skirmishes are part of escalating hostilities.

For those on the right, the threat is the cumulative effect of the changes that have come about since the 1960s, with various civil rights movements insisting on greater inclusion into society. The demands of these entitlement efforts have reshaped how we lead our lives and have shifted power from some groups to others to a certain degree. African-Americans, women, gays and lesbians, Hispanics, "secular humanists," and other constituencies have forced society to recognize their respective rights and talents, causing more established groups to feel left behind or left out. In a sample of writings from a variety of conservatives, an overarching theme uniting them is the sense that America has been steadily sliding into a moral sewer since the 1960s. "Decadent art," the way conservatives so often describe the expression of these newly enfranchised groups, puts additional nails in society's coffin.

The political left has been the beneficiary of many of the transformations the political right abhors. But where the right sees too much change, the left feels that there has not been enough. The left experiences a revolution of rising expectations: change has come, but accompanied by an impatience to speed the process along. Its goal, then, is to wipe out residual traces of prejudice and discrimination as quickly as possible. In the hands of absolutists, this means trying to enforce tolerance by eliminating or altering a wide range of offensive, archaic symbols.

Consider the humble crayon. Binney and Smith, manufacturers of Crayola, decided to "retire" eight traditional colors in 1990 and replace them with eight vibrant new ones. They did not anticipate the public uproar they would elicit by such meddling: scores of disgruntled people complained, and at least three grass-roots movements were initiated to symbolically restore order, the most telling being CRAYON: the Committee to Re-establish All Your Old Norms.

Binney and Smith quickly saw the error of its marketing ways, reviving the old colors in a 1991 commemorative tin. Chastened by this breach, they demonstrated that they are attuned to contemporary sensitivities by next issuing a multicultural "My World Colors" pack. These sixteen hues embody the skin, hair, and eye color of a broad sample of people, supplanting the antiquated, all-purpose "flesh" of the past. The smart shopper can now likewise find "adhesive bandages of color."

### Ideologues Wish to Impose Their Own Sense of Morality onto the Entire Public

Senator Jesse Helms (R-N.C.) has distinguished himself as one of the most relentless crusaders against contemporary art. He declared in his book *Where Free Men Shall Stand,* "Our political problems are nothing but our psychological and moral problems writ large." When he views Robert Mapplethorpe's photograph *Embrace,* in which a white man and a black man tenderly hug one another, it is probably difficult for him to regard this type of affection in positive (or even neutral) terms. Rather than taking this as an alternative, legitimate relationship, he is likely to perceive a dual challenge to the bedrock of his own life: the norms of racial segregation and heterosexuality.

What's merely different can be quickly recast as immoral and unacceptable. Helms's counterparts on the progressive side are legion—Black aldermen in Chicago could not tolerate an extremely unflattering portrait of the late Mayor Harold Washington in a 1988 student show at the School of the Art Institute of Chicago. They had it "arrested" to foreclose the chance it might "spark a riot." African-Americans have similarly censored *The Adventures of Huckleberry Finn, Show Boat,* an outdoor sculpture by David Hammons ("How Ya Like Me Now?"), and a post-Civil War obelisk in downtown New Orleans. In 1991 the female director of the National Museum of American Art attempted to remove *Muybridge* 1 (1964) by Sol LeWitt from an exhibit because it suggested to her the voyeurism of a peep show, what she judged to be "a degrading pornographic experience." In 1988 AIDS activists demonstrated outside the Museum of Modern Art against the work of photographer Nicholas Nixon. They believed that his portraits of people with AIDS (PWAS) captured isolated and defeated individuals. They wished to substitute images of PWAS who are "vibrant, angry, loving, sexy, beautiful, acting up and fighting back."

In all these cases there was a rejection of the belief that viewers in a free society have a fundamental right to draw their own conclusions about what they see. At the very least, this requires that the public has access to a wide range of material. Yet this is a scary proposition for those engaged in a high-stakes battle for hearts and minds. Such preemptive, protective responses reveal deep insecurities about the strength of the moral stances certain advocates espouse, and stem from their urgent need to shore up their defenses lest people be lured away from "the right path."

### The Result of Ideologues at Work: The Restraint of Expression and the Shredding of the Social Fabric

Intergroup relations in America are in a disturbingly fragmented state at present. Those on the extreme right wish to bury their heads in the sands of the past. If they could, they would force the genie of civil rights back into the bottle and restore the verities of yesteryear. But those on the extreme left insist on an "in your face" posture, guaranteeing that their demands must be addressed in some manner or another. Each side shares the sense of these being momentous times, with the very nature of their world at risk at virtually every turn.

Ideologues see everything in black and white. The nuance, contradiction, and complexity that characterize so much contemporary art are destined to trouble them. In fact, a basic property of most of the art that has generated controversy is the *mixture* of sacred and profane elements, blending ingredients that generally are kept apart.

This is evident in Andres Serrano's photograph *Piss Christ,* where a plastic crucifix was submerged in the artist's urine. It is manifest in Robert Mapplethorpe's photographs, and in the work of many other gay as well as feminist artists, where the attributes of "maleness" and "femaleness" may be deconstructed, merged, or reconfigured, and a heterosexual erotic preference cannot be taken for granted. And it is apparent in the work of performance artists who smudge the line between public and private, self and other, decency and morality.

Whereas some viewers enjoy the frisson created by these novel combinations (for them the thrill is in the sense of fresh possibilities), these same efforts may cause immense discomfort for the absolutist. What for one person signals a laudable burst of creativity at most, or silliness at the very least, for another sounds a warning about a world gone terribly awry. It is then that the absolutist frame of mind is activated, engendering the types of results I've enumerated in the examples I've cited.

---

## ➤ Sir Chartres Biron, Chief Magistrate

(1928), United Kingdom

---

### Judgment Regarding *The Well of Loneliness*

The magistrate: . . . I agree that this book has some literary merit, defamed, as I think everybody who has read it will admit, with certain deplorable lapses of taste; but the mere fact that a book is well written can be no answer to these proceedings, because otherwise we should be in this preposterous position, that because it is well written the most obscene book would be free from such proceedings. It is quite obvious to anybody of intelligence that the better an obscene book is written the greater the public to whom the book is likely to appeal. The more palatable the poison the more insidious. . . .

There is one matter which I think should be cleared up, and that is that the mere fact that this book deals with unnatural offences between women would not in itself make it, in my view, an obscene libel. I can imagine a book written dealing with this subject presenting the whole matter as a tragedy, the tragedy being that there may be people so afflicted who try their best to fight against this horrible vice, find themselves impelled in that direction or unable to resist those tendencies, with the result of the moral and physical degradation which indulgence in these vices must necessarily involve; I can imagine a book dealing with the subject on those terms, presenting these women as the prisoners of circumstances which, however much they fight against them, they are unable to resist—I can imagine a book of that kind, whatever one's opinion may be as to whether it is or it is not desirable that these matters should form the subject of a novel for popular reading, having anything but an immoral influence; it might have a strong moral influence. But does that book do it? I am told here by Mr. Melville that the book is presented as a tragedy. It is true that in a sense that is so, but what is the tragedy of the book? It is not the tragedy which I have just indicated at all; it is not the tragedy of people fighting against horrible instincts and being unable to resist them; but, on the contrary, the tragedy as presented here is that people who indulge in these vices are not tolerated by decent people; they are not received in society and they are ostracized by decent people; and the whole note of the book is a passionate and almost hysterical plea for the toleration and recognition of these people who, in the view presented in this book, are people who ought to be tolerated and recognized, and their practices tolerated and recognized, in decent society. That is what is put forward in this book. It is a long book of some 500 pages dealing solely, or at any rate in the main, with unnatural offences. There is not a single word from beginning to end of this book which suggests that anyone with these horrible tendencies is in the least blameworthy or that they should in any way resist them. Everybody, all the characters in this book, who indulge in these horrible vices are presented to us as attractive people and put forward for our admiration; and those who object to these vices are sneered at in the book as prejudiced, foolish and cruel. Not merely that, but there is a much more serious matter, the actual physical acts of these women indulging in unnatural vices are described in the most alluring terms; their result is described as giving these women extraordinary rest, contentment and pleasure; and not merely that, but it is actually put forward that it improves their mental balance and capacity. . . .

[The book] concludes with a very singular hysterical passage in which God is introduced. At the end the last sentence of the book is: "God" she gasped, "we believe; we have told You we believe. . . . We have not denied You, then rise up and defend us. Acknowledge us, oh God, before the whole world. Give us also the right to our existence." There are a good many other passages in which the name of the Deity is introduced in a way which is hardly appropriate. I do not know whether the word "reverence" is introduced in this discussion or whether it is necessary to introduce it, but I confess the way in which the Deity is introduced into this book seems to me singularly inappropriate and disgusting. There is a plea for existence at the end. That of course means a plea for existence in which the invert is to be recognized and tolerated, and not treated with condemnation, which they are at present, by all decent people.

This being the tenor of this book, I have no hesitation whatever in saying that it is an obscene libel, that it would tend to corrupt those into whose hands it should fall, and that the publication of this book is an offence against public decency, an obscene libel, and I shall order it to be destroyed.

Bow Street Police Court.

Friday, 16th November, 1928.

---

The National Archives, HO 144/22547.

## ➤ **Gayatri Gopinath**

(2005), United States

### From "Local Sites/Global Contexts: The Transnational Trajectories of *Fire* and 'The Quilt'"

. . . An analysis of *Fire*'s reception both within and outside India underscores the inadequacy of feminist analyses that seek to destabilize heterosexuality without adequately grappling with the significance of alternative sexualities in the constitution of communal and nationalist collectivities. The film and the controversy it engendered demand that we explore more fully the ways in which challenges to state-sanctioned sexual subjectivities are managed with hegemonic articulations of community and nation, and how they simultaneously threaten to interrupt the coherence of such entities. The violent hostility of religious nationalists in India toward a diasporic film like *Fire* highlights the urgent need for feminist scholarship both in India and in the diaspora to extend its scope of analysis in two directions: first, to view heterosexuality and contemporary nationalisms as overlapping structures of domination; and second, to move beyond the nation-state in order to account for the transnational circuits that both prop *and* challenge contemporary nationalisms. . . .

*Fire* both adheres to and challenges a developmental narrative of gay and lesbian identity, which underlies dominant Euro-American discourses on non-Western sexualities. The film opens with a scene of the adult protagonist Radha's memory/fantasy of herself as a young girl, sitting beside her parents in an open field of yellow flowers. Her mother urges the young Radha to "see the ocean" lying just beyond the landlocked field: "What you can't see you can see, you just have to see without looking." This scene, with its exhortation to "see" without looking, to "see" differently, recurs and resonates throughout the film and suggests an analogy with the ways in which *Fire* interrogates the notion that the proper location of lesbianism is within a politics of visibility in the public sphere. However, the film's counterhegemonic representation of queer female desire is undercut and complicated by its own history of production, distribution, reception, and consumption. Funded largely with Canadian money, *Fire* had circulated from 1996 to 1998 mostly at international film festivals in India, Europe, and North America and had a lengthy art house release in major U.S. cities. Thus, prior to its general release in India in November 1998, it was available to a limited audience in India but gained a significant South Asian diasporic viewership as well as a mainstream lesbian and gay audience in the United States and Canada. Given the trajectory of the film's reception, it is worth asking how the film has become available and legible to its diasporic and international audiences.

*Fire* takes place in the middle-class neighborhood of Lajpat Nagar, in New Delhi, and tells the story of the burgeoning love and desire that emerges between Radha (Shabana Azmi) and her new sister-in-law Sita (Nandita Das), in a joint-family household. [Director Deepa] Mehta quickly establishes the familiar familial violences and compulsions that inhabit the household: the women do most of the labor for the family business while their husbands ignore or abuse them. Radha's husband, Ashok, is tender and attentive not to Radha but to his guru, with whom he spends all his free time and who preaches sexual abstinence, while Sita's husband, Jatin, is too preoccupied with his Westernized Chinese girlfriend to attend to Sita. The two women eventually turn to each other for sex and emotional sustenance. Mehta rather conventionally frames the dilemma of her heroines as one in which "modernity," with its promise of individual freedom and self-expression, pulls inevitably against "tradition," which demands that the women adhere to the roles prescribed for them as good Hindu wives and remain chaste, demure, and self-sacrificing. Indeed, their very names bespeak these roles. In Hindu mythology, Radha is the consort of the god Krishna, who is famous for his womanizing; together Radha and Krishna symbolize an idealized, transcendent heterosexual union. Sita, the heroine of the Hindu epic *Ramayana,* proves her chastity to her husband, Ram, by immersing herself in fire, and thus represents the ideal of wifely devotion and virtue. The image of Sita emerging unscathed from her *agni pariksha,* or trial by fire, is the inescapable motif around which the women's lives revolve throughout the film: for instance, the background noise in their daily lives is the popular serialization of the *Ramayana,* which plays incessantly on the television. Das's Sita, however, refuses to inhabit the overdetermined role of her legendary namesake: with her penchant for donning her husband's jeans instead of her heavy silk saris, and her willingness to pursue her attraction to Radha, she becomes the emblem of a "new India" and its promise of feminist self-fulfillment. Conversely, the stultifying effects of "tradition" are embodied in the character of Biji, the mute, paralytic grandmother who keeps a disapproving eye on the activities of her daughters-in-law.

The dichotomies through which the film is structured—between Biji and Sita, saris and jeans, silence and speech, self-denial and self-fulfillment, abstinence and desire, tradition and modernity—implicate it in a familiar teleological narrative of progress toward the individual freedom offered by the West, against which the "non-West" can only be read as premodern. In fact, a number of U.S. critics have used the film as an occasion to replay colonial constructions of India as a site of regressive gender oppression, against which the West stands for enlightened egalitarianism. Within the dominant discursive production of India as anterior to the West, lesbian or gay identity is explicitly articulated as the marker of full-fledged modernity. After Ashok spies the two women in bed together, Sita comments to Radha, "There is no word in our language to describe what we are to each other," to which Radha responds, "You're right; perhaps seeing is less complicated." Film critics in the United States, most notably Roger Ebert, have taken this exchange (as well as Mehta's own pronouncement in the press notes that "Indians don't talk about sex") as proof of the West's cultural superiority and advanced politicization: "Lesbianism is so outside the experience of these Hindus that their language even lacks a word for it." Indeed, almost all mainstream U.S. reviewers stress the failure of "these Hindus" to articulate lesbianism intelligibly, which in turn signifies the failure of the non-West to progress toward the organization of sexuality and gender prevalent in the West. To these critics, ironically, lesbian or gay identity becomes intelligible and indeed desirable when and where it can be incorporated into this developmental narrative of modernity.

Because *Fire* gains legibility within such narratives for at least some North American, non-South Asian viewers (both straight and gay), it is helpful to resituate it within other discourses of non-heteronormative sexuality that are available to South Asian and South Asian diasporic audiences. . . . *Fire* [can] be read as a diasporic appropriation and transformation of Ismat Chughtai's "The Quilt." Reading the film through the story provides an alternative to the tradition-modernity axis by foregrounding the complex model of queer female desire suggested by the film but foreclosed by its mainstream U.S. reception. . . .

For Radha and Sita, then, like the women in Chughtai's story, queer desire becomes the means by which they are able to extricate themselves from the terms of patriarchal heteronormativity by creating their own circuits of pleasure, desire, and fantasy. While some critics have suggested that *Fire*'s depiction of lesbian sexuality capitulates to the familiar notion of lesbianism as merely a reaction to failed heterosexual marriages, I would argue that, at least in the middle-class urban Indian context that Mehta details, it is precisely within the cracks and fissures of rigidly heteronormative arrangements that queer female desire can emerge. As in Chughtai's text, where queer female desire is routed through and against heterosexuality, the attraction between Radha and Sita is enabled by those spaces of sanctioned female homosociality legislated by normative sexual and gender arrangements. . . .

The reactions to *Fire* within and outside India force us to consider the function of cultural representation as a site of both "promise and peril," a site of both the subversion of nationalist ideologies and the reiteration of homophobic sentiments. *Fire* gains multiple and contradictory meanings as it circulates within India, within the South Asian diaspora, and within film festival circuits and theaters in Europe and North America. As the film circulates within India, it may pose a potent challenge to right-wing Hindu nationalism, yet it is simultaneously available for recuperation within a liberal humanist framework that subsumes sexuality under a human rights rubric. Similarly, as it travels outside India, the film both resists and plays into dominant developmental narratives of modernity. I have focused on *Fire* in particular since it is emblematic of the ways in which South Asian diasporic texts travel along increasingly complex trajectories of production and reception. In a Euro-American context, the film's strategy of disarticulation—where it refuses to collapse female homoerotic acts, desires, and practices into static identities—challenges dominant conceptions of what lesbian and gay identity looks like in the West; yet in an Indian context, this very strategy simultaneously allows for the elision of queer desire and the challenge it poses to dominant conceptions of community, home, and nation. The violent debates that have surrounded *Fire* demand that we develop frames of analysis supple enough to account for these transnational movements and the various discourses of gender and sexuality to which they give rise.

---

Gayatri Gopinath, "Local Sites/Global Contexts: The Transnational Trajectories of *Fire* and 'The Quilt,'" in *Impossible Desires,* pp. 131–160 (excerpts). Copyright, 2005, Duke University Press.

# SECTION IV

# Media

The mass media, including television, movies, the Internet, and underground publication venues, remains a powerful force in both expressing and shaping public opinion and private musing about sex and sexuality. This section prompts students to explore in greater depth the ways in which queer sexuality is constructed, produced, disseminated, and argued about through a variety of mass media.

# CHAPTER 13

# Film and Television

Images of queers in film and TV have had a long and complicated history in the 20th C. The explosion of lesbian and gay images beginning in the 1990s represents a turning point in queer visibility. This chapter examines how visibility can operate as a double-edged sword, diluting the power of underground community while ostensibly promoting mainstream acceptance.

In the early days of moviemaking, Magnus Hirschfeld [λ Chapters 2 and 5] introduced the film *Different from the Others* (1919), a German production by The Scientific Humanitarian Committee, which had been founded in 1897 to help bring about the abolition of Paragraph 175 [λ Chapter 2] by "eliminating false prejudices against homosexuals." Hirschfeld's introduction to the first showing of *Different* contained these lines:

> The matter to be put before your eyes and soul today is one of severe importance and difficulty. Difficult, because the degree of ignorance and prejudice to be disposed of is extremely high. Important, because we must free not only these people from undeserved disgrace but also the public from a judicial error that can be compared to such atrocities in history as the persecution of witches, atheists and heretics. . . . The film you are about to see for the first time today will help to terminate the lack of enlightenment, and soon the day will come when science will win a victory over error, justice a victory over injustice and human love a victory over human hatred and ignorance. (Russo 20)

Almost a century later, Hirschfeld's hopes for the film's impact have not been completely realized. What has happened, however, is that commentary about LGBT presence in film has continued to use Hirschfeld's ideas; critics have repeatedly called for visibility and representation in the same ways that Hirschfeld did when he introduced *Different from the Others.*

Film and television—two of the most important venues of contemporary mass media—serve as sites of intense cultural work. Through film and TV, larger cultures clarify their dominant values and ideological investments, while subcultures and minority groups negotiate their place at the table through posi-

**Figure 13.1** Still from *Different from the Others* (1919).

tive representation or through critical interrogation of negative images. Much of the discourse around queers in film and television has focused on questions of visibility and representation. Do we see LGBT people in film and on TV? How often do we see them? Are these representations of LGBT people positive or negative? What do we mean when we use the terms *positive* and *negative?* Do those representations show LGBT people in realistic ways? In this chapter, we focus on a relatively small number of films and TV shows that feature LGBT characters to raise questions about the "cultural work" of film and television with LGBT content—explicit or not. We begin with some information about the way scholars and critics have talked about film, and then we offer several analyses of recent films, moving from reality-based subject matter to fiction to fantasy. From there we shift to television, analyzing significant moments when shows and characters appeared (or disappeared) and asking what these trends might mean. This chapter does not engage in exhaustive historical listing of LGBT characters in film and TV productions; rather, our focus will be on providing some specific analyses of the cultural work accomplished by a variety of representations of queers in mass media.

## Visibility and Representation

Vito Russo's *The Celluloid Closet: Homosexuality in the Movies,* written in 1981 and revised in 1987, was in its time the most comprehensive discussion of gay characters in U.S. film. In 1990, it was made into a documentary film featuring interviews with people connected to Hollywood. Russo's book covers nearly a century of films with homosexual characters, asking whether they are presented in a positive or a negative light. Russo's account, written before the explosion of queer characters and issues in the mass media of the 1990s, depicts a startling and unsettling reality: when homosexuals were represented on film, they were often sad and suicidal or unstable and psychopathic. One prime example Russo cites is William Friedkin's controversial 1980 film *Cruising,* in which Al Pacino portrays an undercover cop assigned to infiltrate New York's gay leather underworld to catch a serial killer. By the end of the film, Pacino's character is seemingly seduced into becoming homosexual himself. Russo explains, "[T]he unavoidable conclusion is that Pacino becomes a murderer of gays. The audience is left with the message that homosexuality is not only contagious but inescapably brutal" (259). What's more, for Russo, "The fact that Pacino's girlfriend ends up in the last shot trying on his leather gear says that his lifestyle is seductive and contagious, threatening to what's good in the world" (261). Others agreed with Russo's analysis, and at the time of its original release, many gays picketed the film, which ultimately did poorly at the box office: "Usually, when gay people complain about this sort of thing their concerns are dismissed as partisan, but this time everyone complained because the evidence was too overwhelming to ignore" (261).

Certainly, *Cruising* created a stir, but we must remember that moviemakers' intentions only tell part of the story of how films and other mass media work in a

**Figure 13.2**   Al Pacino in *Cruising.*

culture. Stuart Hall's notions of "encoding" and "decoding" are useful here. For Hall, *encoding* refers to the messages deliberately included in cultural products by their makers; *decoding* refers to the messages cultural consumers glean from these products—not necessarily the encoded ones. Russo may be correct in ascribing homophobic intent, or encoding, to *Cruising*'s makers, and the gay picketers who protested the film read it in that way. But since the film's release, many gay video distribution companies, such as Theatre of the Living Arts (TLA), have marketed the film specifically to gay audiences. Many in the contemporary gay world find *Cruising* a rather sexy and provocative look at leathersex, despite the homophobic story that frames it. Different gay viewers thus decode the film in ways that make its message more interesting and complex to them as viewers or "readers."

In the revised 1987 version of *The Celluloid Closet,* Russo discusses the block-buster film *The Color Purple* (Warner Bros. 1985, dir. Steven Spielberg). Russo, like many other LGBT reviewers, criticizes the film harshly for diluting the lesbian material that figured prominently in its inspiration, Alice Walker's 1982 book. The book had already been slammed by black male critics such as Mel Watkins, Courtland Milloy, Tony Brown, and Spike Lee for its unflattering portrayal of black men and for airing "dirty laundry" about domestic and sexual abuse in black households (Iverem, Bobo). Feminists criticized Spielberg's film for rehabilitating the principal abuser to the point where his smiling silhouette dominates the reunion between protagonist Celie and her long-lost sister Nettie. Moreover, as Russo observes, Spielberg "took a sexually explicit love affair in an existing work and, by his own admission, sanitized it into a series of chaste kisses to beg acceptance from a mass audience" (278). Andrea Weiss writes, "The joke in lesbian circles while the film was in production was that Steven Spielberg wasn't intimidated by creatures from outer space [in his 1982 movie *E.T: The Extra-Terrestrial*] but a lesbian relationship was more than he could handle" (79). Molly Hite goes still further, accusing Spielberg of erasing non-hegemonic behavior to the point where, unlike the book, the film insists on "restoring the patriarchal status quo" (141n).

Using Russo's terms, many LGBT viewers have criticized films such as *The Hunger, Bound,* and *Basic Instinct* for their lesbian characters who are portrayed as violent outsiders. Beginning in the late 20th century, as attitudes toward LGBT people began to shift, some filmmakers worked to provide more sympathetic characters. *Longtime Companion, Philadelphia, Claire of the Moon,* and *The Incredibly True Adventures of Two Girls in Love* are probably the best known among these rehabilitative films. Russo himself acknowledged at the end of the revised version of *Celluloid Closet* that "[g]ay visibility has never really been an issue in the movies. Gays have always been visible. It's how they have been visible that has remained offensive for almost a century" (325). But even when such images become markedly less offensive, as in the dramatically increased gay and lesbian mass media visibility of the 1990s, critical questions remain. In our discussion of the following three films—*Monster, Unveiled,* and *Shrek 2*—we probe beyond the binary of good representation versus bad representation to ask the following:

- How are representations of queer lives constructed?
- What complex realities do they depict?
- What biases or blind spots remain?

## Varieties of Queerness in Contemporary Film

*Monster* (KW 2003, dir. Patty Jenkins) stars Charlize Theron, who won an Oscar for her portrayal of lesbian prostitute and serial killer Aileen (Lee) Wuornos. The film is "loosely based" on the two years of Wuornos's life during which she met and became involved with Tyria Moore (renamed Selby Wall in the film) and during which she murdered seven men (Kalwani). *Monster* depicts Wuornos as a psychologically unstable survivor of childhood sexual violence who kills her first victim after being beaten and raped by him. The Selby Wall character is played by Christina Ricci as a doe-eyed and willfully blind young lesbian, who whines, "I just want a normal life" and feigns ignorance of Wuornos's murders. After Wuornos's arrest, Wall sells her out, engaging her in a telephone conversation in which Wuornos, realizing the phone is bugged, implicates herself and exonerates Wall. As Wuornos is sentenced to death in the film's final scene, we begin to see her life as a series of truly tragic circumstances.

As a film, *Monster* replays earlier representations of the man-hating lesbian and the psychopathic homosexual to provide psychological and social class context for the characters. Viewers see how lives can be tortured through a nexus of sexual abuse, devaluation of women, homophobia, and poverty. The film, then, is a complex intersectional portrait of social class, gender, and sexuality, which invites us to understand queer lives made desperate through interlocking oppressions. Regardless of the actual events upon which it is based, the film asks viewers not only to understand but also to sympathize with Wuornos. We begin to understand why she kills the men she does, and we come to see her relationship with Wall as an attempt to achieve intimacy and love. Wall's desire for a "normal life" seems abnormal, as it can only be achieved at Wuornos's expense. At the very least, Wall's return to normalcy is presented as a refusal to understand the systems that can immiserate queer lives, driving them to desperate acts. Ultimately, Wall's idea of normal and Wuornos's rage and violence are presented as equally pathological.

Attempts to negotiate a "normal life" are at the heart of the German film *Unveiled* (Wolfe 2005, dir. Angelina Maccarone), which tells the story of Fariba, an

Iranian woman who flees to Germany to avoid punishment—imprisonment, rape, torture, possibly even death—after the discovery of her affair with a married woman. In Germany, Fariba takes on the identity of Siamak, a fellow (male) Iranian refugee who has committed suicide. She becomes involved with Anne, a coworker at the sauerkraut factory where Siamak/Fariba is an undocumented employee. Germany turns out to be an unsatisfactory sanctuary for Fariba, as a toxic combination of government bureaucracy and threatening working-class men conspire to force her back to Iran. In *The Globalization of Sexuality,* Jon Binnie points out that "movement across national borders is restricted for some sexual dissidents because of heteronormative and homophobic migration policies" (99). *Unveiled* illustrates the impact of immigration policies that discriminate against LGBT people; it does not allow us simply to demonize the repressive country, in this case Iran, for Fariba is persecuted and ultimately denied asylum in "progressive" Germany as well. Fariba is suspended not only between two countries but also between two genders as she seeks her freedom. In fact, the film's intersectional analysis [λ Chapter 8] of sexuality, gender, and class—Fariba must pose as a man among working-class Germans and other immigrants to secure any possibility of sanctuary—depicts the multiple dangers that some queers must negotiate to find freedom from sexual-, gender-, and nation-based repression.

The German title of the film, *Fremde Haut* (*Strange Skin*), foregrounds at once the protagonist's fraught immigrant Iranian condition, her passing as a male, and her removal of the *chador*—a covering of the skin for women in conservative Islamic cultures. It also positions *Unveiled* as a contemporary link to the lurid sensational titles of 1950s pulp novels—*Strange Sisters, Veil of Torment, Three Strange Women, The Black Veil,* and so forth. Interestingly, the portrayal of Fariba as a dark-haired butch and Anne as a light-haired femme also recalls typical pulp covers [λ Chapter 10]. We see this pattern in popular queer films as well; clear examples are the classic lesbian romance *Desert Hearts* (1986), the Brandon Teena bio-pic *Boys Don't Cry* (1999), and the "true-life" German film *Aimée and Jaguar* (1999). The nod to pulp fiction and popular films underscores the apparently intentional derivativeness of *Unveiled;* many reviews of the film and even the publicity poster reproduced on the DVD box mention the similarities to *Boys Don't Cry,* for instance. And these are striking, beginning with the bleak, inhospitable landscapes in Germany and Nebraska but also including the perils of passing in a world populated by menacing, potentially murderous men and institutions.

Filmmakers sometimes treat oppression, including anti-queer intolerance, in subtle and even humorous ways. Right-wing conservative organizations such as the Traditional Values Coalition (TVC) have condemned *Shrek 2* (DreamWorks 2004, dir. Andrew Adamson, Kelly Asbury, Conrad Vernon) mostly because they see the film as an attempt to "mainstream abnormal behaviors" ("A Gender Identity Disorder Goes

Mainstream"). *Shrek 2*, they point out, "features a male-to-female transgender (in transition) as an evil bartender. The character has five o'clock shadow, wears a dress and has female breasts. It is clear that he is a she-male. His voice is that of talk show host Larry King" ("Parents Beware"). The film does indeed contain "subtle sexual messages," as the TVC suggests. But Larry King's MtF ugly stepsister bartender is merely a surface gag (and hardly subtle).

*Shrek 2*'s central story revolves around newlyweds Shrek and Fiona seeking acceptance from the King and Queen, Fiona's parents. In the first *Shrek* movie (2001), Princess Fiona—doomed by a curse to live as a human by day and an ogre by night—"comes out" by choosing full-time ogre identity to be her true self and to marry Shrek. This film, however, mitigates its potential queer theme. For one thing, Fiona was attractively unconventional—athletic, powerful, eccentric—as a human but more conventionally "wifely" as a (married) ogre. For another, the "happily ever after" heterosexual marriage plot defuses and domesticates Fiona's potential queerness. *Shrek 2*, however, places the "coming-out-to-parents" plot squarely in the middle of the filmic message. The King and Queen are confronted with a daughter who has chosen to live openly as an ogre and who brings her ogre husband home to meet the folks. We might observe that, in this case, the ogre identities seem to stand in for race, not necessarily queerness; after all, green skin and bulky physique are clearly marked on the ogres' bodies. Still, as Eve Kosofsky Sedgwick points out in *Epistemology of the Closet* (1990), the tropes of the closet and coming out have become central metaphors in Western, particularly U.S., culture [λ Chapter 11]. Emerging from concealment into a true (even essential) identity symbolically characterizes any number of life trajectories: coming out as an alcoholic, as a Jew or a Muslim or a Christian, as the parent (or child) of a gay person, and so forth. *Shrek 2* finally places queerness at the center of its concerns, and it elaborates on the coming-out theme in ways that resonate powerfully for LGBT people. The Queen, for example, is more accepting of Fiona and Shrek than her husband the King. This not only reflects the general tendency for straight women to be more open to sexual nonconformity than straight men (see, for example, Herek, Kite, Morin and Garfinkle), but it also highlights an interesting subplot in the movie. It turns out that the King is only human on sufferance of the scheming Fairy Godmother, who has threatened to turn him (back) into a frog if Fiona fails to marry her son, Prince Charming. The King's straight masculinity—even his humanity—is thus shown to be fragile and quickly revocable, and we are reminded of queer theorist Judith Butler's *Gender Trouble* (1990), where she observes that gender—particularly masculinity—is a precarious masquerade that can be reinforced only through performance and re-performance [λ Chapter 11]. *Shrek 2*, despite the TVC's focus on its transgender bartender, does far more than simply offer some possibly LGBT images. Rather, it is constructed around the central queer cultural trope of coming out to family, and its final message of acceptance (even of the King who is now a frog) is assumed to resonate with gay and straight people alike.

## Small-Screen Queers

Partly because queers have always had some presence in Hollywood, films are frequently critiqued in terms of type of representation, while television is more often critiqued in terms of number of representations. Bucking this trend, in *All the Rage: The Story of Gay Visibility in America,* Suzanna Danuta Walters critiques the way gays were represented in television shows, films, and advertisements throughout the 1990s, the seeming "golden age" of gay representation, by discussing, for instance, *Ellen, Will & Grace,* and other shows. The sheer number of examples she is able to call upon is surprising: we are, apparently, everywhere. Walters identifies a pervasive "normalizing" trend in these representations: gays as good neighbors, gays placed in situations that highlight the liberal tolerance of straight friends and family, and gays as sick, dying, and alone (76). Lesbians and gay men are represented, but how—and what can be learned from this inclusion?

For decades, shows such as ABC's *The Corner Bar* (1972), *Hot L Baltimore* (1975), and *Soap* (1977–1981) had gay characters, but until the latter part of the 20th century, queer representations on television were rare—so rare, in fact, that beginning around 1990, popular television shows such as *Roseanne* (1988–1997) and *Friends* (1994–2004) made news with episodes that not only featured gay characters but focused on queer behavior. In one episode of the sitcom *Mad about You* (1992–1999), Jamie Buchman observes the gay pride parade from her apartment window and ponders the difficulty of living in a world that proscribes public displays of affection between same-sex romantic partners. In 1993 and 1994, public broadcasting stations in the United Kingdom and the United States screened *Tales of the City,* a miniseries based on Armistead Maupin's novels about gay (and straight) life in San Francisco. *Roseanne* introduced a minor recurring gay character, played mostly for comic relief by a swishy Martin Mull (1991), and followed up in 1994 with TV's first woman-to-woman kiss, between Roseanne and Mariel Hemingway, who had gained popularity among lesbians for her starring role in the now cult film *Personal Best* (1982). Also in 1994, MTV's hugely popular pseudo-reality show *The Real World* featured Pedro Zamora, an HIV+ man who shared a house with other young people for several months. The show offered the United States one of the first "real-life" views of how a gay person lived with HIV and negotiated relationships and intimacies with others. The popular graphic novel *Pedro and Me* (2000), written by *Real World* participant Judd Winick, chronicles the friendship between Zamora and Winick that lasted until Zamora's death and that inspired Winick to devote his energies to AIDS prevention.

The sitcom *Ellen* (1994–1998) is the first network television show to feature a main character who comes out as a lesbian. Noting that the lead character, Ellen Morgan, seemed uninterested in dating, one producer suggested she get a puppy. When that suggestion was cast aside in favor of Ellen's professing her love for a woman, the idea stuck, and still today, the coming-out episode is called "The Puppy Episode." Malinda Lo writes in "Back in the Day: Coming Out with Ellen" that

> [i]t wasn't until March 1997, after the first version of the coming-out script had been rejected, that Disney executives gave the official go-ahead to tape "The Puppy Episode." What followed was a media blitz: DeGeneres went on *The Oprah Winfrey Show,* was interviewed by Diane Sawyer, and was featured on the cover of *Time* with the headline "Yep, I'm Gay." At the same time, DeGeneres had just met Anne Heche, a heretofore heterosexual actress whose career was beginning to take off. DeGeneres and Heche also made the media rounds, even attending the White House Correspondents' Dinner together in late April.

Despite the enormous amount of attention paid to that episode, though, the show survived only one more season. Some claimed that the show lost momentum after "The Puppy Episode," and others said that the show's considerable attention to gay issues undermined it. Ron Miller of the *San Jose Mercury News,* for instance, argued that "DeGeneres is a funny and inventive woman, whose sexual orientation is only an important aspect of her life, not the sole purpose of it. Maybe the *Ellen* writers would have retained more viewers if they had let her gayness take over only when they really had some fresh and funny point to make" ("GLAAD"). Despite the cancellation, the impact of DeGeneres's real-life and fictional coming out prompted other producers to include a growing number of queer characters in their shows. Between 1997 and 2001, the number of recurring gay characters in television shows was consistently in the double digits (Walters 96–97). Such characters were no longer the simple buffoons or suicidal psychopaths depicted in earlier decades; they were, like Ellen in her show's last season, increasingly nuanced and complex characters, confronting discrimination and working on relationships. Seemingly, queers were beginning to achieve the kind of media visibility that critics like Russo had longed for.

For instance, *Will & Grace,* about the friendship between a gay man and a straight woman, began on the heels of *Ellen*'s cancellation; its main characters were gay male Will and his zany, redheaded best (straight) female friend, Grace. The show also featured Jack, a flaming gay man, and Karen, who was wealthy and shallow but campy and served as Jack's foil. Interestingly, the show was touted as "gay," but the visual representations told a fairly heterosexualized story. Though Jack and Will were sometimes shown in scenes where they discussed their sexuality or their romantic exploits, more often Will and Grace appeared together, with Jack and Karen forming another platonic couple. Queer sexuality was often presented either as a kind of joke (as in the campy character, Jack) or erased altogether. For example, one slapstick episode focused on a sexual competition between Will and Grace, who were both attracted to a man who had just moved into their apartment building. The outcome of the competition was that the man in question, while never revealing his sexuality to either Will or Grace, pro-

**Figure 13.3** Ellen DeGeneres and wife, Portia di Rossi.

claimed that he wanted friendship and not romance from them and scolded them for their shallowness. This is meant to be a lesson to Will and Grace to deemphasize sexual attraction as a basis for relationships. A number of other episodes feature Will and Grace's friends, Rob and Ellen, a heterosexually married couple. In one episode, Will and Grace compete as a charades team against Rob and Ellen, a move that allows the writers to present Will and Grace as a heterosexualized couple, a dynamic that plays out in many episodes. *Will & Grace* was wildly popular (according to a blurb on the DVD cover, its final episode in 2006 is estimated to have drawn 18.1 million viewers), and the show kept sexual difference, camp, and interactions between professedly gay characters in the public consciousness. Queer responses to it, though, were not entirely positive. John Lyttle told *The Independent on Sunday* that, "[i]n a few years' time, we will look back on [*Queer Eye, Will & Grace* and a UK version of *Queer Eye* called *Fairy Godfathers*] in the same way we look back on [the book] *Uncle Tom's Cabin.* People will cringe. . . . The thing about camping it up [is that] it's gone from being very subversive—without it we wouldn't have had gay liberation—to being the norm on TV. Gay culture is not all about that stereotype. It's like gay men are only acceptable if they play the court jester" ("Edinburgh").

While complex and nuanced queer characters continue to be somewhat rare on major American broadcast channels such as CBS, NBC, and ABC, cable channels have

**Figure 13.4** The cast of *Will & Grace*.

hosted a variety of long-running series with significant queer content, some focused primarily on lesbian and gay lives. Showtime's *Queer as Folk* (2000–2005), based on a short-lived British TV series, offered a sometimes explicit and frequently controversial look at the lives of several gay and lesbian friends in Pittsburgh. Featuring some of the most graphic same-sex erotic scenes in a television drama, *Queer as Folk* pushed boundaries and showed audiences some of the issues facing contemporary urban gay people, such as drug addiction, nonmonogamy, job discrimination, homophobic assaults, and difficulties encountered by same-sex parents attempting to raise children. A comparable show focusing on lesbian friendships and relationships, *The L Word* (2004–present), also on Showtime, focuses on a group of lesbian-identified friends living in Los Angeles. In 2006, Logo began airing the African-American–themed *Noah's Arc*, which is described in promos in this way: "From new boy-friends to strained friendships to career changes, these men persevere and live their lives with grace and wit" ("*Noah's Arc*"). *Noah's Arc* foregrounds issues common to urban gay men, such as attraction to a man who is coy about revealing his sexuality, living together in a tiny apartment, and adjusting to a new lover's straight friends. The pay-for-TV location of these shows permits them to present queer lives in more depth and complexity than would be permitted on free channels, but it also limits the size and diversity of the audiences they reach and thus the conversations they can prompt about queer lives.

Walters maintains that such increased media visibility is a mixed blessing. On one hand, she argues that it is good because "cultural visibility can really push the envelope, bringing complicated and substantive gay identities into public view. And sometimes these cultural images slowly, almost imperceptibly, chip away around the edges of bigotry, never really getting to the core but perhaps revealing it all too clearly" (15). On the other hand, "We may be seen now, but I am not sure we are known" (10); "visibility does not erase stereotypes nor guarantee liberation" (13); and "[i]f gays are now a regular part of the visual landscape, then they too can be mocked and 'dissed'" (117). In fact, as Walters points out, the newfound media visibility might backfire: "Gay as chic can be used in ways that deflect attention away from more substantive concerns about lesbian and gay civil rights" (17). For instance, the media in general fail to represent homophobia as it moves through and even destroys some queer lives; this may be the most serious shortcoming of the new gay representation.

As we reflect on the films, television shows, and critical commentaries that we have discussed in this chapter, we see that filmic representations of queers, particularly in the past two decades, have been significant for a number of reasons: they provide LGBT people a set of images with which to relate and identify, they serve pedagogically to instruct the larger culture how to respond nonhomophobically to queers, and as in the case of *Shrek 2* and its "queer" storyline, they offer metaphorical ways of thinking critically about culture and difference. While we view these as salutary uses of such images, we also wonder about their limitations. For instance, we find that many contemporary fictional representations of queerness in the movies and on television are freighted with what we might call the "imperative of the happy ending," that is, the insistence that plotlines featuring gay people, queer relationships, or LGBT romances end happily. While such endings serve the pedagogical purpose of showing straights and queers alike that LGBT people can—and should—be able to lead happy, healthy, and productive lives, the happy-ending imperative seems like merely the inverse of the negative representational patterns that Russo observed two decades ago. In the fictional film *Ma Vie En Rose* (1997), for example, the happy ending involves the "conversion" of adults and other children to the protagonist's point of view that "he" is a girl born into a boy's body as a result of the accidental loss of his second X chromosome.

In contrast, the based-on-real-life movies, such as *Boys Don't Cry*, have room for less imperatively happy endings; in some cases, their grounding in reality can license a more complex rendering of queer lives and experiences. Finally, the widespread use of the coming-out narrative that we identified as a key theme in *Shrek 2* allows viewers to build empathy with those who have secrets and are trying to negotiate their differences with the larger culture—a situation many LGBT people face today. At the same time, we wonder whether the extension of the metaphor of the closet to all differences dilutes a more specific consideration of the particular difficulties faced by queer people as they navigate sexist and homophobic systems, institutions, and ideologies.

## QUESTIONS FOR DISCUSSION

1. Traditionally, the assumption has been that there is a clear relationship between visibility—in film, television, and other mass media—and movement toward equality. But is the path from visibility to equality really so direct? How might it proceed by fits and starts? And whose equality, specifically, are we talking about? Gays and lesbians? Bisexuals? The transgendered? White LGBT folk? Middle-class LGBT folk? And to complicate things even further, how do we define equality, and why do we assume that equality is a laudable goal? Think intersectionally about the visibility of LGBT people in the mass media to problematize and nuance your ideas about this issue.

2. We acknowledge that this chapter, by necessity, deals with a very small number of films and television shows. We note, for instance, that well-known feature films *The Adventures of Priscilla, Queen of the Desert; To Wong Foo, Thanks for Everything, Julie Newmar; Hedwig and the Angry Inch;* and *Transamerica* (all focused on transgender characters) did not make it into our narrative. How might you use the critique of representation and visibility that we present in this chapter to understand the cultural work around transgenderism in one or more of these films?

3. In this chapter, we have focused on major motion pictures and television series, ignoring a mixed genre: made-for-television movies. *Consenting Adults* (1985) depicted a mother trying to come to terms with her son's disclosure of his homosexuality, and *An Early Frost* (1985) showed a middle-class family dealing with a gay son's AIDS. Such movies served a pedagogical function in bringing some awareness of queer lives, however limited and sentimental, to the larger American (and Western) culture. Such movies taught the public about queerness by focusing primarily on family members' struggles to deal with homosexuality, as opposed to the individual lives of queers themselves. These movies are currently available on DVD. Locate one or more made-for-television movies, and contrast the cultural work they do with the cultural work done by recurring queer characters in sitcoms or ongoing TV dramas.

## References and Further Reading

Binnie, Jon. *The Globalization of Sexuality.* London: Sage, 2004. Print.

Bobo, Jacqueline. "Sifting through the Controversy: Reading *The Color Purple.*" *Callaloo* 39 (Spring 1989): 332–42. Print.

Butler, Judith. *Gender Trouble: Feminism and the Subversion of Identity.* New York: Routledge, 1990. Print.

Doty, Alexander. *Flaming Classics: Queering the Film Canon.* New York: Routledge, 2000. Print.

———. *Making Things Perfectly Queer: Interpreting Mass Culture.* Minneapolis: U of Minnesota P, 1993. Print.

Duralde, Alonso. "Gay Guide to the Oscars." *The Advocate,* 1 Mar. 2005. Web. 31 Aug. 2012. <http://findarticles.com/p/articles/mi_m1589/is_2005_March_1/ai_n12417610>.

"Edinburgh Festival: Gay Activists Attack TV over 'Poofs in Primetime.'" *The Independent on Sunday,* 15 Aug. 2004. Web. 31 Aug. 2012. <http://findarticles.com/p/articles/mi_qn4159/is_20040815/ai_n12759089>.

"A Gender Identity Disorder Goes Mainstream." *Special Report.* Traditional Values Coalition, Apr. 2005. Web. 6 Aug. 2008. <http://www.jesus-is-savior.com/Evils%20in%20America/Sodomy/homosexual_identity_disorder.pdf>.

"GLAAD Media Round-Up: *Ellen's* Gay, Gay World." N.p., 27 Feb. 1998. Web. 31 Aug. 2012. <http://www .glaad.org/action/al_archive_detail.php?id=1883>.

Hall, Stuart. "Encoding/Decoding." *Media Studies: A Reader.* Eds. Paul Marris and Sue Thornham. New York: NYU P, 2000. 51–61. Print.

Hanson, Ellis. *Out Takes: Essays on Queer Theory and Film.* Durham, NC: Duke UP, 1999. Print.

Herek, G. M. "Assessing Heterosexuals' Attitudes toward Lesbians and Gay Men." *Psychological Perspectives on Lesbian and Gay Issues: Vol. 1. Lesbian and Gay Psychology: Theory, Research, and Clinical Applications*. Eds. B. Greene and G. M. Herek. Thousand Oaks, CA: Sage, 1994. 206–23. Print.

Hite, Molly. "Writing—and Reading—the Body: Female Sexuality and Recent Feminist Fiction." *Feminist Studies* 14.1 (1988): 120–42. Print.

Iverem, Esther. "An Interview with Alice Walker." N.p., 28 Feb. 2002. Web. 6 Aug. 2008. <http://www.seeingblack.com/2003/x022803/walker.shtml>.

Kalwani, Dinesh. "Real-Life Beauty, Reel-Life 'Monster.'" Chicago GSB, 26 Jan. 2004. Web. 6 Aug. 2008. <http://media.www.chibus.com/media/storage/paper408/news/2004/01/26/ArtsEntertainment/RealLife.Beauty.ReelLife.monster-589672.shtml>.

Keeling, Kara. "'Joining the Lesbians': Cinematic Regimes of Black Lesbian Visibility." *Black Queer Studies: A Critical Anthology*. Eds. E. Patrick Johnson and Mae G. Henderson. Durham, NC: Duke UP, 2005. 213–27. Print.

Kite, M. E. "Sex Differences in Attitudes toward Homosexuals: A Meta-Analytic Review." *Journal of Homosexuality* 10.1–2 (1984): 69–81. Print.

Lo, Malinda. "Back in the Day: Coming Out with Ellen." *After Ellen: News, Reviews & Commentary on Lesbian and Bisexual Women in Entertainment and the Media*. N.p., 9 Apr. 2005. Web. 6 Aug. 2008. <http://www.afterellen.com/>.

Morin, S., and E. Garfinkle. "Male Homophobia." *Journal of Social Issues* 34.1 (1978): 29–47. Print.

"*Noah's Arc*—Original Series from MTV's Logo Network Comes to DVD This Summer." N.p., 9 May 2006. Web. 31 Aug. 2012. <http://www.tvshowsondvd.com/newsitem.cfm?NewsID=5626>.

"Parents Beware: 'Shrek 2' Features Transgenderism and Crossdressing Themes." The Traditional Values Coalition, n.d. Web. 6 Aug. 2008. <http://www.traditionalvalues.org/modules.php?sid=1659>.

Russo, Vito. *The Celluloid Closet: Homosexuality in the Movies*. Rev. ed. New York: Harper & Row, 1987. Print.

Sedgwick, Eve Kosofsky. *Epistemology of the Closet*. Berkeley: U of California P, 1990. Print.

Walters, Suzanna Danuta. *All the Rage: The Story of Gay Visibility in America*. Chicago: U of Chicago P, 2001. Print.

Weiss, Andrea. *Vampires and Violets: Lesbians in Film*. New York: Penguin, 1992. Print.

Winick, Judd. *Pedro and Me*. New York: Henry Holt, 2000. Print.

## READINGS

> ## Maria Pramaggiore
(1997), United States

---

### "Fishing for Girls: Romancing Lesbians in New Queer Cinema"

With the underground cinema gaining in strength, with all the publicity and all, the moneybags are beginning to see profitable possibilities in it. All the temptations and the commercial bustle is beginning to surround us. All kinds of clever commercial fishermen are beginning to tempt us with promises, contracts, sweet tongues. It's time to sound a warning.

Jonas Mekas, 1967

The 1990s have brought much less suspicion of the popular.

Cherry Smith, 1995

. . .

### *Little Movies That Could: Independent Cinema, New and Old*

Although the contemporary film industry's search for lucrative independent film projects has created opportunities for the theatrical release of lesbian-themed films like Troche and Turner's *Go Fish* and Maggenti's *The Incredibly True Adventures of Two Girls in Love*, the premises and promise of New Queer Cinema as a radical formal and political weapon are part and parcel of the entertainment industry's commodification of queer identities. As gay "homocore" filmmaker Bruce La Bruce puts it: "The media will tolerate its bad children as long as they entertain and perform within the limitations it dictates; when it is no longer amused, or gets bored, you have to be savvy enough to transform yourself into something else or risk having your head chopped off" (188). When entertainment conglomerates and whiz-kid executives have exhausted the public's desire for a particular version of the "alternative"—"little movies that could" in *Time* film critic Richard Corliss's terms—will New (now Old?) Queer filmmaking face significant and all-too-familiar barriers to financing and distribution? And would that be a bad thing?

As [B. Ruby] Rich points out, New Queer cinema grew out of a particular tradition, whether it knows it or not: the marginal, alienated and avowedly resistant practices of Mekas's New American Cinema. Films associated with a tradition that self-reflexively thrives on its outsider status only reluctantly find bedfellows among the commercial successes of New Queer Cinema. Underground queer film lives on in spirit in the work of Bruce La Bruce and Sadie Benning, two filmmakers whose work is surprisingly widely distributed, given its raw pain, graphic sex and startling formal experimentation. Increasingly, however, the hegemony of the feature-length 35 millimeter film and growing opportunities for mass distribution have lured a number of filmmakers out of the underground closet, enticed as much by the prospect of breaking even or having their films shown as by lucrative commercial deals.

The aesthetic and political ancestors of Rich's New Queer Cinema—the New American Cinema Group—met with a similar fate, although assimilation into Hollywood was carried out by the first generation of film-schooled "Hollywood Renaissance" directors in the late 1960s, not by the practitioners of New American Cinema themselves. Mekas and others championed a radical cinema defined by the improvisation of John Cassavetes and the hand-held camerawork of Robert Frank (techniques which interestingly but not surprisingly reappear with a vengeance in *Go Fish*). The New American Cinema Group rejected the production methods, distribution channels and aesthetic stranglehold of Hollywood, an economic and aesthetic monolith which, despite its dominance in the U.S. and abroad for thirty years, was literally disintegrating as a result of studio divestiture, the increasing competition from television, and the growing appeal of European art cinema.

Self-consciously subversive, New American Cinema distanced itself from the mainstream industry not only by money and miles (Hollywood versus New York and San Francisco) but also by a tangible, self-policed border that neatly divided commerce from art. That no man's land of anti-Establishment attitude spanned the irrecoverable distance between (to be intentionally perverse) Jack Smith's *Flaming Creatures* and Joseph Manckiewicz's *Cleopatra,* both released in 1963.

Today one might argue that *Flaming Creatures* and *Cleopatra* are somewhat aesthetically compatible, that they can be recovered and recycled as camp—and this is precisely the point. Postmodern understandings and practices of politics refuse to set art against commerce, to imagine, as Mekas and others did, an author-driven filmmaking practice unsullied by the society of the spectacle and its commercial encroachments. Today's entertainment corporations large and small are happy to promote films that uncritically embrace the power of the image and its accouterments, delighted to encourage mass audiences to consume a slice of an alternative "lifestyle" on-screen, recognizing queer subjects only when served up as delectable and exotic matinee fare. As a result, the energy behind contemporary independent cinema—itself rapidly becoming the fair-haired child of mainstream film culture—is increasingly directed toward features that look less like the thoughtful *The Return of the Secaucus Seven* (1981) and more like the unthinking *Pulp Fiction* (1993), to, once again perversely, compare films by two vastly different independent directors, John Sayles and Quentin Tarantino.

"Hollywood" is an increasingly problematic framework to use to describe an industry populated by a few voracious entertainment conglomerates, a growing number of small production companies, and the fashionable Indie circuit experiencing a feeding frenzy as a result of profitable (queer and non-queer) small films. Similarly, "New Queer Cinema" is an equally inadequate, if not vacuous, term to use to analyze the economic, political and aesthetic issues surrounding filmmaking by and about lesbians, gays, bisexuals, transsexuals, transvestites and other gender and sexual outlaws, particularly when the films and directors may or may not resist or oppose the genres, formal devices, production methods and distribution channels of traditional film culture.

Unlike the New American Cinema defined by Jonas Mekas, then, New Queer Cinema(s) must stake out its (their?) location(s) upon the heterogeneous map of post-classical, post-Renaissance filmmaking in a context in which "independent" has become a buzz-word for commercial viability rather than, or in addition to, an assertion of an anti-hegemonic aesthetic. Targeting queer markets has paid off, of course, as Gregory Woods writes of Great Britain: "Since the late 1980s it has become increasingly commonplace to speak, not only of the purchasing power of the so-called 'pink economy,' but also of the pink pound's extraordinary resilience during the recession of the early 1990s" (147). Bruce La Bruce's analysis is even more cynical and contradictory:

> [A friend] tells me I should direct the marketing for my new movie towards a "regular" audience and steer clear of the ghettoisation of the gay and lesbian film festival circuit. I'm at a bit of a loss to think how an explicit movie about a washed-up gay porno star who is shown sucking a lot of cocks and getting fucked up the ass could appeal to a heterosexual crowd, but I guess you can market anything these days. And you know, somehow, I think he's right. (191–92)

What puzzles La Bruce, momentarily at least, is the assertion that his film could be made palatable to a wide audience through marketing; the notion that a larger, general audience is preferable to a specialized gay market goes unquestioned. To read La Bruce's predicament in terms of both its economic and aesthetic implications requires not the rubric of New Queer Cinema, but instead, Eve Sedgwick's distinction between universalizing and minoritizing discourses surrounding sexuality. La Bruce's comments clearly show how that distinction operates in an environment of instantaneous and inescapable commodification. Minoritizing and universalizing "tendencies" differ according to whether they view sexuality as relevant for a subculture or for an entire culture, Sedgwick writes:

> I hypothesized in Epistemology of the Closet that modern homo/heterosexual definition has become so exacerbated a cultural site because of an enduring incoherence about whether it is to be thought of as an issue only for a minority of (distinctly lesbian or gay) individuals or, instead, as an issue that cuts across every locus of agency and subjectivity in the culture. ("Forward: T Times" xii)

As Sedgwick points out, it is one of the paradoxes of queernesses, Old and New, that minoritizing and universalizing impulses are interwoven and contained within them. It is no paradox at all that harnessing the universalizing tendency makes for good box office. In other words, the deceptively simple idea of "marketing" La Bruce refers to above encompasses not only blatant advertising ploys but also a film's textual strategies: both help to draw paying customers. Targeting gay and lesbian audiences as a specialized, minority market is one thing; successfully purveying queerness in a universalizing fashion [in the tradition of *The Wedding Banquet* (1993), *The Crying Game* (1992), and *To Wong Foo* (1995)] sends profitability ratios over the top.

Anxieties surrounding the greedy fishermen who calculate profit ratios—the sort Mekas describes in the epigram to this essay—underlie commentaries on authentically political queer film. In an article on the success *Go Fish* met with at the Sundance Film Festival, for example, Ruby Rich includes this disclaimer: "If this article has a hidden agenda, it's the attempt to head off the backlash and argue that this film is far more than any mainstream distributor's fishing expedition" ("Goings and Comings" 14). If Mekas's and Rich's fishermen have gone trolling for catch in New Queer Cinema, and if the resulting commercial success of small films like *Go Fish* no longer disqualifies them from functioning as political art, I would argue that textual analysis becomes an important tool with which to assess the political impact and aesthetic innovation of these films. If queer-made independent and straight-made studio-produced films become virtually indistinguishable in terms of production, marketing and distribution, then narrative and visual expression must carry the burden of the aesthetic-political project of queer, new and/or subversive cinema(s). At this point it is important to ask if the New Queer paradigm gives us greater access to these films in terms of textual address.

In my readings of *Go Fish* and *Two Girls,* aesthetic and political differences can be interpreted more usefully through Sedgwick's universalizing/minoritizing distinction than through the generality of New Queer Cinema because Sedgwick's terms antici- pate the shifty politics of postmodern image-making apparatuses and address issues of audience appeal and political sensibilities without the circular logic implied by New Queerness: "we're here, we're queer, we're doing something with film that you will have to get used to." It seems fair to argue that the distinctive style of some recent queer films—like *Go Fish*—does pose challenges to dominant film aesthetics—in large part because they draw upon the legacy of an underground cinema that never quite stays underground. At the same time such New Queer films are already constructed in the dominant discourses of a mass culture of entertainment geared toward the con- tinued repackaging of novelty for the sole purpose of generating box office receipts. It is not my intention to lambaste either *Go Fish* or *Two Girls*—two appealing and well-made films—as "selling out" to the amorphous specter of "Hollywood" or its fishermen-henchmen but, rather, to find a more productive way to interrogate the politics and aesthetics of and in films yoked together as New and Queer.

There is another shortcoming of the New Queer Cinema rubric which seriously ham- pers any analysis of the economics and aesthetics of lesbian films: it fails to address gender dynamics in independent and mainstream cinema. Analyzing lesbian films in terms of their history, generic patterns, and representational politics provides a per- spective that a New Queer aesthetic vision cannot because the latter fails to explore the implications of the male-domination of the film industry for lesbian cinema.

### *"Decade of the Dyke": Girls, Genre and New Lesbian Cinema?*

Rich alludes to the material realities affecting New Queer feature filmmaking (as opposed to videos and short films) in her 1992 *Sight and Sound* article, where she points out that gender still matters in the film industry:

> Surprise, all the new movies being snatched up by distributors, shown in main- stream festivals, booked into theatres, are by the boys. Surprise, the amazing new lesbian videos that are redefining the whole dyke relationship to popular culture remain hard to find. (32)

Videos, experimental short films such as those of Barbara Hammer, and the now- famous pixelvision of Sadie Benning are staples of lesbian cinema, new and old. The fact remains that gay men have made inroads into both mainstream and independent feature filmmaking with much greater and more visible success off and on-screen.

In 1994, with the long and torturous road to release of *Go Fish* in mind, Rich expresses hope that the time for lesbian cinema has come:

> Finally, critically, not incidentally, a lesbian feature cinema is emerging alongside lesbian video. After years of boys-only filmmaking, *Go Fish* is a dramatic lesbian film to cheer . . . if the papers are to be believed there are already more than a dozen mainstream lesbian films in production or pre-production in Hollywood. If this keeps up, then the 90s may just be the decade of the dyke after all. ("Goings and Comings" 16)

To confirm Rich's always prescient sense of film and culture, evidence for the critical mass necessary for a lesbian cinema is clear from the formidable increase in the number of lesbian features produced in the 1990s. By 1995, lesbian feature film production had nearly doubled that of the entire decade of the 1980s.

Specific industry practices of exclusion—in mainstream film production as well as independent film—and economic and power dynamics have effectively prevented lesbians from making films; thus identifying gendered imbalances further fractures the New Queer Cinema paradigm. Amy Taubin claims that, from the evidence available in 1992, "queer cinema is figured in terms of sexual desire and the desire it constructs is exclusively male . . . [i]ndeed, women are even more marginalised in 'queer' than in heterosexual film; at least in the latter, they function as objects of desire" (37). Because lesbians have had limited access to film-making and because lesbian image making is of critical importance to notions of gender, sexuality, queerness and cultural power, it is important to acknowledge that lesbian cinema participates in New Queer Cinema and to recognize that contemporary lesbian filmmaking is not characterized with enough precision or specificity by such a term.

With reference to the marginalization of women in queer and mainstream films alike, Guinevere Turner, who co-wrote, co-produced and acted in *Go Fish,* speaks with Holly Willis about the personal and community empowerment associated with taking Sundance by storm and reaching a wide audience:

> We didn't imagine any crossover in terms of a heterosexual audience. We didn't think anyone would really pay attention; luckily we also didn't care about that. Also, lesbians are excited not only because it's a lesbian movie but also because it's getting so much attention. It's this affirmation for everyone. We are interesting. We are talented. We are real people. (20)

While an anecdotal statement cannot substitute for a systematic framework for analyzing questions of gender, power and queer film, Turner's comments suggest that for lesbian communities marginality is not a position of strength from which to express or enact resistance, a view which may differ in some ways from Turner's gay male counterparts. For Turner, producing lesbian images that affirm lesbian cultural production and materialize lesbian existence in the heterosexualist imagination is a powerful political act.

Lesbian cinema is, in fact, redefining itself in relation to ideas of community and affirmation, particularly in terms of narrative complexity, visual style, and genre, aspects of filmic form which the rubric of New Queer Cinema is unlikely to discern with appropriate specificity. For that matter, it is arguable whether "lesbian cinema" is nuanced enough to describe *Go Fish* and *Two Girls,* which are romantic comedies. The recurring adoption of the generic conventions of the romantic comedy in films by lesbians, however, suggests an interest— lesbian? queer? cinematic? all three and more?—in remapping romance. If, as Eve Sedgwick argues, heterosexuality "has been permitted to masquerade so fully as History itself—when it has not presented itself as the totality of Romance," it does so nowhere more seamlessly than in the darkened space of the movie theater ("Queer and Now" 11).

Recent lesbian romances go beyond the coming-out narrative to explore lesbian identities, communities and the relationship between lesbian culture and popular culture. One important facet of this increasing complexity is the transition from drama to comedy. *Go Fish* and *Two Girls,* for example, both complicate the coming-out narrative of "lesbian problem pictures" like *Desert Hearts* (1985) and *Claire of the Moon* (1993), partly because the comedies begin from the premise that out lesbians have interesting stories to tell that are not related to their coming out experiences. The origins and impetus for the transition from angst-ridden coming-out to playful outings are not entirely clear: Rich notes that *"Go Fish* is the daughter of [*A Comedy in Six Unnatural Acts* (Oxenberg, 1975)], the living proof that lesbian camp does exist and even has a lineage. Except that Troche and Turner have never seen it" ("Goings and Comings" 15). *Go Fish* and *Two Girls* do, however, speak directly to the fact that lesbians respond critically to the way that the romance genre, when it has represented lesbian characters, has almost exclusively constructed lesbian identity as not only a problem, but the problem.

The expansion and development of recent lesbian cinema in terms of narrative focus and complexity is not necessarily "generational," however, nor does it correlate with release dates. For example, Patricia Rozema's recent *When Night Is Falling* (1995) retells a familiar coming-out narrative, albeit with captivating and lyrical imagery, whereas her earlier *I've Heard the Mermaids Singing* (1987) explores lesbian image-making in a narrative that eschews the coming-out to coupledom scenario and instead situates lesbian desires in a variety of contexts: friendly, romantic, creative, and professional relationships.

Sedgwick's terminology of universalizing and minoritizing understandings of sexual difference (*Epistemology of the Closet* 9) is suited to addressing films that complicate queer identities and address multiplicitous sexual and racial identities. In fact, the tensions circulating among these impulses and lesbian image making are reflected in political and aesthetic differences between *Go Fish* and *Two Girls in Love,* not least because minoritizing and universalizing frames have implications for the use, abuse or transformation of a pre-existing genre. One of the most important distinctions between the films is that they treat the conventions of romantic comedy in very different ways.

It may be that the success of *Two Girls* and *Go Fish* is partly attributable to genre. After all, mass-produced film culture is nothing if not dedicated to the proposition that happily-ever-after is worth millions, expended at eight dollars a head. Mandy Merck places lesbian romance within the European art cinema tradition, a cinema which typically has eschewed Hollywood conventions but also has garnered a small but devoted audience. Merck claims that "lesbian romance is becoming a conventional—and highly conventionalized—narrative in the 'art' cinema of Europe and North America" and argues that, because art cinema emphasizes European cultural specificity and authorial expressivity, it translates into "adult," and, therefore, "sexy" film (377).

[Art film] provides a sufficient degree of difference from dominant heterosexual conventions to be seen as "realistic," "courageous," "questioning"—all terms from British reviews of *Lianna* [Sayles, 1983]—but it does this by offering literally more of the same, more of the traditional cinematic use of the figure of the woman to signify sexual pleasure, sexual problems, sex itself. (378)

Merck contends that *Desert Hearts* was hailed as a remarkable achievement because it transformed lesbian distress into romance, while at the same time reinscribing traditional genre conventions. According to her analysis, lesbian romantic comedies generally rely upon the standard narrative involving the seduction of the reluctant woman and renew the popular romance genre by revitalizing the tired "boy meets girl, loses girl, gets girl back" formula (379). Furthermore,

> In order to succeed as a popular romance, *Desert Hearts* was divested of any social or political ramification or context that would restrict its generality. As Donna Deitch herself argues, "I didn't want to put it in seventies New York. It's not about lesbian custody or any particular issues, it's essentially a love story." This principle of universal applicability is conventionally seen as a mark of artistic success. (380)

Deitch's sentiments are echoed in statements by Maria Maggenti, director of *Two Girls,* who states that "My film is based on my experience falling in love for the first time. I cannot be more emphatic when I say that this has nothing to do with the commodification of lesbian experience nor the so-called current interest in our lives. I am interested in truth as a filmmaker not markets" ("[Transcript of] Conference" 4). While both *Go Fish* and *Two Girls* can be classified as romantic comedies, the former self-consciously interrogates the genre's terms and intervenes in them in minoritizing terms whereas *Two Girls* playfully adapts the classical romance narrative along the universalizing lines suggested by Merck's reading of *Desert Hearts*. . . .

### Terms of Enqueerment

If assessing the radical nature of a non-Hollywood film practice is difficult in postmodern culture, it is nevertheless the case that the terminology of New Queer Cinema poses a number of problems as a framework for economic and textual analysis. It may be the case that the marginal status of queer films is no longer an appropriate measure of political commitment; however, it does seem useful to address the politics of queer films in terms of universalizing or minoritizing understandings of sexual difference. In fact, these terms do have something to contribute in terms of a discussion of commodification—and not in the sense that films exhibiting a universalizing tendency will always be more marketable. Product differentiation in a heterogeneous industry may ensure that both styles of film will be produced and distributed; however, the current independent film scene does favor the production of universalizing queer films such as *Two Girls*. Changes in industrial structure may make the production of films like *Go Fish*—whose minoritizing lesbian politics intervene in heterosexual romance conventions and are embedded in its structure and style—less likely.

While the term "Queer" is useful in many contexts as a term that distinguishes the interests of a coalition of deviants—gay men, lesbians, bisexuals, transsexuals, transvestites, sexual and gender outlaws, non-narrow straights and others—from those who continue to press for discriminatory treatment of non-heterosexuals, the generality of "Queer" in terms of textual analysis poses significant drawbacks. To assess the political and aesthetic dimensions of recent films—lesbian, gay, queer or New Queer—specific attention to genre and gender history is required in order to analyze currents and undercurrents within queer and independent filmmaking.

### Works Cited

Burston, Paul and Colin Richardson, eds. A Queer Romance: Lesbians, Gays, and Popular Culture. London: Routledge, 1995.

Corliss, Richard. "The Little Movies That Could." Time 12 Sept. 1994: np.

Gever, Martha, John Greyson, and Pratibha Parmar, eds. Queer Looks. New York: Routledge, 1993.

Interview 24.5 (1994): 22.

———. 24.6 (1994): 40.

La Bruce, Bruce. "The Wild, Wild World of Fanzines: Notes from a reluctant pornographer." In Burston. 186–95.

Mekas, Jonas. "On How the Underground Fooled Hollywood." Village Voice 21 Dec. 1967. Rpt. in Movie Journal: The Rise of a New American Cinema 1959–71. New York: Macmillan, 1972. 301–2.

———. "On the Commercial Temptations," Village Voice 11 May 1967. Rpt. in Movie Journal: The Rise of a New American Cinema 1959–71. New York: Macmillan, 1972. 278.

Merck, Mandy. "Desert Hearts." In Gever 377–82.

Parmar, Pratibha. "That Moment of Emergence." In Gever 3–11.

Rich, B. Ruby, "New Queer Cinema." Sight and Sound 2.5 (1992): 32.

———. "Goings and Comings." Sight and Sound 4.7 (1994): 14–16.

Sedgwick, Eve Kosofsky. "Queer and Now." Tendencies. Durham: Duke UP, 1993. 1–20.

———. "Forward: T Times." Tendencies. Durham: Duke UP, 1993. xi–xvi.

———. Epistemology of the Closet. Berkeley: U of California P, 1990.

Taubin, Amy. "Beyond the Sons of Scorsese." Sight and Sound 2.5 (1992): 37.

"Transcript of Conference with Writer/ Director Maria Maggenti." The Two Girls Homepage: http://www2.interpath.net/ fineline/twogirls.htm. American Online. 28 June 1995.

Willis, Holly. "Fish Stories: Holly Willis on Go Fish." Filmmaker 2.3 (1994): 18–20.

Woods, Gregory. "We're Here, We're Queer and We're not Going Catalogue Shopping." In Burston. 147–63.

"Fishing for Girls: Romancing Lesbians in New Queer Cinema," by Maria Pramaggiore, *College Literature*, West Chester State College.

## ➢ Kara Keeling

(2005), United States

### "'Joining the Lesbians': Cinematic Regimes of Black Lesbian Visibility"

. . . I offer the following examination of Cheryl Dunye's film *The Watermelon Woman* [First Run, 1996] as an example of a queer interpretative project that begins by interrogating the regime of visibility in which "black lesbian" appears and moves into a consideration of what that regime renders invisible in its efforts to produce the ethico-political subject "black lesbian." . . .

Cheryl Dunye's *The Watermelon Woman* provides . . . insight into the nexus of "needs" and "interests" that a visible "black lesbian" currently serves. The film provides a fictional past for "black lesbian" that Cheryl (the film's main character) ultimately fashions into a past in which she finds "hope," "inspiration," "possibility," and "history." By so doing, *The Watermelon Woman* provides insight into what must be rendered "invisible" in the image "black lesbian" in order for "black lesbian" to become "visible."

*The Watermelon Woman* has been received as a film in which the "typically invisible bodies" of "black lesbians" are "rendered visible in a number of ways."[i] The narrative of the film follows Cheryl (a character who identifies herself as "a black lesbian filmmaker" and who is played by Cheryl Dunye), in her efforts to excavate a story about a black actress who appeared in several "mammy" roles in Hollywood films and who is credited in those films as "the Watermelon Woman." While conducting research, Cheryl uncovers evidence of an erotic relationship between "the Watermelon

Woman" (aka "Fae Richards" and "Faith Richardson") and a white female direc-tor, Martha Page. Based on the evidence she uncovers regarding Richardson's rela-tionship with Page, Cheryl concludes, "I guess we have a thing or two in common, Miss Richards: the movies and women." The interracial relationship between Fae and Martha thus provides the initial context within which "the Watermelon Woman" becomes visible as "black lesbian."

During the course of her research, Cheryl talks to "Shirley Hamilton," a character who remembers Mae Richards as "quite a looker" who "used to sing for all us stone butches." Perhaps most significantly, however, Cheryl's research ultimately leads her to "June Walker," a character played by Cheryl Clarke, a writer whose theoretical and creative work during the late 1970s and early 1980s were part of a movement that provided a vocabulary through which a political articulation of "black lesbian" as a critique of "black," "lesbian," "woman," "patriarchy," and "capitalism" emerged. Clarke's character in the film, June, Fae's lover until her death, writes a letter to Cheryl in which June explains that she thinks that the mammy roles Fae played "troubled [Fae's] soul." In the letter, June implicates Martha Page in that vexed history. June's letter implores Cheryl to leave Page out of the movie on Fae's life. Speaking about Fae as part of a collective "we," June asserts, "She did so much, Cheryl. That's what you have to speak about. She paved the way for kids like you to run around making movies about the past and about how we lived then. Please, Cheryl, make our his-tory before we are all dead and gone. But, if you are really in 'the family,' you better understand that our family will always only have each other."

June's comments draw attention to the way that "black lesbian" might be policed to keep some "in the family" and others out of "our family." Yet, the documentary that Cheryl makes about Fae Richards' life similarly reveals Cheryl's own choices about the value of the information she uncovers and, importantly, about the utility of that information to an enabling construction of "black lesbian." Cheryl tailors the docu-mentary about "the Watermelon Woman" presented at the end of the film in order to provide, as Cheryl explains, "hope," "inspiration," "possibility," and a "history" that would rationalize and support the existence of Cheryl herself, as a "black lesbian filmmaker." Cheryl explains the choices she makes in crafting a historical narrative about Faith Richardson's life in the monologue, which introduces the film within a film. Cheryl explains that the historical narrative June provides of her life with Fae validates a different "world" than that which Cheryl inhabits as a "black lesbian film-maker." In response to June's interrogation into Cheryl's interest in the relationship between Fae and Martha, Cheryl explains, "I know she meant the world to you, but she also meant the world to me, and those worlds are different."

Each world, Cheryl's and June's, is authorized via access to a different sheet of the past,[ii] and Cheryl makes it clear that the narrative she will tell is one that will validate and legitimate her existence, not June's: "What [Fae] means to me, a twenty-five-year-old black woman, means something else. It means hope. It means inspiration. It means possibility. It means history. And, most importantly, what I understand is that I'm gonna be the one who says, I am a black lesbian filmmaker who's just beginning. But I'm gonna say a lot more and have a lot more work to do."

The fictional "biography of the Watermelon Woman" that Cheryl presents at the end of *The Watermelon Woman* legitimates the "black lesbian filmmaker" as "the one" who will become visible as "black lesbian" by invoking a sheet of the past that supports Cheryl's needs and interests as they have been presented throughout *The Watermelon Woman,* a past wherein interracial lesbian desire is part and parcel of "black women's" participation in Hollywood and so continues to inform their entry into it. The world that Cheryl claims is hers, as "a twenty-five-year-old black woman," is one in which her professional aspirations demand that she articulate herself into the emergent market category of "black lesbian filmmaker" in a way that will register within the terms of that market.

With the character Cheryl, Dunye ruminates on the conditions for the success of her own film, *The Watermelon Woman*. The first feature-length "black lesbian film," *The Watermelon Woman* is a conjunction between the previously existing categories of "black film" and "lesbian film." The film's articulation into a category recognizable as "black lesbian film" proceeds according to the logic that currently governs post-70s Hollywood; on the film's promotional poster and video cover, the film is proclaimed to be "*Go Fish* Meets *She's Gotta Have It!*" Cheryl Dunye and Guinevere Turner (from the "lesbian film" *Go Fish*) are singled out in the promotional materials as the film's "stars" and they are named and featured prominently on the poster, both smiling.[iii] The choice to feature both Dunye and Turner in the promotional materials indicates that it is via the logic of an interracial "lesbian" relationship that the first "black lesbian feature film" to be picked up for distribution appears.

The marketing decision to feature Turner instead of Valarie Walker, the black actress who plays "Tamara," the other primary character in the film, is mirrored in the final account of "the Watermelon Woman's" life that Cheryl provides. That film-within-a-film begins with a shot of "Martha Page" and "Faith Richardson." While Fae's relationship with Martha Page, although not described explicitly as "lesbian," is granted an eroticism that provides the governing logic behind the film's embrace of Fae as a "black lesbian" foremother, June Walker's relationship with Fae is relegated via the voice-over narrative to the status of "special friend," a rhetorical move that un-self-consciously reproduces the homophobic discourse through which same-sex erotic attachments are obscured and rendered illegitimate within dominant conceptions of the world. Fae's relationship with June, the way she sang for the "stone butches" in the bar, etc., do not appear to be part of the past that enables Cheryl to find "hope," "inspiration," or her "history." Those who exist on a sheet of the past that might support a narrative that would challenge the construction of "black lesbian" that Cheryl provides are relegated by Cheryl's narrative to a "different" world, one that is incommensurate with that in which "black lesbian" can appear and circulate proudly in films.

Yet, because it re-creates the processes whereby Cheryl chooses what from the available past will support her own needs and interests as a "black lesbian filmmaker" and, hence, what will appear in the image that the film-within-a-film designates and puts into circulation as "black lesbian," *The Watermelon Woman* allows for a different possibility to be perceived in the image that Cheryl calls "black lesbian," one that remains hostile to the world Cheryl claims as hers because it is inassimilable into that world's logic. That possibility might collect the "stone butches," the "special friends," "the studs," "the femmes," "the woman-lovers," and "the queers" that were part of the working-class social milieu to which Fae Richards herself belonged and make those ambivalent, destabilizing, and unstable forces of desire and community cohere as a collective expression of a multifarious "we" that complicates any innocent notion of "the one" who says, "I am a black lesbian filmmaker." The multifarious "we" that challenges formulations of "the one . . . black lesbian" also drags "into the maelstrom of a continuously contingent, unguaranteed, political argument and debate,"[iv] even the conception of the world in which an "I" will be perceived to be writing as a "black queer film scholar" who authoritatively (even if passionately) cautions against "joining the lesbians" in favor of the (re)constitution of a multifarious "we."

## Notes

i. Laura L. Sullivan, "Chasing Fae: *The Watermelon Woman* and Black Lesbian Possibility," *Callaloo* 23:1 (2000): 450. In another analysis of the film, Mark Winokur points out that Cheryl/Dunye (character/filmmaker) "creates a black lesbian body in order to recover her own" in an essay that focuses primarily on the way that Dunye's film "creates a representation of the negative oedipal stage of both identification and desire for the body of the black lesbian mother" (Winokur, "Body and Soul: Identifying (with) the Black Lesbian Body in Cheryl Dunye's *The Watermelon Woman*," in *Recovering the Black Female Body: Self-Representations by African American Women,* ed. Michael Bennett and Vanessa D. Dickerson [New Brunswick: Rutgers University Press, 2001], 244, 245).

ii. For an explanation of "sheets of the past" as they might be accessed through cinema, see Gilles Deleuze, *Cinema 2: The Time-Image,* trans. Hugh Tomlinson and Robert Galeta (Minneapolis: University of Minnesota Press, 1989), 98–125.

iii. Valarie Walker, the black actress who plays Tamara, Cheryl's best friend in the film, and a character that, arguably, is just as significant as Turner's Diana, is not mentioned and does not appear on the poster. Clearly, the promotional materials cannot feature every actress in the film. Yet, the choice not to feature Walker but rather Turner, recognizable from Rose Troche's film *Go Fish* as the "trendy, pretty, young Lesbian who is having trouble finding love," is indicative of, among other things, the extent to which *The Watermelon Woman's* financial success was thought to reside in its ability to be recognizable as a "black lesbian film" according to the contours of existing categories.

iv. Stuart Hall, "New Ethnicities," in *Stuart Hall: Critical Dialogues in Cultural Studies,* ed. David Morley and Chen Kuan-Hsing (New York: Routledge, 1996), 444.

---

# CHAPTER 14

# Queers and the Internet

Contemporary LGBT people find representation and community through many forms of media. The Internet can provide queer community in a virtual world. This chapter discusses myths about the Internet, as well as social networking and activist sites and their uses.

In the previous chapter, we examined the cultural work done by filmic representations of queer identities and lives; those representations have been important to many LGBT people. Nonetheless, they are still static; that is, viewers of films and television have to work with what they are given—not images that they themselves create. In this chapter, we examine the Internet, asking questions about the way it, as a space where viewers are transformed into participants, allows LGBT people the opportunity to exercise some control over their own self-representation at the same time that it uses many of the tools offered by other visual media. The Internet's "webbed" environment poses some unique challenges for us writing in a textbook format, as issues consistently embed themselves in and complicate one another. What appears as a statement at one point reappears as a question, and what seems true when talking about one kind of site seems extraordinarily inaccurate when talking about others.

Some of the emerging scholarship about how LGBT people use the Internet focuses on the seemingly limitless opportunities for queers to connect with each other. Joanne Addison and Michelle Comstock, for instance, point out that many queers are "establishing cyberzines, discussion groups, and support services through the Internet" (371). While we share some of the general enthusiasm about the creation of what Nina Wakeford has called "cyberqueer spaces" (410), we also want to think critically about "queers on the Net." We examine some of the major myths about the Internet and its uses by sexual minorities, focusing on ongoing problems related to access and censorship as well as the capitalist underpinnings of much queer-related Internet content. Taking a look at social networking and activist uses of the Internet allows us to consider not just how queers represent themselves but also how they form communities and launch sites of political resistance and coalition. What's more, taking a global view of Internet usage provides us the richest context for understanding how queers have—and have not—connected via the Internet.

## Access, Connection, and Identity

Since its inception as a public communications tool in the mid-1990s, the Internet has garnered much attention as a means of disseminating information quickly and effectively. Many have hailed the Internet as a powerful source of information, but others have critiqued the inconsistent level of access that potential users have to it. While rates of use in the United States and other countries in the Global North are relatively high—165 to 210 million estimated users in the United States—that access still depends on users being able to afford both computer equipment and Internet Service Provider (ISP) charges necessary to use the Internet (Fallows). Fortunately for many, access is increasingly available in public places, such as libraries and community centers. However, the idea that the Internet provides interaction and information on a global scale and in an unequivocally egalitarian way is problematic; it does not take into account issues such as nationality, social class, and general access to resources—reliable electricity, for instance—needed to use the Internet. It also does not account for the fact that some governments prohibit access to specific sites and information or for the fact that, in the United States, access can be limited for people whose primary Internet usage occurs in schools or libraries.

**Find Out More** in the articles by Heins and Cho, Gottschalk, and Anderson cited in this chapter's References and Further Reading.

For those with access, the Internet, with its multiple venues for textually complex and visually rich expression, offers LGBT people some opportunity to articulate their concerns, interests, and desires. Given the highly interactive nature of the Internet, users can not only represent themselves but also exchange ideas, form a variety of communities, and meet others from around the world. Social networking sites are a significant way for queers to feel connected to a larger community of like-minded people. Working with basic templates that ask users to provide information on personal likes, dislikes, and identities, users can identify their romantic, emotional, and sexual interests and augment this information by uploading images and videos. Users can also create groups to affiliate with others of similar interests. Facebook, for instance, offers hundreds of queer and LGBT interest groups. LGBT affinity subgroups also function in less predictable online locations—within knitting websites such as Ravelry, for instance.

As we look for LGBT community in a digital age, we sometimes find a mixed bag. For instance, the popular blog "A Gay Girl in Damascus" purported to follow the life of a young lesbian living in Syria, whose culture is hostile to homosexuals. However, the site was actually a hoax (Wardrop). At other times, though, the proliferation of legitimate coming-out blogs, sites, and videos can provide a kind of queer "strength in numbers" (Alexander and Losh 48). Such narratives might also save lives. In response to a rash of suicides of gay teens who had been bullied or harassed, Dan Savage and husband Terry Miller created the It Gets Better Project in 2010. Their site (http:www.itgetsbetter.org/) displays, as of this writing, more than 30,000 videos of adult LGBT people and allies who talk about their lives and experiences growing up and who offer encouragement to young queers who may be facing difficult personal circumstances. Even President Barack Obama contributed a video to the site.

While social networking sites offer queers a potential sense of connection and community, they also unfortunately increase the ways in which one can encounter **homophobia**. For instance, when searching for "queer" groups on Facebook, we are just as likely to encounter homophobically tinged groups as LGBT-friendly communities. Users can create communities "for fun," such as "Jerry is SO Gay," to ridicule their friends and others. A surprisingly large number of groups use gay slurs. Moreover, self-identification on social networking sites may leave LGBT people vulnerable not only to virtual assault but also to attacks in physical space. In 2006, Jason Johnson was dismissed from the University of the Cumberlands in Williamsburg, Kentucky, when administrators learned that he had come out as gay on his MySpace page. Johnson wrote the following passage on his site: "I'm just starting out a wonderful dating adventure with a beautiful boy named Zac. I'm excited because I'll be moving close to him soon. Next semester, I'll be transferring to the University of Kentucky to finish my degree in theatre" (Bene).

Officials at the University of the Cumberlands, which is affiliated with the Southern Baptist Convention, told Johnson that he was being expelled because they did not approve of his "gay lifestyle," and even though Johnson had been on the dean's list, his grades were all converted to Fs. The university dismissed him on the basis of a 2005 revision of the student handbook indicating that students participating in premarital sex or promoting homosexuality would face expulsion. The handbook revision was not finalized, however, until after Johnson was already attending the university. Johnson eventually settled with Cumberland, which agreed to allow him to finish his in-progress course work, reinstated his grades, and promised not to characterize his departure as an expulsion (Bene). This story highlights a reality about social networking sites: while they function as important venues for making connections among LGBT people, what appears on them can also be accessed and used maliciously—sometimes years later—to "punish" LGBT people and to control expressions of sexuality.

Beyond the facilitation of social interaction, the Internet can also provide LGBT people with an efficient way to find one another for sexual liaisons. Message boards, Yahoo! groups, craigslist, and a host of other sites enable people to locate others interested in a wide range of sexual practices. Much sexual activity also occurs on the Internet, as individuals use Internet technologies, such as chat and video chat, to engage in virtual sexual behavior. Shaka McGlotten notes that "[i]n video chat, the possibility for constructing alternate intimate scenarios [is] intensified." Furthermore, he argues that "[y]ou might do something a stranger asked you to do without question, an act that carried none of the delay or frustration that might come with having to explain to your partner [for instance] why spanking doesn't necessarily mean you want to be abused" (129). At a time when awareness of HIV and other sexually transmitted infections is heightened, particularly in the West, virtual sex can seem like a safe alternative to risky in-person encounters. And, as McGlotten's example illustrates, participants in virtual sex can explore a variety of nonnormative sexual practices and fantasies. Some queer and queer-friendly groups use the Internet to promote sex-positive practices; women-focused and queer-friendly Good Vibrations, for instance, uses its website to "enhance our customers' sex lives and to promote healthy attitudes about sex" (http://www.good vibes.com/). At the same time, we should note that queer-identified people are not the only ones accessing queer porn and erotica on the Internet. Some observe that many so-called lesbian porn sites are merely "representations of all-female sexuality . . . so inaccurate, and so clearly geared toward a straight male audience, that very few could truly be considered lesbian" ("Pornographic"). More disturbingly, the Internet has been used by those seeking intergenerational sexual encounters to transmit erotica depicting sex with minors [λ Chapter 6].

## Internet Censorship and Corporatization

Issues of access are often complicated by state-supported censorship, through which some governments and legal jurisdictions impose their ideologies. In China, for instance, "censorship, monitoring, rules, and enforcement make for a much more controlled Internet. Within China, maintaining this situation already requires tens of thousands of Internet police and many layers of accountability and potential punishment. (To give one relatively unpublicized example: ISPs convicted of hosting pornographic sites are in principle eligible for the death penalty)" (Fallows). We can catch a glimpse of how limited Internet use is in China when we consider that the Pew Internet Project reports that there are currently 137 million Internet users in that country—approximately one tenth of their population (Fallows). The Iranian Queer Organization (IRQO) features on its website pictures of gay men who have been flogged for hosting queer gatherings in Iran, where sexual acts between men are punishable by death. In the words of its founders, the IRQO site exists "in the hope of building alliances and creating solidarity among Iranian homosexual, Bisexual and Transgender" people (http://www.pglo.net/). The site, however, is banned in Iran, limiting communication and connection among LGBT Iranians.

While such cases may seem extreme, it is important to keep in mind that censorship of queer content on Western ISP servers is not uncommon. Many public servers are programmed to prohibit access to information with LGBT content or to websites with streaming video. This is particularly important because public servers are often the only means of accessing the Internet for people who cannot afford to pay for high-speed lines in their homes. More and more Internet sites that contain information about and facilitate interaction among LGBT people require high-speed connections. Some governments censor the Internet by limiting the kinds of sites that can be offered by ISPs; in the United States, a similar kind of censorship occurs at the local level when public servers such as libraries and schools limit access to sites with LGBT content—ostensibly in the interest of "protecting children" from "sexually explicit" material.

While national governments or local boards of education can suppress some kinds of Internet content for ideological reasons, another form of control occurs when Internet content is shaped by market forces. In the West, the Internet, despite being figured by some as countercultural and even anarchical, betrays at every turn its capitalist underpinnings. It is fairly common knowledge, for instance, that 20-something geeks Steven Chen and Chad Hurley sold their YouTube invention to Google in October 2006 for $1.7 billion. In 2012 Facebook went public with a $5 billion Initial Public Offering (Swartz, Martin, and Krantz). David Kushner, writing about the "Baby Billionaires of Silicon Valley," shows how popular applications, such as MySpace, Firefox, LicketyShip, and others, are inextricably tied to commercialism and commodity capitalism. Even craigslist, which offers "[l]ocal classifieds and forums for 450 cities worldwide" and claims to have a "service mission and non-corporate culture," has been incorporated as a for-profit company since 1999 ("craigslist").

Earlier in this book, we referred to Michel Foucault's *History of Sexuality* and John D'Emilio's "Capitalism and Gay Identity" as works that argue, in different ways, that contemporary gay identity could only develop within a capitalist economic framework that imposes social control through categorization [λ Chapter 2]. While categories allow queers to identify one another and thereby facilitate the creation of community, they also allow marketers to target potential consumers. Take, for example, the growing phenomenon of online "television" networks such as the lesbian- and gay-focused Logo TV site, which proclaims, "Watch Logo on TV. Or online. Or on your iPod. And that's only the beginning!" LGBT people might be excited to know that there is a network whose purpose is to offer "the LGBT world . . . a place all its own . . . [which] brings you the stories, shows and news you won't see anywhere else. From original series and films to groundbreaking documentaries to LGBT news and more" ("About Logo"). The issues of access addressed above come into play here; access to TV shows on the Internet requires high-speed connectivity and up-to-date software. Furthermore, the "free" access to the Logo site that most Internet users expect is supported by corporate sponsors. Again, LGBT people are the subjects of marketing, so the price we pay for virtual queer space is the price we pay for the services and equipment needed to access that space and for the products sold by those who underwrite it.

Even scholarly projects focused on the Internet can have corporate connections. The Annenberg Center for the Digital Future, one of the best-known organizations researching Internet usage worldwide, describes its work in this way: "In addition to its flagship surveys of America's involvement with the Internet and digital media, the Center administers the complementary World Internet Project in two dozen countries, manages the Annenberg School's On-line Communities Project, and is currently surveying Internet use by military personnel for the U.S. Department of Defense" ("Collaboration"). It is difficult to find LGBT-focused research on the Annenberg site, but LGBT and sexuality-related attitudes are part of what Annenberg surveys. Tellingly, Annenberg's research is at least partly funded by its corporate partners, which include Coca-Cola, whose advertising on the Internet has become pervasive, and Microsoft, AT&T, and Time Warner, which have clear investments in encouraging Internet use. As is true of other mass media, then, what we know about and can access on the Internet is often influenced by corporations that stand to benefit from that information.

# Internet Activism

As Jennifer Egan points out, Internet access is crucial for many seeking information, community, and contact with LGBT and queer people: "[F]or homosexual teenagers with computer access, the Internet has, quite simply, revolutionized the experience of growing up gay. Isolation and shame persist among gay teenagers, of course, but now, along with the inhospitable families and towns in which many find themselves marooned, there exists a parallel online community—real people like them in cyberspace with whom they can chat, exchange messages and even engage in (online) sex" (113). However, as Sandip Roy observes, "The very convenience of the Internet can lull people into a sense of 'keyboard activism,' forgetting that the real grassroots organizing still needs to be down on the ground" (189). The question becomes whether a one-to-one substitution can be made between the physical communities of family and town and the "parallel online community" described by Egan. We are inclined to believe that there is no easy equivalence between "real people" in physical communal space and "real people" online. If we also consider Roy's concerns about the possibility that the Internet can create the illusion of social change rather than actual social change, then we must also ask about the impact on "inhospitable families and towns" when community is sought online rather than transformed in physical space. When individuals check out into virtual queer space rather than live openly in the world as LGBT, those families and towns can maintain homophobic biases and sanctions unchallenged.

In terms of LGBT activism, the Internet poses some interesting contradictions. As noted, much of what LGBT people have access to on the Internet is dependent on corporate support and is therefore controlled and normalized in some of the same ways as television and film. At the same time, the Internet provides LGBT people the opportunity to represent themselves in ways that are often creative, insightful, and political. What's more, on the Internet, LGBT people can learn about important sexuality-related activism throughout the world. For instance, Internet users can easily locate sites hosted by the National Gay and Lesbian Task Force (NGLTF), the International Lesbian and Gay Association (ILGA), and the Lambda Legal Defense and Education Fund. Especially in the United States, the proliferation of politically focused LGBT sites has undermined the notion that LGBT people represent a political monolith. While a fairly quick search can lead Internet users to sites like that of the Human Rights Campaign (HRC) or those of student LGBT organizations on high school and college campuses, it can also lead one to sites like that of the Log Cabin Republicans or the Pro-Life Alliance of Gays and Lesbians (PLAGAL). These organizations' websites facilitate membership as LGBT people look for others with similar interests. But they do something else as well: the presence of a carefully constructed site on the Internet can create a sense that an organization is cohesive and powerful, that there are "bodies" behind the name, and that, if need be, they might show up in force at physical locations to engage in loud, even disruptive, protest.

While some LGBT people see the Internet as a means of initiating political connections, others use it as a means of making those connections visible. Since the

**Figure 14.1** Michelangelo Signorile.

1980s, one of the most controversial ways of doing that has been public *outing,* that is, forcefully identifying the presence of queer people in a variety of social, cultural, and political spaces. The practice of media outing of LGBT celebrities and politicians was originally associated with gay anger at the slow and a half-hearted response to the AIDS crisis in mainstream American culture [λ Chapter 4]. Journalist Michelangelo Signorile admits that "ACT UP's rhetoric and shrill tactics fueled many of [his] early columns" in *OutWeek,* where he attacked columnist Liz Smith "for remaining closeted herself and for not reporting on the gay lives of some of the supposedly heterosexual celebrities mentioned in her column" (72). He also warned other closeted celebrities that, if they refused to "[be] part of the solution instead of part of the problem, . . . we're coming through and nothing is going to stop us. And if that means we have to pull you down, well, then, have a nice fall" (73). This was shocking stuff, and *Time* magazine named it "outing." At that time, Signorile made clear that only those "queers who are closeted and harming others" should be outed. For him, outing was more than "mak[ing] the revelation of homosexuality into a punishment" (77). It was simply equalizing—treating homosexuality as equal to heterosexuality in the media.

The ease of posting on the Internet has added a digital dimension to outing. The advent of the Internet, as we have discussed, brought millions of people into what had previously been exclusively journalistic conversations, such as blogs and wikis. Not surprisingly, the Internet flexed to admit eager discussants who created sites specifically designed to produce knowledge through collaborative participation. Wikipedia is probably the best-known online collaborative site, describing itself as "a multilingual, web-based, free content encyclopedia project. Wikipedia is written collaboratively by volunteers from all around the world." As many Web searchers agree, Wikipedia entries tend to contain vastly more (and more interesting) content than typical encyclopedia entries. Still, some believe it susceptible to "vandalism," inaccuracy, or even incivility as contributors argue over content and interpretation ("Wikipedia: About"). For instance, Wikipedia has often served as an easy way to engage in homophobic false outings that assume that the label *gay* or *homosexual* is a slur. A recent example involved *The Sopranos* creator David Chase, whose Wikipedia entry was edited to read, "David Chase . . . is a homosexual American television writer" (TMZ). The article describing this piece of Internet vandalism appeared in an online publication titled *A Critical Look at Wikipedia, the Online "Encyclopedia" That Anyone Can Edit,* and the assumption underlying the news item is that only a *wiki thug* would accuse someone of homosexuality. In the case of David Chase, the false outing seems to have been an expression of anger after the inconclusive ending of *The Sopranos*'s last show in June 2007. Similarly, Tony O'Clery, a disgruntled former devotee of guru Sathya Sai Baba, used *QuickTopic* instant online discussion space to accuse the president of India, a follower of Sai, of being a "gay pedophile" ("Tony"). In these and other cases, the outing appears to have originated with presumably heterosexual accusers who construct homosexuality as obviously negating public credibility.

The Internet is also a venue for organized attacks on the very idea of queerness. The notorious God Hates Fags site, developed by the Reverend Fred Phelps of Westboro Baptist Church in Topeka, Kansas, is a prominent example of how some use the Web to garner support for their antigay sentiments. Phelps and his followers believe that what they perceive as "toleration" of homosexuality dooms the world to divine punishment. Their site features, among other hate propaganda, the "Perpetual Gospel Memorial to Matthew Shepard," which includes a counter indicating the number of days Shepard has been "burning in Hell" and a doctored photo of Shepard with animated flames beneath his face (http://www.godhatesfags.com).

**Find Out More** by reading about Matthew Shepard in Chapter 4.

More generally, pundits, social critics, journalists, and newscasters seem to revel in frightening citizens with the many dangers of the Internet—not only for queers but also for the public at large. It should come as no surprise that the national media often present the Internet as a danger zone. In part, of course, the hostile portrayal of the Internet by national video and print media results from their economic conflict with the Internet, which houses principal alternative news outlets—the Independent Media Center (IMC, or IndyMedia) or the Common Dreams News Center, for example. Both of these news outlets include LGBT issues among the progressive political causes they support. Common Dreams includes the Gay and Lesbian Alliance Against Defamation (GLAAD), the HRC, the NGLTF, and Parents, Families, and Friends of Lesbians and Gays (PFLAG) among their "Links to America's Progressive Community," as well as Planet Out, Gay Financial News, and Women's E-News among the news services from which they gather articles to republish on their websites. By treating LGBT-related stories as newsworthy, these sites underscore how readily the national media elide queer issues, concerns, and politics.

Globally, even in countries where officials censor the Internet to deny users access to LGBT-related sites, some are clearly receiving news of the political work and struggles of LGBT people in other parts of the world. Iranian activist Arsham Parsi, founder of the Persian Gay and Lesbian Organization (PGLO), says,

> We have been in existence for three years, and through this period we have become recognized by many gay and lesbian organizations throughout the world. We based most of our activities through Internet communication. We must communicate solely by Internet as we do not have the freedom to work in a public forum in our country. We do not have any sponsors locally in Iran as the religious extremists do not support gay rights, but would rather see all LGBT people silenced. (Parsi)

Parsi is now living in Canada, and he continues to speak on behalf of the PGLO. His gay advocacy illustrates the global reach of the Internet in that alone, or with a mere handful of like-minded associates living in exile from Iran, he could create an organization, give it a name, and insert it into the global online conversation. To put this in context, Parsi's website (http://www.homanla.org) gives his organization an import beyond its physical numbers, which it could not have had previous to the Internet; it facilitates identification among Iranian LGBT people "inside and outside of their homeland" and makes their existence visible. His tiny organization is then treated by others worldwide as a going concern and taken seriously as a player in queer activist circles.

Chinese LGBT people experience a similar silencing as their counterparts in Iran, and like them, Chinese activists have set up headquarters in exile. For example, the Institute for *Tongzhi* (Gay) Studies, located at the City University of New York, involves Chinese-speaking teachers and researchers in academic studies about LGBT people in China. But as China has gradually liberalized some attitudes toward gays over the past decade or so, more opportunities have arisen for Chinese gays and lesbians to connect with each other; Hong Kong's Court of Final Appeal, for instance, recently "rejected a ban . . . on public gay sex" (Hui). Still, gay and lesbian webmasters exercise extreme caution in openly discussing their online connections. Despite the fact that "there are now hundreds of gay websites in China and the number is growing all the time" (Chan), the November 2001 meeting of Chinese gay webmasters had to be held in secret. In a testament to the dangers associated with gay activism in China, Yuen Chan's article describing the Chinese webmasters' meeting provides no URLs for the websites it discusses.

While these Iranian and Chinese activists are using the Internet to organize politically, much as their counterparts in the United States do, they also struggle with whether to base their queer activism on a U.S. model. Roy asks important questions about what happens when one cultural model is imposed globally:

> Will the very speed of dissemination that the Internet provides create a borderless world where the American concept of a gay movement can spread like a virus and infect all cultures? Does it now just take a modem to start a movement? And once that movement gets off the ground, will it merely borrow from existing movements in the West? Will countries with fledgling GLBT movements risk losing the process of building a movement that is about them and their needs and end up assimilating into Western models because they are more accessible? What happens when the seeds of the movement are sown by members of their diaspora in the West? Is there a danger that the Internet will not only pull together people across oceans but at the same time offer them ready packaged visions of a GLBT movement that does not account for cultural differences? Or will cultural differences cease to matter in a well-homogenized "gay" world? (181)

Roy seems to be seeking a balance between the U.S.-centric notion of what Dennis Altman has called the "global gay" and the unique positioning of homosexuality in individual cultures worldwide. It is important to recognize how the Internet's enabling of communally constructed conversation across national and cultural borders depends on resisting global corporatization, which relies on constructing LGBT people as a monolithic economic market to maximize profit. Roy's questions highlight the need for a new way of thinking about the international LGBT community, one that imagines transnationality as transformational. The Internet's ability to facilitate the building of a diverse, international LGBT community independent from corporate imperatives surely represents its most exciting potential.

## QUESTIONS FOR DISCUSSION

1. If you have access to social networking sites such as Facebook or Tumblr, keep notes on how queer-identified people represent themselves. How do gays and lesbians, for instance, use textual identifiers, images, and even video to mark their identities, their affiliations, their relationships, and their desires? Consider how bisexuality and transgenderism are comparably identified. Based on a number of observations, what might you assert about queer self-fashioning in online spaces, particularly on social networking sites?

2. Fact-check a pro- or antigay website of your choice. What do you learn from your research? Consider not only the content of the sites you examine but also their layout and design. How do different activists use the web—textually, visually, aurally—to muster support for their positions?

3. Debate the value of LGBT pornography on the Internet. In particular, consider the position that the Internet, with its proliferation of millions of sex, erotica, porn, and fetish sites detailing a seemingly infinite diversity of sexual pleasures and possibilities, has done more to "queer" sex than nearly any other medium. Do you agree or disagree? What are the limits of this kind of "queering" of sex?

## REFERENCES AND FURTHER READING

"About Logo: Welcome to Logo." *Logo Online*, n.d. Web. 6 Aug. 2008. <http://www.logoonline.com/about/>.

Addison, Joanne, and Michelle Comstock. "Virtually Out: The Emergence of a Lesbian, Bisexual and Gay Youth Cyberculture." *Generations of Youth: Youth and History in Twentieth-Century America*. Eds. Joe Austin and Michael Nevin Willard. New York: NYU P, 1998. 367–78. Print.

Alexander, Jonathan, and Elizabeth Losh. "'A YouTube of One's Own?': 'Coming Out' as Rhetorical Action." *LGBT Identity and Online New Media*. Eds. Christopher Pullen and Margaret Cooper. New York: Routledge, 2010. 37-50. Print.

Altman, Dennis. *Global Sex*. Chicago: U of Chicago P, 2001. Print.

Anderson, Joseph. "CIPA and San Francisco, California: Why We Don't Filter." *Web Junction*, n.d. 6 Aug. 2008. <http://www.webjunction.org/do/Display Content?id=996>.

Bene Diction (pseud.). "Gay Student Expelled from Baptist University." *Spero News*, 11 April 2006. Web. 27 Aug. 2012. <http://www.speroforum.com/site/print.asp?idarticle=3248>.

Bob Jones Univ. v. United States. Supreme Ct. of the US, 461 U.S. 574. 24 May 1983. Web. 27 Aug. 2012. <http://www.law.cornell.edu/supct/html/historics/USSC_CR_0461_0574_ZS.html>.

Chan, Yuen. "Out of the Closet in China." *BBC News, International Version*, n.d. Web. 6 Aug. 2008. <http://news.bbc.co.uk/2/hi/asia-pacific/3389767.stm>.

"Collaboration Will Deliver Leading-Edge Insights into the Impact of the Internet." *USC Annenberg School Center for the Digital Future*, 26 June 2006. Web. 6 Aug. 2008. <http://www.digitalcenter.org/pages/news_content.asp?intGlobal Id=198>.

"craigslist fact sheet." *craigslist online community*, n.d. Web. 6 Aug. 2008. <http://www.craigslist.org/about/pr/factsheet.html>.

"Cyberbullying." *Stop Bullying Now!*, n.d. Web. 6 Aug. 2008. <http://stopbully ingnow.hrsa.gov/adult/indexAdult.asp?Area=cyberbullying>.

"Dangers on the Internet." *Internet Evangelism Day: A Worldwide Awareness Resource for Christians*, n.d. Web. 6 Aug. 2008. <http://ied.gospelcom.net/dangers.php>.

Egan, Jennifer. "Lonely Gay Teen Seeking Same." *New York Times Magazine* 10 Dec. 2000: 110–13. Print.

Fallows, Deborah. "China's Online Population Explosion: What It May Mean for the Internet Globally . . . and for U.S. Users." *Pew Research Center Publications*, 12 July 2007. Web. 27 Aug. 2012. <http://pewresearch.org/pubs/537/china-online>.

"Fighting for Tomorrow: An Interview with Arsham Parsi." *Homan: The Iranian Gay,*

*Lesbian, Bisexual, and Transgender Organization,* n.d. Web. 6 Aug. 2008. <http://www.homanla.org/New/Arsham_oct06.htm>.

Gottschalk, Lana. "Internet Filters in Public Libraries: Do They Belong?" *Library Student Journal,* Sept. 2006. Web. 27 Aug. 2012. <http://www.librarystudentjournal.org/index.php/lsj/article/view/25/17 >.

Heins, Marjorie, and Christina Cho. "Internet Filters: A Public Policy Report." *National Coalition against Censorship,* n.d. Web. 6 Aug. 2008. <http://www.ncac.org/internet/filters.cfm>.

Hui, Sylvia. "Hong Kong Court Rejects Gay Sodomy Law." *Boston Globe,* 17 July 2007. Web. 6 Aug. 2008. <http://www.boston.com/news/world/asia/articles/2007/07/17/hong_kong_court_ rejects_gay_sodomy_law/>.

"Interactive: Online Predators." *Cincinnati Enquirer,* 7 June 2007. Web. 6 Aug. 2008. <http://news.enquirer.com/apps/pbcs.dll/article?AID=/20070607/NEWS01/306060027>.

*Iranian Queer Organization.* N.p., n.d. Web. 27. Aug. 2012. < http://www.pglo.net/>.

"Irish Boy, 14, Arranges Sex with Adult Men Using Gaydar." *Americans for Truth about Homosexuality,* 6 Mar. 2007. Web. 6 Aug. 2008. <http://americansfortruth.com/news/irish-boy-14-arranges-sex-with-adult-men-using-gaydar.html>.

Karl, Irmi. "On-/Offline: Gender, Sexuality, and the Techno-politics of Everyday Life." *Queer Online: Media, Technology, and Sexuality.* Eds. Kate O'Riordan and David J. Phillips. New York: Peter Lang, 2007. 45–66. Print.

Kushner, David. "The Baby Billionaires of Silicon Valley." *Rolling Stone,* 1 Nov. 2006. Web. 27 Aug. 2012. <http://74.220.215.94/~davidkus/index.php?option=com_content&view=article&id=71:the-baby-billionaires-of-silicon-valley&catid=35:articles&Itemid=54>.

Kumaran, Uttarika. "Disabled, gay, and as normal as you." *Daily News and Analysis,* Jan. 30, 2011. Web. 27 Aug. 2012. <http://www.dnaindia.com/lifestyle/report_disabled-gay-and-as-normal-as-you_1500718>.

Lee, Min. "Chinese Rules Limit Online Teen Gaming." *Cincinnati Enquirer* 18 July 2007: A8. Print.

Leingang, Matt. "Data Theft Reaches 859,800: Number Rises on Device Stolen from State Intern." *Cincinnati Enquirer,* 12 July 2007. Web. 6 Aug. 2008. <http://news.enquirer.com/apps/pbcs.dll/article?AID=/20070712/NEWS01/707120341/-1/back01>.

McGlotten, Shaka. "Virtual Intimacies: Love, Addiction, and Identity @ The Matrix." *Queer Online: Media, Technology, and Sexuality.* Eds. Kate O'Riordan and David J. Phillips. New York: Peter Lang, 2007. 123–38. Print.

"Nevada Couple Blame Internet for Neglect." *Yahoo! News,* 16 July 2007. Web. 27 Aug. 2012. <http://www.westwideweb.com/wp/2007/07/16/nevada-couple-blame-internet-for-neglect-yahoo-news/>.

"Nigerian Dating Scam (aka 419 scam)." *Dangers of Internet Dating,* n.d. Web. 6 Aug. 2008. <http://www.dangersofInternetdating.com/nigeriandatingscam.htm>.

Parsi, Arsham. "Speech to Canadian Gay Groups." PGLO Advocacy Group. 13 June 2006. Web. 27 Aug. 2012. <http://www.homanla.org/New/pgloArsham.htm>.

"Pornographic Film and Video: Lesbian." *GLBTQ: An Encyclopedia of Gay, Lesbian,*

*Bisexual, Transgender, & Queer Culture,* 2002. Web. 6 Aug. 2008. <http://www .glbtq.com/arts/porn_lesbian.html>.

Roy, Sandip. "From Khush List to Gay Bombay: Virtual Webs of Real People." *Mobile Cultures: New Media in Queer Asia.* Eds. Chris Berry, Fran Martin, and Audrey Yue. Durham, NC: Duke UP, 2003. 180–97. Print.

Signorile, Michelangelo. *Queer in America: Sex, the Media, and the Closets of Power.* Rev. ed. Madison: U of Wisconsin P, 2003. Print.

Swartz, Jon, Scott Martin, and Matt Krantz. "Facebook IPO filing puts high value on social network." *USA Today,* 2 Feb. 2012. Web. 27 Mar. 2012. <http://www.usatoday.com/tech/news /story/2012-02-01/facebook-ipo/529 21528/1>.

TMZ Staff. "*Sopranos* Fans Whack Creator's Wiki Entry." *Wikipedia: A Critical Look at Wikipedia, the Online "Encyclopedia" That Anyone Can Edit,* n.d. Web. 6 Aug. 2008. <http://wiki-problem-pedia.blog spot.com/>.

"Tony O'Clery Defames India's President." *Anthony Tony O'Clery Exposed.* N.p., 25 Feb. 2007. Web. 6 Aug. 2008. <http:// tony-oclery-exposed.blogspot.com/ 2007/02/tony-oclery-defames-indias- president.html>.

Wakeford, Nina. "Cyberqueer." *The Cybercul- tures Reader.* Eds. David Bell and Barbara M. Kennedy. London: Routledge, 2000. 403–15. Print.

Wardrop, Murray. "'A Gay Girl in Damascus': extracts from US man's hoax blog." *The Telegraph,* 13 June 2011. Web. 27 Mar. 2012. <http://www.telegraph .co.uk/news/worldnews/middleeast/ syria/8572694/A-Gay-Girl-in-Damascus -extracts-from-US-mans-hoax-blog .html>.

"Wikipedia: About." *Wikipedia: The Free Encyclopedia,* n.d. Web. 6 Aug. 2008. <http://en.wikipedia.org/wiki/Wiki pedia:About>.

## READINGS

> ## Andil Gosine
(2007), Canada

### "Brown to Blond at Gay.com: Passing White in Queer Cyberspace"

I am in love with the image and idea of white manhood, which is everything I am not and want to be, and if I cannot be that at least I can have that, if only for the night, if only for one week or the month. ([Reginald] Shepherd 1991)

I would love to be white. Not forever, but perhaps a weekend. Don't you ever get sick of being a minority? . . . I have posed this question to other minority artists, and get stumped by answers like "No, not ever have I ever wanted to be white." And I just don't buy it. Why would you not want things to be easier? ([Margaret] Cho 2005)

So much social, economic, and cultural capital is invested in the idealization of white bodies (and in the devaluation and denigration of non-white ones) that neither Shepherd's confessional yearnings nor Cho's caustic daydream is surprising—nor are the disapproving reactions from those who find their declarations uncomfortable, even upsetting. Fantasies and anxieties about the realization and loss of whiteness inform the configuration of social relations and production of knowledge in much of the contemporary world. Since at least the fifteenth century, white has connoted purity, virginity, beauty, and even Godliness in European nations, and the accident of white skin has authorized its bearers to claim, conquer, and colonize the lands and cultures of non-white peoples of Africa, Asia, and the Americas. Whiteness, writes Kalpana Seshadri-Crooks, is a "master signifier that establishes a structure of relations, a signifying chain that through a process of inclusions and exclusions constitutes a pattern for organizing human difference" (2000:3–4). Through the production of Orientalism, non-white subjects are characterized as a function of the white subject and are allowed no autonomy and purpose except as a means of knowing the white self (Said 1978). Consequently, white people are systematically privileged and enjoy "unearned advantage and conferred dominance" in Western societies (McIntosh 1992:74). They "create the dominant images of the world and don't quite see that they construct the world in their own image," and "they set standards of humanity by which they are bound to succeed and others bound to fail" (Dyer 1997:9). Frantz Fanon concludes: "Sin is Negro as Virtue is white" (1967:138).

There are longstanding rituals through which white people are able to perform non-white racialized ethnicities (e.g., casting white actors in Asian roles in films, donning kimonos or turbans to play Japanese or Indian at costume parties) and for non-white people to perform exaggerated expressions of racialized identities (e.g., American Minstrel shows, representations in television and film), but not many choices exist for a Korean-American comic like Cho or an African-American like Shepherd to assume white racial identities. The advent of cyberspace provided a new venue for non-white people to experience racial crossing into whiteness—an experience that was part of a parcel of opportunities being trumpeted by queer, feminist, and cyberculture critics anticipating the liberating potential of virtual worlds (Turkle 1995; Plant 1996; Sunden 2001; Gross 2004).

In November 1998, I engaged [in] "race" play in cyberspace as a way of examining claims about its revolutionary promise, and of racial crossing. For five consecutive days, I participated in conversations in the "Toronto" chat rooms at gay.com, and kept a journal of my online interactions. Selecting a gay website feature to consider the operation of "race" in cyberspace made sense for several reasons, including my own ties to and investments in queer culture, and the fact that queer scholars were among those leading the celebration of this technological advance. Many of them, including Larry Gross, for example, imagined that for queer men and women, the net would present more opportunities to inhabit sexual desires and identities, connect and create community, and refuse gender and class restrictions that structured their offline, "real world" lives (2004). A focus on chat rooms also seemed appropriate. As Lisa Nakamura observes, "cyberspace is a place of wish fulfillments and myriad gratifications, material and otherwise and nowhere is this more true than in chat spaces" (2002:32). Textual chat spaces, she says, "encourage users to build different identities, to take on new identities . . . to describe themselves in any way they wish to appear" (Nakamura 2002:32).

My chat room experiences did not prove to be as liberating an event as proclaimed in the cyberutopian rhetoric. Although opportunities to unfix and reconstitute meanings of identities and social markers were certainly available, processes of racialization were evident in and seemed to have an important structuring influence on the organization, flow of dialogues and relationships between users in the chat rooms. Returning to review the site seven years later, in 2005, I also found that whatever potential may have existed for dominant, colonial narratives of "race" to be displaced or undermined in cyberspace are fading (or have faded). Changes to gay.com's chat services since 1998 appear to have further reinforced racial categories and ensure the reproduction of "real life" racism. In this respect, the development of virtual worlds has been shown to be not unlike other technologies, merely mimicking dominant socioeconomic relations rather than challenging them.

What also emerged from this study of the chat rooms were compelling insights about desires for passing white. Very often, racial crossing from non-white to white is read as evidence of investments in racial imagery and symbolism. This presumption underlies the outrage expressed by Cho's friends about her wanting to be white for a weekend and the persistence of epithets to describe non-white people accused of "acting white" (e.g., "coconut" for South Asians, "banana" for East Asians). But analysis of the operation of "race"-racism in the gay.com chat rooms suggests that passing white is not simply the exercise of desires by non-white people to become white or fetishize whiteness, but, rather, to experience the privileges afforded to whiteness. Passing white expresses longing for the experience of racial disembodiment that cyberspace promises, but does not ultimately appear to fulfill. . . .

### Passing White: Resource Access and the Exercise of Agency

In one of her studies on white people engaging [in] racial passing in cyberspace, Nakamura observed that "many users masquerading as racial minorities in chat spaces tend to depict themselves in ways that simply repeat and reenact old racial stereotypes," including, for example, "users masquerading as samurai and geishas, complete with swords, kimonos, and other paraphernalia lifted from older media such as film and television" (2002:107). This type of play, she says, "reenacts an anachronistic version of 'Asian-ness' that reveals more about users' fantasies and desires than it does about what it 'feels like' to be Asian either on- or offline" (2002:107). Passing white, however, may serve a different purpose, not exclusively an exercise in fantasy or anxiety production but an opportunity to experience the material and cultural privileges afforded to white people. Unlike its reverse ritual, racial crossing from non-white to white may not be primarily motivated by fetishistic conscious or unconscious desire, but by struggles for access to resources and for experience of cultural and political agency.

## Accessing Resources

One of the reasons queer scholars cheered the development of cyberspace was their expectation that virtual spaces would be better able than bars or clubs to provide affirmation for "many who do not find themselves welcomed or validated by the increasingly commercialized and mainstreamed institutions of the newly respectable GLBT communities, including marginalized sub-culture groups" (Gross 2004:xi). Keith Dorwick argues,

> One thing online communication has changed radically is that men can now speak to men they'd never speak to in the bars. The social barriers between races, between "hot men" and "dogs" or "trolls" and between younger and older men are much lower online. (Alexander et al. 2004)

But characterizations of chat rooms as more egalitarian spaces do not hold up on more attentive examination. Anxieties about race—held by both white and non-white men—may sometimes determine who is solicited for conversation, friend-ship or sex in bars, but they perform the same function in cyberspace as well, as evidenced by the shutting down of conversations after responses to the "back-ground" question confirm non-white racial identity and, also, by the preferred sta-tus afforded to white men.

Of the many identities I adopted in the Toronto chat rooms at gay.com, blue-eyed and blond haired "Robbie" was easily the most fun to inhabit. Robbie fit my own physical description except, importantly, that he was blond and blue-eyed; I enjoyed the most attention from other online chatters than in any other represen-tation of myself. I was overwhelmed with requests for private window conversa-tions and many times I was chatting separately but simultaneously with five or six of the thirty users in the room. Changing only information about hair and eye color to indicate a white identity, I was invited to participate [in] conversations with many more men and have an altogether different experience than when my descriptor indicated that I was non-white. Others engaged in similar projects have reported similar experiences. For example, one Taiwanese-born college student posting to a Bulletin Board System based in Orange County, California, also found that immediately after changing his ethnic identity from "Chinese" to "Caucasian," he received more queries and invitations to chat (Tsang 2000:435). Tsang also reports that consequent to their experiences of queer spaces on the Web, many non-white users refused to identify themselves, or identified themselves as "Other" or "Mixed" when given a choice, "in the hopes that their chances [to interact with other men] would be improved" (2000:435). In the physical world, non-white men have often been refused entry to white-dominant gay bars and clubs; in cyber-space, self-identification as white often serves as a qualifier to access conversations with other users.

### *Exercising Agency*

Interactions in the Toronto gay.com chat rooms make clear that the act of passing white is also an attempt to experience another kind of privilege of whiteness: the opportunity to be viewed as active, dynamic and complex agents. Dominant processes of racialization fix identities for non-white people in ways that generally do not apply to white people. Writing about gay bars and clubs in the real world, Mercer and Julien observe that representations of non-white men are "confined to a narrow repertoire of types—the supersexual stud and the sexual savage on the one hand, the delicate and exotic 'Oriental' on the other" ([Julien and Mercer] 1991:169). Choices placed to non-white men appear to oscillate between the two:

> Far too many of the white men I see in . . . clubs look at me as if to say, "I couldn't sleep with you. You're black." Or they desire me because I am black. (Shepherd 1991:54)

These representations, rooted in the experience of colonialism and empire, are circulated again in cyberspace. Toronto resident "Marshall," a twenty-six-year-old Asian male who regularly goes online, references a common experience among non-white men:

> I find that a lot of guys won't consider me because of my background . . . a lot of guys are not into Asians, or, if they are, are only into submissive Asians, but I'm a top. . . . I've had guys say to me . . . "if I were into Asians I'd totally get with you." I don't exactly consider those compliments, but they're part of my reality and so I deal. (Cited in Sanders 2005:83)

Similarly, "Big_Wolf" says of his experiences on IRC, "if they suspect or find out you are black MANY immediately go to the penis size thing" (Campbell 2004:79).

Byron Burkhalter makes the important point that racial identification occurs differently online. "Stereotyping in face-to-face interaction follows from an assumed racial identity," but online interaction, he says, "differs in that the imputation tends to go in the other direction—from stereotype to racial identity" (1999:73). In real-life situations, the complex, multidimensional realities of racialized peoples also serve to reveal race as a lie. Online, however, fixed stereotypes are the means through which users are received in interactions. "In online interactions," Burkhalter points out, "perspectives resist modification because participants confront an immutable text" (1999:73). There are of course occasions when the exploration of conversations in cyberspace might engage chatters in critical self-reflection—a user might be surprised about his interactions and be challenged to rethink race-based presumptions. But this happens in the real world bars as well, and I would even suggest that spontaneous acts leading to confrontations with and challenges to "race"-based expectations may be more likely to happen in bars than cyberspace. For example, suppose that I believe that I am not interested in forming friendships or relationships, or having sexual encounters with Japanese men. I might, however, walk into a bar and encounter a Japanese man whose gestures, body, or manner are attractive to me. Such a real-life meeting might challenge my imagination to be less fixed, resolve sub-/unconscious desires and undermine my investments in "race." If I come to a gay.com chat room with the same belief, I simply shut off the possibility of speaking to men identifying themselves as Japanese, allowing no opportunity for challenges to the same investments in "race" [which then] proceed, untroubled.

Insofar as racial identification is concerned, white men are generally not subject to this fixing gaze. As Dyer observes about his study of white representation:

> One cannot come up with a limited range of endlessly repeated images, because the privilege of being white in white culture is not to be subjected to stereotyping in relation to one's whiteness. White people are stereotyped in terms of gender, nation, class, sexuality, ability and so on, but the overt point of such typification is gender, nation, etc. Whiteness generally colonizes the stereotypical definition of all social categories other than those of race. To be normal, even to be normally deviant (queer, crippled), is to be white. White people in their whiteness, however, are imaged as individual and/or endlessly diverse, complex and changing. (1997:11–12)

When I represented myself as any kind of non-white man in the chat rooms, my "race" almost always figured into users' reactions. Whatever kind of non-white man I claimed to be, even opposed reactions referenced "race"; some respondents shut down conversations because I was non-white, others pursued me because I was Black/Indian/Chinese, etc. But as blond, blue-eyed Robbie, I was "normal," a complex human whose behavior and personality were not necessarily read through racial tropes. No longer trapped in my skin, I was neither repulsive nor alluring because of it. I was not a member of a group but an individual. I was not a "type" and I spoke for no community but myself. Raced white, I accomplished what Peggy McIntosh identifies as an ultimate achievement of whiteness: the belief that everything a white person does may be accounted for in his/her individuality (1992:70–81). I was imagined as white people were imagined to be: endlessly diverse, complex, and changing (Dyer 1997:12).

## Conclusion/Epilogue

My experiences as "Robbie" seemed to achieve the kinds of experiences imagined by Shepherd and Cho, and revealed motivations for "passing white" and occupying white identities that were similar to their own. Passing white, whether in a chat room for a few hours, over the course of a trouble-free weekend, or, as Shepherd coyly suggests, for "just one night" if not all eternity, appears to be neither an idle expression of identity play, nor a pronouncement of faith in white supremacist mythologies. Those wishing to "pass white" may have no actual desires to inhabit or be with white bodies; I never imagined what "Robbie" might look like, nor was I motivated to undertake this project by conscious desires for white men in particular. Instead, as demonstrated in the analysis of the Toronto chat rooms at gay.com, this act more likely conveys a longing to experience the cultural, social and political privileges afforded to whiteness.

Although Shepherd introduces his "On Not Being White" essay as a reflection on his "obsessive attraction to white men" (1991:47), he provides no explanation other than a yearning to enjoy the same kinds of liberties enjoyed by them. Shepherd writes, "As a child I would go to sleep wishing that when I awoke I would be white" (1991:48). Yet, his imaginative energies are less spent on visualizing himself in a white body than in fleeing the restrictions placed on his movements because of the cultural meanings attached to blackness:

> The burden of my identity, one of the many burdens of my identity, has always been the burden of not being white. . . . I was the wrong one: wrong lips, wrong nose, wrong self. . . .

I've had notions, negative each one, images of what it is to *seem* black: to look black, to talk black, to walk black. . . . If one did not say those things, wear those things, if one didn't do things that way, then one would never, could never be branded with that word, that awful word; though of course one was. (1991:47–49)

Shepherd may want to sleep with white men, but says nothing about what he likes about their bodies. They are described as "beautiful" but [with] no details describing what exactly he likes about white bodies. No yearning is expressed to touch white skin, no allusions to phenotypes associated with white men.

Sexual desires are the consequence of a complicated mess of personal experiences, social relations, and conscious and subconscious anxieties; for Shepherd, a yearning for political liberation is clearly part of that mix:

If I am seen with a beautiful man, not only am I thus one who can acquire a valuable prize but I am by the same operation (as a man having it both ways) transformed into such a prize myself, sought after and acquired by the man I am with. . . . By being seen with him, I am made an honorary white man for so long as I am with him. Suddenly I am part of the community. So by being with him I manage almost to be him. (1991:54)

Writing two decades later than Shepherd, Cho gets right to the point about what motivates her daydreams of becoming white:

What if I didn't have to bend anything? What if there really was a level playing field? I would love to see how far I could actually go. What if all I had to show off was my mad skills? Wouldn't I really be able to fly then? (margaretcho.com/blog, January 23, 2005)

Cho doesn't actually want to be white, just [to] enjoy access to the privileges it affords. Similarly, Shepherd concludes:

My dream? Finally to be "myself," relieved of the baggage of my history both as an individual and as a member of an oppressed race and caste, relieved of my self-despisal in the shining warmth of the beloved's blond approbation. (1991:56)

Passing white in cyberspace makes a similar promise to Shepherd's beloved blond: temporary comfort from—but no absolution from—the inflictions of "race."

### References

Alexander, J., Barrios, B., Blackmon, S., Crow, A., Dorwick, K., Rhodes, J., et al. 2004. "Queerness, Sexuality, Technology and Writing: How Do We Queers Write Ourselves When We Write in Cyberspace?" Retrieved January 20, 2005, from http://acadiana.arthmoor.com/cuppa

Burkhalter, B. 1999. "Reading Race Online: Discovering Racial Identity in USENET Discussions," in M.A. Smith and P. Kollock (Eds.), *Communities in Cyberspace* (pp. 60–75). London: Routledge.

Campbell, J.E. 2004. *Getting It On Online: Cyberspace, Gay Male Sexuality, and Embodied Identity*. London: Harrington Park Press.

Cho, M. 2005. "I Would Love to Be White." Retrieved January 23, 2005, from http://www.margaretcho.com/blog

Dyer, R. 1997. *White*. London: Routledge.

Fanon, F. 1967. *Black Skin, White Masks*. NY: Grove.

Gross, L. 2004. "Preface," in J.E. Campbell, *Getting It On Online: Cyberspace, Gay Male Sexuality, and Embodied Identity* (pp. ix–xii). London: Harrington Park Press.

Julien, I., and Mercer, K. 1991. "True Confessions," in E. Hemphill (Ed.), *Brother to Brother* (pp. 167–173). Boston: Alyson.

McIntosh, P. 1992. "White Privilege and Male Privilege: A Personal Account of Coming to See Correspondences through Work in Women's Studies," in Margaret L. Anderson and Patricia Hill Collins (Eds.), *Race, Class and Gender: An Anthology* (pp. 70–81). Belmont: Wadsworth.

Nakamura, L. 2002. *Cybertypes: Race, Ethnicity and Identity on the Internet*. NY: Routledge.

Plant, S. 1996. "On the Matrix: Cyberfeminist Simulations," in R. Shields (Ed.), *Cultures of the Internet: Virtual Spaces, Real Histories, Living Bodies* (pp. 170–183). London: Sage.

Said, E. 1978. *Orientalism*. London: Routledge.

Sanders, C. 2005. "M4M Online Chat Rooms: The Use of Gay Websites by Men Seeking Men." MA thesis, York University, York, UK.

Seshadri-Crooks, K. 2000. *Desiring White: A Lacanian Analysis of Race*. NY: Routledge.

Shepherd, R. 1991. "On Not Being White," in J. Beam (Ed.), *In the Life: A Black Gay Anthology* (pp. 46–57). Boston: Alyson.

Sunden, J. 2001. "What Happened to Difference in Cyberspace? The (Re)turn of the She-Cyborg." *Feminist Media Studies* 1(2), 215–232.

Tsang, D. 2000. "Notes on Queer 'n' Asian Virtual Sex," in D. Bell and B. Kennedy (Eds.), *The Cybercultures Reader* (pp. 432–438). NY: Routledge.

Turkle, S. 1995. *Life on the Screen: Identity in the Age of the Internet*. NY: Simon & Schuster.

Andil Gosine, "Brown to Blond at Gay.com: Passing White in Queer Cyberspace." *Queer Online: Media, Technology & Sexuality*. Ed. Kate O'Riordan and David J. Phillips. New York: Peter Lang.

## ➢ **Uttarika Kumaran**

(January 31, 2011), India

### **"Disabled, gay, and as normal as you"**

On Saturday, at the Queer Azadi March in Mumbai, thousands from the Indian LGBT (lesbian, gay, bisexual and transgender) community poured onto the streets to show the city once again—lest it forgets—that they exist. But 37-year-old Dinesh Gupta opted out. "I doubt I'd have been able to walk that far or for that long," he says. Dinesh was born with a genetic disorder called osteogenesis imperfecta, which causes bones to break easily, often with little or no apparent cause. His first fracture was when he was two-months old, and by the time he was 13 Dinesh had suffered 14 fractures on various bones below his waist. One of these fractures left him disabled. But once he reached puberty and his bones matured, the fractures stopped.

Only, something else happened. Dinesh began to feel a distinct attraction towards men and realised he was gay. "The same hormonal changes that halted the fractures also aided my sexual development. In a way, I've always felt I am alive because I'm gay."

### Shared history

Historically, both the gay and the disability rights movements have stemmed from a common resistance to what is considered 'normal' in society. By challenging the acceptance of heterosexuality as the norm, people with alternate sexualities often claim to be 'socially disabled'. Disability rights activists too have struggled to overturn barriers that give preference to a particular social construction of the body. At times, the two movements have crossed paths. In 1983 in Minnesota, US, Karen Thompson began an eight-year-long battle to gain access to her live-in partner Sharon Kowalski who was disabled after a car accident and remanded to the guardianship of her parents who denied Thompson visitation rights. With support from the gay and disabled communities, Thompson finally acquired legal guardianship of her partner in 1991.

In India, the concerns of the gay and disabled movements have been independent of each other. Popular culture too has seen very few and narrowly explored meeting points. In 1964, the Hindi film Dosti, directed by Satyen Bose, portrayed the friendship between two boys rejected by society—one blind and the other a cripple, and has since been appropriated in queer readings of Hindi cinema as a metaphor for homosexual repression, but nothing more. It was another Hindi film in 2008, Dostana that threw homosexuality into the limelight and convinced Dinesh to come out. The media lapped up his story, but neglected to ask a crucial question—does being disabled colour his experience as a gay man?

### Bare truths

Being practically bed-ridden while growing up, it took years before Dinesh could confront his sexuality. Studying at home, he completed his graduation and later underwent a surgery that greatly improved his mobility. It was at 26, when he started to venture outdoors on his own that he began to meet men and slowly gain confidence. Despite the relative openness regarding alternative sexual behaviour in Indian society after the 2009 High Court ruling, there has been a stony silence about sexual practices among the physically disabled. In a society where beauty is held in utmost regard, the physically disabled are at an immediate disadvantage. Priti Prabhughate, research director, Humsafar Trust, says, "Even among able-bodied people in the gay community, self-esteem over body image seems to be an issue. For the disabled gay person, it can be doubly difficult."

Dinesh says matter-of-factly, "I've never had a gay partner. Some are bisexual. Many claim to be straight and say they choose to be with me for a short while out of pity. Even if that's true, I'm okay with it because I do have physical needs." Dinesh maintains that he would prefer an able-bodied partner over a disabled one.

### Invisible men

"I would like to reach out and tell my story so that more people like me know they're not alone. I applied to get on Sach Ka Samna but they didn't select me. Then I wanted to be on Raaz Pichle Janam Ka. I'm still waiting to hear from them," says Dinesh. In March 2006, while still in the closet about his sexuality, Dinesh read about Manvendra Singh Gohil, the prince from Gujarat whose coming out made headlines across the world. In August the same year, Dinesh attended his first community programme at Humsafar Trust, a networking and advocacy group serving the needs of the MSM (males who have sex with males) and transgender communities in Mumbai. He says,

"I felt immediately accepted. I heard their stories. I wasn't aware there were so many like us out there." Yet, five years on, Dinesh has yet to meet another gay man with a disability like his.

Unlike the emergence of gay icons and the concept of 'gay pride' that have given the queer movement media visibility, the disability rights movement has failed to generate the same curiosity. "Forget media visibility, Mumbai is among the most disability-unfriendly cities," says Rohini Ramkrishnan, researcher at the Disability Research and Design Foundation, "How often do you see a physically disabled person comfortably using the train or bus? Right now, it's like they don't exist. We just put them in rehab centres and pretend they're not there."

### United, we stand

Disability points to an obvious bodily impairment which influences every aspect of one's interaction with society. The experience of homosexuality is not as disabling on an everyday basis," explains Srilatha Juvva, associate professor, Centre for Disability Studies and Action, TISS. Other disability experts feel that the immense cost of making structural adjustments—such as installing ramps in public places—has resulted in their rights being ignored, including rights pertaining to sexual health. "I feel that the government's HIV efforts don't consider how a physically disabled person has sex. How then will you tell him/her to be safe?" asks Prabhughate of the Hunsafar Trust.

One of the main reasons for the success of the queer movement has been the alliance of sexuality and gender-identity based communities under one umbrella-term called LGBT. A similar model in the disability rights field, especially in the wake of the framing of the UNCRPD & Disability Act 2010, seems the need of the hour. In the meantime, ask Dinesh whether he identifies with his gay identity or his disabled one, he replies, "I'm proud to say I'm gay." Some day, he might be proud to say he's disabled too.

---

From http://www.dnaindia.com/lifestyle/report_disabled-gay-and-as-normal-as-you_1500718.

# CHAPTER 15

# The Politics of Location

*Alternative Media and the Search for Queer Space*

A variety of media have assisted LGBT people in developing both identity and community. These media have at turns facilitated and hindered political activism and consciousness.

The experience of living queer has typically been located at the crossroads of embodiment and disembodiment. We are defined by our corporeal selves, our sexual desires and affectional preferences. As David Bell and Jon Binnie write, "[E]roticism is the basis of [our] community" (87). We tell each other to come out because we wish to be visible as queer; we wish to embody a real identity. Simultaneously, we are disembodied by our cultures. We are ordered to disappear, to inhabit a closet where we can't be seen by the straights, the young, and the innocent. We are told not to "speak its name," not to "flaunt it." Our experience of culture—our sexual citizenship, as it were—is fraught with this uncomfortable double consciousness. We often engage in commerce, in the arts, in political activism, precisely to find a visible, viable place in our culture, a place where our embodied identities need not feel the erasure of a closeting hegemony. Jeffrey Weeks argues that the sexual citizen "makes a claim to transcend the limits of the personal sphere by going public, but the going public is, in a necessary but nevertheless paradoxical move, about protecting the possibilities of private life and private choice." This way of doing citizenship, Weeks goes on to say, is the only way that "difference can [ever] find a proper home" (37). Let us think about the concept of *home* as it relates to LGBT people.

> Gays and lesbians do not have a "home" to return to, either in territorial/historical terms or in the sense of present-day enclaves; most gays and lesbians live amidst their heterosexual families and neighbors without the promise even of a local community center to find affirmation and support. Most grow up convinced that they are "the only one" in their communities. Urban centers ameliorate this situation for those with the resources and desire to relocate, but such relocation involves a separation from, and often a rejection of, their community of birth. Those who do not want to live in cities, or who cannot so choose, often live their lives in isolation. Even those who create a home or a common culture are in a situation drastically different from that faced by racial, ethnic, or national groups; such cultures and homes are created as adults, after the experience of isolation and rejection from one's family and community. (Phelan 30)

Queer "homes," then, are intensely sought after but (for many) ephemeral spaces, purchased through the *pink economy,* that mythical entity accessible only to rich entitled gay men and lesbians.

In this chapter, we consider how some types of alternative media—as opposed to the more mainstream media products discussed earlier in this book—are used by LGBT people to build community. We classify as "alternative" those media that have two characteristics: they aim to reach a particular (limited) audience, specifically a group that seeks knowledge and validation of a point of view; and they lie outside the realm of "mainstream" media, that is, high-budget, high-visibility productions that stand to gross millions of dollars at the box office, newsstand, or bookstore. Any of the media we discussed earlier—film, television, and the Internet—can have both mainstream and alternative manifestations. For instance, documentary films, unlike feature films, are typically shown in small-seating art theaters. They play to an educated, culturally elite audience, and studios spend little on advertising and promotion. Keeping this distinction between *mainstream* and *alternative* in mind, we begin with the assumption that cultural artifacts—such as comic strips, independent documentary films and music, LGBT newspapers and newsletters, and even festivals such as the Michigan Womyn's Music Festival (MWMF)—are produced and consumed to fulfill particular needs. One of the overriding needs seems to have to do with the search for community, a sense of home.

# Documentary Films

The documentary *Flag Wars* (Zeitgeist 2003, dir. Linda Goode Bryant and Laura Poitras) was advertised as "a poignant account of the politics and pain of gentrification. Working-class black residents in Columbus, Ohio fight to hold on to their homes. Realtors and gay home-buyers see fixer-uppers. The clashes expose prejudice and self-interest on both sides, as well as the common dream to have a home to call your own" ("Flag Wars"). On one level, the opposition is direct: "We didn't have any problems till they moved in here," says a straight black resident. "If you don't want to renovate it, don't live in it," counters a white gay man. But *Flag Wars* is far more complex than this simple juxtaposition might suggest. It elucidates some traditional cultural divides: between rich and poor, gay and straight, black and white, even traditional and contemporary. These divides complicate what can be characterized as the search for community undertaken by many LGBT people. It's not uncommon to think of LGBT people as displaced and disenfranchised, and those characterizations are in many ways accurate, but this film asks what happens when the supposedly disenfranchised have access to the culture's resources—money and the legal system, for example—and use them to enfranchise themselves in new locations. The questions addressed in *Flag Wars* have to do with what transpires when LGBT people begin establishing homes in locations where others are already living and with balancing the benefits to a community when property is materially "improved" at the cost of pricing out those who already live in it.

Jon Binnie reminds us that "[i]t is one of the touchstones of the geographies of sexualities that it is only possible to be queer in certain places and spaces. The search for fixity is one in which gay men and lesbians participate endlessly" (82). *Flag Wars* shows us both the need that gay gentrifiers have for habitable home space and community in an often hostile world, as well as the need current residents of urban neighborhoods have to hold onto the home spaces that sustain them. Both see themselves as the "rightful" inhabitants of the neighborhood—gentrifiers because their work "improves" the area's cultural capital and the current residents because they have built lives for themselves in the very homes others would "improve." Although the film seems at first to lay blame for the community conflict at the feet of gay white people—like a lesbian real estate agent whose attitude could be described as predatory—the filmmakers are finally careful to show "that villain and hero, victim and victimizer, good and bad are aspects of all of us" (Bryant). We see how both groups—black residents and gay gentrifiers—have been victimized by social, cultural, and legal forces. The real estate agent, referring to a string of muggings and robberies, justifies her presence in the neighborhood by saying, "We're all busting our ass out here trying to make a difference." A black community leader fighting to keep a colorful sign over his front door in defiance of housing codes remarks, "They've got a free right to occupy. It's our responsibility to keep our own identity."

In *Flag Wars*, then, the issue of identity for both groups is key to their understanding of home. In some of the same ways, the documentary film *Shinjuku Boys* (20th Century Vixen, 1995, dir. Kim Longinotto and Jano Williams)

**Figure 15.1** Still from *Shinjuku Boys*.

explores the connection between identity—in this case, a number of so-called Onnabes, described by the narrator as "women who have decided to live as men"—and the quest for place. The film is set in Japan and follows several Onnabes working in Tokyo's New Marilyn Club, whose clientele is "almost exclusively heterosexual women who have become disappointed with born men" ("Annabe"). The melancholy tone of the film results primarily from the exclusion experienced by the Onnabes—not only from tradition-bound patriarchal Japanese culture but also from that culture's normative identity categories. Although the women who visit the New Marilyn Club consider the Onnabes "ideal men" and compete for their attention, outside the club, the "boys" themselves, living as men but without the privilege of men-born-men, lack a home in the culture. Another documentary, *Dangerous Living: Coming Out in the Developing World* (After Stonewall Productions 2003, dir. John Scagliotti), offers narratives from lesbian, gay, and transgender-identified people in the Global South who are seeking both physical safety and a sense of home in often extremely hostile environments. Opening with the story of a Cairo resident, Ashraf Zanati, who was "tortured, humiliated, beaten and forced to spend 13 months in prison" ("Dangerous Living"), the film shows how queer visibility in some parts of the world can complicate the move to create community. The film characterizes the search for home in highly personal ways. Zanati powerfully declares, "My sexuality is my own sexuality. It doesn't belong to anybody. Not to my government, not to my brother, my sister, my family. No." Zanati sees the claiming of his sexuality as a move away from his family, perhaps even his country of origin. But the reality of sexuality lies in its embeddedness, not just in personal conceptions of self but in social, cultural, and even political matrices. The search for home, then, can rarely be an individual journey, as personal as it may seem; it is often a collective journey, as groups attempt to form new families, communities, and counter-publics.

# Film and Music Festivals

Film and music festivals have historically been configured as locations where LGBT people can meet to enjoy creative expressions of queer identification. These festivals are venues for viewing and distributing truly independent films whose makers lack the deep pockets for advertising that mainstream filmmakers enjoy. LGBT and queer film festivals are commonplace in many parts of the world. A quick Google search provides links to advertisements for film festivals in many countries—Italy, Australia, the United States, the Canary Islands, Spain, and Canada, to name just a few. In fact, the PlanetOut website lists more than 150 lesbian and gay film festivals, many of which occur annually. This proliferation leads GLBTQ.com to ask whether these film festivals are "still necessary given the significant number of gay-themed films now seeing wider theatrical distribution" [λ Chapter 13]. In many ways, the answer is yes, they are, given that queers are a "complex people yearning for the experience of community—being together, sharing our different realities, exchanging ideas, cruising each other." LGBT film festivals are one of the "relatively few places where we get to experience community" ("Film Festivals").

Like film festivals, music festivals provide spaces for LGBT people to create community through creative expression. GALA (Gay & Lesbian Association) Choruses has as its mission "to support GLBT choruses as we change our world through song." Claiming the Philadelphia-based Anna Crusis Women's Choir, founded in 1975, as their "most-tenured" group, GALA boasts a membership of more than 100 choruses and 10,000 singers worldwide. The organization, which hosts periodic international and regional gatherings, holds concerts that attract not only queer participants but major musical and arts celebrities, such as Maya Angelou, Natalie Cole, Liza Minnelli, Holly Near, and Kate Clinton ("About GALA Choruses").

GALA festival performances are often profound experiences for participants, reflecting the diversity of queer life and community. Catherine Roma, founder of both Anna Crusis and MUSE, Cincinnati's Women's Choir, notes that "every

**Figure 15.2**  MUSE, Cincinnati's Women's Choir.

movement for social change has been accompanied by strong singing." She goes on to say, "We in the gay and lesbian choral movement are really just in a long line of music for social change . . . the labor movement, the civil rights movement, the women's liberation movement" (Roma). A desire for such "social change" has found not just musical expression but also political expression in the work of many LGBT choruses in response to the AIDS crisis. Gay men's choruses in New York and San Francisco, for example, raised significant amounts of money and generated much volunteer time to address AIDS, even as their membership was being decimated by the epidemic ("Gay Men's Chorus").

Unlike film festivals and choral festivals, which inhabit different physical spaces year by year, the MWMF is tied to a particular place in central Michigan (called "The Land" by festie-goers). Boden Sandstrom writes, "The Festival was created as separate . . . 'womyn-only' space isolated from the hegemonic culture" (47). The MWMF first took place in 1976, a time when some lesbians were forming separatist groups [λ Chapter 4] on a communitarian model, based on "feminist political analysis which rejected the patriarchal and capitalist system" (77). The MWMF is the result of a conscious "process of building and creating an environment according to [women's] own vision" (111). Stressing this utopian feel, Bonnie Morris's book about women's music festivals, including Michigan, is titled *Eden Built by Eves*. After nearly 40 years of existence, and despite weathering some intense ideological storms, Michigan still functions as a safe "home" for lesbian (and some other) women [λ Chapter 6]. Sandstrom quotes a Michigan festie-goer talking about her experiences: "Coming into the total women's space of the festival was definitely a culture clash/shock initially. I felt a gradual relaxing of mind and muscle, and when I began to drink [at] this new well, my thirst was insatiable." She speaks of Michigan as "coming back home," contrasting its "warmth and support" with the "straight, patriarchal world [that] shakes and rattles and threatens" (283).

**Figure 15.3**   2008 MWMF poster.

# Queer Music

Certainly, queer music has its mainstream and commercial dimensions, and a number of openly lesbian, gay, and bisexual pop and rock artists have enriched the popular music industry and have served as role models for any number of young queer people. Elton John, Melissa Etheridge, and Michael Stipe of R.E.M (who identifies as a "queer artist") are among the most successful of such musicians. Still, not all of the "out" musicians address queer issues in their music, and if they do, they often do so in covert or subtle ways. At times, gay artists (George Michael, for example) are outed against their will, and other seemingly queer-friendly artists, such as Madonna or, more recently, Lady Gaga, are accused of using homo- and bi-eroticism to be edgy and enhance their notoriety. So we are left with a crucial question: can we count on these artists to directly address the concerns and issues of queer people? To find the music that speaks—or sings—to this question, many look to alternative music and musical venues, which often eschew or limit ties to the corporate music industry in the hopes of maintaining a high degree of autonomy and freedom to pursue particular artistic visions.

Central to the MWMF experience is, of course, the music, a particular subgenre called Women's Music. To some extent a product of the lesbian-feminist genera-tion but also appealing to younger women, the Women's Music phenomenon combines lesbian-feminist politics with intense emotional self-expression. Begin-ning in the early 1970s with the self-consciously feminist music and lyrics of Alix Dobkin, Maxine Feldman, Linda Tillery, and others, Women's Music crossed into the "mainstream" with k.d. lang, Ani DiFranco, Tracy Chapman, the Indigo Girls, and contemporary artists such as the Cliks. Composers including Kay Gardner and Therese Edell have used a contemporary classical style to celebrate spaces women have created, specifically the MWMF. Gardner's ritual music for Michigan and her Wiccan oratorio *Ouruboros* and Edell's Michigan festival anthem "Gather In" all express women's need for safe and empowering community.

The new Women's Music subgenre galvanized many lesbians into seeking and creating venues where all aspects of production—recording, mixing, sound quality, and so forth—were done by women. In 1972, Holly Near began bring-ing out albums on her Redwood label, and the next year, Alix Dobkin inaugu-rated Women's Wax Works. But "the most influential, most quintessential, most lesbionic label" was Olivia Records (Baumgardner). Cofounded in 1973 by Judy Dlugacz and other members of the Furies and Radicalesbians collectives in Washington, DC [λ Chapter 4], its purpose was to record, distribute, and mar-ket women's music. Olivia's first 45-rpm record featured Meg Christian on one side and Cris Williamson on the other; it brought in $12,000, enough to make Christian's first album, *Now You Know,* and then Williamson's blockbuster, *The Changer and the Changed. Changer* sold 60,000 to 80,000 copies in its first year and, as of 2007, had sold more than 300,000 copies. Its success allowed Olivia to outsource its distribution end, which became Goldenrod Music in 1975. In 1976, Laurie Fuchs established Ladyslipper, "a mail order catalog devoted to

**Figure 15.4** Romanovsky and Phillips just moments after receiving the Heritage Award from Outmusic, New York City, 2003.

distributing women's music." Fuchs recalls, "When I first started the catalog, I thought I could cover everything recorded by women"—and ironically, in the mid-1970s, that was not outside the realm of possibility (Baumgardner). Olivia and the other labels established a powerful presence at Michigan and other music festivals in the United States, cementing the relationship between performance venues and alternative labels in the popularization of Women's Music.

Inspired by feminism and its musical offshoots, Mehn's music, written and performed by males, bills itself as anti-patriarchal. According to Ron Romanovsky of the gay music group Romanovsky & Phillips, Mehn's music arises out of a "movement of gay and straight men who are [invested in] creating non-sexist music" ("Mehn's Music").

Believing that most Western music has been patriarchal, with male composers dominating music "his"tory, Romanovsky and others, such as Mark Weigle, Doug Stevens, and the group Pansy Division, promote music that decries sexism and homophobia while celebrating male intimacy and homoerotic sexuality. Michael Callen (1955–1993), among the most famous of gay male songwriters, wrote poignantly about the need to revise normative conceptions of love, family, and community to create a space in which queer people could find respect. In his song "Redefine the Family," Callen composed an anthem in praise of alternative family constructions:

> My lover's name is Richard
> His lover's name is Pat
> We're one big happy family
> Is there a box for that?
> We live here with Pam and Lyn
> They're lesbians and lovers
> Together, we're raising three great kids
> Gertrude, and her two brothers. (Callen)

Recordings of Mehn's music are most readily available through distributors that specialize in women's and lesbian music, such as Ladyslipper.

# LGBT Journalism: Magazines, Newspapers, and Comics

I n *Unspeakable: The Rise of the Gay and Lesbian Press in America,* journalist Rodger Streitmatter contends,

> The most important single contribution lesbian and gay journalism has made—and will continue to make—may be one most straight people simply are not able to fathom. For half a century, reading gay publications has served as a first tenuous step for men and women embarking on the very personal, and often profoundly difficult, journey toward acknowledging their homosexuality to themselves and the world around them. (347)

Like the pulps and pictorials of the post–World War II period, early gay and lesbian newsletters let queers across the country know that they were not alone [λ Chapters 3 and 10]. But beyond providing touchstones for identifications and pleas for tolerance and understanding, gay and lesbian writers for newsletters, magazines, and other periodicals borrowed from the activist energies of the 1960s and 1970s to begin organizing queers communally and politically. Streitmatter notes that "America's alternative media have evolved because groups of people outside the mainstream of society—most notably African Americans and women—historically have been denied a voice in conventional media networks" (308). Gay and lesbian activists claimed journalistic spaces to promote increasingly politicized agendas, and magazines such as *The Advocate* provided journalistic coverage of social, cultural, and political issues of concern to gay and lesbian people. When *The Advocate* was still a local Los Angeles newspaper in the late 1960s, its writers attempted to mobilize queers to fight back against homophobic legal injustice. Writing about how L.A. police broke into a private residence to arrest two men on charges of "lewd conduct," *The Advocate* devoted its front page to urging gays to respond:

> We are bleeding now, and L.A. Gays sit in their big homes and fancy apartments planning their next garden party. Wake up! It isn't just the bar queer and the street walker who is in danger. Our fancy homes and apartments are no longer all that safe. Our lives and our freedom are on the line. (qtd. in Streitmatter 148)

While *The Advocate* continues today, offering U.S. LGBT people a prominent source of news about issues facing queer people, some short-lived publications from the 1960s and 1970s offered more radical advice. For instance, *Come Out!* "urged the annihilation of the nuclear family," and *Killer Dyke* "called for eliminating mental institutions, marriage, private property, and the state" and for all Americans to be given "free food, free housing, free clothing, free education, and free marijuana" (Streitmatter 150). The vision espoused by such publications was often one that agitated for an interrogation or reimagining of the idea of *home* at local and national levels. The advent of the AIDS crisis in the 1980s propelled a growing number of publications, such as *The Advocate* and *Outweek,* to address the homophobia that made the government largely silent about a disease disproportionately affecting gay men [λ Chapter 4]. These publications were not beyond bickering among themselves, with *Outweek,* for instance, criticizing *The Advocate* for advertising porn videos depicting unsafe sex practices (Streitmatter 280–81).

Political journalism relating to LGBT issues continues with *The Washington Blade,* which claims to be the "oldest LGBT newspaper in the United States," having been founded in 1969. Situated in Washington, DC, with versions in other major metropolitan areas, the *Blade* provides detailed coverage of issues such as gay marriage, gays in the military, and politicians who support (or not) a variety of LGBT concerns and issues. Comparable kinds of magazines and newspapers have sprung up throughout the world. Some originate in countries where LGBT organizing has been going on for decades: *Gay Times, QX Magazine, Diva,* and *Capital Gay* in England, for instance, or the *Sydney Star Observer, Bi the Way,* and *Brother Sister* in Australia. Other publications chronicle emerging LGBT consciousness in countries that are just beginning to articulate it: *Masok* from Hungary, *Lambda* from Turkey, *Gay News FILO* and *INACZEJ* from Poland, *O Pothos* from Greece, and *Kekec* from

**Find Out More:** Consider the claim in Michael Sibalis's article on Paris's Marais district at the end of this chapter: "Consommer gay, c'est s'affirmer" (To consume gay is to affirm oneself). Do you agree?

Slovenia represent a few examples. It is clear that, throughout the world, LGBT magazines and newspapers constitute a lifeline, a necessary link and introduction to queer community for those already connected to it and for those seeking such community for the first time.

Today, a number of "lifestyle" magazines, such as *Out, Girlfriends, Genre* (for "smart, stylish, and tuned in" gay men), and *Gay Times,* offer not only political commentary but social and cultural news, fashion advice, and consumer reports. Understanding the increasing buying power of queer markets, these magazines are often loaded with advertisements from corporations that seek a share of the "gay dollar." While such magazines may pander to a middle- and upper-class gay market, they still speak to attempts to create a sense of community, even on a national scale, for many queer people.

Important attractions included in many LGBT magazines and newspapers are gay-themed cartoons and comic strips. Over the past three decades, these publications and, more recently, the Internet have enabled LGBT cartoonists to reach a wide audience with their pointed commentaries on queer life. Eric Orner's "playfully self-reflexive . . . and surrealistic" strips narrating "The Mostly Unfabulous

Social Life of Ethan Green" and Michael-Christopher's series "Living the Life" first became famous after appearing in gay-themed publications. According to Reyhan Harmanci, Orner's Ethan Green appeared in "more than a hundred newspapers and alt-weeklies in America and Europe" before being made into a movie in 2006. "Living the Life" was aimed specifically at black gay men and ran in *WHASSUP!* and *CLIKQUE* magazines. In 1991, Diane DiMassa introduced "Hothead Paisan: Homicidal Lesbian Terrorist," which appeared in Robert Kirby's *Strange-Looking Exile, The Advocate,* and elsewhere. DiMassa describes Hothead Paisan as "comics for the fed-

**Figure 15.5** Panel from DiMassa's "Hothead Paisan," Dyke Strippers.

up, rage therapy for the marginalized. Way cheaper than a shrink." DiMassa's "lesbian terrorist" contrasts sharply with Alison Bechdel's "Dykes to Watch Out For" (DTWOF), whose strips began in the 1980s in such publications as *Chicago Gay Life, Hot Wire, Lesbian Contradiction,* and *Womanews* then moved to paperback collections until Bechdel stopped writing the series in 2008. DTWOF "documents the life, loves, and politics of a fairly diverse group of characters (most of them lesbians) ... featuring both humorous soap-opera storylines and biting topical commentary" ("Dykes").

Set in several domestic locations—a women's bookstore, characters' homes, a commune where four of the characters live—Bechdel's DTWOF makes much of the daily interactions among characters Mo, Sparrow, Ginger, Tony, Sydney, Clarice, Jezanna, and others. Readers of the strip become intimately involved in the lives of these characters as they work their way through the books. When Tony and Clarice and their son Raffi move to the suburbs, we wonder how they will, as an interracial lesbian couple, be received by their new neighbors. And when Clarice locks horns with one of those neighbors over Raffi's insistence that he "can too marry Stone Cold Steve Austin" when he grows up, readers are invited to see the poignancy and humor of the moment when the neighbor child responds (much to his father's chagrin), "You can not, 'cause I'm gonna marry him, and we're gonna kick your butt" (*Post-Dykes* 77). Bechdel's work, like much lesbian and gay literature, also uses specific kinds of inside jokes, many of which have to do with romantic relationships and domestic issues. In one of her earliest collections, *Dykes to Watch Out For: Great Romances That Never Were,* Bechdel's "Guide to the First

**Find Out More** in Alison Bechdel's graphic memoirs *Fun Home* (a 2006 National Book Critics Circle award finalist for autobiography) and *Are You My Mother?* (2012).

Sleepover" provides a number of dos and don'ts for the first date, one of which is "Don't Get Carried Away," a panel that shows one woman asking another, "So, when are you moving in?" This reference is picked up again on the cover of *Split-Level Dykes to Watch Out For,* where Clarice, Tony, and Raffi are shown moving into their suburban home with the aid of the strip's other characters and a truck from "Y'All Haul." These references are to one of the longest-running lesbian inside jokes: what does a lesbian bring on the second date? A U-Haul.

The U-Haul joke reflects lesbians' (and, by extension, LGBT people's in general) desire to establish meaningful home spaces in a world that does not endorse nonnuclear, nonheterosexual families. Queer partners in DTWOF face rejection from their families of origin. Toni, for instance, refuses her father's request that she leave Clarice and "come home with us so Rafael can grow up in a real family" (*Hot Throbbing* 57). Sparrow's parents threaten, "If you expect to inherit a penny from us, we insist you marry this man" (*Dykes and Sundry* 153). In a real sense, much of DTWOF claims the right of queer people to form families of choice and establish "homesteads" in the face of a world that enforces compulsory heterosexuality [λ Chapter 5].

## Many Journeys, Many Homes

**M**any of the alternative media and media venues we have been discussing in this chapter find homes for production and dissemination in what have come to be known as *gay ghettos*—urban areas that LGBT people have claimed as their own in some of the world's largest metropolitan areas. Locales such as the Castro in San Francisco, West Hollywood in Los Angeles, Greenwich Village in New York City, the Via San Giovanni in the Laterano district of Rome, or the Oxford Street area in Sydney, Australia, contain concentrations of queer-owned businesses, stores, entertainment complexes, sex shops, and housing. Often figured as refuges for LGBT people, gay ghettos serve as home for many queers who have migrated to large urban areas in search of greater freedom for self-expression; local and even national gay rights organizations often have headquarters and offices alongside the shops that queers frequent. These areas also support a variety of alternative media, including independent bookstores featuring books from gay and gay-friendly presses, movie theaters offering annual LGBT film festivals, and coffee shops providing access to numerous new weeklies, many of which are free. In these ways, the ghettos offer a sense of home that is often markedly different from that experienced by many queer people who grow up in households that are intolerant of their sexual and affectional desires. But they are more than just places of escape; they offer the opportunity to reinvent the idea of home—in often very queer, non-normative, and unexpected ways.

In the United States, these neighborhoods arose in the decades following World War II, when many men and women found themselves shipped overseas or relocated to metropolitan areas after being drafted into either the army or the wartime workforce. After the war, many lesbians and gays decided to stay in the metropolitan areas that served as their ports of embarkation. As urban areas underwent a variety of changes in the mid to late 20th century, including

**Figure 15.6**    Street scene from Paris, Marais district.

the move of middle-class people into the suburbs, many queers moved into abandoned or decaying urban areas to revitalize them, claiming a home. In some ways, we might describe this movement of queers as a kind of diaspora—perhaps an inverse diaspora in which a group isn't forced to leave a homeland and disperse but rather exists as a dispersed people journeying toward home and community. This search for home is not without cost; the gentrification described in *Flag Wars* can be one of the negative consequences of the development of gay neighborhoods in that some queer people renovate and remodel existing communities into fashionable districts, pricing out previous residents. At the same time, commentator Richard Florida suggests that the presence of a strong and visible gay community is a sign of health in American cities; such communities speak to both a city's acceptance of diversity and its support of creative pursuits, such as alternative media.

One question that might arise concerning this chapter is how film and music festivals, as well as urban neighborhoods where LGBT people tend to live or visit, fit into a chapter about alternative media. Festivals and neighborhoods are, after all, locations rather than artifacts of creative expression. But if we look more closely, we recognize that alternative media depend on a kind of communal sharing, or word of mouth for their distribution and popularity. And more often than not, festivals and neighborhoods where LGBT people congregate are sites for exchange of information about new films, music, news, and ideas. Even this way of understanding festivals and neighborhoods, though, ignores what is perhaps a less obvious reality about these locations—namely, that their communal nature facilitates the exchange and development of creative work by bringing together diverse populations of people who share some similar interests. These places embody the *homing desire* that Anne-Marie Fortier says is "about *motions of attachment*":

> It is lived in motions: the motions of journeying between homes, the motions of hailing ghosts from the past, the motions of leaving or staying put, of "moving on" or "going back," the motions of cutting or adding, the motions of continual reprocessing of what home is/was/might have been. But "home" is also remembered by attaching it, even momentarily, to a place where we strive to *make* home and to bodies and relationships that touch us, have touched us, in meaningful ways. (130–31)

The locations where LGBT alternative creative expressions are nurtured and shared are thus "homes" in this dynamic sense, for they enable attachment to "bodies and relationships that touch us." For LGBT people, reinvented concepts of home and family through alternative spaces, activities, and artifacts can function as lifelines to community. These various aspects of communal experience have allowed many queer people—especially those in prosperous nations who have access to the resources available in large metropolitan centers—to construct a coherent identity-based subculture, a queer home.

## QUESTIONS FOR DISCUSSION

1. The term *alternative media* is most often used to refer to media that fall outside the mainstream and are not corporately supported. In this chapter, we have defined it more broadly as a result of our sense that much media geared directly at an LGBT audience qualify as *alternative* in a world where many mainstream communications corporations are still hesitant to support work that deals with nonnormative sexuality. What do you think about the choices we have made? Write us a letter in which you make a cogent and well-developed case for your agreement or disagreement with our choices in this area. If you can find colleagues in your class with whom to discuss this issue, find out what they think and make your letter a community effort.

2. Throughout this chapter, we have evoked "the search for home" as a significant dimension of LGBT experience. This concept can be problematized in many ways: such a frame can be read as "normalizing" LGBT lives by making them fit a heteronormative model, the diversity of definitions of the word *home* can get lost if the term is used too generally, and the concept of *home* is often used in capitalist societies to encourage uncritical participation in economic acquisition. What do you think about the way a journey toward a sense of home is used in this chapter? Do you accept it as related to alternative media and space? Why or why not?

3. As this is the last chapter, we assume that you have now read all or most of the book. What have you learned? What has surprised you? What has disappointed you? What do you want to know more about? Write a short paper or journal entry in which you explore more fully through careful research an issue you have read about in *Finding Out*. Share the results by preparing a presentation or publication with a specific audience in mind.

**References and Further Reading**

"About GALA Choruses." N.d., n.p. Web. 6 Aug. 2008. <http://www.galachoru ses.org/about/about_gala.html>.

"Annabe." *Women in Suits—Eye Candy,* n.d. Web. 6 Aug. 2008. <http://www.dande liondesign.ca/Ties/ties2.html>.

Baumgardner, Jennifer. "Women's Music 101." *Z Magazine,* 1 Aug. 2007. Web. 6 Aug. 2008. <http://www.zmag.org/ZMag/arti cles/women%20music.htm>.

Bechdel, Alison. *Dykes and Sundry Other Carbon-Based Life-Forms to Watch Out For.* New York: Alyson, 2003. Print.

———. *Dykes to Watch Out For: Great Romances That Never Were.* Ithaca, NY: Firebrand, 1986. Print.

———. *Hot Throbbing Dykes to Watch Out For.* Ithaca, NY: Firebrand, 1997. Print.

———. *The Indelible Alison Bechdel: Confessions, Comix, and Miscellaneous Dykes to Watch Out For.* Ithaca, NY: Firebrand, 1998. Print.

———. *Post-Dykes to Watch Out For.* Ithaca, NY: Firebrand, 2000. Print.

———. *Split-Level Dykes to Watch Out For.* Ithaca, NY: Firebrand, 1998: 79. Print.

Bell, David, and Jon Binnie. *The Sexual Citizen: Queer Politics and Beyond.* Cambridge, UK: Polity, 2000. Print.

Binnie, Jon. *The Globalization of Sexuality.* London: Sage, 2004. Print.

Bryant, Linda Goode. "Filmmaker Interview." N.p., n.d. Web. 6 Aug. 2008. <http://www.pbs.org/pov/pov2003/ flagwars/behind_interview.html>.

Callen, Michael. "Redefine the Family." *Legacy* Lyrics, n.d. Web. 6 Aug. 2008. <http://hometown.aol.com/sigothinc/ topdisc1.htm>.

"Dangerous Living." Al-Fatiha Foundation: The First-Ever Queer Muslim Film Festival Program Guide, n.d. Web. 6 Aug. 2008. <http://www.al-fatiha .org/docs/conference2004films.pdf>.

DiMassa, Diane. "Hothead Paisan: Homicidal Lesbian Terrorist." N.p., n.d. Web. 6 Aug. 2008. <http://hotheadpai san.com/>.

"Dykes to Watch Out For." N.p., n.d. Web. 6 Aug. 2008. <http://en.wikipedia.org/ wiki/Dykes_to_Watch_Out_For>.

Farley, Christopher John. "Michael Stipe and the Ageless Boys of R.E.M." *Time,* 14 May 2001. Web. 6 Aug. 2008. <http:// www.time.com/time/sampler/article /0,8599,109715,00.html>.

"Film Festivals." *GLBTQ: An Encyclopedia of Gay, Lesbian, Bisexual, Transgender, & Queer Culture,* n.d. Web. 6 Aug. 2008. <http://www.glbtq.com/arts/film_fes tivals.html>.

"Flag Wars." N.p., n.d. Web. 6 Aug. 2008. <http://www.pbs.org/pov/pov2003/ flagwars/>.

Florida, Richard. *The Rise of the Creative Class.* New York: Basic Books, 2002. Print.

Fortier, Anne-Marie. "Making Home: Queer Migrations and Motions of Attachment." *Uprootings/Regroundings: Questions of Home and Migration.* Eds. Sara Ahmed, Claudia Castaneda, and Anne-Marie Fortier. New York: Berg, 2003. 115–36. Print.

"Gay Men's Chorus Carries on after Death of 257 Members." *A Cappella News,* 5 June 2006. Web. 27 Aug. 2012. <http://www .acappellanews.com/archive/001199 .html>.

Halberstam, Judith. *In a Queer Time and Place: Transgender Bodies, Subcultural Lives.* New York: NYU P, 2005. Print.

Harmanci, Reyhan. "Pioneer Gay Comic Strip Hero Ethan Green Finally Snags a Date with the Big Screen." *San Francisco Chronicle,* 29 June 2006. Web. 6 Aug. 2008. <http://sfgate.com/cgi-bin/article.cgi?file=/c/a/2006/06/29/DDG3FJLBDO1.DTL>.

"Mehn's Music." *Ladyslipper Music Online Catalogue,* n.d. Web. 6 Aug. 2008. <http://www.ladyslipper.org/rel/v2_home.php?storenr=53&deptnr=58>.

Michael-Christopher. *Living the Life,* n.d. Web. 6 Aug. 2008. <http://productionsfirehorse.com/ltl-gne.html>.

Morris, Bonnie. *Eden Built by Eves.* New York: Alyson, 1999. Print.

Orner, Eric. "The Mostly Unfabulous Social Life of Ethan Green." N.p., n.d. Web. 6 Aug. 2008. <http://www.ethangreen.com/books.html>.

Phelan, Shane. *Sexual Strangers: Gays, Lesbians, and Dilemmas of Citizenship.* Philadelphia: Temple UP, 2001. Print.

Roma, Catherine. "Interview: *Why We Sing.*" N.p., n.d. Web. 6 Aug. 2008. <http://www.cetconnect.org/msie_video.asp?id=1371>.

Sandstrom, Boden. *Performance, Ritual and Negotiation of Identity in the Michigan Womyn's Music Festival.* Diss. Ethnomusicology, University of Maryland at College Park, 2002. Print.

Streitmatter, Rodger. *Unspeakable: The Rise of the Gay and Lesbian Press in America.* Boston: Faber & Faber, 1995. Print.

Weeks, Jeffrey. "The Sexual Citizen." *Love and Eroticism.* Ed. Mike Featherstone. London: Sage, 1999. 35–52. Print.

# READINGS

> ## Michael Sibalis

(August 2004), Canada

---

### From "Urban Space and Homosexuality: The Example of the Marais, Paris' 'Gay Ghetto'"

#### *Gay Men and Urban Space in Paris*

. . . Gay men have a special relationship to urban space. Only in cities are there enough homosexually inclined men to permit the emergence of a self-aware community with its own commercial venues, social and political organisations and distinctive sub-culture. In the words of the Danish sociologist Henning Bech, "being homosexual is a way of *being*, a *form of existence.*" Homosexuals belong to one of a number of social worlds (Bech does not identify the others) that are all essentially urban: they are largely worlds of strangers and not just of personal acquaintances; they depend in part upon the non-personal, urban free flow of signs and information, as well as upon the pool of strangers, for recruitment and reproduction; they occupy time-space slices of the city and need urban stages to be enacted on (Bech 153–156).

We know a great deal about the urban spaces used by Parisian homosexuals (generally called "sodomites" or "pederasts" before 1900) since the early 1700s, both outdoor ones (parks, gardens, riverbanks, quays and streets) and indoor ones (taverns, bars, clubs and restaurants). In the 18th and 19th centuries, these were spread across the city, but were usually situated on its margins, either literally (on its physical periphery) or figuratively (in poorer and seamier districts). Beginning in the 1880s, however, commercial venues catering to homosexuals clustered in the Montmartre quarter of northern Paris, known for bohemianism and illicit sexuality, including female prostitution. In the 1920s and 1930s, other districts, like the Rue de Lappe near the Bastille or Montparnasse in the south, also became important to Paris' homosexual sub-culture. After the Second World War, homosexuals frequented the bars, clubs and cafés of the Left Bank district of Saint-Germain-des-Prés, the centre of post-war intellectual life and non-conformity. In the 1970s, homosexual nightlife migrated across the Seine to the streets between the Palais-Royal and the Opera House and, most famously, to the Rue Sainte-Anne. In marked contrast to Montmartre and Saint-Germain, this was a quiet residential and business neighbourhood, almost deserted after the workday ended; the possibility of going out in relative secrecy is probably what attracted gay customers to its venues.

The popularity of the Rue Sainte-Anne lasted hardly more than a decade. In June 1983, a gay journalist observed that the homosexual geography of the capital has changed dramatically. Saint-Germain and the Rue Sainte-Anne are out. Les Halles and especially the Marais are in.

Several factors explain the shift. First of all, there was the accessibility of the Marais, which is centrally located and easily reached by public transport. A few hundred metres to the west lies Les Halles, former site of Paris' wholesale food market, which was transferred to the suburbs in 1969. In the 1970s, Les Halles underwent major commercial redevelopment, which included construction of an underground station (opened in December 1977) to link the subway system and the RER (Réseau Express Régional), a network of suburban trains that served 60 per cent of the population of the Paris region (Michel). The nearby Avenue Victoria, running between City Hall and Châtelet, is also the main terminus for the city's night buses, which operate from 1:30 AM to 5:30 AM.

Secondly, the renovated Marais had an undoubted aesthetic appeal. In the over-blown rhetoric and rather stilted English of a recent bilingual guidebook:

> No other area of Paris has such a strong personality in spite of its [architectural] diversity. The same beauty of its dwellings can be seen in every street, the same refinement of the stones, the same warmth of the thoroughfares and every-where the same poetic poetry [*sic*]. The Marais has a spirit, a soul, an immaterial existence beyond the mirror of life. (Auffray 8)

The attractiveness increased in the 1970s and 1980s, when the Marais was turned into an important cultural and artistic quarter. The Pompidou Centre (a new national museum of contemporary art) opened on its western edge in 1977 and the opening or refurbishing of other museums and the proliferation of commercial art galleries soon followed.

But there is a third factor that explains how and why the Marais became the centre of Parisian gay life. Gay businessmen recognised that the Marais, with its low rents and real-estate prices, was ripe for investment. In this respect, the gay Marais, like gay villages and ghettos in Britain and North America, developed spontaneously in response to favourable market conditions. But gay investors in Paris were concerned with more than the balance sheet. They consciously set out to create a new gay quarter as much because of their personal convictions as from their desire to benefit financially from an evident commercial opportunity. . . .

### *The Marais and the Emergence of a Community*

The Marais has thus become a clearly delineated gay space in the heart of Paris, where gay men and lesbians can stroll hand-in-hand or kiss in the street without embarrassment or risk of harassment. In the convoluted jargon of a geographer, such public displays of affection constitute an "appropriation and territorialisation [of a quarter] through the street behaviour of the clientele of gay establishments [who] challenge the hetero-centric character of public spaces and thus give the Marais a conspicuous territoriality" (Bordet 119).

The average homosexual would put it more simply. According to one gay man, "One feels more among family here [in the Marais] than anywhere else in Paris. Perhaps that's what we mean by the [gay] community" (Darne 8).

And for another, who recently moved from Lille to Paris, the Marais represents his community's financial clout: "I was glad to see that *les pédés* ['fags' or 'poof-ters'] had money and could open stylish establishments. I was glad to belong to something organized, which represented a certain economic power" (Laforgerie [1998] 20).

Their enthusiastic appreciation of the ghetto is a relatively recent attitude and even today is not shared by all gays and lesbians. As long ago as 1964, the monthly magazine *Arcadie,* organ of France's politically conservative "homophile" associa-tion, the Club Littéraire et Scientifique des Pays Latin (Literary and Scientific Club of the Latin Countries), warned French homosexuals against copying what was occurring in the US by creating

> a little artificial world, enclosed and suffocating, where everything would be homosexual: not only the bars, restaurants and movie theatres, but also the houses, the streets (in New York several streets are already almost entirely inhabited by homosexuals), the neighbourhoods. A world where one could live one's entire life without seeing anything other than homosexuals, without knowing anything other than homosexuality. In Europe that is called *ghettos*. We hate this false, harmful and grotesque conception of homosexuality. (Daniel 387)

Radical gay militants of the 1970s had little in common with their homophile elders, but they too denounced gay ghettos—both the "commercial ghetto," meaning the bars at Saint-Germain-des-Prés or on the Rue Sainte-Anne, and the "wild ghetto" constituted by the parks, gardens and public urinals where homosexual men hunted for sexual adventure (Martel 77).

Radicals believed that ghettos encouraged a separatist homosexual identity (J. Girard 132–133), whereas they wanted homosexuals to participate in the revolutionary transformation of society as a whole: "Instead of shutting everybody up in their own space, we need to change the world so that we find ourselves all mixed together" (Boyer 74).

Some gay radicals, however, eventually changed their minds and came to recognise the political potential of the gay ghetto. Guy Hocquenghem (1946–88), the emblematic radical militant of the 1970s, told an American interviewer in 1980:

> We don't have a gay community in France. That is, we have a gay movement—with several organisations actively working for political rights, as in all the Western countries—but people do not feel part of a *community*, nor do they live together in certain parts of the city, as they do here in New York City or in San Francisco—for example. And this is the most important difference and the most significant aspect of gay life in the U.S.: not only having a "movement," but having a sense of community—even if it takes the form of "ghettos"—because it is the basis for anything else. (Blasius 36)

The relationship evoked here by Hocquenghem—linking territory, collective identity and political activism—is a complex one. Veteran militant Jean Le Bitoux, for instance, has argued that the gay community appeared first and then produced the gay Marais:

> The homosexual community that was successfully emerging most likely wanted to complete this social emergence in the 1980s with a space "for expressing an identity" [*un espace "identitaire"*]. An emergent community needed a new geographical anchorage. (Le Bitoux 49)

Other analyses invert the equation, however, insisting that the Marais created a gay community and not the other way around. For example, Yves Roussel has noted that, whatever their political camp, homosexual activists of the 1950s–1970s rejected the formation of a distinct gay community (conservatives advocating assimilation into society, radicals wanting to overthrow it), but that by the 1990s a new generation had come to embrace "identity politics."

> Many are the men and women who see themselves as belonging to a minority group, which is the victim of a process of exclusion; this sentiment of exclusion has combined with the intense desire to constitute and to structure a homosexual community. (Roussel 85)

He has attributed this shift to several factors, including the need to mobilise against the AIDS epidemic, but one particularly significant determinant has been "the emergence of a vast ensemble of gay commercial enterprises [that] have allowed for the constitution of a community of homosexual consumers with characteristic lifestyles" (Roussel 107). Jan-Willem Duyvendak has similarly concluded that "in the middle of the 1980s, the concentration of gay clubs and bars, such as in the Marais in Paris, provided a certain 'infrastructure' for a community," although he minimises this community's political activism: "the militants took the occasion to go dancing rather than to demonstrate" (Duyvendak 79).

Gay businessmen share this view that their venues have contributed to the growing sense of community among French gays. In the mid 1980s, the gay entrepreneur David Girard (1959–90) responded to those activists who criticised him for his brazen capitalist spirit by declaring that "[t]he bar owner who, in the summer, opens an outdoor terrace where dozens of guys meet openly, is at least as militant as they are. I think that I have done more for gays than they ever have" (D. Girard [1986] 164).

He even told his customers: "This gay life that is ever more present and diversified in Paris, it is first of all you who create it by consuming" (D. Girard [1983]). This was precisely the message put out in an advertising campaign by the SNEG in 1996: "To consume gay is to affirm one's identity" ("*Consommer gay, c'est s'affirmer*"). The campaign's avowed purpose was to promote its members, but "it is equally a communitarian campaign, a way to bring home to people the visibility of gay establishments" (Primo).

Arguments like these are certainly self-interested on the part of the businessmen who advance them, but that does not mean that they are without merit. As Scott Gunther has recently pointed out,

> The transformed Marais of the 80s provided a space for the development of a gay identity that had not existed before in France. As the community grew, gays themselves gained a reputation as respectable, resourceful, and affluent. Throughout the 80s, the emerging gay identity and geographical space of the Marais became increasingly inseparable and by the early 90s it seemed impossible to imagine the existence of one without the other. The resulting community, which may initially have been defined by a sexual orientation, became increasingly united by shared tastes, cultural preferences in music and food, and even by a distinct "Marais look" among the gay male inhabitants. (Gunther 34)

Not surprisingly, the proliferation and increasing visibility of gay establishments in the Marais and the concomitant development of a self-conscious gay community have resulted in conflict with some long-time residents who resent the on-going influx of gays and the dramatic changes that they have brought about in the quarter. There is also discord among homosexuals and lesbians themselves, many of whom disapprove of the Marais or feel excluded by its dominant cultural values.

## Disputed Territory

Sudden change in a neighbourhood often alarms its residents, a problem that has by no means been unique to the Marais. In the Butte-aux-Cailles district in Paris' 13th *arrondissement,* the artists, writers and middle class who took over this once working-class neighbourhood in the 1980s now complain that it "has become one of the new meeting places for Parisian youth. All year long, music coming from the bars and noisy laughter invade the streets into the early hours of the morning. This nightlife has become a nightmare for certain inhabitants" (Chenay).

In the Popincourt district of the 11th *arrondissement,* it is the "Chinese invasion" by Chinese-born wholesalers in the clothing trades that upsets residents, who find the immigrants "discreet, kind, likeable," but insist that "they have killed the quarter" by taking over every shop that comes onto the market, with the result that there are fewer stores, bakeries and restaurants (Goudet). But nowhere in Paris has the changing character of a neighbourhood aroused more sustained animosity and acrimony than in the Marais.

Homosexuals have had relatively little trouble with the Marais' other significant minority, the orthodox Jews who live on and around the Rue des Rosiers on the very edge of the gay neighbourhood. When the only Jewish tobacconist's on the Rue Vieille-du-Temple became a gay bar in 1983, "[the Jews] were furious that we had taken over this sacred place on their territory," Maurice McGrath has recalled, but "very quickly, we fraternized." Gay businesses even lent their support to protect the quarter in 1986 during a wave of anti-Semitic terrorism (Chayet). In contrast, there has been a long-festering dispute with some of the Marais' middle-class residents who, unhappy with the gay influx, have sometimes expressed themselves in words that carry an explicit or implicit homophobic message.

The Association Aubriot-Guillemites has been at the forefront of the struggle against gay businesses. Residents founded the association, named for two small streets in the Marais, in 1978 to protect the area from damage to the architectural quality of buildings and to the environment, noise, especially at night, nuisances, various inconveniences, and generally anything that might trouble the peace and comfort of the inhabitants of the aforementioned area. (Association circular, c. 1996, reproduced in Méreaux)

By the mid 1990s, the association was denouncing "the major alteration in the atmosphere of the quarter brought about by the proliferation of homosexual businesses" and calling on its members to report "the multiple incidents that bear witness to the accelerated degradation of daily life in our quarter: noise pollution, solicitation of young boys, prostitution, sexual relations on the public street." (There is in fact little or no evidence for most of these charges.) The association warned that "a small group dreams of making this quarter the equivalent of the homosexual quarters of certain large American cities, which the inhabitants do not want at any price" (Razemon and Galceran, 1996a and 1996b; Rémès). In 1997, it went so far as to declare that no normally constituted citizen, whether homosexual or heterosexual, can approve of the multiplication of these specialised bars the inevitable result of which is segregationist and discriminatory and the sole purpose of which is nothing other than the economic exploitation of homosexuality. (e-m@le magazine)

Under pressure from the Association Aubriot-Guillemites, the mayor of the 4th *arrondissement,* Pierre-Charles Krieg, told his constituents in 1996 that "a structured homosexual community has recently received coverage in the media that is disproportionate and dangerous to the harmony of local life." While deploring the "simplistic and racist ideas of thoroughgoing homophobes," he also criticised the "proselytism, ostentation or virulence" allegedly manifested by the neighbourhood's gay men (Krieg). Krieg was a conservative gaullist, but even a socialist municipal councillor declared herself "generally hostile to communitarianism, *a fortiori* if there is risk of [creating] a ghetto" (Pitte 51–52). The dispute crystallised in the "Affair of the Flags." In July 1995, Bernard Bousset, as president of SNEG, suggested that gay and gay-friendly businesses in the Marais display the "rainbow flag" (the internationally recognised symbol of gays) on their façades and some 15 businesses did so. The Association Aubriot-Guillemites objected and in April 1996 the police invoked an ordinance issued by the prefect of police in 1884 and ordered the removal of the flags (which Mayor Krieg contemptuously dismissed as "multicoloured rags") on the grounds that the grouped and quasi-systematic display of overly large emblems risks arousing hostile reactions. And in these circumstances it is not necessary to wait for trouble to occur before imposing a ban. (Baverel; Berthemet; Razemon and Galceran 1996a)

The flags soon reappeared or were replaced with more discreet rainbow decals stuck on windows and doors, but the dispute was symbolic of deeper and more persistent concerns. In late 1990, a new police commissioner, determined to put an end to "ten years of laxness," began a crack-down on noise in the quarter which, bar owners claimed, amounted to "police harassment" of their establishments (Rouy; *Illico*). In 1995/96, gay bars in the Marais deplored another round of harassment by police, including reports for "disturbing the peace at night" actually drawn up in the late morning or early evening (Rémès). A series of meetings held in early 1997 by police, municipal officials and representatives of SNEG produced an agreement for concerted efforts "to diminish the nuisances for residents from 'nighttime' establishments" (*Paris Centre*). Another series of discussions followed in the spring of 1999, after renewed complaints about noisy bars and customers who gathered outside the doors of certain establishments, blocking the pavement and sometimes impeding the circulation of automobiles in the street. The Association of Co-owners in the Marais Quarter (Association des Copropriétaires du Quartier du Marais) even advocated closing bars at 11 PM (instead of 2 AM). One gay publication observed that "these problems raise the issue of a veritable redevelopment of the quarter by residents, businesspeople, police and administrators," but its proposed solution ("the creation of districts designated for partying, leisure and places for socializing") was probably unrealistic (Abal). In 2003, the municipality had to put metal rivets in the pavement to delimit the outdoor terraces of restaurants and cafés that were encroaching too far onto the pavement along the Rue des Archives (Laforgerie 2003, 31–32).

Although in the past decade or so the French press has been generally favourable to gay demands for equal rights, coverage of gay issues has rarely been free of unconscious prejudice, especially where the Marais is concerned. As David Caron has pointed out, the heading above one newspaper article about the Marais—"The gay flag hangs over the Rue Sainte-Croix-de-la-Bretonnerie"—typically used "a metaphor for foreign invasion" to describe the gay presence in the Marais (Caron 151). Newspapers tend to ignore lesbians, portray gay men as hedonistic and sex-obsessed revellers, equate homosexual "visibility" with "provocation" (of heterosexuals) and depict the Marais as a geographical and metaphorical "ghetto" and the headquarters of gay "corporatism," "communitarianism" or "militant *apartheid*" (Huyez). As these charges indicate, the conflict within the neighbourhood over the use of urban space has much broader ideological implications arising from the particular way that the French conceptualise their society.

## References

Abal, O. (1999) Trop de bruits dans le Marais?. *CQFG* 3:(22 April), p. 12.

Auffray, M.-F. (2001) Le Marais: la légende des pierres, if stones could speak.—trans. by E. Powis. Paris: Hervas

Baverel, P. (1996) Le Drapeau gay flotte rue Sainte-Croix-de-la-Bretonnerie. *Le Monde* p. 11.—22 June

Bech, H. (1997) When Men Meet: Homosexuality and Modernity.—trans. by T. Mesquit and T. Davies. Chicago, IL: University of Chicago Press

Berthemet, T. (1996) Querelle de drapeau dans le Marais. *Le Figaro* p. 24.—25 April

Blasius, M. (1980) Interview: Guy Hocquenghem. *Christopher Street* 4:(8), p. 36.

Bordet, G. (2001) Homosexualité, altérité et territoire: les commerces gais sur le bas des pentes de la Croix-Rousse et dans le Marais.—Unpublished Mémoire de maîtrise de géographie, Université Lumière-Lyon 2

Boyer, J. (1979/80) Quand les homosexuels se lancent à la conquête de l'espace. *Masques* 3:(Winter), p. 73.

Caron, D. (2001) AIDS in French Culture: Social Ills, Literary Curses.—Madison, WI: University of Wisconsin Press

Chayet, S. (1996) Marais, le triangle rose. *Le Point* 1232:(27 April), p. 96.

Chenay, C. de (2003) A Paris, la Butte-aux-Cailles, des communards aux 'bobos'. *Le Monde* p. 9.—29 July

Daniel, M. (1964) Le plus grave danger. *Arcadie* 11:(129), p. 385.

Darne, R. (1995) Ghetto? Milieu? Communauté? Un débat ouvert. *Exit, le journal* p. 8.—21 July

Duyvendak, J.-W. (1993) Une 'communauté' homosexuelle en France et aux Pays-Bas? Blocs, tribus et liens. *Sociétés: Revue des Sciences Humaines et Sociales* 39, p. 75.

———. (1998) Pas de quartier pour les gays!. *e-m@le magazine* 23:(12 March), p. 15.—e-m@le magazine

Girard, D. (1983) Édito. *5 sur 5* 1:(September), p. 1.

Girard, D. (1986) Cher David: les nuits de citizen gay.—Paris: Ramsey

Girard, J. (1981) Le Mouvement homosexuel en France 1945–1980.—Paris: Syros

Goudet, A. (2003) Pas de racisme, mais trop de Chinois dans le sape. *Marianne* 329:(11–17 August), p. 59.

Gunther, S. (1999) The indifferent ghetto. *Harvard Gay and Lesbian Review* 6:(1), p. 34.

Huyez, G. (2002) Dix ans de 'ghetto': le quartier gay dans les hebdomadaires français. *ProChoix* 22:(Autumn), p. 59.

———. (1991) Le Marais en alerte. p. 7.—Illico; 3 January

Krieg, P.-C. (1996) Éditorial. *Paris Centre: Le Journal du IVème* 93:(October/November), p. 3.

Laforgerie, J.-F. (1998) Dehors, dedans: mon ghetto. *Ex Aequo* 14:(January), p. 16.

Laforgerie, J.-F. (2003) Le Marais est-il en crise?. *Illico* 78:(6 June), p. 30.

Le Bitoux, J. (1997) Marcher dans le gai Marais. *Revue h* 1:(July), p. 47.

Martel, F. (1999) The Pink and the Black: Homosexuals in France since 1968.—Stanford, CA: Stanford University Press

Méreaux, J. (2001) Le "Marais": l'espace homosexuel comme métaphore du groupe: éléments pour une socio-anthropologie d'une culture territorialisée.—Unpublished Mémoire de Diplôme d'Études Approfondies, Université de Paris X-Nanterre

Michel, C. (1988) Les Halles: la renaissance d'un quartier 1966–1988.—Paris: Mason

———. (1997) 'Gays' dans le IVème. 95:(April/May), p. 7.—Paris Centre: Le Journal du IVème

Pitte, J.-R. (1997) L'avenir du Marais. *Cahiers du Centre de Recherches et d'Études sur Paris et l'Ile-de-France* 59, p. 49.

Primo, T. (1998) Bernard Bousset: de la mémoire avant toute chose. *e-m@le magazine* 17:(29 January), p. 18.

Razemon, O. and Galceran, S. (1996a) La bataille du Marais. *Ex Aequo* 2: (December), p. 16. Razemon, O. and Galceran, S. (1996b) Marais: la guérilla. *Illico* 73:(December), p. 6.

Rémès, E. (1996) Les policiers harcèlent les bars gays du Marais. *Libération* p. 15.—18–19 May

Roussel, Y. (1995) Le mouvement homosexuel français face aux stratégies identitaires. *Les Temps Modernes* 50:(582), p. 85.

Rouy, P. (1990) Bars gais: nuisances policières. *Gai Pied Hebdo* 449/450:(20 December), p. 15.

Sibalis, Michael. "Urban Space and Homosexuality: The Example of the Marais, Paris' 'Gay Ghetto.'" *Urban Studies* 41.9 (2004): 1739–58.

# ➢ Sergio Arguello

(2011), United States

## "They Were Here First: LGBTQ Seniors in Los Angeles"

You walk towards the bar. You're about to order a drink when you notice the ravishing strager near the counter. As the two of you make eye contact and you open your mouth to mumble a cheesy pick up line, the lights go off. It's pitch black, people begin the mutter. This is not part of the show, nor a blown fuse. Instinctively, you make your way towards the nearest exit, but it is locked from the outside. The crowd panics. You hear glass shattering somewhere, someone tries to climb out the window, a scream, followed by sirens. The police are outside waiting to arrest each person climbing down through the window, for "masquerading" or wearing clothes of the opposite gender. The year is 1970, and this is another raid of another gay bar. This seems like a horror story from the distant past, yet there are people among us who remember living through this.

As Kathleen Sullivan, the director for seniors programs at the L.A. Gay & Lesbian Center, said: "This is the number one thing people don't know about LGBT seniors. They lived through so many traumatic events during such an important time of their lives." But after enduring so many difficulties that we will never understand, today's LGBT seniors still face many more.

Few of us think about old age and its hardships, let alone those faced by LGBT- and queer-identified seniors. However, with more openly gay and lesbian seniors than ever in the history of the US, this once mute section of society has begun to voice its needs, injuries and hopes.

Despite the social and political progress the queer community has made in the last few decades, the statistics for the remaining members of what is sometimes known as the "Lost Generation" are still heart-wrenching: according to a study by the National Association of Social Workers, over 75% of LGBT seniors live alone, a figure twice as high as their straight counterparts. 90% of LGBT seniors do not have the support of children, since adoption by same-sex couples was nearly unheard of until about twenty years ago. Most alarmingly, 20% of LGBT seniors have no one to contact in case of emergency.

| 67% | 90% | 80% | 51% | 20% |
|---|---|---|---|---|
| Of medical professionals report that LGBT seniors receive substandard care | Of LGBT seniors are childless | Of LGBT seniors enter old age without a partner | Of LGBT seniors lack wills and explicit end-of-life plans | Of LGBT seniors lack an emergency contact |

**Figure 15.7**

*Source:* Catherine Thurston/National Association of Social Workers

Perhaps more nuanced than the numbers are other factors such as estrangement from their natal families and psychological trauma from the AIDS epidemic, which took the life of so many of their peers. Even those fortunate enough to age with a partner must face the fact that upon the death of one, the other will obtain no benefits from social security, pension, or inheritance laws. The death of a partner might very well leave a senior unable to support him- or herself economically. Without warning, the hunger for human warmth might yield to the pressure of actual hunger.

It is not uncommon to hear about discrimination, whether subtle or blatant, against LGBT seniors in the healthcare industry. Many seniors are simply too uncomfortable to claim the bare minimum level of resources provided to them by law, due to lack of trust or fear of ill treatment. This is unfortunate, since LGBT seniors are twice as likely to lack health insurance. The threat of physical and emotional abuse, a cruel truth for the elderly, is all the more present for LGBT seniors. While the crisis of bullying against LGBT youth has come into the media spotlight in recent times, the abuse against LGBT seniors continues to be an issue on the most remote margins of the agenda.

But there are many resources available, the most important of which are the people who give their time and energy for the benefit of LGBT seniors. The people factor is the key component of the seniors program of the L.A. Gay & Lesbian Center because, as Sullivan explains, "For so long the establishment, be it the public or whatever, was openly discriminatory against {LGBT individuals}." Because of the long-seated distrust that accompanies such trauma, "many seniors who reach out to conventional resources feel the need to closet themselves." Ironically, many of these seniors seek out an opportunity to socialize, but if they do not feel safe, they will shut themselves in, thereby sinking lower into their feelings of depression and isolation.

Therefore, the importance of programs focused on welcoming queer seniors cannot be overstated, especially resources for those that are not gay, white, and male. The seniors program at the L.A. Gay & Lesbian Center has made reaching out to marginal groups a top priority goal, and has already seen many improvements in its representations of these traditionally overlooked people. Its current gender demographics break down to 55% men and 45% women – a huge improvement in the latter over the past few years, largely due to a number of programs exclusively for women that have been created in an effort to reach out to the lesbian community. Similarly, the center provides services for both bilingual and monolingual Spanish speakers. This is no accident; Sullivan explains, "It is estimated that by the year 2030, 40% of the population 65 and over [in California] will be composed of Latina women."

The seniors program is set on providing services and programs to as many subsections as possible, especially marginal groups, since it is those people who are least willing to reach out to resources who need them the most. Unfortunately, transgender seniors are rare among the program clientele. "We have one or two transgender regulars," admits Sullivan.

Yet the center does not limit itself to mahjong and counseling: one of its greatest contributions is sensitivity training to institutions, from healthcare facilities to governmental offices. "We are a five-person office; we know we won't be able to reach out to every senior citizen who needs us, so we try to educate as many people as possible." The training sessions usually begin with a screeing of Glenne McElhinney's 2009 breakthrough film "On These Shoulders We Stand," a documentary about the stories of eleven LGBT seniors through the earliest years of the gay rights movement in Los Angeles. As one of these seniors says: "[Today's youth] need to know that there's people that survived all that shit." The hope for people like Sullivan is that once people know, they will be more inclined to listen to the voices that have been silent for so long.

---

*Source:* Sergio Arguello, "They Were Here First: LGBTQ Seniors in Los Angeles." *OutWrite*. Fall 2011.

# Glossary

**Aesthete:** a person who has an extreme appreciation for art and nature; a so-called fleshly poet.

**Asexuality:** lacking interest in or desire for sex.

**Assimilationist:** an LGBT activist who prioritizes civil rights, arguing the similarity of LGBT people to the heterosexual mainstream.

**BCE (Before the Common Era):** a synonym for BC (Before Christ) used in the fields of archaeology and anthropology.

**BDSM:** bondage, dominance, sadomasochism (see **Sadomasochist**).

**Beat culture:** a 1950s counterculture movement, including writers such as Jack Kerouac, Allen Ginsberg, and Diane DiPrima. The term *Beat* describes both a sense of being "beaten down" by conservative forces and a desire to march to the beat of a different drummer.

*Belle Époque:* French for "Beautiful Era." A period of relative peace and stability in Europe beginning in the late 19th century and lasting until World War I. This era saw advances in technology and the first "modern" art.

**Bestiality:** use of an animal for human sexual gratification.

*Bildungsroman:* a novel of personal development, describing the protagonist's journey from youth to maturity.

**Biological determinism:** the theory that a person's behavior is determined by inherited physical characteristics.

**Bisexual:** a person who is sexually attracted to people of both sexes.

**Black Panthers:** a progressive political organization formed by Huey Newton in the 1960s to fight for equality of all socially oppressed minorities. The Black Panthers differed from many black civil rights organizations in that they were armed and advocated the overthrow of the U.S. government.

**Buggery:** anal intercourse.

**Butch:** a lesbian gender characterized by performing stereotypical masculinity; also refers to gay men.

**Congenital:** inborn.

**Cross-dressing:** the wearing of clothing characteristic of a different gender; one who cross-dresses is sometimes referred to as being *in drag*.

**Culture wars:** a term used primarily in the 1980s in the United States to describe the conflict between conservative or traditional views and those considered liberal or progressive.

**Decadence:** a period of perceived "decay" or decline, specifically within a generation or society; most often used to describe the European 1890s.

**Diaspora:** ancient Greek for "scattering." Refers to a group expelled from their homeland and scattered throughout the world, specifically Jews and Africans.

**Dildo:** a penis-shaped object used for sexual stimulation.

**Drag king:** a woman who dresses as a man and performs masculinity (see also **Drag queen**).

**Drag queen:** a man (usually gay) who dresses as a woman and performs femininity (see also **Drag king**).

**Essentialism:** a theory that a trait is innate rather than acquired.

**Etiology:** the study of origins and causes.

**Eugenics:** the study of how to improve a population through selective breeding.

**Eunuch:** a castrated male.

**Femme:** a lesbian gender characterized by performing stereotypical femininity; also refers to gay men.

**Fetishism:** sexual arousal using inanimate objects.

**Fin de siècle:** French for "end of the century." A term referring to the last decade of the 19th century.

**FtM or F2M:** a female-to-male transsexual.

**Fundamentalism:** a religious movement where followers adhere strictly to a literal interpretation of sacred texts.

**Gender:** learned behaviors and attitudes supposed to correspond with biological sex.

**Gender dysphoria:** another name for gender identity disorder.

**Gender identity disorder (GID):** a clinical psychological diagnosis marking a person who is strongly identified with the "other" sex.

**Gender inversion:** see **Inversion**.

**Hegemony:** influence of a dominant and normalized group over other groups.

**Heteronormative:** characterized by the presumed hegemony of heterosexuality over other forms of sexual expression.

**Homophile movement:** a movement in the mid-1900s in which gay men and lesbians refused to accept that homosexuality was a sickness. Through groups such as the Mattachine Society and the Daughters of Bilitis (DOB), they embraced their homosexuality and worked to gain acceptance from society.

**Homophobia:** the fear of homosexuals or homosexuality.

**Hysteria:** a vague and ill-defined mental disorder commonly diagnosed in women; its etymological association with the Greek word *hystera* ("womb") led to a tendency among 19th-century doctors to associate femaleness with illness.

**Intersectionality:** a theory that seeks to examine the ways in which socially and culturally constructed categories interact on multiple levels to manifest themselves as inequality in society. Intersectionality holds that the classical models of oppression within society, such as those based on race or ethnicity, gender, religion, nationality, sexual orientation, class, or disability, do not act independently of one another.

**Intersex:** born with genitalia that cannot be definitively classified as male or female; hermaphrodite.

**Inversion:** a term used by late 19th-century sexologists to describe performance of gender behavior or sexual desire thought to be appropriate only for the "other" sex.

**Masochism:** the derivation of pleasure from pain.

**Misogynist:** a person who hates women.

**Monogamy:** having a single sexual partner during a period of time.

**Monolithic:** characterized by uniformity and resistance to change.

**Monosexuality:** identifying as a single (hetero- or homo-) sexuality as opposed to more fluid constructions (bi-, pan-, etc.).

**MtF or M2F:** a male-to-female transsexual.

**Paroxysm:** obsolete term for a female orgasm.

**Pederasty:** a sexual relationship between an adult man and a boy.

**Pedophile:** an adult who is sexually attracted to children.

**Progressive:** favoring reform or change.

**Queer:** a word once used as a taunt against homosexuals, now reclaimed as an umbrella term to signify the diversity of LGBT identities and to assert the value of difference.

**Sadism:** the derivation of sexual gratification through the infliction of pain on others.

**Sadomasochist:** one who derives sexual gratification through inflicting or receiving pain; the word *sadomasochist* combines the words sadism and masochism.

**Self-actualization:** a psychological term for realizing one's full potential.

**Separatism:** separation from an established group, especially referring to groups of lesbians who wished to establish all-female communities.

**Sexologist:** a medical doctor specializing in the study of sexual behavior.

**Sexology:** the pseudo-scientific study of human sexual behavior and identity.

**Sex-positive:** embracing sexual openness without ethical distinction among sexual expressions or identities.

**Sexual inversion:** see **Inversion**.

**Sexual libertarianism:** the view that it is not wrong to engage in any noncoercive sexual conduct.

**Snuff:** pornography that depicts the killing of a human being.

**Social constructionism:** a theory that assumes that many personal identifications—homosexuality, for instance—develop through interaction with the surrounding environment.

**Sodomy:** oral or anal sexual intercourse.

**Sodomy laws:** laws criminalizing non-procreative sexual acts, especially between members of the same sex.

**Splice:** to cut and manipulate DNA in order to insert genetic material.

**Strategic essentialism:** the conscious deployment of essentialism as an argument against discrimination; in terms of queer activism, using the assumption that homosexuality is innate to argue for gay rights.

**Teleological:** assuming that everything has an inherent purpose and a final cause.

**Tommy:** late 19th-century term for a boyish or passing woman.

**Transgender:** having a gender identity that does not align with physical sex; a willingness to challenge dominant gender norms in one's behavior or presentation.

**Transman:** a person who was born female but who identifies as male.

**Transsexual:** having a gender identity that does not align with physical sex; changing one's self-presentation or one's body in order to arrive at a more satisfactory gender expression.

**Transvestite:** an obsolete term for a cross-dresser; a person who derives erotic gratification from dressing in clothing presumed by the dominant culture to be that of the opposite sex.

**Urnings:** a term invented by Karl Heinrich Ulrichs to describe a third sex comprising homosexuals, whom he theorized displayed visible physical differences from heterosexuals.

**Zap:** a quick and unexpected direct action designed to cause disruption or discomfort to make a political point.

# Photo Credits

## Chapter 1

Figure 1.1 page 3 Illustration Greg Reeder, 2008.

Figure 1.2 page 5 Artist unknown, seventeenth century, Reza Abbasi Museum.

Figure 1.3 page 6 Appeared in *The Zuñi Man-Woman*. Albuquerque: U of NMP, 1991.

Figure 1.4 page 8 Originally from the Monastery of St. Catherine on Mt. Sinai, now in Kiev Museum of Eastern and Western Art.

Figure 1.5 page 11 Lithograph by James Henry Lynch after Lady Leighton, 1887. (National Portrait Gallery, London)

## Chapter 3

Figure 3.1 page 55 Time From Sachsenhausen Memorial Site, by Gen Baugher.

## Chapter 4

Figure 4.1 page 71 Bettmann/Corbis.

Figure 4.2 page 91 Bettmann/Corbis.

Figure 4.3 page 74 Original album cover, Alix Dobkin's *Lavender Jane Loves Women*.

Figure 4.4 page 76 Scott DeWitt & Trauman.

Figure 4.5 page 79 © epa/Corbis.

## Chapter 5

Figure 5.1 page 103 The New Yorker Collection 1948 Peter Arno from cartoonbank.com. All rights reserved.

Figure 5.2 page 104 From Kinsey, Alfred C., Wardell B. Pomeroy, and Clyde E. Martin. *Sexual Behavior in the Human Male*. Philadelphia: W. B. Saunders, 1948.

Figure 5.3 page 105 Michelle Gibson.

Figure 5.4 page 107 Fritz Klein.

Figure 5.5 page 108 Michael Storms.

Figure 5.6 page 126 From Albert Mohler, Jr. (March 2, 2007), United States "Is Your Baby Gay? What If You Could Know? What If You Could Do Something About It?" Blog posting by R. Albert Mohler Jr. (http://www.albertmohler.com/2007/03/02/is-your-baby-gay-what-if-you-could-know-what-if-you-could-do-something-about-it-2/)

## Chapter 7

Figure 7.1 page 154 Michelle Gibson.

Figure 7.2 page 154 Michelle Gibson.

## Chapter 8

Figure 8.1 page 181 Photo by Duane Cramer.

Figure 8.2 page 183 Carmen Vazquez.

Figure 8.3 page 186 From M. Gibson, M. Marinara, D. Meem, "Bi, Butch, and Bar Dyke: Pedagogical Performances of Class, Gender, and Sexuality," *College Composition and Communication*, 52:1 (Sept. 2000), 69–95. Copyright 2000 by the National Council of Teachers of English. Used with permission.

Figure 8.4 page 187 From G. Rubin, "Thinking Sex: Notes for a Radical Theory of the Politics of Sexuality" in Abelove, Barale, Halperin, et al. (Eds.), *The Lesbian and Gay Studies Reader*. (1992).

# Chapter 9

Figure 9.2 page 213 Eakins, Thomas, *The Swimming Hole*, 1884-85, Oil on canvas, 27 3/8 x 36 3/8 in. (69.5 x 92.4 cm), Amon Carter Museum, Fort Worth.

Figure 9.4 page 217 © 2012 Tamara Art Heritage / ADAGP, Paris / ARS, NY.

Figure 9.8 page 221 Linda J. Russell.

Figure 9.10 page 223 Claude Cahun, "Self portrait (reflected in mirror)", 1928. Courtesy of the Jersey Heritage Collections.

# Chapter 10

Figure 10.1 page 238 Time & Life Pictures/Getty.
Figure 10.2 page 239 Bettmann/Corbis.

Figure 10.3 page 240 Tom of Finland.

Figure 10.4 page 243 By Tereska Torres.

Figure 10.5 page 244 By Ann Bannon.

Figure 10.6 page 245 Photo portrait of Ann Bannon by Tee Corinne.

Figure 10.7 page 245 Sophie Bassouls/Sygma/Corbis.

Figure 10.8 page 246 Cover Image of *Twilight Men* by Marvin J. Taylor.

Figure 10.9 page 247 Photo: Harold Halma.

Figure 10.10 page 248 © Sophie Bassouls/Sygma/Corbis.

# Chapter 12

Figure 12.2 page 281 Hulton-Deutsch Collection/Corbis.

Figure 12.3 page 282 Image of 1928 Well of Loneliness Cover by Radclyffe Hall published by Jonathan Cape.

# Chapter 13

Figure 13.2 page 304 John Springer Collection/ Corbis.

Figure 13.3 page 311 Axel Koester/Corbis.

Figure 13.4 page 312 Brad Barket/Getty.

# Chapter 14

Figure 14.1 page 334 Jodi Buren/Time & Life Pictures/ Getty.

# Chapter 15

Figure 15.1 page 353 Image courtesy of Vixen Films.

Figure 15.2 page 355 By Dorothy Smith.

Figure 15.3 page 356 Designed by Cynthia Clabough.

Figure 15.4 page 358 From Outmusic, New York City 2003.

Figure 15.5 page 361 By Roz Warren. Cleis, 1995, p. 59.

Figure 15.6 page 363 Michelle Gibson.

# Index

Note: In page references, f indicates figures.

# About the Authors

**Michelle A. Gibson** is Professor Emerita of the Department of Women's, Gender, and Sexuality Studies at the University of Cincinnati. Her scholarship focuses on Sexuality Studies and pedagogy. Her most recent writing applies queer and postmodern identity theories to pedagogical practice and popular culture. In retirement, she writes and publishes poetry and maintains a blog called ProfSpazz at http://profspazz.com. With Jonathan Alexander, she edited *QP: Queer Poetry*, an online poetry journal, and she and Alexander also edited a strain of *JAC: Journal of Advanced Composition* titled "Queer Composition(s)." With Deborah Meem, she coedited *Femme/Butch: New Considerations of the Way We Want to Go* (2002) and *Lesbian Academic Couples* (2005).

**Jonathan Alexander** is Professor of English and Chancellor's Fellow at the University of California, Irvine. He is a three-time recipient of the Ellen Nold Award for Best Articles in the field of computers and composition studies and, in 2011, was awarded the Charles Moran Award for Distinguished Contributions to the Field of Computers and Writing. His books include *Literacy, Sexuality, Pedagogy: Theory and Practice for Composition Studies* (2008) and *Digital Youth: Emerging Literacies on the World Wide Web* (2005); the coedited collections *Bisexuality and Queer Theory: Intersections, Connections and Challenges* (2011), *Bisexuality and Transgenderism: InterSEXions of the Others* (2004), and *Role Play: Distance Learning and the Teaching of Writing* (2006); and the coauthored books *Argument Now: A Brief Rhetoric* (2005) and *Understanding Rhetoric: A Graphic Guide to Composition* (forthcoming, 2013).

**Deborah T. Meem** is Professor and Head of the Department of Women's, Gender, and Sexuality Studies at the University of Cincinnati. Her academic specialties are Victorian literature, Lesbian Studies, and the 19th-century woman's novel. She earned a PhD from Stony Brook University in 1985. Her

411

work has appeared in *Journal of the History of Sexuality, Feminist Teacher, Studies in Popular Culture*, and elsewhere. She has edited three works by Victorian novelist and journalist Eliza Lynn Linton: *The Rebel of the Family* (Broadview, 2002), *Realities* (Valancourt, 2010), and *The Autobiography of Christopher Kirkland* (Victorian Secrets, 2011). With Michelle Gibson, she coedited *Femme/Butch: New Considerations of the Way We Want to Go* (2002) and *Lesbian Academic Couples* (2005), both published by Haworth Press. With Jonathan Alexander, she wrote "Dorian Gray, Tom Ripley, and the Queer Closet" (CLCWeb, 2003).

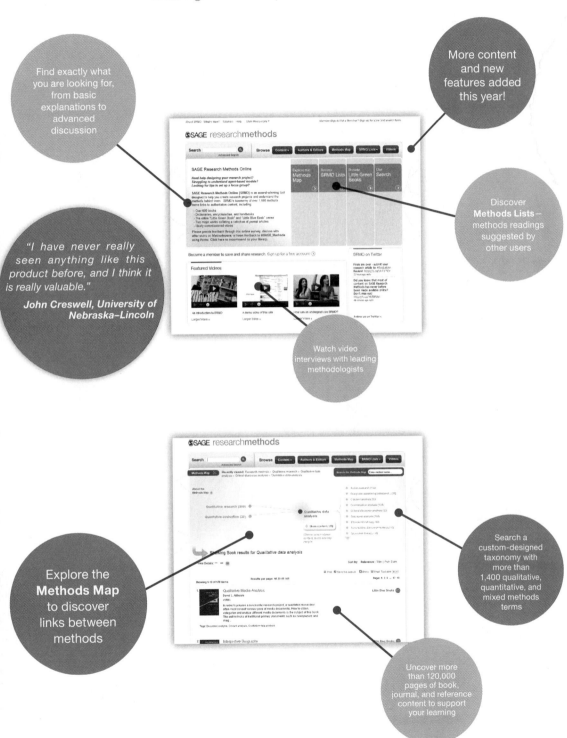

# SAGE researchmethods

The essential online tool for researchers from the world's leading methods publisher

Find exactly what you are looking for, from basic explanations to advanced discussion

More content and new features added this year!

"I have never really seen anything like this product before, and I think it is really valuable."

**John Creswell, University of Nebraska–Lincoln**

Discover **Methods Lists**—methods readings suggested by other users

Watch video interviews with leading methodologists

Explore the **Methods Map** to discover links between methods

Search a custom-designed taxonomy with more than 1,400 qualitative, quantitative, and mixed methods terms

Uncover more than 120,000 pages of book, journal, and reference content to support your learning

# Find out more at
www.sageresearchmethods.com